Conflict Management in Law Enforcement

THIRD EDITION

James Pardy

2012
Emond Montgomery Publications
Toronto, Canada

Emond Montgomery Publications Limited
60 Shaftesbury Avenue
Toronto ON M4T 1A3
http://www.emp.ca/college

Printed in Canada.
17 16 15 14 13 12 11   1 2 3 4 5

We acknowledge the financial support of the Government of Canada through the Canada Book Fund for our publishing activities.

Acquisitions editor: Bernard Sandler
Developmental editor: Sarah Gleadow
Marketing manager: Christine Davidson
Director, sales and marketing, higher education: Kevin Smulan
Supervising editor: Jim Lyons
Copy editor: David Handelsman
Typesetter: Nancy Ennis
Proofreader and Indexer: Paula Pike
Text and cover designer: Tara Wells
Cover image: DNY59/iStockphoto

Library and Archives Canada Cataloguing in Publication

Pardy, James, 1958-
   Conflict management in law enforcement / James Pardy. — 3rd ed.

Includes index.
ISBN 978-1-55239-391-8

   1. Police—Canada—Textbooks.   2. Conflict management—Textbooks.
3. Crisis management—Textbooks.   I. Title.

HV7936.P75P37 2011   363.2'3   C2011-905279-2

Contents

CHAPTER 4   CHILD ABUSE

CHAPTER 5   SPOUSAL ABUSE

CHAPTER 6   ELDER ABUSE

CHAPTER 7   MENTAL ILLNESS AND PERSONALITY DISORDERS

Preface

Policing has the unenviable reality of being, in many situations, the last intervention option available. When other crisis intervention professionals are unable to effectively deal with an escalating situation, they have the option of withdrawing and calling for assistance from police. Police do not have the option of dialing 911 when situations intensify.

Police are required to respond in circumstances where no other professional will attend. Police officers are expected to have the ability to effectively communicate, counsel, mediate, advise, empathize, protect, and console. Officers are expected to be knowledgeable and possess a thorough understanding of federal and provincial legislation and its application. They must also have the physical capacity and willingness to forcibly intervene, and to do so without malice. Police are expected to calmly and compassionately render assistance to the public and at the same time deal firmly with the criminal element of society. This may seem an impossible endeavour, but to make the task even more daunting, police officers are asked to perform these feats several times each day without complaint, and many times without thanks.

Policing is a profession that does not have an established daily routine—each day will bring different occurrences, challenges, and problems. It is therefore impossible for a text to address every situation that a police officer may encounter. Rather than make such a vain attempt, this text will examine several of the most difficult occurrences faced by police officers. Two problem-solving models, CAPRA and PARE, are used in much of this text. Although there are other problem-solving models that may also be effective, both of these models have proven to be particularly effective in policing situations. By understanding how the CAPRA and PARE models are used in the situations described in the text, officers can later apply that knowledge to situations they encounter in their professional future.

This text is written for those who wish to enter the profession of policing, and who have a thorough knowledge of federal and provincial statutes and their applications. No attempt has been made to identify the "facts in issue" of any particular offence, although there are some procedural explanations. Students are expected to have an understanding of evidence and investigative procedures, as well as an understanding of what is required to effectively communicate with the persons involved in a conflict.

The goal of this text is to expose students to relevant situations that they will encounter in their future policing career and to provide examples of safe procedures to follow to enhance the likelihood of successful interventions.

The first two chapters of the text deal with factors that precipitate a conflict or crisis situation, followed by a chapter on problem-solving and intervention techniques. The next three chapters deal with child, spousal, and elder abuse, followed by a chapter addressing psychological and emotional disorders.

Next is a chapter on suicide intervention—often one of the most emotionally difficult situations faced by police officers. Intervention techniques and recognition of risk are discussed in this chapter along with elements of officer safety. The final chapter deals with victims of crime and also examines some potentially emotional situations, such as the aftermath of a break-and-enter, and the difficult task of providing injury and death notifications.

The text includes self-study exercises that will assist students in applying their understanding of the course material. Many of the scenarios used in the self-study exercises are taken from actual occurrences and represent common situations that police officers will encounter.

James Pardy

Stress in Conflict and Crisis Situations

INTRODUCTION

This book looks at issues of conflict and crisis. A **conflict** is a dispute in which the goals or motives of the involved parties are incompatible. A conflict may not require police intervention—for example, a dispute between siblings that does not become violent will not require police assistance. This does not mean that police intervention will never be required in a conflict situation. Intervention may be required to prevent the conflict from escalating or to keep the public peace.

If the conflict does escalate, it may develop into a crisis. A **crisis** occurs when the involved parties can no longer effectively deal with the stress of the conflict. Stress is a major contributor to many crisis situations. See the figure below.

A person pushed beyond his or her ability to cope with stress from any source is a **person in crisis**. The person's equilibrium has been upset and his or her coping skills have become ineffective. Such persons may, under normal circumstances, be non-violent and non-confrontational, but under severe stress become unpredictable and display inappropriate behaviour toward others or pose a danger to themselves. Immediate assistance is needed, although not always from the police. Community and social service agencies may be the best source of help.

CHAPTER OBJECTIVES

After completing this chapter, you should be able to:

- Describe the physical and mental changes produced by stress.
- Describe the signs and symptoms of a person in crisis.
- Identify the three models of police intervention and understand the limits of police intervention.
- Describe how stress can impair the performance of a police officer.
- Explain how post-traumatic stress disorder arises and describe its potential effects.

conflict
a dispute in which the goals or motives of the involved parties are incompatible; a conflict may not require police intervention

crisis
a situation in which the parties involved in a conflict can no longer effectively deal with the stress of the conflict

person in crisis
a person pushed beyond his or her ability to cope with stress from any source

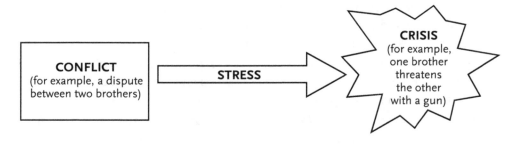

CONFLICT (for example, a dispute between two brothers) → STRESS → CRISIS (for example, one brother threatens the other with a gun)

PERSONS PRONE TO CRISIS

Some people are more crisis prone than others. Several factors are associated with people prone to crisis:

- lack of long-lasting personal relationships;
- little support from family or friends;
- a history of continually making the same or similar mistakes (this may result in frequent incarceration for similar offences);
- a history of mental health issues or lack of emotional control;
- low self-esteem;
- impulsive behaviour (this may result in frequent interactions with law enforcement officers);
- abuse of alcohol or other drugs;
- a history of sporadic employment; and
- frequent changes in residence.

Because of the personal nature of the majority of these factors, police are not able to readily identify which people are more prone to crisis, with a possible exception. Correctional officers generally have access to the person's history of interactions with law enforcement and to the person's personal history. This is vital information in a correctional institution and necessary for effective and safe interactions between the inmate and the correctional officers. Other law enforcement officers are likely to have contact only when the person is already experiencing a crisis.

THE NATURE OF STRESS

stress
a response to a perceived threat or challenge or change; a physical or psychological response to a demand

stressor
something that causes a stress reaction or response

Stress, defined for the purposes of this text as "a response to a perceived threat or challenge or change ... a physical or psychological response to a demand" (Mitchell & Bray, 1990), is an inherent part of policing.

Stress affects everybody at one time or another. It is an ordinary part of our daily lives. When handled properly, stress can be a positive force that enhances our physical and mental capabilities. It may, however, lead to problems when **stressors**—sources of stress—overpower our ability to cope.

There are three main types of stressors: environmental stressors, psychosocial stressors, and personality stressors.

- *Environmental stressors* are sources of stress that are external to the individual and may include noises, weather conditions, and external demands, such as the need to make rapid decisions.
- *Psychosocial stressors* are sources of stress related to social relationships and may include conflicts in family relationships and work relationships, abuse from a suspect, and feeling underappreciated by others.
- *Personality stressors* are sources of stress that are within the individual and may include an inability to say no to requests, a need to be liked by everyone, a pessimistic approach to life, and a lack of confidence in one's abilities. Personality stressors are sometimes called intrapersonal stressors.

Reactions to Stress

Police involvement with people experiencing a stress reaction is required when they are unable to deal with the stress in their lives and react inappropriately. These people are experiencing a crisis.

Members of the public do not call the police when their lives are in order. In the majority of first response occurrences, police become involved only when the stress of the situation exceeds the coping abilities of the involved persons.

Police must remember that persons pushed beyond their abilities to effectively deal with stressful situations may react totally out of character. The stress reaction they experience causes physical and psychological changes that can manifest in the form of unpredictable behaviours.

Police officers are not immune to these stress reactions. Policing is a stressful occupation. Officers perform their duties under circumstances that exist only in the television imaginations of most.

Imagine that you are a police officer on lunch break. You're just about to bite into a sandwich when the phone rings. It's a fellow officer and he needs urgent assistance. You drop your lunch and spring into action. Your muscles tense, your pupils dilate to enhance your vision, your heart rate increases, forcing extra blood flow to your muscles to cope with the threat, your digestion shuts down so that blood can be directed to more important bodily tasks in response to the threat, and your mind begins to process information more quickly.

The changes in the above scenario are all part of the acute stress reaction, and are only a few of the many complex responses exhibited by the body as it adapts to stressors. As long as this reaction is not triggered too often and does not become permanent, it will help you survive stressful situations. But if it becomes permanent, it can cause physical, emotional, and mental health problems. (The effects of stress are discussed in greater detail in the sections below.)

In modern society our high-pressure, fast-paced daily environment produces a continual triggering of the acute stress reaction. Adverse emotional, physical, and cognitive changes can occur when improper means are used to handle this stress. Angry outbursts, abuse of sick time, and alcohol abuse are all common results of improper stress management. One may begin to lose one's mental efficiency, have difficulty remembering details, become more easily distracted, lose the ability to focus on a particular task, and begin to distrust others. One may appear to be detached and unapproachable. A simple question or action can result in an exaggerated emotional response.

Effective interventions by police officers depend upon recognizing these symptoms of stress and learning how to function effectively while experiencing stress or interacting with persons who are experiencing levels of stress beyond their ability to manage.

This chapter will identify and discuss some of the more common types of stress and stress reactions. Stress management techniques will be briefly discussed.

TYPES OF STRESS

Cumulative Stress

Cumulative stress, or chronic stress, is caused by long-term, frequent, low-level stress. Cumulative stress reactions result from the buildup of work-related and non-work-related stressors. These stressors may accumulate over a period of months or years before becoming problematic.

Police officers often perform their duties under extremely stressful conditions and suffer greatly from accumulated stress. Compounding the problem are the improper coping techniques common in policing. Angry outbursts, abuse of sick leave, and alcohol abuse are all common police reactions to stress and examples of improper coping. Physical and cognitive reactions to constant stress result in poor concentration, loss of objectivity, and, if allowed to continue, apathy.

Cumulative stress is preventable if the signs and symptoms are recognized early and corrective action is taken. However, recognizing cumulative stress is difficult. The condition usually develops slowly over several years and the subtle signs and symptoms are not easily recognizable as reactions to stress.

Cumulative stress reactions are generally experienced in four distinct phases. Table 1.1 summarizes the phases of the cumulative stress reaction, and outlines their signs and symptoms and treatment.

1. Warning Phase

During the warning phase, the reactions are usually emotional in nature. Unfortunately, the sufferer may not be able to readily identify stress as the cause of these symptoms. If recognized at this stage, the reactions may be reversed by actions as simple as taking a vacation, changing exercise habits, or discussing feelings.

2. Worsening Symptoms

Failure to recognize and address a person's warning signs may lead to more serious stress reactions. In this phase, the initial emotional symptoms may now be accompanied by physical symptoms.

At this stage, the reaction may be treated through a lifestyle change that reduces stressors. Also, short-term professional counselling may help the person recover.

3. Entrenched Stress

This phase occurs when the initial stages of the stress reaction are ignored or not adequately addressed. Once entrenched, stress is very difficult to recover from without assistance from mental and other medical health professionals.

4. Debilitating Stress

Ignoring or failing to identify and treat the symptoms of stress for a long period of time may lead to debilitating stress.

It is extremely unlikely that a person suffering from debilitating stress will be able to participate in the workforce. At this stage, the sufferer is physically and emotionally incapable of interacting with society. The sufferer's increased potential for self-destructive behaviour and inability to interact socially make it impossible for him or her to be an effective participant in the community. The most likely method of intervention at this stage is psychotherapy and medication to control symptoms. Full recovery is unlikely.

Table 1.1   Cumulative Stress: Phases, Signs and Symptoms, and Treatment

Phase	Signs and Symptoms	Treatment
Warning Phase *(emotional symptoms)*	• vague anxiety • depression • apathy • emotional fatigue	• taking a vacation • changing exercise habits • discussing feelings
Worsening Symptoms *(emotional and physical symptoms)*	• sleep disturbances • frequent headaches • muscle aches • fatigue • irritability • increased depression	• lifestyle change that reduces stressors • short-term professional counselling
Entrenched Stress	• physical and emotional fatigue • intense depression • increased use of alcohol or other drugs • heart problems • elevated blood pressure • migraine headaches • loss of sexual drive • intense anxiety • withdrawal • sleeplessness	• assistance from mental and other medical health professionals
Debilitating Stress	• heart attack • severe depression • low self-esteem • low self-confidence • inability to manage daily activities • uncontrolled emotions • suicidal thoughts • agitation • poor concentration and attention span • carelessness • paranoia • thought disorders	• psychotherapy • treatment of symptoms through medication

Acute Stress

acute stress
a reaction to one or more specific critical incidents that are beyond the individual's ability to cope

Acute stress, also called critical incident stress, is more easily identified than cumulative stress. Acute stress is a reaction to one or more specific critical incidents that are beyond the individual's ability to cope. Law enforcement officers respond to many incidents that can cause acute stress reactions:

- the death of a fellow worker,
- the suicide of a friend or family member,
- a natural or other disaster,
- a severe accident,
- a violent assault, or
- the death or serious injury of a child.

The signs and symptoms of acute stress are shown in Table 1.2.

Acute stress reactions may begin at the time of the incident or shortly afterward, although it is not unusual for the reaction to occur days, weeks, or even years after the incident. A delayed reaction can make it difficult to identify the nature of the symptoms experienced. In many cases, professional help is required to ascertain and address the problem.

The acute stress reaction is divided into three phases: alarm, resistance, and exhaustion. During the alarm phase, the threat, real or perceived, is identified and the body initiates the fight or flight response. During the resistance phase, the person resists the threat through disengagement (flight) or through a physical or verbal encounter (fight). Resistance continues until the threat is eliminated or the person is not capable of further resistance. The person then enters the exhaustion phase, when the body attempts to recover from the encounter. See Figure 1.1.

fight or flight response
the body's physiological response to a perceived threat; chemicals are released into the bloodstream, producing mental and physical changes that increase the person's ability to fight or flee from the threat

The **fight or flight response** is a physiological reaction to stress. It likely developed as a survival mechanism in humans to help ensure survival by increasing the ability to flee from or fight a threat. In primitive times, the threat might have been a tiger or other wild animal; today, work pressures can trigger the same response. Tigers or work, the body recognizes only a stressor, and responds accordingly.

The fight or flight response produces a series of physical reactions:

- The body releases epinephrine (adrenalin). This hormone alerts the brain that a stressor has been or will be encountered.
- The brain prepares the body for the encounter through stimulation of the pituitary gland. The pituitary releases a chemical called adrenocorticotropic hormone. This hormone prepares the body for fight or flight.
- The muscles tighten.
- The pupils dilate.
- Breathing rate increases.
- Heart rate increases.
- Blood pressure increases.
- Fat cells are released into the bloodstream to be used by the liver to increase the amount and rate of glucose production.
- Protein and antibody levels in the blood increase.

Certain cognitive, emotional, and behavioural changes may occur in conjunction with the fight or flight response, such as:

- confusion and loss of mental efficiency,
- loss of short-term memory,
- loss of ability to focus,
- changes in perception (for example, minor obstacles may be seen as major hurdles),
- excessive use of humour in the face of real or perceived threat (consciously or unconsciously),
- loss of trust, and
- detachment.

Table 1.2   Signs and Symptoms of Acute Stress

Signs and symptoms that require immediate corrective action

Physical	*Cognitive*
Chest pain	Decreased alertness or hyperalertness
Difficulty breathing	Difficulty making decisions
Excessive blood pressure	Mental confusion
Collapse from exhaustion	Disorientation to surroundings
Excessive dehydration	Slowed thinking
Dizziness	Problem recognizing familiar people
Vomiting	
Emotional	*Behavioural*
Panic reactions	Change in speech patterns
Shock-like state	Excessive angry outbursts
Phobic reaction	Crying spells
General loss of control	Antisocial acts
Inappropriate emotions	Extreme hyperactivity

Signs and symptoms that require timely, but not immediate, action

Physical	*Cognitive*
Upset stomach	Confusion
Profuse sweating	Lowered attention span
Chills	Memory problems
Sleep disturbance	Distressing dreams
Muscle aches	Disruption in logical thinking
Fatigue	Reliving an event over and over
Emotional	*Behavioural*
Denial	Withdrawal
Grief	Becoming suspicious of everything
Feeling hopeless	Increased or decreased food intake
Feeling overwhelmed	Excessive humour
Feeling lost	Excessive silence
Feeling worried	Increased alcohol intake and smoking
Wanting to hide	Change in interaction with others

Figure 1.1   The Acute Stress Reaction

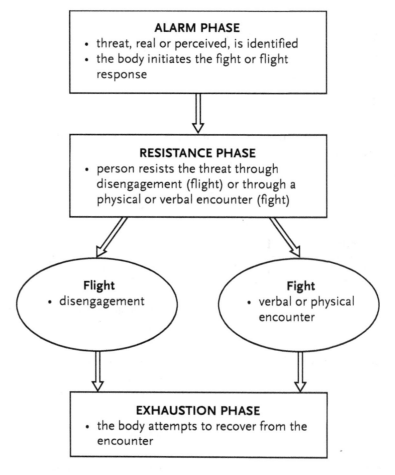

These changes, together with the fight or flight response, may make the behaviour of a person experiencing a high level of stress very unpredictable. They may believe that they are being threatened and react accordingly. A person who has no previous record of violence may lash out violently at a perceived threat. The person's judgment may be further impaired through the use of alcohol or other drugs taken in an attempt to deal with their stress.

In modern society, most people seldom experience the fight or flight response. This is not true in the law enforcement profession. The response may be evoked several times during one shift. The officer may not have the opportunity to enter the recovery stage. The response, while advantageous in some situations, is a definite health hazard if evoked too frequently. Severe physical, psychological, and emotional problems may develop within persons functioning for extended periods in the alarm and resistance stages.

DEVELOPMENT AND STAGES OF A CRISIS

A crisis is a serious interruption in a person's equilibrium. Stress is generally the underlying issue that precipitates a crisis situation. A person functioning normally within his or her individual stress threshold may experience an occurrence of unusual stress caused by a single incident or by multiple incidents. The person attempts to deal with the stress by using his or her usual coping mechanisms. If the coping mechanisms prove ineffective and the person cannot effectively deal with the stressors, a crisis occurs. The person begins a downward spiral of maladaptive behaviours.

A crisis develops in three stages.

- *Stage 1.* An incident occurs. This may be a critical incident, such as the death of a fellow worker, or a seemingly trivial incident that evokes a disproportionate response. This disproportionate response could be the result of cumulative stress. The person may experience disorientation or shock-like symptoms. Some feel surges of energy, likely from the fight or flight response. The person is focused on the present event that upset his or her equilibrium.

- *Stage 2.* The person's ability to deal with the incident is compromised. He or she is unable to effectively deal with the acute or cumulative stress evoked by the incident. The person may focus only on the stressful event and may experience emotions such as hostility, uncertainty, and detachment. Until the person can distance himself or herself from the event (the person is now able to see the event as something that has occurred, but is no longer occurring), the person will remain in a state of crisis.

- *Stage 3.* The person has been able to distance himself or herself from the event that precipitated the crisis. The person is able to think more clearly and seeks to regain control of his or her situation. The person may require additional resources to deal with the stress response.

RECOGNIZING A PERSON IN CRISIS

Recognizing the characteristics of a person in crisis is a critical skill that police officers must possess. Ideally, you will possess background information about the person and any symptoms the person has been exhibiting; this will help you determine whether the person is experiencing or will experience a crisis. This information may be obtained from family members, friends, or co-workers if they are available and time permits. The following are typical symptoms of a person in crisis:

- personality changes,
- general anxiety,
- feeling overwhelmed with everyday life,
- irritability,
- difficulty making decisions,
- nightmares,
- increased fatigue,
- excessive use of sick leave,
- diminished job performance,
- alcohol or other drug abuse,

- change in level of talkativeness (more talkative or less talkative),
- change in appetite, and
- loss of trust.

Unfortunately, the often abrupt nature of the engagement with the subject usually does not allow an opportunity to obtain background information, and most of these indicators are observable only by persons in regular close contact with the subject. Furthermore, although there are identifiable acute incidents that could cause a crisis, it is more likely that the events precipitating the subject's behaviour have evolved over a period of time. For these reasons, it is difficult to accurately predict whether a person will enter into a crisis. It is therefore important to learn to recognize the verbal and non-verbal cues of a person in crisis, which include:

- a distorted view of reality (the person imagines that certain events are taking place);
- in serious cases, unresponsiveness;
- feelings of anger or fear;
- chest pains or other physical discomfort, shortness of breath, and excessive perspiration;
- crying or explosive verbal or physical outbursts;
- poor attention span and poor concentration (these characteristics increase the officer's difficulty in communicating with the subject); and
- agitation, extreme restlessness, and hyperactivity (these characteristics further increase communication difficulties).

There are some indicators of a crisis state that may be readily identifiable during a brief conversation with the person:

- Apathy. "Nothing can help me now."
- Helplessness. "I can't take care of myself."
- Confusion. "I can't think clearly."
- Urgency. "I need help now!"

Personal safety is a major concern when dealing with persons in crisis. Although you want to help, you must not forget the need for your safety. A person in crisis can be extremely dangerous, and may be experiencing a temporary loss of control over his or her thoughts and actions. Recognizing such potentially dangerous persons depends on your ability to interpret verbal and non-verbal messages. The appropriate response depends on the situation.

In many cases, it will be immediately obvious that a person is in crisis. At other times, you'll need to ask yourself the following questions to determine whether the person is in crisis:

1. Are any of the physical, cognitive, behavioural, or emotional crisis indicators discussed above present?

2. Are there any readily identifiable events immediately preceding the intervention that may indicate the person is in crisis? For example, has the person been involved in a fight or a heated argument?

3. Do the person's verbal and non-verbal cues suggest that he or she is in crisis?

Law enforcement officers on scene must then decide whether they can assist the person or whether the problem is beyond their abilities. They also need to ask: is it safe to leave the person alone? If not, an appropriate, legally sanctioned response must be determined, such as arrest or apprehension of the person, to prevent harm or the commission or continuation of an offence.

INTERVENTION

When interacting with a person in crisis, an officer must attempt to identify the problem(s) that caused the crisis. In situations where the problem is not readily identifiable, it is unlikely that police intervention will be of much assistance in alleviating the stress. **Intervention** may be defined, for the purpose of this text, as any verbal or physical interference by police for the purpose of managing the course of events in an effort to change or modify any negative outcome.

It is imperative that the officer listen actively and effectively to ascertain whether the problem can be addressed through police intervention. Responding to the person may be a delicate process. Care must be taken not to judge. Judging the person's words or actions usually serves only to sever communications. Persons in crisis may cease to reveal their feelings or express their problems if they believe that the officer has prejudged them. Advice should not be given until the basis of the problem is understood and the person in crisis asks for assistance in dealing with the problem.

intervention
for the purposes of this text, any verbal or physical interference by police for the purpose of managing the course of events in an effort to change or modify any negative outcome

Crisis Intervention Models

There are three fundamental crisis intervention models: the cognitive model, the psychosocial transition model, and the equilibrium model.

1. The Cognitive Model

The cognitive model is based on the premise that crises originate from unsound thinking about the environment in which the person interacts. First, the person has negative thought patterns that distort his or her view of reality. Then, his or her thoughts become self-fulfilling prophecies. Finally, the person begins a continuously downward spiral.

The cognitive model seeks to remedy the person's behaviours through therapies designed to change thought patterns. The person learns to view his or her environment more realistically and positively. This model is best applied after the person has reached a state of balance.

Unfortunately, the time commitment and expertise required to use this model make it impractical for police.

2. The Psychosocial Transition Model

The psychosocial transition model presumes that people are a product of their learning experiences in the social environment. When people lack adequate coping mechanisms, they are unable to adapt to everchanging social environments. The psychosocial transition model considers all elements of the person's life in seeking to address the state of crisis. Effective treatment may require changes to the person's internal coping mechanisms, thought patterns, and social supports. Like the cognitive model, this model is best applied after the person in crisis has reached a state of balance. Due to time constraints and required expertise, this model, too, is unsuitable for police intervention.

3. The Equilibrium Model

The equilibrium model is the model most suited to police intervention. This model is based on the premise that a person in crisis is operating in a state of disequilibrium. His or her usual coping mechanisms and problem-solving methods have failed. The person may feel, and may act, out of control and disoriented.

The goal of the equilibrium model is to return the person to a state of stability through contextual discussions of the problem. The officer may, through effective communication, try to assist the person in identifying the cause of his or her crisis. Once the source of the problem is identified, the officer may be able to suggest a short-term solution. This allows the person to deal with his or her crisis until a more permanent solution can be found. Finally, a follow-up referral to a community agency is generally required to complete the intervention.

The Limits of Police Intervention

This chapter has examined cumulative and acute stress and the effects of exceeding a person's ability to deal with stress. Persons unable to deal with the stressors in their lives experience episodes of crisis. Left untreated, these episodes may become continuous, causing irreparable physical, emotional, and psychological damage.

With the exception of the use of the equilibrium model of crisis intervention, police generally have limited ability to effectively assist a person with issues of cumulative or acute stress.

Police may provide a short-term management strategy, but long-term solutions usually require professional counselling.

Learning Activity 1.1

Read the following scenario. Then answer the questions that follow.

You are a police officer responding to a disturbance call at 777 Colwell Drive. The residence is quiet upon arrival. You ring the doorbell. The door is answered by Mike Buck. He appears to have been crying. You ask if you can come in.

Buck replies: "Come in. I'm sorry about the mess. I suppose that you are here about the noise. I'm sorry."

You and your partner enter the home. You observe broken dishes throughout the living room along with various pieces of broken furniture.

Mr. Buck says: "Be careful. There is a lot of broken glass on the floor. I guess I lost it."

You ask him if there is anyone else in the home.

He tells you, "My wife left me six months ago. She took the kids. She went to live with some rich guy that she had been seeing for a while behind my back! I have to pay child support for our three children. I want to take care of them, but I just can't make it!"

You ask if you can have a quick look around, just to be sure that no one else is in the home.

He responds, "Look all you want. There's no one here except me!"

You look throughout the house. Your partner stays with Mr. Buck. There is a lot of damage throughout the home. No other persons are found. You return to Mr. Buck. You ask Mr. Buck to explain what he meant by "I just can't make it."

He replies, "I work as a sanitary engineer, that's the job title anyway. I'm a garbage collector. I make $18 an hour. I work 40 hours a week. My take-home pay is $1,148 every two weeks. The money is good and, until recently, I liked my job. We always had food on the table and were able to get a mortgage to buy this place. We had decided that I would work and Cindy, my wife, would stay home with the kids, at least until they were in school. I thought we were happy. Everything seemed to be fine until six months ago."

You ask Mr. Buck to tell you what happened six months ago.

He continues, "I came home from work. Cindy was waiting at the door. There was a suitcase by the door. I asked her what was going on. She told me that she was leaving. She was tired of living a middle-class life and wanted more. I didn't know what to say. She told me that she was leaving me for another man that she had met while taking night classes at the local college. Then she just walked out. I didn't know what to do or say. I just stood there and watched her get into a cab and drive away."

You ask Mr. Buck to tell you what happened tonight.

He tells you, "I guess I lost it. I have been giving Cindy $900 a month for child support. I am paying the mortgage and taxes on the house, that's almost $900 a month, and all the bills Cindy and I had when we were together. It has been very difficult to pay all the bills. Bill collectors call me every day looking for money. Today when I came back from my route, my car was gone. I called the police to report that it had been stolen from the lot at work. They told me that they had received notice that the car was to be repossessed. I hadn't made a payment in four months, but I didn't think that the bank would repossess the car."

You ask him to tell you more about what happened tonight.

Mr. Buck replies, "Like I said, I guess I lost it. I lost control."

You ask him to explain "I lost it."

He replies, "I came home from work, put a frozen dinner in the microwave and sat in the living room to watch television until dinner was ready. I was watching something on television. I can't remember what was on. My head has been aching for the past four days. I had taken some painkillers at work but my head was still aching. I got up to get some more. I haven't been sleeping much, that's probably why I have a headache. I have been having a hard time at work. I used to like my job, but now everything bugs me! Anyway, I went to get some more painkillers. As I was walking to the bathroom, my cellphone rang. It was Cindy. She told me that she was leaving her new boyfriend and that she would be seeking alimony in addition to the child support. I told her that there was no way that I could give her more money. I can hardly feed myself now! She told me that I would have to sell the car. I told her that the car had been repossessed. She said, 'That's too bad. I guess I will have to go after the house.' She hung up.

"My chest began to hurt and I felt dizzy and sick in my stomach. I went to the bathroom to get something for my headache. There were no painkillers in the bottle. It seems like a dream, but I guess that I just started smashing things. I feel better now."

1. Identify the type of stress that evoked the stress response and the stage to which the stress has progressed.

2. Identify the type of police response most suited to this scenario.

STRESS AND POLICING

Sources of Stress in Policing

Police function within an environment where they experience high levels of acute and cumulative (chronic) stress unique to policing. Sources of stress for officers include:

- *Exposure to the realities of violence, abuse, trauma, and poverty.* Exposure to these social ills may challenge officers' belief systems about themselves and the world.

- *The risk of physical assault while on duty.* Research by K. Pedro (2003) found that in some Canadian jurisdictions almost 50 percent of patrol officers were physically assaulted while on duty over a one-year period.

- *Other common risks.* These include injury or death from high-speed accidents and car chases; trauma from attending at critical incidents; and exposure to air-borne or blood-borne diseases.

- *Vicarious trauma.* This refers to the acute and cumulative stress experienced when witnessing or hearing about the pain and suffering of others (Fisher, 2003). Sources of vicarious trauma include attending accident scenes, witnessing injury, dealing with traumatized witnesses, being continuously exposed to human misery, witnessing the assault or death of a fellow officer, and participating in investigations of assault, abuse, and homicide.

- *Not being able to discuss problems.* Most of the population does not understand the stressors associated with law enforcement work. Officers' experiences with offenders and victims may only be completely understood by colleagues, limiting officers' ability to discuss their problems.

- *Feeling judged or stigmatized by the public.* Uniformed members present a highly visible public profile. Policing obligations and duties are not always valued by society and officers often experience social stigma and negative judgments. The community may project their feelings onto the uniform rather than responding to the person wearing it.

Police personnel and others subjected to similar stressors may experience increased rates of clinical depression, suicide, anxiety disorders, post-traumatic stress disorder, substance abuse, addictions, and diminished self-esteem. Behavioural and interpersonal effects include social isolation and withdrawal, relationship problems, and increased rates of family dysfunction.

At a psychological level, these challenges may cause stress, personal identity conflicts, isolation, and alienation from society as a whole.

These effects may contribute to increased rates of absenteeism, sick-leave, long-term disability, early retirement or attrition, and labour–management friction.

Unseen Stressors

The duties of police officers may be dangerous and require bravery and heroism; or they may be tedious and require inordinate patience. The obvious stressors such as physical confrontations or gunplay are more easily recognized as being harmful. But the unseen social and psychological stressors can be equally debilitating. These unseen stressors are many-faceted. They include intrapersonal and interpersonal stressors; organizational stressors; and operational stressors that are inherent to the very nature of police duties.

Intrapersonal stress can occur when a person believes that his or her abilities do not coincide with his or her position in life. For example, an officer may believe that she should be working at a higher rank but, for some reason, has not achieved that rank. The greater the discrepancy between the person's perceived deserved status and his or her actual status, the greater will be the intrapersonal stress.

intrapersonal stress
stress that can occur when a person believes that his or her abilities do not coincide with his or her position in life

To address the problem of intrapersonal stress, realistic personal evaluation and objective, informed, outside opinions are used to identify unrealistic goals or performance levels beyond a person's ability. Strategies that may assist in alleviating intrapersonal stress include lowering of unrealistic expectations or raising the level of performance to be closer to the individual's perceived potential.

Organizational stress often emanates from the police service itself, including policies and procedures that govern and direct the officer's actions. These procedures often require copious and onerous amounts of paperwork. In many police services, street-level officers do not have much input into policies or procedures, even though these regulations directly affect them. Other organizational stressors include insufficient in-service training, compounded with a lack of promotional opportunities or rewards. Officers may perceive that they do not receive adequate organizational support and that the only time they are noticed is when they make a mistake and are reprimanded.

organizational stress
stress that emanates from the police service itself, including policies and procedures that govern and direct the officer's actions

The introduction of an expedited, simplified public complaints process may reinforce this perception of lack of organizational support. This process could be viewed by some officers as a betrayal of the traditionally internalized complaints process, where problems are resolved out of the public eye. Further, the public complaints process may be seen as an effort by administrative bodies to encourage the public to complain about trivial matters.

A study of municipal and provincial police officers in Ontario (Kohan & Mazmanian, 2003) focused on the organizational and operational stressors of police officers. Participants had an average age of 36.5 years and an average of 13 years' policing experience in a wide range of functions. There was no discernible difference in the replies of municipal or provincial police officers.

The study revealed that, as a group, officers were more stressed by operational stressors (dealing with the public) than by organizational stressors (dealing with the department). This overall finding was different when the officers' replies were divided into subgroups of patrol and supervisory officers. Patrol officers reported more operational stressors while supervisory officers reported more organizational stressors.

Part of the study identified some of the negative aspects of operational and organizational stressors. The most obvious was "burnout," which the study defined as "an extreme state of depleted resources that can result from chronic exposure to work stress." Burnout was examined from the perspective of emotional exhaustion (depleted mental energy and fatigue), depersonalization (cynicism toward the organization), and diminished personal accomplishment.

Officers who reported having more organizational hassles felt more emotionally exhausted and cynical toward the organization. The study concluded that these employees may be more inclined to leave policing or take more time off and that, when on the job, their contributions and efforts may be minimal.

Conversely, officers who reported positive organizational experiences tended to be more loyal employees who were willing to participate in organizational betterment.

This study, while not definitive, may indicate that organizational stress is a controllable variable in the cumulative stress experienced in policing. Fewer organizational stressors may reduce stress-related organizational problems such as absenteeism and poor work effort.

Although operational stress cannot be eliminated, there are stress reduction techniques that may assist officers.

One of the best strategies to reduce acute stress is to thoroughly prepare officers for situational encounters, such as armed suspect encounters or multiple victim occurrences. Training is one aspect where organizational behaviour can have a positive influence on the reduction of operational stress. An officer receiving adequate technical and interpersonal training may be less likely to suffer from critical incident stress and will likely be more confident and less indecisive in operational situations. Although it is not possible to prepare police officers for all potential encounters, preparation through classroom and scenario-based training can greatly assist with stress reduction and enhance officer safety. When faced with highly stressful situations, officers will most often revert to behaviours ingrained through training.

Health and Stress

Although training may assist with short-term stress reduction, it will not reduce the effects of long-term stress. Long-term coping strategies are the responsibility of individual officers. Proper eating habits and regular exercise are two of the most controllable and effective strategies available. Officers in good physical condition are usually more confident in their physical ability to effectively control a situation. Good health also allows the officer to recover more quickly from the unavoidable stressful encounters experienced in policing.

Good health benefits officers in another way. As discussed earlier, when an officer encounters a stressful situation, the stress response is triggered. The stress response prepares the body for intense physical activity through chemical and hormonal stimulation. However, stressful encounters in policing rarely result in all-out physical exertion, and the chemical compounds that the body produced are not significantly reduced after the encounter. These compounds, described earlier, may be caustic and cause damage at a cellular level. Physical exercise will help reduce this overabundance of unused compounds and help return the body to a more balanced state. Aerobic exercise appears to be best for this purpose.

The following are some suggestions to help officers keep their stress within tolerable levels (Greenstone & Leviton, 2002):

- Ensure proper nutrition.
- Get adequate sleep and don't rely on caffeine to get through the shift.
- Exercise regularly.
- Reduce intrapersonal stress through realistic assessments of your abilities and expectations.
- Schedule regular recreational and vacation times. Quality time spent on recreation can greatly reduce stress.
- Try to maintain an optimistic outlook.
- Set realistic goals for yourself.
- Recognize that you are responsible for your well-being.

Post-Traumatic Stress Disorder

Post-traumatic stress disorder (PTSD) occurs when a person is unable to recover from the physical, emotional, and psychological stress caused by exposure to a "psychologically traumatic event involving actual or threatened death or serious injury to self or others" (Canadian Mental Health Association, 2011). The event that triggers the disorder may be a violent personal assault, a car or plane accident, military combat, an industrial accident, or a natural disaster, such as an earthquake or hurricane. In other cases, seeing another person injured or killed has brought on the disorder.

The symptoms of PTSD usually appear within three months of the traumatic event. More rarely, they surface many years later. Recovery times vary. Some people recover in six months; other people require much longer. Symptoms of PTSD fall into three categories:

1. *Re-experiencing the event.* This is the chief characteristic of PTSD. The person experiences powerful, recurrent memories of the event, recurrent nightmares, or flashbacks that make him or her relive the traumatic experience.

2. *Avoidance and emotional numbing.* Persons with PTSD avoid scenarios that could remind them of the trauma. This behaviour is accompanied by

post-traumatic stress disorder (PTSD)
a disorder in which a person is unable to recover from physical, emotional, and psychological stress caused by exposure to a "psychologically traumatic event involving actual or threatened death or serious injury to self or others"

emotional numbing, which usually begins very soon after the traumatic event. The person may withdraw from friends and family members, lose interest in activities they used to enjoy, and have difficulty feeling emotions, especially emotions associated with intimacy. It is also common for sufferers to experience feelings of extreme guilt. In extreme cases, a person may enter a dissociative state, in which the person believes that he or she is reliving the event. The dissociative state may be as short as a few minutes or as long as several days. During this time, the person may act as if the event is happening all over again.

3. *Changes in sleeping patterns and increased alertness.* Insomnia is a common symptom. Some sufferers have difficulty concentrating and completing tasks. Increased aggression may also be a consequence of these changes.

The American Psychiatric Association identifies a diagnosis of PTSD as meeting the following conditions and symptoms.

1. The person must have been confronted with an event involving actual or threatened death or serious injury.

2. The traumatic event is re-experienced in at least one of the following ways:
   - recurrent, distressing recollections of the event;
   - recurrent nightmares of the event;
   - flashback episodes involving sensory perceptions of the incident; and
   - intense psychological distress upon exposure to cues resembling some aspect of the event.

3. The person persistently attempts to avoid re-experiencing the incident and exhibits at least three of the following signs and symptoms:
   - attempts to avoid thoughts, dialogues, or feelings associated with the event;
   - inability to recall important aspects of the traumatic event;
   - significantly diminished interest in previously enjoyed activities;
   - emotional and social detachment;
   - inability to react to situations within normal emotional ranges; and
   - pessimistic outlook on all aspects of life.

4. The person displays increased nervous system arousal indicated by
   - difficulty falling or staying asleep, and
   - irritability or angry outbursts.

5. The person is unable to maintain employment and social relationships, or engages in substance abuse brought about by psychological disturbances as a result of the disorder.

Who Can Develop Post-Traumatic Stress Disorder?

Post-traumatic stress disorder can be experienced by anyone who has gone through or witnessed an extremely traumatic event. In Canada, the risk of a person developing PTSD when exposed to trauma is estimated to be between 10 and 25 percent

(Whitney, 2010). There are differences in the types of traumas experienced by each gender. Women are more likely to experience interpersonal trauma such as sexual assault and childhood sexual assault, while men are more likely to experience physical violence, accidents, and witnessed violence.

Policing and Post-Traumatic Stress Disorder

Traumatic incidents that may lead to PTSD occur frequently in policing. They include losing a partner in the line of duty, having to take a life in the line of duty, being violently assaulted, attending occurrences where children have been killed, intervening in or witnessing a suicide, and attending motor vehicle collisions where severe injury or death resulted. This list is far from exhaustive.

Police officers vicariously and personally experience these types of traumatic events on a regular basis. Police are more likely to be exposed to such traumatic events than are others not involved in law enforcement. It is likely that at some point in their career, all police officers will be violently attacked. It is also likely that all officers will witness violent criminal acts. This frequent exposure to traumatic events increases the possibility that police officers will experience PTSD.

These traumatic events may be referred to as "critical incidents." One or more of these critical incidents may precipitate the initial stages of PTSD. The effects of PTSD may be difficult to identify as they are often accompanied by other conditions. The most common of these conditions are major depression, other anxiety disorders, and alcohol abuse or dependence.

As well, dizziness, chest pain, gastrointestinal complaints, and immune system problems may be linked to PTSD. These are often treated as self-contained illnesses; the link with PTSD will be revealed only if a patient volunteers information about a traumatic event, or if a doctor investigates a possible link with psychological trauma.

Without treatment, the condition is often permanent. The condition is extremely serious and may lead to personality changes, illness, and, if ignored, suicide. Proper treatment must be provided by a knowledgeable and skilled mental health professional.

Treatments for Post-Traumatic Stress Disorder

Treatment for PTSD can involve psychological intervention as well as medications. Psychological intervention is particularly helpful in treating "re-experiencing" symptoms and social or vocational problems caused by PTSD.

The main treatment for PTSD is **cognitive behavioural therapy**. This involves examining the thought processes associated with the trauma, the way memories return, and how people react to them. The goal of therapy is to accelerate the natural healing or forgetting process. Discussing memories of the trauma in a safe environment may help the sufferer become less frightened or depressed by those memories. This is called desensitization, which is often combined with cognitive behavioural therapy.

Exposure therapy, in which the patient relives the experience under controlled conditions in order to work through the trauma, can also be beneficial.

cognitive behavioural therapy
psychological treatment to change maladaptive thoughts, feelings, beliefs, and habits

Most people with PTSD will benefit from taking antidepressant medications, whether or not clinical depression accompanies their PTSD. These medications are particularly helpful in treating the avoidance and arousal symptoms, such as social withdrawal and angry outbursts, as well as any anxiety and depression. Other medications may be used to assist the person in re-establishing regular sleep patterns.

Factors That Contribute to Post-Traumatic Stress Disorder

For PTSD to occur, the stress caused by the critical incident must be severe and exceed the officer's coping abilities. The severity required to induce PTSD varies from person to person. A situation that one officer may find overwhelming, intolerable, disgusting, or terrifying may not have such a severe effect on another. Note that PTSD does not always manifest itself immediately. The symptoms may not become noticeable until several months after the traumatic event.

The factors that may contribute to PTSD include the following:

- *The proximity of the person to the event.* The more involved the person is in the event, the more likely it is that the person will be affected by the disorder.
- *The person's mental, emotional, and physical state.* If the person enters the traumatic situation in a weakened state, he or she is more likely to suffer serious negative effects from the resulting stress.
- *The significance of the event to the person.* Some events may have special significance to the officer. For example, the event may awaken a childhood memory of a traumatic event or arouse latent responses in the officer that stem from unresolved losses or traumas of a similar type.
- *The person's general character.* A person who can effectively handle large amounts of stress has probably developed his or her coping mechanisms to the point that susceptibility to PTSD is diminished.
- *The amount of help that the person receives after experiencing the traumatic event.* Support from fellow workers, superiors, and, if required, mental health professionals can help alleviate the symptoms before they become problematic.

Reducing the Effects of Post-Traumatic Stress Disorder

To help reduce the effects of critical incident stress and PTSD, police services have developed critical incident stress debriefings. These debriefings are primarily confidential discussions about the critical incident that emphasize emotional venting and expression of reactions to the incident. Advice on how to handle the stress may be given, or the officer may simply elect to express his or her feelings about the incident. The major goals of these debriefings are to reduce the impact of the incident, expedite the officer's recovery, and reduce the possibility of PTSD.

Over the past decade, psychologists have evaluated treatments for PTSD. The popular one-session procedure, referred to as a critical incident debriefing, appears to be of little benefit in reducing psychological distress. However, brief cognitive behavioural therapy (five to six sessions) provided to very distressed people shortly after a traumatic event appears helpful in reducing PTSD symptoms. Also, short-term (8 to 30 hours) behavioural and cognitive therapies have been shown to alleviate PTSD symptoms in chronic sufferers.

Common therapeutic components of successful treatments include giving people the opportunity to repeatedly describe the traumatic event and their emotional responses to it. Assistance with stress-coping skills helps patients examine concerns about personal safety ("I can never be safe again") and allows them to gradually re-establish more realistic beliefs about personal safety through changes in thinking patterns ("It is safe to go into tall buildings again").

PTSD does not disappear by itself. If you recognize the symptoms in yourself or a fellow officer, get help. Ignoring PTSD may lead to the loss of a job, relationship problems, personality changes, alcohol and drug abuse, and even suicide.

Strategies for Coping with Post-Traumatic Stress Disorder

If an officer has been diagnosed with PTSD and has received the appropriate professional assistance, there are still some strategies he or she can use to deal with the condition (National Centre for War-Related PTSD, 2006):

- *Eat healthy foods.* A poor diet contributes to increased stress.
- *Get regular exercise.* Exercise, especially aerobic exercise, reduces harmful chemicals in the officer's body and helps him or her relax.
- *Follow a daily routine.* Establishing a daily routine helps the officer feel in control and function well.
- *Set realistic goals and establish priorities.* Some people find it helpful to keep lists of tasks, which they can check off as they complete them. This provides a sense of accomplishment. Establishing priorities helps the sufferer be realistic about what is and what is not achievable.
- *Set aside a specific time each day to think about the trauma.* The officer should give himself or herself permission to think about the event at a designated time—and not think about it at other times. Otherwise, the sufferer may find himself or herself dealing with upsetting thoughts and feelings the entire day.
- *Ask for support.* The officer should seek support from family, friends, or the community. Asking for help is not a sign of weakness.
- *Learn more about PTSD.* Understanding the condition will help sufferers deal with their experiences and problems.
- *Care for loved ones and ensure they know they are valued.* The officer should clarify feelings and assumptions with loved ones to avoid misunderstandings. He or she should be supportive and patient with their children.
- *Acknowledge any unresolved issues that relate to the condition.* For example, admissions of fear and anger will aid in recovery.
- *Focus on strengths.* Drawing on strengths and coping skills will help the officer deal with ongoing problems.
- *Take responsibility.* The officer should not use the PTSD condition as an excuse for mistreating others.

- *Remember that there are other people with PTSD.* There is comfort in knowing that there are others who are dealing with the same problems.

Learning Activity 1.2

Many police services use critical incident stress debriefings as a method of assisting officers with dealing with stressors encountered within the execution of their duties. The process uses peer counsellors at the initial stage of intervention. Professional assistance, if needed, is available through an employee assistance plan.

1. There has been some evidence to suggest that peer counsellors are often more effective when intervening in the early stages of stress reactions than are professional counsellors. Based on your understanding of the chapter, do you believe that this suggestion is true? Explain.

2. The financial costs of peer and professional counselling are borne by police services through employee assistance plans. Based on your understanding of the chapter, why would police services bear the cost of such services? Explain.

KEY TERMS

acute stress

cognitive behavioural therapy

conflict

crisis

cumulative stress

fight or flight response

organizational stress

intervention

intrapersonal stress

person in crisis

post-traumatic stress disorder (PTSD)

stress

stressor

REFERENCES

American Psychiatric Association. (2000). *Diagnostic and statistical manual of mental disorders* (4th ed.). Washington, DC: Author.

Canadian Mental Health Association. (2011). *Post traumatic stress disorder.* Retrieved from http://www.cmha.ca/bins/content_page.asp?cid=3-94-97.

Canadian Psychological Association. Koch, W.J. (1994). *Did you know that ... Psychology works for posttraumatic stress disorder (PTSD).* Retrieved from Oshawa Psychological and Counselling Services website: http://www.oshawapsychologist.com/pdf/ptsd.pdf.

Fisher, P. (2003). *Workplace stress & trauma in policing: Sources, outcomes & implications.* Review document prepared for the Canadian Professional Police Association (CPPA) Annual General Meeting. Edmonton, AB.

Greenstone, J.L., & Leviton, S.C. (2002). *Elements of crisis intervention: Crises and how to respond to them.* Toronto: Thomson Learning.

Kohan, A., & Mazmanian, D. (2003). Police work, burnout, and pro-organizational behavior: A consideration of daily work experiences. *Criminal Justice and Behavior, 30,* 559–583.

Mitchell, J., & Bray, G. (1990). *Emergency services stress.* Scarborough, ON: Prentice Hall.

National Centre for War-Related PTSD. (2006). *Post-traumatic stress disorder (PTSD) and war related stress.* Retrieved from Veteran Affairs Canada website: http://www.veterans.gc.ca/pdf/mental-health/ptsd_warstress_e.pdf.

Pedro, K. (2003, March 30). Assaults worrying city cops; more than half of city patrol officers have been assaulted on duty in the last year. *The London Free Press,* p. A1.

Whitney, D. (2010). *Post traumatic stress disorder.* Discussion paper prepared for the Workplace Safety and Insurance Appeals Tribunal. Retrieved from http://www.wsiat.on.ca/english/mlo/index.htm.

EXERCISES

TRUE OR FALSE

_F_ 1. Stress reactions are always obvious.

_F_ 2. Stress cannot cause serious health problems.

_F_ 3. Stress affects only the body, not the mind.

_F_ 4. Work-related stress cannot affect one's home life.

_F_ 5. The effects of stress can be eliminated from one's life.

_T_ 6. The effects of stress may not be felt for several months.

_F_ 7. Persons in crisis situations will exhibit predictable behaviours.

_F_ 8. Only mentally unstable police officers suffer from the effects of stress.

MULTIPLE CHOICE

1. Stress is

    a. a response to a real danger

    b. a response to a perceived danger

    (c.) a response to a real or imagined danger

    d. a response to poor physical conditioning

2. The acute stress reaction is

    a. an emotional reaction

    b. a physical reaction

    (c.) a psychological reaction

    d. a physical and psychological reaction

3. The best way to handle stress is to
   a. use alcohol and illegal drugs
   b. learn proper stress reduction techniques
   c. ignore it
   d. use prescription drugs such as tranquilizers

4. The fight or flight response allows the body to
   a. perform at a higher level mentally and physically
   b. combat a threat
   c. escape from a threat
   d. all of the above

5. The intervention model most suited to police interventions is
   a. the cognitive model
   b. the psychosocial transition model
   c. the equilibrium model
   d. the anti-psychotic model

6. Which of the following physical symptoms of acute stress requires immediate corrective action?
   a. chest pain
   b. difficulty breathing
   c. excessively high blood pressure
   d. collapse from exhaustion
   e. all of the above

7. Which of the following cognitive signs of acute stress requires immediate corrective action?
   a. decreased alertness
   b. difficulty making decisions
   c. hyperalertness
   d. mental confusion
   e. all of the above

8. Which of the following emotional signs of acute stress requires immediate corrective action?
   a. panic reactions
   b. shock-like state
   c. phobic reaction
   d. general loss of control
   e. all of the above

9. Which of the following behavioural changes resulting from acute stress requires immediate corrective action?

   a. change in speech patterns

   b. excessive angry outbursts

   c. crying spells

   d. antisocial acts

   e. all of the above

SHORT ANSWER

1. Is police intervention always the best way to help a person in crisis? Explain your answer.

2. List five behaviours that may indicate that a person is in crisis.

3. Why is officer safety a major concern when dealing with a person in crisis?

4. Briefly describe post-traumatic stress disorder (PTSD).

5. List five factors that may contribute to PTSD.

6. How do critical incident stress debriefings help officers cope with the after-effects of highly stressful situations?

7. Explain intrapersonal stress.

8. Identify two strategies that may be used to reduce levels of intrapersonal stress.

9. Explain organizational stress.

10. Explain operational stress.

The Nature of Conflict

2

INTRODUCTION

Recall from Chapter 1 that a conflict occurs when the goals or motives of the involved parties are incompatible. The incompatibility of differing values, attitudes, or personalities may lead to a conflict. A conflict may occur between a law enforcement officer and one or more parties involved in a dispute, or it may occur between two or more parties not involving an officer.

A conflict may follow a predictable course, progressing from frustration to annoyance to anger to rage to violence. These stages may be identified, although not with complete accuracy, by noting the verbal and non-verbal cues of the subject. Frustration may be demonstrated by a subject's lack of verbal and non-verbal responses. Annoyance may be demonstrated by verbal expressions such as "You're bothering me. Go away." Anger may be demonstrated through more forceful verbal and non-verbal messages such as "Get away from me now!" Rage may be identified through verbal and non-verbal messages. Verbal threats such as "Get away from me now or I will hurt you!" accompanied by threatening physical gestures such as fist shaking indicate rage. Violence may be identified when a physical confrontation has occurred, either between two or more subjects or between an officer and one or more subjects. In some situations, particularly those involving people with short tempers, no verbal warning will be given and a conflict will move from frustration immediately to violence.

Not all consequences of conflict are negative. The conflict can have positive outcomes if managed properly and not allowed to develop into a crisis. Recall from Chapter 1 that a crisis occurs when the involved parties are no longer able to deal with the stress of the situation and need assistance to prevent further escalation. Proper conflict management can bring about the following positive outcomes. The opposing parties may change their perspectives or develop a greater respect for differing perspectives. The

CHAPTER OBJECTIVES

After completing this chapter, you should be able to:

- Understand the nature of anger and the techniques that police officers can use to manage their anger.
- Identify the five conflict management styles and know how to select the conflict management style or styles best suited to a particular conflict situation.
- Identify basic criteria for effective communication in a conflict or crisis situation, including the use of proxemics and effective listening.
- Identify effective verbal communication techniques for intervention in a crisis or conflict situation.
- Describe the common personality traits of violent persons and the visible signs of a potentially violent person.
- Understand the potential causes of violence and know how to predict, prepare for, and defuse violent encounters.
- Apply effective communication techniques for de-escalating conflict and crisis situations.
- Understand the role of mediation in conflict resolution.

conflict may reveal underlying issues that may be discussed. Discussion may lead to enhanced interpersonal communication skills. This could lead to decreased incidents of future conflict.

Positive outcomes rely on the ability of the involved parties or, where intervention is necessary, the abilities of the intervening officer, to prevent escalation of the conflict.

Failure to effectively manage the conflict may lead to negative consequences. The involved parties may be more concerned with defending their positions than resolving the dispute, leading to a deterioration in the relationship between the parties. If the conflict is allowed to escalate to the point where the fight or flight response is evoked, detrimental physical, cognitive, and emotional consequences may occur. Even if this response is not experienced, prolonged conflict is fatiguing.

During a conflict, many emotions are experienced. Frustration occurs when one of the involved parties is unable to influence the position of another party involved in the conflict. Frustration can eventually, or in some cases, immediately, lead to anger. The potential for violent reactions as a result of anger increases with prolonged and unresolved conflict.

Anger

Anger is a normal human emotion. It is an emotional state that can vary from mild irritation to rage. Anger can be caused by both external and internal events. Like other emotions, it is accompanied by physiological and biological changes similar to critical incident stress reactions. It is a natural response to threats. Anger often evokes aggressive feelings and behaviours similar to those evoked by the fight or flight response.

Some people are easily and intensely angered. They may display their anger by shouting, screaming, gesturing, or committing violent acts. There are also those who don't show their anger but are chronically irritable. People who are easily angered generally have a low tolerance for frustration. They feel that they should not have to be subjected to frustration, inconvenience, or annoyance. They may become infuriated if the situation seems somehow unjust—for example, if they are corrected for a minor mistake. Angry people tend to be demanding. When their demands aren't met, their disappointment turns to anger, which is often communicated through swearing or speaking in highly descriptive terms that reflect their thoughts.

The causes for such low tolerance have not been clearly identified. It may be genetic or physiological. Family background may play a role. It may be a learned response. Easily angered persons may come from families that are chaotic and not skilled at emotional communication and have difficulty controlling their angry responses.

Anger Management for Police Officers

People use a variety of both conscious and unconscious processes to deal with their angry feelings. The three main approaches are expressing, suppressing, and calming. Expressing your anger in an assertive manner is the healthiest way to express anger. Being assertive doesn't mean being pushy or demanding; it means being respectful of yourself and others and communicating clearly what your needs are and how they can be met. However, expressing anger is seldom the best course of action for law enforcement officers. Expressing anger, even assertively, may be viewed by the involved parties as being partial or biased. This view will interfere with effective communication.

It may be necessary at times to suppress anger to help foster a more effective communication atmosphere. The objective of this tactic is to convert your suppressed anger into more constructive behaviour. However, there are problems with this approach. Suppressed anger may accumulate within and cause health problems such as hypertension or depression. It can lead to unreasonable expressions of anger, or the suppressed anger can cause the bearer to develop a personality that seems perpetually cynical and hostile.

A healthier way to deal with anger involves calming your outward behaviour and internal responses. The goal is to reduce both the emotional feelings and the physiological arousal that anger causes. Taking immediate steps such as using deep breathing and relaxing imagery can help manage the feelings of anger. Such actions should be undertaken only when safety concerns have been satisfied. The primary concern must be officer safety.

The nature of law enforcement makes it unlikely that officers will be able to avoid the situations that cause anger but they can learn to control their angry reactions.

Relaxation tools, such as deep breathing and relaxing imagery, can help calm down angry feelings. Here are some simple steps you can try:

- Breathe deeply from your diaphragm; breathing from your chest won't relax you. Your midsection should expand and contract as you breathe.
- Slowly repeat a calming word or phrase. Repeat it to yourself while breathing deeply.
- Use imagery; visualize a relaxing experience, from either your memory or your imagination.
- Use slow rhythmic exercises such as those used in yoga and tai chi to relax your muscles. These can make you feel much calmer.
- Make sure you have some personal time scheduled each day when you will have time to relax.

There is a belief within the law enforcement culture that every problem has a solution. This isn't true. In fact, law enforcement officers cannot provide solutions for the vast majority of problems they encounter. There are many situations where the conflict is deeply ingrained or the involved persons are not serious about finding a solution for their problems.

Intervention by law enforcement officers is often referred to as a "band-aid solution." The immediate conflict may be addressed on the surface, but the problem has not been healed. This inability to solve problems can lead to frustration, possibly leading to anger. A good method to help manage this frustration is to not focus on finding the solution to the problem, but rather to focus on how well you handled and faced the conflict. Resolve to do your best; do not punish yourself if a solution cannot be reached. If you deal with each incident with your best intentions and efforts, you will be less likely to lose patience and become frustrated.

CONFLICT MANAGEMENT STYLES

The Thomas-Kilmann Conflict Mode Instrument, frequently used in conflict resolution training, identifies five different modes, or styles, that people use to handle conflict (Thomas & Kilmann, 1974). Sometimes, people use more than one style in a given conflict situation. The styles we choose depend on many variables, including our basic disposition, our personality, our environment, and where we are in our professional careers. No matter which mode is used, effective communication is essential to manage a conflict. Effective communication requires that you pay attention to the verbal and non-verbal messages that you are relaying. Pay close attention to your own messages and to the verbal and non-verbal messages of the involved parties. This will greatly assist in identifying problems and de-escalating the potential for violence.

In addition, we each have a dominant conflict management style. A self-assessment instrument is provided in the Exercises section at the end of the chapter to help you identify your dominant style.

The five conflict management styles are as follows: avoiding, accommodating, competing, compromising, and collaborating. Table 2.1 compares these five styles, outlines the advantages and disadvantages of each, and describes the situations in which they may be used in policing.

SELECTING SUITABLE CONFLICT MANAGEMENT STYLES

As noted above, you may need to use different styles within the same situation. The following are some factors that influence which styles you should choose:

1. *Self-concept.* Do you think your thoughts, feelings, and opinions are worth being heard? Your opinion of yourself affects how you approach conflict.

2. *Expectations.* Do you believe that the other person wants to resolve the conflict?

3. *Situation.* Where is the conflict occurring? Is the conflict personal or professional?

4. *Position.* What is your relationship status with the person with whom you are in conflict? For example, is the person a peer, subordinate, friend, or client?

5. *Knowledge.* Which styles do you know? Knowledge of conflict management techniques developed through study and practice will aid your ability to determine which conflict management styles are appropriate in a particular situation.

6. *Practice.* Which styles have you practised? In the course of your duties you will gain conflict management experience. Practice will enhance your ability to use all five conflict modes effectively and will help you to determine which conflict styles are most effective to resolve the conflict.

Table 2.1   Comparison of Conflict Management Styles

	Avoiding	Accommodating	Competing	Compromising	Collaborating
Description	The avoider • is usually low on the assertiveness scale and low on the cooperativeness scale • doesn't take care of his or her needs and/or the needs of others involved in the conflict.	The accommodator • is usually low on the assertiveness scale and high on the cooperativeness scale • doesn't take care of his or her needs • sacrifices personal needs to cooperate and satisfy the other person.	The competitor • is usually high on the assertiveness scale and low on the cooperativeness scale • takes care of his or her needs first • cares very little for the needs of others • does not try to cooperate • wants to win.	The compromiser • is usually at the midpoint on the assertiveness scale and the cooperativeness scale • tries to find a middle ground by taking care of his or her needs as well as the needs of others • tries to cooperate, but not at his or her personal expense.	The collaborator • is usually high on the assertiveness scale and high on the cooperativeness scale • takes care of his or her needs as well as the needs of others without compromising, or giving something up • tries to understand where the other person is coming from so that a win–win situation is achieved, where neither party loses anything • tries to achieve an optimum result so that both sides get what they want and negative feelings are minimized.

(Table 2.1 is concluded on the next page.)

Table 2.1   Concluded

	Avoiding	Accommodating	Competing	Compromising	Collaborating
Appropriateness for use in policing/ Advantages	Sometimes appropriate, as in the following situations: • when the issue is trivial • when confrontation will hurt a working relationship • when disruption outweighs benefit of conflict resolution • when gathering information is more important than immediate action • when others can more effectively resolve the conflict • when time constraints demand a delay.	Generally ineffective for law enforcement purposes, but may be used in situations when it may be appropriate to feign accommodation to achieve specific purposes, such as situational control. Advantages: • minimizes emotional injury when an individual is outmatched • helps to maintain relationships.	Not an effective style to resolve conflict, but may be necessary in some law enforcement situations, as in the following situations: • when there is a potential for violence • when the conflict involves personal differences that are difficult to change • when developing intimate or supportive relationships is not critical • when conflict resolution is urgent and it is vital that a decision be made quickly • when unpopular decisions need to be implemented.	If there is no risk of escalation and an offence has not been committed, could be used in the following situations: • when important or complex issues leave no clear or simple solutions • when conflicting parties are equal in power and have strong interests in different solutions.	Appropriate for use in the following situations: • when maintaining relationships is important • when time is not a concern • when trying to gain commitment through consensus building. Advantage: • can be very effective.
Disadvantages	• conflicts remain unresolved	• the accommodator may feel resentment because his or her own needs are not satisfied	• may breed hostility among those whose needs have not been met	• no one is ever really satisfied • less than optimal solutions get implemented	• requires a lot of time and energy

Note: This table is not the Thomas-Kilmann Conflict Mode Instrument (TKI). For more information on the TKI, visit www.kilmann.com/conflict.html.

Source: Adapted from Thomas & Kilmann (1974).

Practice will also augment your ability to change styles as necessary while engaged in a conflict.

7. *Communication skills.* Do you posses the necessary communication skills to use a particular style? The essence of conflict resolution and conflict management is the ability to communicate effectively. People who use effective communication will resolve their conflicts with greater ease and success. This topic is discussed in greater detail under the heading "Communication in a Conflict Situation," below.

DECIDING WHETHER TO INTERVENE

Conflict may be viewed as either something positive that can be worked through or something negative to be avoided and ignored at all costs. In your job, you will experience both the negative and positive outcomes of conflicts. Experience will help you predict the likelihood of positive and negative outcomes in given situations. Such predictions are never completely accurate. However, an experienced officer who is knowledgeable and skilled in conflict management techniques can usually predict outcomes with better than average certainty. There are times when you have a choice whether to engage in or to avoid a conflict. Consider the following variables when deciding whether to intervene or to not intervene in a conflict.

Relationship with the Involved Parties

The importance of the working/personal relationship often dictates whether you will engage in a conflict. If you value the person and/or the relationship, going through the process of conflict resolution may be important. Conversely, avoiding a confrontation, particularly when the issue is trivial, may preserve the relationship. It is possible that the conflict may involve a colleague, but police officers are more likely to be involved in a conflict with parties previously unknown. In these situations, the long-term relationship is likely to be unimportant to you. Engagement in such conflicts is generally not optional, unless it is unsafe to engage.

Requirement or Obligation to Intervene

During personal interactions, you may choose to not engage in a conflict regarding issues that are not personally important. However, in your job you may be required to intervene in conflicts, even if the issues in conflict are not meaningful to you. For example, if the issue is a breach of a regulation or law that it is your job to enforce, ethical and professional obligations require that you intervene.

Time and Energy Constraints and Considerations

The reality of law enforcement is that conflict is a common occurrence. In fact, conflict will likely occur at some point during each shift. The conflict management styles that you choose to deal with the situation may depend upon how much time is available and how much energy you have to focus on the conflict. Prioritizing your efforts may be necessary. This does not mean that you should try to assist in only select situations, but that you may have to choose the styles of conflict management that are appropriate to the seriousness and complexity of the situation. If, after obtaining information about the situation, you determine that the conflict is trivial or not a matter that can be managed by intervention, you may not want to futilely expend your energies.

However, you must consider whether you are avoiding the conflict for other reasons. If your avoidance is based on reasons such as being too tired to bother with trivial conflicts, or because the matter is unimportant to you personally, carefully consider the consequences. The stress caused by such actions may cause you future problems.

Potential Consequences of Intervention

Prior to engaging in a conflict, try to think about anticipated consequences of your intervention, both positive and negative. After analyzing potential consequences, determine whether you are prepared to engage in the conflict. Do you foresee more positive consequences than negative? Identification of mostly positive outcomes with little chance of negative outcomes may indicate that it is appropriate to engage in the conflict. A negative consequence that is always possible is a violent reaction toward you. Thorough preparation and training in recognizing potentially violent persons will help reduce the likelihood or severity of a violent response. If your safety cannot be satisfied and there are no immediate safety concerns for the involved parties, you may choose to not engage. Furthermore, if you determine that the situation is too dangerous to continue engagement, disengagement is always an option while awaiting assistance.

COMMUNICATION IN A CONFLICT SITUATION

Police officers rely on their communication skills to define and defuse problems in conflict situations. The most important tool in such instances is your ability to observe what is happening and relay accurate information to the parties involved. Your verbal and non-verbal communication skills are important tools for controlling the incident and mediating disagreements.

The following are some basic criteria for more effective communication in a conflict or crisis situation:

- *Use of proxemics.* Proxemics is the study of the spatial separation between individuals within the context of communication. Understanding and paying attention to the use of space as a communication and safety tool can lead to more effective management of conflict situations. Proxemics identifies four kinds of space or distance:
  - □ *Intimate distance* ranges from contact to approximately 18 inches. This distance is reserved for intimate relationships. When a stranger enters into this intimate zone, a person may feel threatened. Deliberate invasion of intimate space may result in an angry reaction.
  - □ *Personal space* ranges from 18 inches to 4 feet. This is the space in which friends are allowed. Uninvited strangers may increase the person's stress level and hinder communication.

☐ *Social distance* is the space ranging from 4 feet to 12 feet and is the distance in which impersonal communication takes place.

☐ *Public distance* is a physical separation of 12 feet or more. This distance allows the subject to safely decide whether or not he or she will interact with persons within this zone.

The distance you use to communicate with a subject will depend greatly upon the level of threat that may be present and observations of the level of comfort being exhibited by a non-combative subject. If the subject does not exhibit indications of stress when approached by an officer, and safety issues have been addressed, personal space may be the distance that will be most effective for conflict management purposes. Communication from a social distance may be required if there are indications of stress when entering the subject's personal space. For your own safety, you must always be aware of your physical proximity to the involved parties.

• *Calmness.* The presence of police officers can sometimes escalate a conflict. Because the parties feel safe and protected with officers present, they may resort to violence against their antagonist. You must ensure that nothing is said or done that may inadvertently arouse antagonism or provoke further conflict. If a party is shouting, you may decide to allow him or her to continue as long as the shouting will not inflame the situation. Such venting may allow some of the party's hostility to be harmlessly alleviated.

• *Honesty.* Tell the parties why you are present. Explain that you are there to help if possible and will use all reasonable means to resolve the situation, but will physically intervene if necessary.

• *Positive atmosphere.* Whenever possible, try to create a positive atmosphere. People are more likely to discuss their disagreements if they believe that a solution to the problem exists. You should maintain a professional bearing and treat everyone present with equal respect and in as dignified a manner as possible.

• *Non-verbal communication.* Your body language should communicate as much openness as safety allows. Openness may encourage dialogue. Assess your own body language: Are your fists clenched? Are your arms crossed across your chest? Are you staring directly at the person? Eye contact can convey support, interest, or authority, but prolonged direct eye contact may be viewed as threatening. Reducing direct eye contact may decrease your position from that of a figure of authority to that of a helper. This sometimes may be helpful by allowing the parties to communicate directly with each other rather than through you. Never compromise your safety by completely turning your attention away from the subject.

Remember to monitor your behaviour to ensure that your non-verbal messages are consistent with your verbal messages. If your non-verbal behaviour is conveying a message that is inconsistent with your verbal message, your non-verbal message will usually be taken as a more reliable indication of your feelings and intentions.

Keep in mind that the non-verbal portion of your message may be used by the involved parties to evaluate your ability as an officer to assist in the dispute. If your body language does not tell the persons that you are in control and able to assist with the dispute, your intervention will not be successful. You must present a calm, authoritative demeanour, ensuring that your behaviour toward the involved parties is not aggressive or condescending.

This may be a difficult task. Situations of conflict intervention are emotionally charged with people often on the edge of losing control. There may be shouting and abusive language. As a result, you may experience a stress reaction, which may manifest itself physically and visibly through symptoms such as a cracking voice, flushed face, pounding heart, increased breathing rate, and shaking hands. These symptoms may mistakenly be interpreted by those involved as signs that you are unable to effectively deal with the situation. Although the reaction is not controllable, some of the symptoms of the reaction may be controlled (but not alleviated) through recognition that the reaction is normal and through the application of deep-breathing techniques where the situation allows. Take slow, deep, deliberate breaths to assist in controlling your voice and your breathing rate. Inhale and exhale slowly, taking care not to hyperventilate. A few breaths should suffice. Controlling the volume and pitch of your voice demonstrates that you are in control of a situation, and can be used to convey empathy, a positive attitude, or authority.

However, if the situation has become violent or violence is imminent, your first priority is to intervene and you may not have the time to use this breathing technique.

- *Control.* Be sure that you do not argue with the parties. Arguing may suggest a loss of objectivity. Arguments directed toward you should be dealt with by a calm reply such as "My beliefs are irrelevant in this situation." As an officer, you must remain in command of the situation and should maintain control of the conversation. This may be accomplished through verbal direction and non-verbal communication such as eye contact.

- *Information gathering.* Your questions should be clear and directed to the person who possesses the information that you require.

  You are there to provide help. Therefore, you must clearly understand the subject's responses. Paraphrase a subject's responses to determine whether you have understood the responses correctly, but at the same time avoid interpreting or explaining the feelings of the other person. You may cause the person to become defensive or frustrated if you incorrectly interpret his or her feelings. Such interpretations, even if correct, may cause the involved parties to believe that you are feeling sympathetic toward one of the parties and therefore may have a biased opinion. The other parties involved in the conflict may not offer further information if it is thought that you have a predetermined opinion of the incident.

- *Unbiased perspective.* Be careful not to judge the parties. As long as their actions and ideas are legal, you should not criticize them or interject personal opinions. Control your non-verbal forms of expression. Non-verbal messages can relay information to a person more quickly than verbal messages and can send mixed messages that disclose your beliefs, biases, or prejudices. Do not stereotype groups of people on the basis of their behaviour or physical appearance. Stereotyping may lead to prejudicial attitudes and behaviours toward the identified group. If you display any type of prejudice, it is not possible to develop a positive communication atmosphere.

Learning Activity 2.1

In the following scenario, you are a police officer responding to a disturbance call. You are responding to the call with another police officer.

Upon arrival you are invited into the home by the homeowner, Mike Mains. Mr. Mains tells you, "I am glad to see you. Perhaps you can help settle this disagreement." You tell him that you will help if you can. You ask Mr. Mains if there is anyone else in the home. He tells you that his wife, Shelia Mains, is in the living room. There is no one else in the home.

You ask if you can look around to satisfy yourself that there is no one else in the home. Mr. Mains tells you, "Go ahead. There's no one else here."

You look around. Your partner stays with Mr. and Mrs. Mains. You do not find any other persons in the home. You return to the living room. You ask Mr. and Mrs. Mains to tell you what had happened before your arrival.

Mr. Mains tells you, "Like I said. Can you help me with this problem?" You ask him to describe the problem. Mr. Mains begins. "My wife has a problem with me smoking cigars. I buy a cigar every Friday after work and smoke it on Saturday evening while I watch the hockey game. She told me that it stinks and that I should be more considerate. I work sixty hours a week in a hardware store. I don't drink alcohol or smoke cigarettes. Once a week I like to smoke a cigar. Is that too much to ask?"

Mrs. Mains interjects. "You are polluting my air. You have been smoking a cigar every week for the past forty years. You have probably given me cancer!"

You glance at your partner. He is looking out a window at the street.

Mrs. Mains continues to speak. "You have been glued to that television every Saturday night for the past twenty years. Don't you think that I would like to go out sometime?"

Mr. Mains replies. "I'm not stopping you from going out. Leave right now if you want to!"

Mrs. Mains replies. "A husband should be with his wife. He should want to take her out in public!"

Mr. Mains replies. "My days of going out are long over. I don't drink and I don't like music, so where would we go? I have asked you many times to go to a hockey game with me but you always say no!"

Mrs. Mains replies. "Then I will have to find a male companion to escort me in public."

Mr. Mains replies. "Go ahead! That would be a load off my mind. Maybe I will find a young lady that likes to watch hockey games and invite her over when you go out with your companion!"

Mrs. Mains replies. "You're sixty-two years old! What would a young girl want with you?"

Mr. Mains replies. "I'm in pretty good shape for my age. I know that I'm about a hundred pounds overweight and have no hair, but if it wasn't for this hernia, I could have any young girl that I wanted!"

Mrs. Mains replies. "Don't be so stupid. With your heart condition you would die if a young girl paid any attention to you!"

Mr. Mains replies. "I'm doing fine with my heart medication! I could show any girl a good time!"

You are having a difficult time concealing your reaction to the humour of the situation. Your partner has turned away and is audibly trying to stifle a laugh.

Mr. Mains looks at you and then at your partner. He asks, "What the hell is wrong with you? Do you think this is a joke? This is not why I allowed you into my home! Get out before I throw you out!"

You try to compose yourself, but are only partially successful.

Mrs. Mains states, "You are a disgrace to the police service! You are laughing at people that asked for your help. I have never been so insulted!"

Mr. Mains gets out of his chair and shouts at you. "Get out of my home! You are both disgraceful and insolent!"

You apologize and tell him that you are sorry that you behaved as you did. As you speak, your partner audibly laughs.

Mr. Mains picks up a knife that was sitting on a plate beside his chair. He shouts. "I told you to get out of my house! You have insulted me and my wife! Get out! Get out!"

You shout at Mr. Mains. "Put down the knife! Do it now!"

He replies. "Get out of my house!"

He continues to approach you with the knife in his hand. Mrs. Mains picks up a lamp and joins her husband shouting, "Get out! Get out!"

The family dog that until now was sitting at the entrance door begins to growl. You turn and see the dog slowly walking toward you. It has its teeth bared and is growling.

You and your partner take out pepper spray. You face Mr. and Mrs. Mains while your partner faces the dog.

You again shout at Mr. and Mrs. Mains. "Put the weapons on the floor! Do it now!" You hear a dog yelp. Your partner shouts, "I sprayed the dog!"

Mr. Mains shouts. "You killed my dog!" He lunges toward you. You spray him with pepper spray.

He falls to the floor. Mrs. Mains drops the lamp and kneels on the floor beside her husband.

"You killed him! You killed him!"

You tell her that he will be all right. She is crying. "He's not breathing!"

You look for your partner. He tells you that the dog ran outside through the dog door. You turn to Mr. and Mrs. Mains. You check Mr. Mains. He is not breathing. You start to administer CPR.

Mrs. Mains starts pulling you by your hair. She shouts, "You killed him!" Your partner restrains Mrs. Mains. He calls for an ambulance. You administer CPR until the arrival of the paramedics.

The paramedics attend to Mr. Mains, but are unable to revive him. He is transported to the hospital. He is pronounced dead upon arrival. An autopsy reveals that Mr. Mains died from a heart attack.

1. What did the body language of the two officers communicate to the Mains in this scenario?

2. Was the force used in this scenario excessive?

3. Do you believe that the officers would be held criminally or civilly liable in this scenario?

4. What other communication or procedural "mistakes" were made by the officers in this scenario?

Effective Listening

You must employ active listening techniques to obtain accurate information. **Active listening** means devoting complete attention to a message to ensure full and accurate understanding. The techniques for active listening are as follows:

active listening
devoting complete attention to a message to ensure full and accurate understanding

- *Concentrate on the message.* It may be necessary to make a conscious effort to concentrate on verbal messages. Because we think faster than we speak, we tend to try to predict what a person will say, instead of focusing solely on the information being relayed.

- *Show empathy and acceptance.* Empathy is an attempt to see the situation from the perspective of those involved in the conflict. Empathy allows you to view the problem from the viewpoint of another person.

  Empathy must not be confused with sympathy. Feeling sorry for someone involved in a conflict may taint your opinion, resulting in a loss of objectivity. Empathy can be demonstrated through nodding in response to comments, or acknowledging the person by using phrases such as "I see" or "I understand that you are angry," or by using responses such as "mm hmm." The content of the response is not as important as the context of the message. The response should demonstrate acceptance of the person's feelings and the message that he or she is trying to convey. It does not initially matter whether you agree with the opinion of the person, only that the person has been acknowledged. If your response is neutral, detached, or silent, the subject may assume that you are not listening or that their message is trivial or unimportant. This will likely evoke a defensive response. He or she may feel that you are minimizing their opinion and their attempt to communicate the nature of the problem.

- *Don't jump to conclusions.* It is critical that you do not jump to conclusions and form an opinion before the person has finished expressing himself or herself. It is acceptable to try to predict the outcome of a person's physical actions, but it is nearly impossible to accurately predict the thoughts of another.

- *Take responsibility for accurately understanding the completed message.* Verify that your understanding of the message is accurate by summarizing it and then asking the subject for feedback. Use "I" responses. "I believe that the problem is ..." "Have I correctly identified the problem?" If you correctly identify the problem, the involved parties receive affirmation of their communication skills. If you were not correct in identifying the problem, the involved persons are given the opportunity to restate the problem allowing them more time to consider the problem in a different context. The subject will have to re-explain the problem in a non-emotional context that may allow them to re-evaluate their perspective on the problem. The use of "I" does not criticize the communication skills of the involved parties.

Verbal Intervention

Effective verbal communication is an essential skill that you as a law enforcement officer must possess when intervening in a conflict or crisis situation. Effective verbal intervention techniques can help you to

- prevent escalation of a conflict situation into a crisis, or
- assist in de-escalating a situation that has escalated into a crisis.

However, the use of verbal intervention techniques requires a non-violent atmosphere of cooperation, and your safety is the main concern. If violence or the threat of violence is present, you may need to take immediate action and forgo the use of verbal intervention techniques.

Remember that communication is the *exchange* of information: it consists of both the messages you send and the messages you receive. To communicate effectively, you need to be able to understand and interpret the messages that others send to you. There are three types of messages that you can expect to receive during verbal communications. These are content, feelings, and behaviours and responses:

- *Content* refers to the facts of the situation. Assuming that you and the other person are not trying to be deceptive, content should be relatively easy to obtain and understand. Keep in mind that accurate content is obtained only when all the available information regarding the incident is obtained and analyzed.
- *Feelings* are emotions such as anger, fear, hurt, and trust. Feelings may often be identified without being verbally communicated.
- *Behaviours and responses* are the reactions of the subject to what you say. These may be difficult to accurately identify. The person may be attempting to deceive you, or trying to manipulate your emotions. An accurate interpretation of the person's behaviours and responses to your verbal messages is necessary to verify the content of their response to your message. Remember that the person's non-verbal response will be more accurate than his verbal response. Although the person may indicate verbally that he is calm and in control of his actions, his non-verbal expression may contradict the verbal message. If verbal and non-verbal

responses conflict, the non-verbal responses will be more accurate. Non-verbal behaviours are discussed later in this chapter.

Influence Versus Coercion

The ideal outcome of verbal intervention is for you to **influence**, rather than **coerce**, the actions of the involved parties. *Influencing* allows the objective of defusing a situation with the least possible interference with the involved parties. Through persuasive and effective communication, you will be able to influence the parties enough that they will adhere to your wishes (not your orders). If done effectively, the involved parties will believe that they have independently made their own decision to change their situational behaviour. This technique will likely avoid resentment directed toward you.

Coercion involves more direct control by you. It may involve direction or orders to carry out certain acts. Some professionals believe that they should be aggressive when intervening in conflict and crisis situations. Their attitude is: Take charge! Take control! Solve the problem! Tell the subject what they are to do! This is not communication; there is no exchange of information. The tendency to tell the subject what to do may stem from the confusing of **aggressiveness** with **assertiveness**.

Assertive behaviour allows you to confidently state your position and have a positive influence on the situation. Assertive persons communicate in a direct, non-provoking manner. Using aggressive behaviour may be viewed as provoking or showing a readiness to attack the behaviour and person of the involved parties. Aggressive persons tend to be argumentative, critical, and resistant to personal criticism.

People become defensive when being told what to do. They may resist your commands. By keeping your language and behaviour assertive rather than aggressive, you can keep communication channels open. You will be able to provide an environment that will be supportive, allowing the subjects to identify their issues. If you respond in demeaning language or are hurried with your responses, it is unlikely that the subject will openly communicate their issues.

A supportive environment requires that you consider the nature of your communication with the subjects. A common error made by police officers in the course of communicating with subjects is the conveyance, consciously or unconsciously, of officer superiority. The subjects may sense that you believe that you are more intelligent and that they are inferior because they could not handle their problems on their own. This lack of situational equality hinders effective communication.

Another common communication error that hinders a supportive environment is the tendency of some police officers to strategize the outcome of the exchange before the exchange is completed. This is not to say that there should not be a strategy in place for your protection and the protection of the subjects, but that the goal of the strategy should not be blatant. The persons involved in a conflict believe that their conflict is the only situation that is important. It is unlikely that the involved parties have developed effective conflict resolution methods and may be acting emotionally rather than strategically.

A supportive environment may also be hindered by your need to control the outcome of the situation by asserting that only your solutions are acceptable. From

influence
use effective communication techniques to affect another person's thought process and behaviours with the objective of persuading the person to change his or her perspective

coerce
use threats or force to require another person to do something against his or her will

aggressiveness
in the context of conflict situations, attacking a person's perspective in an antagonistic manner

assertiveness
in the context of conflict situations, confidently stating a position in a forceful but non-aggressive manner

the viewpoint of the subjects involved, your attitude may be viewed as exploiting your superiority and could be perceived as aggressive behaviour.

Achieve a rapport with the subject through active listening and positive communication as quickly as possible. Listen for the content of the message and observe the emotions and behaviours. Show interest in the subject's predicament. To obtain information and assist with de-escalating the situation use phrasings such as "Tell me what happened. I'm here to help. I want to work with you. Let's try to resolve this together."

Although aggressive behaviour will likely negate effective communication, there are situations involving officer safety *and* public safety that may require aggressive action or perhaps the use of force. You must remain in control of the situation. In some situations it may be necessary, for safety or duty requirements, to order the person to comply, or to use force if legally authorized and necessary to ensure compliance. The use of effective communication techniques to persuade the subject to comply is the desired outcome, but physical control may be required if verbal persuasion fails. In these situations, communication may be ineffective or time constraints will likely prohibit establishing a rapport. Use force only when all other options fail and it becomes necessary for protective or compliance purposes.

Your safety and effectiveness can be enhanced by learning and practising the styles of communication discussed above. Learn the appropriate style that would most likely be effective in defusing a conflict situation and what style of communication would likely de-escalate a crisis situation.

Keep in mind that some phrasings, however well meaning, may be offensive to the people that they are directed toward. A command such as "You! Come here!" instantly tells the person that they are being singled out (in a demeaning way) and that they have likely done something wrong. This may lead to an unnecessary confrontation that could have been avoided by safely approaching the person and politely asking the person to speak with you. There is little difference in the final outcome of the exchange; if you remain in control of the conversation, the likelihood of a defensive reaction by the subject is decreased.

A tactic commonly used is to tell the person involved in a conflict or altercation to "calm down" or "remain calm." This tactic is almost always ineffective. Telling a person to "calm down" won't alleviate whatever is upsetting them. A state of calm must be first achieved. Such phrasings may be perceived as a criticism of their behaviour and may suggest that they have no legitimate right to be upset.

To assist with de-escalation, be prepared to listen to the subject. If safety is not a concern, active listening may convey a mutual agreement on one or more points of view or perceptions of the subject. This strategy is particularly useful in dealing with irate or irrational individuals, where rapid de-escalation is necessary to prevent injury to the officer or the individuals. Present the view of real or feigned "agreement for now," no matter how bizarre the point of view. Always ensure that your safety will not be compromised. Use responses such as "You are absolutely right to feel that way. I'd probably feel the same way if that happened to me. Why don't we try to solve this problem?" Acknowledge that you recognize the legitimacy of the subject's problem and are willing to assist.

Telling someone to "be reasonable" may have the same ineffective result as telling someone to "calm down." A person in crisis is not thinking reasonably; they are dealing with the situation in a manner that may seem "reasonable" to them. When you tell them to "be reasonable," you are in effect saying, "You can't deal with your problems! You are behaving inappropriately!" This approach may be viewed as condescending and will likely evoke a defensive response, thereby shutting down communication channels.

Using language such as "What's your problem?" may be interpreted as a flippant comment that tells the person that you do not care about their problem or that their problem is frivolous. Such comments also imply that they are failures at managing their problem. "What's your problem?" does not offer assistance, but merely identifies the person's inadequacy at controlling their behaviour. Rather than reassuring them that things will improve, which should be your goal, you have created a communication barrier.

There are more effective phrases that may be used. Phrases such as "What's wrong?" or "How can I help you?" or "Tell me what is upsetting you" acknowledge that you recognize that the person is upset and that you are willing to provide assistance. These types of phrases invite open communication and do not criticize or belittle the person's state of mind or the person's inability to control their problem.

Regardless of which positive phrasing you choose, be sure that your response addresses the problem, not the person. This may be difficult with a frustrated subject. Quite often, persons under stress make verbal attacks to vent their frustration or anger. Their frustration may be directed toward you. A professional response is required to maintain control of the situation. Belittlement or negative put-downs are unacceptable. All words and phrases should be supportive and encouraging, assisting the subject to be able to visualize a satisfactory solution to his or her problem.

Use reassuring language such as "Let me see if I understand ... ." Paraphrase what the subject has said and repeat it back to them in your own words. Paraphrasing may calm the person down and make them more receptive to discussion because your words will be more professional and less emotional. The subject is likely to pay attention to your paraphrasing of what they have said. People are interested in having someone mirror their thoughts.

This communication technique puts you in control and gets the subject listening. If you are inaccurate in your paraphrasing and the subject believes that you are trying to understand their view, they will tend to listen to you closely to ascertain whether you understand their position. When you paraphrase what you heard, in calmer language, the subject is more likely to amend their original emotionally charged attitude and be less defensive. This approach helps alleviate tension and allows the person to focus on the problem rather than their emotional response to the problem. This tactic allows you to help the person step back and see the problem in context.

In a situation where a person is not complying with your directions, you may be tempted to issue a command such as "Do what I say or else ... you will get hurt" or "... you will be restrained" or "... you will regret it." Whatever the phrasing, you are warning the subject that you intend to take action. The subject may comply or may decide to take a stand against you. You have given the person time to prepare, physically and psychologically, to respond to your demand. In effect, you have issued a threat and indicated that you will take action. You have removed the element of communication from the situation. If you are not prepared to act, or if your demand cannot be legally enforced, you will lose credibility. The loss of credibility could lead to the loss of control and, possibly, pose a threat to your safety. Such aggressive phrases give the person an ultimatum to comply and may trigger their fight or flight response.

More effective communication may be established in such situations by using a phrasing such as "For your safety and for mine, please do what I say." Providing a reasonable explanation gives the person a rational reason to comply. The use of "your" and "mine" involves the person in the decision. It contextualizes the situation to one of officer *and* subject safety. You are ultimately in control of the situation. The subject will, willingly or unwillingly, comply with your demands. It is always better if compliance can be achieved through non-violent means. If the subject believes that they are making the choice to acquiesce to your demand, does it really matter whether the subject believes that they had a choice, so long as compliance is obtained?

Other effective phrasings include, "It is important that you pay close attention to what I'm about to tell you" or "I would like to resolve this issue without using force. Is there anything we can do to help resolve the issue?" If the answer is no, or the person indicates that they are not going to be cooperative and you are acting with legal justification, take action immediately, likely while the subject is still answering and off-guard. Do not telegraph your actions. It is safer to act without allowing the subject to prepare.

If force must be used, try to continue using non-confrontational language throughout the intervention process. Although this is difficult to accomplish when dealing with an irate, resistant, or combative subject, aggressive and demeaning language can have a psychological effect on the subject's demeanour and reaction during and after the encounter. Such tactful language will also greatly assist in reducing the negative perceptions of witnesses or other involved parties.

When the person, willingly or unwillingly, complies with your directive, continue to use non-confrontational phrases such as "I appreciate that you are doing what you were asked." This will allow the subject to save face in front of others, particularly in situations of subject posturing. Such phrasings are effective because the subject will be able to diminish the appearance of acquiescing to your commands. The subject can justify, psychologically and in the view of their peers, that compliance was their choice, again assisting with de-escalation of the subject's resistive behaviour.

VIOLENCE

violence
any unwanted act of aggression resulting in physical contact

For the purpose of this section, **violence** may be defined as any unwanted act of aggression resulting in physical contact. Violent behaviour can be a consequence of stress that has overwhelmed a person's ability to cope. This part of the chapter is directed toward fostering a better understanding of violent behaviour and how to handle it.

Physical confrontations are an inevitable part of law enforcement. You may be called to respond to highly volatile situations where people have lost control, physically and emotionally. There may be a risk of a violent reaction toward you from a normally peaceful, law-abiding person who has been pushed to his or her limit. In such situations it can be difficult to determine the proper course of action. Your ability to read the situation and use proper intervention and communication skills will determine whether the person is helped with his or her problem or whether they lose control and possibly resort to violence.

Chronically Violent Persons

A small number of persons make violence a way of life. Throughout their lives, they have used violence as a way of handling problems or taking what they want. In their encounters with law enforcement officers, they will not hesitate to use violence to achieve their goals or to demonstrate to others that they have no regard for the law. They may be well prepared—they may be carrying a weapon, have training in martial arts, or be skilled in street fighting. They may be looking for a confrontation that will give them status in their eyes or in the eyes of their peers. Injuring you may, in their view, help them achieve this status. For some subjects, there is nothing to lose by violently attacking an officer. The subject and his or her peers know that officers are trained in self-defence and control tactics. You are expected to be able to control the subject, with assistance if necessary. With no expectation of "winning," the subject will gain peer status through violent resistance, even if he or she is unsuccessful in eluding you.

This type of person often enjoys violence and has little fear of being injured. The legal repercussions of violence are not a consideration for this personality type. They know that you are bound by law to use only as much force as is necessary to control a subject. Because the violent person does not act with such constraint, they may believe that their lack of restraint may be advantageous. Any such advantage can be negated, however, by a well-prepared and well-trained police officer who can react immediately and effectively.

Violent tendencies are not inherited. They can, however, be a product of one's environment, which may explain why they seem to run in families. In such families it may be a learned behaviour that is considered an acceptable alternative to peaceful conflict resolution.

Common Characteristics of Violent Persons

There appear to be some common personality traits possessed by violent persons:

- *Below-average intelligence.* Persons of below-average intelligence may resort to violence more frequently than others in the general population. This does not mean that lower intelligence is a cause of violence. Instead, these individuals may lack the ability to adequately solve problems and may see violence as their only viable option.

- *Impulsivity and a lack of self-control.* People who are impulsive and lack self-control show a greater potential for violence.

- *An inflated sense of self-worth.* Individuals with this characteristic may consider the views of others as being beneath their consideration. Such persons may react aggressively and violently in situations where they believe their superiority is being challenged.

- *An intense craving for social power and esteem.* Persons with this trait demonstrate rigid, egocentric thought patterns, prejudicial beliefs, and an intense focus on obtaining power. They may treat those of perceived lower social standing with disdain, and may react aggressively and violently during confrontations with these persons.

Potential Causes of Violence

There are a variety of factors that may increase an individual's potential for violence (Hafen & Frandsen, 1985):

- *Stress.* Chronic stress may lead to violence. The stressor need not be the object or target of the violent behaviour, and may be related to work, family, or finances.
- *Personality disorders.* Violence related to personality disorders is usually explosive. The person may have a long record of violence, as a victim or a perpetrator.
- *Alcohol and drugs.* Alcohol and drugs can impair a person's ability to control impulsive responses to stress.
- *Threats.* Physical, emotional, or financial circumstances, as well as many other kinds of circumstances, can be perceived by the body as a threat and trigger a violent response.
- *Panic.* Persons may feel that they are losing control over their lives. Violent reactions can restore a sense of control.
- *Societal influences.* A sense of power may be gained through violence and intimidation. Certain groups in society grant respect, money, and prestige to those who gain power this way.

Preparation for Violent Encounters

Mental preparation is the most important tool that you as an officer possess in any type of encounter. In violent encounters, you must be prepared not to back down from an encounter even when your instinct tells you to run away. Although disengagement may be an option in some circumstances, other situations require that you physically intervene to gain control of the situation or to defend yourself or others. In such situations, your mental preparation is crucial to your safety and effectiveness.

Prepare yourself by mentally rehearsing reactions to likely situations. Try to rehearse appropriate reactions to situations that you have not yet encountered and, where necessary, consider what appropriate reactions worked best in situations that you have already encountered. The more automatic your responses, the more confidence you will have when confronting a conflict. You must also be aware of your strengths and weaknesses when mentally rehearsing. It is unrealistic, for example, for an officer in poor physical condition to imagine chasing a criminal for several kilometres and then using physical strength to forcibly restrain him or her.

There are some other factors that will influence how you react to a potentially violent situation:

- *Size and strength of the subject.* Does the subject appear to be much larger and stronger than you?
- *Your abilities and skill level.* Do you possess the ability to defuse the situation through effective communication techniques or will it be necessary to forcibly subdue the subject? Are you confident in your abilities?
- *Fears and perceptions.* Do you have the perception that you are able to, or unable, to control the subject?
- *Equipment.* Are weapons available to you? Do you possess the knowledge and skill to use the weapons effectively in order to defend yourself?
- *Personal experiences.* Have you ever engaged in a physical confrontation?

It is important to recognize that when you are involved in a violent or potentially violent situation, you are likely to experience physical and emotional reactions to the threat. Typical reactions include:

- a natural fear of injury;
- the stress reaction—rapid breathing, increased heart rate, increased perspiration, etc.;
- a sick feeling;
- a shaky or cracked voice; and
- tunnel vision (focusing only on the direct threat).

You must learn to recognize and accept these reactions as normal responses to a stressful situation.

During a stressful encounter, you may need to react immediately, and may not have time to think. In such situations, you will need to rely on your training and physical and mental preparation. This is why mental and physical preparation is essential. If you have never before encountered the situation and have not mentally and physically prepared yourself, you will be forced to determine an effective course of action on the spot. Time constraints may not allow the opportunity to formulate a proper response.

Maintaining the Proper Level of Awareness

The proper level of awareness is crucial to your survival in hostile situations, which often arise suddenly and require an immediate reaction. The following is an explanation of levels of awareness.

Level 1. You are completely relaxed and not fully aware of your surroundings. This is the level of awareness maintained while, for example, at home watching television and eating pizza. You feel completely safe and see no possibility of danger. This level of awareness is never acceptable while on duty. If you function at this level while working, potential or actual threats may not be recognized. A person functioning at this level of awareness is almost completely oblivious to the surrounding environment and is in a daydream state. If you allow yourself to enter this state while on duty, you become a potential victim.

Level 2. You are cautious and alert, even if no immediate danger is present. You are aware of your surroundings and of potential hazards. Level 2 is not a state of tension, but of relaxed awareness. Potential hazards have been identified and assessed. Level 2 is the level of awareness that should be maintained while responding to occurrences and while on duty.

You can enhance this level of awareness by paying more attention to details in your daily routine. This can include, for example, noting the colour and type of a vehicle that just passed or committing to memory the physical characteristics of a person on the sidewalk. Upon entering a building, increase your awareness by identifying potential hazards or items that could be used as weapons. Also, look for all entrances and exits that could allow persons who might be a threat an opportunity to suddenly appear or to make an escape. Another enhancement training strategy is to pay attention to the non-verbal communication of friends and acquaintances, and to note your surroundings while not on duty. This practice of increased awareness will make it easier for you to remain in a state of level 2 awareness for longer periods of time.

Level 3. You have identified an immediate and specific threat. If you are able to maintain a level 2 state of awareness while on duty, you will be able to quickly shift to level 3. A confrontation is about to take place or some other immediate danger exists and you are preparing yourself physically and mentally to respond. Your body initiates the fight or flight response. This stress reaction temporarily enhances your physical and mental capabilities. You will likely process information much more quickly. As the information is processed and analyzed, a response based on experience, training, and judgment is formulated.

Level 4. A confrontation is taking place and there is immediate danger. Fight or disengage; there are no other options. When you are well prepared, you will likely react automatically and know what to do. Your training and general mental and physical preparation will help you through the encounter, ideally without injury.

Level 4 awareness involves situations that may be life threatening or result in serious bodily harm to you or the assailant. This is a state of hyperawareness and is very physically and mentally taxing, and cannot be maintained indefinitely. Level 4 reactions can create certain problems. There may be a tendency to focus only on the direct threat (the tunnel vision effect). Tunnel vision is part of a normal stress reaction, but can be a liability. Focusing only on the direct threat may prevent you from noticing other dangers. For example, you may see only the gun or knife in front of you and not the person approaching from another direction with a baseball bat. Recognition that tunnel vision is occurring is the key to overcoming the problem and being able to see potential hazards. Remember to scan the area for dangers while still paying attention to the immediate threat. Your enhanced mental processing and physical ability to handle the stress reaction will be an asset in this situation.

Some physical difficulties may occur while you are in a state of level 4 awareness. Loss of fine motor control is one problem. You may feel clumsy and your fingers may not work as they normally would, making it more difficult for you to control a firearm. The trigger pull on police-issue firearms is heavier than that on competition-type firearms for this reason. A firearm with a light trigger pull may be difficult to control in stressful circumstances.

Another physical reaction that can occur during level 4 awareness is the distortion of time and distance. Although the cause is not yet known, it has been theorized that a temporarily increased ability to process information may occur. This increased ability to process information may make events appear to occur in slow motion. Another theory is that during states of level 4 awareness, memories are recorded in much more vivid detail.

Regardless of which theory is correct, accurate recall of the sequence of events is highly unlikely. Immediate recollection of the incident will probably be inaccurate because of the inability to recognize the degree of the distortion of time and distance that occurred during the incident. With time to consider the incident in perspective, you may be able to more accurately describe the incident. This is one situation in which time may enhance the accuracy of recall.

After experiencing a level 4 state of awareness, you may experience a heightened state of arousal for a short time following the incident. Because the body cannot maintain this level of arousal for extended periods, it will be followed by a "crash" as the body exits this state of awareness, and you may feel physically and psychologically exhausted. Recovery time varies depending upon your state of physical and psychological preparedness preceding the incident.

Learning Activity 2.2

As a police officer, it is inevitable that you will be involved in violent encounters. However, if you maintain the appropriate level of awareness while on duty and understand the physical and emotional reactions you are likely to experience in a violent encounter, you can minimize or prevent injury to yourself and others, and possibly avoid the violent encounter altogether.

This learning activity will allow you to identify common reactions to violent encounters.

Read the scenario below. Then answer the questions that follow.

The time is 1:55 a.m. It is a very warm night. A male enters a convenience store and approaches the clerk. He draws a knife and demands the money in the cash register. While complying with the male's demand, the clerk triggers the silent alarm.

A nearby police station receives the call and two officers are dispatched. While the officers are en route, another police officer on regular patrol duties, who is unaware of the holdup, enters the convenience store at 2 a.m. to buy a cold drink. The male, wielding the knife in his hand and screaming, immediately runs toward the officer. The officer immediately draws his firearm and shoots, hitting the male in the chest. The male collapses face down on the ground.

The officer shouts to the male, "Stay down! Put your hands to your sides!" The male does not move or verbally respond. The officer again shouts to the male, "Put your hands to your sides! Do it now!" The male does not respond.

The officer approaches the male. He does not appear to be breathing.

The officer holsters his firearm and handcuffs the male. The officer then checks for a pulse. The officer is unable to find any pulse. The officer turns the male over onto his back to render CPR and sees blood on the centre of the male's chest. The officer decides not to perform CPR.

The clerk calls 911 to report that shots have been fired by a police officer. The clerk says he doesn't know whether the officer has been injured, but tells the dispatcher that the officer is covered with blood. Dispatch advises the two officers responding to the silent alarm that an officer is on scene and may be injured. Paramedics are also dispatched to the scene.

The two officers arrive at the store. They enter, firearms drawn.

One of the officers assists with the downed male.

Paramedics arrive on scene and examine the officer. The officer is not injured. The robbery suspect is presumed dead by the paramedics. Medical assistance is not rendered.

The suspect is later transported to the hospital where he is pronounced dead by a doctor.

The officer involved in the shooting is asked by an "internal affairs" investigator to make a statement about the incident. The officer agrees and provides a statement at the scene.

Q. Why were you in the store?
A. To buy a cold drink.

Q. Describe what you saw when you first entered the store.
A. I saw a male running at me. He had a knife with a serrated edge in his left hand. The knife had a brown wooden handle. The blade was approximately ten inches long. I believe it was a bread knife, the kind that is used to slice bread. The blade was narrow at the tip and wider at the base near the handle. There was writing on the blade. It looked like a new knife.

Q. Describe the male.
A. He was wearing a black T-shirt.

Q. Continue.
A. That's all I remember.

Q. How far away was the male from you when you entered the store?
A. It took him a while to cross the store, so I guess that he must have been twenty-five to thirty feet away.

Q. How many shots did you fire?
A. I don't remember.

Q. Did the male say anything to you before you shot?
A. No.

Q. Approximately how long were you in the store before the incident took place?
A. I think it happened as soon as I came in. Wait; maybe not. I remember looking toward the cooler where the Pepsi is kept. I noticed that there were a few different kinds of Pepsi. So I must have been in the store for a few seconds at least.

Q. When did the male come toward you?

A. I guess that it must have been several seconds after I entered the store. I saw him running toward me with the knife in his left hand. The blade was pointed toward me. I remember thinking that my body armour would not stop the blade.

Q. What did you do when you saw the male running toward you?

A. I remembered that I was supposed to try to get out of the way and to seek cover. I don't remember taking my firearm from my holster, but I obviously must have taken it out. I remember thinking that this guy is going to kill me. I don't know why he wanted to kill me. I don't even know him. I aimed at the centre of his chest and shot. He fell down. I didn't hear my firearm go off. I might have had a misfire. I felt relieved that he had tripped and fallen before he got to me. I told him to stay down. I think I handcuffed him. He was covered in blood.

Q. How much time passed from the time that you went into the store until the male was on the floor?

A. Let me think. It was a few seconds after I came in before I noticed the male. He had to cross the store with the knife. That must have taken ten or twenty seconds. I remember thinking about what I was supposed to do, and about the knife going through my body armour, so that must have taken twenty or thirty seconds. I took out my firearm, aimed, and squeezed the trigger; that must have taken ten seconds. I saw him fall to the floor and I told him to stay down; that must have taken twenty or thirty seconds. I guess the whole incident took about a minute.

The initial questioning concludes. The officer is told to go to the station to "clean up."

The investigator then speaks to the store clerk.

Q. Tell me what happened here tonight.

A. That cop got it all wrong. The guy that was robbing me saw the cop car pull up. He told me to hurry up with the money or he would cut me. I gave him all the money in the cash register. The button for the holdup alarm is inside the cash register. I pushed it. He took the money and said, "I'm gonna kill me a cop!" As soon as the cop started to open the door, the dead guy was running at him with the knife in his hand. The guy was crazy—screaming all the time he was running at the cop! The cop took out his gun and shot the guy! The whole thing didn't take five seconds! Good riddance I say. That guy robbed me before, but you didn't catch him!

The investigator tells the clerk that he is finished. He asks if he wants to be checked by the paramedics. The clerk replies, "No. I'm all right. I've been robbed eight times before. No problem with me. It's not my money!"

1. a. Identify and explain the levels of awareness experienced by the officer in this scenario.

    b. What led you to conclude that the officer experienced these levels of awareness?

2. Which of the two persons interviewed likely provided more accurate information regarding the timelines of the incident? Explain your answer.

Predicting Violent Behaviour

Certain kinds of violent behaviour are specific to police work, such as the violence displayed by a person who postures or reacts violently toward officers in an attempt to gain respect from peers or onlookers. It is impossible to predict with complete accuracy whether or not a person will respond violently to an encounter with you. Situations, personalities, and personal experiences vary too widely. It is recommended that you always respond to incidents involving members of the public as if the potential for violence exists.

Although anyone has the potential for violent behaviour, males are generally more likely than females to use violence in a conflict situation. Statistics over the past several decades indicate that males are charged with violent offences approximately 6.5 times more frequently than females. According to Statistics Canada, in 2009 there were 443,284 violent crimes reported to police across Canada. "Violent crimes," for statistical purposes, included criminal harassment, uttering threats, and threatening or harassing phone calls. Adult males were charged with approximately 87 percent of these crimes (Statistics Canada, 2010).

Certain common indicators can help an officer determine whether a subject is violence prone. To determine whether these indicators are present, an officer should try to answer the questions below before engaging with the subject. Note, however, that this information may not be attainable before the encounter.

- Has the person ever been charged with committing a violent act, including an assault or other violent act committed during the course of an offence such as robbery, disturbing the peace, or harassment?
- Have complaints of violence that did not result in a conviction been lodged against the person? Although complaints of violence may be unfounded or lack sufficient evidence to prosecute or obtain a conviction, they may indicate a history of violent behaviour.
- Has the person ever threatened violence? The threat of violence is sometimes the result of an emotional outburst, but should not be taken lightly. Did the person carry out the threat? If so, the person poses a substantial risk of further violence. The threat was a preconceived idea showing that the person did not act on impulse.
- Does the person abuse alcohol or drugs? Alcohol and drugs affect a person's ability to reason, and sometimes lead a person to commit acts that are out of character.
- Does the person's history include being a victim of child abuse, a history of cruelty to animals, or symbolic acts of aggression such as the violent destruction of photographs or clothing? These and certain other acts and experiences greatly increase the possibility of violence, although they may be difficult for you to uncover.

You will also need to learn the outward signs of a potentially violent person. Recognition can allow you to handle a situation more safely, by giving you more time to remove or lessen the impact of whatever is agitating the person. Common signs include:

- Loud, aggressive speech.
- Lack of emotion or, conversely, extreme emotion and volatility.
- Tense and alert posture (for example, sitting on the edge of a chair and appearing ready to move).
- Irritability. Everything is "bugging" the person in question.
- Short attention span. The person's mind is wandering and unable to focus, which can cause frustration and make the person lash out.
- Threatening gestures (for example, clenching or shaking fists, hitting the table with fists, or slamming doors) or destroying the person's own property.
- Refusal to discuss the situation. The person who remains silent and expressionless may be contemplating his or her next move or have already decided what to do next.

Some other indicators of potential violence include:

- Pacing.
- Finger drumming, wringing of hands, or other restless, repetitive movements.
- Change in voice or subject matter.
- Staring, or avoiding eye contact.
- Change in facial colour and expression.
- Trembling.
- Shallow, rapid breathing.

The most important indicators of possible violence are non-verbal. You must use your judgment to interpret non-verbal communication. If the person's body language does not match what he or she is saying, rely on the body language. Body language usually reflects a person's true emotions and can account for approximately 70 to 90 percent of the information transmitted in an interaction.

Dealing with Potentially Violent or Violent Persons

Most officers try to avoid using violent responses to conflict or crisis situations. However, you may experience an adrenalin rush when a potentially violent situation is encountered—for example, when a suspect taunts or otherwise verbally abuses you. This may affect your judgment. Therefore, you must not react to rudeness, aggression, sarcasm, or any other provocation. It will only escalate the situation.

You must act within the bounds of the law and use good judgment at all times. It may be difficult to control your emotions, but control is an ability that you *must* possess.

You should not hurry into any situation or try to solve the problem in a few minutes. Move and speak slowly when engaging a subject. Physical contact should be avoided unless you, the subject, or anyone else is in immediate danger.

Try to determine the problem by engaging the person in conversation. Speak in a calm and rational manner. Try to use short, simple sentences when addressing a person displaying signs of potential violence. The person may be in a state of heightened arousal. His or her mind may be experiencing high levels of stress and may not be able to focus on messages with complex meanings.

The person may be irrational and may not respond to spoken words. Instead, he or she may react to any non-verbal messages that you may be sending. Therefore, avoid using body language that can be perceived as threatening, such as placing your hands on your hips, crossing your arms, or pointing. It is normal to feel fear when confronted with a potentially violent situation, but try not to allow the fear to show in your voice or in your body language.

Personal space should be considered. A hostile or agitated person may react violently if his or her personal space is invaded.

Try to reduce the potential for violence by attempting to persuade the person to put away any weapons and move away from any areas where there is ready access to weapons. Eye contact with the person should never be broken. When the person has moved to a "neutral" area, he or she can be offered a non-alcoholic drink, food, or a cigarette. This may temporarily distract the person's attention from the problem. After the person has become calm, you will then have time to decide on a further course of action.

Of course, protecting yourself and the public from violence takes precedence over allowing a person to vent his or her emotions. Accordingly, immediate physical intervention may be necessary and you may have to forgo the process described above.

Learning Activity 2.3

This learning activity will allow you to identify some indicators that could signal that a subject may react violently.

Indicate whether the following statements are true or false. Explain your answer.

_____ 1. Persons with below-average intelligence levels are more likely to react violently in stressful situations.

_____ 2. Stress is a contributing factor to violent behaviour.

_____ 3. Depressive drugs, such as alcohol, do not increase the risk of violent behaviour.

_____ 4. Males are more likely to be charged with a violent crime than are females.

_____ 5. The most consistent predictor of violent behaviour is the subject's use of alcohol or other drugs.

_____ 6. The subject's avoidance of eye contact is an accurate indicator of potential violence.

_____ 7. Threatening gestures are an accurate indicator of potential violence.

_____ 8. Refusal to discuss the situation occurring is an accurate indicator of potential violence.

DEFUSING CONFLICT SITUATIONS

Calm, persuasive communication may reduce the risk of violence in a confrontation. Remember, you should try to influence an individual's behaviour rather than coerce that person. The following are some actions that may help to de-escalate a situation and reduce the potential for violence:

- *Respond in a calm, reassuring manner.* This will help defuse the situation by allowing the disputants to see that you are ready to help in an unemotional and unbiased manner, and that you are in control of the situation. Should you display any emotional outbursts, you will likely exacerbate the situation.

- *Separate the parties to alleviate tensions.* Try to keep the parties separate so that their eye contact is broken. At the same time, maintain eye contact with fellow officers.

- *If separating the parties does not de-escalate the situation, take a greater degree of verbal or physical command of the situation.* However, do not give ultimatums or make assurances that cannot be kept. Statements such as "Do what I say or else" may aggravate the situation. Your voice, demeanour, and actions should communicate the fact that an opportunity to solve the problem or to withdraw from the conflict with dignity is available, but that escalation of the conflict will not be tolerated.

- *Maintain an authoritative demeanour.* The most important factor in defusing a conflict or crisis situation and preventing an escalation of violence is your outward behaviour and attitude. Use-of-force tactics have their place, but with the appropriate non-violent intervention techniques, most situations can be defused without resorting to force.

- *Address the concerns of the parties as soon as possible.* Ascertain the nature of the problem and determine whether intervention is appropriate. If intervention is not possible, referrals to appropriate agencies should be made.

- *Where a situation escalates and there is a potential for violence, remove the parties.* The police have a duty to protect the person and property of all citizens. Knowledge of the appropriate provincial and federal arrest powers is essential at this point to enable the officer to legally apprehend the person or persons responsible for the escalation.

  If arrest is deemed necessary and is legal, it should be carried out. Although an arrest may not solve a problem, it may be necessary to prevent violence. Arrestees should be clearly told that they are being arrested for their actions, not for failure to obey an officer's directions. If force must be used to stop or prevent violence, the action taken should commence without warning and be as non-invasive as possible. This denies the arrestee time to plan a response to the police intervention and thus reduces the need for greater force on the part of the police.

- *Do not use the threat of force or arrest to compel obeyance.* It is hypocritical to use the threat of force to prevent another person from using force. Arrest should not be threatened if there are no legal grounds to make an arrest; you can appear inept if the threat is made but cannot be legally executed.

Problem Identification

A solution to a problem cannot be reached until the problem is accurately identified. The problem may be obvious to the parties involved but not to an outsider. Perception is reality: if the person believes there is a problem, then there is one.

Be careful when attempting to determine the cause of a problem. The immediate occurrence may merely be evidence of a deeper problem. Addressing the current problem is necessary, but may do little to resolve the fundamental cause of the conflict. Careful observation and active listening may help identify the fundamental cause of the conflict and increase your chances of resolving it.

To accurately diagnose the fundamental causes of a problem, be methodical and collect all pertinent information relating to the conflict. You must use your best judgment to determine what information is important and what is not. Accurate analysis of the conflict will allow you to more precisely identify the problem. This analysis requires good judgment, an understanding of verbal and non-verbal modes of communication, and the ability to remain objective.

If the person describes his or her problem vaguely, makes ambiguous statements, or presents non-verbal behaviour that does not agree with his or her verbal message, seek clarification. The person is more likely to elaborate and clarify when asked non-intrusive, non-threatening questions. However, use this technique carefully and sparingly. Continually asking the person to clarify his or her statements could make him or her feel uneasy and distrust your ability to assist.

Another effective method of identifying the problem is to ask the person to restate or rephrase the problem. The person will often respond positively to you if the problem has been identified or will explain the problem more clearly if he or she believes that you are sincerely trying to understand.

If you are unsure whether he or she has accurately identified the problem, admit to being confused and ask the person for clarification. As with restating and rephrasing, this method shows the person that you are interested in what is being said.

You may also need to ask questions in addition to requesting clarification. Pose questions in a non-accusatory manner for the purpose of clarification and not interrogation. The questions may be closed or open. A closed question elicits a brief response (for example, "yes" or "no"), whereas an open question encourages further discussion in order to narrow the focus of the problem.

When seeking clarification, direct your attention to the person's non-verbal behaviours. As stated earlier, if the non-verbal behaviours are incongruous with the spoken message, the non-verbal message will generally be more reliable. Even so, the non-verbal message must always be contextually considered. It is possible that the action is a habit or nervous behaviour with no significant meaning.

To identify a problem and determine whether intervention is appropriate, you must be alert to the specific attitude that the person presents. The following are examples of common attitudes that people present and the behaviours that indicate each attitude.

- Openness
  - ☐ open hands
  - ☐ hands spread apart
  - ☐ palms up
  - ☐ body leaning forward during conversation

- Defensiveness
  - ☐ arms crossed
  - ☐ legs crossed
  - ☐ hands closed into fists

- Cooperation
  - ☐ head tilted
  - ☐ significant eye contact (may differ culturally)
  - ☐ hand-to-face gestures
  - ☐ body leaning forward

- Evaluating
  - ☐ head tilted
  - ☐ pacing
  - ☐ chin stroking
  - ☐ pinching the bridge of the nose

- Readiness
  - ☐ hands on hips
  - ☐ body leaning forward
  - ☐ moving into another person's personal space

- Suspicion
  - ☐ avoiding eye contact (may differ culturally)
  - ☐ rubbing the eyes
  - ☐ rubbing the ears
  - ☐ sideways glance

- Confidence
  - ☐ elevated position on chair or platform
  - ☐ hands clasped behind the back
  - ☐ body leaning back with hands behind the neck
  - ☐ fingers steepled (fingertips touching).

By using effective communication skills, clarifying issues, and observing non-verbal behaviours, you should be able to decide whether the problem should be addressed through officer intervention.

When you believe you have identified the problem, ask the parties whether your assessment is accurate. Parties involved in a heated exchange may not immediately recognize whether or not you are correct. Try to build a consensus with the parties and try to make reaching an agreement the priority.

Determine what response is appropriate at this stage. Mediation (discussed in the next section) may be applicable.

In some situations it will not be possible for an officer to accurately identify the underlying problem. For example, in the case of domestic strife that has lasted 25 years, there may be issues that cannot be identified in the time the officer has available, or that are beyond the officer's expertise. Likewise, in situations involving the abuse of alcohol or drugs, the officer may not have the ability to help. In such instances the officer must at least be able to identify the immediate problem and refer the parties to the appropriate community or social service agencies.

Always remain aware that physical intervention may be necessary to prevent an offence or halt the continuance of one. Such intervention may have to be at the expense of determining the underlying cause of the problem.

MEDIATION

mediation
assisted negotiation in which a third party helps the disputants resolve their disagreement themselves

Mediation may be defined as assisted negotiation or third-party intervention. It may be used when the involved parties ar2e unable to reach a mutually agreeable solution to their problem without assistance. The goal of mediation is to have the disputants resolve their disagreement themselves with some guidelines and assistance. The intervening officer, in most cases, cannot solve a problem that was created by others.

Effective mediation relies on several assumptions:

- the parties voluntarily agree to mediation;
- the parties agree to discuss their issues in a non-adversarial manner;
- the mediator will act as a neutral third party;
- the parties agree to hear the submissions of each party involved in the conflict; and
- the parties agree to allow you, as mediator, to help them reach a consensus (if possible).

Conflicts more likely to be resolved through mediation by an officer are those isolated incidents where the parties are unlikely to have future contact with each other, or situations where police were involved at the first instance of the conflict.

If the problem is a recent one, you may be able to offer assistance or advice. But solving a long-term problem is likely to be beyond the scope of your responsibilities.

Determine whether the problem is a one-time, acute problem or an ongoing, chronic problem. To determine whether the problem is acute or chronic, analyze the information acquired through investigation. A chronic problem may require long-term intervention and/or counselling by professionals who are better equipped to deal with the nature of the problem. Referral to an appropriate community or social service agency may be your best response to chronic problems if you have concluded that your immediate presence is of little value in helping solve the problem. However, referral should not be the first option for chronic problems where you believe that the conflict could escalate to the point where public or personal safety is threatened. Your first priority, after ensuring your own safety, is to protect all involved parties.

Some situations, such as child custody disputes, family property disputes, or similar disputes, are better dealt with through means other than police mediation. In such situations, it is not possible for police to reach a legal agreement between the parties. Police may give advice on how to proceed to civil or family court or may refer the disputants to the services of a lawyer. The role of police in such matters is that of a peacekeeper.

After determining the nature of the problem, decide whether you are able to mediate the problem or whether the problem is beyond immediate help and should be referred to an appropriate agency.

If the decision is to mediate, formulate a plan for the mediation. The following suggestions may help you achieve a successful outcome:

- *Reiterate the nature of the problem.* All parties should clearly understand and agree on the nature of the problem.

- *State the intended outcome of the mediation.* All parties should understand and agree on the goals and purpose of the mediation.

- *Physically separate the parties, but ensure that they are within speaking distance.* Keeping the parties separate reduces the probability of physical confrontations.

- *Ensure that one officer is in charge of the mediation.* Conflicting comments by different officers can confuse the parties and hinder the mediation process.

- *Establish the ground rules for the interaction.* The parties will each be allowed to speak and explain their views on the dispute. Allow both parties to state their positions. Do not interrupt unless necessary. Each party will be asked to listen to the concerns of the other party without interrupting. Everyone concerned will be asked to agree on the ground rules. If agreement is not reached, the mediation may be a wasted effort, because the parties may not be sincere in their commitment to resolve the problem.

- *Separate personalities from the problem to avoid bias and help speed up the process.* The parties should be directed to address the problem, not personalities. Personal bias, if allowed to enter into the process, may negate any advantage of mediation. For example, if a particular individual is perceived to be the problem and is treated as such, the other parties may not be willing to listen to his or her suggestions about resolving the issues, because they already "know" who the problem is. Their bias may predetermine the outcome of the mediation and doom it to failure.

- *Summarize the parties' understandings of the problem once they have had the opportunity to speak.* Your summary should be presented to the parties, and each party should be asked whether the problem has been clearly stated. There should be a consensus among the parties about the accuracy of your interpretation of the problem. The summary should be clear and descriptive. Descriptive language helps convey that you understand the party's summary of the problem. Care must be taken not to use negative descriptors such as "I understand that the problem is your failure to ..." or "I understand that the problem is that you do not understand ... ." Negative descriptions, even if accurate, may interfere with the parties' perception of your objectivity, lessening the chances of a positive outcome from the mediation.

- *Ask the parties for solutions once the problem has been identified.* They created the problem, and only they can resolve it. If solutions are not proposed, identify common goals shared by the disputing parties. Identification of common goals may assist the parties in directing their focus toward their commonalities and away from their differences. Effective listening skills are essential to being able to identify common goals. You will need to be able to identify commonalities, if any, from earlier conversations and observations. There will generally be some commonalities unless the parties have entered into a dispute during their first contact. Such a dispute is possible, such as in the case of a dispute over a parking space. Mediation is not likely to be effective in such cases. It is more likely that you will direct the solution to the problem.
- *Take care not to ridicule any proposed solutions.* Remember that the dispute is not your problem, and therefore that it is not your place to belittle proposed solutions. Remain respectful.
- *When a solution is proposed, ask the other parties whether the proposal is viable.* Care must be taken not to interject personal opinion. If asked for an opinion, politely decline. Do not offer solutions.
- *When an adequate compromise is reached, ask each person whether he or she is willing to abide by the agreement.* Once a consensus is reached, confirm that all parties are satisfied and that your presence is no longer required, and then leave. This is called the reconciliation phase.

It may not always be possible for the parties to reach a consensus within a reasonable time. What is a reasonable time? There is no single answer. It depends on the complexity of the problem, the time available, and the willingness of the disputants to work toward a consensus. Use your judgment to determine what is reasonable. You may have to concede that you are unable to effectively mediate the situation and are unable to help the parties reach an agreement within a reasonable time.

PERSONAL ANGER MANAGEMENT IN MEDIATION

Mediation may be a frustrating process for those who think that they are the problem solvers. This frustration may lead to feelings of anger, either about the initial circumstances of the problem or about the inability of the involved parties to reach a consensus or to follow the mediation rules as outlined above. There are some preparatory steps that you can take to reduce the likelihood of angry reactions.

Develop an action plan that is professional and non-antagonistic before entering the mediation process.

- *Avoid an all-or-nothing approach.* Mediation is a process of compromise. There is no winner. The objective is to reach a consensus that results in no one feeling that he or she is the losing party.

- *Decide that you will allow the parties to speak their minds and state their positions.* You cannot predict what they are going to say, nor should you jump to conclusions.

- *Do not exacerbate the problem.* No matter how serious you believe the problem may be, the problem is not yours. There is no need to identify the magnitude of the problem as seen from your perspective. If the parties are able to manage the problem through mediation, and the danger of violent reactions has been averted, the mediation was successful.

- *Do not display your anger during mediation.* Such displays may show that you are not in control and this will serve to aggravate the situation.

After the occurrence, evaluate your handling of the situation. Doing so will help you recognize and overcome anger in future mediations, or at least prevent those feelings of anger from becoming apparent. Ask yourself the following questions:

1. Did I avoid linear thinking? Did I resort to all-or-nothing solutions, anticipate the thoughts and responses of the parties involved, or magnify the problem or perceived personality "problems" of the parties involved?

2. How did I react to confrontation by the parties? Did I take the confrontational situation personally? Did I remain calm and in control?

3. How well did I recognize and control my anger? Did I recognize my own body signals (tense muscles, increased heart rate, agitation, etc.)? Did I use breathing and internal relaxation techniques to control my feelings?

4. Did I deal with my feelings after the occurrence? Did I talk to someone about stress management? Have I made a plan to alleviate my anger in future situations—for example, control my overall stress through healthy physical and relaxation activities? It is important that you have a healthy outlet for suppressed anger. Physical exercise and use of relaxation techniques are the best solutions to controlling levels of cumulative anger.

KEY TERMS

active listening

aggressiveness

assertiveness

coerce

influence

mediation

violence

REFERENCES

Hafen, B., & Frandsen, K. (1985). *Psychological emergencies and crisis intervention.* Scarborough, ON: Prentice Hall.

Statistics Canada. (2010). Police-reported crime statistics, 2009. *The Daily,* Tuesday, July 20, 2010.

Thomas, K.W., & Kilmann, R.H. (1974). Thomas-Kilmann conflict mode instrument. Mountain View, CA: Xicom and CPP.

EXERCISES

SELF-ASSESSMENT INSTRUMENT

Listed below are 15 statements. Read each statement and assign each a numerical value from 1 to 5 reflecting how you react in a conflict. Answer as you actually behave, not as you think you should react.

1 Always   2 Very often   3 Sometimes   4 Not very often   5 Rarely

_5_ a. I argue with peers and colleagues to defend the merits of my views.

_2_ b. I try to reach compromises through negotiation.

_3_ c. I attempt to meet the expectations of others.

_2_ d. I seek to find mutually acceptable solutions.

_3_ e. I am firm when it comes to defending my beliefs.

_3_ f. I try to avoid being singled out, keeping conflict with others to myself.

_3_ g. I uphold my solutions to problems.

_2_ h. I compromise in order to reach solutions.

_2_ i. I exchange information with others so that problems can be solved together.

_3_ j. I avoid discussing my differences with others.

_3_ k. I try to accommodate the wishes of my peers and colleagues.

_23_ l. I seek to bring everyone's concerns out into the open to resolve disputes.

_4_ m. I put forward middle positions in an effort to break deadlocks.

_2_ n. I accept the recommendations of colleagues and peers.

_3_ o. I avoid hard feelings by keeping my disagreements with others to myself.

The 15 statements you just read are listed below in five categories. Each category contains the letters of three statements. Record the number you placed next to each statement. Your dominant style will be your lowest score.

Style   *Total*

Competing	a.	5	e.	3	g.	3	11
Collaborating	d.	2	i.	2	l.	3	7
Avoiding	f.	3	j.	3	o.	3	9
Accommodating	c.	3	k.	3	n.	2	8
Compromising	b.	2	h.	2	m.	4	8

TRUE OR FALSE

_____ 1. The attitude of the attending officer has no bearing on the outcome of an intervention.

_____ 2. A non-violent situation can become violent upon of the arrival of officers.

_____ 3. Non-violent disputants should be physically separated and their eye contact with each other broken.

_____ 4. Delivering an ultimatum is a good way for officers to defuse a situation.

_____ 5. In mediation, a solution to a dispute should come from the disputants themselves.

MULTIPLE CHOICE

1. Mediation is an effective problem-solving technique
   a. in most of the situations encountered by police officers
   b. in only a few situations encountered by police officers
   c. in none of the situations encountered by police officers
   d. only in domestic disturbance situations

2. Appropriate options in a conflict or crisis situation include
   a. arrest
   b. inaction
   c. mediation
   d. all of the above

3. The most important ability that you must possess in a conflict or crisis situation is
   a. the ability to defend yourself
   b. the ability to communicate
   c. the ability to use common sense and good judgment
   d. none of the above

4. If you cannot assist a person with a problem, you should
    a. tell the person that you cannot help, and then leave the scene
    b. call a relative of the person
    c. refer the person to an appropriate community or social service agency
    d. remain at the scene as long as the person wishes

SHORT ANSWER

1. Outline the differences between the terms "influence" and "coerce" in the context of verbal communication techniques.

2. Outline the differences between the terms "aggressiveness" and "assertiveness" in the context of verbal communication techniques.

3. Explain proxemics in the context of communication techniques.

4. Why is it more advantageous to influence a person's decision through effective communication than to coerce the person's decision?

5. Explain the four levels of awareness and which levels may be experienced by police officers in the course of their duties.

6. Identify some strategies that may be used to help you control the stress reaction experienced when facing potentially violent situations.

7. Explain why it is important for an officer to remain calm when intervening in an emotionally charged dispute.

8. Explain why the potential for violence between the disputants arises when officers enter a previously non-violent situation.

9. What is the fundamental obligation of police officers when intervening in a conflict situation?

10. Briefly describe five potential causes of violent behaviour.

11. List five outward signs of a possibly violent person.

12. Briefly explain the procedure for dealing with a potentially violent person.

13. Explain active listening and why it is an important skill for police officers.

14. Explain the phrase "perception is reality" in the context of problem identification.

CASE ANALYSIS

You are called to the corporate headquarters of Salter Industries to investigate a complaint of harassment. You speak to the complainant, Ruthie Smith. She tells you that Joe Schmoe sprayed her with pepper spray. Her eyes are watering, there are large quantities of mucus running from her nose, and her face is red. She does not appear to have any breathing difficulty.

Ruthie tells you that Joe sprayed her for no reason. You advise her to wash her face and eyes with large quantities of fresh water. She proceeds to do so.

You speak with Joe Schmoe. He tells you that Ruthie Smith continually bothers him about being homosexual and constantly tells him that she can "convert" him.

About 15 minutes ago they met in the hallway, where she again began to taunt him about his sexuality and reiterated that she can convert him. She proceeded to touch his genitals through his pants.

He sprayed her with pepper spray. He tells you that he keeps a small container in his shirt pocket for protection.

What will you do in this situation?

Problem Solving

3

INTRODUCTION

Problem solving is an integral part of policing. Problem solving and improvisational skills are paramount in allowing police officers to successfully and safely complete their duties. Your problem-solving skills will determine how successful you will be.

The previous chapter discussed communication techniques and conflict management styles. This chapter will expand your understanding of the nature of conflict through discussion of problem-solving models that have proven to be effective in a law enforcement context.

The generic term "problem solving" is used in many of the popular problem-solving models. However, in the context of intervention by police officers, it may be a misnomer. A more accurate term would be "problem management."

In many instances, you as a police officer cannot solve the problem. Most conflicts begin long before your arrival. You likely have had no involvement in the circumstances leading to the conflict, and therefore have no knowledge of the situation that led to the conflict. The information you are able to obtain usually comes from the parties involved in the dispute, who are not always objective and unbiased. Although you are unlikely to be able to solve their problem, you may, by using the proper techniques, be able to assist the parties in resolving their dispute. At the least, you may be able to prevent the problem from escalating.

There are also some situations where successful intervention is impossible. There are situations, as well, where conflict management may require removal of one or more of the involved parties through arrest or other means, such as enforcement of the provisions of the Ontario *Trespass to Property Act*. In other cases, a party may be persuaded to leave voluntarily. Although removal may appear to bring an end to the dispute, in many instances it only postpones it. Nevertheless, removal may be necessary to protect the parties or public safety.

The problem management models discussed below are designed to allow you to consider the needs of all concerned parties before proposing or facilitating a response. Because it is unlikely that your response will satisfy the interests of all

CHAPTER OBJECTIVES

After completing this chapter, you should be able to:

- Understand the importance of an officer's attitude in problem solving.
- Identify, explain, and apply each component of the SARA, CAPRA, and PARE problem-solving models.

parties involved, you must decide the best response based upon your analysis of the information available at the time that your decision needs to be made.

The responses available to you will depend on your ability to intervene in the situation. If the problem is between the involved parties and not between the public and the parties, the number of response options will be reduced. In situations where you are not duty-bound to intervene, your role may be best described as that of a facilitator. Recognition of these limitations is an essential component of effective problem solving.

Failure to recognize the nature of the problem through a thorough analysis of the situation will lead to frustration and an inability to assist the involved persons. The inability to ensure that the involved parties take ownership of their problem is a common reason for failure to manage the problem. You may believe that you are required to resolve any situation.

Another common fallacy is that you are expected to provide expert solutions to any problem. You must be able to recognize when it is appropriate to refer the problem to a person or organization with more subject-specific expertise—for example, a colleague, social worker, or addiction support group.

Problem-solving skills can be learned by almost anyone. All that is required is a positive attitude, a willingness to learn, and a desire to help.

ATTITUDE

In any conflict situation, you must remain professional and objective. The persons involved in the conflict look to you to provide unbiased responses. You should remain as polite as possible under the circumstances, but always remember the possible need for forceful verbal or physical intervention if safety issues arise.

You should be patient and allow the parties time to adequately explain their problem. Questions should be focused on the problem only. You should attempt to respect the parties' privacy by not searching for unnecessary personal details.

The attitude you project will have a substantial effect on the attitude of the parties. A positive attitude should be displayed even if you are unsure of the outcome of the intervention. The parties may be more likely to engage in meaningful conversation if you display the attitude that the situation is solvable.

Motivating the parties to address the situation in a positive manner can alleviate tension. If a solution is not immediately reached, remain patient and continue to seek a resolution. You must remain calm even if the conversation among the parties becomes heated. Any emotional outbursts on your part may reinforce the parties' perception that the situation is out of control and that you cannot help.

Intervene with empathy, but not sympathy. Recall from Chapter 2 that "empathy" means trying to see a situation from another's perspective. It can be displayed by accepting emotions and by displaying respect for the worth of another. "Sympathy" means feeling sorry for someone. A display of sympathy may lead one party in a dispute to believe that you are on his or her side.

Offer cautious guidance, but not solutions, to individuals involved in a dispute. You can be helpful, but cannot solve someone else's problems. Remain aware that the need for non-verbal intervention can arise at any time. Always be prepared for a possible escalation to violence.

PROBLEM-SOLVING PROCESSES

Along with the proper attitude, you must have a method of sequentially addressing a problem—that is, a way to break down the process into steps. Although the following problem-solving models were developed for law enforcement purposes, each can be adapted to any conflict situation when you understand the sequential nature of the components of the models.

One such problem-solving process, known by the acronym **SARA** (scanning, analysis, response, and assessment), is used by many law enforcement services throughout Canada. The SARA problem-solving model was first used in Virginia in the early 1980s. The SARA process is not as detailed as the processes discussed later in this chapter, but it is easy to use and allows quick and effective intervention. Many of the later problem-solving models are based on the SARA model.

SARA
a problem-solving process with four components: scanning, analysis, response, and assessment

The SARA model consists of four steps:

1. *Scanning.* The purpose of scanning is to determine whether the problem may benefit from intervention. If more than one problem is identified, the problems must be prioritized.

2. *Analysis.* The analysis considers all aspects of the problem—the victim, the offender, the circumstances leading to the occurrence, etc.

3. *Response.* The response is a strategy based on the analysis of the problem and implementation of the strategy.

4. *Assessment.* The assessment evaluates the response strategy. Was the response effective? Why? Why not? What could be done to make it more effective and easier to implement?

The SARA model can be quickly adapted to most situations but, as with all police interventions in conflict situations, the officer must be ready to interrupt the process and arrest an offender if necessary. See Figure 3.1.

There are other popular problem-solving models that may require more time than the SARA model, but generate more in-depth information and response options. That being said, these problem-solving models are substantially based on the concepts of the SARA model.

The two most popular of these models are the CAPRA problem-solving model, used by the Royal Canadian Mounted Police as its operational model, and the PARE model, used by the Ontario Provincial Police as its community policing operational model.

THE CAPRA CONFLICT MANAGEMENT SYSTEM

This book uses an adaptation of the **CAPRA** system of problem solving, similar to the RCMP operational policing model. The system can be successfully applied to any conflict or crisis situation once its components are fully understood. The following is a description of the system's components. Each letter in the acronym CAPRA relates to a different aspect of the system.

CAPRA
a problem-solving system with five components: clients (and communication skills), acquiring and analyzing information, partnerships, response, and assessment

Figure 3.1   The SARA Problem-Solving Model

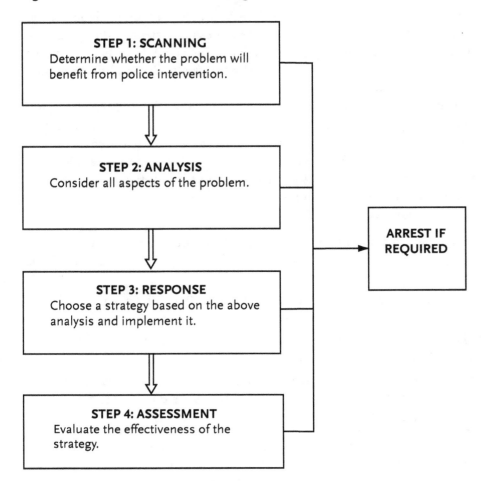

Components of the CAPRA System

C   Clients

client
anyone directly or indirectly
involved in an occurrence, or
in any way affected by it

The C in CAPRA stands for client. You must be able to identify the client—the person in need, or the person that should be addressed. The person may have a problem or may be creating a problem. A **client** may be anyone directly or indirectly involved in an occurrence, or in any way affected by it. "Direct clients" are the persons with whom you come into contact in everyday occurrences. They include suspects, victims, witnesses, and concerned citizens. "Indirect clients" are persons with whom you may not have direct contact but who are affected by your actions. Indirect clients include business communities, special interest and cultural groups, and the general public. Getting to know a client's needs and expectations greatly promotes efficiency when problems arise and may assist in appropriately allocating resources for the client.

The C in CAPRA also refers to the communication skills that you must possess in order to successfully intervene.

IMPORTANCE OF KNOWING YOUR CLIENTS

The better you understand a client, the more quickly and effectively you can

- meet the client's needs, demands, and expectations;
- defuse potentially violent situations;
- resolve community safety problems;
- generate workable and sustainable preventive action; and
- mobilize the community to assist in achieving a safe environment (Royal Canadian Mounted Police, 2009).

EXPECTATIONS OF CLIENTS

The following are some examples of what clients expect from law enforcement personnel in various contexts:

- *Call for assistance.* Be polite, caring, and respectful. Provide referral and followup where appropriate.
- *Call to an incident in progress.* Attend to victims. Apprehend the suspect. Where property has been stolen, have the goods returned. Reduce the likelihood of recurrence.
- *Call to an incident after the fact.* Increase the likelihood of successful prosecution through appropriate collection of evidence according to law and policy.
- *Interaction with a suspect.* Control the suspect to ensure public and police safety. Treat him or her with respect and dignity.
- *Testimony in court.* Provide concise, objective, honest, and accurate testimony to ensure the fair outcome of the trial.
- *Community group call for assistance.* Show sensitivity and ensure the full participation of community members in preventive problem solving to arrive at a mutually agreed upon strategy (Royal Canadian Mounted Police, 2009).

A   Acquiring and Analyzing Information

You must be able to acquire and analyze relevant information not only to help resolve an incident, but also to investigate possible offences. Acquiring and analyzing information may also help you in your determination of who the primary client should be. Gathering and analyzing information requires knowledge of procedure, legislation, and investigative techniques, as well as an open mind unclouded by prejudice or bias. Information can be obtained from many sources. Your task is to determine where information can be found, which information is relevant, and which sources are the most credible. Sources of information include victims, witnesses, and fellow officers. Don't dismiss pertinent information obtainable through unpleasant activities such as interviewing belligerent witnesses or searching garbage containers.

To acquire and analyze information effectively, you must use your skills in crime analysis, leadership, communication, and time management. A combination of these skills will permit quicker identification of problems, allowing a more immediate response.

P Partnerships

Remember that problem solving requires partnerships. You may determine that a person's problem is beyond the scope of your ability or authority to solve. You must be able to direct your client to an agency or to a community-based organization that may be able to help. Knowing what services the relevant community-based organizations and agencies offer is essential to making a proper referral. Some examples of available partners include:

- *Experts in the field*—for example, social workers and colleagues with experience or expertise in a particular area.
- *Community groups*—for example, cultural groups, addiction support groups, and organizations supporting battered women and other victims.
- *Individual citizens*—volunteers or individuals who may be privy to information that can help solve the problem.

"Partnership" also refers to the relationships that you may build with the parties to a conflict or with witnesses. You may decide to partner with one or more of the involved parties if the party is genuinely interested in resolving the conflict. This strategy may be used in non-violent situations when the conflict involves only differing perspectives and you believe that you can influence the reasoning of those involved.

In some situations, witnesses may provide an unbiased perspective that could be helpful in managing the situation. Involvement of individuals not directly concerned in the conflict should be limited to voluntary involvement, and only in non-violent situations.

To establish a working partnership, you need to use effective interpersonal communication skills and display qualities such as integrity and respect for others. Such partnerships may help immensely in acquiring information. By working together, the partners may be able to remove the source of the problem.

Should you choose to establish a working relationship with one or more parties, you must remain in control of the situation. You are present because the parties are unable to resolve the conflict. The partnership extends only so far and its purpose is to allow a fuller disclosure of the problem and the possibility of a solution. You must set clear boundaries that establish the limits of allowable participation by the partners.

IMPORTANCE OF ESTABLISHING AND MAINTAINING PARTNERSHIPS

Officers should attempt to establish and maintain partnerships. Establishing and maintaining partnerships on an ongoing basis has several benefits (Royal Canadian Mounted Police, 2009):

1. It develops trust to ensure that partners are available when they are needed.

2. It ensures that you are aware of all the potential partners that do exist so that the best available information or assistance can be provided to clients as soon as possible.

3. It ensures that there are contingency plans in place for cases where a preferred partner is unavailable, so that when assistance is required, it is still immediately available from another partner.

4. It ensures that clients receive assistance and follow-up through partners when police have other priorities that require their attention.

R Response

"Response" encompasses incident and risk management, officer and public safety, decision making, and handling of suspects and prisoners. It can include arrest, use of force, mediation, referral, non-involvement, and a number of other incident-specific responses. The type of response depends on your skills in areas such as communication, negotiation, and the use of force, and on your physical condition. Responses will vary, but must remain within the confines of legislation and the policies of your police service.

Four categories of response are available:

1. *Service.* Referral of the client to partner agencies.

2. *Protection.* Protection of the public interest and safety through appropriate action.

3. *Enforcement.* Enforcement of the law by arrest or other means. (Enforcement is not always the ideal response but it is sometimes necessary.)

4. *Prevention.* Prevention of conflicts. This is the ultimate goal. If workable community strategies are in place and you possess the knowledge and ability to implement these strategies, all of society benefits.

A Assessment

You must continually assess your actions. Self-evaluation can improve your ability to intervene in conflict situations. Mistakes may have serious consequences, but should be viewed as opportunities to learn. A single mistake is a learning experience—a repeated mistake displays incompetence. Self-assessment gives you the opportunity to continually enhance your skills and knowledge.

To assess your actions, begin by establishing some criteria for self-evaluation, such as whether the chosen response met the needs of the client and whether the response fell within the guidelines of your police service. Compare your performance against recognized standards of performance.

"Assessment" also encompasses your ability to assess the outcome of a decision before any action is carried out. The ability to predict the likely outcome of an action enhances your ability to make better choices in a given situation.

Application of the CAPRA System

Effective application of the CAPRA system requires an in-depth and comprehensive knowledge of what information must be obtained, how to obtain the information, and how to determine and assess a client's response. The following are some questions that may help you to work through the process:

- *Clients.* Who are the clients (direct and indirect)?
- *Acquiring and analyzing information.* What is the apparent problem? What are the underlying issues in the dispute? What are the clients' expectations, needs, and demands? What sources of information are available?
- *Partnerships.* Who are the potential partners that may help define the problem or resolve the issue?
- *Response.* Which type of response does this situation require: service, protection, enforcement, or prevention?
- *Assessment.* What are the possible consequences of the chosen response? Are the identified consequences acceptable in this situation? Was the chosen response correct for this situation? What can be learned from the occurrence?

Learning Activity 3.1

The scenarios in this learning activity are not police related. They are designed to allow you to recognize that the CAPRA problem-solving model is applicable to any situation.

The problem-solving process allows you to consider all concerned parties before proposing or facilitating a response. It is likely not possible to satisfy all interests identified in the application of the problem-solving model. You must decide the "best" response based upon your analysis of the information available at the time the decision is to be made.

Case 1

You are the owner of a small fitness club. Several patrons have approached you to complain that they have to wait too long to use the exercise equipment during the busy noon-hour period. You tell them that you will look into the matter. Your staff tells you that there is indeed a problem. Some patrons are waiting as long as 20 minutes to use some of the equipment. In the opinion of the staff, six new pieces of equipment are required to alleviate the problem. The cost of the new equipment is about $60,000, which is beyond your financial capabilities.

Using the CAPRA system, propose some solutions to this problem. Assess the possible outcomes of each solution.

Case 2

You are an employee at a fast-food restaurant. Three other employees work the late shift with you. For the past four Fridays, two employees, John and Jane, have been highly intoxicated when they came to work. Because of this, they have been unable to work, so you and the remaining employee, Abe, have had to do their share of the work.

You arrive at the restaurant for your Friday shift and meet Abe in the parking lot. The two of you discuss the situation. Abe is tired of having to work harder because of John and Jane, and says, "We should do something about it." You agree.

John and Jane arrive about 30 minutes late. They are again highly intoxicated. They stagger to the employee change room, telling you that they will be right out. The restaurant is quite busy. After 30 minutes they have still not come out of the room. You check the room and find them both passed out on the floor. Attempts to revive them are unsuccessful. You go back to serving customers while Abe is busy in the kitchen.

About four hours later, John walks out of the change room and asks, "What's going on?" He is still intoxicated. Luckily the restaurant is closed. You tell him, "It's time to clean up around here." He tells you he is too sick and is going home. He also tells you that he has been having problems at home and that he is in financial trouble and may lose his car. He then walks out the door. Jane is still sleeping in the change room. You and Abe have to work an extra three hours to finish cleaning.

Using the CAPRA system, propose some solutions to this problem. Assess the possible outcomes of each solution.

Case 3

You are teaching a law class of 45 students. Not for the first time, two students in particular are having difficulty grasping an advanced concept. You therefore take a few minutes in class to re-explain the concept. After class you are approached by three students who complain that the class is going too slowly. They are becoming bored and want the class to progress faster. They are tired of you always having to stop and re-explain concepts to the same two students. They are paying a lot of money to take this course and want an immediate change. You explain that the two students in question are working full-time and raising families, and that they can't stay after class for extra help. The response is, "We don't care. If they can't afford to be in college, they shouldn't be here."

Using the CAPRA system, propose some solutions to this problem. Assess the possible outcomes of each solution.

THE PARE PROBLEM-SOLVING MODEL

PARE
a problem-solving system
with four components:
problem identification,
analysis, response,
and evaluation

The **PARE** model is a sequential problem-solving model that was developed in 1997 by the Ontario Provincial Police. Its fundamental components are similar to those of the CAPRA model.

The PARE model was developed with the goals and philosophies of community policing in mind. It may be more applicable to community-type problems than the CAPRA model, which has been adapted for use in occurrences involving specific individuals and more "personalized" problems.

Components of the PARE Model

The PARE problem-solving model consists of four parts: problem identification; analysis; response; and evaluation. See Figure 3.2.

Problem Identification

The most crucial step in problem solving is accurately identifying the problem. When trying to ascertain the true nature of a problem, you should do the following:

- *Consider all perceptions of the problem.* Does everyone see the same problem?
- *Determine whether the problem is longstanding.* Is the identified problem overshadowing an underlying issue? Longstanding problems usually cannot be solved through intervention by police officers. A referral may be of assistance.
- *Examine the problem using the "five Ws."* Ask Who? What? When? Where? Why?
- *View the problem in context with the available information.* Who is involved? Who has contributed to the problem?

A   Analysis

In analyzing the problem, you should

- try to determine the underlying causes of the problem;
- gather all available information on the victim, offender(s), and the situation—the information may be obtained on scene, through previous contact with the parties, from occurrence reports, from other officers, or from other sources; and
- numerically rate (prioritize) the problem.

The Ontario Provincial Police have developed a scale to numerically rate problems based on the impact, seriousness, complexity, and solvability of the problem. This numeric ranking system may be helpful in determining how to allocate resources in situations of multiple, simultaneous occurrences. Problems ranking numerically higher may be more easily resolved, or should receive immediate attention depending on the overall context of the problem. The scale is designed to

Figure 3.2   The PARE Problem-Solving Model

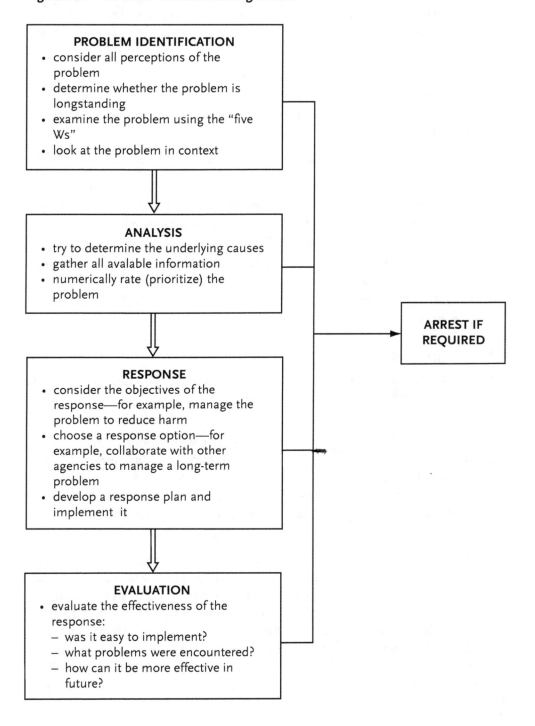

PROBLEM IDENTIFICATION
- consider all perceptions of the problem
- determine whether the problem is longstanding
- examine the problem using the "five Ws"
- look at the problem in context

ANALYSIS
- try to determine the underlying causes
- gather all avalable information
- numerically rate (prioritize) the problem

RESPONSE
- consider the objectives of the response—for example, manage the problem to reduce harm
- choose a response option—for example, collaborate with other agencies to manage a long-term problem
- develop a response plan and implement it

EVALUATION
- evaluate the effectiveness of the response:
  - was it easy to implement?
  - what problems were encountered?
  - how can it be more effective in future?

ARREST IF REQUIRED

ensure that the least complex and most easily solved problem is given the highest priority. However, situations involving injury or the threat of violence should receive first priority regardless of their numerical ranking. The ranking system is set out below.

1. Impact   1 least–5 most
2. Seriousness   1 least–5 most
3. Complexity   1 most–5 least
4. Solvability   1 difficult–5 easy

To determine the numerical ranking for each of these criteria, ask yourself the following questions:

- *Impact of the problem.* Is it a big problem? Who is affected by the problem?
- *Seriousness of the problem.* Would it be dangerous to not address the problem? Is the public concerned?
- *Complexity of the problem.* Are resources available to address the problem? Is it a "law enforcement problem"?
- *Solvability of the problem.* Can the problem be solved by officers with the resources available?

OPP RANKING SYSTEM: AN EXAMPLE

The following example shows how police might use the OPP ranking system to deal with two simultaneous calls for assistance.

Call one
Several youths are loitering in front of a convenience store. They are not impeding customers, but the store owner wants them removed from the area. He doesn't think they are good for business.

Call two
A store owner reports that approximately ten minutes ago two persons broke his store window, took several smartphones that were on display, and fled on foot.

Both calls originate in the same commercial area. After applying the numerical ranking system to these simultaneous calls, the officers decide that call one should be addressed first. Why not call two? Because call two will consume considerably more police time and will be difficult to solve. Further, there is no immediate danger and there is little chance that the suspects can be immediately apprehended. Call one, on the other hand, is in the general area of call two and will likely consume very little police time. More importantly, addressing call one first may prevent a violent escalation of the situation. Police might rank these occurrences as follows:

Call one
Impact	1
Seriousness	2
Complexity	5
Solvability	5

Call two
Impact	2 (no injury)
Seriousness	1
Complexity	1
Solvability	1

R   Response

In responding to a problem, you must consider the objectives of your response and your response options.

OBJECTIVES OF RESPONSE

- *Eliminate the problem.* Usually, you will be able to eliminate only simple problems. It is difficult to eliminate more complex problems.
- *Reduce the harm.* Manage problems in a manner that reduces the harm.
- *Improve the response through improved community services to victims.* Police can establish programs such as the Victim Crisis Assistance and Referral Service (VCARS). (See Chapter 9.)
- *Redefine responsibility for the problem.* Determine whether other community agencies may be better equipped to address the problem.

RESPONSE OPTIONS

Depending on the objectives identified, a number of response options are available:

- *Investigation and enforcement.* Arrest and charging may manage and, in some situations, eliminate the problem. Enforcement is usually only a short-term solution, but in some situations it is necessary.
- *Focused strategies.* Usually a small number of criminals are responsible for a large number of offences. Removing these offenders may greatly reduce crime. The provisions of the *Trespass to Property Act* may be applicable in situations where a few individuals cause an inordinate number of problems on private property.
- *Interagency strategies.* Collaboration with other agencies (for example, a Children's Aid Society or a branch of the Canadian Mental Health Association) may be an effective way to manage long-term problems. Community agencies often have more problem-specific expertise and time than police.
- *Referral to provincial or municipal government agencies in non-criminal matters.* Examples include the Ontario Landlord and Tenant Board (which resolves complaints that come under the Ontario *Residential Tenancies Act, 2006*) and Investigation Services, Municipal Licensing and Standards Division (which ensures compliance with Toronto bylaws, among other matters).
- *More discriminating use of law enforcement.* A stronger focus on prevention rather than enforcement can be a more effective way to deal with problems.
- *Community education.* Educating the community can help to reduce the occurrence of certain crimes. Fraud prevention programs are a good example.
- *Community mobilization and crime prevention programs.* The Neighbourhood Watch and Block Parent programs are two examples.

- *Environmental design.* Community design features, such as well-lit areas, can assist in crime reduction. Consultation on environmental design with the aim of crime prevention can be an effective strategy.

At this point, the problem has been identified and analyzed, and a response option has been chosen. An intervention plan is now developed and implemented based on the information obtained through the process. The response must now be evaluated.

E   Evaluation

To evaluate the effectiveness of your response, ask the following questions:

- Was the response easy to implement?
- What problems were encountered?
- What can be done to make this response more effective in future similar situations?

Application of the PARE Problem-Solving Model

To effectively apply the PARE problem-solving model, ask yourself the following self-directed questions. These questions are adapted to the format of the model to allow self-assessment.

Problem Identification

- Can the problem be solved or managed through intervention, or is it a long-term problem that cannot be effectively addressed by police?
- Do all involved parties agree that the problem has been accurately identified?

Analysis

- Does anyone require medical assistance?
- Is there any threat of violence?
- Has all information available about the victim, the offender, and the situation been considered?
- Does the description of the problem by the victim and the offender match the available evidence?
- Are the statements of the victim and the offender credible?
- Has information obtained through previous occurrences been considered?
- If more than one problem has been identified, have the problems been prioritized?
- How complex is the problem?
- Can the problem be solved or managed through the necessarily brief law enforcement intervention?

Response

- Would there be any repercussions if you do not intervene?
- Is the problem a law enforcement problem or are the parties responsible for the solution?
- Is enforcement through charging an appropriate response?
- Is mediation an appropriate response?
- Would referral to a community agency be an effective response?
- Is arrest necessary?

Evaluation

- Was the response appropriate in light of the circumstances and information available at the time?
- What difficulties were encountered when implementing the response?
- In hindsight, was there a better option available?
- What resources could have been used that were not used or available initially?
- How could these resources be accessed in the future?
- Was the overall outcome of this intervention positive or negative?
- Was the intervention a learning experience?
- Will knowledge gained enhance the effectiveness of interventions in future similar incidents?

Learning Activity 3.2

You are a police officer responding to a complaint at the public library. You obtain the following information.

There are three picnic tables at the rear of the building that are used as a place of relaxation by library staff and families with their children. The last six mornings in a row, there were human feces in the middle of each table. The area is open to the public. There is no fence. The feces were deposited sometime between closing at 10 p.m. and 6 a.m., when staff arrive. Cleaning staff cleaned and disinfected the tables each morning after the incidents occurred, but neither the library staff nor the public has been made aware of the situation.

Video cameras had been set up, but captured only a grainy image of a person committing the act. The person could not be identified from the video. His face was covered. The library manager is irate and wants something done immediately.

What will you do? Apply the PARE problem-solving model to this problem.

SUMMARY

A thorough understanding of the components of the problem-solving models will allow you to develop a model of problem management that you can effectively apply. Your method of problem solving may not exactly follow the previously outlined process of problem management. As discussed in Chapter 2, there are differing styles of conflict management that may be applicable in various situations or that you may find better suited to your personality. After assessing your effective responses, you will likely observe that you have applied, intentionally or unintentionally, many of the components of the problem-solving models discussed in this chapter.

KEY TERMS

CAPRA   PARE
client   SARA

REFERENCES

Royal Canadian Mounted Police. (2009). *Incident management/intervention model*. Retrieved from http://www.rcmp-grc.gc.ca/index-eng.htm.

Trespass to Property Act. (1990). RSO 1990, c. T.21.

EXERCISES

TRUE OR FALSE

_____ 1. It is important to offer several solution options to individuals involved in a dispute.

_____ 2. Under the CAPRA system of problem solving, a "client" is anyone directly or indirectly involved in an occurrence.

_____ 3. Acquiring and analyzing relevant information is important for investigating possible offences, as well as helping to resolve an incident.

_____ 4. The CAPRA system is applicable only to law enforcement.

_____ 5. It is important to select one system or model for problem solving and apply it consistently.

_____ 6. When intervening in a conflict situation, a police officer will never partner with one of the parties.

_____ 7. Properly applying the CAPRA system will allow a police officer to solve any problem.

_____ 8. Arrest is an option provided for by the CAPRA system.

_____ 9. With some guidance, most parties can solve their own problems.

MULTIPLE CHOICE

1. As a police officer, it is your responsibility to
    a. resolve all disputes between individuals that arise on your watch
    b. show sympathy to gain trust
    c. recognize the nature of the problem and the limits of your authority
    d. both a and c
    e. all of the above

2. Police intervention may be required
    a. in domestic disputes
    b. in landlord and tenant disputes
    c. in property ownership disputes
    d. all of the above

3. When dealing with an incident, you should
    a. be patient and allow the parties sufficient opportunity to explain their problem
    b. never use forceful or physical intervention
    c. remain objective
    d. both a and c
    e. all of the above

4. The acronym SARA means
    a. Scenario/Analysis/Response/Assessment
    b. Scanning/Analysis/Result/Assessment
    c. Scanning/Action/Response/Assessment
    d. Scanning/Analysis/Response/Assessment
    e. Scanning/Analysis/Response/Actualize

5. The acronym PARE means
    a. Problem identification/Analysis/Response/Evaluation
    b. Police notification/Analysis/Response/Evaluation
    c. Problem identification/Action/Response/Evaluation
    d. Problem identification/Analysis/Result/Evaluation
    e. Problem identification/Analysis/Response/Entry in notebook

6. The acronym CAPRA means

    a. Crisis/Acquiring and analyzing information/Partnerships/Response/ Assessment

    b. Clients/Acquiring and analyzing information/Partnerships/Response/ Assessment

    c. Clients/Analysis/Partnerships/Response/Assessment

    d. Clients/Acquiring and analyzing information/Performance/Response/ Assessment

    e. Clients/Acquiring and analyzing information/Partnerships/Response/ Actualize

Short Answer

1. Briefly describe the four components of the SARA problem-solving model.

2. Briefly describe the four components of the PARE problem-solving model.

3. Briefly describe the five components of the CAPRA conflict management system.

CASE ANALYSIS

Case 3.1

You are a police officer dispatched to a call for assistance at an apartment building. You are met at the entrance by Mr. Smith. He tells you that the building owner refuses to rent him an apartment because he is collecting social assistance. The owner, Mr. Collins, comes to the entrance to speak with you. He tells you he doesn't want to rent the apartment to someone on social assistance because the last time he did, the tenants wrecked the apartment.

Using the CAPRA system, answer the following questions:

1. Who are the clients in this scenario?

2. What information do you need? From which sources can you obtain this information?

3. What partners are available to assist you in this situation?

4. What is an appropriate response?

5. Assess your response. What are some possible outcomes?

Case 3.2

You are a police officer responding to a complaint at the residence of the local community college. You are met in the lobby by a young female student. She complains that one of her professors, Professor Doe, has been harassing her. She explains that Professor Doe has continually been making comments rife with sexual innuendoes. Professor Doe has never called her at home but takes every opportunity to comment on her looks and actions.

Using the CAPRA system, answer the following questions:

1. Who are the clients in this scenario?

2. What information do you need? From which sources can you obtain this information?

3. Which partners are available to assist you in this situation?

4. What is an appropriate response?

5. Assess your response. What are some possible outcomes?

Case 3.3

You are a police officer in charge of community policing. You are participating in a public meeting regarding community problems.

Several residents of Birch Street complain about the noise on the street after closing time at a nearby college bar. There is shouting, swearing, fighting, and cars "squealing" their tires. One complainant tells you that his two children, ages two and three, are awakened by the noise on Thursday, Friday, and Saturday nights. They are afraid to go to sleep because of the loud noises that awaken them.

Others complain of drunken students walking through their yards. One person, living directly behind the college, tells you that some of them are urinating in her garden. They want something done about the problem.

Apply the PARE problem-solving model to this problem.

Case 3.4

During the same meeting, the Residential Safety Committee brings forth a complaint that children are not wearing helmets while riding their bicycles. The chair of the committee, Dr. Bain, states that this complaint was brought to the Police Services Board on three consecutive meetings. The board advised police to enforce the helmet bylaw. The committee has checked the number of bylaw charges regarding bicycle helmets. In the past three months, no charges have been laid. They demand that something be done to rectify the situation. They warn that if nothing is done, they will make a complaint to the Ontario Civilian Commission on Policing Services regarding the inability of the police service to provide adequate services.

Apply the PARE problem-solving model to this problem.

Case 3.5

The final complaint brought to your attention at the meeting regards pedestrians standing in the turning lane on the highway. The Residential Safety Committee cites several incidents where pedestrians have been observed standing in the turning lane during periods of heavy traffic.

The area in question has two lanes on either side of the turning lane. Pedestrians have been running from the sidewalk to the turning lane, where they wait for a break in the traffic before running across the other two lanes of traffic. Dr. Bain tells you that on three occasions (times and dates were noted), a police cruiser drove past the pedestrians as they stood in the turning lane. She asks you: "Will you address the problem of the pedestrians and the officers neglecting their duty or will you also neglect to do your duty?"

Apply the PARE problem-solving model to this problem.

Child Abuse

4

INTRODUCTION

Children of all ages, from babies to teenagers, and from all kinds of homes and from all types of ethnic, religious, social, and economic backgrounds, suffer from abuse. There are many kinds of abuse and these are not specific to certain age groups. Infants may be sexually abused and teenagers may be emotionally abused by humiliation and rejection.

Children may be abused by family members or by persons who are not family members. Family members include parents, spouses (current and former), children, siblings, or other individuals related to the victim by blood, marriage, or another legal relationship, such as adoption. All other relationships are considered to be non-family relationships (Ogrodnik, 2010).

STATISTICAL DATA: CHILD ABUSE IN CANADA

Quantifying the incidence of violent victimization against children and youth continues to be a challenge. In Canada, detailed information about police-reported violent incidents committed against children and youth is collected through Statistics Canada's Incident-Based Uniform Crime Reporting Survey (UCR2). However, police-reported violence represents only a portion of the abuse suffered by young persons. Children and youth can also be victims of maltreatment or neglect. While some of these harmful behaviours come to light when charges are laid under the *Criminal Code* of Canada and provincial/territorial child welfare legislation, their prevalence is more difficult to measure.

In order to obtain a more comprehensive picture of criminal victimization in Canada, Statistics Canada also collects self-reported victimization data through the General Social Survey on Victimization (GSS). However, because the GSS does not survey persons under the age of 15, our knowledge of self-reported victimization is lacking for child victims.

CHAPTER OBJECTIVES

After completing this chapter, you should be able to:

- Identify different types of child abuse.
- Differentiate between punishment and abuse.
- Recognize and understand general investigation techniques regarding child abuse.
- Explain the application of the *Child and Family Services Act* of Ontario.
- Identify possible criminal offences and applicable criminal law relating to child abuse.
- Develop effective responses to scenarios involving child abuse.

child
generally, a person under the age of 18; under some legislation, a person under the age of 16 or 14

This chapter will use statistics from the UCR2 unless otherwise noted.

The UCR2 survey found that just over 75,000 children and youth were victims of police-reported violent crime in 2008 (Ogrodnik, 2010). That is, for every 100,000 children and youth in Canada, 1,111 were victims of a violent offence.

The rate of violence against children and youth tends to increase as children get older. The lowest rate of violence reported was for children under 3 years of age (162 per 100,000). The rates for subsequent age groups were substantially higher (see Figure 4.1). Note, however, that the youngest victims (those under 3 years of age) must rely on others in their immediate vicinity to report violence against them. In the case of these victims, the perpetrators of the violence are most often family members. As a result, incidents of violence against children in this category are often underreported compared with other age groups, who have greater exposure to the outside world through attendance at school and participation in other activities.

Teens aged 15 to 17 reported the highest rate of violence (2,710 per 100,000) among all age categories. The higher violent victimization among teens may be attributed to the propensity of teens to engage in high-risk behaviours.

According to the International Youth Survey (IYS), over one-third of students in grades 7 to 9 in Toronto reported having engaged in delinquent behaviours, including behaviours involving violence, acts against property, and drugs.

The International Youth Survey is the Canadian portion of the International Self-Report Delinquency study (ISRD) that examined the behaviour of students in grades 7 to 9 in about 30 European countries, the United States, and Canada.

The survey was representative of each of the three grades (7 to 9) and, at the grade level, of both sexes. In April 2006, about 3,200 students in 176 schools completed the IYS.

For students under the age of 8, reported rates of violent crime were generally higher for female victims. For students between ages 9 and 12, male rates of abuse exceeded those of females. However, by the age of 13, the rate of abuse for females once again exceeded that of males, peaking at age 17 (see Figure 4.2). This increase is chiefly a result of higher rates of sexual violence against girls.

Physical Assault

Physical assaults are the most common type of violent crime experienced by children and youth. Almost 42,000 physical assaults against children and youth were reported to police in 2008 (Ogrodnik, 2010).

The UCR2 identifies four categories of physical assault. These are described below, along with their applicable *Criminal Code* section(s).

1. *Level 1: common assault.* This is the least serious form of assault. It includes pushing, slapping, punching, and face-to-face verbal threats (s. 266).

2. *Level 2: assault with a weapon or causing bodily harm.* This more serious form of assault involves carrying, using, or threatening to use a weapon against someone or causing someone bodily harm (s. 267).

Figure 4.1   Rates of Violent Victimization Highest Among Youth Aged 15 to 17

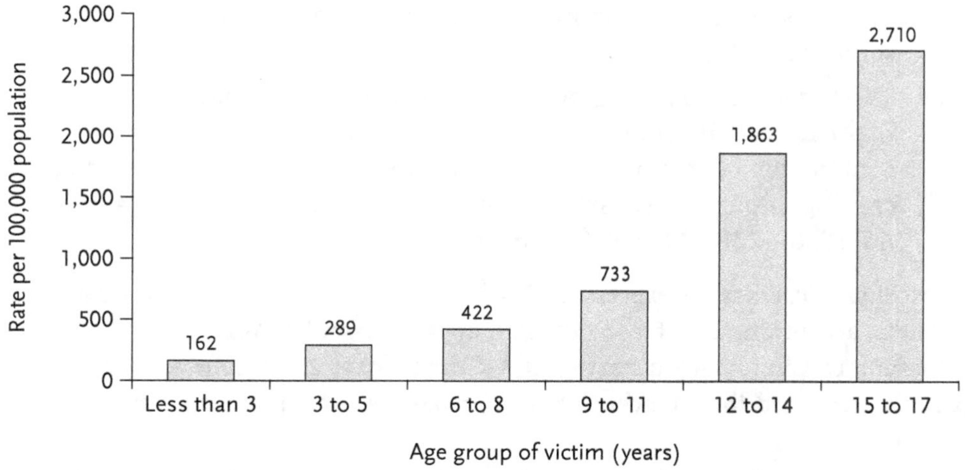

Notes: Excludes incidents where the sex and/or age of the victim were unknown. The Incident-Based Uniform Crime Reporting Survey collected data from 155 police services, representing approximately 98 percent of the Canadian population in 2008. Rate per 100,000 population under 18 years of age for the geographic areas policed by the Incident-Based Uniform Crime Reporting Survey respondents.

Sources: Statistics Canada, Canadian Centre for Justice Statistics, Incident-Based Uniform Crime Reporting Survey. Adapted from Ogrodnik (2010).

Figure 4.2   Rates of Violence Steadily Increase, Peaking at Age 17 for Both Females and Males, 2008

Notes: Excludes incidents where the sex and/or age of the victim were unknown. The Incident-Based Uniform Crime Reporting Survey collected data from 155 police services, representing approximately 98 percent of the Canadian population in 2008. Rate per 100,000 population under 18 years of age for the geographic areas policed by the Incident-based Uniform Crime Reporting Survey respondents.

Sources: Statistics Canada, Canadian Centre for Justice Statistics, Incident-Based Uniform Crime Reporting Survey. Adapted from Ogrodnik (2010).

3. *Level 3: aggravated assault.* This is the most serious type of assault. It involves wounding, maiming, disfiguring, or endangering the life of someone (s. 268).

4. *Other assaults.* This category of assault includes unlawfully causing bodily harm, discharging a firearm with intent, using a firearm during the commission of an offence, pointing a firearm, assaulting a peace officer, criminal negligence causing bodily harm, and other forms of assault (ss. 85, 87, 221, 244, 269, 270, and others).

Most physical assaults experienced by children and youth in 2008 were common assaults, accounting for 76 percent of all physical assaults. Assault with a weapon or assault causing bodily harm accounted for another 22 percent, and aggravated assault accounted for 1 percent of all reported physical assaults against children and youth.

Some additional facts about physical assaults against children in 2008 are provided below (Ogrodnik, 2010):

- in assaults against children and youth under 18, a weapon was typically not used;
- when the victims sustained injuries, the injuries were most often the result of physical force (47 percent) rather than the use of a weapon (15 percent);
- when a weapon was used, it usually fell into the category of an "other weapon," such as a motor vehicle, poison, or an object that could be used for strangulation;
- 1 percent of physical assaults against children and youth involved a firearm;
- among young victims of physical assault, teens aged 15 to 17 were the most likely to sustain injuries (57 percent sustained minor injuries and 3 percent sustained major injuries), followed by children under 3 years of age (43 percent sustained minor injuries and 13 percent sustained major injuries);
- overall, males, regardless of age, were more likely than females to be victims of physical assault. Males under the age of 18 suffered physical assault at a rate that was nearly one and a half times higher than their female counterparts (707 compared to 525 per 100,000);
- 81 percent of police-reported physical assaults against children under the age of 6 were committed by a person known to the victim;
- for the youngest victims (children under 6 years of age), 64 percent of physical assaults were committed by a family member;
- of family members accused of physically assaulting a child under 6, roughly eight in ten (85 percent) were parents;
- fathers were the perpetrator in 59 percent of physical assaults, followed by mothers (27 percent) and other male family members (10 percent);
- children aged 9 to 11, and youth aged 12 to 14 and 15 to 17, were most likely to be assaulted by an acquaintance (33 percent, 40 percent, and

33 percent, respectively), or a stranger (11 percent, 14 percent, and 17 percent);

- a larger proportion of male victims (23 percent) than female victims (10 percent) aged 15 to 17 were physically assaulted by a stranger, possibly reflecting increased risk-taking behaviours among males; and
- peers were most often responsible for physical assaults against teens (44 percent for 12 to 14 year olds, 43 percent for 15 to 17 year olds).

Sexual Assault

In 2008, there were over 13,600 children who were victims of sexual offences reported to police. Over half (59 percent) of all victims of sexual assault were children and youth under the age of 18.

The UCR2 identifies four categories of sexual assault. These are described below, along with their applicable *Criminal Code* section(s).

1. *Level 1: sexual assault.* These sexual assaults involve minor physical injuries or no injuries to the victim (s. 271).
2. *Level 2: sexual assault with a weapon or causing bodily harm.* These sexual assaults include sexual assault with a weapon, threats, or causing bodily harm (s. 272).
3. *Level 3: aggravated sexual assault.* These sexual assaults result in wounding, maiming, disfiguring, or endangering the life of the victim (s. 273).
4. *Other sexual crimes.* These are offences that are primarily meant to address incidents of sexual abuse directed at children, including sexual interference, invitation to sexual touching, sexual exploitation, incest, corrupting children, luring a child via a computer, anal intercourse, bestiality, and voyeurism.

The most common sexual offence committed against victims under 18 years old was level 1 sexual assault (80 percent of incidents). Other sexual crimes committed against children included sexual interference (s. 151), sexual touching (s. 152), and sexual exploitation of children (s. 153). These offences accounted for 19 percent of all sexual offences against children and youth. The more serious forms of sexual assaults against young people, including sexual assault with a weapon or aggravated sexual assault, accounted for about 1 percent of incidents.

The vast majority of child victims of sexual offences were female (82 percent). Females under the age of 18 are victims of sexual violence nearly five times more often than males under the age of 18.

Females under the age of 18 experience the highest rates of sexual victimization during their teenage years, especially at ages 13 through 15 (see Figure 4.3).

In 75 percent of cases, sexual violence against children and youth is perpetrated by someone known to the victim, usually an acquaintance or a family member. However, as the age of the victim increases, the proportion of sexual assaults committed by a family member decreases—youth aged 12 to 14 and 15 to 17 were more likely to be sexually abused by persons outside the family (59 percent and 63 percent, respectively) than were children under the age of 12. Strangers were implicated in

Figure 4.3   Sexual Assault Rates Highest Among 13- to 15-Year-Old Females, 2008

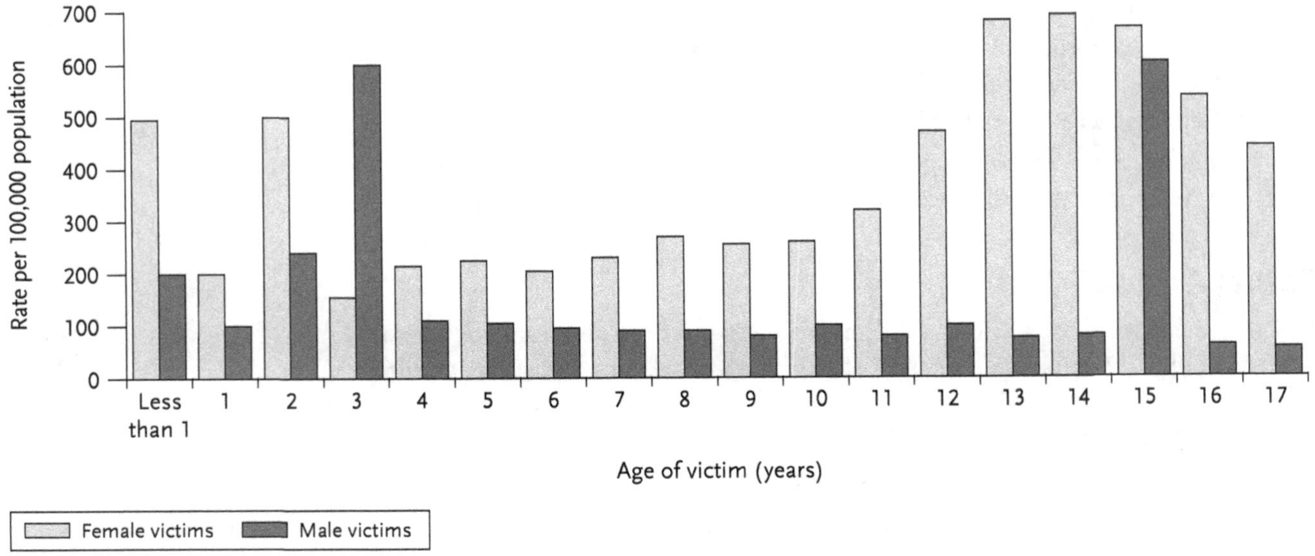

Notes: Excludes incidents where the sex and/or age of the victim were unknown. The Incident-Based Uniform Crime Reporting Survey collected data from 155 police services, representing approximately 98 percent of the population of Canada in 2008. Rate per 100,000 population under 18 years of age for the geographic areas policed by the Incident-Based Uniform Crime Reporting Survey respondents.

Sources: Statistics Canada, Canadian Centre for Justice Statistics, Incident-Based Uniform Crime Reporting Survey. Adapted from Ogrodnik (2010).

10 percent of police-reported sexual violence against children. The majority (80 percent) of child victims who were sexually assaulted by a stranger were aged 12 to 17.

Over one-quarter of all reported sexual assaults against youth were committed by casual acquaintances. Of these victims, 29 percent were aged 12 to 14 and 27 percent were aged 15 to 17. The age of the persons accused of the assaults suggests that many of them were peers—39 percent of the accused were between 12 and 17 years of age, and another 23 percent were between 18 and 24 years of age.

In cases where a family member was accused of sexually abusing a child or youth (33 percent), the violation was almost always perpetrated by a male relative (97 percent). Over one-third (37 percent) of family-related sexual incidents involved male extended family members. This category includes uncles, cousins, grandfathers, and others related to the victim by blood, marriage, foster care, or adoption. Fathers, including biological, step, foster, and adoptive fathers, were responsible for 35 percent of the sexual violence, followed by brothers of the victim, who were responsible for 27 percent of the incidents.

In 2008, minor injuries were sustained in 12 percent of incidents of sexual abuse against children. Among female child victims of sexual assault, teen girls aged 15 to 17 (16 percent) and younger children under the age of 3 (15 percent) sustained the highest proportion of physical injuries.

Physical force—for example, choking or punching—was the most common method used to injure child and youth victims of sexual abuse (see Table 4.1).

Child Pornography and Luring

Trend data from the UCR Trend Data file, which contains information from 63 police services and represents 54 percent of the population of Canada in 2008, show that between 1999 and 2008, there was a nine-fold increase in the number of reported incidents of child pornography: from 78 reported incidents in 1999 to 730 reported incidents in 2008. The trend data also reveal that there was a significant increase in child luring via computer: from 20 reported incidents in 2003 to 149 reported incidents in 2008.

Other Violent Offences

Following physical assault and sexual assault, the UCR2 identified several other violent offences committed against children and youth. Of these, uttering threats, robbery, and criminal harassment were the most common (see Table 4.2). Youth aged 12 to 14 and 15 to 17 reported the highest rates of other types of violent offences compared with the younger age groups. This reflects the fact that teens may be more likely to be in situations that put them at risk of being victims of these types of crimes.

Males were victims in 6 out of 10 incidents of police-reported other violations involving violence or the threat of violence—mainly robberies and uttering threats. Females were more likely to be victims of uttering threats and criminal harassment.

Children were victims in nearly one-quarter (24 percent) of all reported robberies in 2008 (just under 7,000 robberies). Youth aged 12 to 14 and 15 to 17 reported robbery rates that were 1.8 to 3 times higher than the rate for all children and youth. The higher rate may be because teens are more likely to carry expensive items such as laptop computers, cellphones, and portable music and gaming devices.

The majority of persons accused of robbing children were males (88 percent), either strangers (58 percent) or acquaintances (26 percent). Most persons accused of robbing teens (aged 15 to 17) were themselves teens (59 percent) or young adults aged 18 to 24 (24 percent). Most incidents of robbery against teens did not involve a weapon (71 percent); rather, physical force (21 percent) was predominantly used, followed by knives (2 percent).

Uttering threats against children accounted for 17 percent of all police-reported threats in 2008. Youth aged 15 to 17 reported the highest rate (328 per 100,000), a rate considerably higher than that for young adults. Seven in ten persons accused of uttering threats against teens were males. Nearly half of threats against teens were made by casual acquaintances (49 percent), followed by friends (9 percent), strangers (7 percent), and ex-boyfriends or ex-girlfriends (6 percent). Most persons accused of threatening teens were their peers. Over half of those accused of threatening teens were 15 to 17 (37 percent) or 18 to 24 (19 percent).

There were nearly 2,000 child and youth victims of criminal harassment or stalking in 2008. The majority of child victims of stalking were female (73 percent), particularly girls aged 12 to 14 and 15 to 17. Adolescent girls aged 12 to 17 were most likely to be stalked by a casual acquaintance (32 percent), an ex-girlfriend or ex-boyfriend (18 percent), or a stranger (12 percent). Adolescent girls and boys were more likely to be stalked by a male (72 percent) than by a female (28 percent). Persons accused of stalking teens were often teens themselves aged 15 to 17 (36 percent), or young adults aged 18 to 24 (24 percent).

Table 4.1   Child and Youth Victims of Violence by Method of Violence Causing Injury and Sex of Victim, Reported to a Subset of Police Services, 2008

| | | | Sex of victim | | | |
| | Total | | Female | | Male | |
Method of violence	Number	Percent	Number	Percent	Number	Percent
Total violent violations	**75,333**	**100**	**36,864**	**100**	**38,469**	**100**
No weapon[a]	42,632	57	22,127	60	20,505	53
Physical force[b]	24,504	33	11,552	31	12,952	34
Weapons—total	**8,197**	**11**	**3,185**	**9**	**5,012**	**13**
Firearm[c]	568	1	139	0	429	1
Knife/other cutting instrument[d]	1,171	2	328	1	843	2
Club, blunt instrument[e]	949	1	272	1	677	2
Other weapon[f]	3,215	4	1,152	3	2,063	5
Unknown[g]	2,294	3	1,294	4	1,000	3
Physical assault—total	**41,926**	**100**	**17,339**	**100**	**24,587**	**100**
No weapon[a]	15,872	38	6,572	38	9,300	38
Physical force[b]	19,850	47	8,694	50	11,156	45
Weapons—total	**6,204**	**15**	**2,073**	**12**	**4,131**	**17**
Firearm[c]	470	1	120	1	350	1
Knife/other cutting instrument[d]	924	2	254	1	670	3
Club, blunt instrument[e]	869	2	255	1	614	2
Other weapon[f]	2,972	7	1,063	6	1,909	8
Unknown[g]	969	2	381	2	588	2
Sexual assault—total	**13,641**	**100**	**11,141**	**100**	**2,500**	**100**
No weapon[a]	9,887	72	8,042	72	1,845	74
Physical force[b]	2,800	21	2,356	21	444	18
Weapons—total	**954**	**7**	**743**	**7**	**211**	**8**
Firearm[c]	4	0	3	0	1	0
Knife/other cutting instrument[d]	19	0	17	0	2	0
Club, blunt instrument[e]	0	0	0	0	0	0
Other weapon[f]	52	0	40	0	12	0
Unknown[g]	879	6	683	6	196	8
Other violent violations—total	**19,766**	**100**	**8,384**	**100**	**11,382**	**100**
No weapon[a]	16,873	85	7,513	90	9,360	82
Physical force[b]	1,854	9	502	6	1,352	12
Weapons—total	**1,039**	**5**	**369**	**4**	**670**	**6**
Firearm[c]	94	0	16	0	78	1
Knife/other cutting instrument[d]	228	1	57	1	171	2
Club, blunt instrument[e]	80	0	17	0	63	1
Other weapon[f]	191	1	49	1	142	1
Unknown[g]	446	2	230	3	216	2

(The table is concluded on the next page.)

Table 4.1   Concluded

Notes: Percentages may not add up to 100 percent due to rounding. Includes victims under 18 years of age. Excludes incidents where the age and/or sex of the victim was unknown. The Incident-Based Uniform Crime Reporting Survey collected data from 155 police services, representing approximately 98 percent of the Canadian population in 2008.

[a] No weapon was involved, or no injury was caused.

[b] The use of body strength and/or action that is used to cause bodily injury or death (for example, choking, punching, pushing).

[c] Firearms include fully automatic firearms, sawed-off rifles, handguns, rifles, and other firearm-like weapons.

[d] Includes knives and other cutting/piercing instruments that would cut or pierce.

[e] Includes any tool or article that is used to cause injury using a hitting or bludgeoning action.

[f] Other weapons might include motor vehicles, poison, and other objects that may be used for strangulation.

[g] There is no indication of what type of weapon caused an injury to the victim.

Sources: Statistics Canada, Canadian Centre for Justice Statistics, Incident-Based Uniform Crime Reporting Survey. Adapted from Ogrodnik (2010).

CHILDREN AT RISK

The *Child and Family Services Act* (CFSA) of Ontario affirms the fervent desire of society to protect the well-being of its most vulnerable members. Section 79(1) of the Act defines **abuse** as "a state or condition of being physically harmed, sexually molested or sexually exploited." Section 37(2) defines the conditions under which a child may be in need of protection. It expands on the definition of abuse by including neglect and emotional and psychological abuse. It also states that a child is in need of protection when there exists the risk of abuse.

The term "risk" allows child protection workers and police to use their best judgment in determining whether the child is at risk of harm. If they are in doubt and if there is any reasonable possibility of risk, child protection workers are encouraged to first consider the best interests of the child. It is preferable to remove the child through the use of authorized apprehension authorities, and inconvenience or upset the person in care of the child, than to have the child injured in any way.

Although any child that interacts with adults has the potential to be abused, some children are at greater risk, including:

- children with behavioural problems or other special needs that consume a great deal of the parent's time;
- children of teenage mothers (stressors on teenage mothers, including full-time childcare obligations and financial problems due to limited employment opportunities, may be contributing factors);
- children who continually demand attention or, conversely, children who do not communicate; and
- children who fall short of the parent's expectations—for example, in athletics or academic achievement.

abuse

in the *Child and Family Services Act*, a state or condition of being physically harmed, sexually molested, or sexually exploited

Table 4.2   Victims of Violence by Age Group and Offence Type, Reported to a Subset of Police Services, 2008

Offence	Age group (years)							
	Less than 3		3 to 5		6 to 8		9 to 11	
	Number	Rate	Number	Rate	Number	Rate	Number	Rate
Physical assault—total	**1,010**	**95**	**1,195**	**115**	**2,206**	**210**	**4,636**	**418**
Aggravated assault (level 3)	67	6	8	1	2	0	7	1
Assault with a weapon or causing bodily harm (level 2)	204	19	202	20	531	51	1,102	99
Common assault (level 1)	703	66	968	93	1,639	156	3,451	311
Other assaults[a]	36	3	17	2	34	3	76	7
Sexual assault—total	**252**	**24**	**1,459**	**141**	**1,711**	**163**	**2,066**	**186**
Aggravated sexual assault (level 3)	1	0	2	0	4	0	2	0
Sexual assault with a weapon or causing bodily harm (level 2)	0	0	4	0	10	1	17	2
Sexual assault (level 1)	149	14	1,138	110	1,283	122	1,554	140
Other sexual crimes[b]	102	10	315	30	414	39	493	44
Other violations involving violence—total	**457**	**43**	**335**	**32**	**519**	**49**	**1,424**	**128**
Homicide/attempts	20	2	9	1	8	1	7	1
Robbery	20	2	8	1	33	3	228	21
Extortion	0	0	3	0	3	0	5	0
Criminal harassment	12	1	11	1	37	4	126	11
Uttering threats	241	23	169	16	297	28	850	77
Forcible confinement/ kidnapping	24	2	18	2	30	3	57	5
Abduction—non-parental	34	3	23	2	37	4	64	6
Abduction—parental	40	4	55	5	43	4	30	3
Other violent violations[c]	66	6	39	4	31	3	57	5
Total violent violations	**1,719**	**162**	**2,989**	**289**	**4,436**	**422**	**8,126**	**733**

(The table is concluded on the next page.)

Table 4.2   Concluded

	Age group (years)							
	Less than 3		3 to 5		6 to 8		9 to 11	
Offence	Number	Rate	Number	Rate	Number	Rate	Number	Rate
Physical assault—total	**12,375**	**1,015**	**20,504**	**1,572**	**41,926**	**619**	**53,204**	**1,694**
Aggravated assault (level 3)	60	5	278	21	422	6	1,010	32
Assault with a weapon or causing bodily harm (level 2)	2,409	198	4,603	353	9,051	134	12,831	409
Common assault (level 1)	9,766	801	15,389	1,180	31,916	471	37,635	1,198
Other assaults[a]	140	11	234	18	537	8	1,728	55
Sexual assault—total	**4,241**	**348**	**3,912**	**300**	**13,641**	**201**	**4,071**	**130**
Aggravated sexual assault (level 3)	6	0	13	1	28	0	31	1
Sexual assault with a weapon or causing bodily harm (level 2)	28	2	52	4	111	2	72	2
Sexual assault (level 1)	3,347	274	3,456	265	10,927	161	3,816	122
Other sexual crimes[b]	860	71	391	30	2,575	38	152	5
Other violations involving violence—total	**6,106**	**501**	**10,925**	**838**	**19,766**	**292**	**23,704**	**755**
Homicide/attempts	19	2	53	4	116	2	365	12
Robbery	2,180	179	4,376	336	6,845	101	7,811	249
Extortion	37	3	88	7	136	2	157	5
Criminal harassment	520	43	1,156	89	1,862	27	3,268	104
Uttering threats	2,874	236	4,282	328	8,713	129	8,855	282
Forcible confinement/kidnapping	150	12	435	33	714	11	1,366	43
Abduction—non-parental	69	6	14	1	241	4	0	0
Abduction—parental	20	2	0	0	188	3	0	0
Other violent violations[c]	237	19	521	40	951	14	1,882	60
Total violent violations	**22,722**	**1,863**	**35,341**	**2,710**	**75,333**	**1,111**	**80,979**	**2,578**

Notes: The Incident-Based Uniform Crime Reporting Survey collected data from 155 police services, representing approximately 98 percent of the Canadian population in 2008. Excludes incidents where the sex and/or age of the victim was unknown. Includes a small number of cases where the age of the victim and age of the accused may have been reversed. Rates are calculated on the basis of 100,000 population under 18 years of age for the geographic areas policed by the Incident-Based Uniform Crime Reporting Survey respondents.

[a] "Other assaults" includes unlawfully causing bodily harm, discharge firearm with intent, using firearm during commission of offence, criminal negligence causing bodily harm, and other assaults.

[b] "Other sexual crimes" includes sexual interference, invitation to sexual touching, sexual exploitation, incest, corrupting children, luring a child via a computer, anal intercourse, bestiality, and voyeurism.

[c] Includes hostage taking, human trafficking, explosives causing bodily harm, arson, and other violent violations.

Sources: Statistics Canada, Canadian Centre for Justice Statistics, Incident-Based Uniform Crime Reporting Survey. Adapted from Ogrodnik (2010).

IDENTIFYING CHILD ABUSE

Section 37(2) of the *Child and Family Services Act* identifies situations where a child is in need of protection. In many of these situations, police can offer only initial intervention, such as child apprehension or referral to an appropriate community agency, because they lack the required expertise and resources.

Child in Need of Protection: Child and Family Services Act, Section 37(2)

37(2) A child is in need of protection where,

(a) the child has suffered physical harm, inflicted by the person having charge of the child or caused by or resulting from that person's,

(i) failure to adequately care for, provide for, supervise or protect the child, or

(ii) pattern of neglect in caring for, providing for, supervising or protecting the child;

(b) there is a risk that the child is likely to suffer physical harm inflicted by the person having charge of the child or caused by or resulting from that person's,

(i) failure to adequately care for, provide for, supervise or protect the child, or

(ii) pattern of neglect in caring for, providing for, supervising or protecting the child;

(c) the child has been sexually molested or sexually exploited, by the person having charge of the child or by another person where the person having charge of the child knows or should know of the possibility of sexual molestation or sexual exploitation and fails to protect the child;

Note: On a day to be named by proclamation of the Lieutenant Governor, clause (c) is repealed by the Statutes of Ontario, 2008, chapter 21, section 2 and the following substituted:

(c) the child has been sexually molested or sexually exploited, including by child pornography, by the person having charge of the child or by another person where the person having charge of the child knows or should know of the possibility of sexual molestation or sexual exploitation and fails to protect the child;

. . .

(d) there is a risk that the child is likely to be sexually molested or sexually exploited as described in clause (c);

(e) the child requires medical treatment to cure, prevent or alleviate physical harm or suffering and the child's parent or the person having charge of the child does not provide, or refuses or is unavailable or unable to consent to, the treatment;

(f) the child has suffered emotional harm, demonstrated by serious,

(i) anxiety,

(ii) depression,

(iii) withdrawal,

(iv) self-destructive or aggressive behaviour, or

(v) delayed development,

and there are reasonable grounds to believe that the emotional harm suffered by the child results from the actions, failure to act or pattern of neglect on the part of the child's parent or the person having charge of the child;

(f.1) the child has suffered emotional harm of the kind described in sub-clause (f)(i), (ii), (iii), (iv) or (v) and the child's parent or the person having charge of the child does not provide, or refuses or is unavailable or unable to consent to, services or treatment to remedy or alleviate the harm;

(g) there is a risk that the child is likely to suffer emotional harm of the kind described in subclause (f)(i), (ii), (iii), (iv) or (v) resulting from the actions, failure to act or pattern of neglect on the part of the child's parent or the person having charge of the child;

(g.1) there is a risk that the child is likely to suffer emotional harm of the kind described in subclause (f)(i), (ii), (iii), (iv) or (v) and that the child's parent or the person having charge of the child does not provide, or refuses or is unavailable or unable to consent to, services or treatment to prevent the harm;

(h) the child suffers from a mental, emotional or developmental condition that, if not remedied, could seriously impair the child's development and the child's parent or the person having charge of the child does not provide, or refuses or is unavailable or unable to consent to, treatment to remedy or alleviate the condition;

(i) the child has been abandoned, the child's parent has died or is unavailable to exercise his or her custodial rights over the child and has not made adequate provision for the child's care and custody, or the child is in a residential placement and the parent refuses or is unable or unwilling to resume the child's care and custody;

(j) the child is less than twelve years old and has killed or seriously injured another person or caused serious damage to another person's property, services or treatment are necessary to prevent a recurrence and the child's parent or the person having charge of the child does not provide, or refuses or is unavailable or unable to consent to, those services or treatment;

(k) the child is less than twelve years old and has on more than one occasion injured another person or caused loss or damage to another person's property, with the encouragement of the person having charge of the child or because of that person's failure or inability to supervise the child adequately; or

(l) the child's parent is unable to care for the child and the child is brought before the court with the parent's consent and, where the child is twelve years of age or older, with the child's consent, to be dealt with under this Part.

In some of these situations, it is obvious that police, beyond initial intervention, cannot adequately address the needs of the child. Intervention by child protection authorities is needed. The Act requires that, in situations of suspected abuse, child protection authorities be apprised of the possibility that a child may be in need of protection.

Duty to Report Child in Need of Protection: Child and Family Services Act, Section 72(1)

72(1) Despite the provisions of any other Act, if a person, including a person who performs professional or official duties with respect to children, has reasonable grounds to suspect one of the following, the person shall forthwith report the suspicion and the information on which it is based to a society:

The Act then lists the situations where a child is in need of protection. See s. 37(2), above.

Although police officers may not have the expertise or resources to address the verbal, emotional, or psychological aspects of child abuse, they do have the expertise and legislative authority to address the criminal aspects. Physical abuse, sexual abuse, and neglect may be effectively dealt with through police intervention in conjunction with child protection authorities.

IDENTIFYING PHYSICAL ABUSE

Child physical abuse can take the form of punches, kicks, or any other method of striking a child. Where small children are concerned, it may involve shaking or throwing. The abuse may produce extreme injuries such as burns, scalds, broken bones, concussions, bites, and severe bruising. Such abuse can cause the child's death.

Signs of Physical Abuse in Children

There are many behavioural and physical clues to possible abuse (Children's Aid Society of Algoma, 1998). Behavioural signs include the following:

- The child is unable to recall how injuries suggestive of abuse occurred.
- The child is very aggressive or extremely withdrawn.
- The child has a vacant stare, as if unaware of his or her surroundings.
- The child indiscriminately seeks affection.
- The child is compliant and eager to please.
- The child caters to his or her parent's needs (role reversal).
- The child models negative behaviour when playing, such as using violence to deal with disagreements or shouting at playmates.
- The child dresses inappropriately in an attempt to hide injuries.
- The child runs away from home or expresses a fear of going home.
- The child describes incidents of abuse.
- The child behaves in a way that provokes punishment.
- The child flinches or pulls away if touched unexpectedly.

Physical signs of abuse include unexplained bruises, welts, or lacerations. Most physical signs involve injuries to parts of the body that, among children, typically tend not to be injured. Children frequently injure themselves while playing or when involved in sports. These common injuries usually take the form of bruises, lacerations, or abrasions at the joints or on the hands. By contrast, abusive injuries often appear at suspicious locations, such as the lips, mouth, and other parts of the face. They are also common on the backs of the legs, the buttocks, and soft tissue areas such as the abdomen. Abusive injuries may have a regular pattern, as in the case of tooth marks, handprints, or the imprints of objects such as belts, cords, and rulers. As time passes, the injuries suffered by the child may become more severe or obvious.

Bruises

Common areas where children bruise include shins, elbows, knees, and to a lesser extent the forehead. When investigating potential abuse, look for bruising in areas uncommonly injured in daily activities. Children rarely bruise themselves in areas such as the small of the back, buttocks, or abdomen.

Bruises seen in infants, especially on the face and buttocks, are suspicious and should be considered non-accidental until proven otherwise. Very young children, not yet walking or crawling, very rarely have accidental bruising. "If they don't cruise, they don't bruise!"

Medical personnel at the Hospital for Sick Children in Toronto have observed that less than 0.5 percent of children under 6 months of age had any type of bruising, whereas 11.5 percent of children between 9 and 12 months of age had bruising. (Note: This was not a study of possible abuse, merely observations of the presence of bruising.)

Injuries to children's upper arms (caused by efforts to defend themselves), the trunk, the front of their thighs, the sides of their faces, their ears and neck, genitalia, stomach, and buttocks are more likely to be non-accidental. Injuries to their shins, hips, lower arms, forehead, hands, or the bony prominences (the spine, knees, nose, chin, or elbows) are more likely to signify accidental injury.

Pattern bruises may also indicate abuse. The bruising may be in the pattern of a hand with bruising from the abuser's thumb and fingers. Bruising from bite marks may be present. Human bite marks may be easily distinguished from those of common house pets such as dogs or cats. The animals' teeth are designed to tear flesh, whereas the human bite mark will compress the flesh, leaving a distinct bruise pattern.

As shown in the table below, the age of a bruise may be estimated by its colour. This will be an estimate only, as some children heal faster than others and a child may have an underlying medical condition that hinders healing.

Colour	Estimated age of bruise
Red and swollen	Usually less than 2 days old
Red, blue, or dark purple	Usually 1–3 days old
Green	Usually 4–7 days old
Yellow	Usually 7–14 days old
Brown	Usually more than 14 days old

Although estimates of the age of the bruise may not be completely accurate, such dating may be useful in the course of an investigation. For example, suppose that a child has a soft tissue bruise that the parent says is two weeks old. The bruise is reddish-purple in colour. Although there cannot be a completely accurate dating of the bruise, the parent's statement is likely inaccurate. A bruise that is two weeks old will likely not be reddish-purple in colour. The statement should elicit further investigation as to why the bruise has not healed in two weeks. It may be discovered that the child has a medical condition that slows healing. More likely, the parent is not being truthful about the age of the bruise.

Burns

Burn injuries should arouse suspicion if the parent's or caregiver's explanation does not fit with the extent and category of the burn. There are three main categories of burns: scalding burns, contact burns, and flame burns.

- *Scalding burns* are caused by spilling, splashing, or immersion in a hot liquid. Spill and splash burns are characterized by irregular margins and inconsistent burn depth. They may exhibit an inverted arrow pattern with the narrow area of the pattern at the bottom. Immersion burns are caused by immersing part of the child in hot water. The burn is evidenced by the distinct burn line dividing the immersed from the non-immersed parts of the body. A child who "accidentally pulled a boiling pot from the stove" will not have the distinct burn pattern consistent with an intentional immersion burn.

- *Contact burns* are caused by contact with hot objects or acidic substances. Burns from hot objects often mirror the shape of the object used. For example, small circular burns on the hands or soles of the feet may indicate a cigarette burn. The investigating officer should consider the age of the child when weighing the probability of the explanation provided. For example, it is extremely unlikely that an infant who is not yet able to crawl will accidentally incur a contact burn.

    Not all contact burns are the result of abuse. There are pattern burns that may occur in diapered babies where the shape of the burn will resemble the edge of the diaper. This could be an acidic burn caused by urine or stool where the baby's diet is high in fruit products. Such burns should be categorized only by qualified medical personnel.

- *Flame burns* are caused by contact with direct flame. Such burns have random patterns, depending on the source of the flame.

The injury resulting from a burn depends on:

- the cause of the burn,
- the temperature of the mechanism of the burn, and
- the duration of exposure.

Burns are classified as first, second, and third degree burns.

- First degree burns involve the epidermis, or outer layer of skin. A first degree burn exhibits as redness of the epidermis.
- Second degree burns extend into the dermis, the layer of skin below the epidermis.

Partial thickness burns extend into the outer layers of the dermis. Such burns are painful and generally blister, but they heal well, often without scarring.

Deeper second degree burns extend deeper into the dermis and cause a great deal of pain. Such burns heal more slowly and often leave a scar.

- Third degree burns involve burning of the entire dermis, and possibly the underlying tissues. These burns are not painful because all the pain sensors have been destroyed. However, the damage caused by third degree burns is serious and possibly life-threatening if the burned area is large.

The table below provides estimates of the amount of time required at a given temperature to produce a third degree burn of a child's bare skin. Officers can use this information to evaluate the credibility of information they receive from a parent or caregiver regarding the cause of the burn injury.

Temperature	Time
49 degrees Celsius	300 seconds
54.5 degrees Celsius	30 seconds
60 degrees Celsius	5 seconds
65 degrees Celsius	1.5 seconds

When investigating cases of accidental burns, attention should be directed to the standard of care provided by the parent or caregiver. If there is any indication that the child was accidentally burned as a result of neglect, a Children's Aid Society must be informed (s. 72 of the CFSA).

The degree of burn may indicate abuse. Suspicion should arise if the degree of the burn does not match the circumstances of the explanation given by the parent or caregiver.

It is important to examine the potential temperature and time of exposure when considering the validity of the explanation. For example, suppose that the caregiver reports that the child burned his hand under the running water in the bathroom sink while washing before dinner. Your observations indicate third degree burns. The average temperature of household hot water, from a hot water heater, is approximately 52 to 54 degrees Celsius. Referring to the table above, it would take over 30 seconds of constant exposure to inflict a third degree burn. It is unlikely that a child would hold his or her hand under 52 to 54 degree water for this period of time. It is more likely that the child's hand was held by someone else.

Head and Neck Injuries Detected During Dental Examinations

Section 72 of the CFSA requires that all health-care professionals, including dentists, report suspected cases of child abuse.

Physical abuse, sexual abuse, and neglect may be revealed through dental examination. Through a program called PANDA (Prevent Abuse and Neglect through Dental Awareness), dentists throughout Ontario have been provided with information to assist them in identifying child abuse ("Reporting Suspicions of Child Abuse," 1999).

Studies have indicated that approximately 65 percent of child physical abuse injuries occur in the head and neck area; these are areas easily viewed and examined by dental health-care professionals (Stechey, 2001).

Injuries readily identified by dental health-care professionals include:

- gag marks caused by the abuser tying something around the child's mouth to muffle sounds;
- injuries caused by direct trauma to the facial area;
- bruising of the hard and soft palate from forced oral sex;
- injuries on the soft tissues inside the mouth caused by forcefully holding the child's mouth shut, usually to quiet the child;
- venereal warts, which may indicate sexual abuse;
- multiple abscesses and caries as a result of neglect;
- tongue lacerations, which may indicate physical abuse; and
- marks on the neck, which may indicate strangulation by hands, rope, or similar means.

Bite Marks

In inflicting abuse, a perpetrator may bite his or her victim. The resulting bite pattern can serve as a unique identifier of the aggressor. As discussed above, human bite marks are distinct from the bite marks of other animals. This distinctiveness may assist in the apprehension and prosecution of the abuser.

Officers should keep in mind that a child can suffer bite marks through interactions with other children. However, if there is any doubt as to the origin of the bite mark, officers should err on the side of safety and take steps to protect the child.

A dental health-care professional experienced in the field of forensic odontology can assess bite mark patterns to implicate or exonerate suspects. The odontologist can compare the bite marks with the suspect's dental records or impressions of the suspect's teeth.

Bite mark analysis can also be used to determine whether the suspect was at the crime scene and whether the suspect inflicted the injury. Investigators should ask the victim whether he or she was bitten by the assailant as well as whether the victim bit the assailant. Bite marks on the victim could contain the DNA of the suspect. Bite marks on the suspect that match those of the victim could put the suspect at the scene.

Section 487.092(1) of the *Criminal Code* allows police to obtain a warrant requiring a suspect to provide an impression of his or her teeth to be used for comparison purposes:

> A justice may issue a warrant in writing authorizing a peace officer to do any thing, or cause any thing to be done under the direction of the peace officer, described in the warrant in order to obtain any handprint, fingerprint, footprint, foot impression, teeth impression or other print or impression of the body or any part of the body in respect of a person if the justice is satisfied

(a) by information on oath in writing that there are reasonable grounds to believe that an offence against this or any other Act of Parliament has been committed and that information concerning the offence will be obtained by the print or impression; and

(b) that it is in the best interests of the administration of justice to issue the warrant.

Telltale Injuries

There are other injuries that are more definite indicators of physical abuse. These include:

- *Injuries to the face.* Common examples are broken teeth or a black eye. These injuries may have been caused by schoolyard fights or sporting activities, but warrant an investigation into the origin of the injury.
- *Fractures.* Infants rarely fracture bones. Look for signs of deformities of limbs, swelling, or inability to move the limb. In older children, there may be a reasonable explanation for the injury. Police should investigate the explanation. Fractures that do not receive immediate medical attention should be treated as suspicious.
- *Fractures of the chest area.* These may be more difficult for police to detect. Look for signs of breathing distress and deformities in the area of the rib cage.
- *Abdominal injuries.* These are also difficult to detect. Look for distention, bruising, or swelling of the abdominal area. Abdominal injuries can result in death due to internal bleeding.

When questioning the parent or other involved parties about the injuries, look for discrepancies in their explanations. Compare the explanations with the injuries observed to identify possible inconsistencies.

If there is any risk that the child is being abused, consider the child to be "in need of protection."

Shaken Infant Syndrome

The term "shaken infant syndrome" describes a classic injury pattern seen in shaken infants and very young children. The victim is held around the chest by an adult and violently shaken back and forth. This causes the extremities and the head to whiplash back and forth. Violent shaking creates shearing forces on the extremities, which may cause fractures of the growth plate (skull). These fractures are highly specific to this type of abuse.

The violent shaking causes similar shearing forces in and on the brain. This may cause large amounts of brain matter to tear and may also cause bleeding to occur on the surface of the brain if the brain strikes the skull during shaking. With violent shaking, serious brain damage may occur. In fact, infants have died after being violently shaken.

The tight grasp around the chest that accompanies this shaking may also cause rib fractures (these are also highly specific for abuse). These rib fractures may be incidentally found on chest X-rays performed for other reasons, such as to diagnose pneumonia.

Facts About Shaken Infant Syndrome

Officers should know the following facts about shaken infant syndrome to aid them in their investigations:

- It is a non-accidental trauma caused by violently shaking the infant.
- It usually occurs in children less than three years old, although the majority of victims are less than one year old.
- The most common perpetrators are (in order) the father, boyfriend of the mother, female babysitter, and mother of the child.
- Injuries occur as the result of severe back and forth motion of the infant's head.
- It usually causes brain injuries.
- It may also cause retinal hemorrhages.
- Approximately 50 percent of severely injured victims die from the abuse.
- Most victims are left with a severe disability.
- Victims that appear to fully recover are often left with developmental difficulties.

Some common explanations put forth by the perpetrators of this crime include:

- the baby suffered an accidental fall;
- the injuries were inflicted by chest compressions from CPR;
- another child in the home caused the injuries;
- the injuries are the cumulative result of several accidents; or
- the injuries are the result of an illness, such as meningitis, a bleeding disorder, or a genetic disease.

Thorough investigation by medical practitioners and police generally reveals the fallacy of these "defences."

CRIMINAL OFFENCES RELATED TO THE PHYSICAL ABUSE OF CHILDREN

The definition of assault is found in s. 265 of the *Criminal Code*.

Assault: Criminal Code, Section 265(1)

265(1) A person commits an assault when

(a) without the consent of another person, he applies force intentionally to that other person, directly or indirectly;

(b) he attempts or threatens, by an act or a gesture, to apply force to another person, if he has, or causes that other person to believe on reasonable grounds that he has, present ability to effect his purpose; or

(c) while openly wearing or carrying a weapon or an imitation thereof, he accosts or impedes another person or begs.

The degree of injury caused by the assault will determine the section of the *Criminal Code* that has been violated and the severity of the punishment for the assault. Several different kinds of assault and physical abuse are described in the sections of the *Criminal Code* listed below.

Assault: Criminal Code, Section 266

266. Every one who commits an assault is guilty of

(a) an indictable offence and is liable to imprisonment for a term not exceeding five years; or

(b) an offence punishable on summary conviction.

This section can be used where the assault was not severe and there is evidence that the child was assaulted. A child's statement that he or she was assaulted can be enough to support a charge under this section.

Assault with a Weapon or Causing Bodily Harm: Criminal Code, Section 267

267. Every one who, in committing an assault,

(a) carries, uses or threatens to use a weapon or an imitation thereof, or

(b) causes bodily harm to the complainant,

is guilty of an indictable offence and liable to imprisonment for a term not exceeding ten years or an offence punishable on summary conviction and liable to imprisonment for a term not exceeding eighteen months.

Section 267 may be used in situations where the child was struck with an object or suffered bodily harm. Bodily harm has been defined as injuries that are not transient in nature.

Aggravated Assault: Criminal Code, Section 268(1)

268(1) Every one commits an aggravated assault who wounds, maims, disfigures or endangers the life of the complainant.

If the child's injuries are severe (as in the case of broken bones) or life-threatening, aggravated assault may be an appropriate charge.

Excision: Criminal Code, Section 268(3)

268(3) For greater certainty, in this section, "wounds" or "maims" includes to excise, infibulate or mutilate, in whole or in part, the labia majora, labia minora or clitoris of a person, except where

(a) a surgical procedure is performed, by a person duly qualified by provincial law to practise medicine, for the benefit of the physical health of the person or for the purpose of that person having normal reproductive functions or normal sexual appearance or function; or

(b) the person is at least eighteen years of age and there is no resulting bodily harm.

Section 268(3) of the *Criminal Code* recognizes the practice of female genital mutilation as a criminal offence if the procedure is carried out upon a female under the age of 18 years. Excision may be legally performed as an approved surgical procedure for medical reasons or upon consent when the person is 18 years of age.

Correction of Child by Force

There may be instances where the parent claims that force was applied to a child as a corrective punishment. The *Criminal Code* of Canada, since its inception in 1892, has included a provision granting permission to parents, and persons standing in place of parents, to use force to correct a child's behaviour. The provision in the 1892 legislation is reproduced below.

Criminal Code of Canada 1892: Section 55

55. It is lawful for every parent, or person in the place of a parent, schoolmaster or master, to use force by way of correction towards any child, pupil or apprentice under his care, provided that such force is reasonable under the circumstances.

The authority has evolved over the past century but remains substantially the same. The provision for corrective punishment in the current *Criminal Code* is reproduced below.

Correction of Child by Force: Criminal Code, Section 43

43. Every schoolteacher, parent or person standing in the place of a parent is justified in using force by way of correction toward a pupil or child, as the case may be, who is under his care, if the force does not exceed what is reasonable under the circumstances.

Challenges to the Validity of Section 43

The validity of s. 43 of the *Criminal Code* has been challenged by the Canadian Foundation for Children, Youth and the Law. The issue was brought before the Supreme Court of Canada in the case of *Canadian Foundation for Children, Youth and the Law v. Canada (Attorney General)*. The court was asked to invalidate s. 43 of the *Criminal Code* on a number of constitutional violations.

The judgment of the court was delivered by Chief Justice Beverley McLachlin on January 30, 2004. Below are sections of the judgment applicable to law enforcement. A summary of the judgment follows the excerpt.

[1] THE CHIEF JUSTICE: The issue in this case is the constitutionality of Parliament's decision to carve out a sphere within which children's parents and

teachers may use minor corrective force in some circumstances without facing criminal sanction. The assault provision of the *Criminal Code*, RSC 1985, c. C-46, s. 265 prohibits intentional, non-consensual application of force to another. Section 43 of the *Criminal Code* excludes from this crime reasonable physical correction of children by their parents and teachers.

. . .

[19] The purpose of s. 43 is to delineate a sphere of non-criminal conduct within the larger realm of common assault. It must, as we have seen, do this in a way that permits people to know when they are entering a zone of risk of criminal sanction and that avoids *ad hoc* discretionary decision making by law enforcement officials. People must be able to assess when conduct approaches the boundaries of the sphere that s. 43 provides.

. . .

[21] Section 43 delineates *who may access* its sphere with considerable precision. The terms "schoolteacher" and "parent" are clear. The phrase "person standing in the place of a parent" has been held by the courts to indicate an individual who has assumed "*all* the obligations of parenthood": *Ogg-Moss*, [[1984] 2 SCR 173], at p. 190 (emphasis in original). These terms present no difficulty.

[22] Section 43 identifies less precisely *what conduct* falls within its sphere. It defines this conduct in two ways. The first is by the requirement that the force be "by way of correction." The second is by the requirement that the force be "reasonable under the circumstances." The question is whether, taken together and construed in accordance with governing principles, these phrases provide sufficient precision to delineate the zone of risk and avoid discretionary law enforcement.

[23] I turn first to the requirement that the force be "by way of correction." These words, considered in conjunction with the cases, yield two limitations on the content of the protected sphere of conduct.

[24] First, the person applying the force must have intended it to be for educative or corrective purposes: *Ogg-Moss*, *supra*, at p. 193. Accordingly, s. 43 cannot exculpate outbursts of violence against a child motivated by anger or animated by frustration. It admits into its sphere of immunity only sober, reasoned uses of force that address the actual behaviour of the child and are designed to restrain, control or express some symbolic disapproval of his or her behaviour. The purpose of the force must always be the education or discipline of the child: *Ogg-Moss*, *supra*, at p. 193.

[25] Second, the child must be capable of benefiting from the correction. This requires the capacity to learn and the possibility of successful correction. Force against children under two cannot be corrective, since on the evidence they are incapable of understanding why they are hit (trial decision (2000), 49 OR (3d) 662, at para. 17). A child may also be incapable of learning from the application of force because of disability or some other contextual factor. In these cases, force will not be "corrective" and will not fall within the sphere of immunity provided by s. 43.

[26] The second requirement of s. 43 is that the force be "reasonable under the circumstances." The Foundation argues that this term fails to sufficiently delineate the area of risk and constitutes an invitation to discretionary *ad hoc* law enforcement. It argues that police officers, prosecutors and judges too often as-

sess the reasonableness of corrective force by reference to their personal experiences and beliefs, rendering enforcement of s. 43 arbitrary and subjective. In support, it points to the decision of the Manitoba Court of Appeal in *R v. K.(M.)* (1992), 74 CCC (3d) 108, in which, at p. 109, O'Sullivan JA stated that "[t]he discipline administered to the boy in question in these proceedings [a kick to the rear] was mild indeed compared to the discipline I received in my home."

[27] Against this argument, the law has long used reasonableness to delineate areas of risk, without incurring the dangers of vagueness. But reasonableness as a guide to conduct is not confined to the law of negligence. The criminal law of negligence, which has blossomed in recent decades to govern private actions in nearly all spheres of human activity, is founded upon the presumption that individuals are capable of governing their conduct in accordance with the standard of what is "reasonable." But reasonableness as a guide to conduct is not confined to the law of negligence. The criminal law also relies on it. The *Criminal Code* expects that police officers will know what constitutes "reasonable grounds" for believing that an offence has been committed, such that an arrest can be made (s. 495); that an individual will know what constitutes "reasonable steps" to obtain consent to sexual contact (s. 273.2(b)); and that surgeons, in order to be exempted from criminal liability, will judge whether performing an operation is "reasonable" in "all the circumstances of the case" (s. 45). These are merely a few examples; the criminal law is thick with the notion of "reasonableness."

[28] The reality is that the term "reasonable" gives varying degrees of guidance, depending upon the statutory and factual context. It does not insulate a law against a charge of vagueness. Nor, however, does it automatically mean that a law is void for vagueness. In each case, the question is whether the term, considered in light of principles of statutory interpretation and decided cases, delineates an area of risk and avoids the danger of arbitrary *ad hoc* law enforcement.

· · ·

[30] The first limitation arises from the behaviour for which s. 43 provides an exemption, simple non-consensual application of force. Section 43 does not exempt from criminal sanction conduct that causes harm or raises a reasonable prospect of harm. It can be invoked only in cases of non-consensual application of force that results neither in harm nor in the prospect of bodily harm. This limits its operation to the mildest forms of assault. People must know that if their conduct raises an apprehension of bodily harm they cannot rely on s. 43. Similarly, police officers and judges must know that the defence cannot be raised in such circumstances.

[31] Within this limited area of application, further precision on what is reasonable under the circumstances may be derived from international treaty obligations. Statutes should be construed to comply with Canada's international obligations: *Ordon Estate v. Grail*, [1998] 3 SCR 437, at para. 137. Canada's international commitments confirm that physical correction that either harms or degrades a child is unreasonable.

· · ·

[36] Determining what is "reasonable under the circumstances" in the case of child discipline is also assisted by social consensus and expert evidence on what constitutes reasonable corrective discipline. The criminal law often uses the

concept of reasonableness to accommodate evolving mores and avoid successive "fine-tuning" amendments. It is implicit in this technique that current social consensus on what is reasonable may be considered. It is wrong for caregivers or judges to apply their own subjective notions of what is reasonable; s. 43 demands an objective appraisal based on current learning and consensus. Substantial consensus, particularly when supported by expert evidence, can provide guidance and reduce the danger of arbitrary, subjective decision making.

[37] Based on the evidence currently before the Court, there are significant areas of agreement among the experts on both sides of the issue (trial decision, at para. 17). Corporal punishment of children under two years is harmful to them, and has no corrective value given the cognitive limitations of children under two years of age. Corporal punishment of teenagers is harmful, because it can induce aggressive or antisocial behaviour. Corporal punishment using objects, such as rulers or belts, is physically and emotionally harmful. Corporal punishment which involves slaps or blows to the head is harmful. These types of punishment, we may conclude, will not be reasonable.

[38] Contemporary social consensus is that, while teachers may sometimes use corrective force to remove children from classrooms or secure compliance with instructions, the use of corporal punishment by teachers is not acceptable. Many school boards forbid the use of corporal punishment, and some provinces and territories have legislatively prohibited its use by teachers: see, e.g., *Schools Act, 1997*, SNL 1997, c. S-12.2, s. 42; *School Act*, RSBC 1996, c. 412, s. 76(3); *Education Act*, SNB 1997, c. E-1.12, s. 23; *School Act*, RSPEI 1988, c. S-2.1, s. 73; *Education Act*, SNWT 1995, c. 28, s. 34(3); *Education Act*, SY 1989-90, c. 25, s. 36. This consensus is consistent with Canada's international obligations, given the findings of the Human Rights Committee of the United Nations noted above. Section 43 will protect a teacher who uses reasonable, corrective force to restrain or remove a child in appropriate circumstances. Substantial societal consensus, supported by expert evidence and Canada's treaty obligations, indicates that corporal punishment by teachers is unreasonable.

· · ·

[40] When these considerations are taken together, a solid core of meaning emerges for "reasonable under the circumstances," sufficient to establish a zone in which discipline risks criminal sanction. Generally, s. 43 exempts from criminal sanction only minor corrective force of a transitory and trifling nature. On the basis of current expert consensus, it does not apply to corporal punishment of children under two or teenagers. Degrading, inhuman or harmful conduct is not protected. Discipline by the use of objects or blows or slaps to the head is unreasonable. Teachers may reasonably apply force to remove a child from a classroom or secure compliance with instructions, but not merely as corporal punishment. Coupled with the requirement that the conduct be corrective, which rules out conduct stemming from the caregiver's frustration, loss of temper or abusive personality, a consistent picture emerges of the area covered by s. 43. It is wrong for law enforcement officers or judges to apply their own subjective views of what is "reasonable under the circumstances"; the test is objective. The question must be considered in context and in light of all the circumstances of the case. The gravity of the precipitating event is not relevant.

Summary of the Judgment

Below are summaries of the sections of the judgment reproduced above.

Use of Force for Corrective Purposes: Paragraphs 24, 25

The court clearly stated that the use of force must be for corrective purposes. Striking a child out of anger or frustration does not meet the requirement of s. 43 of the *Criminal Code* that the force be "by way of correction." Paragraph 25 states another condition: The child must be capable of learning from the corrective force. If the child is too young or lacks the ability to understand why he or she is being punished, the use of force is not permissible.

Force That Is "Reasonable Under the Circumstances": Paragraphs 26, 27, 28, 40

In interpreting "reasonable under the circumstances," the court clearly stated that police officers must not base their opinions only on subjective views. Instead, they must determine whether criminal behaviour has occurred by using an objective test (discussed below). The court was satisfied that police officers could determine what is "reasonable for the circumstances" by applying the objective test, and could reach an accurate conclusion of what actions constitute criminal behaviour.

Paragraph 27 of the decision refers to the ability of police to determine a standard of reasonableness such as the determination of "reasonable grounds" as found in s. 495 of the *Criminal Code*.

Paragraph 40 refers to the need for police to objectively consider their opinion of "reasonable under the circumstances."

The objective test is described in the decision of *R v. Storrey*. Although the subject of the decision is the validity of an arrest, the objective test that it proposes for determining reasonable grounds also applies to the issue of the reasonable use of force.

> [A]n arresting officer must subjectively have reasonable and probable grounds on which to base the arrest. Those grounds must, in addition, be justifiable from an objective point of view. That is to say, a reasonable person placed in the position of the officer must be able to conclude that there were indeed reasonable and probable grounds for the arrest.

Force Cannot Cause Bodily Harm: Paragraph 30

The application of corrective force cannot cause bodily harm. The court went further by adding the words "or raises a reasonable prospect of harm." If the force used causes bodily harm or raises the reasonable prospect of bodily harm, s. 43 cannot be relied upon for a defence by the person who administered the punishment.

Restrictions on the Use of Corporal Punishment: Paragraph 37

Paragraph 37 sets out several restrictions:

- The use of force to correct a child under the age of two has no demonstrated corrective value and has been shown to be harmful. Therefore, corrective force will not be authorized in such circumstances.
- Corporal punishment of teenage children can cause aggressive and/or antisocial behaviour and therefore will not be permitted.
- Corporal punishment using objects will not be permitted.
- Blows to the head, including slaps, are not reasonable and therefore are not permitted.

Use of Force by Teachers: Paragraphs 38, 40

A teacher may only use force to restrain a child, to ensure compliance with instructions, or to remove a child from the classroom in appropriate circumstances. The use of corporal punishment by teachers is not acceptable.

PUNISHMENT VERSUS ABUSE

This section addresses situations where a person legally authorized to use force to correct a child has used force, and the child has been harmed or a complaint has been made. It may be used as a guide for determining whether a child is in "need of protection" within the meaning of s. 37 of the CFSA.

These guidelines, along with the above discussion of *Canadian Foundation for Children, Youth and the Law v. Canada*, should assist officers in determining whether the force used against a child is an appropriate punishment or a criminal offence.

Abusive (inappropriate) physical punishment includes the following:

- The use of generally accepted types of physical punishment, such as slapping hands or buttocks, that is unduly prolonged or that is applied with an excessive amount of force.
- The use of generally unaccepted or inappropriate types of physical punishment, such as continual or lengthy beating, striking with fists, kicking, burning, scalding, or suffocating.

The decision in *Canadian Foundation for Children, Youth and the Law v. Canada* provides the following guidelines on the use of force:

- The force used must be for corrective purposes.
- The child must be capable of understanding why he or she is being punished.
- The child must be over the age of 2 and under the age of 13.
- The force used must be reasonable. Unreasonable force includes:
  - ☐ causing bodily harm,
  - ☐ administering strikes to the head, and
  - ☐ using objects to strike a child.

Descriptions of Physical Punishment

The descriptions of physical punishment in the following sections are from the Ontario Association of Children's Aid Societies *Ontario Child Welfare Eligibility Spectrum* (OACAS, 2006). They are designed to assist Children's Aid Society staff in determining whether a child is in need of protection in situations where a child has been physically harmed as a result of a direct physical action by a caregiver against a child. Protection of the child rather than consideration of proof of a criminal offence was the overriding concern in their drafting. However, police officers must also know when physical punishment constitutes a criminal offence so that they can act accordingly. Child protection should be foremost when determining whether to apply criminal or provincial legislation in child abuse cases.

The punishment identified in the following descriptions is in order of most to least amount of force used.

1. Excessive or Inappropriate Physical Force Used, Resulting in Severe Injury

Severe injuries are those requiring immediate medical attention, including bone fractures, internal injuries (such as those caused by shaking), intentional burns, brain or spinal cord injury, and deep wounds or punctures. This level of injury meets the definition of a child in need of protection. A criminal offence has likely been committed.

2. Excessive or Inappropriate Physical Force Used, Resulting in Moderately Serious Injury

Moderate injuries are those that are not life-threatening even in the absence of medical treatment. Examples include sprains, mild concussions, broken teeth, bruising, and small fractures. This level of injury also meets the definition of a child in need of protection. A criminal offence has likely been committed.

3. Excessive or Inappropriate Physical Force Used, Resulting in Superficial Injury

Superficial injuries involve no more than broken skin. These injuries include localized bruises, welts, cuts, and abrasions. This level of injury may meet the definition of a child in need of protection. A criminal offence may have been committed, depending on the circumstances in which the force was applied. A welt from a single slap on the buttocks may not constitute a criminal offence, but a strike to the head or face has been found by the Supreme Court of Canada to be unreasonable. The entirety of the situation must be considered.

CASE LAW: SUPREME COURT OF CANADA 1995

In *R v. Halcrow* (1993), 80 CCC (3d) 320, 40 WAC 197 (BCCA), aff'd. [1995] 1 SCR 440, 95 CCC (3d) 94, 90 WAC 72, 179 NR 63, Southin JA in her opinion (dissenting in part) considered that the word "reasonable" in this section means "moderate" or "not excessive" and what is or is not excessive should depend solely upon the age and physical condition of the child. Factors such as the gravity of the offence, the character of the child, and the likely effect on the character of the child are relevant only to the issue of the accused's purpose, whether the force was applied by way of correction. [*Martin's Annual Criminal Code, 1999*]

CASE LAW: SUPREME COURT OF CANADA 2004

In *Canadian Foundation for Children, Youth and the Law v. Canada*, Chief Justice Beverley McLachlin, in delivering the court's ruling, stated: "Corporal punishment which involves slaps or blows to the head is harmful. These types of punishment, we may conclude, will not be reasonable."

4. Excessive or Inappropriate Force Used, but No Resulting Injury

The child is not physically injured but may experience considerable temporary pain. The potential for injury is present. An example is several slaps on the buttocks. This level of injury may meet the definition of a child in need of protection. A criminal offence may have been committed, depending on the circumstances in which the force was applied.

5. Physical Force Used, but Not Excessive or Inappropriate

The person in care of the child uses a generally accepted method of physical punishment—for example, a slap on the buttocks. The force used does not ordinarily leave any marks on the child. It is unlikely that the child is in need of protection, nor is it likely that a criminal offence has been committed. The punishment is allowed under s. 43 of the *Criminal Code* in cases where the person has used the punishment to correct the child's behaviour.

6. No Physical Force Used with Child

Non-physical, non-assaultive methods of correction are used on the child. Examples are taking away privileges and verbal disapproval. The child is not in need of protection. A criminal offence has not been committed unless the person in care of the child fails to provide the necessities of life, which is an offence under s. 215 of the *Criminal Code*. This offence would be established in only the most extreme cases such as locking a child in a room and not providing food or water for several days. In rare circumstances such as this, the child would also be in need of protection.

Police officers must use their expertise and judgment in establishing whether the punishment rendered was permissible and reasonable and whether an offence was committed. By referring to the preceding descriptions and by using the objective test, the officer should be able to reach a defensible conclusion as to whether a child has been abused. If the officer is unsure whether a criminal offence has taken place, but still suspects abuse, he or she must adhere to the provisions of s. 72 of the CFSA and report the suspected abuse to a Children's Aid Society.

Learning Activity 4.1

Referring to the previous reading of the decision of the Supreme Court of Canada and the descriptions of physical punishment, classify the following actions as "legal" or "illegal" or "questionable" punishment. Be sure you can explain your answer.

Your answer choices are: Legal or Illegal or Questionable (Not Specifically Defined by Law).

1. A parent slapping an 18-month-old child on the buttocks because he put his hand on the hot stove.

2. A parent slapping her 6-year-old child across the face because she spilled her milk.

3. A parent slapping his 18-year-old son across the face for skipping school.

4. A parent locking her 16-year-old daughter in her room until she cleans it properly.

5. A teacher slapping a 9-year-old child across the buttocks for not paying attention in class.

6. A parent shaking his 10-month-old child to stop his crying.

7. A parent immersing the hand of her 10-year-old daughter into boiling water as a punishment for stealing.

8. A teacher forcibly removing a disruptive child from a classroom.

9. A parent correcting his 6-year-old child by striking her three times across the buttocks with a belt.

10. A parent lightly biting her 3-year-old child on the forearm to correct the child's biting behaviour toward other children.

SEXUAL ABUSE

child sexual abuse
any activity or behaviour that is sexual in nature and directed toward a child

Child sexual abuse includes any activity or behaviour that is sexual in nature and directed toward a child. Generally speaking, the *Criminal Code* defines a child as a person under the age of 18.

Children who are victims of sexual abuse may experience disruptions in their developing view of themselves and the world (Department of Justice Canada, 2005). These disruptions can bring about significant emotional and behavioural changes as the victims find ways to cope with these events. Victims feel that their sense of personal integrity, safety, and security has been violated. They may also experience feelings of shame and guilt. Opportunities to play, learn, and have healthy relationships with others may be lost.

Sexual abuse in childhood may have far-reaching effects that may not be apparent until later in the child's life. Some research (Wilken, 2002) suggests that child sexual abuse experiences may, along with other factors, contribute to experiences of sexual exploitation later in life. Many young people who are sexually exploited and have run away come from home environments where they have been physically, sexually, and emotionally abused. The effects of sexual abuse and exploitation may continue into adulthood. Adolescent and adult women who were sexually molested as children are more likely than non-victims to suffer from both physical and psychological problems.

Less research has been done on male victims of child and youth sexual abuse and exploitation, but the research that is available (Purcell, Malow, Dolezal, & Carballo-Dieguez, 2004) indicates that male victims are also more likely than non-victims to experience physical and psychological problems. Male victims may experience depression, anxiety, and suicidal thoughts and behaviours. They may also adopt inappropriate coping strategies, such as drug and alcohol use.

Pedophiles

Pedophiles are people who are sexually attracted to children. A pedophile is most often male and may be attracted to both male and female children. Pedophiles sometimes know that their actions are wrong but may be unable to control their urges. They are aroused sexually by young, usually prepubescent children. They may be further stimulated by engaging in or observing violent sexual acts with children.

pedophile
a person who is sexually attracted to children

There are sexual predators who are opportunistic and will randomly abduct a child for sexual purposes. These predatory offences are investigated in the same way as any other random act of sexual violence. It is unlikely that the predatory pedophile will attack the same child again. The majority of pedophiles, however, are known to the child and are usually family members or family friends.

Some of the commonalities that pedophiles may share are family histories marked by physical, sexual, and emotional abuse as well as frequent experiences of failure, problems in social functioning, and unsatisfactory peer relationships (Department of Justice Canada, 2005).

Modus Operandi of a Pedophile

There are similarities in the methods that pedophiles use to gain access to children for sexual purposes. Box 4.1 summarizes a conversation between an undercover police officer and a pedophile in which the pedophile reveals his modus operandi for finding and sexually abusing child victims. The officer, who was posing as a person who could provide access to children for sexual purposes, recorded the conversation on audiotape. The perpetrator in this case was successful in gaining access to approximately 20 children (established through investigation; the number could be greater). The information is specific to the case but has many commonalities that may assist police in understanding the modus operandi of a pedophile.

In the remainder of this section, note the following commonalities of pedophiliac behaviour identified in Box 4.1:

- secrecy
- exposure to pornography
- personal use of pornography
- grooming.

Box 4.1   A Conversation with a Pedophile

Below is a summary of a conversation between an undercover police officer and a pedophile, with quotations from the pedophile:

- He spoke of the desire to create sexual videos involving himself and children.
- He said he often masturbated while watching child pornography.
- He explained how he sat in parks, not far from his home, and waited for kids to approach him. He stated that having a puppy dog was a good idea, that it "brings the kids to you." He said that it was not a good idea to approach kids because "everyone is telling them to stay away from strangers."
- He stated: "You have to groom them gradually. Not too fast."
- He described how he brought children to his home, where he provided candy and soft drinks, and possibly alcohol for the older kids under 14.
- He discussed his age limits, saying it was too difficult with kids over 13. As part of the conversation, he identified a situation where he tried to have sexual contact with a 14-year-old male. The male reported to police. This created a "bad situation."
- He explained how, as part of the grooming process, he allowed the children to use his computer to play games.
- He described how he gradually exposed the children to sexual images on his computer.
- He said he progressed to child pornography on his computer and through the use of pornographic books that he "left around" his home.
- He explained how the exposure to child pornography escalated using books and video to the point of becoming constant.
- He said he used child pornography to "show them what to do."
- He advised: "Don't force them. I had bad luck with that. The kid fought back and told his parents."

Child Pornography and Luring

Child pornography victimizes children and youth through the creation of images depicting them in a sexually explicit manner and the distribution of these materials for profit or other purposes. In 2002, the *Criminal Code* was amended to broaden the scope of the offences relating to child pornography and to prohibit the use of a computer to communicate with a child for the purpose of facilitating the commission of a sexual offence against that child. The relevant provisions are reproduced below.

Luring a Child: Criminal Code, Section 172.1

172.1(1) Every person commits an offence who, by means of a computer system within the meaning of subsection 342.1(2), communicates with

(a) a person who is, or who the accused believes is, under the age of eighteen years, for the purpose of facilitating the commission of an offence under subsection 153(1), section 155 or 163.1, subsection 212(1) or (4) or section 271, 272 or 273 with respect to that person;

(b) a person who is, or who the accused believes is, under the age of 16 years, for the purpose of facilitating the commission of an offence under section 151 or 152, subsection 160(3) or 173(2) or section 280 with respect to that person; or

(c) a person who is, or who the accused believes is, under the age of 14 years, for the purpose of facilitating the commission of an offence under section 281 with respect to that person.

Punishment

(2) Every person who commits an offence under subsection (1) is guilty of

(a) an indictable offence and liable to imprisonment for a term of not more than ten years; or

(b) an offence punishable on summary conviction and liable to imprisonment for a term not exceeding eighteen months.

Presumption re Age

(3) Evidence that the person referred to in paragraph (1)(a), (b) or (c) was represented to the accused as being under the age of eighteen years, sixteen years or fourteen years, as the case may be, is, in the absence of evidence to the contrary, proof that the accused believed that the person was under that age.

No Defence

(4) It is not a defence to a charge under paragraph (1)(a), (b) or (c) that the accused believed that the person referred to in that paragraph was at least eighteen years of age, sixteen years or fourteen years of age, as the case may be, unless the accused took reasonable steps to ascertain the age of the person.

In 2005, additional reforms were made that broadened the definition of child pornography and created a new offence against the advertisement of child pornography.

Definition of "Child Pornography": Criminal Code, Section 163.1

163.1(1) In this section, "child pornography" means

(a) a photographic, film, video or other visual representation, whether or not it was made by electronic or mechanical means,

(i) that shows a person who is or is depicted as being under the age of eighteen years and is engaged in or is depicted as engaged in explicit sexual activity, or

(ii) the dominant characteristic of which is the depiction, for a sexual purpose, of a sexual organ or the anal region of a person under the age of eighteen years;

(b) any written material, visual representation or audio recording that advocates or counsels sexual activity with a person under the age of eighteen years that would be an offence under this Act;

(c) any written material whose dominant characteristic is the description, for a sexual purpose, of sexual activity with a person under the age of eighteen years that would be an offence under this Act; or

(d) any audio recording that has as its dominant characteristic the description, presentation or representation, for a sexual purpose, of sexual activity with a person under the age of eighteen years that would be an offence under this Act.

Making Child Pornography

(2) Every person who makes, prints, publishes or possesses for the purpose of publication any child pornography is guilty of

(a) an indictable offence and liable to imprisonment for a term not exceeding ten years and to a minimum punishment of imprisonment for a term of one year; or

(b) an offence punishable on summary conviction and liable to imprisonment for a term not exceeding eighteen months and to a minimum punishment of imprisonment for a term of ninety days.

Distribution, etc. of Child Pornography

(3) Every person who transmits, makes available, distributes, sells, advertises, imports, exports or possesses for the purpose of transmission, making available, distribution, sale, advertising or exportation any child pornography is guilty of

(a) an indictable offence and liable to imprisonment for a term not exceeding ten years and to a minimum punishment of imprisonment for a term of one year; or

(b) an offence punishable on summary conviction and liable to imprisonment for a term not exceeding eighteen months and to a minimum punishment of imprisonment for a term of ninety days.

Possession of Child Pornography

(4) Every person who possesses any child pornography is guilty of

(a) an indictable offence and liable to imprisonment for a term not exceeding five years and to a minimum punishment of imprisonment for a term of forty-five days; or

(b) an offence punishable on summary conviction and liable to imprisonment for a term not exceeding eighteen months and to a minimum punishment of imprisonment for a term of fourteen days.

Accessing Child Pornography

(4.1) Every person who accesses any child pornography is guilty of

(a) an indictable offence and liable to imprisonment for a term not exceeding five years and to a minimum punishment of imprisonment for a term of forty-five days; or

(b) an offence punishable on summary conviction and liable to imprisonment for a term not exceeding eighteen months and to a minimum punishment of imprisonment for a term of fourteen days.

Interpretation

(4.2) For the purposes of subsection (4.1), a person accesses child pornography who knowingly causes child pornography to be viewed by, or transmitted to, himself or herself.

Aggravating Factor

(4.3) If a person is convicted of an offence under this section, the court that imposes the sentence shall consider as an aggravating factor the fact that the person committed the offence with intent to make a profit.

Defence

(5) It is not a defence to a charge under subsection (2) in respect of a visual representation that the accused believed that a person shown in the representation that is alleged to constitute child pornography was or was depicted as being eighteen years of age or more unless the accused took all reasonable steps to ascertain the age of that person and took all reasonable steps to ensure that, where the person was eighteen years of age or more, the representation did not depict that person as being under the age of eighteen years.

Defence

(6) No person shall be convicted of an offence under this section if the act that is alleged to constitute the offence

(a) has a legitimate purpose related to the administration of justice or to science, medicine, education or art; and

(b) does not pose an undue risk of harm to persons under the age of eighteen years.

Question of Law

(7) For greater certainty, for the purposes of this section, it is a question of law whether any written material, visual representation or audio recording advocates or counsels sexual activity with a person under the age of eighteen years that would be an offence under this Act.

The Phases of Abuse

Child sexual abuse may be categorized into five phases: engagement, sexual interaction, secrecy, disclosure, and suppression (Murphy, 1985). Each phase is discussed below.

Engagement

In the engagement phase, the abuser communicates with the child with the objective of engaging the child in sexual activity. The abuser may entice the child into sexual activity through the use of trickery or rewards. Entrapment may be used to manipulate the child into feeling that he or she has no choice but to participate. The abuser may use his adult authority to impose feelings of guilt and convince the child that he or she is responsible for the abuse. Threats of harm may be used to force the child into participating in sexual activity. The threat may be to the child or a family member. The abuser, most often a family member, may convince the child that he will commit suicide if the child does not participate. The abuser may use alcohol or other drugs to subdue the child or may simply use his superior size and strength to overpower the child.

The majority of abusers rely on enticement or entrapment to engage the child in sexual activity. The engagement strategy, if successful, is likely to be repeated and not escalate into violent strategies. Pedophiles tend to repeat their modus operandi, often for many years, until they are discovered or the child grows up and the pedophile loses interest.

Pedophiles often prey on children who have recently begun using the Internet and who complain of not having many real friends. These children are easy prey. They are more susceptible to someone trying to befriend them and they are less likely to talk about their online conversations with anyone. They're lonely, and the pedophile poses as a much-needed friend. Pedophiles look for kids who are having problems at home. The pedophile tries to win the child over and further separate the child from his or her family by complaining about parents generally. A common modus operandi for the online pedophile is to first gain the trust of the child and then make arrangements to meet him or her some place where they can talk privately. The child has no way of knowing whether he or she is meeting with a 14-year-old peer to discuss teenage problems or with a 44-year-old pedophile.

Sexual Interaction

Sexual interaction is the second phase of child sexual abuse. Types of abuse may include masturbation, fondling, digital penetration, oral or anal penetration, intercourse, and pornography.

Secrecy

In the secrecy phase, the objective of the abuser is to continue with the activity. This necessitates his avoiding detection and maintaining access to the child. The abuser may use threats or guilt to coerce the child into keeping the abuse a secret.

Disclosure

In the disclosure phase, the abuse may be discovered accidentally, or the child may intentionally disclose the abuse. When a child discloses abuse, it is usually to a family member. This can cause tremendous emotional turmoil within the family if the family member refuses to believe that the abuse occurred.

Suppression

In the suppression phase, the family attempts to keep the secret of the abuse within the family and chooses not to disclose it to police and child welfare authorities. This phase may begin as soon as disclosure takes place and may continue through investigation by police and child welfare authorities. There are many reasons for suppression:

- desire to protect the family's reputation, to protect the child, or to protect the abuser;
- fear of legal repercussions;
- fear of involvement with the legal system, particularly of being a witness;
- avoidance of responsibility; or
- feelings of inadequacy as a result of failure to protect the child.

A subsequent police investigation may reveal that failing to act immediately upon disclosure may have allowed the abuse to continue.

Identifying Signs of Sexual Abuse in Children Through Sexual Behaviours

A sexually abused child may not have any readily visible physical signs of abuse. However, the abused child may exhibit changes in behaviour. There are some common behaviours that a child who has experienced or is experiencing sexual abuse may exhibit. These behaviours are age-related, although there is no definite age at which they are exhibited.

All police services have officers specifically trained in the identification of child sexual abuse. Trained officers will have significantly more subject knowledge than is presented in this chapter. The information in this chapter is intended to be used as a guide to facilitate a basic understanding of the identification of child abuse.

Identifying sexual abuse may be more difficult than identifying physical abuse. There may not be any physical indicators readily apparent to the investigating officers. The indicators most often examined, beyond physical indicators, are behavioural patterns. See Tables 4.3 and 4.4.

The behaviours in Table 4.3 are mostly seen in toddlers and preschoolers, but may also be seen in older children. Table 4.4 looks at behaviours common in older children. Older children, for the purpose of this discussion, are children between the ages of 5 and 15 years.

A child aged 16 years or older is not considered to be a child within the scope of provincial legislation such as the Ontario *Child and Family Services Act*.

In the tables, behaviours are classified as normal, caution, and attention.

- "Normal" indicates that the behaviours are not out of context with the behaviours of other children in this age range.
- "Caution" indicates that the behaviours are not generally observed in children of this age group and could be indicative of possible sexual abuse.
- "Attention" indicates that the behaviours should not be present in children of this age group, and should be investigated for the possibility of past or present sexual abuse.

Police officers investigating complaints of child sexual abuse should be aware that the preceding behaviours will not be easily observed during the first intervention. Identification of behavioural indicators will more likely be revealed through interviews with family, friends, and the child. These interviews are generally conducted by child protection workers in the presence of or with the assistance of police officers. However, these interviews may be unproductive and frustrating. Statistically, the perpetrator of the crime is likely to be a family member or a person known to the child. The child, as a result of the perpetrator's perceived position of authority, will likely have difficulty discussing the occurrence.

There are some other behaviours that could indicate sexual abuse including:

- The child engages in age-inappropriate sexual play with toys, in which the toys are used to mimic sex acts.
- The child touches himself or herself sexually at inappropriate times.

Table 4.3   Appropriateness of Sexual Behaviours: Toddlers and Preschoolers

	Normal	Caution	Attention
Curiosity behaviours	• asks appropriate questions about sex (for example, "Where do babies come from?") • shows interest in learning the names of parts of the body	• shows fear when talking about anything to do with sex	• does not stop asking questions about sex • knows too much about sexuality for age and stage of development
Self-exploration	• likes to be naked • has erections • is curious and enjoys exploring own body • touches own genitals as a self-soothing behaviour (for example, when going to sleep, or when feeling sick, tense, or afraid) • is very aware of genital area during toilet training • puts objects in own genitals or buttocks without it feeling uncomfortable	• self-stimulates using furniture, toys, and other objects • imitates sexual behaviour with dolls or toys • continues to self-stimulate in public after being told that this behaviour should take place in private • puts objects in genitals and buttocks even when it feels uncomfortable	• self-stimulates in public or in private instead of playing in other activities • self-stimulates on other people • harms own genitals or buttocks
Behaviour with others	• explores the bodies of other children when playing • likes to look at naked people • wants to touch genitals, to see what they feel like • may show his or her genitals or buttocks to others • may take off clothes in front of others • sees the above behaviours as fun and silly	• continues to play games like "doctor" after being asked not to • always wants to touch other people • tries to engage in adult sexual behaviours • copies adult sexual activity with clothes on	• forces or bullies other children to take their clothes off or do sexual things • in dramatic play, acts out sad, angry, or aggressive scenes • demands to see the genitals of other children or adults • tricks or forces other children into touching genitals, engaging in adult sexual behaviours, copying sexual acts with clothes off, or performing oral sex
Bathroom, toileting, and sexual functions	• is interested in "peeing" and "pooing" • is curious about and tries to see what people are doing in the bathroom • wants privacy in the bathroom and when changing (applies to some preschoolers) • uses unacceptable words for toileting and sexual functions	• spreads feces • purposefully urinates in places he or she shouldn't • is often caught watching others who want privacy in the bathroom • continues to use unacceptable words after being asked not to	• continues spreading feces after being told to stop • continues to urinate in places he or she shouldn't • does not allow others privacy in the bathroom or bedroom • does not care about the rules set for unacceptable language and continues to use it

(The table is concluded on the next page.)

Table 4.3   Concluded

	Normal	Caution	Attention
Relationships	• plays house with other children • kisses and hugs people who are important to him or her • may share what he or she has found out about sex	• when talking about adult relationships, refers to sex a lot • is afraid of being kissed or hugged • talks or acts in a sexual way with others • uses sexual language even after being asked not to • talks about sex or includes sex in play instead of doing other things	• imitates adult sexual behaviour in detail • shows fear when touched • talks in a sexual way even with people he or she does not know
Behaviour with animals	• is curious about how animals have babies	• touches genitals of animals	• engages in sexual behaviour with animals

Source: Adapted from Johnson (1999).

Table 4.4   Appropriateness of Sexual Behaviours: School-Aged Children

	Normal	Caution	Attention
Relationships	• thinks children of the opposite sex are "gross" • chases children of the opposite sex • talks about sex with friends, talks about having a boyfriend/girlfriend • plays games with peers about sex (applies to older children) • likes telling and listening to dirty jokes	• refuses contact with specific individual(s) • uses sexual language to insult or scare others • wants to play games related to sex with much younger or older children • continues to tell dirty jokes after being asked not to • makes sexual sounds	• hurts and/or avoids certain types of people (for example, the opposite sex, or people with certain features such as facial hair) • cannot seem to stop talking about sex and sexual acts • sees all relationships in a sexual way • forces others to play sexual games • continues to tell dirty jokes even after being disciplined
Nature of sexual awareness	• includes genitals on drawings of people • looks at pictures of naked people • makes fun of the opposite sex • shows that he or she wants privacy respected • hates being a boy or girl • hates own genitals • demands privacy in an aggressive or overly upset way	• includes genitals in drawings of one sex and not the other • in pictures, makes genitals a main feature or makes them larger than other body parts • is overly curious with pictures of naked people • masturbates while looking at pictures of naked people • becomes very upset when privacy is not respected	• in drawings, may depict adult sexual activity or sexual abuse of a child • hates being a boy or girl • hates own genitals • wants to be the opposite sex

Source: Adapted from Johnson (1999).

- The child produces age-inappropriate sexually explicit drawings or descriptions.
- The child shows evidence of sophisticated sexual knowledge, beyond that of children of the same age.
- The child refuses, for no apparent reason, to go home or to the home of a relative or family friend.
- The child fears being in a particular area of the home.
- The child fears being left alone with a person of a particular sex.
- The child hints that he or she is engaged in sexual activity or has been abused.

Older children, including but not limited to teens, may exhibit behavioural changes in addition to those noted above:

- depression;
- self-destructive behaviour such as alcohol or drug abuse;
- aggressive or sexually suggestive behaviour;
- unusual or out-of-context sexual statements;
- promiscuity or prostitution;
- recurring physical complaints without a physiological basis;
- recurring references to sexual abuse in school projects or essays; or
- sudden interest in sex, sexually transmitted diseases, or pregnancy.

When an officer responds to a complaint of sexual abuse, the complainant, often a teacher or family member, may initially be the best source of information. The responding officer, having no prior knowledge of the child's behaviour, will have no basis for comparing the child's past and present behaviour. Consultation with others familiar with the child may reveal behavioural changes that indicate sexual abuse.

There may be some physical indicators, too, although most cannot be readily identified by the responding officer (Children's Aid Society of Algoma, 1998):

- the presence of a sexually transmitted disease;
- unusual or excessive itching or pain in the genital or anal area;
- blood in the stool or urine;
- bruises, lacerations, redness, swelling, or bleeding in the genital or anal area;
- torn, stained, or bloody underclothing; or
- pregnancy.

Physical force is rarely necessary to prompt a child to engage in sexual activity. The abuser is often in a position of trust toward the child. The child can be tricked, bribed, threatened, or pressured into sexual activity, or may willingly engage in such activity because he or she trusts and depends on the abuser and wants to gain his or her approval. The goal of the abusive act, as in most sex crimes, is not sexual gratification but power and control. The abuser takes advantage of his or her position of trust for personal gratification.

In most instances where the child is under 14, his or her consent is irrelevant and cannot be used by the abuser as a defence.

Consent by a Child

Consent No Defence: Criminal Code, Section 150.1

150.1(1) Subject to subsections (2) to (2.2), when an accused is charged with an offence under section 151 or 152 or subsection 153(1), 160(3) or 173(2) or is charged with an offence under section 271, 272 or 273 in respect of a complainant under the age of 16 years, it is not a defence that the complainant consented to the activity that forms the subject-matter of the charge.

Exception—Complainant Aged 12 or 13

(2) When an accused is charged with an offence under section 151 or 152, subsection 173(2) or section 271 in respect of a complainant who is 12 years of age or more but under the age of 14 years, it is a defence that the complainant consented to the activity that forms the subject-matter of the charge if the accused

(a) is less than two years older than the complainant; and

(b) is not in a position of trust or authority towards the complainant, is not a person with whom the complainant is in a relationship of dependency and is not in a relationship with the complainant that is exploitative of the complainant.

Exception—Complainant Aged 14 or 15

(2.1) When an accused is charged with an offence under section 151 or 152, subsection 173(2) or section 271 in respect of a complainant who is 14 years of age or more but under the age of 16 years, it is a defence that the complainant consented to the activity that forms the subject-matter of the charge if

(a) the accused

(i) is less than five years older than the complainant; and

(ii) is not in a position of trust or authority towards the complainant, is not a person with whom the complainant is in a relationship of dependency and is not in a relationship with the complainant that is exploitative of the complainant; or

(b) the accused is married to the complainant.

Exception for Transitional Purposes

(2.2) When the accused referred to in subsection (2.1) is five or more years older than the complainant, it is a defence that the complainant consented to the activity that forms the subject-matter of the charge if, on the day on which this subsection comes into force,

(a) the accused is the common-law partner of the complainant, or has been cohabiting with the complainant in a conjugal relationship for a period of less than one year and they have had or are expecting to have a child as a result of the relationship; and

(b) the accused is not in a position of trust or authority towards the complainant, is not a person with whom the complainant is in a relationship of dependency and is not in a relationship with the complainant that is exploitative of the complainant.

Exemption for Accused Aged Twelve or Thirteen

(3) No person aged twelve or thirteen years shall be tried for an offence under section 151 or 152 or subsection 173(2) unless the person is in a position of trust or authority towards the complainant, is a person with whom the complainant is in a relationship of dependency or is in a relationship with the complainant that is exploitative of the complainant.

Mistake of Age

(4) It is not a defence to a charge under section 151 or 152, subsection 160(3) or 173(2), or section 271, 272 or 273 that the accused believed that the complainant was 16 years of age or more at the time the offence is alleged to have been committed unless the accused took all reasonable steps to ascertain the age of the complainant.

Idem

(5) It is not a defence to a charge under section 153, 159, 170, 171 or 172 or subsection 212(2) or (4) that the accused believed that the complainant was eighteen years of age or more at the time the offence is alleged to have been committed unless the accused took all reasonable steps to ascertain the age of the complainant.

Mistake of Age

(6) An accused cannot raise a mistaken belief in the age of the complainant in order to invoke a defence under subsection (2) or (2.1) unless the accused took all reasonable steps to ascertain the age of the complainant.

Within the realm of consent, an accused may rely on the defence of mistake of age to explain sexual interactions with a person under 16 years of age. The accused must have taken all reasonable steps to determine the age of the person before engaging in sexual activity with him or her. Otherwise, the accused cannot rely on mistake of age as a defence. The following court decisions address the issue of mistake of age.

Mistake of Age: R v. Osborne

The accused, in order to rely on the defence of mistake, need only raise a reasonable doubt. The accused must, however, have made an earnest inquiry or there should be some compelling factor that obviates the need for such an inquiry. Thus, the accused must show what steps he took and those steps were all that could be reasonably required of him in the circumstances: *R v. Osborne* (1992), 17 CR (4th) 350, 102 Nfld. & PEIR 194 (Nfld. CA). [*Martin's Annual Criminal Code, 2012*, p. 292]

Mistake of Age: R v. P.(L.T.)

In *R v. P.(L.T.)*, the court identified some criteria for determining whether the mistake of age was reasonable in the circumstances.

Where the accused raises the defence of honest but mistaken belief in the complainant's age, the Crown must prove beyond a reasonable doubt that the accused did not take all reasonable steps to ascertain the complainant's age or did not have an honest belief as to the complainant's age. The issue to be determined is what steps would have been reasonable for the accused to take in the circumstances. While in certain circumstances a visual observation may suffice, where it does not, further reasonable steps should be considered having regard to the complainant's physical appearance, her behaviour, the ages and appearance of those in whose company the complainant was found, the activities engaged in, the times, places and other circumstances in which the accused observes the complainant and her conduct. The accused's subjective belief is relevant but not conclusive of this determination: *R v. P.(L.T.)* (1997), 113 CCC (3d) 42, 142 WAC 20 (BCCA). [*Martin's Annual Criminal Code, 2012*, p. 292]

No Consent Where Fear of Physical Harm: R v. Ewanchuk

The issue of consent in cases of sexual assault was addressed by the Supreme Court of Canada in the 1999 decision of *R v. Ewanchuk*. This case did not involve a child but may be referred to when investigating situations where the victim is 16 years of age or older. The decision refers to a situation where the accused alleges that the victim consented to the sex act through the victim's non-response or non-refusal to participate.

There is no defence of implied consent to sexual assault. The absence of consent is subjective and must be determined by reference to the complainant's subjective internal state of mind towards the touching at the time it occurred. The complainant's statement that she did not consent is a matter of credibility to be weighed in light of all of the evidence including any ambiguous conduct. If the trier of fact accepts the complainant's testimony that she did not consent, no matter how strongly conduct may contradict her claim, the absence of consent is established. The trier of fact need only consider s. 265(3) if the complainant has chosen to participate in sexual activity or her ambiguous conduct or submission has given rise to doubt regarding the absence of consent. There is no consent where the complainant consents because she honestly believes that she will otherwise suffer physical violence. While the plausibility of the alleged fear and any overt expressions of it are relevant in assessing the complainant's credibility that she consented out of fear, the approach is subjective: *R v. Ewanchuk*, [1999] 1 SCR 330, 131 CCC (3d) 481, 22 CR (5th) 1. [*Martin's Annual Criminal Code, 2012*, p. 582]

This decision removes a measure of ambiguity from the concept of consent. If the victim acquiesces through an honest belief that he or she may suffer physical harm if he or she resists, consent is not given. In the information presented to the court in the *Ewanchuk* case, the victim did not adamantly refuse the advances of the accused. The court ruled that the victim could have honestly believed that such refusal could result in physical harm. This may often be the case in situations of child sexual assault. The perpetrator of the crime is most likely to be physically larger than the victim, leading the victim to fear for his or her safety.

Sexual Offences Involving Children

There are specific sections in the *Criminal Code* that address the sexual abuse of children.

Sexual Interference: Criminal Code, Section 151

151. Every person who, for a sexual purpose, touches, directly or indirectly, with a part of the body or with an object, any part of the body of a person under the age of 16 years

(a) is guilty of an indictable offence and liable to imprisonment for a term not exceeding ten years and to a minimum punishment of imprisonment for a term of forty-five days; or

(b) is guilty of an offence punishable on summary conviction and liable to imprisonment for a term not exceeding eighteen months and to a minimum punishment of imprisonment for a term of fourteen days.

This offence is made out when a person touches a child under the age of 16, directly or indirectly, for a sexual purpose.

The following provincial court ruling confirms the inability of a child to consent to sexual activities.

No Consent Where Child Suggests Sexual Interaction: R v. Sears

An accused who intends sexual interaction of any kind with a child and with that intent makes contact with the body of a child, "touches" the child within the meaning of this section, even where the sexual interaction is suggested by the child: *R v. Sears* (1990), 58 CCC (3d) 62 (Man. CA). [*Martin's Annual Criminal Code, 2012*, p. 297]

Invitation to Sexual Touching: Criminal Code, Section 152

152. Every person who, for a sexual purpose, invites, counsels or incites a person under the age of 16 years to touch, directly or indirectly, with a part of the body or with an object, the body of any person, including the body of the person who so invites, counsels or incites and the body of the person under the age of 16 years,

(a) is guilty of an indictable offence and liable to imprisonment for a term not exceeding ten years and to a minimum punishment of imprisonment for a term of forty-five days; or

(b) is guilty of an offence punishable on summary conviction and liable to imprisonment for a term not exceeding eighteen months and to a minimum punishment of imprisonment for a term of fourteen days.

Section 152 applies "regardless of whether the accused invites the touching of his or herself or another person or incites the person under 16 to touch their own body" (*Martin's Annual Criminal Code, 2012*, p. 298).

No Proof of Physical Contact Required: R v. Fong

This offence does not require proof of actual physical contact between body parts or an invitation to engage in that level of contact. This section covers not only actual touching but "indirect" touching and thus includes an invitation by the accused to the complainant to hold a tissue onto which the accused ejaculated: *R v. Fong* (1994), 92 CCC (3d) 171 (Alta. CA), leave to appeal to SCC refused 94 CCC (3d) vii. [*Martin's Annual Criminal Code, 2012*, p. 299]

Sexual Exploitation: Criminal Code, Section 153

153(1) Every person commits an offence who is in a position of trust or authority towards a young person, who is a person with whom the young person is in a relationship of dependency or who is in a relationship with a young person that is exploitative of the young person, and who

(a) for a sexual purpose, touches, directly or indirectly, with a part of the body or with an object, any part of the body of the young person; or

(b) for a sexual purpose, invites, counsels or incites a young person to touch, directly or indirectly, with a part of the body or with an object, the body of any person, including the body of the person who so invites, counsels or incites and the body of the young person.

Punishment

(1.1) Every person who commits an offence under subsection (1)

(a) is guilty of an indictable offence and liable to imprisonment for a term not exceeding ten years and to a minimum punishment of imprisonment for a term of forty-five days; or

(b) is guilty of an offence punishable on summary conviction and liable to imprisonment for a term not exceeding eighteen months and to a minimum punishment of imprisonment for a term of fourteen days.

Inference of Sexual Exploitation

(1.2) A judge may infer that a person is in a relationship with a young person that is exploitative of the young person from the nature and circumstances of the relationship, including

(a) the age of the young person;

(b) the age difference between the person and the young person;

(c) the evolution of the relationship; and

(d) the degree of control or influence by the person over the young person.

Definition of "Young Person"

(2) In this section, "young person" means a person 16 years of age or more but under the age of eighteen years.

Definition of "Dependency": R v. Galbraith

The term "dependency" is to be read *ejusdem generis* [of the same class] with two other categories of trust or authority and contemplates a relationship in which there is a *de facto* [in reality, actual] reliance by a young person on a figure who has assumed a position of power, such as trust or authority over the young person along non-traditional lines. The disentitling condition of dependency must exist independently of a sexual relationship: *R v. Galbraith* (1994), 90 CCC (3d) 76, 30 CR (4th) 230 sub nom. *R v. G.(C.)*, 18 OR (3d) 247, 71 OAC 45 (CA), leave to appeal to SCC refused 92 CCC (3d) vi. [*Martin's Annual Criminal Code, 2012*, p. 301]

Incest: Criminal Code, Section 155

155(1) Every one commits incest who, knowing that another person is by blood relationship his or her parent, child, brother, sister, grandparent or grandchild, as the case may be, has sexual intercourse with that person.

Punishment

(2) Every one who commits incest is guilty of an indictable offence and liable to imprisonment for a term not exceeding fourteen years.

Defence

(3) No accused shall be determined by a court to be guilty of an offence under this section if the accused was under restraint, duress or fear of the person with whom the accused had the sexual intercourse at the time the sexual intercourse occurred.

Definition of "Brother" and "Sister"

(4) In this section, "brother" and "sister," respectively, include half-brother and half-sister.

There is a rarely used section of the *Criminal Code* that addresses the corruption of children. Note that police may commence proceedings only with the permission of the attorney general. However, the charge may be brought forth by a Children's Aid Society without the permission of the attorney general.

Corrupting Children: Criminal Code, Section 172

172(1) Every one who, in the home of a child, participates in adultery or sexual immorality or indulges in habitual drunkenness or any other form of vice, and thereby endangers the morals of the child or renders the home an unfit place for the child to be in, is guilty of an indictable offence and liable to imprisonment for a term not exceeding two years.

(2) [Repealed]

Definition of "Child"

(3) For the purposes of this section, "child" means a person who is or appears to be under the age of eighteen years.

Who May Institute Prosecutions

(4) No proceedings shall be commenced under subsection (1) without the consent of the Attorney General, unless they are instituted by or at the instance of a recognized society for the protection of children or by an officer of a juvenile court.

This section makes it an indictable offence to indulge in behaviour, in a *child's home*, which corrupts children. Children are defined in s. 172(3) as being *under or apparently under* the age of *18*. The prohibited activities listed in the section are expansively defined by adultery, sexual immorality, habitual drunkenness, or *any other form of vice*. However, it must be shown that the *result* of this behaviour is to *endanger the morals* of a child or to make the house unfit for a child to live in. [*Martin's Annual Criminal Code, 2012*, p. 331]

Sexual Immorality and the Corruption of Children: R v. E.(B.)

The offence of engaging in sexual immorality in the home of a child requires proof that the accused intentionally engaged in the prohibited conduct including knowledge or at least wilful blindness that the children were aware of the sexually immoral conduct. 'Sexual immorality' requires an objective consideration of conduct by reference to community standards of tolerance that are tied directly to the harm caused or threatened by the conduct. 'Participation' requires proof of some form of conduct. 'Morals' refers to those core values that are central to the maintenance of a free and democratic society. The morals of a child will be endangered by sexual immorality where: (1) the sexual conduct presents a real risk that the child will not develop an understanding that exploitive or non-consensual sexual activity is wrong; (2) the conduct degrades or dehumanizes women such that the child will not develop an understanding that all persons are equal and worthy of respect regardless of gender; (3) the conduct imperils the child's understanding of parents' responsibilities to protect and nurture their children; and (4) to the extent that the conduct actively involves the child, it may endanger the child's morals by leaving him or her without a proper sense of his or her own self-worth or autonomy: *R v. E.(B.)* [(1999), 139 CCC (3d) 100, 29 CR (5th) 51 (Ont. CA)]. [*Martin's Annual Criminal Code, 2012*, pp. 331-332]

Although the offence of engaging in sexual immorality in the home of a child violates s. 2(b) of the Charter, it is a reasonable limit within the meaning of s. 1 and is therefore valid: *R v. E.(B.)* (1999), 139 CCC (3d) 100, 29 CR (5th) 51 (Ont. CA). [*Martin's Annual Criminal Code, 2012*, p. 331]

Sexual Assault

Sections of the *Criminal Code* relating to sexual assault are discussed below.

The offence of sexual assault does not include any age limitations, as demonstrated by the use of the term "Every one" in s. 271(1).

Sexual Assault: Criminal Code, Section 271(1)

271(1) Every one who commits a sexual assault is guilty of

(a) an indictable offence and is liable to imprisonment for a term not exceeding ten years; or

(b) an offence punishable on summary conviction and liable to imprisonment for a term not exceeding eighteen months.

The facts in issue that constitute assault, as set forth in s. 265 of the *Criminal Code*, must first be established before a charge of sexual assault can be pursued.

Assault: Criminal Code, Section 265

265(1) A person commits an assault when

(a) without the consent of another person, he applies force intentionally to that other person, directly or indirectly;

(b) he attempts or threatens, by an act or a gesture, to apply force to another person, if he has, or causes that other person to believe on reasonable grounds that he has, present ability to effect his purpose; or

(c) while openly wearing or carrying a weapon or an imitation thereof, he accosts or impedes another person or begs.

Application

(2) This section applies to all forms of assault, including sexual assault, sexual assault with a weapon, threats to a third party or causing bodily harm and aggravated sexual assault.

Consent

(3) For the purposes of this section, no consent is obtained where the complainant submits or does not resist by reason of

(a) the application of force to the complainant or to a person other than the complainant;

(b) threats or fear of the application of force to the complainant or to a person other than the complainant;

(c) fraud; or

(d) the exercise of authority.

Once the facts in issue constituting assault have been established, the nature of the assault (sexual versus non-sexual) must be determined.

To establish that an assault is sexual in nature, certain tests must be met. The Supreme Court of Canada has addressed this question in *R v. Chase* and *R v. V.(K.B.)*.

Sexual assault is an assault, within any one of the definitions of that concept in s. 265(1), which is committed in circumstances of a sexual nature such that the sexual integrity of the victim is violated. The test to be applied in determining whether the impugned conduct has the requisite sexual nature is an objective one: whether viewed in the light of all the circumstances the sexual or carnal context of the assault is visible to a reasonable observer. The part of the body touched, the nature of the contact, the situation in which it occurred, the words and gestures accompanying the act, and all other circumstances surrounding the conduct, including threats, which may or may not be accompanied by force, will be relevant. The intent or purpose of the person committing the act, to the extent that this may appear from the evidence, may also be a factor in considering whether the conduct is sexual. If the motive of the accused is sexual gratification, to the extent that this may appear from the evidence it may be a factor in determining whether the conduct is sexual. The existence of such a motive is, however, merely one of many factors to be considered: *R v. Chase*, [1987] 2 SCR 293, 37 CCC (3d) 97, 59 CR (3d) 193 (6:0). [*Martin's Annual Criminal Code, 2012*, p. 578]

Sexual assault does not require proof of sexuality or sexual gratification, which are merely factors. The conduct of the accused in grabbing his young child's genitals as a form of 'discipline' was an aggressive act of domination which violated the sexual integrity of the child which could be found to be a sexual assault: *R v. V.(K.B.)* (1992), 71 CCC (3d) 65, 13 CR (4th) 87, 8 OR (3d) 20 (CA), aff'd. [1993] 2 SCR 857, 82 CCC (3d) 382. [*Martin's Annual Criminal Code, 2012*, p. 578]

As the Supreme Court indicated, sexual gratification is not a necessary element in a charge of sexual assault. Touching of parts of the body that is deemed to violate sexual integrity appears to be enough to pursue a charge of sexual assault, particularly in light of the court's decision in *R v. V.(K.B.)*.

When the elements of a charge of sexual assault have been established, the degree of force used will determine the section of the *Criminal Code* that has been violated.

If there has been bodily harm or if a weapon has been used, the charge may be sexual assault with a weapon or sexual assault causing bodily harm, as defined in s. 272 of the *Criminal Code*.

Sexual Assault with a Weapon, Threats to a Third Party or Causing Bodily Harm: Criminal Code, Section 272

272(1) Every person commits an offence who, in committing a sexual assault,

(a) carries, uses or threatens to use a weapon or an imitation of a weapon;

(b) threatens to cause bodily harm to a person other than the complainant;

(c) causes bodily harm to the complainant; or

(d) is a party to the offence with any other person.

Punishment

(2) Every person who commits an offence under subsection (1) is guilty of an indictable offence and liable

(a) if a restricted firearm or prohibited firearm is used in the commission of the offence or if any firearm is used in the commission of the offence and the offence is committed for the benefit of, at the direction of, or in association with, a criminal organization, to imprisonment for a term not exceeding 14 years and to a minimum punishment of imprisonment for a term of

(i) in the case of a first offence, five years, and

(ii) in the case of a second or subsequent offence, seven years;

(a.1) in any other case where a firearm is used in the commission of the offence, to imprisonment for a term not exceeding 14 years and to a minimum punishment of imprisonment for a term of four years; and

(b) in any other case, to imprisonment for a term not exceeding fourteen years.

Subsequent Offences

(3) In determining, for the purpose of paragraph (2)(a), whether a convicted person has committed a second or subsequent offence, if the person was earlier convicted of any of the following offences, that offence is to be considered as an earlier offence:

(a) an offence under this section;

(b) an offence under subsection 85(1) or (2) or section 244 or 244.2; or

(c) an offence under section 220, 236, 239 or 273, subsection 279(1) or section 279.1, 344 or 346 if a firearm was used in the commission of the offence.

However, an earlier offence shall not be taken into account if 10 years have elapsed between the day on which the person was convicted of the earlier offence and the day on which the person was convicted of the offence for which sentence is being imposed, not taking into account any time in custody.

Sequence of Convictions Only

(4) For the purposes of subsection (3), the only question to be considered is the sequence of convictions and no consideration shall be given to the sequence of commission of offences or whether any offence occurred before or after any conviction.

An abuser's threats to harm a third party, covered by s. 272(1)(b), can impede the investigation of a child sexual abuse case. The child may be intimidated by the abuser's threats of harm to a person such as the child's mother. The seriousness with which the law views such threats is apparent in the fact that the punishment for making such threats during a sexual assault is the same as the punishment for using a weapon during a sexual assault.

Aggravated Sexual Assault: Criminal Code, Section 273

273(1) Every one commits an aggravated sexual assault who, in committing a sexual assault, wounds, maims, disfigures or endangers the life of the complainant.

Aggravated Sexual Assault

(2) Every person who commits an aggravated sexual assault is guilty of an indictable offence and liable

(a) if a restricted firearm or prohibited firearm is used in the commission of the offence or if any firearm is used in the commission of the offence and the offence is committed for the benefit of, at the direction of, or in association with, a criminal organization, to imprisonment for life and to a minimum punishment of imprisonment for a term of

(i) in the case of a first offence, five years, and

(ii) in the case of a second or subsequent offence, seven years;

(a.1) in any other case where a firearm is used in the commission of the offence, to imprisonment for life and to a minimum punishment of imprisonment for a term of four years; and

(b) in any other case, to imprisonment for life.

Subsequent Offences

(3) In determining, for the purpose of paragraph (2)(a), whether a convicted person has committed a second or subsequent offence, if the person was earlier convicted of any of the following offences, that offence is to be considered as an earlier offence:

(a) an offence under this section;

(b) an offence under subsection 85(1) or (2) or section 244 or 244.2; or

(c) an offence under section 220, 236, 239 or 272, subsection 279(1) or section 279.1, 344 or 346 if a firearm was used in the commission of the offence.

However, an earlier offence shall not be taken into account if 10 years have elapsed between the day on which the person was convicted of the earlier offence and the day on which the person was convicted of the offence for which sentence is being imposed, not taking into account any time in custody.

Sequence of Convictions Only

(4) For the purposes of subsection (3), the only question to be considered is the sequence of convictions and no consideration shall be given to the sequence of commission of offences or whether any offence occurred before or after any conviction.

Contact and Non-Contact Offences

The *Criminal Code* offences that involve the sexual abuse of children may be divided into offences involving physical contact and offences where physical contact is not required:

Contact offences
- sexual interference (s. 151)
- sexual exploitation (contact) (s. 153(1)(a))
- incest (s. 155)
- sexual assault (s. 271)
- sexual assault with a weapon, threats to a third party or causing bodily harm (s. 272)
- aggravated sexual assault (s. 273)

Non-contact offences
- invitation to sexual touching (s. 152)
- sexual exploitation (invitation) (s. 153(1)(b))

All of these offences may be considered indictable for the purpose of arrest. Other criminal offences may also apply, depending on the nature of the incident.

RULING OUT CHILD ABUSE: SUDDEN INFANT DEATH SYNDROME

Every year infants die suddenly, unexpectedly, and for no apparent reason in their sleep. Yet they all have something in common: they are all victims of **sudden infant death syndrome (SIDS)**. SIDS, sometimes called "crib death," is not preventable or predictable. These infant deaths remain unexplained after all known causes have been ruled out through autopsy, death scene investigation, and medical history.

sudden infant death syndrome (SIDS)
the sudden, unexpected, and unexplained death of an infant during sleep

SIDS affects families of all races, religions, and income levels. Its victims appear to be healthy. Neither parents nor doctors can tell which infants will die. The first year of life is a time of rapid growth and development when any infant may be vulnerable to SIDS.

Of every 1,000 infants born, one will die of SIDS before the age of one year. Most SIDS deaths occur when an infant is between two and four months of age. In fact, 95 percent of all SIDS victims are under six months of age. The risk of SIDS then diminishes during the first year of life. The diagnosis of SIDS is not used when the victim is more than one year old.

What Causes SIDS?

We do not yet know exactly how or why SIDS happens, although researchers are making great progress in identifying deficits, behaviours, and other factors that may put an infant at higher risk. Scientists are exploring many areas to determine the causes of SIDS: the development and function of the nervous system, the brain, and the heart; breathing and sleep patterns; body chemical balances; autopsy findings; and environmental factors. It is likely that SIDS is caused by some subtle developmental delay, an anatomical defect, or a functional failure. SIDS, like many other medical disorders, may eventually be found to have more than one explanation and more than one means of prevention. This may explain why the characteristics of SIDS babies are so varied.

SIDS can be determined as the cause of death only after an autopsy, an examination of the death scene, and a review of the child's medical history.

Although researchers have not yet discovered the causes of SIDS, they do know that

- SIDS is not caused by vomiting and choking;
- SIDS is not contagious;
- SIDS is not child abuse;
- SIDS does not cause pain or suffering for the infant; and
- SIDS is not caused by routine immunizations.

Risk Factors

We do not know which infants will die of SIDS, but we do know that there are certain risk factors that make a SIDS death more likely:

- The mother used alcohol or drugs or smoked during pregnancy.
- The infant is exposed to cigarette smoke in the home.
- The infant sleeps on soft bedding surfaces, such as quilts, sheepskins, and pillows.
- The infant sleeps with soft pillows, a beanbag cushion, or stuffed animals.
- The infant sleeps on his or her belly.

Police Intervention

Police investigating the death of an infant should treat the scene as a sudden death of undetermined cause. The coroner must be notified as stated in s. 10(1) of the *Coroners Act*. As previously stated, only an autopsy can identify whether the cause of death was SIDS. The family will be going through an extremely emotional period and may be unable to provide information regarding the death. In substantiated SIDS cases, the family is not being uncooperative; instead, they probably do not have any information to provide.

Things can still go wrong even when parents do everything right. The fact is that many SIDS victims have no known risk factors; and most infants with one or more risk factors will not die of SIDS. Because the causes of SIDS remain unknown, police must refrain from concluding that childcare practices caused the infant's death. The investigating officers should treat the scene as they would a crime scene while trying to take into account the emotional distress of the family. The investigation is an integral part of a SIDS diagnosis: it rules out accidental, environmental, and unnatural causes of death.

But, there is always the possibility that the death was not caused by SIDS. Look for signs of suffocation or physical signs that indicate accidental, abusive, or environmental causes of death. Remember that a victim of SIDS will show no outward signs of abuse. Death occurs during sleep. There is no evidence that the victim suffers any pain or discomfort. There should not be any sign of a struggle. Only a small number of children die of SIDS. Far more die as a result of abuse, often at the hands of a parent.

SUDDEN UNEXPLAINED DEATH SYNDROME

Sudden unexplained death syndrome (SUDS) describes cases of sudden mortality for which a coroner has been unable to determine the exact cause of death. In incidents of SUDS, the coroner may find that there is a possibility that the person did not die of natural causes.

In making this diagnosis, the coroner will apply the criteria for SIDS, plus the following additional criteria:

- unexplained healed injury,
- unexplained toxicology, and
- history of abuse.

NEGLECT

The Canadian Incidence Study of Reported Child Abuse and Neglect (CIS—2008) examined 15,980 investigations of child maltreatment carried out by 112 child welfare agencies in Canada in the autumn of 2008.

The CIS tracked only reports investigated by child welfare agencies. It did not include reports that were screened out or cases that were investigated by the police only.

The study is based on assessments provided by the investigating child welfare workers. These assessments have not been independently verified. For example, the investigating child protection workers determined whether the child subject demonstrated functioning concerns such as depression or anxiety. Because these assessments were not verified by an independent source, they cannot be considered to be 100 percent accurate.

The CIS—2008 identified that of 235,842 child maltreatment investigations conducted in Canada in 2008, 74 percent of the investigations focused on abuse or neglect and 26 percent of the investigations dealt with concerns about risk of future maltreatment (Public Health Agency of Canada, 2010).

The CIS further identified that

- 36 percent of all investigations were substantiated (85,440 investigations);
- in 8 percent of investigations (17,918 investigations) there was insufficient evidence to substantiate maltreatment;
- 30 percent of investigations (71,053 investigations) were unfounded;
- In 5 percent of investigations, the worker concluded there was a risk of future maltreatment;
- in 17 percent of investigations, no risk of future maltreatment was indicated; and
- in 4 percent of investigations, workers did not know whether the child was at risk of future maltreatment.

Note: Many of these behaviours are addressed in the *Child and Family Services Act* in s. 37(2)—Child in Need of Protection. These behaviours are generally not readily identifiable by officers responding to calls for assistance. Further investigation is required to substantiate many of the following forms of neglect.

Investigation may reveal that the child may be in need of protection as defined in s. 37(2) of the CFSA although no offence has been committed.

The CIS—2008 defines neglect as follows:

The child has suffered harm or the child's safety or development has been endangered as a result of a failure to provide for or protect the child.

The following are categories of behaviours considered to be neglect by the CIS—2008:

- **Failure to supervise: physical harm:** The child suffered physical harm or is at risk of suffering physical harm because of the caregiver's failure to supervise or protect the child adequately. Failure to supervise includes situations where a child is harmed or endangered as a result of a caregiver's actions (e.g., drunk driving with a child, or engaging in dangerous criminal activities with a child).
- **Failure to supervise: sexual abuse:** The child has been or is at substantial risk of being sexually molested or sexually exploited, and the caregiver knows or should have known of the possibility of sexual molestation and failed to protect the child adequately.
- **Permitting criminal behaviour:** A child has committed a criminal offence (e.g., theft, vandalism, or assault) because of the caregiver's failure or inability to supervise the child adequately.

- **Physical neglect:** The child has suffered or is at substantial risk of suffering physical harm caused by the caregiver(s)' failure to care and provide for the child adequately. This includes inadequate nutrition/clothing, and unhygienic, dangerous living conditions. There must be evidence or suspicion that the caregiver is at least partially responsible for the situation.

- **Medical neglect (includes dental):** The child requires medical treatment to cure, prevent, or alleviate physical harm or suffering and the child's caregiver does not provide, or refuses, or is unavailable, or unable to consent to the treatment. This includes dental services when funding is available.

- **Failure to provide [psychiatric] treatment:** The child is suffering from either emotional harm demonstrated by severe anxiety, depression, withdrawal, or self-destructive or aggressive behaviour, or a mental, emotional, or developmental condition that could seriously impair the child's development. The child's caregiver does not provide, or refuses, or is unavailable, or unable to consent to treatment to remedy or alleviate the harm. This category includes failing to provide treatment for school-related problems such as learning and behaviour problems, as well as treatment for infant development problems such as non-organic failure to thrive. A parent awaiting service should not be included in this category.

- **Abandonment:** The child's parent has died or is unable to exercise custodial rights and has not made adequate provisions for care and custody, or the child is in a placement and parent refuses/is unable to take custody.

- **Educational neglect:** Caregivers knowingly permit chronic truancy (5+ days a month), or fail to enroll the child, or repeatedly keep the child at home. If the child is experiencing mental, emotional, or developmental problems associated with school, and treatment is offered but caregivers do not cooperate with treatment, classify the case under failure to provide treatment as well.

Neglect is established by a pattern of behaviour over a period of time, which can make detection difficult for police officers. Note that the definition of neglect varies from one piece of legislation to the next. A general definition of **neglect** for the purposes of this chapter is caregiver omissions in providing adequate care that result in actual or potential harm to a child. The question arises: What is "adequate care"? The term is hard to define because it is subjective. This makes establishing a standard of adequate care difficult.

neglect
for the purposes of this chapter, caregiver omissions in providing adequate care that result in actual or potential harm to a child

Neglect of a child may be devastating to his or her physical, emotional, and psychological well-being. The physical form of neglect, failing to provide the necessities of life (referred to as "necessaries of life" in the *Criminal Code*), may result in criminal prosecution. Anyone who has the responsibility to provide such necessaries and fails to do so can be charged with an offence under the *Criminal Code*. The sections of the *Criminal Code* pertaining to neglect are reproduced below.

Duty of Persons to Provide Necessaries: Criminal Code, Section 215

215(1) Every one is under a legal duty

(a) as a parent, foster parent, guardian or head of a family, to provide necessaries of life for a child under the age of sixteen years;

(b) to provide necessaries of life to their spouse or common-law partner; and

(c) to provide necessaries of life to a person under his charge if that person

(i) is unable, by reason of detention, age, illness, mental disorder or other cause, to withdraw himself from that charge, and

(ii) is unable to provide himself with necessaries of life.

Offence

(2) Every one commits an offence who, being under a legal duty within the meaning of subsection (1), fails without lawful excuse, the proof of which lies on him, to perform that duty, if

(a) with respect to a duty imposed by paragraph (1)(a) or (b),

(i) the person to whom the duty is owed is in destitute or necessitous circumstances, or

(ii) the failure to perform the duty endangers the life of the person to whom the duty is owed, or causes or is likely to cause the health of that person to be endangered permanently; or

(b) with respect to a duty imposed by paragraph (1)(c), the failure to perform the duty endangers the life of the person to whom the duty is owed or causes or is likely to cause the health of that person to be injured permanently.

Punishment

(3) Every one who commits an offence under subsection (2)

(a) is guilty of an indictable offence and is liable to imprisonment for a term not exceeding two years; or

(b) is guilty of an offence punishable on summary conviction and liable to imprisonment for a term not eceeding eighteen months.

This section places a legal obligation on parents to provide the necessaries of life until a child reaches age 16. Necessaries include food, clothing, shelter, and medical treatment.

This offence imposes liability on an objective basis. On a charge contrary to subsec. (2)(a)(ii), the Crown must prove a marked departure from the conduct of a reasonably prudent parent in circumstances where it was objectively foreseeable that the failure to provide the necessaries of life would lead to a risk of danger to the life, or a risk of permanent endangerment to the health, of the child: *R v. Naglik*, [1993] 3 SCR 122, 83 CCC (3d) 526, 23 CR (4th) 335. [*Martin's Annual Criminal Code, 2012*, p. 436]

Neglect of a child is also identified in s. 37(2) of the CFSA as one of the situations where a child may be in need of protection:

(2) A child is in need of protection where,

    (a) the child has suffered physical harm, inflicted by the person having charge of the child or caused by or resulting from that person's,

        (i) failure to adequately care for, provide for, supervise or protect the child, or

        (ii) pattern of neglect in caring for, providing for, supervising or protecting the child;

    (b) there is a risk that the child is likely to suffer physical harm inflicted by the person having charge of the child or caused by or resulting from that person's,

        (i) failure to adequately care for, provide for, supervise or protect the child, or

        (ii) pattern of neglect in caring for, providing for, supervising or protecting the child;

The need to establish a pattern of neglect probably removes the probability of police obtaining sufficient grounds to remove the child from the home. Patterns of neglect are more likely to be established through the observations and investigations of dedicated child protection workers.

Signs of Neglect

The following are some signs that may indicate neglect (Children's Aid Society of Algoma, 1998). These signs do not necessarily establish neglect and should be viewed in the context of the child's usual standard of care:

- The child is inappropriately dressed for the season.
- The child is extremely dirty.
- The child suffers from poor dental or medical care.
- The child is left with inappropriate caregivers or is left unattended for periods of time that are excessive in light of the child's age.

Section 79(3) of the CFSA identifies the age at which a child may be left unattended. The section does not define what is reasonable care or an inappropriate caregiver. Investigating officers must use their judgment to determine whether reasonable care is being provided by an appropriate caregiver.

Leaving Child Unattended: Child and Family Services Act, Section 79(3)

79(3) No person having charge of a child less than sixteen years of age shall leave the child without making provision for his or her supervision and care that is reasonable in the circumstances.

Note that this section of the Act discusses adequate supervision but does not define it. In fact, adequate supervision has not been objectively defined by legislation; instead, it is situationally established. Thus, the standard of adequate supervision will vary with the child's age, development, and behaviour. Also, the standard of adequate supervision will vary with the area in which the child lives. For example, the degree of supervision required for a child living in a rural area may differ from the degree of supervision required for a child in an urban area.

Parents must provide a basic level of care in order to meet any standard of "adequate supervision." Parents must take precautions that minimize the risk of moderate or serious harm to a child and ensure that the child's basic needs have been met: food, clothing, shelter, and medical treatment.

Reverse Onus: Child and Family Services Act, Section 79(4)

79(4) Where a person is charged with contravening subsection (3) and the child is less than ten years of age, the onus of establishing that the person made provision for the child's supervision and care that was reasonable in the circumstances rests with the person.

If the officer deems that the lack of care or the care provided is inadequate in the circumstances, the child may be considered to be a child in need of protection as defined in s. 37(2) of the CFSA.

Some signs of neglect may be more difficult for police officers to detect but come to police attention when reported by child protection workers or other concerned parties:

- The child lacks adequate shelter (including but not limited to unsafe, inadequately heated, or unsanitary living conditions).
- The child is malnourished. Signs include low body weight, an extremely low body fat to lean tissue ratio (in infants), sallow complexion, skin conditions caused by dehydration, and prolonged diarrhea.
- The child suffers from severe diaper rash or other skin disorders caused by lack of proper hygiene.

Behavioural signs of neglect include the following (Children's Aid Society of Algoma, 1998):

- Slowness in development of speech and motor skills, without any apparent physical cause.
- Lack of attachment to parents.
- Inappropriate attachment to other adults.
- Excessive demands for affection and attention.
- Poor school performance.
- Illegal activity or abuse of alcohol and drugs.

OTHER FORMS OF NEGLECT

There are other instances of neglect that require the intervention of police or child protection workers. The CIS—2008 identified the following as being the most common forms of neglect (Public Health Agency of Canada, 2010):

- failure to supervise: physical harm
- failure to supervise: sexual abuse

- permitting criminal behaviour
- physical neglect
- medical neglect (includes dental)
- failure to provide psychiatric treatment
- abandonment
- educational neglect.

Failure to Supervise: Physical Harm

When this form of neglect exists, the child is in need of protection. Police or child protection workers may intervene.

Child in Need of Protection: Child and Family Services Act, Section 37(2)(a)

37(2) A child is in need of protection where,

(a) the child has suffered physical harm, inflicted by the person having charge of the child or caused by or resulting from that person's,

(i) failure to adequately care for, provide for, supervise or protect the child, or

(ii) pattern of neglect in caring for, providing for, supervising or protecting the child.

Failure to Supervise: Sexual Abuse

In this situation, a child has been or could be sexually abused, and the parent, due to neglect or wilful blindness, did nothing to stop the abuse. Section 37(2)(c) of the CFSA allows intervention where

(c) the child has been sexually molested or sexually exploited, by the person having charge of the child or by another person where the person having charge of the child knows or should know of the possibility of sexual molestation or sexual exploitation and fails to protect the child.

> Note: On a day to be named by proclamation of the Lieutenant Governor, clause (c) is repealed by the Statutes of Ontario, 2008, chapter 21, section 2 and the following substituted:
>
> (c) the child has been sexually molested or sexually exploited, including by child pornography, by the person having charge of the child or by another person where the person having charge of the child knows or should know of the possibility of sexual molestation or sexual exploitation and fails to protect the child;

Permitting Criminal Behaviour

This type of neglect falls within the parameters of s. 37(2) of the CFSA. The child is in need of protection. Police may intervene. Under ss. 37(2)(j) and (k) of the CFSA, a child is in need of protection where

(j) the child is less than twelve years old and has killed or seriously injured another person or caused serious damage to another person's property, services or treatment are necessary to prevent a recurrence and the child's parent or the person having charge of the child does not provide, or refuses or is unavailable or unable to consent to, those services or treatment;

(k) the child is less than twelve years old and has on more than one occasion injured another person or caused loss or damage to another person's property, with the encouragement of the person having charge of the child or because of that person's failure or inability to supervise the child adequately.

Physical Neglect

Physical neglect includes not adhering to the duty to provide the necessities of life. The child is also in need of protection.

Medical Neglect

A situation of medical neglect allows police or a child protection worker to apprehend the child as a result of the parent's neglect in providing medical treatment. Section 37(2)(e) of the CFSA allows police or child protection workers to apprehend the child where

(e) the child requires medical treatment to cure, prevent or alleviate physical harm or suffering and the child's parent or the person having charge of the child does not provide, or refuses or is unavailable or unable to consent to, the treatment.

The *Criminal Code* refers to failure to provide medical treatment as a form of neglect. The *Child and Family Services Act* also refers to failure to provide medical treatment and describes it as a situation where a child could be in need of protection. The CFSA expands on the *Criminal Code* provisions by further stating that the parent must take steps to prevent physical harm or suffering.

The parent must provide adequate health care in the following respects:

- Reasonable efforts must be made to treat minor problems—for example, by cleaning a child's cut.
- Professional care must be obtained for moderate to severe problems, such as difficulty breathing.
- Preventive health care must be provided. This may be a contentious issue where the observer believes that preventive health care is necessary, but such care may not be economically feasible for the parent—for example, preventive dental care.
- The health care provided must meet accepted health-care standards.

Failure to Provide Psychiatric Treatment

In situations where the parent does not provide treatment to alleviate or prevent any emotional or psychological damage to the child, the child may be considered to be in need of protection. Under ss. 37(2)(f) to (h) of the CFSA, police and child protection workers have authority to intervene where

> (f) the child has suffered emotional harm, demonstrated by serious,
>> (i) anxiety,
>> (ii) depression,
>> (iii) withdrawal,
>> (iv) self-destructive or aggressive behaviour, or
>> (v) delayed development,
>
> and there are reasonable grounds to believe that the emotional harm suffered by the child results from the actions, failure to act or pattern of neglect on the part of the child's parent or the person having charge of the child;
>
> (f.1) the child has suffered emotional harm of the kind described in subclause (f)(i), (ii), (iii), (iv) or (v) and the child's parent or the person having charge of the child does not provide, or refuses or is unavailable or unable to consent to, services or treatment to remedy or alleviate the harm;
>
> (g) there is a risk that the child is likely to suffer emotional harm of the kind described in subclause (f)(i), (ii), (iii), (iv) or (v) resulting from the actions, failure to act or pattern of neglect on the part of the child's parent or the person having charge of the child;
>
> (g.1) there is a risk that the child is likely to suffer emotional harm of the kind described in subclause (f)(i), (ii), (iii), (iv) or (v) and that the child's parent or the person having charge of the child does not provide, or refuses or is unavailable or unable to consent to, services or treatment to prevent the harm;
>
> (h) the child suffers from a mental, emotional or developmental condition that, if not remedied, could seriously impair the child's development and the child's parent or the person having charge of the child does not provide, or refuses or is unavailable or unable to consent to, treatment to remedy or alleviate the condition.

Abandonment

A situation of abandonment could constitute neglect and is a criminal offence as defined in s. 218 of the *Criminal Code*.

Abandoning Child: Criminal Code, Section 218

> 218. Every one who unlawfully abandons or exposes a child who is under the age of ten years, so that its life is or is likely to be endangered or its health is or is likely to be permanently injured,
>
> (a) is guilty of an indictable offence and liable to imprisonment for a term not exceeding five years; or
>
> (b) is guilty of an offence punishable on summary conviction and liable to imprisonment for a term not exceeding eighteen months.

Abandonment and Endangering a Child: R v. Holzer

While the Crown, to prove this offence, must prove not only that the child was abandoned but that, *inter alia*, its life was likely to be endangered, the offence was made out where the accused abandoned her child in a motor vehicle for an indefinite period of time in an environment which posed a threat to its life due to the cold temperatures and risk of abduction. It was no excuse that the accused intended to return several hours later at a time, when according to expert evidence, the child would still be alive. It is the act of endangering that constitutes the offence: *R v. Holzer* (1988), 63 CR (3d) 301 (Alta. QB). [*Martin's Annual Criminal Code, 2012*, p. 439]

Abandonment Under the Child and Family Services Act

The CFSA also includes abandonment as one of the situations where a child is in need of protection. While the *Criminal Code* specifies a child for the purpose of abandonment as being under 10 years of age, a child within the meaning of the CFSA is a person under 16 years of age. Police or child protection workers may intervene in situations of abandonment. According to s. 37(2)(i) of the CFSA, police or child protection workers may intervene where

(i) the child has been abandoned, the child's parent has died or is unavailable to exercise his or her custodial rights over the child and has not made adequate provision for the child's care and custody, or the child is in a residential placement and the parent refuses or is unable or unwilling to resume the child's care and custody.

Protection of the Officer from Personal Liability

Neglect is often difficult for police officers to identify because of their limited interaction with the neglected child. If there is any risk of immediate danger to the child's well-being, the officer should apprehend the child and contact the appropriate child protection authorities. If the officer's actions are not malicious and are carried out in good faith, the CFSA protects the officer against any civil liability. This protection is congruent with the paramount purpose of the Act, child protection.

Protection from Personal Liability: Child and Family Services Act, Section 40(14)

40(14) No action shall be instituted against a peace officer or child protection worker for any act done in good faith in the execution or intended execution of that person's duty under this section or for an alleged neglect or default in the execution in good faith of that duty.

Learning Activity 4.2

In the following situations, determine whether "child neglect" has been established. Apply the definitions found in the *Criminal Code* and the Ontario *Child and Family Services Act*.

Scenario 1

The parents of a 16-year-old girl leave her at home while they tour Europe for four weeks. All the relatives live in different cities. She is alone in the home. Her parents left her with money for food and told her to keep the door locked when she is at home.

Scenario 2

The parents of twin 14-year-old boys work the night shift at a factory. As a result, the boys are often left alone in the family apartment from 10 p.m. to 6 a.m. The boys are told to stay inside and call their Uncle Fred if they need anything. Uncle Fred lives in the adjoining apartment. He checks on the boys each night at 10:30 p.m. and ensures that they are in bed. The parents arrive home at approximately 6:45 a.m. The usual routine is that the boys are awakened for school at 7:30 a.m. after their father makes breakfast. Their mother gets their clothes ready. The boys are then driven to school at 8:45 a.m. The parents then sleep.

Scenario 3

You are a police officer responding to a call of possible child abuse.

A teacher reports that a student in his class may be neglected. The teacher bases his opinion on the physical appearance and behaviour of the child. The child is ten years old. He is often tired and sometimes falls asleep in class. His clothes are tattered but clean. You investigate the family situation.

The child's mother is a single mother. She works two jobs, six days a week, from 9 a.m. to 5 p.m., then from 6 p.m. to 10 p.m. Both jobs pay $10.25 per hour. Her monthly pay after deductions is $2,060.

After school, the boy is supervised by his 15-year-old sister. She feeds him dinner and puts him to bed.

You speak with the boy's mother. She gives you the following information.

She tries to take care of her children the best that she can. The children have tattered clothing because she does not have money to buy new clothing. She gets their clothing at thrift stores. Her daughter does the shopping for clothes. She herself shops for groceries after work.

They moved into a two-bedroom apartment a few months ago. She thought that it was important that her son and daughter live in a safe building, close to public transit. The children have their own rooms. She sleeps on the couch in the living room. The rent for the apartment is $1,300 per month. Transit passes for her to go to work cost $121 per month, cheaper than daily transit fees because she has to travel to both jobs. The children pay transit fees daily because it is cheaper than a monthly pass since they only use public transit to go to school. The total cost of public ransit for the children is $160 per month. The remaining $479 per month is spent on food, clothing, electricity, telephone, and other necessities. She tells you that she knows that they don't often have fresh fruit or vegetables and rarely have meat or dairy products, but there just isn't enough money for everything.

She tells you that she has applied for more hours with both her employers but the only available hours are on Sunday. She would like to spend one day a week with her children but may have to take the extra hours to pay all the bills.

INVESTIGATING CHILD ABUSE

Regulation 3/99 of the Ontario *Police Services Act* requires that police services develop policies and procedures for investigating incidents of child abuse. Police officers must follow the policies of their police service. The following information is generic in content.

The role of the police in an investigation of child abuse is twofold. Police conduct the investigation to determine whether the child is in need of protection and to determine whether there are reasonable grounds to believe that a criminal offence has been committed.

The investigation involves gathering evidence in order to establish the facts, and preparing for criminal proceedings where appropriate. These activities include:

- preserving the crime scene,
- obtaining the child's account of events,
- obtaining a statement from the alleged offender,
- obtaining statements from other witnesses,
- arranging to obtain and preserve any physical evidence,
- obtaining medical and other expert opinions if needed, and
- determining the need to arrest a suspect.

Characteristics of Child Abusers

Perpetrators of child abuse frequently share many of the following character traits and past experiences:

- *They abuse others.* Investigation will likely reveal that the child abuser has also carried out abusive acts or exhibited abusive behaviours toward others.
- *They like to have power and control.* The need to control his or her immediate environment may lead the abuser to use violence or demeaning verbal abuse as a method of maintaining control of his or her surroundings.
- *They live isolated from society.* The pattern of demeaning and abusive behaviour generally does not endear the abuser to society in general.
- *They have few friends or family connections.* The egocentric nature of the abuser's personality does not lend itself well to friendship or close family ties.

- *They are part of a cycle of child abuse.* The abuser may have been abused as a child. Childhood abuse may be a contributing factor but it is not present in all child abusers.
- *They abuse alcohol/drugs.* These are contributing factors but not the sole cause of the abusive behaviour.
- *They suffer from severe postpartum depression.* This is a legally recognized mental disorder that affects a small number of women. Although it is a factor contributing to child abuse, based on the percentage of women who abuse children, it is not a very significant factor.
- *They have poor coping skills.* The abuser is often unable to effectively deal with daily stressors.
- *They have low self-esteem, likely due to an abusive childhood.* Abusive mothers tend to be battered wives.
- *They are unable to effectively communicate with the child.* The abuser may believe that the child is not listening because the child does not understand the expectations of the abuser.
- *They believe in corporal punishment for children.* Abusive parents may believe that harsh physical punishment is necessary to control the child. (See the section entitled "Punishment Versus Abuse," above.)

Although the above information may help focus an investigation, officers must continue to think laterally and not rule out possible suspects until all available evidence is obtained.

Maintaining Objectivity

Investigating child abuse can be very emotionally difficult for many police officers. Feelings of anger and disgust may emerge. But regardless of his or her emotions, the investigating officer has to be objective and gather the necessary information and evidence. Emotional reactions should not be allowed to interfere with an officer's professionalism or cause an officer to say or do anything that could harm the investigation. An officer may be outraged by what he or she learns, but must remain calm and in control. Loss of emotional control by the officer may have a negative effect on the child. The child has probably seen a substantial amount of anger and inappropriate behaviour in his or her life, and a display of police exasperation or anger may lead the child to believe that he or she is the cause.

Accessing the Child Victim

One of the most valuable sources of evidence in an investigation is the victim. Unfortunately, it may be difficult to gain access to a child who is being abused. In many instances an immediate family member is the abuser and will deny the authorities access to protect himself or herself. If access is denied, an officer must use other means to establish contact with the child. The reporting requirements of the CFSA can be a starting point. If the suspected abuse has been reported by a person designated in s. 72 of the Act, that person may be able to provide evidence of abuse, allowing the officer to establish that the child is in need of protection as defined in s. 37(2) of the Act. If there is reason to believe that the child is in need of protection, a Children's Aid Society must be contacted.

The CFSA authorizes three methods of bringing a child before the court to determine whether the child is in need of protection. The following sections will address these methods sequentially from least to most invasive.

Section 40(4) of the CFSA, below, allows child protection workers, which include police officers, as defined in s. 40(13), to apply to the court to have the person in charge of the child bring the child before the court. The court will determine whether the child is in need of protection.

This section may be used when the danger to the child is not immediate, but there is cause to believe that the child may be in need of protection. Note that in the CFSA, the word "society" means a Children's Aid Society.

Order to Produce or Apprehend Child: Child and Family Services Act, Section 40(4)

40(4) Where the court is satisfied, on a person's application upon notice to a society, that there are reasonable and probable grounds to believe that

(a) a child is in need of protection, the matter has been reported to the society, the society has not made an application under subsection (1), and no child protection worker has sought a warrant under subsection (2) or apprehended the child under subsection (7); and

(b) the child cannot be protected adequately otherwise than by being brought before the court, the court may order

(c) that the person having charge of the child produce him or her before the court at the time and place named in the order for a hearing under subsection 47(1) to determine whether he or she is in need of protection; or

(d) where the court is satisfied that an order under clause (c) would not protect the child adequately, that a child protection worker employed by the society bring the child to a place of safety.

If a child protection worker has reasonable grounds to believe that the danger to the child is not immediate but likely imminent, an application may be made to the court to have a warrant issued allowing the immediate apprehension of the child and delivery to a place of safety. The child will be brought before the court to determine whether the child is in need of protection, and to determine the appropriate method of child protection.

Warrant to Apprehend Child: Child and Family Services Act, Section 40(2)

40(2) A justice of the peace may issue a warrant authorizing a child protection worker to bring a child to a place of safety if the justice of the peace is satisfied on the basis of a child protection worker's sworn information that there are reasonable and probable grounds that

(a) the child is in need of protection; and

(b) a less restrictive course of action is not available or will not protect the child adequately.

The most invasive apprehension authority contained within the CFSA is the authorization of immediate, warrantless apprehension of a child in need of protection. Apprehension without a warrant is generally carried out by police officers in situations where the danger to the child is immediate. Because of the immediacy of circumstances, it would not be expeditious for the officer to apply for pre-authorization in the form of a warrant or court order.

Apprehension Without Warrant: Child and Family Services Act, Section 40(7)

40(7) A child protection worker who believes on reasonable and probable grounds that

(a) a child is in need of protection; and

(b) there would be a substantial risk to the child's health or safety during the time necessary to bring the matter on for a hearing under subsection 47(1) or obtain a warrant under subsection (2),

may without a warrant bring the child to a place of safety.

Legislators have recognized that the immediate apprehension of a child without a warrant may be a situation in which the person in charge of the child may not be cooperative. Because the safety of the child is paramount, the legislation authorizes child protection workers to use force to enter and search for a child in need of protection.

Right of Entry, etc.: Child and Family Services Act, Section 40(11)

40(11) A child protection worker who believes on reasonable and probable grounds that a child referred to in subsection (7) is on any premises may without a warrant enter the premises, by force, if necessary, and search for and remove the child.

The CFSA offers a degree of legal protection for persons carrying out their duty to protect children. If the child protection worker was acting in good faith, and without malicious intent, no legal action will be taken against the worker, even if the court finds that he or she lacked reasonable grounds to apprehend the child.

If, after investigation or apprehension, the child protection worker determines that the child is or may be in need of protection, the child must be brought before the court to determine how to best protect the child. "Court," for the purpose of the CFSA, means the Ontario Court of Justice or the Family Court of the Superior Court of Justice.

Application: Child and Family Services Act, Section 40(1)

40(1) A society may apply to the court to determine whether a child is in need of protection.

Child Protection Hearing: Child and Family Services Act, Section 47(1)

47(1) Where an application is made under subsection 40(1) or a matter is brought before the court to determine whether the child is in need of protection, the court shall hold a hearing to determine the issue and make an order under section 57.

Where the court determines that the child is in need of protection, s. 57 of the CFSA, below, sets out the options available to the court. The court will select the option that will best protect the child in the circumstances.

Order Where Child in Need of Protection: Child and Family Services Act, Section 57(1)

57(1) Where the court finds that a child is in need of protection and is satisfied that intervention through a court order is necessary to protect the child in the future, the court shall make one of the following orders or an order under s. 57.1, in the child's best interests:

Supervision order
1. That the child be placed in the care and custody of a parent or another person, subject to the supervision of the society, for a specified period of at least three months and not more than 12 months.

Society wardship
2. That the child be made a ward of the society and be placed in its care and custody for a specified period not exceeding twelve months.

Crown wardship
3. That the child be made a ward of the Crown, until the wardship is terminated under section 65.2 or expires under subsection 71(1), and be placed in the care of the society.

Consecutive orders of society wardship and supervision
4. That the child be made a ward of the society under paragraph 2 for a specified period and then be returned to a parent or another person under paragraph 1, for a period or periods not exceeding an aggregate of twelve months.

In addition to the previous options, the court may also prohibit access to the child. These orders may prohibit access absolutely or may allow supervised access.

Restraining Order: Child and Family Services Act, Section 80(1)

80(1) Instead of making an order under subsection 57(1) or section 65.2 or in addition to making a temporary order under subsection 51(2) or an order under subsection 57(1) or section 65.2, the court may make one or more of the following orders in the child's best interests:

1. An order restraining or prohibiting a person's access to or contact with the child, and may include in the order such directions as the court considers appropriate for implementing the order and protecting the child.

2. An order restraining or prohibiting a person's contact with the person who has lawful custody of the child following a temporary order under subsection 51(2) or an order under subsection 57(1) or clause 65.2(1)(a) or (b).

Interviewing the Victim

The nature of child abuse and the likelihood that the abuse took place in the family home make investigation very difficult. There may be little physical evidence available. The child may not exhibit any visible sign of injury at the time of the interview. The abuser, being in complete control of the child, will generally ensure that the child's injuries are healed to the point of not being visible before the child is allowed to appear in public.

The lack of prominent physical evidence means that the police have only the interview with the child to try to determine whether abuse took place.

But the victim's young age and immaturity may hinder the police in obtaining information through an interview and may present the following problems:

- The concept of abuse may not be understood by the victim because of his or her trust in and dependence on the abuser, which may lead him or her to believe that the abuser did not do anything wrong.
- The victim may believe that he or she caused the abuse, or that no one will believe his or her story.
- The victim may not want to talk about the abuse. He or she may fear the abuser or be embarrassed to reveal the details to strangers.
- The victim may not be able to express himself or herself well and may be embarrassed about using slang or "bad" words.
- The victim may believe that everyone will be angry with him or her for revealing the abuse or, if the abuser is a family member, that the family will break up.
- The victim may feel worthless because of the abuse, and may believe that what happens to him or her does not matter.

Police services are required to have officers trained in child abuse response. If possible, an officer with this special training should conduct the interview. The interview may be carried out jointly by the officer and a child protection worker. Each may prompt the other in an unobtrusive manner to solicit pertinent information from the victim.

The same officer and child protection worker should conduct all the interviews. This allows the child to become acquainted with the interviewers. It also helps the police to piece together the fragments of information that may emerge over many sessions.

The interviewers must use language that is appropriate to the child's age and stage of development. The child's understanding of sexual touches or disciplinary spankings may be limited, and he or she may have no concept of right and wrong.

For younger children, notions such as "good touches" and "bad touches" may be more suitable for interview use than advanced concepts such as right and wrong.

Treating the child sensitively is a priority. The interview should take place as soon as possible following the disclosure or report of abuse. Several brief interviews may be necessary to allow the child to overcome his or her fear and reluctance. Brief sessions also accommodate children's short attention spans. The number and duration of interviews should be confined to the minimum necessary. Where the child has difficulty communicating, the interviewers should make arrangements to have a competent and unbiased interpreter or communication specialist, or a person skilled in communicating with the particular child, present for the interview. The questions posed to the child should be simple enough for him or her to understand and respond to.

When interviewing witnesses or victims, interviewers should use open-ended questions. Open-ended questions are those that do not have simple "yes" or "no" answers. These questions are helpful in that they

- do not suggest an idea or answer to the witness or victim;
- invite witnesses or victims to talk in their own words;
- act as memory prompts;
- get people talking;
- encourage full answers;
- help to get accurate information; and
- let the witness or victim talk 80 percent of the time.

The interviewers should also paraphrase the victims' or witnesses' words when they ask subsequent questions. Also, when a conversation goes off topic, the interviewers should

- wait for a break;
- bring the conversation back to the topic;
- use another open-ended question;
- not interrupt a statement;
- ask questions to confirm points later; and
- if possible, ask the witnesses or victims to write their own statements.

Interviewers should avoid closed-ended questions when interviewing witnesses or victims. Close-ended questions are those that often require only a "yes" or "no" answer. Courts may consider them as leading questions. The interviewers must be careful not to use leading questions or a repetitive, badgering style of questioning when speaking with the child. The need to please may prompt the child to say what he or she thinks the interviewers want to hear. Closed-ended questions are often unproductive because they

- suggest an idea to the witness or victim;
- may lead the witness or victim to repeat what the interviewers said; and
- elicit little information because they often take only one word to answer.

The officer should make a verbatim record of the interview using videotape or audiotape.

The interview should take place in an area where the child feels safe and not intimidated, such as an interview room filled with toys or a similar neutral environment. The child's home is not the best interview environment, especially if it is suspected that the abuse occurred there.

Careful observation of the child's non-verbal reaction may alert the interviewers to potential areas of conflict or avenues of investigation. If, for example, mention of a specific place or person causes a negative non-verbal reaction from the child, further investigation may be indicated.

These interviews, due to the age of the victim and his or her lack of sophistication, require that the interviewing officers have an understanding of the thought and communication processes of children.

Interviewing the Victim of a Pedophile

The interview should be carried out in the same manner as any other investigation of child sexual abuse. There may be more hesitation on the part of the child if there has been an ongoing relationship with the offender. The offender is probably a person whom the child has seen regularly and with whom the child has developed a trust relationship. This relationship will have been fostered by the offender's constant reminders of the supposed need for secrecy. The child will naturally be hesitant about disclosing the private details of this relationship.

This hesitancy may be overcome through patient interviewing of the child. As in other child sexual abuse cases, several brief interviews may be necessary to obtain all the details. The child may be worrying about the safety of his or her family. Reassuring the child that the offender will not be allowed to harm him or her and the family may help alleviate the child's fear of reprisals.

There are some techniques and considerations used by trained child abuse investigators that may assist with overcoming the child's hesitancy to provide information. These techniques and considerations are age related and may not be effective with older children.

Some of these considerations include:

- Who should conduct the interview? A uniformed officer? A plainclothes officer? A child protection worker?
- How many people should be present?
- Where should the interview be conducted? A neutral area, away from the abusive environment, is preferable.

Some of the techniques used include:

- Using short interviews to accommodate for the short attention spans of younger children.
- Taking the time to get acquainted. This would include telling the child your first name.
- Talking about other subjects and engaging in small talk to put the child at ease.

- After becoming acquainted, explaining to the child that he or she is not "in trouble" and that you are there to talk about what happened.
- Keeping it simple to avoid overwhelming or confusing the child.
- Using the terms "good feelings" and "bad feelings" and "good touches" and "bad touches" to identify abuse.
- Using words and questions appropriate to the child'a age and understanding.
- Avoiding leading questions.
- Videotaping and/or audiotaping the interview.

There may be some tools that could assist with the investigation. These "tools" are best used by properly trained personnel who have the requisite knowledge to be able to interpret the child's behaviour. Children could be given:

- a plastic telephone to anonymously call someone and tell their story;
- pencils, crayons, and paper to draw and colour their family and house;
- puppets to act out their story;
- doll houses to show good and bad rooms;
- comics describing good and bad touches and feelings; and
- anatomical drawings and/or dolls to allow the child to show good and bad touches.

Family support of the child is crucial to healing. If the family blames the child for the attention that his or her plight has attracted, the child may decide that silence is the best option and blame himself or herself for the family's troubles. When speaking with the child, the interviewing officer must clearly communicate the message that the abuser, not the child, was in the wrong, and that the child is in no way responsible for what has happened to the abuser or to the family. Others who seek to help the child must reinforce the same message.

STAGES OF CHILD DEVELOPMENT AND THEIR IMPLICATIONS FOR POLICING

How Children Learn

School curriculums have been based on an understanding of how children learn. Learning and understanding are a developmental process in human beings. Children learn at different rates, and often in different ways during their development. Experts in the field of education, however, have determined that certain characteristics in learning patterns can be generally related to the student's age and grade.

Teachers use different techniques and methodologies to instruct children at different ages. Children respond and learn better when the means of communicating is appropriate to their level of understanding. Thus, the language that teachers use must reflect what the child is capable of understanding.

These factors are important for police officers. Police must be aware that children not only express themselves differently from adults, but are incapable of grasping certain information and concepts at certain ages as well.

Interviewing children then, should be guided by this knowledge. In law, too, this factor has been recognized. Legal professionals stress the importance of explaining, in appropriate language, legal rights to young people suspected of crimes. Children cannot be held legally accountable for their actions until the age of 12, a further recognition that a child's sense of personal responsibility for his or her actions develops slowly. The testimony of a child under the age of 14 is weighed in terms of whether the child understands his or her requirement to tell the truth.

Interviewing child victims, witnesses, and suspects, then, should be conducted using this understanding of how children learn, and where appropriate, using the techniques and methodologies that have proven effective in the classroom.

The following sections address the ability of specific age groups to understand situations and to convey their understanding. Knowledge of the child's abilities and age-related perspectives may help the officer formulate appropriate questions that will allow the child to relate his or her experiences clearly.

Age 2 to 5: Preschool-Aged Children

Children in this age group are highly dependent on their parents or guardians. They understand their parents and other adults much better than their peer group. They understand simple instructions, and tend to pick up general instructions more than specific details. Children this age are egocentric and unaware of the perspectives of others. Language is highly adaptive, sometimes only understood by the children themselves. Children learn at this stage by trial and error, and memory only gradually develops. They judge things on the basis of appearance. They do not have any true understanding of time. Time is understood as "now." Past, present, and future are not understood.

Age 5 to 7: Kindergarten, Grade 1

Children in this age group often have a well-developed vocabulary (20,000 words), although some "baby words" may linger in speech. Children this age are often highly imaginative, and enjoy telling stories. They will express ideas in loosely connected sentences and will have trouble with abstract terms such as ask/tell, more/less, and older/younger. These children like to imitate adults, and need praise, warmth, patience, and success. They also need supervision and guidance. Friendship with peers is important, but the source of authority comes from parents and other adults. Children this age idolize their favourite people.

Age 7 to 9: Grades 2, 3, 4

Children in this age group are more self-assured and outgoing. They communicate well with peers and adults, and are able to carry on organized conversations with both. They can assume responsibility for simple tasks. Although same-sex friendships flourish at this age, parents and parental approval are still very important. Concepts of time, distance, speed, size, shape, and quantity have meaning. These children have a developed ability to express themselves through pictures, words, and numbers.

Age 9 to 10: Grade 5

Children in this age group are able to use past experiences when considering their actions. Generally, however, they can handle only concrete concepts and their ability to perceive abstract ideas is limited. Their primary influence remains with their families. Children in this age group seek adults other than parents with whom to identify. They have a basic sense of right and wrong.

Age 10 to 11: Grade 6

Children at this age can understand some problem solving and decision making but generally only in concrete terms. They are developing a strong sense of loyalty and peer identity. They are beginning to show interest in their future options. Children at this stage are beginning to apply logical thinking.

Age 11 to 12: Grade 7

Children in this age group are now able to generalize about cause and effect, and can assume some responsibility for their actions. Twelve-year-old children are legally culpable for their actions according to law. They are intensely interested in themselves and in moral or value decisions. They are deeply concerned about fairness, and peer influence is becoming a powerful influence in their lives.

Age 12 to 13: Grade 8

Children in this age group experiment with ideas, fashions, etc. They usually work well within groups, teams, and clubs, and often look to their peers more than their families to provide support. They are at an age when they are vulnerable to role models, good and bad.

Age 13 to 14: Grade 9

Children at this age are able to absorb a wealth of information and are able to think in abstract terms. They tend to be argumentative with their families, their friends, and even with themselves. They are interested in personal relationships as well as peer groups. They are attempting to understand their place in the world, and have a deep-rooted desire for individual recognition.

Age 15 to 16: Grade 10

Generally, at this age, the young person has a good understanding of right and wrong and is able to express himself or herself in clearly understood language. These young people may be experimenting sexually and may be subject to peer pressure. They may be rebellious within the family group and may push their societal limits.

Clearly, very young children (under the age of seven) are difficult interview subjects, and often are ideal victims of such crimes as sexual abuse. The child's inability to determine time and space, or to describe incidents in detail make interviews difficult. Also, young children's state of dependency and trust in adults poses many problems.

Older children also have limitations—factors that the interviewers must be aware of if they are to be successful. Appropriate language, questioning techniques, props, guides, and anatomically correct dolls are useful aids when applied to the correct age groupings.

TESTIFYING

If an investigation reveals that a child has been abused and that criminal charges are warranted, the next issue is the presentation of the child's evidence in court.

If the child is mature enough to understand that part of the process will involve testifying in court, the interviewers may explain, in appropriate language, the provisions of the *Criminal Code* that allow testimony to be given from a private location. This may assist in alleviating some of the child's fears of facing his or her abuser.

Evidence of Victim or Witness Under 18: Criminal Code, Section 715.1

715.1(1) In any proceeding against an accused in which a victim or other witness was under the age of eighteen years at the time the offence is alleged to have been committed, a video recording made within a reasonable time after the alleged offence, in which the victim or witness describes the acts complained of, is admissible in evidence if the victim or witness, while testifying, adopts the contents of the video recording, unless the presiding judge or justice is of the opinion that admission of the video recording in evidence would interfere with the proper administration of justice.

Order Prohibiting Use

(2) The presiding judge or justice may prohibit any other use of a video recording referred to in subsection (1).

A question arises regarding the admissibility of a video recording: What is "within a reasonable time"? The Supreme Court of Canada addressed this question in *R v. L.(D.O.)*, [1993] 4 SCR 419, 85 CCC (3d) 289, 25 CR (4th) 285.

The court held that the trial judge did not err in admitting a videotaped interview under this section, notwithstanding the delay of five months from the time disclosure was first made by the nine-year-old complainant. In her concurring opinion, L'Heureux-Dubé held that what is a reasonable time depends entirely on the circumstances of the case and that in making the determination the judge may take into consideration the fact that children often delay disclosure. As well, it may be necessary to conduct a prior investigation to ensure the seriousness of the allegations. On the other hand, such determination must also take into account empirical data which makes clear that recollection decreases in accuracy with time and that children's memories fade faster than those of adults. There is thus a clear advantage to gathering evidence from a child as early as possible. [*Martin's Annual Criminal Code, 2012*, pp. 1416-1417]

Reasonable time therefore is dependent upon the situation and when the child disclosed the abuse. It may not be reasonable for police to wait for a period of time after the disclosure of abuse before recording a statement. Such a delay could raise the possibility of "coaching" the child before the statement was recorded. The statement should be recorded as soon as possible in the investigation.

Videotaped Statements: R v. F.(C.C.)

A statement is "adopted" within the meaning of this section where the witness recalls giving the statement and testifies that they were attempting to be honest and truthful when they gave the statement. A videotaped statement is admissible even if a witness has an independent present memory of the events or if the witness cannot remember the events discussed in the videotape. In the latter case, there are several factors in this provision which guarantee the reliability of the videotaped statement including the requirement that the statement be made within a reasonable time, that the trier of fact will have an opportunity to observe the demeanour and assess the personality and intelligence of the child in the videotape, and that the child attest that she was attempting to be truthful at the time that the statement was made. The test for adoption is not a final determination of reliability, but rather a test for determining the threshold degree of reliability required for the admission of the video. Once a trial judge rules that the statement has been adopted, the videotaped statement together with the *viva voce* evidence given at trial comprises the whole of the evidence-in-chief. Even if evidence which contradicts the videotaped statement is elicited in cross-examination, this does not render those parts of the videotape inadmissible. The circumstances in which the video was made, the veracity of the witness's statements and the overall reliability of the evidence are factors which are relevant to weight rather than the admissibility of the statement: *R v. F.(C.C.)* [[1997] 3 SCR 1183, 120 CCC (3d) 225, 11 CR (5th) 209]. [*Martin's Annual Criminal Code, 2012*, p. 1416]

Exclusion of Public in Certain Cases: Criminal Code, Section 486(1)

486(1) Any proceedings against an accused shall be held in open court, but the presiding judge or justice may order the exclusion of all or any members of the public from the court room for all or part of the proceedings if the judge or justice is of the opinion that such an order is in the interest of public morals, the maintenance of order or the proper administration of justice or is necessary to prevent injury to international relations or national defence or national security.

Protection of Witnesses Under 18 and Justice System Participants

(2) For the purposes of subsection (1), the "proper administration of justice" includes ensuring that

(a) the interests of witnesses under the age of eighteen years are safeguarded in all proceedings; and

(b) justice system participants who are involved in the proceedings are protected.

Reasons to Be Stated

(3) If an accused is charged with an offence under section 151, 152, 153, 153.1, 155 or 159, subsection 160(2) or (3) or section 163.1, 171, 172, 172.1, 173, 212, 271, 272, 273, 279.01, 279.011, 279.02 or 279.03 and the prosecutor or the accused applies for an order under subsection (1), the judge or justice shall, if no such order is made, state, by reference to the circumstances of the case, the reason for not making an order.

The child victim can also provide testimony outside of the courtroom away from public view.

Testimony Outside Court Room—Witnesses Under 18 or Who Have a Disability: Criminal Code, Section 486.2

486.2(1) Despite section 650, in any proceedings against an accused, the judge or justice shall, on application of the prosecutor, of a witness who is under the age of eighteen years or of a witness who is able to communicate evidence but may have difficulty doing so by reason of a mental or physical disability, order that the witness testify outside the court room or behind a screen or other device that would allow the witness not to see the accused, unless the judge or justice is of the opinion that the order would interfere with the proper administration of justice.

Other Witnesses

(2) Despite section 650, in any proceedings against an accused, the judge or justice may, on application of the prosecutor or a witness, order that the witness testify outside the court room or behind a screen or other device that would allow the witness not to see the accused if the judge or justice is of the opinion that the order is necessary to obtain a full and candid account from the witness of the acts complained of.

Application

(2.1) An application referred to in subsection (1) or (2) may be made, during the proceedings, to the presiding judge or justice or, before the proceedings begin, to the judge or justice who will preside at the proceedings.

Factors to Be Considered

(3) In making a determination under subsection (2), the judge or justice shall take into account the factors referred to in subsection 486.1(3).

Specific Offences

(4) Despite section 650, if an accused is charged with an offence referred to in subsection (5), the presiding judge or justice may order that any witness testify

    (a) outside the court room if the judge or justice is of the opinion that the order is necessary to protect the safety of the witness; and

    (b) outside the court room or behind a screen or other device that would allow the witness not to see the accused if the judge or justice is of the opinion that the order is necessary to obtain a full and candid account from the witness of the acts complained of.

Offences

(5) The offences for the purposes of subsection (4) are

(a) an offence under section 423.1, 467.11, 467.12 or 467.13, or a serious offence committed for the benefit of, at the direction of, or in association with, a criminal organization;

(b) a terrorism offence;

(c) an offence under subsection 16(1) or (2), 17(1), 19(1), 20(1) or 22(1) of the *Security of Information Act*; or

(d) an offence under subsection 21(1) or section 23 of the *Security of Information Act* that is committed in relation to an offence referred to in paragraph (c).

Same Procedure for Determination

(6) If the judge or justice is of the opinion that it is necessary for a witness to testify in order to determine whether an order under subsection (2) or (4) should be made in respect of that witness, the judge or justice shall order that the witness testify in accordance with that subsection.

Conditions of Exclusion

(7) A witness shall not testify outside the court room under subsection (1), (2), (4) or (6) unless arrangements are made for the accused, the judge or justice and the jury to watch the testimony of the witness by means of closed-circuit television or otherwise and the accused is permitted to communicate with counsel while watching the testimony.

No Adverse Inference

(8) No adverse inference may be drawn from the fact that an order is, or is not, made under this section.

Use of a Screen in Testifying: R v. Levogiannis

[T]he circumstances under which a judge may make an order under the predecessor to this subsection did not require that exceptional and inordinate stress be caused to the child. The trial judge has substantial latitude in deciding whether the use of the screen should be permitted and the evidence in support of the application need not take any particular form. In exercising the discretion under the section, the trial judge may consider evidence of the capabilities and demeanour of the child, the nature of the allegations and the circumstances of the case. It may well be that the trial judge may also consider the fact that the accused is unrepresented in determining whether or not to permit the use of the screen: *R v. Levogiannis*, [1993] 4 SCR 475, 85 CCC (3d) 327, 25 CR (4th) 325 (9:0). [*Martin's Annual Criminal Code, 2012*, pp. 877-878]

MISSING CHILDREN

Police services, as required by regulation 3/99 of the *Police Services Act*, will have specific policies and procedures that deal with missing children. Officers are required to follow the procedures of their respective police service.

Statistics compiled by the RCMP Missing Children's Registry indicate that, in 2009, there were 50,492 reported cases of missing children under the age of 18 in Canada (National Missing Children Services, 2010). By far, the most common type of missing child reported is in the "runaway" category. For whatever reason, the child has chosen to leave the family home. The second most common type of missing child is in the "unknown" category. This label is applied to missing children when there was no previous indication that the child would leave the home. "Unknown" does not necessarily indicate foul play, but only that police have not definitively categorized the missing child as a runaway or voluntarily missing.

The different categories of missing children are described below.

- *Runaway.* Includes children under 18 years of age who have run away from home or substitute home care (foster home, group home, or Children's Aid Society home or shelter). The causes may include a previous history of running away or a particular circumstance that leads to the subject's disappearance (for example, a family fight, or breakup with a boyfriend or girlfriend).

- *Unknown.* This category is used when the police agency has no previous record on the missing child. The child has never run away, walked out, or wandered off before the incident was reported to police. The child has "no previous history."

- *Other.* This category is used when the child or youth has not returned to a detention home or institution housing young offenders.

- *Wandered off.* This category is used in the following cases: where the child is presumed to have wandered away in a confused state from a hospital, mental institution, or chronic care facility; where a child has become lost in the woods or has not returned when expected from hiking, camping, or hunting; where the child has wandered away or is lost from the family location; or where the child has not returned when expected from school, a friend's house, a meeting, etc.

- *Abduction by parent.* Defined as when the subject is a child and he or she has been abducted by a parent. This category is divided into cases where a custody order has been granted, and cases where a custody order has not been granted.

- *Abduction by stranger.* Defined as an abduction by individuals other than the subject's parents or guardian. The abductor may be an uncle, sister, cousin, grandfather, neighbour, or close family friend. This definition also includes a child who has been briefly restrained from his or her intended destination. An example is a child who has been sexually assaulted and then released.

- *Accident.* This category is chosen when the probable cause for the child's disappearance is an accident of some kind and the body has not been recovered. This includes accidental drowning, fire/avalanche/hiking disappearance, and other types of accidents.

The number of reported missing children in Canada in 2009 in each category is shown in Figure 4.4.

Figure 4.4   Reported Missing Children in Canada, 2009

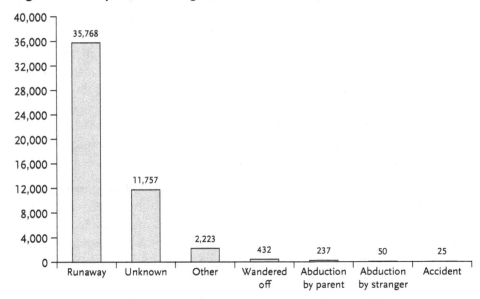

Note: The total number of reported missing children in Canada in 2009 was 50,492.

Source: Based on data from National Missing Children Services, *2009 missing children reference report: National Missing Children Services*, 2010. Ottawa: Minister of Public Works and Government Services.

Voluntarily Missing Children

In abusive situations there are instances where the child feels he or she has no choice but to leave the abusive home. This does not mean that all runaways are products of an abusive environment. The majority of runaways leave home for other reasons. Boredom may entice the child to seek excitement elsewhere or on the street. Refusal to abide by house rules is an often encountered reason for leaving. Users of illicit drugs may leave home to seek out areas where drugs are readily available.

There are legislative avenues available to assist in the apprehension and returning of runaways. The CFSA contains provisions that allow the apprehension of runaway children. A child within the meaning of this legislative authority is a person under the age of 16.

Although the child may be voluntarily missing, the parent, as defined in s. 43(1) of the CFSA, has the option of appearing before a justice of the peace to obtain a warrant authorizing police to apprehend the missing child and return him or her to the parent. The parent must appear before a justice. Police cannot appear on behalf of the parent.

The conditions for obtaining the warrant are specific:

- the parent must swear an information before a justice using the following form: Information in Support of a Warrant to Apprehend and Return a Child Who Has Withdrawn from a Parent's Control (see Appendix 4A at the end of this chapter);
- the child must be under the age of 16;
- the child must have left the custody of the parent without parental consent; and
- the parent must believe that the child's health and safety may be at risk.

If the justice accepts the information of the parent, a Warrant to Apprehend and Return a Child Who Has Withdrawn from a Parent's Control will be issued (see Appendix 4B at the end of this chapter). The warrant authorizes all police in the province of Ontario to apprehend the named child and return the child to the custody of the parent, or if not possible or immediately impractical, to a place of safety as defined in s. 37(1) of the CFSA. Section 43 of the Act is reproduced below.

Runaways: *Child and Family Services Act, Section 43*

43(1) In this section,

"parent" includes,

      (a) an approved agency that has custody of the child,

      (b) a person who has care and control of the child.

Warrant to Apprehend Runaway Child

(2) A justice of the peace may issue a warrant authorizing a peace officer or child protection worker to apprehend a child if the justice of the peace is satisfied on the basis of the sworn information of a parent of the child that,

      (a) the child is under the age of sixteen years;

      (b) the child has withdrawn from the parent's care and control without the parent's consent; and

      (c) the parent believes on reasonable and probable grounds that the child's health or safety may be at risk if the child is not apprehended.

Idem

(3) A person who apprehends a child under subsection (2) shall return the child to the child's parent as soon as practicable and where it is not possible to return the child to the parent within a reasonable time, take the child to a place of safety.

Notice to Parent, etc.

(4) The person in charge of a place of safety to which a child is taken under subsection (3) shall make reasonable efforts to notify the child's parent that the child is in the place of safety so that the child may be returned to the parent.

Where Child Not Returned to Parent Within Twelve Hours

(5) Where a child taken to a place of safety under subsection (3) cannot be returned to the child's parent within twelve hours of being taken to the place of safety, the child shall be dealt with as if the child had been taken to a place of safety under subsection 40(2) and not apprehended under subsection (2).

Where Custody Enforcement Proceedings More Appropriate

(6) A justice of the peace shall not issue a warrant under subsection (2) where a child has withdrawn from the care and control of one parent with the consent of another parent under circumstances where a proceeding under section 36 of the *Children's Law Reform Act* would be more appropriate.

No Need to Specify Premises

(7) It is not necessary in a warrant under subsection (2) to specify the premises where the child is located.

The legislation recognizes that the safety of the runaway child is at risk. The Warrant to Apprehend and Return a Child Who Has Withdrawn from a Parent's Control allows police to enter any premises at any time, by force if necessary, to search for and remove the child.

Authority to Enter, etc.: Child and Family Services Act, Section 44(1)

44(1) A person authorized to bring a child to a place of safety by a warrant issued under subsection 41(1) or 43(2) may at any time enter any premises specified in the warrant, by force, if necessary, and may search for and remove the child.

Protection from Personal Liability: Child and Family Services Act, Section 44(7)

44(7) No action shall be instituted against a peace officer or child protection worker for any act done in good faith in the execution or intended execution of that person's duty under this section or section 41, 42 or 43 or for an alleged neglect or default in the execution in good faith of that duty.

If, upon apprehension, police believe that the child may be in need of protection as defined in s. 37(2) of the CFSA, and the person presenting the possible danger is the parent, the child may be taken to a place of safety. In situations where the child is brought to a place of safety, s. 72 requires that police report their suspicion that the child may be in need of protection to a Children's Aid Society. Child protection workers will carry out an investigation, along with police if appropriate, to determine whether the child may be in need of protection. If the investigation determines that the child may be in need of protection, court proceedings may be initiated to determine how to best protect the child. Police may conduct a parallel or subsequent investigation to determine possible offences.

Child Protection Proceedings: Child and Family Services Act, Section 43(8)

43(8) Where a peace officer or child protection worker believes on reasonable and probable grounds that a child apprehended under this section is in need of protection and there may be a substantial risk to the health or safety of the child if the child were returned to the parent,

(a) the peace officer or child protection worker may take the child to a place of safety under subsection 40(7); or

(b) where the child has been taken to a place of safety under subsection (5), the child shall be dealt with as if the child had been taken there under subsection 40(7).

In situations where the child has left parental custody voluntarily and there is no reason to believe that the child is in need of protection, the child will be returned to the parent.

Involuntarily Missing

In situations of identified child abduction, an AMBER alert may be issued. The Ontario AMBER Alert Program is a voluntary cooperative plan between the Ontario Association of Broadcasters, law enforcement agencies, and the Ontario Ministry of Transportation. The program is used to alert the public in child abduction cases where police believe the child is in danger of bodily harm or death.

The Ontario Provincial Police facilitate the program. The OPP provide media outlets with critical information concerning confirmed child abductions. The program is available to all police agencies in Ontario.

The AMBER Alert Program uses highway message signs, radio, and television to immediately broadcast descriptions of kidnap victims, their abductors, and suspect vehicles (Ontario Provincial Police, 2009). Radio and television stations immediately interrupt their programming to provide information about the AMBER Alert. This is done as a public service without commercial endorsement. The AMBER Alert allows police to quickly notify the public of the details of the abduction during the early stages of the investigation. Members of the public who have information about the case are encouraged to contact police.

Before an AMBER Alert is activated, the following criteria must be met:

1. a law enforcement agency must believe that a child under the age of 18 has been abducted;

2. the law enforcement agency must believe that the child is in danger; and

3. enough descriptive information must be available about the child, abductor, and/or vehicle for the law enforcement agency to believe that an immediate broadcast alert will help in locating the child.

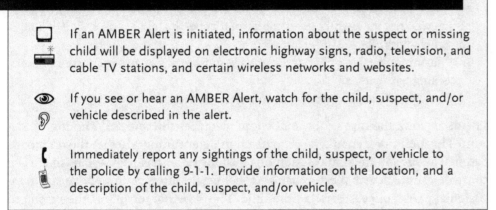

What to Do if You See or Hear an AMBER Alert

If an AMBER Alert is initiated, information about the suspect or missing child will be displayed on electronic highway signs, radio, television, and cable TV stations, and certain wireless networks and websites.

If you see or hear an AMBER Alert, watch for the child, suspect, and/or vehicle described in the alert.

Immediately report any sightings of the child, suspect, or vehicle to the police by calling 9-1-1. Provide information on the location, and a description of the child, suspect, and/or vehicle.

An AMBER Alert is not intended for cases involving parental abductions or runaways except in life-threatening situations. The duration of an alert will depend on the circumstances surrounding the abduction and will vary from case to case. In most cases, five hours is the maximum amount of time that an alert will stay in effect.

If the child is missing or has been missing for a lengthy period—which will be dictated by individual circumstances—there are organizations that may be helpful in locating the child. The following organizations post information about missing children on their websites:

- Our Missing Children (hosted by the RCMP): www.rcmp-grc.gc.ca/omc-ned/index-accueil-eng.htm
- National Center for Missing and Exploited Children: www.missingkids.org
- Child Find Canada: www.childfind.ca

The information may be posted by the police or by the person who is reporting the missing child.

Parental Abduction

Missing child statistics identify that it is more likely that a parent, rather than a stranger, will abduct a child. Parental abductions often occur as a result of a custody dispute or as a means of punishing the child's "other" parent.

Parental abduction is a criminal offence. The *Criminal Code* identifies two types of parental abduction: abduction where a custody order exists and abduction where a custody order does not exist.

Abduction in Contravention of Custody Order: Criminal Code, Section 282(1)

282(1) Every one who, being the parent, guardian or person having the lawful care or charge of a person under the age of fourteen years, takes, entices away, conceals, detains, receives or harbours that person, in contravention of the custody provisions of a custody order in relation to that person made by a court anywhere in Canada, with intent to deprive a parent or guardian, or any other person who has the lawful care or charge of that person, of the possession of that person is guilty of

(a) an indictable offence and is liable to imprisonment for a term not exceeding ten years; or

(b) an offence punishable on summary conviction.

The decision in the case of *R v. McDougall* identifies the court's definition of "detain." This definition should be considered in determining whether the offence of parental abduction in contravention of a custody order has been established. The court determined that there must be a deliberate attempt to deprive the noncustodial parent of possession of the child. This does not mean that the person in custody of the child has not violated the terms of the custody order, but only that a criminal offence may not have been committed.

Detention and Possession: R v. McDougall

The term "detain" in this section means "withhold" and thus the mere fact that a parent keeps a child longer than the prescribed access period would not necessarily constitute a withholding and thus a detention of the child. Further, to prove the requisite intent for the offence, there must be proof that the act was done for the express purpose of depriving the other parent of possession of the child. Mere recklessness would not suffice. There must be an intention to somehow put the child beyond the reach of the other parent's custody or control. An intention not to assist or co-operate in the regaining of physical control of the child by the other parent cannot be equated with the intention to deprive that parent of possession of the child: *R v. McDougall* (1990), 62 CCC (3d) 174, 3 CR (4th) 112, 1 OR (3d) 247, 42 OAC 223 (CA). [*Martin's Annual Criminal Code, 2012*, pp. 615-616]

Police should be careful when considering arrest for a breach of a custody order. The orders may be varied by the court and it may take time for the varied order to be obtained by the involved parties. Police may not have immediate access to the most recent variance of the custody order. The Ontario Provincial Court in *R v. McCoy* advised police to be cautious and make inquiries about the accuracy of the custody order.

Accuracy of the Custody Order: R v. McCoy

Every custody order is subject to variation and particularly where the order is only an interim custody order, police officers before attempting to arrest a parent for abduction in contravention of such an order should take reasonable steps and make such inquiries as are appropriate and possible to ensure that the order accurately reflects the true legal relationship between the parties: *R v. McCoy* (1984), 17 CCC (3d) 114 (Ont. Prov. Ct.). [*Martin's Annual Criminal Code, 2012*, p. 616]

If there are reasonable grounds for believing that a child is being unlawfully withheld in violation of a custody order issued under the authority of the *Children's Law Reform Act*, and there is no reason to believe that the child is in danger, the person having custody of the child may appear before the court and request an order to apprehend the child.

Order Where Child Unlawfully Withheld: Children's Law Reform Act, Section 36(1)

36(1) Where a court is satisfied upon application by a person in whose favour an order has been made for custody of or access to a child that there are reasonable and probable grounds for believing that any person is unlawfully withholding the child from the applicant, the court by order may authorize the applicant or someone on his or her behalf to apprehend the child for the purpose of giving effect to the rights of the applicant to custody or access, as the case may be.

An order under s. 36(2) of the CLRA directs police to apprehend and deliver the child to the person named in the order.

Order to Locate and Take Child: Children's Law Reform Act, Section 36(2)

36(2) Where a court is satisfied upon application that there are reasonable and probable grounds for believing,

(a) that any person is unlawfully withholding a child from a person entitled to custody of or access to the child;

(b) that a person who is prohibited by court order or separation agreement from removing a child from Ontario proposes to remove the child or have the child removed from Ontario; or

(c) that a person who is entitled to access to a child proposes to remove the child or to have the child removed from Ontario, and that the child is not likely to return,

the court by order may direct a police force, having jurisdiction in any area where it appears to the court that the child may be, to locate, apprehend and deliver the child to the person named in the order.

An order under s. 36(5) of the CLRA authorizes police to enter any place, by force if necessary, and search for and remove the child.

Entry and Search: Children's Law Reform Act, Sections 36(5) and (6)

36(5) For the purpose of locating and apprehending a child in accordance with an order under subsection (2), a member of a police force may enter and search any place where he or she has reasonable and probable grounds for believing that the child may be with such assistance and such force as are reasonable in the circumstances.

Time

36(6) An entry or a search referred to in subsection (5) shall be made only between 6 a.m. and 9 p.m. standard time unless the court, in the order, authorizes entry and search at another time.

Abduction Where a Custody Order Is Not in Effect

It is very difficult for police officers to ascertain the rightful custodial parent of a child without a court order. The *Criminal Code* addresses the issue of parental abduction of a child under 14 years of age through the provisions of s. 283.

Abduction: Criminal Code, Section 283

283(1) Every one who, being the parent, guardian or person having the lawful care or charge of a person under the age of fourteen years, takes, entices away, conceals, detains, receives or harbours that person, whether or not there is a custody order in relation to that person made by a court anywhere in Canada, with intent to deprive a parent or guardian, or any other person who has the lawful care or charge of that person, of the possession of that person, is guilty of

(a) an indictable offence and is liable to imprisonment for a term not exceeding ten years; or

(b) an offence punishable on summary conviction.

(2) No proceedings may be commenced under subsection (1) without the consent of the Attorney General or counsel instructed by him for that purpose.

Note that s. 283(2) directs that proceedings shall not be commenced without the permission of the Crown.

CRIMINAL CODE OFFENCES RELEVANT TO CHILD ABUSE: SUMMARY

Physical Abuse of Children

The *Criminal Code* contains numerous offences related to physical abuse of children, some of which apply to victims of all ages and others that are specific to children, including:

- assault (s. 266);
- assault causing bodily harm or with a weapon (s. 267);
- aggravated assault (s. 268);
- aggravated assault excision (s. 268(3)) (genital mutilation to a female child under 18);
- unlawfully causing bodily harm (s. 269);
- administering a noxious thing (s. 245);
- criminal negligence (ss. 219 to 221);
- murder (ss. 229 to 231);
- manslaughter (s. 234);
- infanticide (s. 233) (child under 1 year);
- killing an unborn child in the act of birth (s. 238); and
- homicide from injury before/during birth (s. 223(2)) (child born alive who later dies).

Sexual Abuse of Children

The *Criminal Code* contains sexual offences that apply to victims of all ages as well as offences specific to children. In addition, there are significant differences in how offences in the former category apply to sexual activity among adults, between adults and children, and among children. The *Criminal Code* offences concerning the sexual abuse of children include:

- sexual interference (s. 151) (child under 16);
- invitation to sexual touching (s. 152) (child under 16);
- sexual exploitation (s. 153) (by adult in position of trust or authority; child 16 to 17);
- luring a child (s. 172.1) (child 14 to 17);
- sexual assault (ss. 271 to 273);
- incest (s. 155);
- indecent acts and exposure (s. 173) (of genitals for sexual purpose; child under 16);
- child pornography (s. 163.1) (child under 18);
- procuring (ss. 212(2), (2.1), and (4)) (child under 18);

- parent or guardian procuring sexual activity (s. 170) (child under 18); and
- householder permitting sexual activity (s. 171) (child under 18).

Neglect of Children

Although the *Criminal Code* does not establish a specific criminal offence of child neglect, the criminal law recognizes the responsibility of parents and guardians to provide care and protection for children through several related offences, including:

- failure to provide necessaries of life (s. 215);
- criminal negligence (ss. 219 to 221) (child under 16);
- abandoning child (s. 218) (child under 10);
- neglect to obtain assistance in childbirth (s. 242); and
- corrupting children (s. 172) (child under 18).

Emotional and Psychological Abuse of Children

The *Criminal Code* does not include specific offences concerning emotional or psychological abuse of children. What it does include are several offences, applicable to victims of all ages, with respect to threatening or intimidating behaviour by others:

- criminal harassment (s. 264);
- uttering threats (s. 264.1);
- intimidation (s. 423);
- making indecent or harassing telephone calls (s. 372);
- extortion (s. 346); and
- culpable homicide (s. 222(5)) (causing death by wilfully frightening a human being, in the case of a child or sick person).

Kidnapping and Abduction of Children

The *Criminal Code* has specific offences addressing parental and non-parental abductions. These offences include:

- kidnapping and forcible confinement (s. 279) (any person);
- trafficking of a person under the age of 18 (s. 279.011);
- abduction of person under 16 (s. 280(1)) (by any person);
- abduction of person under 14 (s. 281) (by person not parent, guardian, or person having lawful charge of person under 14);
- abduction in contravention of custody order (s. 282(1)) (by parent or guardian; child under 14);
- abduction (s. 283) (by parent or guardian; child under 14); and
- removal of child from Canada (s. 273.3) (for the purpose of committing certain offences against the child; different provisions for specified offences against children under 16, 16 to 17, and under 18).

Other Criminal Code Provisions

By virtue of s. 7(4.1) of the *Criminal Code*, sexual offences against children committed outside Canada by Canadian citizens or permanent residents are deemed to have been committed in Canada.

KEY TERMS

abuse	neglect
child	pedophile
child sexual abuse	sudden infant death syndrome (SIDS)

REFERENCES

Canadian Foundation for Children, Youth and the Law v. Canada (Attorney General). 2004 SCC 4.

Child and Family Services Act. (1990). RSO 1990, c. C.11.

Children's Aid Society of Algoma. (1998). *Handbook on child abuse.* Sault Ste. Marie, ON: Author.

Children's Law Reform Act. (1990). RSO 1990, c. C.12.

Coroners Act. (1990). RSO 1990, c. C.37.

Criminal Code. (1985). RSC 1985, c. C-46, as amended.

Department of Justice Canada. (2005). *Sexual abuse and exploitation of children and youth: A fact sheet from the Department of Justice Canada.* Ottawa: Author.

Johnson, T.C. (1999). *Understanding your child's sexual behavior: What's natural and healthy.* Oakland, CA: New Harbinger Publications.

Martin's annual Criminal Code, 1999. (1999). Aurora, ON: Canada Law Book.

Martin's annual Criminal Code, 2012. (2011). Aurora, ON: Canada Law Book.

Murphy, W.D. (1985). The dynamics and phases of sexual abuse. Sexual Abuse Treatment Project, Department of Human Services, University of Tennessee.

National Missing Children Services. (2010). *2009 missing children reference report: National Missing Children Services.* Ottawa: Minister of Public Works and Government Services.

Ogrodnik, Lucie. (2010). *Child and youth victims of police-reported violent crime, 2008.* Ottawa: Statistics Canada, Canadian Centre for Justice Statistics. Catalogue no. 85F0033M, no. 23.

Ontario Association of Children's Aid Societies (OACAS). (2006). *Ontario child welfare eligibility spectrum.* Toronto: OACAS.

Ontario Provincial Police. (2009). *AMBER alerts.* Orillia, ON: Queen's Printer for Ontario.

Police Services Act. (1990). RSO 1990, c. P.15.

Public Health Agency of Canada. (2010). *Canadian incidence study of reported child abuse and neglect—2008: Major findings.* Ottawa: Author.

Purcell, D.W., Malow, R.M., Dolezal, C., & Carballo-Dieguez, A. (2004). Sexual abuse of boys: Short- and long-term associations and implications for HIV prevention. In L.J. Koenig, L.S. Doll, A. O'Leary, & W. Pequegnat (Eds.), *From child sexual abuse to adult sexual risk: Trauma, revictimization, and intervention* (pp. 93-114). Washington, DC: American Psychological Association.

Reporting suspicions of child abuse. (1999). *Dispatch, 13*(2), 6–7.

Stechey, F.M. (2001). PANDA: A dentist's introduction to recognizing child abuse. *Dental Practice Management* (Summer), 26–28.

Storrey, R v. (1990). [1990] 1 SCR 241.

Wilken, Thomas. (2002). *Adult survivors of child sexual abuse.* Retrieved from Public Health Agency of Canada: http://www.phac-aspc.gc.ca.

EXERCISES

TRUE OR FALSE

_____ 1. Physical contact between the abuser and the child must occur before the police can intervene in a case of child sexual abuse.

_____ 2. The colour of a bruise provides an exact way to determine when the bruising occurred.

_____ 3. A police officer cannot remove a "child in need of protection," as identified in s. 37(2) of the CFSA, unless a warrant has been obtained.

_____ 4. A victim of child abuse always wants to talk about the abuse he or she has endured.

_____ 5. Proving sexual assault requires proof that the assailant experienced sexual gratification.

_____ 6. Child neglect is not a criminal offence.

SHORT ANSWER

1. List the types of professionals who are required by the *Child and Family Services Act* to report reasonable suspicions of child abuse. What are the possible repercussions for failure to report?

2. List the types of situations under s. 37(2) of the *Child and Family Services Act* that may lead to a child being identified as "in need of protection."

3. Under what circumstances does a police officer have the right to bring a child in need of protection to a "place of safety" without the authority of a warrant?

4. What problems might a police officer encounter when trying to interview a child abuse victim? Be sure to discuss why it might be necessary to hold several brief interview sessions.

5. List four behavioural signs of possible child sexual abuse.

   a.

   b.

   c.

   d.

6. List four physical signs of possible child sexual abuse.

    a.

    b.

    c.

    d.

7. List two sexual offences that can involve children and do not require physical contact between the abuser and the victim to support a conviction.

    a.

    b.

8. List four behavioural signs of possible child physical abuse.

   a.

   b.

   c.

   d.

9. List four physical signs of possible child physical abuse.

   a.

   b.

   c.

d.

10. List four signs of possible child neglect.

    a.

    b.

    c.

    d.

11. Explain the circumstances under which the *Criminal Code* allows correction of a child by force (s. 43).

12. Summarize the circumstances under which the neglect provisions of s. 215 of the *Criminal Code* apply.

Case Analysis

Case 4.1

You are a police officer called to a local school regarding an abuse complaint. You speak to Ms. Smith, who tells you that one of her students, ten-year-old Jack, is being beaten by his parents. Jack confirms her account.

You then speak to Jack's parents, and discover that both have been drinking beer. They tell you that Jack misbehaves. They punish him by spanking him about five or six times a week. Just today they had to spank him because he kicked the cat. Jack tells you that his parents spank him almost every day for practically no reason at all.

What should you do? Can charges be laid? Be sure to refer to the *Criminal Code* in your answer.

Case 4.2

You are a police officer responding to a complaint of assault at a local school. You speak to the suspect, an 11-year-old named Joe. He tells you that his father, Joe Sr., told him to beat up Bill, an 8-year-old at the same school, because Bill's father got a promotion at work that Joe Sr. thought he himself deserved. Joe Sr. told Joe Jr. that beating up Bill was the only way to redeem their family's honour. He also said that Joe Jr. did not have to worry about the police because he was only 11 years old.

What should you do? Can charges be laid? Be sure to refer to the appropriate legislation in your answer.

Case 4.3

You are a police officer responding to a call for assistance at 135 Main Street. Upon arrival you are met by 13-year-old Sally Smith. She tells you that she is being abused by her father. He yells at her for the least little thing she does and won't allow her to go out with her friends. She is now grounded for two weeks for drinking beer and not allowed to leave the house except to go to school. She feels like she is being forcibly confined to the house like a prisoner. She hates her father and is thinking about running away or killing herself.

What will you do in this situation? Explain your authorities.

Case 4.4

You are a police officer. It is 11 p.m. when you receive information from Mrs. Noseworthy that her neighbours, the Simpsons, often leave their children alone when they go to work. Mrs. Noseworthy saw both parents leave the residence about two hours ago. They work the night shift at a factory. She heard some shouting and swearing coming from the Simpson residence. She asks you to attend the residence and see whether the children are all right.

You attend at the Simpson residence, where Amanda Simpson meets you at the door. She is 16 years old. She asks you to come into the house. You enter the living room where you notice a wine bottle on the coffee table. You tell her that you are there to determine whether everything is all right. She tells you that everything is fine. You ask whether her parents are at home. She tells you they work from 10 p.m. to 8 a.m. at the car plant. They are part of the cleaning staff. She looks after the house and her two brothers, 14-year-old John and 12-year-old Patrick, while her parents are at work.

You hear some shouting from the rear of the house. Amanda shouts: "Go back to sleep, you have to get up at six-thirty for school!" The voice tells her: "Shut up! Who made you the f'n queen!"

She shouts back, "The police are here, they are going to take you away if you keep swearing!"

Patrick Simpson, who is 12, enters the living room. He is in his underwear. He appears startled and exclaims, "Holy shit, it's the police!" Amanda tells him to watch his language. He apologizes and sits in a chair. The front door opens and a teenage male, later identified as 14-year-old John Simpson, walks into the living room. Amanda shouts at him, "Where were you? You are supposed to be in by ten-thirty. It's now twenty to twelve. You have school in the morning. You just wait until Mom and Dad are home. Now get to bed!"

John starts to say something but stops when he sees you. He asks, "Why are the police here?" Amanda tells him. John replies, "That nosy Mrs. Noseworthy! She is always spying on us!" Amanda tells the two boys to go to bed. They walk down the hallway, presumably to go to their bedrooms.

Amanda tells you that everything is all right. She has to make lunches for school tomorrow and finish her studying before going to bed. She tells you that she has to get up at 6 a.m. to make breakfast for the boys so that they will be ready to catch their bus at 7:15. She asks you if you would please leave now.

What will you do in this situation? Be sure to quote authorities.

Case 4.5

You are a police officer investigating a complaint of a child with a slingshot. You attend 67 Bruhau Street, the home of the child in question. You speak to Mr. Jones, the father of the child. A ten-year-old boy comes into the room.

Mr. Jones speaks to the boy: "Billy Jones, have you been shooting your slingshot at cars or windows?" The boy replies: "No sir, I shot a few birds and hung them in the barn with the rest, but I didn't hit no cars or houses!"

Mr. Jones asks you, "Exactly what is the problem, officer?" You tell him of the complaint, which was rather vague, and that you were concerned that the boy might inadvertently cause property damage. Mr. Jones tells you that he taught his son how to shoot a slingshot. He invites you to come to the barn to see his son's shooting abilities.

You attend the barn where you see approximately 100 birds hanging from the roof by strings. The birds are in varying states of decay and dismemberment. Mr. Jones proudly tells you that his son killed them all with his slingshot in just two weeks. He boasts that his son's skills are improving—Billy had killed only 50 in the previous two weeks.

Billy is holding a bird in his hand. He tells you, "I just shot this one while you were walking to the barn. See, still twitching!" Mr. Jones tells his son not to let the bird suffer. "Kill it the way I showed you." Billy then breaks the bird's neck by twisting its head.

Mr. Jones tells his son, "Hang it over in the corner with the others that you shot today. If you keep up the good shooting, today could be your record." He turns to you and states, "I'm real proud of that boy. A real killer. He'll be a great soldier, just like his old man."

What will you do in this situation? Be sure to quote authorities (if any). Your answer must demonstrate a thorough understanding of any pertinent legislation.

Case 4.6

You are a police officer responding to a call for assistance at a local shopping mall. Upon arrival you are met by security guard Jay Star. He tells you that there is a disturbance going on in front of a restaurant at the other end of the mall. While en route to the restaurant, Star tells you what he knows about the incident. He received a call from another security guard that two females were shouting at each other about an incident that happened in the restaurant. That is all the information he has to provide.

You arrive on the scene. There appears to be an argument between two females as described by Star. There are two other security guards present. They tell you that they have been keeping the females separated, but that they continue to shout and swear at each other. There are three small children beside one of the females. They are crying.

Security tells you that they told the females to leave the mall but one of them, identified as Linda Truman, refused to leave, telling them to call the police.

When you approach the females, Linda Truman tells you that she is glad to see you. She is angry and exclaims, "This bitch is abusing her children!" She is referring to the other female in the incident, identified as Sally Smith. Sally shouts, "Shut your mouth! I wanted to leave, but that bitch threatened to call the Children's Aid Society and report that I was abusing my kid. I said I would stay until the police arrived because the CAS is a pain in the butt!" You tell them to stop shouting and ask them to explain what happened.

Linda tells you that she and Sally were in the restaurant drinking beer. Sally had her three children, ages three, four, and five, with her. Linda had about 6 or 7 bottles of beer. Sally had about 11 or 12 beers. One of the children asked for a glass of pop. Sally said she wouldn't waste money on pop and gave the child a drink of beer. The children complained that they were hungry and asked for some French fries. Smith again said she wouldn't waste money on restaurant food; there was food at home.

When one of the children began to cry, Sally slapped the child on the shoulder and told him to stop crying. Linda became upset and told Sally that she is not allowed to slap her children. She read something in a school policy that her child brought home from school about not being allowed to hit a child. Sally then called her a stupid cow, and said she didn't know anything about children. Sally added, "You have to hit them once in a while when they get out of line; not hard, just enough to let them know who's the boss!"

The two then began to argue. They were told to leave the restaurant, which they did. When security told them to leave the mall, Sally agreed but Linda refused, telling security to call the police. The security guards confirm that when Sally tried to leave, Linda threatened to call the Children's Aid Society and report the abuse. Sally said she would stay until the police arrived because the CAS is a pain in the butt.

Smith tells you that she did nothing wrong and that she wants to leave now.

What will you do in this situation? Explain your answer. Be sure to quote authorities.

APPENDIX 4A   INFORMATION IN SUPPORT OF A WARRANT TO APPREHEND AND RETURN A CHILD WHO HAS WITHDRAWN FROM A PARENT'S CONTROL

 **Ontario**   Ministry of Children and Youth Services

Information in Support of a Warrant to Apprehend and Return a Child Who has Withdrawn From a Parent's Control
Subsection 43 (2) of the *Child and Family Services Act*

Name of Court		Court file no.

at

Unit No.	Street No.	Street Name		PO Box

City/Town		Province	Postal Code

This is the Information of

Name of Informant

Last Name		First Name	Middle Initial

of

Address

Unit No.	Street No.	Street Name		PO Box

City/Town		Province	Postal Code

1. I am

☐ a parent of

☐ an authorized officer of an approved agency that has custody of

☐ a person who has care and control of

Name of Child

Last Name		First Name	Middle Initial

Date (yyyy/mm/dd)

who was born on [   ]

2.   On or about the [Day] day of [Month] [Year],

Name of Child

Last Name		First Name	Middle Initial

withdrew from my care and control without consent by: (describe circumstances)

3. I have reasonable and probable grounds to believe and do believe that if

Child's Name

Last Name	First Name	Middle Initial

is not apprehended his/her health or safety may be at risk, for the following reasons:
(set out reasons)

4. Name of Child

Last Name	First Name	Middle Initial

has not withdrawn from the care and control of one parent with the consent of another parent in circumstances where a proceeding under section 36 of the *Children's Law Reform Act* would be more appropriate.

(Do not complete if not applicable)

5. I have reasonable and probable grounds to believe that

Name of Child

Last Name	First Name	Middle Initial

may be found at

Address

Unit No.	Street No.	Street Name	PO Box

City/Town	Province	Postal Code

Sworn (or affirmed) before me this [Day   ] day of [Month   ] [Year   ]

at the [   ] of [   ]

in the [   ] of [   ]

A justice of the peace in and for the Province of Ontario

Signature of Informant

Information on this form is collected under the legal authority of the *Child and Family Services Act*, R.S.O. 1990 for the purpose of administering Ministry of Children and Youth Services programs and/or services. For more information contact: Director, Child Welfare Secretariat, Ministry of Children and Youth Services, 3rd Fl., 101 Bloor St. W., Toronto ON M5S 2Z7 or call 416 314-9462.

Source: Ontario Central Forms Repository: www.forms.ssb.gov.on.ca.

APPENDIX 4B   WARRANT TO APPREHEND AND RETURN A CHILD WHO HAS WITHDRAWN FROM A PARENT'S CONTROL

Ontario   Ministry of Children and Youth Services

Warrant to Apprehend and Return a Child who has withdrawn from a Parent's Control
Subsection 43 (2) of the *Child and Family Services Act*

Name of Court	Court file no.

at

Unit No.	Street No.	Street Name		PO Box

City/Town		Province	Postal Code

To all Child Protection Workers and Peace Officers in the Province of Ontario:

On the basis of an Information under subsection 43 (2) of the *Child and Family Services Act*, which information is laid before me on oath of

Last Name	First Name	Middle Initial

☐   a parent of the child named or described on the back of this warrant,

☐   an authorized officer of an approved agency that has custody of the child,

☐   a person who has care and control of the child,

I am satisfied that the child is under sixteen years of age.

I am also satisfied, on the basis of that information, that the child has withdrawn from the care and control of a person described above without that person's consent. I am also satisfied, on the basis of that information, that the person described above believes on reasonable and probable grounds that the child's health or safety may be at risk if the child is not apprehended.

I am further satisfied, on the basis of that information, that the child has not withdrawn from the care and control of one parent with the consent of another parent in circumstances where a proceeding under Section 36 of the *Children's Law Reform Act* would be more appropriate.

Check this box only if child's whereabouts are known

☐   I am further satisfied, on the basis of that Information, that the child may now be found at (Give a municipal address or a precise description of the premises where the child may be found.)

Unit No.	Street No.	Street Name		PO Box

City/Town		Province	Postal Code

I therefore authorize you to return the child to the child's parent

Last Name	First Name	Middle Initial

at	Unit No.	Street No.	Street Name		PO Box

City/Town		Province	Postal Code

as soon as practicable and, where it is not possible to return the child to the parent within a reasonable time, to take the child to a place of safety as defined in the *Child and Family Services Act.*

0034E (2011/05)   ©Queen's Printer for Ontario, 2011   Disponible en français   Page 1 of 2

This warrant further authorizes you to enter by force if necessary and to search

Name and Location of Premises

Name of Premises

Unit No.	Street No.	Street Name		PO Box
City/Town			Province	Postal Code

and to remove the child from it.

	Day	Month	Year
This warrant expires on the		day of	

Date (yyyy/mm/dd)	Signature of justice of the peace

City, town, etc. where this Warrant signed

Print or type name of justice of the peace

Last Name	First Name	Middle Initial

Insert all available information

Full name of child

Last Name	First Name	Middle Initial
Birth date (yyyy/mm/dd)	Sex	Aliases or nicknames

Residential address

Unit No.	Street No.	Street Name		PO Box
City/Town		Province	Postal Code	Telephone No. (incl. area code)
Present location of child				Telephone No. (incl. area code)

Height	Weight	Hair colour	Hair style	Eye colour	Complexion

Other features

Name and address of person to be contacted for further information

Last Name	First Name	Middle Initial
Unit No.	Street No.	Street Name		PO Box
City/Town		Province	Postal Code	Telephone No. (incl. area code)

Information on this form is collected under the legal authority of the *Child and Family Services Act*, R.S.O. 1990 for the purpose of administering Ministry of Children and Youth Services programs and/or services. For more information contact: Director, Child Welfare Secretariat, Ministry of Children and Youth Services, 3rd Fl., 101 Bloor St. W., Toronto ON M5S 2Z7 or call 416 314-9462.

Source: Ontario Central Forms Repository: www.forms.ssb.gov.on.ca.

Spousal Abuse

5

INTRODUCTION

Incidents of spousal abuse are some of the most challenging and frustrating calls that police officers attend. Investigations of the abuse can be challenging because of the reluctance of some victims to provide information about the incident. Another challenge is the adherence to the very detailed "Domestic Violence Occurrences" section of the provincial *Policing Standards Manual* and the officer's police services policies. The investigation and accompanying documentation can take several hours to complete.

Often the call for assistance does not come from the victim but from a concerned friend or neighbour. On many occasions, officers will attend the same residence several times, responding to incidents involving the same parties. This can lead to frustration as a result of the officer's perceived lack of effectiveness in convincing the victim (statistically, the female spouse) of the seriousness of the previous incidents of abuse.

Despite these challenges and frustrations, officers must respond appropriately and with empathy. The ultimate objective of the response is to protect the victim from further abuse.

FAMILY VIOLENCE IN CANADA: A STATISTICAL OVERVIEW

Self-Reported Violence

In 2009, Statistics Canada conducted its fifth victimization survey of the General Social Survey (GSS). Previous cycles were conducted in 1988, 1993, 1999, and 2004. The survey provides estimates of Canadians' personal experiences of eight offence types, examines risk factors associated with victimization, examines reporting rates to police, measures the nature and extent of spousal violence, measures Canadians' fear of crime, and examines public perceptions of crime and the criminal justice system (Statistics Canada, 2011).

CHAPTER OBJECTIVES

After completing this chapter, you should be able to:

- Describe the types of spousal abuse.
- Identify the provisions of the *Criminal Code*, the Ontario *Family Law Act*, and the Ontario *Children's Law Reform Act* that apply to spousal abuse cases.
- Describe the various restraining orders available in situations of spousal abuse.
- Describe techniques for police intervention in spousal abuse situations.
- Describe criminal harassment and identify the provisions of the *Criminal Code* that apply to criminal harassment.
- Describe dating violence and identify drugs commonly used in date rape.

Households were contacted using a random digit dialing method. Once a household was contacted, an individual 15 years or older was randomly selected to respond to the survey. Households without telephones or those with only cellphone service were excluded from the survey.

Of the 31,510 households that were selected for the 2009 GSS sample, 19,422 usable responses were obtained, for a response rate of 61.6 percent, a decrease from 2004 (74.5 percent). Non-responses included respondents who refused to participate, could not be reached, or could not speak English or French.

spouse
any person involved in a relationship of cohabitation

The survey found that nearly 19 million Canadians had a current or former **spouse** in 2009. Of these, 6.2 percent or 1.2 million reported they had been victimized physically or sexually by their partner or spouse during the five-year period prior to the survey. This proportion was largely unchanged from 2004 (6.6 percent), the last time the victimization survey was conducted, and down from 1999 (7.4 percent).

The survey disclosed that a similar proportion of men and women reported experiencing spousal violence during the previous five years. Among men, 6 percent, or about 585,000, encountered spousal violence during this period, compared with 6.4 percent or 601,000 women.

Both female and male victims of spousal violence said that the violence had occurred more than once. About 57 percent of women and 40 percent of men who had experienced an incident of spousal violence in the five years prior to the survey reported that it had occurred on more than one occasion.

spousal abuse
the physical, sexual, emotional/psychological, or financial abuse of one spouse by another

Spousal violence was highest among certain segments of the population. The survey indicated that younger adults aged 25 to 34, those in common-law relationships, and those living in blended families were more likely to be the victims of **spousal abuse**. (In previous surveys, those aged 15 to 24 were estimated to have the highest rate of spousal abuse, but this estimate was subject to sampling error and readers were advised to use the data with caution. In the current survey, the information obtained regarding those aged 15 to 24 years was considered to be too unreliable to be published.) See Table 5.1.

About 22 percent of spousal violence victims stated that they had been sexually assaulted, beaten, choked, or threatened with a gun or a knife. See Table 5.2.

Consistent with previous surveys, females reported more serious forms of spousal violence than did males. For example, 34 percent of females who reported spousal violence on the survey said they had been sexually assaulted, beaten, choked, or threatened with a gun or a knife by their partner or ex-partner in the previous five years. This represents three times the proportion for males (10 percent). See Figure 5.1.

Other socio-demographic characteristics of spousal violence victims were examined. These included sexual orientation, presence of an activity limitation, Aboriginal identity, visible minority status, and immigrant status. (However, due to small numbers, the proportion of victims who experienced spousal violence in the 12 months preceding the survey was not publishable for these categories. Therefore, the proportions discussed below are based on five-year estimates of spousal violence by a current or former partner.)

Respondents who self-identified as gay or lesbian were more than twice as likely as heterosexuals to report having experienced spousal violence, while those who

Table 5.1 Victims of Self-Reported Spousal Violence in Current Relationships Within the Past 12 Months, by Sex and Selected Demographic Characteristics, 1999, 2004, and 2009

Type of demographic characteristic	1999		2004		2009	
	Number (thousands)	Percent	Number (thousands)	Percent	Number (thousands)	Percent
Age group of victim						
15 to 24	23[E]	4.7[E]	21[E]	4.5[E]	F	F
25 to 34[1]	87	3.1	70	2.5	69[E]	2.3[E]
35 to 44	82	2.0	65	1.6	72[E]	1.9[E]
45 and over	57	0.8*	74	0.9*	74	0.7*
Marital status						
Married[1]	172	1.3	142	1.1	142	1.0
Common-law	77	3.8*	88	3.3*	90[E]	2.8[E]*
Family type						
Intact[1]	120	1.7	105	1.5	104	1.3
Blended[2]	27[E]	3.7[E]*	17[E]	1.8[E]	33[E]	3.1[E]*
Couple without children	96	1.4	105	1.4	89	1.1
Lone parent	F	F	F	F	F	F
Household income						
Less than $30,000[1]	58	2.8	27[E]	1.7[E]	22[E]	1.8[E]
$30,000 to $59,999	85	1.9	76	1.8	52[E]	1.5[E]
$60,000 or more	66	1.3*	104	1.5	144	1.4
Not stated/don't know	41[E]	1.2[E]*	22[E]	0.8[E]	14[E]	0.5[E]
Education of victim						
High school diploma or less[1]	83	1.6	66	1.3	42[E]	0.9[E]
Some post-secondary[3]	112	2.0	95	1.5	117	1.6
University degree	49	1.6	62	1.6	73[E]	1.4[E]
Not stated/don't know	F	F	F	F	F	F
Education of spouse or partner						
High school diploma or less[1]	125	1.8	94	1.3	75	1.1
Some post-secondary[3]	68	1.7	79	1.8	80	1.6
University degree	49	1.7	49[E]	1.3[E]	75[E]	1.5[E]
Not stated/don't know	F	F	F	F	F	F
Victim's place of residence						
Census metropolitan area	..	..	146	1.5	172	1.5
Non-census metropolitan area	..	..	84	1.4	60[E]	1.0[E]
Total violence by current partner	**250**	**1.7**	**230**	**1.4**	**232**	**1.3**

Notes: Includes legally married, common-law, and same-sex spouses. Values may not add up to totals due to rounding.

[1] Reference group.

[2] A blended family contains children of both spouses (married or common-law) from one or more previous unions or one or more children from the current union and one or more children from previous unions.

[3] Some post-secondary includes diploma, a certificate from a community college, or a trade/technical school.

[E] Use with caution—may be unreliable.

F Too unreliable to be published.

* significant difference from reference group (p < 0.05).

.. Not available.

Sources: Statistics Canada, General Social Survey, 1999, 2004, and 2009. Adapted from Statistics Canada (2011).

Table 5.2   Victims of Self-Reported Spousal Violence Within the Past Five Years, by Type of Violence, 1999, 2004, and 2009

Type of violence	1999		2004		2009[a]	
	Number (thousands)	Percent	Number (thousands)	Percent	Number (thousands)	Percent
Threatened to hit, threw something	158	12.7[b]	152	12.7[b]	213	18.0
Pushed, grabbed, shoved, slapped	375	30.3	448	37.4	411	34.7
Kicked, bit, hit, hit with something	311	25.1	251	20.9	290	24.5
Sexually assaulted, beaten, choked, threatened with a gun or knife	388	31.3[b]	342	28.5	262	22.1
Total	1,239	100	1,200	100	1,186	100

Notes: Includes legally married, common-law, same-sex, separated, and divorced spouses.
[a] Reference group.
[b] Significant difference from reference group (p < 0.05).

Sources: Statistics Canada, General Social Survey, 1999, 2004, and 2009. Adapted from Statistics Canada (2011).

self-identified as bisexual were four times more likely than heterosexuals to report spousal violence.

Of those who reported having a limitation such as a physical or mental condition or health problem, 8 percent said they had been a victim of spousal violence in the previous five years compared with 6 percent who did not have an activity limitation.

The 2009 General Social Survey indicated that those who self-identified as an Aboriginal person were almost twice as likely to be a victim of spousal violence (10 percent versus 6 percent) as those who did not self-identify as being Aboriginal. (Recall that households were selected for the GSS by random digit dialing and respondents were interviewed by telephone. It should be noted that the proportion of households with a landline telephone may be below the national average on some First Nation settlements; therefore, the accuracy of the results may be questionable.)

Self-identification as a visible minority or an immigrant was not found to be associated with increased levels of spousal violence. A similar proportion of visible and non-visible minorities reported experiencing spousal violence (5 percent versus 6 percent), while immigrants were less likely to report being a victim of spousal violence than non-immigrants (4 percent versus 7 percent).

Socio-demographic factors such as household income and education levels were found to have little impact on the rate of spousal violence. Likewise, educational attainment had little effect: victims and perpetrators of spousal violence were no more likely to be university graduates than to be high school dropouts. Similarly, there was little difference in the proportions of spousal violence victims across various income groups.

Figure 5.1   Victims of Self-Reported Spousal Violence, by Most Serious Form of Violence, by Sex, 2009

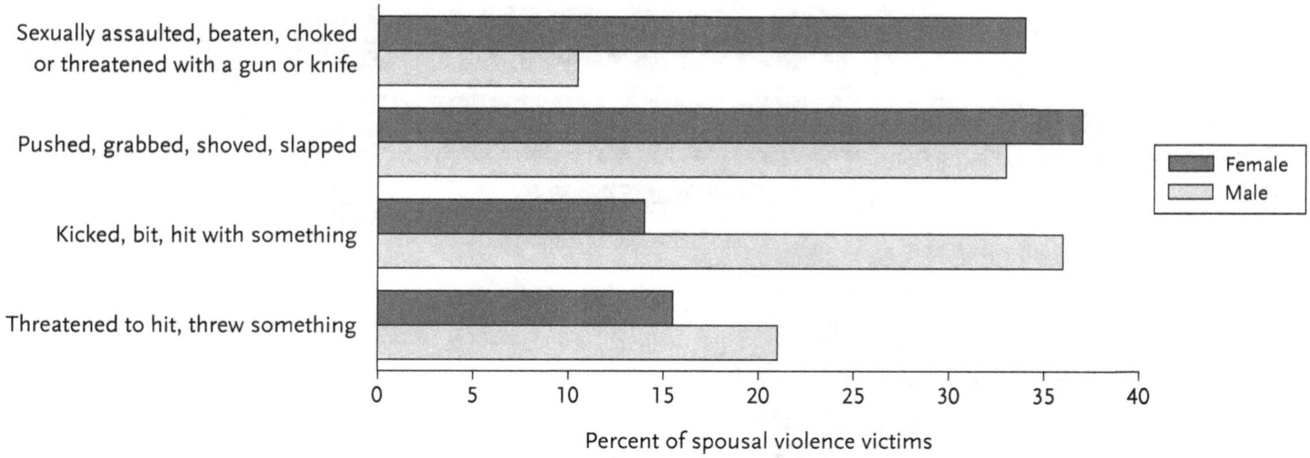

Percent of spousal violence victims

Notes: Includes legally married, common-law, same-sex, separated, and divorced spouses who reported having experienced violence within the five-year period preceding the survey.

Sources: Statistics Canada, General Social Survey, 2009. Adapted from Statistics Canada (2011).

Police-Reported Violence

In 2007, there were 40,165 incidents of spousal violence (that is, violence against legally married, common-law, separated, and divorced partners) reported to police. See Table 5.3. This represents about 12 percent of all police-reported violent crime in Canada, but does not accurately reflect the actual number of spousal abuse incidents that occur because many are not reported to police.

As in previous surveys, the 2009 GSS found that many victims of spousal violence had been victimized multiple times before turning to the police for help. For example, almost two-thirds of spousal violence victims (63 percent) said that they had been victimized more than once before they contacted the police (Statistics Canada, 2011). Almost three in ten (28 percent) stated that they had been victimized more than ten times before they contacted the police.

People choose not to report incidents of spousal violence for a variety of reasons. Among spouses who did not report spousal violence to police in 2009, the most common reason was their belief that the incident was a personal matter and it did not concern the police (82 percent). Other reasons included a preference to deal with the situation in another way (81 percent) and a belief that the incident was not important enough to report (70 percent). See Figure 5.2.

The majority of incidents of spousal violence that were brought to the attention of police were reported by victims themselves. Female victims were about three times more likely than male victims to state that they had reported the incident to police (23 percent versus 7 percent), but both groups gave similar reasons for choosing to report.

The most common reason given by spouses for reporting incidents of spousal violence to police was a desire to halt the violence and to receive protection (89 percent). Spouses provided a number of other reasons: some felt a sense of duty (49 percent), some wanted their partner arrested and punished (31 percent,) and some reported the incident because someone else had recommended they do so

Figure 5.2   Reasons for Not Reporting Spousal Violence to Police, by Sex, 2009

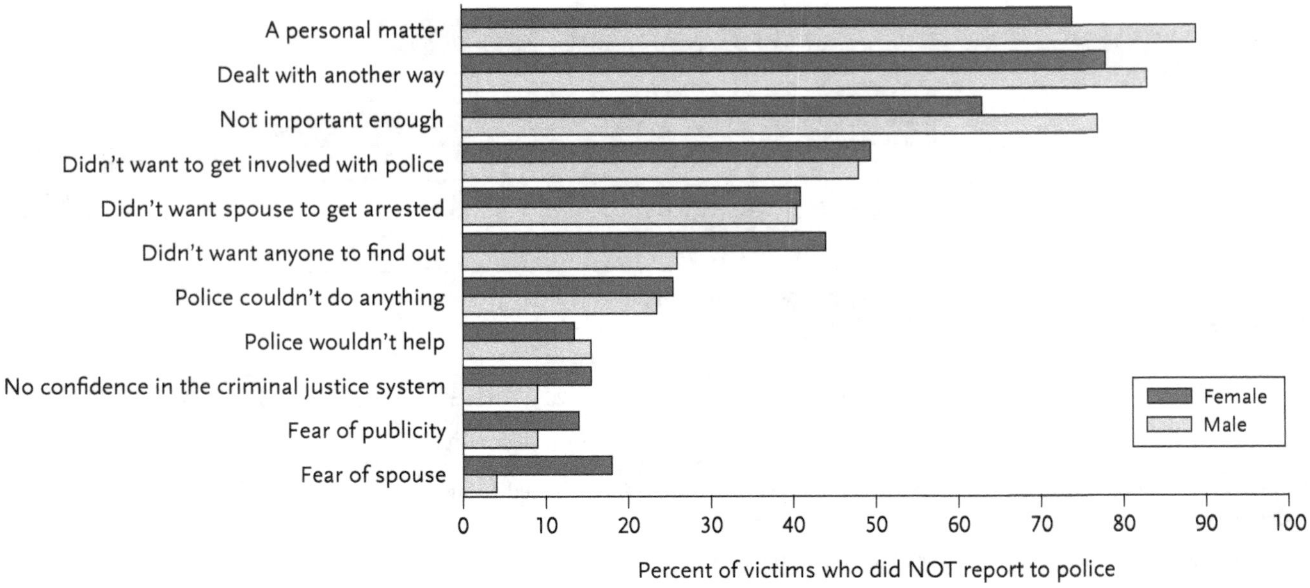

Percent of victims who did NOT report to police

Notes: Includes legally married, common-law, same-sex, separated, and divorced spouses.
Figures do not add to 100 percent due to multiple responses.

Sources: Statistics Canada, General Social Survey, 2009. Adapted from Statistics Canada (2011).

(26 percent). Of victims who did report the violence to the police, more than six in ten said they were satisfied with the police response.

In some cases, victims of spousal violence, primarily women, sought and obtained a restraining or protective order from a criminal or civil court. Such orders are granted to protect victims who fear for their safety or the safety of their children. To achieve this aim, the order may include removing the abuser from the home, giving the victim exclusive occupation of the home, or restricting the abuser's communication with the victim.

During 2009, one in ten victims of spousal violence stated that they obtained a restraining or protective order against their abuser. Women were three times more likely than men to state that they had obtained such an order against their spouse or ex-spouse (15 percent versus 5 percent).

Violation of restraining or protective orders was frequently reported. Of those who had obtained an order, almost one-third (30 percent) reported that their abuser violated its terms. Just over two-thirds (67 percent) of victims stated that they reported the breach to police.

The Uniform Crime Reporting Survey 2 (UCR2)

In 2009, 153 police services in all ten provinces and three territories supplied data for the complete year to the UCR2 survey, representing approximately 99 percent of the population of Canada. The coverage provided by these services in the 2009 database is distributed as follows: 38.6 percent from Ontario, 23.3 percent from Quebec, 13.2 percent from British Columbia, 11 percent from Alberta, 3.6 percent from Manitoba, 3 percent from Saskatchewan, 2.8 percent from Nova Scotia, 2.2

percent from New Brunswick, 1.5 percent from Newfoundland and Labrador, 0.4 percent from Prince Edward Island, and approximately 0.1 percent from each of the three territories (Yukon, Northwest Territories, and Nunavut). Note that coverage is expressed as the proportion of the Canadian population covered by the UCR2 survey. The data contained in the survey results are not geographically representative at the national or provincial level. The UCR data does not contain a count of all crimes committed in Canada. The UCR survey collects information only on those crimes that come to the attention of the police.

In 2007, the majority of victims of spousal violence were females, accounting for 83 percent of victims. Spousal violence was nearly twice as common between current partners (legally married or common-law) as ex-partners in the categories of common assault and major assault. See Figure 5.3.

Police laid charges in more than three-quarters of spousal violence incidents reported. Incidents involving female victims were more likely to result in charges being laid than those involving male victims. Common assault (s. 266 of the *Criminal Code*) was the most frequent type of spousal violence according to police-reported data, followed by major assault, uttering threats, and criminal harassment.

Among victims who reported being injured by their spouse, bruises were the most common form of injury for both female (95 percent) and male (75 percent) victims. Male victims were more likely than female victims to report suffering cuts, scratches, or burns (59 percent versus 30 percent). About 10 percent of females reported bone fractures.

Violence Among Current and Former Spouses

In 2009, the GSS found that spousal violence was four times more likely to occur between ex-spouses or partners than between current spouses or partners. Of adults who had contact with an ex-spouse or partner in the previous five years, 17 percent reported they had been physically or sexually assaulted by their partner at least once. Among those with a current spouse or partner, 4 percent were physically or sexually assaulted during the same time period.

Reconciling Differences Between the 2009 GSS and the UCR2

There appears to be a large discrepancy in the proportion of male and female victims of spousal violence as reported by the UCR2 and the 2009 GSS. Recall that the 2009 GSS disclosed that a similar proportion of men and women (6 percent and 6.4 percent, respectively) reported experiencing spousal violence, whereas the UCR2 disclosed that the majority of victims of spousal violence in 2007 were women (83 percent). This discrepancy may be a result of the manner in which information is gathered by each survey. The UCR2 identifies only those occurrences reported to police, while the GSS is an anonymous survey that relies on self-disclosure of information. Male victims may be more hesitant than female victims in reporting spousal violence to police.

Table 5.3 Victims of Spousal Violence by Offence Type and Sex of Victim, Reported to a Subset of Police Services, 2007

Offence type	Total number	Percent	Sex of victim			
			Female		Male	
			Number	Percent	Number	Percent
Homicide/attempts	127	0	105	0	22	0
Sexual assault[a]	708	2	692	2	16	0
Major assault (levels 2 and 3)[b]	5,889	15	4,266	13	1,623	23
Common assault (level 1)[c]	25,074	62	20,836	63	4,238	61
Criminal harassment	2,891	7	2,565	8	326	5
Uttering threats	4,109	10	3,545	11	564	8
Other violent offences[d]	1,367	3	1,218	4	149	2
Total offences	**40,165**	**100**	**33,227**	**100**	**6,938**	**100**

Notes: Percentages may not add up to 100 percent due to rounding. Excludes incidents where the sex and/or the age of the victim were unknown. Includes victims aged 15 to 98. Spousal violence refers to violence committed by legally married, common-law, separated, and divorced partners. Data are not nationally representative.

[a] Includes sexual assault, classified as one of three levels according to the seriousness of the incident, as well as other sexual crimes. Level 1 sexual assault is the category of least physical injury to the victim; level 2 includes sexual assault with a weapon, threats to use a weapon, or causing bodily harm; and level 3 includes aggravated sexual assault that wounds, maims, disfigures, or endangers the life of the victim.

[b] Includes assault with a weapon or causing bodily harm (level 2) and aggravated assault, defined as assault that wounds, maims, disfigures, or endangers the life of the victim (level 3).

[c] Common or level 1 assault is the least serious form of assault and includes pushing, slapping, punching, and face-to-face verbal threats.

[d] Includes robbery, unlawfully causing bodily harm, discharge firearm with intent, assault against peace-public officer, criminal negligence causing bodily harm, other assaults, kidnapping, hostage-taking, explosives causing death/bodily harm, arson, and other violent violations.

Sources: Statistics Canada: Canadian Centre for Justice Statistics, Incident-Based Uniform Crime Reporting Survey. Adapted from Statistics Canada (2009).

Why Men Are Less Likely to Report Abuse

There are several possible reasons why men may not report being abused:

- *They fear that they won't be believed.* Men are stereotypically the abusers and it is difficult for many people, including the police, to believe that men can be the victims of their female partners.
- *They are ashamed.* Men are regarded as the physically stronger sex. Society sees a man who is beaten by his wife as weak.
- *They adopt a macho, "I can handle it" attitude.* Men who are abused by their intimate partners typically do not seek help in dealing with the emotional and physical impact of the violence because they feel that doing so is unmasculine.
- *They keep silent to avoid embarrassment and ridicule.* Not confiding in a friend, relative, or professional is a common reaction of both male and female victims of domestic abuse because it is embarrassing to be

Figure 5.3   Level 1 Assault the Most Common Offence Against Current and Former Spouses, Criminal Harassment and Threats More Common Among Ex-Spouses, 2007

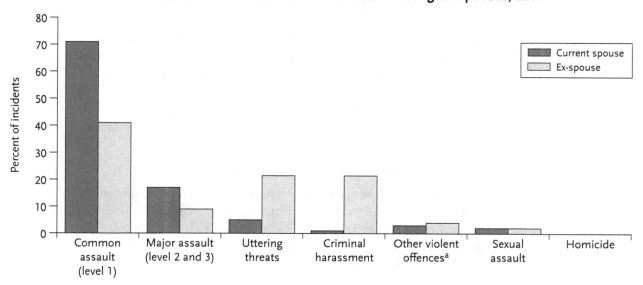

Notes: Percentages may not total 100 percent due to rounding. Includes victims aged 15 to 98. Current spouse includes legally married and common-law partners. "Ex-spouse" includes separated and divorced partners.

[a] Includes robbery, unlawfully causing bodily harm, discharge firearm with intent, assault against peace officer or public officer, criminal negligence causing bodily harm, other assaults, kidnapping, hostage-taking, explosives causing death/bodily harm, arson, and other violent violations.

Sources: Statistics Canada, Canadian Centre for Justice Statistics, Incident-Based Uniform Crime Reporting Survey. Adapted from Statistics Canada (2009).

victimized. But men typically face a greater degree of disbelief and ridicule than do most women in this situation, which helps enforce the silence.

- *They cope by avoiding the abuser.* Men often escape a bad home life that they are afraid of by spending extra time at work, staying in "their" space at home (for example, the garage or den), or even sleeping in the car or at a friend's place.

CAUSES OF ABUSE

Explanations for the causes of abusive behaviour tend to fall into two main categories: psychopathological theory and social learning theory (O'Connor, 2004).

The key ideas of each theory are summarized below.

Psychopathological Theory

According to psychopathological theory, the offender is a mentally disturbed individual who also may be suffering from alcohol or drug addiction. The offender may be venting frustration or anger at a substitute target. The victim may be seen as mentally or emotionally disturbed through his or her tolerance of such behaviour. The victim may also be suffering from guilt, and may believe that he or she induced the spouse to inflict the abuse.

Two opponents of this theory, Richard M. Tolman and Larry W. Bennett (1992), reject the premise that the abuser is mentally disturbed:

The psychological characteristics of batterers are extremely diverse, so much so that no one pathology can be linked to battering. Research shows that no personality traits or clinical factors set abusive men apart from the general population. This is supported by a recent study in which one in five Canadian men living with a woman admitted to using violence against his partner. Most men who assault their partners are not violent outside the home. They do not hit their bosses or colleagues. When abusive men hit their partners, they often aim the blows at parts of the body where bruises don't show. If [abusive] men were truly mentally ill, they could not selectively limit and control their violence.

Social Learning Theory

According to social learning theory, people learn social behaviours by observing the behaviours of others. Social learning theory addresses both the behaviour learned by the abuser and the behaviour learned by the victim. There are three variations of this theory: intergenerational transmission of violence, learned helplessness, and cycle of violence.

Intergenerational Transmission of Violence

The intergenerational transmission of violence version of learning theory asserts that adults learn violence by having seen abusive relationships as a child.

There are those who believe that statistical data do not support this version of social learning theory. For example, Margaret Cooper and Cathy Widom conducted research with the assistance of the Correctional Service of Canada (CSC) and found little support for the theory. Violent offenders were interviewed in an attempt to compile statistical data. The CSC, in its report *The Impact of Experiencing and Witnessing Family Violence During Childhood* (Alksnis & Taylor, 2002), refers to the findings of Cooper (1992):

> Based on the few prospective studies that do exist, numerous reviewers maintain that the majority of abused children do not continue the cycle of violence as adults. Even in childhood, the proportion of children who exhibit clinical levels of emotional/behavioural problems as a result of living with family violence is lower than one might expect: about one-third of boys and one-fifth of girls are in the clinical range.

The CSC report also discusses the findings of Widom (1989):

> Estimates of the proportion of abused children who then go on to abuse their own offspring are around 30 percent. Witnessing violence between parents is thought to be only modestly related to marital aggression in the second generation; about 16–17 percent of witnesses report aggression in their own intimate relationships.

Learned Helplessness

According to the learned helplessness version of social learning theory, the victim stays in the relationship because of perceived or real economic and emotional dependency.

Cycle of Violence

The cycle of violence version of social learning theory states that the victim makes excuses for the offender's behaviour and believes that the offender will change. The abuser promises that the abuse will never happen again, and the victim wants to believe that this is true. But because the victim does not adamantly condemn the behaviour, the abuser concludes that the behaviour will not lead to a relationship breakdown. The abuser then continues the abuse (even though he or she may see the abuse as situationally wrong) and a cycle of violence is created.

CHARACTERISTICS OF ABUSIVE SPOUSES

Abusers come from all social groups and backgrounds, and from all personality profiles. However, some characteristics fit a general profile of an abusive spouse. Abusive spouses often

- are jealous—they imagine that the other spouse is having affairs;
- need to control the relationship and the other spouse;
- project personal faults onto the other spouse;
- have an explosive temper;
- seek to isolate the other spouse;
- tend not to trust other people and therefore tend not to share their inner world with others;
- have a limited or no social network (the partner is the closest person they know);
- are subject to depression, known only to the family;
- get their needs met by exerting control, often through violence and threats;
- may threaten suicide if their partner leaves;
- are frequently demanding and assaultive in sexual behaviour; and
- lack sympathy for their partner's physical and emotional pain.

A study by the Solicitor General of Canada, conducted through the Correctional Service of Canada, identified some additional common characteristics of abusers (Hanson & Wallace-Capretta, 2000):

1. *Traditional sex-role expectations.* The abuser holds very traditional, stereotyped views of male–female roles and relationships. The abuser tends to be preoccupied with a macho ideal of manhood. He feels a need to dominate and control women and often expects it as his right and privilege. He tends to associate weakness with femininity and fears intimacy, which makes him feel vulnerable.

2. *A tendency to objectify women.* The abuser does not see women as people. He sees women as property or sexual objects.

3. *Communication deficits.* The abuser is frequently lacking in assertive communication skills and is more inclined to resolve problems through violence.

4. *Poor impulse control.* The abuser tends to express all negative feelings as anger, which he initially suppresses. Finally, he "explodes" and releases his anger, primarily through violent behaviour.

5. *Low self-esteem.* Despite the bravado that many abusers display, abusers characteristically suffer from low self-esteem. The abuser often feels that he has not lived up to his concept of the male sex role and consequently overcompensates with hyper-masculinity. He becomes emotionally dependent on his partner and feels threatened by the possibility of his partner's departure. This is often evident in his excessive jealousy and possessiveness.

6. *Alcohol and/or drug problems.* There is a high incidence of alcohol and drug abuse among abusers. The alcohol acts to reduce inhibitions, intensifying abusive incidents.

7. *Abusive childhood.* Often, the abuser has been exposed to abusive behaviour in the home at a young age. He may defend his behaviour as normal, although in most situations he tries to hide his actions.

8. *Denial.* The abuser tends to minimize and deny the abuse. Very much like the alcoholic, the abuser denies that there is a problem and refuses to accept responsibility for the abusive behaviour. The abuser blames everyone else for making him angry, thereby excusing his actions.

9. *False genuineness.* The abuser may be pleasant and charming to his partner between periods of violence, and is often seen as a nice guy to outsiders.

Some of these characteristics, such as poor communication skills, lack of impulse control, and alcohol/drug abuse, will often create problems for the abuser outside the spousal relationship. Abusers, for example, may have a history of brushes with the law because of their inability to control their anger. These brushes with the law are sometimes violent and can take the form of "disturbance incidents," in which the abuser is verbally and physically aggressive.

ASSESSING THE RISK OF ABUSE

Predicting violent behaviour has been, and is still, extremely difficult. Police officers at the scene of an incident may be able to make an assessment of the immediate risk of further violence, based upon the kinesics (body movements and gestures) of the involved parties. This type of assessment is often made at the scene by the responding officers. Although such an assessment may be of value in predicting the likelihood of immediate violence, it cannot accurately predict future episodes of spousal abuse.

There have been some attempts to develop models that will more accurately predict future violence. The Ontario Domestic Assault Risk Assessment (ODARA) is a domestic violence risk assessment tool that assesses the risk of future wife assault, as well as the frequency and severity of these assaults. (This model will be discussed in greater detail later in the chapter.)

Statistical data are currently being collected by police officers within the scope of their investigation of domestic violence incidents. The data are recorded on a Domestic Violence Supplementary Report, which is completed by investigating officers in situations where charges are laid. A portion of the report requires that victims voluntarily provide personal information regarding their assailant and their interactions with the assailant.

This information may assist in the development of a more accurate method of predicting spousal abuse. Until an accurate method of predicting violence is developed, officers will have to rely upon their observations in protecting themselves and victims from further violence while on scene.

Assessing the Risk of Spousal Homicide and Assault

Studies of the characteristics of individuals who are at risk of murdering their spouses, conducted by Jacquelyn Campbell (2001), identified nine factors that increased the risk of future homicide:

- access to or ownership of guns,
- use of weapons in prior abusive incidents,
- threats with weapons,
- infliction of serious injury in prior abusive incidents,
- threats of suicide,
- threats to kill,
- drug or alcohol abuse,
- forced sex with a female partner, and
- obsessive behaviour (such as extreme jealousy or dominance).

Campbell also developed a questionnaire to help individuals assess whether they are at risk of being killed by a current or former partner: the Danger Assessment instrument (2004). See Figure 5.4. It has been widely tested and forms the basis for many of the informal assessment methods currently used. One current risk assessment and management tool is that developed by Randall Kropp, Stephen D. Hart, Christopher D. Webster, and Derek Eaves (1995) at the BC Institute Against Family Violence. It is called the Spousal Assault Risk Assessment Guide (SARA).

The Spousal Assault Risk Assessment Guide

The Spousal Assault Risk Assessment Guide (SARA) consists of questions covering criminal history, psychological functioning, and current social adjustment (Department of Justice Canada, 2010). It is designed to assess the risk of future abuse in adult male offenders. In addition, it incorporates the evaluators' professional judgment as part of the assessment. This type of risk assessment model may be referred to as a "structured professional judgment assessment." Items in such instruments are primarily identified from the literature on characteristics of male abusers, predictors of violent crime, and clinical experience. An advantage of this approach is that a list of items and scoring criteria can be easily generated. The total item scores are used to assess the probability of spousal violence recidivism. Subsequent empirical validations are required for data on reliability and accuracy of the assessment. A disadvantage to this approach, for the purposes of law enforcement use, is the need for clinical training and the lengthy time required to conduct a risk assessment.

Figure 5.4   Danger Assessment Instrument

DANGER ASSESSMENT
Jacquelyn C. Campbell, PhD, RN, FAAN
Copyright, 2003; www.dangerassessment.com

Several risk factors have been associated with increased risk of homicides (murders) of women and men in violent relationships. We cannot predict what will happen in your case, but we would like you to be aware of the danger of homicide in situations of abuse and for you to see how many of the risk factors apply to your situation.

Using the calendar, please mark the approximate dates during the past year when you were abused by your partner or ex partner. Write on that date how bad the incident was according to the following scale:

_____ 1. Slapping, pushing; no injuries and/or lasting pain

_____ 2. Punching, kicking; bruises, cuts, and/or continuing pain

_____ 3. "Beating up"; severe contusions, burns, broken bones

_____ 4. Threat to use weapon; head injury, internal injury, permanent injury, miscarriage, choking

_____ 5. Use of weapon; wounds from weapon

(If **any** of the descriptions for the higher number apply, use the higher number.)

Mark **Yes** or **No** for each of the following. ("He" refers to your husband, partner, ex-husband, ex-partner, or whoever is currently physically hurting you.)

_____ 1. Has the physical violence increased in severity or frequency over the past year?

_____ 2. Does he own a gun?

_____ 3. Have you left him after living together during the past year? If you have never lived with him, check here.

_____ 4. Is he unemployed?

_____ 5. Has he ever used a weapon against you or threatened you with a lethal weapon? If yes, was the weapon a gun?

_____ 6. Does he threaten to kill you?

_____ 7. Has he avoided being arrested for domestic violence?

_____ 8. Do you have a child that is not his?

_____ 9. Has he ever forced you to have sex when you did not wish to do so?

_____ 10. Does he ever try to choke you?

_____ 11. Does he use illegal drugs? By drugs, I mean "uppers" or amphetamines, Meth, speed, angel dust, cocaine, "crack," street drugs or mixtures.

_____ 12. Is he an alcoholic or problem drinker?

(The figure is concluded on the next page.)

_____ 13. Does he control most or all of your daily activities? (For instance: does he tell you who you can be friends with, when you can see your family, how much money you can use, or when you can take the car?) If he tries, but you do not let him, check here.

_____ 14. Is he violently and constantly jealous of you? For instance, does he say "If I can't have you, no one can."

_____ 15. Have you ever been beaten by him while you were pregnant? If you have never been pregnant by him, check here.

_____ 16. Has he ever threatened or tried to commit suicide?

_____ 17. Does he threaten to harm your children?

_____ 18. Do you believe he is capable of killing you?

_____ 19. Does he follow or spy on you, leave threatening notes or messages, destroy your property, or call you when you don't want him to?

_____ 20. Have you ever threatened or tried to commit suicide?

_____ Total "Yes" Answers:

Thank you. Please talk to your nurse, advocate or counselor about what the Danger Assessment means in terms of your situation.

Sources: Campbell (2004); Campbell, Webster, & Glass (2009).

The SARA includes the following 20 categorized indicators (Department of Justice Canada, 2010):

Criminal History
1. Past Assault of Family Members
2. Past Assault of Strangers or Acquaintances
3. Past Violation of Conditional Release or Community Supervision

Psychosocial Adjustment
1. Recent Relationship Problems
2. Recent Employment Problems
3. Victim of and/or Witness to Family Violence as a Child or Adolescent
4. Recent Substance Abuse/Dependence
5. Recent Suicidal or Homicidal Ideation/Intent
6. Recent Psychotic and/or Manic Symptoms
7. Personality Disorder with Anger, Impulsivity, or Behavioural Instability

Spousal Assault History
1. Past Physical Assault
2. Past Sexual Assault/Sexual Jealousy
3. Past Use of Weapons and/or Credible Threats of Death
4. Recent Escalation in Frequency or Severity of Assault

5. Past Violation of "No Contact" Orders

6. Extreme Minimization or Denial of Spousal Assault History

7. Attitudes that Support or Condone Spousal Assault

Alleged (Current) Offence

1. Severe and/or Sexual Assault

2. Use of Weapons and/or Credible Threats of Death

3. Violation of "No Contact" Order

The nature of a current offence committed by the male adult offender can also indicate risk—for example, whether the assault was severe and/or involved sexual assault, whether weapons were used, or whether a no-contact order was violated (Department of Justice Canada, 2001). It is important to note that the assessment must never be limited to the 20 indicators described above—factors unique to a particular case must always be examined. For example, has the individual shown violence toward animals? Does he come from a country where he has been the victim of political persecution?

The Ontario Domestic Assault Risk Assessment

The Ontario Domestic Assault Risk Assessment (ODARA) is a domestic violence risk assessment tool that is used to assess risk of future wife assault, as well as the frequency and severity of these assaults. It was developed through the collaborative efforts of the Ontario Provincial Police and the Mental Health Centre based in Penetanguishene, Ontario (Hilton et al., 2004).

The ODARA risk assessment tool was developed and tested only for male-to-female domestic assaults, and only among current or former cohabiting or marital relationships.

The ODARA consists of 13 questions based on factors that are most likely to predict future spousal violence. The questions can be reliably assessed by police officers in predicting future spousal assault.

The risk of assault can be predicted with high accuracy using these questions alone, reducing the need for a comprehensive assessment in order to evaluate risk of re-offending. The 13 yes/no questions elicit information on the subject's history of violence and antisocial behaviour. The questions cover the following topics:

1. Prior domestic assault (against a partner or the children).

2. Prior non-domestic assault (against any person other than a partner or the children).

3. Prior sentence for a term of 30 days or more.

4. Failure to follow conditional release; bail, parole, probation, no-contact order.

5. Threat to harm or kill anyone during an incident of domestic assault.

6. Confinement of victim during an incident of domestic assault.

7. Victim fears future assault.

8. Victim and/or subject has more than one child.

9. Victim has a biological child from a previous partner.

10. Violence against others.

11. More than one indicator of substance abuse problem: alcohol consumption, use of other drugs, increased use of alcohol or other drugs.

12. Assaulted the victim when she was pregnant.

13. The victim faces at least one barrier to support: children, no phone, and no access to transportation, geographical isolation, alcohol/drug consumption or problem.

A score of 0 places the subject in the lowest risk category; a score of 7 or more places the subject in the highest risk category. Higher scores on the ODARA also indicate that the subject will commit more violent acts toward his spouse in a shorter time frame than a subject with a lower score.

Note: Do not use these questions to assess risk of violent behaviour without the full scoring instructions as published by the Research Department of the Waypoint Centre for Mental Health Care, Penetanguishene, Ontario, in collaboration with the Ontario Provincial Police.

The ODARA may be referred to as an actuarial risk assessment, defined as an instrument that provides weightings and empirically based scores to predict future behaviour.

The actuarial approach allows assessors to make decisions based on data that focus on relatively small numbers of known risk factors. The ODARA does not include measures of psychological assessment, although these assessments may reveal strong predictors of future violent behaviours.

The strength of this approach is that it improves upon the poor reliability and validity of unstructured psychological assessments carried out by non-professionals. The use of actuarial risk assessment reduces the requirement of psychological assessment.

The instrument was designed to be easily scored by police officers with no statistical training.

TYPES OF ABUSE

There are four categories of abuse: physical abuse, sexual abuse, emotional/psychological abuse, and financial abuse. The following sections will describe these types of abuse.

Physical Abuse

Although emotional and psychological abuse may be as destructive as, or more destructive than, physical abuse, physical abuse is the type most commonly responded to by the police. It may occur just once or it may happen repeatedly. **Physical abuse** is the use of physical force in a way that injures a person or poses a risk of injury to a person. It includes beating, hitting, shaking, pushing, choking, biting, burning, kicking, or assaulting with a weapon. Other forms of physical abuse may include rough handling, confinement, or any dangerous or harmful use of force or restraint. Below are types of abuse that constitute an offence under the *Criminal Code*:

physical abuse
the use of force in a way that injures a person or poses a risk of injury to a person

- assault (s. 266),
- assault with a weapon or causing bodily harm (s. 267),
- aggravated assault (s. 268),
- forcible confinement (s. 279(2)).

Sexual Abuse

sexual abuse
engagement in any form of sexual activity with a person without the full consent of that person; includes all forms of sexual assault, sexual harassment, or sexual exploitation

Sexual abuse is engagement in any form of sexual activity with a person without the full consent of that person. It includes all forms of sexual assault, sexual harassment, or sexual exploitation. Forcing someone to participate in unwanted, unsafe, or degrading sexual activity, or using ridicule or other tactics to try to denigrate, control, or limit a person's sexuality is sexual abuse.

Sexual abuse also includes:

- treating a spouse as a sex object;
- forcing a spouse to look at pornography;
- being rough (may constitute an offence);
- forcing a spouse to engage in sexual activity in certain positions; and
- forcing a spouse to have sex (may constitute an offence).

Note that many of the above actions and behaviours do not constitute an offence.

Possible Criminal Offences: Sexual Abuse

Some members of the public mistakenly believe that a person cannot be charged with sexual assault when the complainant is that person's spouse. Section 278 of the *Criminal Code* is very specific in addressing this issue.

Spouse May Be Charged: Criminal Code, Section 278

278. A husband or wife may be charged with an offence under section 271, 272 or 273 in respect of his or her spouse, whether or not the spouses were living together at the time the activity that forms the subject-matter of the charge occurred.

Note that ss. 271, 272, and 273, cited in s. 278, describe the following offences: sexual assault; sexual assault causing bodily harm or with a weapon or third-party threats; and aggravated sexual assault.

No Consent Where Fear of Physical Violence: R v. Ewanchuk

The issue of spousal consent is often raised in cases of sexual abuse, especially where the spouse did not adamantly refuse sexual advances. Under s. 265 of the *Criminal Code*, consent is not given if there is a threat or fear of harm. Further, the decision in *R v. Ewanchuk*, discussed below, affirms that consent is not given where there is a fear of physical violence.

There is no defence of implied consent to sexual assault. The absence of consent is subjective and must be determined by reference to the complainant's subjective internal state of mind towards the touching at the time it occurred. The complainant's statement that she did not consent is a matter of credibility to be weighed in light of all of the evidence including any ambiguous conduct. If the trier of fact accepts the complainant's testimony that she did not consent, no matter how strongly conduct may contradict her claim, the absence of consent is established. The trier of fact need only consider s. 265(3) if the complainant has chosen to participate in sexual activity or her ambiguous conduct or submission has given rise to doubt regarding the absence of consent. There is no consent where the complainant consents because she honestly believes that she will otherwise suffer physical violence. While the plausibility of the alleged fear and any overt expressions of it are relevant in assessing the complainant's credibility that she consented out of fear, the approach is subjective: *R v. Ewanchuk*, [1999], 1 SCR 330, 131 CCC (3d) 481, 22 CR (5th) 1. [*Martin's Annual Criminal Code, 2012*, p. 582]

Emotional/Psychological Abuse and Financial Abuse

The 2009 General Social Survey (GSS) reports that close to 1 in 5 Canadians aged 15 years and older (17 percent) said their current or ex-partner had been emotionally abusive at some point during their relationship (Statistics Canada, 2011).

Results from the survey indicate that emotional abuse and financial abuse often accompany physical and sexual spousal violence. Nearly 7 in 10 respondents who reported being a victim of spousal violence said that they had also experienced emotional abuse.

Victims reported that the most common form of emotional abuse was being put down or called names by their partner to make them feel bad (53 percent). Other forms of emotional abuse included having their partner not wanting them to talk to others, having their partner demand to know where they were at all times, and efforts by their partner to limit their contact with family and friends. See Figure 5.5.

Emotional/Psychological Abuse

Emotional/psychological abuse is behaviour intended to control or instill fear in a person, cause a person to fear for his or her safety, or diminish a person's sense of self-worth. It can take the form of verbal attacks, verbal threats, criticism, social isolation, intimidation, or exploitation to dominate another person. Several examples of these abusive acts are listed below:

- intimidating (may constitute an offence);
- ignoring (silence);
- name-calling;
- yelling;
- being sarcastic or critical;
- degrading a spouse and family;
- inappropriately expressing jealousy;
- lying;

emotional/psychological abuse
behaviour intended to control or instill fear in a person, cause a person to fear for his or her safety, or diminish a person's sense of self-worth

- falsely accusing;
- walking away during a discussion;
- finding and verbalizing faults;
- commenting negatively about spouse's physical appearance;
- ignoring spouse's feelings;
- ridiculing spouse's beliefs;
- insulting or humiliating spouse in public;
- refusing to allow spouse's family and friends to visit;
- threatening to leave spouse;
- punishing children because of anger toward spouse (may constitute an offence);
- bragging to spouse about affairs;
- threatening suicide if spouse leaves;
- threatening to harm spouse (may constitute an offence);
- threatening to destroy property (may constitute an offence);
- threatening to take children if spouse leaves (may constitute an offence);
- engaging in actions intended to terrorize spouse, such as playing with firearms or knives and driving dangerously when the spouse and children are in the car (may constitute an offence);
- forcing spouse to perform degrading acts (may constitute an offence); and
- attempting to exert control over spouse—for example, by depriving spouse of sleep, food, or sex.

Note that many of the above actions and behaviours do not constitute an offence.

Possible Criminal Offences: Emotional/Psychological Abuse

The actions listed below constitute emotional/psychological abuse, and may be an offence under the *Criminal Code*:

- abduction (s. 283),
- assault (ss. 266, 267, and 268),
- sexual assault (ss. 271, 272, and 273),
- uttering threats (s. 264.1),
- intimidation (s. 423),
- criminal harassment (s. 264),
- mischief (s. 430),
- cruelty to animals (s. 446), and
- harassing or indecent phone calls (s. 372).

Financial Abuse

financial abuse
actions that result in financial loss or financial harm to a person

Financial abuse encompasses a wide range of activities that result in financial loss or harm to a person. Financial abuse includes stealing from or defrauding a partner; withholding money; manipulating or exploiting a person for financial gain; denying a person access to financial resources; or preventing a person from working.

Figure 5.5   Victims of Self-Reported Emotional and Financial Abuse, by Sex and Type of Abuse, 2009

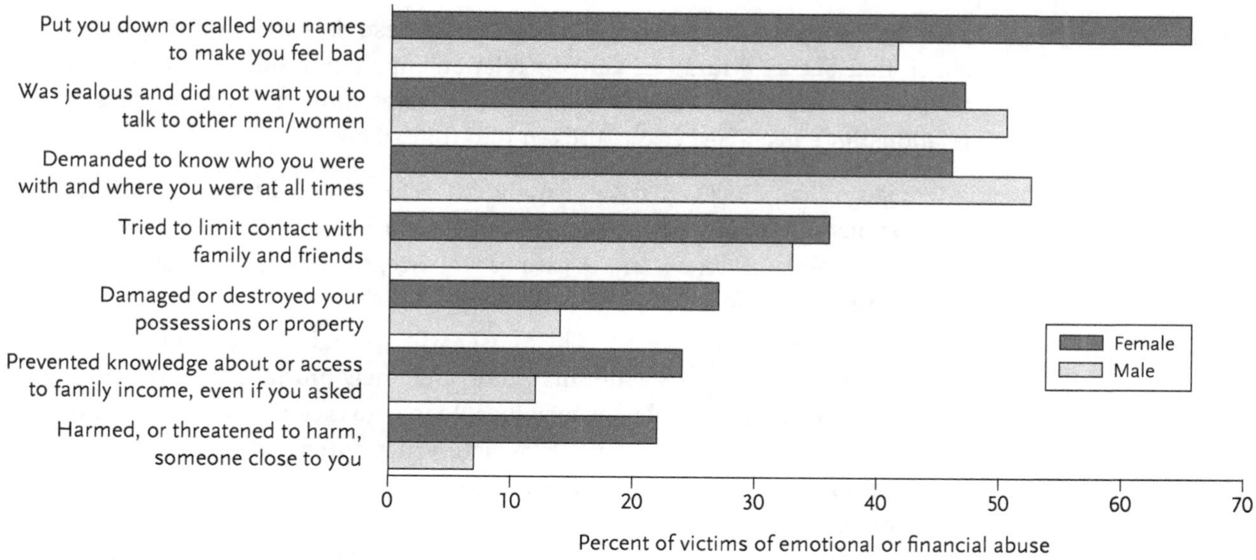

Percent of victims of emotional or financial abuse

Notes: Includes legally married, common-law, same-sex, separated, and divorced spouses. Figures do not add to 100 percent due to multiple responses.

Sources: Statistics Canada, General Social Survey, 2009. Adapted from Statistics Canada (2011).

Possible Criminal Offences: Financial Abuse

The actions listed below constitute financial abuse, and they may constitute an offence under the *Criminal Code*:

- theft (s. 334),
- fraud (s. 380),
- false pretense (s. 362), and
- use, trafficking, or possession of forged document (s. 368).

Other Possible Offences Relating to Spousal Abuse

The following is a list of other possible *Criminal Code* offences applicable to spousal abuse. The list is not exhaustive. The investigating officer must use his or her knowledge and judgment to identify which offences, if any, have been committed and determine an appropriate response:

- use of a firearm during the commission of an offence (s. 85),
- careless use of a firearm (s. 86),
- pointing a firearm (s. 87),
- possession of a weapon for a dangerous purpose (s. 88), and
- dangerous operation of motor vehicles, vessels, and aircraft (s. 249).

These offences are indictable for the purpose of arrest.

The abuse suffered by the victim is often a combination of abusive behaviours. Physical and sexual abuse is likely to be cyclical. Emotional/psychological abuse may be constant. The abusive situation generally follows the pattern described in the cycle of violence, discussed below.

THE CYCLE OF VIOLENCE

The cycle of violence model of spousal abuse describes the continuous cycle of abuse that occurs within an abusive relationship. The model identifies that the abuse will continue unless there is outside intervention or, for some reason, the relationship ends. The cycle is broken into four stages:

- *Stage One: The Occurrence.* An abusive act has been carried out against the spouse. This act may not invoke police action—for example, emotional or psychological abuse. In the case of violence, the police will respond as directed by the solicitor general.

- *Stage Two: Reconciliation.* The abuser will apologize to the victim. He may profess deep regrets about his actions. He may promise to never be abusive again. The abuser may be able to convince the victim that the abuse was the victim's fault. The victim may agree and promise not to provoke the abuser again. The abuser may also deny that any abuse took place or may claim that he doesn't remember committing the abuse.

- *Stage Three: The Calm or Honeymoon Period.* The abuser and the victim put the incident behind them. The abuser has been forgiven for his actions or the victim has accepted responsibility, absolving the abuser of blame. The abuser will not be abusive during this stage. There may be romantic encounters and promises of a better life to come.

- *Stage Four: Tension-Building.* The abuser begins to exhibit signs of abusive behaviour. Stress is building in the abuser's life. There has been no change in the abuser's psyche nor an intervention to address the initial problem of abuse. Whatever reason the abuser had for the previous abusive acts has not been dealt with. The abuser has not suffered any repercussions for his abusive behaviour. Minor incidents such as becoming upset over trivial matters may begin to occur. The tension (stress) begins to increase until the abuser lashes out and commits abuse again. See Figure 5.6.

The cyclical nature of the abusive relationship is generally consistent. The only variable is the time frame between each stage of the cycle. The violence is not always present but is "recycled" throughout the relationship.

Police are usually not involved until the "occurrence" stage of the cycle. It is more likely that police will be called by a complainant other than the victim. In situations where the complainant is the victim, it is likely that she has been abused numerous times before calling police.

Due to the manipulative and controlling behaviours exhibited by the abuser during the reconciliation phase of the cycle, the victim may be convinced that, this time, the abuse will stop. The calm or honeymoon phase reinforces this belief. The abuse will not stop. There has been no change in the fundamental psyche of the abuser. He may feel immediate remorse for perpetrating the abuse, but the feeling will subside.

There needs to be a change in the thought process of the abuser. The abuser must be told that his behaviour is not acceptable. This may be brought about through public condemnation of the abuse using the criminal courts to relay the message. If needed, the courts may require that the abuser obtain professional assistance.

Figure 5.6   The Cycle of Violence

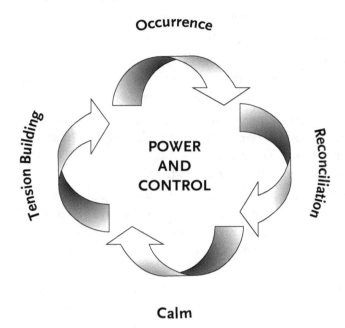

Occurrence

Tension Building

POWER AND CONTROL

Reconciliation

Calm

WHY DO WOMEN STAY?

Officers may find it difficult to understand why a spouse chooses to remain in the home with an abuser. But there are many explanations, ranging from fear of leaving to love for the spouse (Ochberg, 1998):

1. *Fear.* Many women fear that they will suffer even worse abuse if they leave their partner. Their fears are well founded. Women have a heightened risk of spousal homicide after marital separation.

2. *Shame.* Some women who bear the marks of physical abuse cannot bear to be seen in public. They would rather stay in the home than suffer the humiliation.

3. *Lack of resources.* Because of their isolation, battered women often lack a support system. Their family ties and friendships have been destroyed, leaving them psychologically and financially dependent on the abusive partner:

   a. Many women become isolated from friends and families. Either the jealous and possessive abuser isolates them, or the women avoid friends and family to hide the signs of the abuse. The isolation contributes to a sense that there is nowhere to turn.

   b. Many women have at least one dependent child. They stay in the abusive home for fear they will not be able to support the child on their own.

   c. Many women are not employed outside of the home. They fear not being able to support themselves.

   d. Many women have no property that is solely theirs. They fear they will not be able to find adequate housing.

    e. Some women lack access to cash or bank accounts. These women must depend on their spouse for the necessities of life.

    f. Many women fear that if they leave they will lose the children and joint assets.

    g. Many women fear they will face a decline in living standards for themselves and their children if they leave.

4. *Lack of finances/economic reality.* Economic dependence on the abuser is a very real reason for remaining in the relationship. Public assistance programs have been drastically reduced in some jurisdictions, and the programs that remain provide inadequate benefits.

5. *Lack of housing once the victim has to leave a shelter.* Although many women are able to escape immediate danger by fleeing to a shelter, this is not a permanent housing solution. Many women end up returning to their home and to the abuse because there is a real lack of housing available to them.

6. *Children.* Being a single parent can be a strenuous experience in the best of circumstances, and for most battered women, conditions are far from ideal. The enormous responsibility of raising children alone can be overwhelming. Often, the abuser may threaten to take the children away from her if she even attempts to leave.

7. *Feelings of guilt.* Some abused women feel a sense of guilt:

    a. These women may believe that their husbands are sick or need their help. The idea of leaving produces feelings of guilt.

    b. Many battered women feel that the violence is their fault. They may feel that their behaviour somehow provokes the abuser's violence. If they would only be a better wife, they tell themselves, then he would change.

8. *Promises of reform.* The abuser promises that the abuse will never happen again, and the victim wants to believe that this is true.

9. *Sex-role conditioning.* Some women hold beliefs about sex roles that discourage them from leaving:

    a. Some women are taught to be passive and dependent on men.

    b. Some women do not believe that divorce is an appropriate alternative.

    c. Some women believe that a single-parent family is unacceptable. They choose to endure the abuse rather than deprive their children of a father in the home.

    d. The abuser rarely is abusive all the time. During the non-violent phases, he may fulfill the abused woman's dream of romantic love. She believes that he is basically a "good man." She may also rationalize that her abuser is basically good until something bad happens to him and he has to "let off steam."

10. *Religious beliefs.* Religious beliefs reinforce the commitment to marriage. Many faiths hold that the husband is head of the family and that it is a wife's duty to be submissive to him. This may be a powerful reason for staying in a destructive relationship.

11. *The sanctity of marriage.* Clergy and secular counsellors may see only the goal of saving the marriage at all costs, rather than the goal of stopping the violence.

12. *Societal acceptance/reinforcement of violence.* Many people turn a "deaf ear" to spousal abuse and believe that what goes on behind closed doors is a private matter.

13. *Love for spouse.* Most people enter a relationship for love, and that emotion does not simply vanish in the face of difficulty:

    a. After a battering, the abuser often is apologetic. The apologies and promises of reform are often perceived as the end of the abuse.

    b. Many women rationalize their abuser's behaviour by blaming stress, alcohol, problems at work, unemployment, or other factors.

Note that the above reasons for why women stay in abusive homes do not lessen the duty of police to intervene. An officer's duty is to assist the victim in any way legally possible. A victim's decision to stay in the home should have no bearing on an officer's response.

Learning Activity 5.1

The following learning activity will enhance your understanding of the cycle of violence. Identify the following statements as being true or false.

_____ 1. Police are most likely to respond to an occurrence of spousal abuse during the reconciliation stage of the cycle of violence.

_____ 2. During the reconciliation stage of the cycle of violence, the victim may accept responsibility for the abuse.

_____ 3. If the victim accepts the abuser's apology and continues into the calm or honeymoon period of the cycle of violence, future abuse is unlikely to occur.

_____ 4. The stages of the cycle of violence follow a predictable pattern and remain consistent, with the abusive behaviour following each stage of the cycle.

_____ 5. During the occurrence stage of the cycle of violence, police will usually be contacted and will take legal action against the abuser.

_____ 6. Police will intervene in situations of spousal abuse only when the victim agrees to end the relationship with the abuser.

PARENTAL ABDUCTION OF CHILDREN AS A FORM OF PSYCHOLOGICAL ABUSE

In domestic disputes children are often used as pawns. Often, one partner will threaten to take the children away from the partner who has legal custody of them. Using children this way is a form of psychological abuse and may involve the commission of a criminal act, as described in ss. 283 and 282 of the *Criminal Code*.

Abduction: Criminal Code, Section 283

283(1) Every one who, being the parent, guardian, or person having the lawful care or charge of a person under the age of fourteen years, takes, entices away, conceals, detains, receives or harbours that person, whether or not there is a custody order in relation to that person made by a court anywhere in Canada with intent to deprive a parent or guardian, or any other person who has the lawful care or charge of that person, of the possession of that person, is guilty of

(a) an indictable offence and is liable to imprisonment for a term not exceeding ten years; or

(b) an offence punishable on summary conviction.

(2) No proceedings may be commenced under subsection (1) without the consent of the Attorney General or counsel instructed by him for that purpose.

The intent to deprive of possession will exist whenever the taker knows or foresees that his or her actions would be certain or substantially certain to result in the parent being deprived of the ability to exercise control over the child. ... : *R v. Dawson*, [1996] 3 SCR 783, 111 CCC (3d) 1. [*Martin's Annual Criminal Code, 2012*, p. 617]

Abduction in Contravention of Custody Order: Criminal Code, Section 282

282(1) Every one who, being the parent, guardian or person having the lawful care or charge of a person under the age of fourteen years, takes, entices away, conceals, detains, receives or harbours that person, in contravention of the custody provisions of a custody order in relation to that person made by a court anywhere in Canada, with intent to deprive a parent or guardian, or any other person who has the lawful care or charge of that person, of the possession of that person is guilty of

(a) an indictable offence and liable to imprisonment for a term not exceeding ten years; or

(b) an offence punishable on summary conviction.

(2) Where a count charges an offence under subsection (1) and the offence is not proven only because the accused did not believe that there was a valid custody order but the evidence does prove an offence under section 283, the accused may be convicted of an offence under section 283.

The term "detain" in this section means "withhold" and thus the mere fact that a parent keeps a child longer than the prescribed access period would not necessarily constitute a withholding and thus a detention of the child. Further, to prove the requisite intent for the offence, there must be proof that the act was done for

the express purpose of depriving the other parent of possession of the child. ... :
R v. McDougall (1990), 62 CCC (3d) 174, 3 CR (4th) 112, 1 OR (3d) 247 (CA).
[*Martin's Annual Criminal Code, 2012*, pp. 615-616]

Defences for Abduction

Certain statutory and common-law defences are available to the accused in parental abduction cases. Section 284 of the *Criminal Code* allows a defence based on the accused having obtained the permission of the custodial parent. However, s. 286 prohibits abduction based on the consent of the child.

Section 285 allows the defence of necessity (also a common-law defence). The accused must establish that it was necessary to abduct the child in order to protect him or her from imminent harm, or that the accused was escaping imminent danger.

The officer investigating alleged parental abduction of children should try to establish whether a valid custody order is in place. It may be difficult to establish the order's validity because such orders are often amended and the complainant might fail to produce the amended copy. It is always possible that a complainant is trying to use the police to inflict damage on a former partner by maliciously reporting contravention of a custody order. This, of course, does not relieve the officer of his or her duty to ensure the safety and well-being of the child.

SPOUSAL ASSAULT POLICIES, PROCEDURES, AND GUIDELINES

In May 1982, the House of Commons Standing Committee on Health, Welfare and Social Affairs tabled its *Report on Violence in the Family: Wife Battering* (1982). In the report, the committee noted that police were being trained to generally avoid the arrest of a batterer unless he was found actually hitting the victim or unless the victim had suffered injuries that were severe and required a certain number of stitches.

Later that year, on July 8, 1982, the House of Commons unanimously adopted a motion encouraging all Canadian police forces to have their officers regularly lay charges in cases of wife beating.

Four years later, in 1986, the attorneys general and solicitors general of all jurisdictions in Canada issued directives or guidelines to police and Crown prosecutors concerning spousal abuse cases. These directives shared essentially the same objective: ensuring that spousal assaults were treated as a criminal matter. Police policies generally required officers to lay charges where they had reasonable grounds to believe that an assault had taken place. Crown policies generally required the prosecution of cases of spousal assault where sufficient evidence existed to support the prosecution. The victim's wishes were not considered.

The primary objectives of the charging policy for cases of spousal assault are:

- to remove from the victim the responsibility and blame for the decision to lay charges;
- to increase the number of charges that are laid in reported cases of spousal abuse;

- to increase the reporting of incidents where spousal abuse occurred; and
- to reduce the number of incidents of reoffence.

This directive included provisions requiring that police lay charges in incidents of spousal abuse if reasonable grounds existed. Further to this policy, the Ontario *Police Services Act* requires that police services implement procedures regarding domestic violence. Regulation 3/99 of the *Police Services Act* states:

> 12(1) Every chief of police shall develop and maintain procedures on and processes for undertaking and managing general criminal investigations and investigations into ...
>> (d) domestic occurrences; ...

After the development of the directive in 1986, the Ministry of the Solicitor General of Ontario developed the Domestic Violence Justice Strategy (DVJS). It was developed in response to the inquest and 1998 recommendation of the May/Iles coroner's jury. The inquest dealt with the deaths of Randy Iles, who had a history of spousal violence, and his wife's cousin, Arlene May, with whom Iles had an intimate relationship. The DVJS includes a policing component, which sets out guidelines for the handling of domestic violence occurrences. These guidelines, contained in Appendix 5A, supersede previous guidelines.

The DVJS, released in 2000, coordinates police response and the prosecution of domestic violence occurrences where offences have been identified. Not all of these strategies are yet implemented.

The policing component of the DVJS sets out guidelines that may enhance the effectiveness of police response to domestic violence occurrences. Within the content of the strategy is a requirement that police complete a Domestic Violence Supplementary Report. The report is used to identify risk factors for domestic violence and may be used to develop a risk assessment procedure, based on the circumstances of identified situations of domestic violence. This report is also used during a show-cause hearing as evidence to support pre-trial detention.

Note that police services are required to have domestic violence policies in place. Officers should follow the policies and procedures of their respective police services. The following information is general in content.

POLICE INTERVENTION IN SPOUSAL ABUSE SITUATIONS

The following information on police intervention in spousal abuse situations is an overview only. The content is generic and not specific to any police service. Police officers must follow any orders, procedures, and directives of their respective police services when responding to an occurrence.

The information on officer safety is generic and is discussed as one concern of many in situations of spousal abuse.

Entry into a Dwelling

The most practical method of entry without warrant is by invitation. Police may be invited into the dwelling by any person having authority to extend the invitation, usually a resident of the dwelling.

Recognizing that not all persons involved in situations of spousal abuse may be accommodating or in a position to extend an invitation, our legislators and courts have authorized police to enter a dwelling, without warrant, where the safety of possible victims outweighs the individual's right to privacy.

Section 529.3 of the *Criminal Code* authorizes police to enter a dwelling, without warrant, to effect an arrest in exigent circumstances where it would not be practical to obtain a warrant. These circumstances are set out in s. 529.3(2). Exigent circumstances are circumstances in which police have reasonable grounds to believe that

- entry is necessary to prevent immediate death or bodily harm to any person, or
- entry is necessary to prevent immediate loss of evidence.

Authority to Enter Dwelling Without Warrant: Criminal Code, Section 529.3

529.3(1) Without limiting or restricting any power a peace officer may have to enter a dwelling-house under this or any other Act or law, the peace officer may enter the dwelling-house for the purpose of arresting or apprehending a person, without a warrant referred to in section 529 or 529.1 authorizing the entry, if the peace officer has reasonable grounds to believe that the person is present in the dwelling-house, and the conditions for obtaining a warrant under section 529.1 exist but by reason of exigent circumstances it would be impracticable to obtain a warrant.

Exigent Circumstances

(2) For the purposes of subsection (1), exigent circumstances include circumstances in which the peace officer

    (a) has reasonable grounds to suspect that entry into the dwelling-house is necessary to prevent imminent bodily harm or death to any person; or

    (b) has reasonable grounds to believe that evidence relating to the commission of an indictable offence is present in the dwelling-house and that entry into the dwelling-house is necessary to prevent the imminent loss or imminent destruction of the evidence.

Entry Without Warrant: R v. Godoy and R v. Sanderson

Section 529.3 requires that police establish reasonable grounds before entering the dwelling without first having obtained a warrant. This section also refers to arresting or apprehending a person. It does not authorize entry for investigative purposes.

In cases where police have **articulable cause** or reasonable grounds to believe that an occupant of a dwelling is in immediate physical danger, police may immediately enter the dwelling without the need to obtain a warrant. Articulable cause means suspicion based on some discernible fact.

articulable cause
suspicion based on some discernible fact

This premise has been upheld by the Supreme Court of Canada in *R v. Godoy*, [1999] 1 SCR 311, and more recently by the Ontario Court of Appeal in *R v. Sanderson*, 2003 CanLII 20263.

In *Sanderson*, MacPherson JA referred to *R v. Godoy* in his analysis:

Lamer CJC was of the view that the question of police entry into a dwelling house for investigatory purposes needed to be determined "on the circumstances of each case" (at p. 318) and in accordance with the general principles for evaluating the common law powers and duties of police officers as set out in the leading English case, *R v. Waterfield*, [1963] 3 All ER 659 (CCA). Lamer CJC said, at pp. 318-19:

> The accepted test for evaluating the common law powers and duties of the police was set out in *Waterfield*, *supra* (followed by this Court in *R v. Stenning* ... , *Knowlton v. The Queen*, [1974] SCR 443, and *Dedman v. The Queen* ...). If police conduct constitutes a *prima facie* interference with a person's liberty or property, the court must consider two questions: first, does the conduct fall within the general scope of any duty imposed by statute or recognized at common law; and second, does the conduct, albeit within the general scope of such a duty, involve an unjustifiable use of powers associated with the duty.
>
> . . .

In *Godoy*, Lamer CJC stated, at pp. 321-22:

> There is unquestionably a recognized privacy interest that residents have within the sanctity of the home. In *R v. Plant*, 1993 CanLII 70 (SCC), [1993] 3 SCR 281 ... this Court recognized that the values underlying the privacy interest protected by s. 8 of the *Canadian Charter of Rights and Freedoms* are (per Sopinka J at p. 292) "dignity, integrity and autonomy." In *R v. Edwards*, 1996 CanLII 255 (SCC), [1996] 1 SCR 128, at para. 50, Cory J elaborated that one aspect of this privacy interest is "[t]he right to be free from intrusion or interference." However, dignity, integrity and autonomy are the very values engaged in a most immediate and pressing nature by a disconnected 911 call. In such a case, the concern that a person's life or safety might be in danger is enhanced. *Therefore, the interest of the person who seeks assistance by dialing 911 is closer to the core of the values of dignity, integrity and autonomy than the interest of the person who seeks to deny entry to police who arrive in response to the call for help.* [Emphasis added.]

In my view, those observations by Lamer CJC are applicable to this case. The police had been called to assist a distraught young woman in the middle of the night who, after being assaulted twice, had been forced to flee her boyfriend's residence, without any shoes, and wearing only her pajamas.

The Court of Appeal further noted that the powers and duties of a peace officer have been set out in the Ontario *Police Services Act*:

> The powers and duties of a peace officer emanate from common law and statute. The general duty of a peace officer is to preserve the peace as it relates to the protection of life and property: see *R v. Stenning*, [1970] SCR 631 and *R v. Dedman*, 1985 CanLII 41 (SCC), [1985] 2 SCR 2. In Ontario, these common law duties have been codified in ss. 42(1) and (3) of the *Police Services Act*, RSO 1990, c. P.15.

Duties of Police Officer: Police Services Act, Section 42

42(1) The duties of a police officer include,

(a) preserving the peace;

(b) preventing crimes and other offences and providing assistance and encouragement to other persons in their prevention;

(c) assisting victims of crime;

(d) apprehending criminals and other offenders and others who may lawfully be taken into custody;

(e) laying charges and participating in prosecutions;

(f) executing warrants that are to be executed by police officers and performing related duties;

(g) performing the lawful duties that the chief of police assigns;

(h) in the case of a municipal police force and in the case of an agreement under section 10 (agreement for provision of police services by O.P.P.), enforcing municipal by-laws;

(i) completing the prescribed training.

Power to Act Throughout Ontario

(2) A police officer has authority to act as such throughout Ontario.

Powers and Duties of Common Law Constable

(3) A police officer has the powers and duties ascribed to a constable at common law.

The application of these decisions and reference to the duties imposed by the *Police Services Act* substantiate the authority granted to police to enter a dwelling, without warrant, to investigate *if* reasonable grounds or articulable cause exists to believe that a person may be in immediate danger.

Officer Safety

The most important issue in any situation is officer safety. Injured officers cannot be of any assistance to persons in need. The need to ensure the safety of persons involved in a situation of spousal abuse must be weighed with the need to ensure that the officer returns home at the end of each shift.

This chapter previously addressed legal entry into a dwelling. Once the officers are in the residence, there are many safety issues to be addressed including, but not limited to:

- The aggressor is probably still present.
- There has likely been a violent incident. The aggressor may be in a state of high stress.
- The aggressor is in his home, putting the officer(s) at a strategic disadvantage.
- The aggressor knows where weapons, firearms, and avenues of escape are located.
- The victim may also become aggressive with the officer(s).
- There may be other persons present, unknown to the officer(s).

- There may be aggressive pets in the residence that may assist the suspect in a struggle with police. For example, a family dog may attack police to protect its owner.

Attending officers must be in a constant state of alertness when intervening in situations of potential violence. Watch for indicators of violence, found in Chapter 2. Pay particular attention to the non-verbal cues of the involved parties.

If there is reason to believe that firearms are present and reasonable grounds exist to believe that possession of the firearm could pose a danger to the safety of any person, police may search the dwelling without warrant and seize any firearms found.

When officer safety has been reasonably assured, the safety of the victim is the next concern. Note: "reasonably assured"—safety cannot be 100 percent ensured.

Separating the victim from the suspect through the use of verbal commands is preferable to the use of physical force. The victim may come to the aid of the aggressor if there is a physical confrontation. Police may be required to use physical control techniques to restrain the victim.

Ideally, two officers will attend domestic violence occurrences, but this is not always possible. For example, in remote OPP detachments, a back-up officer may not be available. Here, one officer will attend to protect the involved parties. However, the officer must assess the risk to his or her safety and determine whether he or she can safely intervene. In such cases, intervention beyond physical protection of the parties is generally not feasible.

Responding officers should assess the level of danger at each of the following phases of the response:

- *Approach.* Officers must ask themselves: Is backup available? How long until backup arrives? Officers must also watch the area for danger. Is the abuser outside the premises? Does the abuser possess a weapon? During the approach phase, officers must also consider issues of lighting, adapting to the dark, silhouetting, obstacles, and cover and concealment.

- *Entry.* Officers should use care in their positioning at doors. They should pay attention to windows, the roof, and any areas where someone could be concealed. Officers should not enter when directed by voice only; instead, they must wait for someone to come to the door. They must enter legally; observe the premises for dogs, weapons, and other dangers; be alert to the number of persons on the premises; and look for signs of alcohol and drug use (which can diminish inhibitions and increase the potential for violence). Officers should be aware that the potential for violence may increase because of their presence. The abused spouse may feel safer with the police around and lash out at the abuser because she knows that the police will not allow the abuser to retaliate.

- *Inside the premises.* Once inside, the officers should pay attention to the number of persons on the premises and their location. The officers should carefully observe their surroundings, looking for broken articles or other evidence of a struggle, potential weapons, and "blind" areas where someone could jump out at them. They must also check for injuries to any of the parties.

Other Concerns

Does the abused spouse require medical assistance? Does the abused spouse wish to leave the home? Also, the consumption of alcohol or drugs by one or both spouses may mean that the officer will not be able to engage the parties in rational discussion. Obtaining information from an emotionally traumatized victim of abuse or a victim who believes that he or she has caused the abuse can also be difficult.

THE INTERVENTION PROCESS

The following is an example of an intervention in a domestic dispute. It is an example only and may not apply to every situation. The intervening officer should be ready to improvise at any time. The officer can bring the process to a halt at any time by making an arrest.

The following guide is based on the assumption that the officer has safely and legally entered a residence where spousal abuse has been or is taking place. The intervention process has four parts: defusing the potential for violence, interviewing, mediating, and making a referral.

Defusing the Potential for Violence

The officer's first course of action is to defuse the potential for violence:

- The officer must use as little force as possible to intervene. Physical force and verbal commands directed toward one of the spouses may lead the other spouse to believe that the officer is on his or her side and may cause tempers to flare. (The officer also risks losing the image of impartiality that he or she may need to rely on at later stages of the intervention.)

- The spouse expressing the most anger should immediately be addressed. This may be an unpleasant task for the officer, but it will help defuse the situation more quickly.

- The parties must be separated and their eye contact with each other broken. The officer must not lose sight of his or her partner. The separation should be as brief as possible—simply long enough to gather the information required to understand the immediate problem. The parties may become agitated if separated too long, and this can exacerbate the situation. When separating the parties, the officer should avoid taking them to the kitchen (where weapons are available) or the bedroom (an intimate area where the abuse may have occurred). These are commonly recognized as the two most dangerous rooms in a residence for police officers to speak to disputing spouses.

- The officer should allow the parties to vent. Letting them shout or otherwise relieve their stress non-violently may assist at later stages when the parties are together. The officer should respond to their venting in a calm, reassuring manner. This shows them that the officer is in control and may be able to help.

When the threat of violence is no longer high, the parties should be brought back together. There is no particular time frame within which this should happen. The officer must use his or her judgment to determine whether the threat has sufficiently diminished. The parties should be brought within speaking and eye contact distance, but not allowed physical contact at this point, because violence is still a possibility.

The officer should remember that control of the situation, including the flow of conversation, can be influenced by his or her demeanour. Speaking to the parties in a calm, controlled manner will help give them confidence in the officer's abilities.

Interviewing

The potential for violence has been defused and the parties have been brought together to discuss their problem. The officer must remember that he or she is there to resolve a conflict as well as to gather information about a possible offence. This is where interviewing skills are important. The ability to defuse a situation and advise the parties of what resources are available to help them, and at the same time investigate a possible offence, is something that is learned through problem solving and lateral thinking. The following interview techniques may help the officer obtain the information necessary to decide on a course of action:

- *Direct the flow of conversation.* One officer should direct the flow of conversation. Who this will be should be decided before the interviewing starts. A pre-arranged signal will allow other officers at the interview to tell the interviewing officer that a detail is unclear, that further information is required, or that there are discrepancies in the information.

- *Control the conversation.* The interviewing officer should be firm and in control of the conversation, but not to the point of being authoritarian. If the officer treats the parties as suspects or tells them what they should be doing about their problem, they may feel as if they are being interrogated.

- *Place the more aggressive spouse in the most comfortable seat, with his or her hips below the knees if possible.* This makes it more difficult for the spouse to get up quickly, and thus enhances officer safety.

- *Set the rules of the conversation beforehand.* The officer should tell the parties that no interruptions or hostile words or actions will be tolerated.

- *Listen actively during the conversation* (see Chapter 2, under the heading "Effective Listening"). The interviewing officer should speak only when necessary to direct the flow of the conversation or to clarify points that need immediate clarification. Care must be taken not to ask leading questions, which can damage the credibility of a statement that might later be needed as evidence. The interviewing officer must maintain absolute impartiality throughout the entire process.

- *Maintain the focus of the conversation on the problem.* The parties should direct their conversation toward solving their problem. The officers should politely decline to answer if asked for personal opinions.

- *Observe non-verbal communication.* Watching the body language of one spouse when the other is speaking can help an officer gauge the truthfulness of the spoken message or the degree of fear or intimidation that one spouse exerts over the other.

- *If the parties resume arguing, ensure that the situation does not become violent.* If it does, immediate arrest may be necessary.

Here are some tactics that can be used to interrupt an argument that threatens to escalate into violence. Most of these tactics rely on a temporary distraction.

- *Make a surprise request or comment.* Questions such as "May I have a glass of water?" or "What's cooking on the stove?" can focus the parties' attention on the officer.
- *Use eye contact to control the flow of conversation.* Through eye contact, the officer may be able to express displeasure with a spouse's conduct.
- *Consider shouting at the parties.* This tactic may work, but it is risky. They may see the officer's shouting as a loss of control and think that the situation is beyond help.
- *Interject with a summary of the problem.* When each party has had an opportunity to speak, the officer should summarize his or her understanding of the problem. The parties should then be asked whether the officer's understanding is accurate.
- *Do nothing.* Most people will expect the police to intervene. If the officer does nothing, the parties may feel uncomfortable arguing in front of an audience. The officer can use this tactic only if he or she is sure that neither party will assault the other. If the parties are separated, as described above, and properly positioned, they should not be able to make physical contact.

The officer must now decide whether the problem can be adequately addressed by the police or is beyond the scope of police intervention. The officer may decide to mediate if he or she believes that the problem can be satisfactorily handled on the spot.

Mediating

The majority of situations that involve police intervention are not conducive to effective mediation by officers. Estimates suggest that less than 10 percent of problems between spouses can be successfully mediated by police. In most situations, the problem has become entrenched into the lives of the involved people long before police have been called. In the majority of such situations, police are called when the parties are no longer able to deal with the stress of their problems. Police officers generally do not have the time or expertise to successfully mediate such problems.

If the responding officers choose to mediate after interviewing the parties, they may have some success in managing the problem until a referral can be made. Short-term problem management may be considered to be a successful outcome of police mediation. Referral to the appropriate community agency for follow-up discussions may assist the parties in resolving their problem.

However, in the presence of evidence of an assault, mediation is not an appropriate response. If there is evidence of an assault, the suspect must be arrested.

If mediation is deemed appropriate, the following are some suggestions that may enhance the success of the mediation process:

- *Use mediation when arrest is inappropriate or the problem is vague and the parties express an interest in resolving it.* Mediation can also be useful when the parties are still angry. It may not help resolve their problem, but it may give them time to get rid of their anger.
- *Remember that the parties caused the problem, and therefore they are the ones who must solve it.* The police can offer help, but cannot solve the problem. Police must not accept responsibility for the problem. It is possible that the parties will resist police attempts to get them to suggest their own solutions to their problem. There may be a perception that the police will solve the problem. The officer must therefore be persistent in advising the parties that they are responsible for arriving at a solution to their problem.
- *Address the less cooperative spouse.* This can be unpleasant but it is more effective than devoting a lot of attention to the more cooperative spouse.
- *Accept the ideas proposed by the parties.* It is not the officer's place to criticize proposed solutions. The ideas may appear ludicrous, but at least the parties are talking.
- *Settle for partial agreement between the parties.* Total agreement between the parties is not necessary. A degree of compromise is at least a step in the right direction. Even if the officer cannot help the parties find a solution to their problem, they may still feel better because they have had an opportunity to discuss their problem.

Making a Referral

Mediation, whether successful or unsuccessful, is often followed by a referral to a community or social service agency. The officer should do the following before making a referral:

- *Determine whether the parties want assistance.* A forced referral is a waste of effort. The parties must genuinely want assistance if the agency is to be of any use.
- *Inform the parties about the agency's capabilities and limits.* The parties should be told that the agency may be able to help, not that the agency can solve their problem. If possible, the agency's address and telephone number should be provided, as well as information about any costs the parties might incur.
- *Obtain a commitment from the parties that they will seek help.* A commitment by the parties affirming that they will seek help places the onus on them to ensure that they do. It also corrects any perception they may have that it is the officer's responsibility to solve their problem.

When Mediation Is Not Appropriate

Many times, mediation is not the appropriate response. In situations where violent behaviour is evident, arrest is necessary. If arrest of the abuser is the appropriate response, the officer should explain to the abused spouse that removal of the abuser is a temporary reprieve. The abuser will be released from custody in the majority of cases. The abused spouse may use this temporary reprieve to make a decision. The officer should not offer legal advice, only information concerning criminal charges. Requests for an officer's opinion should be met with facts. For example, if the abused spouse asks, "Will he do it again?," an appropriate response is, "In most cases the abuser assaults the spouse again." It can be difficult to avoid becoming emotionally caught up in spousal abuse cases, but if the officer fails to be objective when assessing the situation and gathering evidence, the investigation may be hampered. It can be difficult to be objective and at the same time empathetic, but effective use of interpersonal skills makes this possible.

The abused spouse may not understand the process of charging the abuser. The abused spouse needs to be told that the police lay the charges and that the abused spouse does not have to initiate criminal proceedings. It is also important to mention that s. 4(5) of the *Canada Evidence Act* allows the abused spouse to be a competent witness for the Crown. The officer should explain that the abused spouse may have to testify in court if the abuser pleads not guilty. Sections 4(2) and (4) of the *Canada Evidence Act* identify situations where the wife or husband of a person charged with any of the identified offences is both a competent and compellable witness. The identified offences are offences of violence or offences against children.

The officer must ensure that he or she has gathered the necessary evidence to support the charges. Recording all pertinent information in the officer's notebook and having the abused spouse read and sign the notebook are one form of insurance against later recantation by the abused spouse. Obtaining a formal statement from the abused spouse after the abuser is in police custody is also desirable. Medical reports and photographs of injuries may be useful if the case goes to trial.

If charges are to be pursued, sometimes the abused spouse will contact the officer after a few days have passed to request that charges be withdrawn. This typically happens during the reconciliation stage or honeymoon period mentioned earlier, when the abuser may have said that the abuse will stop and never happen again. The officer will have a difficult and possibly unpopular decision to make. Recalling statistics on spousal abuse and homicide may assist the officer with his or her decision.

If there is sufficient evidence to substantiate a charge, the solicitor general's directive requires the police to lay an information.

If police are attending in situations where one spouse has decided to leave, their role is to ensure the safety of the involved parties. They may advise that the personal property of another may not be taken from the home. They may also recommend that only personal items be immediately removed and that the courts decide the legal entitlement to any joint property. The officers should not assist in the lawful removal of any personal property unless its removal is being interfered with. The officers' assistance should be rendered only to ensure the safety of all parties. The officers should not physically assist in the removal of any property. It may seem like the correct course of action to assist the distressed spouse but it is not. The officers should try to remain impartial and allow the parties to accept responsibility for their decisions. Physical assistance may be interpreted as confirmation of one spouse's decision and, therefore, as a loss of objectivity.

ENHANCING VICTIM SAFETY

The most effective method of stopping the abuser from causing further injury to the victim is to prevent the abuser from having contact with the victim. There are several court orders that can assist with this objective. Some require that both the victim and accused appear before the court. Such orders, although effective, may take some time to obtain.

Restraining orders may be issued by criminal or family courts. The restraining orders issued by family courts are generally issued using s. 46 of the Ontario *Family Law Act* (FLA) or s. 35 of the Ontario *Children's Law Reform Act* (CLRA). Restraining orders made by the criminal courts are issued under the authority of s. 810 of the *Criminal Code*. Police, in most instances, will not be involved in the issuing of orders under the provisions of the *Family Law Act* or the *Children's Law Reform Act*.

In the context of spousal abuse, the orders are intended to protect a person, her children, and her property from harm by such means as removing the abuser from the home, giving the victim exclusive occupation of the home, or placing restrictions on the abuser's communication with the victim.

The issuance of a restraining order does not mean that the person to whom the order is directed has been charged with an offence. The intent of the order is to prevent the commission of an offence against the person seeking protection through the order. This is not to say that a person may not be concurrently charged with an offence, only that the order itself is not a charge. A violation of any of these orders does constitute an offence.

Officers may face potential problems when enforcing restraining orders issued under the *Family Law Act* and the *Children's Law Reform Act*.

The orders are often varied (modified) after the initial issuance. It is difficult for police to determine the validity of these orders if one of the parties contests the content of the order. Police may rely only upon the order produced and verification of the date of issue when determining their course of action.

If there is any doubt about the degree of accuracy of the order presented, police should err on the side of safety and act to protect the persons named in the order. This should be the officer's first priority.

So long as police have reasonable grounds to believe that the order presented is accurate, there should be no legal repercussions for their actions.

In the case of restraining orders issued by the criminal courts under s. 810 of the *Criminal Code*, conditions and modifications to the orders are more readily accessible to police through the Canadian Police Information Centre (CPIC).

The *Family Law Act*, *Children's Law Reform Act*, and the *Criminal Code* contain provisions that allow the victim to apply for orders of protection. The *Family Law Act* also has provisions that allow an order for possession of the matrimonial home. The relevant sections of each of these Acts are discussed below.

FAMILY LAW ACT

Orders Concerning Possession of the Home

One of the many concerns of an abused spouse is housing. The thought of leaving the family home may make the victim reluctant to leave the abusive environment. However, the courts have the ability to grant the victim interim possession of the home through the provisions of the FLA. By informing victims of this possibility, officers may be able to alleviate some of this fear. One of the factors that the court will consider in determining possession of the home is any occurrence of spousal or child abuse.

If spousal or child abuse has occurred, a court might give the applicant the exclusive right to live in the home. This order does not mean that the applicant now owns the home, only that he or she has the right to live there without the abusive partner until other arrangements are made.

Safety issues must be considered when contemplating a request for an interim possession order. The abuser will know where the victim lives. It may be advisable that the victim seek a no-contact order in conjunction with the interim possession order. The most common of these orders is a recognizance (also known as a peace bond), which is issued by a justice under the authority of s. 810 of the *Criminal Code*. This order is discussed below under the heading "*Criminal Code.*"

Order for Possession of Matrimonial Home: Family Law Act, Section 24

24(1) Regardless of the ownership of a matrimonial home and its contents, and despite section 19 (spouse's right of possession), the court may on application, by order,

(a) provide for the delivering up, safekeeping and preservation of the matrimonial home and its contents;

(b) direct that one spouse be given exclusive possession of the matrimonial home or part of it for the period that the court directs and release other property that is a matrimonial home from the application of this Part;

(c) direct a spouse to whom exclusive possession of the matrimonial home is given to make periodic payments to the other spouse;

(d) direct that the contents of the matrimonial home, or any part of them,

(i) remain in the home for the use of the spouse given possession, or

(ii) be removed from the home for the use of a spouse or child;

(e) order a spouse to pay for all or part of the repair and maintenance of the matrimonial home and of other liabilities arising in respect of it, or to make periodic payments to the other spouse for those purposes;

(f) authorize the disposition or encumbrance of a spouse's interest in the matrimonial home, subject to the other spouse's right of exclusive possession as ordered; and

(g) where a false statement is made under subsection 21(3), direct,

(i) the person who made the false statement, or

(ii) a person who knew at the time he or she acquired an interest in the property that the statement was false and afterwards conveyed the interest, to substitute other real property for the matrimonial home, or direct the person to set aside money or security to stand in place of it, subject to any conditions that the court considers appropriate.

Temporary or Interim Order

(2) The court may, on motion, make a temporary or interim order under clause (1)(a), (b), (c), (d) or (e).

Order for Exclusive Possession: Criteria

(3) In determining whether to make an order for exclusive possession, the court shall consider,

(a) the best interests of the children affected;

(b) any existing orders under Part I (Family Property) and any existing support orders;

(c) the financial position of both spouses;

(d) any written agreement between the parties;

(e) the availability of other suitable and affordable accommodation; and

(f) any violence committed by a spouse against the other spouse or the children.

. . .

Offence

(5) A person who contravenes an order for exclusive possession is guilty of an offence and upon conviction is liable,

(a) in the case of a first offence, to a fine of not more than $5,000 or to imprisonment for a term of not more than three months, or to both; and

(b) in the case of a second or subsequent offence, to a fine of not more than $10,000 or to imprisonment for a term of not more than two years, or to both.

Arrest Without Warrant

(6) A police officer may arrest without warrant a person the police officer believes on reasonable and probable grounds to have contravened an order for exclusive possession.

Orders Concerning Harassment

The FLA also includes provisions allowing a spouse, former spouse, or same-sex partner to apply for an interim or final order prohibiting harassment.

"Court," in the sections of the FLA below, means the Ontario Court of Justice, the Family Court of the Superior Court of Justice, or the Superior Court of Justice.

Restraining Order: Family Law Act, Section 46

46(1) On application, the court may make an interim or final restraining order against a person described in subsection (2) if the applicant has reasonable grounds to fear for his or her own safety or for the safety of any child in his or her lawful custody.

Same

(2) A restraining order under subsection (1) may be made against,

(a) a spouse or former spouse of the applicant; or

(b) a person other than a spouse or former spouse of the applicant, if the person is cohabiting with the applicant or has cohabited with the applicant for any period of time.

Provisions of Order

(3) A restraining order made under subsection (1) shall be in the form prescribed by the rules of court and may contain one or more of the following provisions, as the court considers appropriate:

1. Restraining the respondent, in whole or in part, from directly or indirectly contacting or communicating with the applicant or any child in the applicant's lawful custody.

2. Restraining the respondent from coming within a specified distance of one or more locations.

3. Specifying one or more exceptions to the provisions described in paragraphs 1 and 2.

4. Any other provision that the court considers appropriate.

CHILDREN'S LAW REFORM ACT

The *Children's Law Reform Act* contains provisions authorizing restraining orders, orders where a child is unlawfully withheld, and orders to locate and take a child being unlawfully withheld.

Restraining Orders

The purpose of this order is to protect the applicant and his or her children from any person. The order is usually issued to protect a spouse or common-law spouse from the unwanted contact of his or her spouse or common-law spouse.

Restraining Order: Children's Law Reform Act, Section 35

35(1) On application, the court may make an interim or final restraining order against any person if the applicant has reasonable grounds to fear for his or her own safety or for the safety of any child in his or her lawful custody.

Provisions of Order

(2) A restraining order made under subsection (1) shall be in the form prescribed by the rules of court and may contain one or more of the following provisions, as the court considers appropriate:

1. Restraining the respondent, in whole or in part, from directly or indirectly contacting or communicating with the applicant or any child in the applicant's lawful custody.

2. Restraining the respondent from coming within a specified distance of one or more locations.

3. Specifying one or more exceptions to the provisions described in paragraphs 1 and 2.

4. Any other provision that the court considers appropriate.

Transition

(3) This section, as it read immediately before the day section 15 of the *Family Statute Law Amendment Act, 2009* came into force, continues to apply to,

(a) any prosecution or other proceeding begun under this section before that day; and

(b) any order made under this section that was in force immediately before that day.

Orders Where Child Is Unlawfully Withheld

The following two orders contained in the CLRA address situations where a child has not been returned to the parent having legal custody of a child.

Note: This could also be a criminal offence as defined in s. 282 of the *Criminal Code.*

Order Where Child Unlawfully Withheld: Children's Law Reform Act, Section 36(1)

36(1) Where a court is satisfied upon application by a person in whose favour an order has been made for custody of or access to a child that there are reasonable and probable grounds for believing that any person is unlawfully withholding the child from the applicant, the court by order may authorize the applicant or someone on his or her behalf to apprehend the child for the purpose of giving effect to the rights of the applicant to custody or access, as the case may be.

Order to Locate and Take Child: Children's Law Reform Act, Sections 36(2) to (7)

The court may issue an order to locate directed to police officers in the jurisdiction where the child is likely to be located. This order requires the police to locate, apprehend, and deliver the child to the location specified.

The order also authorizes police to enter any place, including a dwelling, by force if necessary, when reasonable grounds have been established to believe that the child is present.

36(2) Where a court is satisfied upon application that there are reasonable and probable grounds for believing,

(a) that any person is unlawfully withholding a child from a person entitled to custody of or access to the child;

(b) that a person who is prohibited by court order or separation agreement from removing a child from Ontario proposes to remove the child or have the child removed from Ontario; or

(c) that a person who is entitled to access to a child proposes to remove the child or to have the child removed from Ontario and that the child is not likely to return,

the court by order may direct a police force, having jurisdiction in any area where it appears to the court that the child may be, to locate, apprehend and deliver the child to the person named in the order.

Application Without Notice

(3) An order may be made under subsection (2) upon an application without notice where the court is satisfied that it is necessary that action be taken without delay.

Duty to Act

(4) The police force directed to act by an order under subsection (2) shall do all things reasonably able to be done to locate, apprehend and deliver the child in accordance with the order.

Entry and Search

(5) For the purpose of locating and apprehending a child in accordance with an order under subsection (2), a member of a police force may enter and search any place where he or she has reasonable and probable grounds for believing that the child may be with such assistance and such force as are reasonable in the circumstances.

Time

(6) An entry or a search referred to in subsection (5) shall be made only between 6 a.m. and 9 p.m. standard time unless the court, in the order, authorizes entry and search at another time.

Expiration of Order

(7) An order made under subsection (2) shall name a date on which it expires, which shall be a date not later than six months after it is made unless the court is satisfied that a longer period of time is necessary in the circumstances.

CRIMINAL CODE

Upon establishing reasonable grounds to believe that an assault has been committed, the officer will lay a criminal charge. If appropriate, the accused will be arrested. If there are grounds to believe that the accused poses a danger to the victim, the officer in charge should seek to have the accused held in custody. The accused must be brought before a justice. The Crown (police) must demonstrate to the court why it is necessary to hold the accused in custody until the trial date. This process is called a show-cause hearing.

The information that may be used to substantiate the opinion of the Crown is found in s. 515(10) of the *Criminal Code*.

Justification for Detention in Custody: Criminal Code, Section 515(10)

515(10) For the purposes of this section, the detention of an accused in custody is justified only on one or more of the following grounds:

(a) where the detention is necessary to ensure his or her attendance in court in order to be dealt with according to law;

(b) where the detention is necessary for the protection or safety of the public, including any victim of or witness to the offence, or any person under the age of 18 years, having regard to all the circumstances including any substantial likelihood that the accused will, if released from custody, commit a criminal offence or interfere with the administration of justice; and

(c) if the detention is necessary to maintain confidence in the administration of justice, having regard to all the circumstances, including

(i) the apparent strength of the prosecution's case,

(ii) the gravity of the offence,

(iii) the circumstances surrounding the commission of the offence, including whether a firearm was used, and

(iv) the fact that the accused is liable, on conviction, for a potentially lengthy term of imprisonment or, in the case of an offence that involves, or whose subject-matter is, a firearm, a minimum punishment of imprisonment for a term of three years or more.

The court has the option of:

- detaining the accused in custody until the trial date, if the Crown shows cause for detention;
- releasing the accused using an undertaking given to a justice or judge, with or without conditions; or
- releasing the accused using a recognizance, with or without sureties, and with or without conditions.

If the officer does not establish reasonable grounds, he or she will not pursue charges. However, if the victim fears harm from the abuser, then the victim, or any person, may appear before a justice to request that a recognizance to keep the peace be issued. This recognizance is commonly referred to as a "peace bond."

A copy of the Information form used to obtain a s. 810 recognizance (peace bond) is reproduced in Figure 5.7. Note: This recognizance is sometimes confused with the above-mentioned recognizance—hence, the often-used term "peace bond."

Sworn testimony must be presented to the justice to establish the belief that harm will occur. When the information is accepted, the justice will issue a summons requiring that the accused appear before the court to answer to the allegations. Note that this is not a criminal proceeding. There is no determination of guilt or innocence of a criminal offence. The sections of the *Criminal Code* dealing with the recognizance and summons are reproduced below.

Figure 5.7   Information

CANADA
PROVINCE OF ONTARIO
PROVINCE DE L'ONTARIO

_____
(Region / *Région*)

Information of / *Dénonciation de :* _____

of / *de* _____

(occupation / *profession*) _____

The informant says that he/she has reasonable grounds to fear and does fear that
Le dénonciateur déclare qu'il a des motifs raisonnables de craindre et craint que

_____, hereinafter called the defendant,
ci-après appelé le défendeur

*will cause personal injury to/damage the property of _____
ne cause des lésions/un préjudice personnels à

on account of a threat made on or about/between* the _____ day of _____ , 20 _____ ,
*à cause d'une menace faite le ou vers le/entre le** *jour de*

at the _____ of _____ , in the words or to the effect following, that is to say,
à(au) *de* *dans les termes qui suivent ou qui peuvent avoir l'effet suivant :*

_____

_____

_____

_____

and therefore prays that the defendant may be ordered to enter into a recognizance, with or without sureties, to keep the peace and be of good behaviour for a period not exceeding twelve months with the conditions fixed by the judge or justice, or committed to prison for a term not exceeding twelve months if he/she fails or refuses to enter into the recognizance, and the informant also says that he/she does not make this complaint from any malice or ill will but merely for the fear, set out aforesaid, pursuant to the *Criminal Code* section 810.

et demande, par conséquent, qu'il soit ordonné au défendeur de contracter un engagement assorti des conditions que le tribunal fixe, avec ou sans caution, de ne pas troubler l'ordre public et d'observer une bonne conduite pour une période maximale de douze mois ou que le défendeur soit envoyé en prison pour une période maximale de douze mois, si le défendeur omet ou refuse de contracter l'engagement. Le dénonciateur déclare de plus qu'il dépose la présente plainte sans malveillance ni intention de nuire, mais seulement à cause des craintes précisées ci-dessus, conformément à l'article 810 du Code criminel.

_____
Informant's Signature / *Signature du dénonciateur*

Sworn before me at the _____ of _____ in the said region
Déclare sous serment devant moi à *de* *dans ladite région*

this _____ day of _____ , 20 _____
le *jour de*

_____
A Justice of the Peace in and for the Province of Ontario
Juge de paix dans et pour la province de l'Ontario

Date				
	Recognizance *Engagement*	☐ Consented to *Accepte*	☐ Opposed *Conteste*	☐ Application withdrawn *Demande retirée*	☐ In absentia *Par défaut*

Finding ☐ Recognizance Ordered   ☐ Recognizance not Ordered
Décision *Engagement ordonné* *Engagement non ordonné*

(1) The Court being satisfied upon the evidence adduced that the informant has reasonable grounds for his/her fears,
La cour étant convaincue, d'après les preuves soumises, que le dénonciateur a des motifs raisonnables d'avoir des craintes,

IT IS ORDERED that the defendant enter into a recognizance with/without* sureties in the amount of $ _____
*IL EST ORDONNÉ que le défendeur contracte un engagement avec/sans** *caution d'un montant de* $

dollars to keep the peace and be of good behaviour for a period of _____ from this day.
dollars pour garder la paix et bien se conduire pour une période de (not exceeding twelve months / *a partir de ce jour.*
ne doit pas dépasser douze mois)

☐ See attached Appendix for other conditions / *Voir annexe ci-jointe pour les autres conditions*

(2) The defendant having failed/refused* to enter into the recognizance, he/she is committed to prison for a term of
*Le défendeur ayant omis/refuse** *de prendre un engagement, il sera incarcéré pour une période de*

_____ from this day, unless he/she sooner enters into a recognizance as aforesaid.
(not exceeding twelve months / *à compter de ce jour, à moins qu'il ne contracte un engagement comme il*
ne doit pas dépasser douze mois) *est précisé ci-dessus.*

_____
Judge or Justice of the Peace in and for the Province of Ontario
Juge ou juge de paix dans et pour la province de l'Ontario

Sec.810 CC – Where Injury or Damage Feared
Article 810 du c. cr. – En cas de crainte de blessures ou dommages

* **Strike out inapplicable /** *Rayer ce qui ne s'applique pas*
CCO-2-810-1 (rev. 10/11) CSD

(The figure is concluded on the next page.)

Figure 5.7 Concluded

CCO-2-810-1 (rev. 10/11) CSD

☐ Language Notification issued / *Langue de notification*
☐ Interpreter / *interprète*

Date	Defendant Appears Adjournment *Le défendeur comparaît Ajournement*	Parties Consent *Consentement des parties*	Bail and/or other action *Cautionnement et/ou autre mesure*	Reason for Adjournment *Raison de l'ajournement*	Fails to Appear *Omet de comparaître*	Bench Warrant *Mandat du tribunal*	*Certificat de défaut*

Return Date of Summons / *Sommation rapportée le*
, yr. / *an*

INFORMATION Against / *DÉNONCIATION visant*

Address / *Adresse*

CHARGE / *ACCUSATION*

Where injury or Damage Feared
code, Sec.810
En cas de crainte de blessures ou dommages
article 810 du c. cr.

☐ Summons / *Sommation* ☐ Warrant / *Mandat* ☐ Arrest / *Arrestation*

☐ Reportable M.V. Offence (H.T.A. 199) / *Infraction V.M. à déclarer (Code de la route 199)*

C.V.O.R. No (Commercial Vehicles Only) / *N° d'immatriculation UVU (véhicules utilitaires seulement)*

Sex / *Sexe*

Birth Date / *Date de naissance*: Day / *Jour* Month / *Mois* Year / *Année*

Was defendant owner? / *Le défendeur était-il propriétaire?* ☐ Yes / *Oui* ☐ No / *Non*

Driver's License Number / *Numéro du permis de conduire*

Plate No. / *Numéro de plaque*

☐ Involves a Collision / *Infraction reliée à un accident*

Informant / *Dénonciateur*

Date Sworn / *Date d'assermentation*

Officer / *Agent de police* No. / *N°*

Div. Dist.

Courtroom / *Salle d'audience*

At / *À(Au)*

Date	Clerk *Greffier*	Reporter *Sténographe*	Prosecutor *Poursuivant*	For Defendant *Pour le défendeur*	Justice's Initia *Initiales du ju*

Where Injury or Damage Feared: Criminal Code, Section 810(1)

810(1) An information may be laid before a justice by or on behalf of any person who fears on reasonable grounds that another person will cause personal injury to him or her or to his or her spouse or common-law partner or child or will damage his or her property.

Duty of Justice

(2) A justice who receives an information under subsection (1) shall cause the parties to appear before him or before a summary conviction court having jurisdiction in the same territorial division.

Adjudication

(3) The justice or the summary conviction court before which the parties appear may, if satisfied by the evidence adduced that the person on whose behalf the information was laid has reasonable grounds for his or her fears,

(a) order that the defendant enter into a recognizance, with or without sureties, to keep the peace and be of good behaviour for any period that does not exceed twelve months, and comply with such other reasonable conditions prescribed in the recognizance, including the conditions set out in subsections (3.1) and (3.2), as the court considers desirable for securing the good conduct of the defendant; or

(b) commit the defendant to prison for a term not exceeding twelve months if he or she fails or refuses to enter into the recognizance.

Conditions

(3.1) Before making an order under subsection (3), the justice or the summary conviction court shall consider whether it is desirable, in the interests of the safety of the defendant or of any other person, to include as a condition of the recognizance that the defendant be prohibited from possessing any firearm, cross-bow, prohibited weapon, restricted weapon, prohibited device, ammunition, prohibited ammunition or explosive substance, or all such things, for any period specified in the recognizance and, where the justice or summary conviction court decides that it is so desirable, the justice or summary conviction court shall add such a condition to the recognizance.

Surrender, etc.

(3.11) Where the justice or summary conviction court adds a condition described in subsection (3.1) to a recognizance order, the justice or summary conviction court shall specify in the order the manner and method by which

(a) the things referred to in that subsection that are in the possession of the accused shall be surrendered, disposed of, detained, stored or dealt with; and

(b) the authorizations, licences and registration certificates held by the person shall be surrendered.

Reasons

(3.12) Where the justice or summary conviction court does not add a condition described in subsection (3.1) to a recognizance order, the justice or summary conviction court shall include in the record a statement of the reasons for not adding the condition.

Idem

(3.2) Before making an order under subsection (3), the justice or the summary conviction court shall consider whether it is desirable, in the interests of the safety of the informant, of the person on whose behalf the information was laid or of that person's spouse or common-law partner or child, as the case may be, to add either or both of the following conditions to the recognizance, namely, a condition

(a) prohibiting the defendant from being at, or within a distance specified in the recognizance from, a place specified in the recognizance where the person on whose behalf the information was laid or that person's spouse or common-law partner or child, as the case may be, is regularly found; and

(b) prohibiting the defendant from communicating, in whole or in part, directly or indirectly, with the person on whose behalf the information was laid or that person's spouse or common-law partner or child, as the case may be.

Breach of Recognizance: Criminal Code, Section 811

811. A person bound by a recognizance under section 83.3, 810, 810.01, 810.1 or 810.2 who commits a breach of the recognizance is guilty of

(a) an indictable offence and liable to imprisonment for a term not exceeding two years; or

(b) an offence punishable on summary conviction.

A breach of a recognizance issued under s. 810 of the *Criminal Code* is a dual procedure offence. For the purpose of arrest, the breach may be treated as an indictable offence. Under s. 495 of the *Criminal Code*, the accused may be arrested without a warrant. The release provisions of ss. 496 through 503 apply, as in any criminal offence.

THE EFFECTIVENESS OF RESTRAINING ORDERS

The 2009 GSS data regarding violations of restraining orders were gathered from self-reporting surveys. The orders were not identified by statute and included restraining orders issued under the provisions of the *Family Law Act*, the *Children's Law Reform Act*, and the *Criminal Code*.

One in ten victims of spousal abuse reported that a restraining order was obtained to prohibit the abuser from contacting the victim. One-third of the victims reported that the abuser violated the terms of the restraining order. Two-thirds of these violations were reported to police. Anecdotally, it appears that restraining orders are not particularly effective.

There has been at least one study examining the effectiveness of restraining orders issued under the provisions of s. 810 of the *Criminal Code*. Dr. George Rigakos conducted a study for the Department of Justice Canada on the effectiveness of s. 810 "peace bonds" after the implementation of Bill C-42. Bill C-42 amended the *Criminal Code* to include the provisions presently governing s. 810.

The study provides at least some empirical evidence to suggest that s. 810 peace bonds are not particularly effective in protecting victims of domestic violence from future incidents of domestic violence.

The following are excerpts from the study's final report (Rigakos, 2003):

> Interviews were conducted by telephone, with eight participants in Ontario, eleven in Nova Scotia, and seven in Manitoba. Interviewees included judges, lawyers, police officers, shelter workers, and justices of the peace. ...
>
> In the province of Nova Scotia, peace bonds are still used in cases of domestic violence, but according to all of the informants, this is becoming an increasingly rare occurrence due to changing enforcement policies. As in Nova Scotia, most Ontario police services, including Hamilton, have adopted a pro-arrest and charge policy in cases of spousal or partner violence. This policy relegates peace bonds to a "last resort" tool that often signifies a criminal justice system failure (i.e., inability to lay a criminal charge) rather than a success. Zero tolerance toward violence against women in the home in Manitoba has resulted in a decreased use of peace bonds in cases of domestic violence. Current policy dictates that the police should arrest or lay charges for assault where reasonable grounds exist. ...
>
> In tracking those issued peace bonds in the Halifax police information system and onto the RCMP's Canadian Police Information Centre (CPIC) criminal record history database, we found that *8.2 per cent of respondents committed an offence while under conditions of a peace bond, and another 8.2 per cent thereafter. In the particular case of domestic violence, the breach rate was 7.1 per cent during and 10.7 per cent after its term of effect* [italics added]. Of those persons issued peace bonds in cases of domestic violence in Winnipeg between 1993-1997, *ten per cent committed an offence while under conditions of the section 810 Recognizance. Another 27.9 per cent committed an offence after the peace bond had lapsed* [italics added]. In Winnipeg, male respondents had a higher likelihood of re-offending than female respondents both during (12.1% vs. 5.1%) and after the peace bond (33.5% vs. 12.7%).
>
> In Nova Scotia, almost all key informants that expressed an opinion believed that sentences for breaching an order were weak and ineffectual. Justice personnel in Hamilton reported that they had not seen any significant change in sentencing practices since Bill C-42 was enacted. Similar sentiments were expressed in Winnipeg.
>
> Without question, the major hurdle for battered women who wished to obtain a peace bond appeared to be operational rather than a problem that could have been ameliorated by amendments to the *Criminal Code*. In all three jurisdictions, obtaining a peace bond by direct application to a Justice of the Peace was reportedly a time-consuming process wrought with delays, making section 810 Recognizance a poor choice for battered women in need of immediate protection.
>
> This difficulty in obtaining, combined with its questionable effectiveness in cases of spousal abuse, relegate the use of a section 810 Recognizance by police to that of a "last option."

As the report shows, a significant percentage of offenders reoffend either while under the conditions of a peace bond or after the peace bond has expired. This suggests that the use of s. 810 is not particularly effective in preventing the recurrence of criminal acts. In light of these findings, and in accordance with the directives and recommendations of the solicitor general (discussed earlier in the chapter), charges should be laid where reasonable grounds exist.

Seizure of Firearms and Other Weapons

If the accused possesses firearms, and there are reasonable grounds to believe that the possession of firearms could pose a danger to the victim, and there is time to appear before a justice to obtain a warrant to seize the firearms, the provisions of s. 117.04(1) of the *Criminal Code* will apply.

Application for Warrant to Search and Seize: Criminal Code, Section 117.04(1)

> 117.04(1) Where, pursuant to an application made by a peace officer with respect to any person, a justice is satisfied by information on oath that there are reasonable grounds to believe that the person possesses a weapon, a prohibited device, ammunition, prohibited ammunition or an explosive substance in a building, receptacle or place and that it is not desirable in the interests of the safety of the person, or of any other person, for the person to possess the weapon, prohibited device, ammunition, prohibited ammunition or explosive substance, the justice may issue a warrant authorizing a peace officer to search the building, receptacle or place and seize any such thing, and any authorization, licence or registration certificate relating to any such thing, that is held by or in the possession of the person.

Note also that if there is an immediate danger to the victim, police may seize the firearms without a warrant.

Search and Seizure Without Warrant: Criminal Code, Section 117.04(2)

> 117.04(2) Where, with respect to any person, a peace officer is satisfied that there are reasonable grounds to believe that it is not desirable, in the interests of the safety of the person or any other person, for the person to possess any weapon, prohibited device, ammunition, prohibited ammunition or explosive substance, the peace officer may, where the grounds for obtaining a warrant under subsection (1) exist but, by reason of a possible danger to the safety of that person or any other person, it would not be practicable to obtain a warrant, search for and seize any such thing, and any authorization, licence or registration certificate relating to any such thing, that is held by or in the possession of the person.

In either situation, police must appear before a justice to determine the disposition of the items seized. If the seizure was made without a warrant, the officer must also establish the reasonable grounds for the seizure as set out in s. 117.04(3) of the *Criminal Code*.

Return to Justice: Criminal Code, Section 117.04(3)

> 117.04(3) A peace officer who executes a warrant referred to in subsection (1) or who conducts a search without a warrant under subsection (2) shall forthwith make a return to the justice who issued the warrant or, if no warrant was issued, to a justice who might otherwise have issued a warrant, showing

(a) in the case of an execution of a warrant, the things or documents, if any, seized and the date of execution of the warrant; and

(b) in the case of a search conducted without a warrant, the grounds on which it was concluded that the peace officer was entitled to conduct the search, and the things or documents, if any, seized.

Authorizations, etc., Revoked: Criminal Code, Section 117.04(4)

117.04(4) Where a peace officer who seizes any thing under subsection (1) or (2) is unable at the time of the seizure to seize an authorization or a licence under which the person from whom the thing was seized may possess the thing and, in the case of a seized firearm, a registration certificate for the firearm, every authorization, licence and registration certificate held by the person is, as at the time of the seizure, revoked.

If the suspect does not currently possess weapons and police want to prevent the suspect from obtaining them in the future, police can apply to a provincial court judge for an order under s. 111 of the *Criminal Code*, below. This order prohibits the person from possessing weapons where the court has reasonable grounds to believe that it is not in the interests of public safety for the person to possess weapons. This prohibition may last up to five years.

Application for Prohibition Order: Criminal Code, Section 111(1)

111(1) A peace officer, firearms officer or chief firearms officer may apply to a provincial court judge for an order prohibiting a person from possessing any firearm, cross-bow, prohibited weapon, restricted weapon, prohibited device, ammunition, prohibited ammunition or explosive substance, or all such things, where the peace officer, firearms officer or chief firearms officer believes on reasonable grounds that it is not desirable in the interests of the safety of the person against whom the order is sought or of any other person that the person against whom the order is sought should possess any such thing.

Police may consider an application under s. 117.011(1) of the *Criminal Code*, below. When persons are prohibited from possessing weapons, this provision is designed to limit their access to weapons belonging to someone with whom they live or associate.

Application for Order: Criminal Code, Section 117.011(1)

117.011(1) A peace officer, firearms officer or chief firearms officer may apply to a provincial court judge for an order under this section where the peace officer, firearms officer or chief firearms officer believes on reasonable grounds that

(a) the person against whom the order is sought cohabits with, or is an associate of, another person who is prohibited by any order made under this Act or any other Act of Parliament from possessing any firearm, cross-bow, prohibited weapon, restricted weapon, prohibited device, ammunition, prohibited ammunition or explosive substance, or all such things; and

(b) the other person would or might have access to any such thing that is in the possession of the person against whom the order is sought.

In situations where the accused has been arrested and there is no immediate danger to the victim, police may ask that the accused be prohibited from possessing firearms as a condition of release. A justice, within the authority of s. 515(4.1) of the *Criminal Code*, may prohibit the accused from possessing firearms in situations where a violent offence has been committed.

Condition Prohibiting Possession of Firearms, etc.: Criminal Code, Section 515(4.1)

515(4.1) When making an order under subsection (2), in the case of an accused who is charged with

(a) an offence in the commission of which violence against a person was used, threatened or attempted,

(a.1) a terrorism offence,

(b) an offence under section 264 (criminal harassment),

(b.1) an offence under section 423.1 (intimidation of a justice system participant),

(c) an offence relating to the contravention of subsection 5(3) or (4), 6(3) or 7(2) of the *Controlled Drugs and Substances Act*,

(d) an offence that involves, or the subject-matter of which is, a firearm, a cross-bow, a prohibited weapon, a restricted weapon, a prohibited device, ammunition, prohibited ammunition or an explosive substance, or

(e) an offence under subsection 20(1) of the *Security of Information Act*, or an offence under subsection 21(1) or 22(1) or section 23 of that Act that is committed in relation to an offence under subsection 20(1) of that Act,

the justice shall add to the order a condition prohibiting the accused from possessing a firearm, cross-bow, prohibited weapon, restricted weapon, prohibited device, ammunition, prohibited ammunition or explosive substance, or all those things, until the accused is dealt with according to law unless the justice considers that such a condition is not required in the interests of the safety of the accused or the safety and security of a victim of the offence or of any other person.

COURT PROCESS

Although the victim may be initially relieved to know that police are required to lay charges, the prospect of facing their assailant in court may be daunting for some. This fear often manifests itself through the victim's hesitancy to testify. As the case moves into prosecution, the onus for successful prosecution is put on the shoulders of the victim. Because the courts consistently use a "best evidence rule," which requires that the most persuasive evidence available be put forward, most trials have relied on the victim's testimony. This practice has resulted in situations where, as a result of the pressures, threats, fear, and intimidation experienced by victims, many have refused to testify or have recanted their original story. Thus, although more assault charges have been laid by police since the introduction of provincial directives regarding domestic violence, increasing numbers of cases are being withdrawn by the Crown.

The Domestic Violence Court Program

To address the specific problems of prosecuting domestic violence cases, the Domestic Violence Court program was introduced. The program also allows the victim to have more input into the court's disposition of the offence.

This project first started in Toronto with the testing of two different specialized courts in an attempt to create a more effective criminal justice system response to spousal abuse. These courts have four objectives:

- to intervene early in domestic violence situations;
- to provide better support to victims throughout the criminal justice process;
- to more effectively prosecute domestic violence cases; and
- to hold offenders accountable for their behaviour.

There are two levels of court: a "plea court" and a criminal court. Which court will be used depends on the severity of the offence. Note: The term "levels" is for the purpose of this discussion only. It is not a legal term.

Level 1: The Plea Court

The plea court may be used where the offender and the victim wish to reconcile. A judge hears the domestic violence case in plea court if four conditions are met:

1. it is the first time that the accused has been charged with a domestic violence offence;
2. there are no visible injuries to the victim;
3. weapons were not used during the offence; and
4. the victim agrees to the court's disposition of mandatory treatment for the offender.

In the plea court process, a specialized Crown prosecutor does the screening. The Victim/Witness Assistance program consults with the victim and provides information and referrals to community resources. The accused then pleads guilty and is ordered to attend a Partner Assault Response (PAR) program. At the conclusion of the PAR program, a report is provided to the Crown. If satisfactory, that report can be considered as a mitigating factor in sentencing. But, the Crown usually recommends a conditional discharge. If the accused does not successfully complete the program, the criminal process is resumed.

Level 2: The Criminal Court

Level 2 is a regular criminal court. This court is used when any of the four conditions for participation in level 1 court have not been met, or when the offender did not satisfactorily complete the PAR program.

Expanding the Domestic Violence Court Process

Ontario has made a commitment to expand the Domestic Violence Court program. As of January 2005, 16 court jurisdictions had instituted specialized domestic violence processes. The provincial government has committed that all 54 court jurisdictions will have either a specialized court with designated staff to handle domestic violence cases or a regular court with a specialized process for doing so. All jurisdictions, regardless of size, will have a specialized process with the following components:

- a Domestic Violence Court Advisory Committee to support the work of the specialized domestic violence court process;
- interpreters to help non-English and non-French speakers communicate with police, Crown prosecutors, and victim support staff;
- enhanced investigative procedures for police (including use of a risk indicator tool, currently under development and initial testing);
- designated victim/witness assistance staff specially trained to give support and information to victims;
- designated Crown prosecutors specially trained in prosecuting domestic violence cases, to produce consistency and continuity;
- specialized counselling programs for abusive partners; and
- specialized processing to expedite cases and ensure coordination of services.

At medium-sized and small rural sites, these components may be implemented differently based on the volume of cases and the size of the jurisdiction. For example, rather than designated staff or a dedicated courtroom, specially trained staff may be used.

Learning Activity 5.2

After reading the following scenario, determine what you would do.

You are a police officer responding to a complaint of a disturbance at 100 Hutch Avenue. The disturbance involves shouting and swearing coming from Apartment 301. The complaint came from 100 Hutch Avenue, Apartment 303.

When you enter the hallway of the third floor, shouting can be heard. The shouting is coming from Apartment 301. It is quite loud.

You ring the doorbell of Apartment 301. A young male, later identified as Rodney Todd, 11 years old, answers the door. You can hear shouting from the back area of the apartment.

You ask Rodney about the shouting.

He tells you that his father, Alphred Todd, is shouting at his mother, Jane Todd, because dinner was too hot when she served it.

You ask if you can come in.

Rodney replies, "Of course you may come in. Any male in authority is welcome in our home. The female with you is also welcome as a guest in my father's house.

Perhaps you can straighten out Jane's thinking. My father and Jane are in the kitchen. My father is quite upset. He had to wait for his dinner to cool. Jane knows that the males in this family eat at 1725 each day. Not at 1727!"

You enter the apartment and proceed to the kitchen area.

You see a male, identified as Alphred Todd, sitting at a table in the kitchen.

A female, identified as Jane Todd, is sitting on a stool in the corner of the room. She is looking at the floor. She has no obvious injuries.

Alphred Todd speaks to you.

"Why are you here? You are welcome, of course, but why are you here? Is the female with you a police officer? Of course she is. That is one of the main problems in society today; females don't know their place. Nonetheless, she is an invited guest in my home."

You tell him that you received a complaint of a disturbance at this address.

Alphred appears to be annoyed and replies, "There is no disturbance. I was merely disciplining my wife. She did not fulfill her duties properly. Such problems must be immediately addressed."

Jane begins to speak.

Rodney immediately interrupts her, saying, "Jane. You know that you may speak only when given permission by the head of the house. Don't embarrass my father with your rude behaviour."

Alphred thanks his son for "looking after" Jane's outburst.

He then speaks to Jane. "Apologize to the officer. Your behaviour and demeanour are unacceptable!"

Jane continues to look at the floor and states, "I am sorry for speaking without permission. Please forgive me."

Alphred tells Jane, "I accept your apology. Don't let it happen again."

You ask Jane if you may speak with her alone.

Alphred replies, "You may."

Alphred tells Rodney that they are to leave the room and go to the entertainment room to watch football. As he is leaving he tells Jane: "When you are finished with the police officer, cook some steaks for myself and Rodney. Mine rare. Rodney will have his medium rare. He is not yet ready for rare steak. You may eat the ill-prepared meal you served."

Alphred and Rodney then leave the room.

You speak with Jane.

You ask her whether she is being abused.

She replies, "No. I have a good life. I sometimes mess up and do not fulfill my duties properly. I deserve to be disciplined when I mess up."

You ask her to explain "disciplined."

Jane replies, "Alphred will sometimes shout at me and tell me where I went wrong. If Rodney is home from school, he will tell me if I am doing anything that would displease Alphred. I really appreciate his help. Sometimes I don't know that what I am doing is wrong. He is a good young man. He will grow up to be just like Alphred: a good, strong man. I am so lucky to have them guide my life."

You ask Jane about any physical violence toward her.

She replies, "Never! Alphred says that violence is for intellectually weak persons who cannot control themselves. He says that the civilized way to control a household, and the world, is for the more intelligent men of the world to be appointed as the societal leaders for life. Elections only allow the less intelligent the opportunity to elect one of their own. The less intelligent men could be taught to handle the day-to-day operations of the workplace and to teach the women how they should behave and to continually reinforce the teachings of the intellectual elite. When everyone follows Alphred's teachings, there will no longer be any violence in the world. Alphred is such an intelligent man!"

You ask Jane whether she ever feels physically threatened by Alphred or Rodney.

She replies, "Alphred would never harm a person in anger. He only teaches me how to behave correctly. Rodney is trying to follow Alphred's example."

You ask Jane whether she wants to leave the residence and seek assistance to deal with her abusive situation.

She replies, "I am not being abused! I have a great life!"

What will you do in this situation? Be sure to consider legislative requirements and authorities.

CRIMINAL HARASSMENT

criminal harassment
conduct that makes a person
fear for his or her safety or
for the safety of someone he
or she knows; also called
stalking

Criminal harassment, also known as stalking, may be perpetrated by any person. Although there is no definite or conclusive indicator of the personality that will engage in harassing behaviours, there are some commonalities among stalkers. They may:

- have a history of violence against the victim,
- have a history of violence against persons other than the victim,
- possess or have access to weapons,
- exhibit threatening behaviour,
- exhibit destructive behaviour,
- have a substance abuse problem,
- have been raised in an abusive family environment, or
- be a loner.

Criminal harassment can include a number of different behaviours intended to control and frighten the person being stalked, including:

- making repeated telephone calls to the victim, or repeatedly sending letters or emails;
- sending unwanted gifts (flowers, candy, etc.) to the victim;
- showing up uninvited at the work or home of the victim;
- stealing the victim's mail;
- following, watching, or tracking the victim;

- threatening harm to the victim or the victim's family, friends, or pets;
- harassing the victim's employer, colleagues, or family;
- vandalizing the victim's car or home;
- harming the victim's pets; or
- assaulting the victim physically or sexually.

Reports of criminal harassment should be taken seriously. The stalker has shown by his or her actions that he or she intends to intimidate, harass, or in some instances harm the person being stalked or the person's family or property. In cases of spousal abuse, the stalker has already shown a propensity toward violence. Stalking behaviour should be treated as a serious threat to the well-being of the spouse. The abuser is expressing contempt for the spouse through premeditated criminal behaviour. He or she has constructed a plan of intimidation. Relevant sections of the *Criminal Code* concerning criminal harassment are set out below.

Criminal Harassment: Criminal Code, Section 264

264(1) No person shall, without lawful authority and knowing that another person is harassed or recklessly as to whether the other person is harassed, engage in conduct referred to in subsection (2) that causes that other person reasonably, in all the circumstances, to fear for their safety or the safety of anyone known to them.

Prohibited Conduct

(2) The conduct mentioned in subsection (1) consists of

(a) repeatedly following from place to place the other person or anyone known to them;

(b) repeatedly communicating with, either directly or indirectly, the other person or anyone known to them;

(c) besetting or watching the dwelling-house, or place where the other person, or anyone known to them, resides, works, carries on business or happens to be; or

(d) engaging in threatening conduct directed at the other person or any member of their family.

Punishment

(3) Every person who contravenes this section is guilty of

(a) an indictable offence and is liable to imprisonment for a term not exceeding ten years; or

(b) an offence punishable on summary conviction.

Criminal harassment may be considered to be an indictable offence for the purpose of arrest.

Statistics on Criminal Harassment in Canada

The most current Statistics Canada police and court data relating to criminal harassment are given below:

Table 5.4 Criminal Harassment, by Province and Territory, 2008 and 2009

Province or territory	2008		2009		Percent change in rate from 2008 to 2009
	Number	Rate	Number	Rate	
Newfoundland and Labrador	197	39	226	44	14
Prince Edward Island	99	71	116	82	16
Nova Scotia	441	47	488	52	10
New Brunswick	596	80	603	80	1
Quebec	4,220	54	4,366	56	2
Ontario	8,711	67	9,372	72	6
Manitoba	326	27	267	22	−19
Saskatchewan	569	56	530	51	−8
Alberta	1,649	46	1,819	49	8
British Columbia	1,650	38	2,127	48	27
Yukon	24	72	13	39	−47
Northwest Territories	47	108	55	127	18
Nunavut	21	66	25	78	17
Canada	18,550	56	20,007	59	7

Notes: Counts are based upon the most serious violation in the incident. One incident may involve multiple violations. Rates are calculated on the basis of 100,000 population. Percent change based on unrounded rates.

Source: Statistics Canada, Canadian Centre for Justice Statistics, Uniform Crime Reporting Survey. Adapted from Milligan (2011).

Canadian police services reported just over 20,000 incidents of criminal harassment in 2009 (Milligan, 2011). Table 5.4 compares incidents of criminal harassment in Canada in 2008 and 2009.

Most often, women are the victims of criminal harassment. In 2009, just over three-quarters of all victims (76 percent) of criminal harassment were women. In comparison, women made up roughly half (51 percent) of the victims of overall violent crime.

The relationship of the accused harasser to the victim tends to differ depending on the victim's sex (see Figure 5.8). In 2009, women were most likely to be criminally harassed by a former intimate partner (45 percent of cases), while men were most likely to be harassed by a casual acquaintance (37 percent of cases).

Weapons, such as firearms or knives, were rarely used in incidents of criminal harassment, as is the case in most violent crimes. In 2009, only 3 percent of incidents involved the use of a weapon; more common was the use of threats (38 percent) and physical force (12 percent). However, almost half the time, none of these methods were used: 48 percent of all incidents of criminal harassment did not involve weapons, threats, or physical force.

Notably, 27 percent of incidents of criminal harassment involved other offences. The most common other offence was uttering threats.

Figure 5.8 Criminal Harassment, by Relationship of Accused to Victim, Canada, 2009

Relationship of accused to victim

Notes:
[a] Includes spouse (married or common-law), boyfriend, girlfriend, and other intimate relationship.
[b] Includes separated spouse (married or common-law), divorced spouse, ex-boyfriend, or ex-girlfriend.
[c] Includes non-spousal family members related by blood, marriage or adoption (for example, parents, siblings, extended family members).
[d] Includes acquaintances and authority figures.

Sources: Statistics Canada, Canadian Centre for Justice Statistics, Incident-Based Uniform Crime Reporting Survey. Adapted from Milligan (2011).

Types of Stalkers

Most stalkers fit into one of three broad categories: intimate partner stalkers, delusional stalkers, and vengeful stalkers (O'Connor, 2005).

Intimate Partner Stalkers

The intimate partner stalker is usually the person who "can't let go." About 50 percent of all stalkers fall into this category. Most of these stalkers have been in some form of relationship with the victim. The contact may have been minimal, such as a blind date, but more commonly the contact involved a prolonged dating relationship, common-law union, or marriage. These are people (usually male) who refuse to believe that a relationship has really ended. Often the victim feels sorry for them and unwittingly encourages them by trying to "let them down easy," or agreeing to talk "just one more time." This type of stalker mounts a campaign of harassment, intimidation, and psychological terror. In many respects, intimate partner stalking is an extension of domestic violence and relates to a desire to control a former partner.

Delusional Stalkers

Delusional stalkers frequently have little, if any, contact with their victims. They may be casual acquaintances (27.9 percent) or unknown to the victim (8 percent) (Statistics Canada, 2000). They may have a serious mental illness such as schizophrenia.

Delusional stalkers hold tight to some false belief that keeps them tied to their victims.

The stalker may have come from a physically or emotionally abusive family background. Delusional stalkers are usually unmarried and socially immature loners, unable to establish or sustain close relationships with others. They rarely date and have had few, if any, sexual relationships. Because they are both threatened by and yearn for closeness, they often pick victims who are unattainable—for example, a married woman, a clergyman, a therapist, a doctor, or a teacher. Those in the helping professions are particularly vulnerable to delusional stalkers. Any kindness may be converted into a delusion of intimacy.

Two forms of delusions experienced by this type of stalker are erotomania and love obsessional delusions. In erotomania stalking incidents, the majority of stalkers are male. The stalker's delusional belief is that the victim loves him and is having a relationship with him, although they might never have met. The person about whom this conviction is held is usually of a higher status than the stalker. The victim could be his supervisor at work, his child's pediatrician, his church minister, or the police officer who stopped him for a traffic violation but did not charge him. Sometimes it can be a complete stranger.

The love obsessional stalkers, on the other hand, can be obsessed in their love without possessing the belief that the victim loves them. These stalkers know they are not having a relationship with their victim, but firmly believe that if they pursue him or her hard enough and long enough, he or she will come to love them in return.

Vengeful Stalkers

Vengeful stalkers are angry with their victims over something, real or imagined. Politicians, for example, are harassed by many of these types of stalkers, who become angry over, say, some piece of legislation that the politician supports. Disgruntled ex-employees may stalk their former bosses, co-workers, or both. Some vengeful stalkers are psychopaths; others are delusional (and often paranoid), and all are convinced that they are the true victims. They stalk to "get even." In general, the less of a relationship that actually existed prior to the stalking, the more mentally disturbed the stalker.

Cyber-Stalking and Online Harassment

Criminal harassment can be conducted through the use of a computer or other electronic device. Not all such complaints of cyber-stalking fall within the definition of criminal harassment. For example, "cyber-stalking" or "online harassment" may refer to the following actions (Department of Justice Canada, 2004):

- direct communication with the victim through email;
- publication of offensive or threatening information about the victim on the Internet; and
- unauthorized use or control of the victim's computer, or sabotage of the victim's computer.

Cyber-stalking can include delivering threatening or harassing messages through one or more of the following online mediums:

- email,
- text messages sent via an electronic device such as a cellphone,
- chat rooms,
- message boards,
- newsgroups, and
- forums.

Cyber-stalking can also take other forms (Department of Justice Canada, 2004):

- sending the victim inappropriate electronic greeting cards;
- posting personal ads in the victim's name;
- making websites that contain threatening or harassing messages to the victim or that contain provocative or pornographic photographs that are related in some way to the victim;
- attempting to infect the victim's computer with a virus;
- using spyware to track websites that the victim visits, or recording keystrokes that the victim makes;
- sending harassing messages to the victim's employer, co-workers, fellow students, teachers, friends, customers, family, or place of worship; or
- sending harassing messages that have been forged in the victim's name to others.

In some situations, criminal harassment charges may be appropriate. Depending on the activity involved, *Criminal Code* charges under s. 342.1 (unauthorized use of a computer), s. 342.2 (possession of device to obtain computer service), and s. 430(1.1) (mischief in relation to data) should also be considered.

Harassing and Indecent Telephone Calls

Some stalkers use the telephone in their attempts to maintain control over their victims. Calling and then hanging up, making repeated calls, and making indecent calls can be criminal offences under ss. 372(2) and 372(3) of the *Criminal Code*.

Indecent Telephone Calls: Criminal Code, Section 372(2)

372(2) Every one who, with intent to alarm or annoy any person, makes any indecent telephone call to that person is guilty of an offence punishable on summary conviction.

Harassing Telephone Calls: Criminal Code, Section 372(3)

372(3) Every one who, without lawful excuse and with intent to harass any person, makes or causes to be made repeated telephone calls to that person is guilty of an offence punishable on summary conviction.

summary conviction offence
a crime that is less serious than an indictable offence and that is tried without a jury or preliminary hearing

indictable offence
a crime that is more serious than a summary conviction offence, that carries heavier penalties, and that may be tried by a judge or a judge and jury

Because indecent and harassing telephone calls are both **summary conviction offences**, the police must find the suspect committing the offence before they can arrest, according to s. 495 at the *Criminal Code*. The frequency and content of the telephone calls determine what action the police will take. Calls can be traced, although this may be more difficult if the suspect is calling from a cellphone or pay phone. The victim should be asked to keep a record of calls received. Alternatively, the victim can change his or her telephone number or use a call display feature to screen calls. Any call that meets the definition of the **indictable offence** of threatening in s. 264.1 of the *Criminal Code* may provide a basis for arrest if there is proof of the identity of the person who conveyed the message or caused it to be conveyed.

Intervention in Cases of Criminal Harassment

When deciding on a method of intervention, police must remember that the safety of the victim is paramount at all times and is a higher priority than evidence gathering (Department of Justice Canada, 2004). To determine the appropriate level or type of intervention in a given case, a threat assessment or risk assessment is first made.

A threat assessment assesses the risk of violence that the suspect poses to the victim and assesses the potential impact of the type of intervention on the victim's safety.

A risk assessment evaluates individuals to determine the risk that they will commit violent acts. The aim of research in this area is to develop intervention strategies to reduce this risk. Risk assessments are contextual and only relevant for a specific period of time. The absence of violence or threats of violent behaviour does not mean that violence will not occur in the future. Note that the terms "threat assessment" and "risk assessment" are often used interchangeably.

The assessment should include the following information: the type of stalker, and the history or nature of the relationship between the stalker and the victim (for example, a history that includes acts of violence, threats, and damage to property). A history of violent behaviour is a strong indicator of the stalker's potential for future violence. Threat assessments should consider all available evidence, as well as all records of police action.

After the threat assessment has been completed, an investigation and case management strategy should be devised and put into action. Several such strategies are discussed below. Note that they can be used alone or in combination, depending on the specifics of the case.

(The Department of Justice Canada is currently supporting the development of a revised risk assessment tool, which will be piloted at three sites. This revised tool is designed to assess risk for spousal assault in criminal and civil justice settings, but it will likely also provide useful information for criminal harassment cases involving former domestic relationships.)

Intervention Options

Police Warning

A police warning may consist of a face-to-face meeting between the stalker and police, and/or a written warning (Department of Justice Canada, 2004). This type of intervention should be carried out only after police have considered all the facts and evidence, and only at the appropriate stage of the investigation. Warning the alleged offender serves two purposes: it shows the victim that the police have taken their complaint seriously, and it informs the offender that his or her behaviour is unacceptable. A warning also gives the offender an opportunity to explain his or her conduct at an early stage, so that police can make well-informed case management decisions in the future.

Stalkers are often deterred by a face-to-face meeting with police in which the police lay out the consequences of continuing the behaviour. In a small number of cases, particularly those involving mentally disordered stalkers, the best option may be to not take action and instead monitor the situation. In these cases, if the victim or police respond, the stalker may escalate his or her stalking behaviour.

When police are monitoring a situation, they must consider consulting mental health professionals, who may provide additional information and insight into possible behaviours that may emerge in the mentally ill person. Note that with this option, police are not ignoring the situation. Instead, they have simply decided that a warning may not be the best option.

On the other hand, if a warning is to be given, the suspect should be cautioned before the interview and the interview documented so that the information is accessible to future investigators, should the warning prove to be ineffective. The interview can provide information about the suspect's thought processes and behaviour patterns. It can also provide admissions or corroboration. The most common psychological defences of a stalker involve minimization, denial, and projection of blame onto the victim. Investigators should keep this in mind as they develop interrogation themes and attempt to establish a rapport with the offender.

Whenever possible, the warnings should be written. Police must carefully consider the content of the warning. A written warning establishes boundaries for the offender and provides a record and evidence of the exact wording used to warn the accused. The written warning, although not legally binding, could be used to establish that the accused understood that the victim was harassed, or that the accused was reckless or wilfully blind to this fact.

Peace Bonds and Civil Protection Orders

These no-contact orders were discussed earlier in this chapter. In situations of criminal harassment, these orders may be an effective deterrent.

The seeking of peace bonds and civil protection orders as a method of intervention should be considered when the victim fears for his or her safety and the suspect poses a risk of physical violence, but there is insufficient evidence to charge the suspect. Peace bonds and civil protection orders are not substitutes for criminal charges. Charges should be laid where there is evidence to support the charges.

Seizure of Firearms

Police may choose to intervene by seeking an order to seize any firearms that the harasser owns. With the safety of the victim being paramount, police should consider applying the same firearms prohibition and seizure provisions of the *Criminal Code* that are applicable in spousal abuse situations:

- s. 117.04,
- s. 111,
- s. 117.011, and
- s. 515(4.1) (if suspect is arrested).

Arrest and Charges

A strong and consistent response to criminal harassment requires that all allegations of criminal harassment be taken seriously. If there are reasonable and probable grounds to believe that the suspect has committed the offence of criminal harassment, arrest and charges are applicable.

Where one or more of the incidents giving rise to the complaint of criminal harassment can be construed as a single criminal offence other than criminal harassment, police should consider laying both the separate charge and the inclusive count of criminal harassment. Examples of other criminal offences under the *Criminal Code* include, but are not limited to, the following:

- intimidation (s. 423),
- uttering threats (s. 264.1),
- mischief (s. 430),
- indecent or harassing telephone calls (s. 372),
- trespassing at night (s. 177),
- assault (s. 265),
- sexual assault (s. 271),
- failure to comply with a condition of an undertaking or a recognizance (s. 145(3)),
- breach of a recognizance (s. 811), and
- failure to comply with a probation order (s. 733.1).

An accused who has outstanding charges against him or her and has contravened, or was about to contravene, his or her form of release should be arrested for criminal harassment, and the provisions of s. 524(2) of the *Criminal Code* should also be applied.

Arrest of Accused Without Warrant: Criminal Code, Section 524(2)

524(2) Notwithstanding anything in this Act, a peace officer who believes on reasonable grounds that an accused

(a) has contravened or is about to contravene any summons, appearance notice, promise to appear, undertaking or recognizance that was issued or given to him or entered into by him; or

(b) has committed an indictable offence after any summons, appearance notice, promise to appear, undertaking or recognizance was issued or given to him or entered into by him,

may arrest the accused without warrant.

The accused will be brought before a justice (generally) or judge, depending on the original offence, as described in s. 524(3) of the *Criminal Code*.

Hearing: Criminal Code, Section 524(3)

524(3) Where an accused who has been arrested with a warrant issued under subsection (1), or who has been arrested under subsection (2), is taken before a justice, the justice shall

(a) where the accused was released from custody pursuant to an order made under subsection 522(3) by a judge of the superior court of criminal jurisdiction of any province, order that the accused be taken before a judge of that court; or

(b) in any other case, hear the prosecutor and his witnesses, if any, and the accused and his witnesses, if any.

Under s. 524(8) of the *Criminal Code*, the justice will cancel the original release document and order that the accused be detained in custody unless the accused can show cause why he should be released (reverse onus).

Powers of Justice After Hearing: Criminal Code, Section 524(8)

524(8) Where an accused described in subsection (3), other than an accused to whom paragraph (a) of that subsection applies, is taken before the justice and the justice finds

(a) that the accused has contravened or had been about to contravene his summons, appearance notice, promise to appear, undertaking or recognizance; or

(b) that there are reasonable grounds to believe that the accused has committed an indictable offence after any summons, appearance notice, promise to appear, undertaking or recognizance was issued or given to him or entered into by him,

he shall cancel the summons, appearance notice, promise to appear, undertaking or recognizance and order that the accused be detained in custody unless the accused, having been given a reasonable opportunity to do so, shows cause why his detention in custody is not justified within the meaning of subsection 515(10).

This section may be useful in detaining the accused in custody, thus enhancing the pre-trial safety of the victim.

SENTENCING CONSIDERATIONS IN SPOUSAL ABUSE CASES

The denunciation and deterrence of criminal acts motivated by hatred or through betrayal of trust may be achieved through the availability and application of increased penalties. The *Criminal Code* identifies the abuse of a spouse as a situation where the court shall consider the aggravating or mitigating factors during sentencing. Mitigating means lessening the culpability or deserving blame of an action. It would be unusual for the court to consider mitigating circumstances in sentencing a person convicted of "spousal abuse," but s. 718.2 of the Code does allow the court the leeway to consider any mitigating circumstances.

Other Sentencing Principles: Criminal Code, Section 718.2

718.2 A court that imposes a sentence shall also take into consideration the following principles:

(a) a sentence should be increased or reduced to account for any relevant aggravating or mitigating circumstances relating to the offence or the offender, and, without limiting the generality of the foregoing,

(i) evidence that the offence was motivated by bias, prejudice or hate based on race, national or ethnic origin, language, colour, religion, sex, age, mental or physical disability, sexual orientation, or any other similar factor,

(ii) evidence that the offender, in committing the offence, abused the offender's spouse or common-law partner,

(ii.1) evidence that the offender, in committing the offence, abused a person under the age of eighteen years,

(iii) evidence that the offender, in committing the offence, abused a position of trust or authority in relation to the victim,

(iv) evidence that the offence was committed for the benefit of, at the direction of or in association with a criminal organization, or

(v) evidence that the offence was a terrorism offence

shall be deemed to be aggravating circumstances;

(b) a sentence should be similar to sentences imposed on similar offenders for similar offences committed in similar circumstances;

(c) where consecutive sentences are imposed, the combined sentence should not be unduly long or harsh;

(d) an offender should not be deprived of liberty, if less restrictive sanctions may be appropriate in the circumstances; and

(e) all available sanctions other than imprisonment that are reasonable in the circumstances should be considered for all offenders, with particular attention to the circumstances of aboriginal offenders.

In *R v. McDonnell*, 1997 SCC 948, 114 CCC (3d) 436, 6 CR (5th) 231, the court cautioned that although there may be aggravating or mitigating factors, the sentencing court must be careful not to create a class of offence that was not envisioned by the legislators.

The court in this case, the Alberta Court of Appeal, opined that the offence in question, sexual assault, was not a "major sexual assault." The Supreme Court of Canada, in hearing the appeal of *R v. McDonnell*, stated: "It is not open to the appellate court to create a category of offence within a statutory offence for the purposes of sentencing." That is, the court may not categorize sexual assault into minor or major sexual assaults. These offences do not exist in law.

This ruling appears to prohibit the sentencing of an offender for the offence of "spousal abuse" because the offence does not exist in law. The court must not differentiate from the facts in issue of the legislatively defined offence and create a category of offence not defined in law.

This decision does not prohibit the courts from considering aggravating or mitigating factors when the offender is being sentenced upon conviction of an offence where the victim is a spouse.

Sections 718.2(a)(ii) and (ii.1) of the Code identify circumstances that are applicable to the consideration of aggravating or mitigating circumstances. These sections identify circumstances where the victim is a spouse, common-law partner, or child. The Ontario Court of Appeal, in its decision in the appeal of *R v. McLeod*, 2003 CanLII 4393, appears to have expanded this definition to include boyfriend–girlfriend relationships as being applicable to s. 718.2(a)(ii). The court stated: "Although section 718.2(a)(ii) speaks of spouses and does not mention a boyfriend-girlfriend relationship the same principle is applicable."

The Supreme Court concurred, in the application of s. 718.2 by the Ontario Court of Appeal in *R v. McLeod*, that the inclusion of other relationships of trust and intimacy not specifically identified in s. 718.2 would be proper. The application of this decision would allow the courts the opportunity to increase, or decrease, the range of sentencing options available in similar situations.

In the *opinion* of the author of this text, I do not believe that the court intended that every instance of dating should be considered to be a relationship of trust and intimacy. For example, a 15-minute, one-time "date" over a cup of coffee would not be considered a relationship of trust and intimacy. I believe that the court intended that the definition be applied to present relationships or previous relationships where violence had occurred. I also believe that the definition could be expanded to instances where the break-up of a relationship resulted in future violence.

The nature of the relationship between the accused and the victim in occurrences of relationship violence should be included in court briefs. Such information may be useful during sentencing if the accused enters a plea of guilty without trial, although it is likely that a victim impact statement (see Chapter 9) will be introduced before sentencing.

Note: The *Policing Standards Manual* in Appendix 5A of this chapter defines a "domestic violence occurrence" as including a relationship of current and former dating.

DATING VIOLENCE

Dating relationships are defined as those between current or former boyfriends and girlfriends as well as "other intimate relationships," but do not include those between boyfriends and girlfriends living together in a common-law relationship.

In 2008, nearly 23,000 incidents of dating violence were reported to police (Mahony, 2010). See Table 5.5. These incidents represented 7 percent of all violent crimes in 2008 and over one-quarter of all violent incidents between intimate partners. As is the case with spousal violence, former partners are often the perpetrator. In 2008, 57 percent of dating violence incidents were committed by former partners.

Table 5.5   Victims of Violent Crime Perpetrated by Dating Partners, by Sex of Victim and Relationship to Accused, 2008

| Relationship of accused to victim | Total | | Sex of victim | | | |
| | | | Female | | Male | |
	Number	Percent	Number	Percent	Number	Percent
Total victims of dating violence	22,798	100	18,745	100	4,053	100
Boyfriend or girlfriend	9,572	42	7,981	43	1,591	39
Ex-boyfriend or girlfriend	13,018	57	10,635	57	2,383	59
Other intimate relationship[a]	208	1	129	1	79	2

Notes: Percentages may not total 100 percent due to rounding. Excludes incidents where the sex and/or age of the victim was unknown. The Incident-Based Uniform Crime Reporting (UCR2) Survey collected data from 155 police services representing approximately 98 percent of the population of Canada in 2008. Only victims aged 15 to 98 are included in this analysis. Violent crimes include violations causing death, attempted murder, sexual assaults, assaults, robbery, criminal harassment, uttering threats, and other violations involving violence or the threat of violence.

[a] Includes a person with whom the victim had a sexual relationship or a mutual sexual attraction but to which none of the other relationship options apply.

Source: Statistics Canada, Canadian Centre for Justice Statistics, Incident-Based Uniform Crime Reporting (UCR2) Survey. Adapted from Mahony (2010).

In 2008, the majority of victims of police-reported dating violence were women. Just over 80 percent of the victims of dating violence were female (see Figure 5.9). This was true in both current boyfriend–girlfriend relationships and former boyfriend–girlfriend relationships. In the category of "other intimate relationships," women were still most often the victims, although at a lower rate (62 percent). This lower rate may be attributable in part to the relatively high proportion of same-sex relationships classified as "other intimate relationships."

Police-reported data show that approximately 10 percent of male victims (265) and 1 percent of female victims (179) of dating violence were involved in same-sex dating relationships. Male victims accounted for approximately 60 percent of these violent incidents, while female victims accounted for approximately 40 percent. The types of offences committed in same-sex and opposite-sex dating relationships were similar. They predominantly involved common assault, uttering threats, major assault, and criminal harassment.

Physical and Sexual Abuse in Dating

Physical abuse against a person includes shoving, slapping, choking, punching, kicking, biting, burning, hair pulling, using a weapon, threatening with a weapon, or forcibly confining.

Typically, men use physical force to assert control, whereas women use it to protect themselves, to retaliate, or to prevent an attack that they fear their partner is about to commit.

Sexual abuse includes unwanted sexual touching, using force or pressure to get a partner to consent to sexual activity, rape and attempted rape, and attempting or having intercourse with a person who, due to the influence of alcohol or drugs,

Figure 5.9 Females Most Likely Victims of Dating Violence, 2008

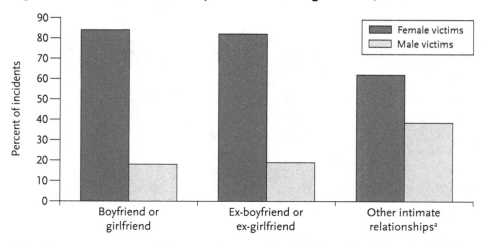

Notes: Percentages may not total 100 percent due to rounding. Excludes incidents where the sex and/or age of the victim was unknown. The 2008 data are based upon information reported by police services covering 98 percent of the population of Canada.

a Includes a person with whom the victim had a sexual relationship or a mutual sexual attraction but to which none of the other relationship options apply.

Source: Statistics Canada, Canadian Centre for Justice Statistics, Incident-Based Uniform Crime Reporting (UCR2) Survey. Adapted from Mahony (2010).

cannot fully consent to the act. These kinds of abuse are more often directed at women.

Police-reported data for 2008 show that the most frequently committed violent *Criminal Code* offence in dating relationships was common assault (50 percent) (s. 266). Following common assault, other offences included criminal harassment (14 percent) (s. 264), uttering threats (12 percent) (s. 264.1), major assault (11 percent) (ss. 267 and 268), indecent or harassing phone calls (6 percent) (s. 372), forcible confinement and related offences (3 percent) (s. 279), and sexual assault (3 percent) (s. 271). See Table 5.6.

Date Rape Drugs

Some sexual offenders use drugs to subdue a victim. The use of drugs to overcome the victim may make investigation of the offence more difficult. The victim may not recall much of the incident due to the amnesic effects of the drug. The following information describes some of the drugs used by sexual offenders.

"Date rape" drugs are substances such as Rohypnol (pill form), gamma hydroxybutyrate (GHB) (liquid form), and ketamine. They're usually slipped unnoticed into drinks at bars, clubs, and parties. The drugs are used to incapacitate or reduce the inhibitions of the victim. Some drugs leave the victim weakened, helpless, or unconscious—unable to escape or resist or to call for help. When the drug wears off, memory may be impaired.

The most commonly used drug is alcohol. Alcohol may be combined with other drugs to assist in overcoming any resistance by the victim.

These drugs are discussed in more detail below.

Table 5.6   Victims of Dating Violence by Offence Type and Sex of Victim, 2008

| | Total | | Sex of victim | | | |
| | | | Female | | Male | |
Offence type	Number	Percent	Number	Percent	Number	Percent
Homicide/attempts	14	0	10	0	4	0
Sexual assault[a]	648	3	638	3	10	0
Major assault (levels 2 & 3)[b]	2,415	11	1,742	9	673	17
Common assault (level 1)[c]	11,438	50	9,301	50	2,137	53
Forcible confinement and related offences[d]	735	3	719	4	16	0
Criminal harassment	3,235	14	2,830	15	405	10
Uttering threats	2,669	12	2,263	12	406	10
Indecent or harassing phone calls	1,354	6	1,003	5	351	9
Other violent offences[e]	290	1	239	1	51	1
Total offences	22,798	100	18,745	100	4,053	100

Notes: Percentages may not add up to 100 percent due to rounding. Excludes incidents where the sex of the victim was unknown. Includes victims aged 15 to 98. Dating violence refers to violence committed by current and former boyfriends/girlfriends and other intimate partners. The 2008 data are based on information reported by police services covering 98 percent of the population of Canada.

[a] Includes sexual assault, classified as one of three levels according to the seriousness of the incident, as well as other sexual crimes. Level 1 sexual assault is the category of least physical injury to the victim; level 2 includes sexual assault with a weapon, threats to use a weapon, or causing bodily harm; and level 3 includes aggravated sexual assault that wounds, maims, disfigures, or endangers the life of the victim.

[b] Includes assault with a weapon or causing bodily harm (level 2) and aggravated assault, defined as assault that wounds, maims, disfigures, or endangers the life of the victim (level 3).

[c] Common or level 1 assault is the least serious form of assault and includes pushing, slapping, punching, and face-to-face verbal threats.

[d] Includes kidnapping, forcible confinement, and hostage-taking.

[e] Includes robbery, unlawfully causing bodily harm, discharge firearm with intent, assault against peace officer or public officer, criminal negligence causing bodily harm, other assaults, explosives causing death/bodily harm, arson, and other violent violations.

Source: Statistics Canada, Canadian Centre for Justice Statistics, Incident-Based Uniform Crime Reporting (UCR2) Survey. Adapted from Mahony (2010).

Ketamine

Ketamine has many street names, including purple, Special K, kit kat, and Super K. The drug takes effect very soon after ingestion, and the effects last approximately six hours. It causes a dissociative state, which has been described as a "near death" experience. The drug also affects balance, judgment, and the ability to communicate. An overdose causes the victim to experience difficulty breathing. It can be fatal if mixed with alcohol or other drugs.

Ketamine is used as a veterinary and medical anesthetic. Legally produced ketamine comes in liquid form that is usually injected. The illegally produced version is sometimes produced as a grainy white powder, commonly mixed with ephedrine. The powder is usually snorted but it may also be pressed into tablet form.

Ketamine depresses the nervous system and causes a temporary loss of body sensation and can also cause perceptual changes or hallucinations. It can give the user a floating feeling as if the mind and body have been separated. Users may be physically incapable of moving while under the influence. High doses, especially when combined with other depressant drugs like alcohol, can suppress breathing and heart function and can lead to unconsciousness.

During recovery, which may take as long as 48 hours, the individual may experience reactions such as vivid dreams, confusion, excitement, and, occasionally, hallucinations. The individual may also display irrational behaviour.

Rohypnol

Rohypnol is the brand name for flunitrazepam, a benzodiazepine drug—the same family of medications as Valium, Halcion, and Xanax. Benzodiazepines have been used for the treatment of anxiety and sleep disturbances and in anesthesia. It is illegal to make or sell Rohypnol in Canada or the United States.

The drug has no detectable taste or colour. The effects include feelings of intoxication, visual disturbances, and loss of control. While using the drug a person may experience a relaxed, mellow feeling and less anxiety. Drowsiness will likely occur along with lack of motor control, slurred speech, and clumsiness.

Other effects include the inability to think clearly, loss of judgment and inhibition, and loss of memory while under the effect of the drug.

In an attempt to reduce misuse of the drug, the manufacturer of Rohypnol, Hoffmann-La Roche Ltd., now adds a blue dye to the product, making it visible in clear liquids.

The drug is usually sold in tablets and taken by mouth, but it can also be purchased in liquid form. A standard dose is from 0.5 milligrams to 2 milligrams. Effects begin approximately 15 to 30 minutes after taking it, and last from two to eight hours.

Rohypnol is known by several street names, including Ruffies, Roofies, Rophies, Roches, Roaches, Forget Pill, Poor Man's Quaalude, R-2s, Circles, Mind-Erasers, and Mexican Valium.

Gamma Hydroxybutyrate

Gamma hydroxybutyrate (GHB) is a powerful, rapidly acting central nervous system depressant. GHB is usually taken orally. It is sold as a light-coloured powder that easily dissolves in liquids or as a liquid packaged in vials or small bottles. In liquid form, it is clear, odourless, tasteless, and almost undetectable when mixed in a drink. The average dose is 1 to 5 grams and the drug takes effect in 15 to 30 minutes. The effects last from three to six hours. The drug is rarely used for medicinal purposes in Canada, but is sometimes used to treat narcolepsy (prescribed as sodium oxybate).

Consumption of less than 1 gram of GHB acts as a relaxant, causing a loss of muscle tone and reduced inhibitions. Consumption of 1 to 2 grams causes a strong feeling of relaxation and slows the heart rate and respiration. At this dosage level, GHB also interferes with blood circulation, motor coordination, and balance. In stronger doses, 2 to 4 grams, pronounced interference with motor and speech control occurs. A coma-like sleep may be induced, requiring intubation to wake the user. When mixed with alcohol, the depressant effects of GHB are enhanced. This can lead to respiratory depression, unconsciousness, or coma.

Side effects associated with GHB include nausea, vomiting, delusions, depression, vertigo, hallucinations, seizures, respiratory distress, loss of consciousness, slowed heart rate, lowered blood pressure, amnesia, and coma.

The anesthetic effect of GHB can physically paralyze an individual and impair short-term memory. These effects are intensified when the drug is combined with alcohol.

Date Rape Drugs and the Criminal Code

Intentionally drugging a person to prevent or reduce the possibility of resistance to unwanted sexual activity is a criminal offence. Section 246 of the *Criminal Code*, set out below, describes the offence. This offence appears to be more prevalent in dating situations than in spousal abuse situations.

Overcoming Resistance to Commission of Offence: Criminal Code, Section 246

246. Every one who, with intent to enable or assist himself or another person to commit an indictable offence,

(a) attempts, by any means, to choke, suffocate or strangle another person, or by any means calculated to choke, suffocate or strangle, attempts to render another person insensible, unconscious or incapable of resistance, or

(b) administers or causes to be administered to any person, or attempts to administer to any person, or causes or attempts to cause any person to take a stupefying or overpowering drug, matter or thing,

is guilty of an indictable offence and liable to imprisonment for life.

Emotional Abuse in Dating

Emotional abuse may occur in dating relationships. It can include insults, profanity, belittling remarks, and threats. It may also include destroying a dating partner's property or possessions, isolating him or her from relatives and friends, and treating him or her with extreme possessiveness or jealousy. Emotional abuse reflects the abuser's desire to control the dating partner's behaviour. The abuser seeks to erode the partner's self-confidence and thereby lessen his or her ability to act independently (Thorne-Finch, 1992).

Both women and men may use emotional abuse to control their dating partners. Men, however, are more likely to escalate the abuse if they believe that they are losing control. When the emotional abuse is no longer effective, abusers will sometimes turn to physical violence in an attempt to reassert control.

KEY TERMS

articulable cause

criminal harassment

emotional/psychological abuse

financial abuse

indictable offence

physical abuse

sexual abuse

spousal abuse

spouse

summary conviction offence

REFERENCES

Alksnis, C., & Taylor, J. (2002). The Impact of experiencing and witnessing family violence during childhood: Child and adult behavioural outcomes. Retrieved from http://www.csc-scc.gc.ca/text/pblct/fv/fv04/toce-eng.shtml.

Campbell, J. (2001). Issues in risk assessment in the field of intimate partner violence: What practitioners need to know. Paper presented at an International Conference on Children Exposed to Domestic Violence, Our Children Our Future: A Call to Action, London, ON.

Campbell, J.C. (2004). *Danger assessment.* Retrieved from Johns Hopkins School of Nursing: http://www.dangerassessment.org.

Campbell, J.C., Webster, D.W., & Glass, N. (2009). The danger assessment: Validation of a lethality risk assessment instrument for intimate partner femicide. *Journal of Interpersonal Violence, 24*(4): 653–674.

Canada. House of Commons. Standing Committee on Health, Welfare and Social Affairs. (1982). *Report on violence in the family: Wife battering.* Ottawa: Author.

Canada Evidence Act. (1985). RSC 1985, c. C-5.

Canadian Centre for Justice Statistics. (2004). *Family violence in Canada: A statistical profile 2004* (catalogue no. 85-224-XIE). Ottawa: Statistics Canada.

Canadian Centre for Justice Statistics. (2004). *Uniform crime reporting survey.* Ottawa: Statistics Canada.

Children's Law Reform Act. (1990). RSO 1990, c. C.12.

Cooper, M. (1992). Current and future effects on children witnessing parental violence: An overview and annotated bibliography series on interpersonal violence report no. 1. Vancouver: BC Institute Against Family Violence.

Criminal Code. (1985). RSC 1985, c. C-46, as amended.

Department of Justice Canada. (2001). Family violence initiative: Second federal/ provincial/territorial forum on spousal abuse cases. Retrieved from http:// www.justice.gc.ca.

Department of Justice Canada. (2004). *Criminal harassment: A handbook for police and crown prosecutors.* Retrieved from http://canada.justice.gc.ca/en/ps/fm/ pub/harassment/index.html.

Department of Justice Canada. (2010). *Inventory of spousal violence risk assessment tools used in Canada.* Retrieved from http://www.justice.gc.ca.

Family Law Act. (1990). RSO 1990, c. F.3.

Hanson, R.K., & Wallace-Capretta, S. (2000). *A multi-site study of treatment for abusive men. User report 2000-05.* Ottawa: Department of the Solicitor General of Canada.

Hilton, N.Z., Harris, G.T., Rice, M.E., Lang, C., Cormier, C.A., & Lines, K.J. (2004). A brief actuarial assessment for the prediction of wife assault recidivism: The Ontario Domestic Assault Risk Assessment. *Psychological Assessment, 16,* 267–275.

Kropp, P.R., Hart, S.D., Webster, C.D., & Eaves, D. (1995). *Manual for the spousal assault risk assessment guide,* 2nd ed. Vancouver: BC Institute Against Family Violence.

Mahony, T.H. (Summer 2010). Police-reported dating violence in Canada, 2008. *Juristat, 30*(2), 1–26. Ottawa: Minister of Industry.

Martin's Annual Criminal Code, 2012. (2012). Aurora, ON: Canada Law Book.

Milligan, S. (2011). Criminal harassment in Canada, 2009. *Juristat: Bulletin* (catalogue no. 85-005-X). Ottawa: Statistics Canada.

Ochberg, F. (1998). *Understanding the victims of spousal abuse.* http://www .giftfromwithin.org/html/spousal.html.

O'Connor, T.R. (2004). *Intimate violence.* http://faculty.ncwc.edu/ toconnor/300/300lect05.htm.

O'Connor, T.R. (2005). *The psychology of violence, intimidation and hate.* http:// faculty.ncwc.edu/toconnor/psy/psylect08.htm.

Ontario. Ministry of the Solicitor General and Correctional Services. (1994). *Policing standards manual.* Toronto: Author.

Police Services Act. (1990). RSO 1990, c. P.15.

Provincial Offences Act. (1990). RSO 1990, c. P.33.

Rigakos, G. (2002). Peace bonds and violence against women: A three-site study of the effect of Bill C-42 on process, application and enforcement: Final report. Retrieved from Department of Justice Canada, Research and Statistics Division: http://www.justice.gc.ca/eng/pi/rs/rep-rap/2003/rr03_1/ rr03_1.pdf.

Roberts, J. (1994). Criminal justice processing of sexual assault cases. *Juristat: Service Bulletin, 14*(7), 1–19. Ottawa: Canadian Centre for Justice Statistics.

Rodgers, K. (1994). Wife assault: The findings of a national survey. *Juristat: Service Bulletin, 14*(9), 1–22. Ottawa: Canadian Centre for Justice Statistics.

Statistics Canada. (2000). *1999 general social survey on victimization.* Ottawa: Author.

Statistics Canada. (2009). *Family violence in Canada: A statistical profile 2009* (catalogue no. 85-224-X). Ottawa: Minister of Industry.

Statistics Canada. (2011). *Family violence in Canada: A statistical profile* (catalogue no. 85-224-X). Ottawa: Minister of Industry.

Thorne-Finch, R. (1992). *Ending the silence: The origins and treatment of male violence against women*. Toronto: University of Toronto Press.

Tolman, R.M., & Bennett, L.W. (1992). A review of quantitative research on men who batter. In R.K. Hanson and L. Hart (Eds.), *Evaluation of treatment programs for male batterers: Conference*. Ottawa: Ministry of Solicitor General.

Tutty, L. (1999). *Husband abuse: An overview of research and perspectives*. Ottawa: Health Canada, Family Violence Prevention Unit.

Widom, C.S. (1989). Does violence beget violence? A critical examination of the literature. *Psychological Bulletin, 106*, 3–28.

EXERCISES

TRUE OR FALSE

_____ 1. The majority of abused spouses call the police the first time they are abused.

_____ 2. Psychological spousal abuse is not as damaging as physical spousal abuse.

_____ 3. Abusive spouses are unlikely to stop their abusive behaviour without police intervention.

_____ 4. A person cannot be convicted of sexually assaulting his or her spouse.

_____ 5. Within the provisions of the *Family Law Act*, a police officer may apply for a restraining order on behalf of an abused spouse.

_____ 6. The arrival of the police on the scene of a domestic dispute can trigger an escalation of violence between the spouses.

_____ 7. The *Family Law Act* authorizes restraining orders only for those who are legally married.

MULTIPLE CHOICE

1. Section 265 of the *Criminal Code* relates to the following type or types of abuse:

   a. physical

   b. emotional

   c. psychological

   d. all of the above

2. A restraining order under s. 46 of the *Family Law Act* of Ontario may be obtained by:

   a. the officer investigating the case

   b. the accused

   c. the victim

   d. a social worker on behalf of the victim

3. A restraining order under s. 35 of the *Children's Law Reform Act* of Ontario may be obtained by:

   a. the officer investigating the case

   b. the accused

   c. the victim

   d. a social worker on behalf of the victim

4. A "peace bond" under s. 810 of the *Criminal Code* may be obtained by:

   a. the officer investigating the case

   b. the victim

   c. a social worker on behalf of the victim

   d. all of the above

5. A violation of s. 810 of the *Criminal Code* is an offence of the following kind for arrest purposes:

   a. summary conviction

   b. indictable

   c. dual

   d. provincial

SHORT ANSWER

1. What are some common characteristics of abusive spouses?

2. List three actions characteristic of persons who commit emotional spousal abuse.

3. List three actions characteristic of persons who commit psychological spousal abuse.

4. Explain the four stages of the cycle of violence in cases of spousal abuse.

5. When there is insufficient evidence to pursue criminal charges in a case of spousal abuse, what possible alternatives does the justice system offer?

6. Describe the tools provided by the *Criminal Code* and other statutes for halting the actions of stalkers.

7. Explain the directive of the solicitor general regarding the laying of charges by police in domestic violence situations.

CASE ANALYSIS

Case 5.1

You are a police officer responding to a complaint of harassment. You attend the residence of Maggie Jones, who tells you that her boyfriend, Don Smith, has been harassing her. Don was living with her until three days ago, when, during an argument about her teenage daughter, he struck her in the face several times. Maggie called her brothers, who threw Don out of the house and told him not to return. Since then Don has been calling her constantly. During the past two days he has called her about 50 times to ask her forgiveness and tell her that he wants them to be together again. Maggie also tells you that Don has been sitting in his car outside her house on several occasions, but drives away when she comes out of the house. She is afraid that Don is unstable and may try to hurt her or her daughter.

Using the CAPRA system, describe what you would do in this situation.

Case 5.2

You are a police officer responding to a disturbance call at 123 Robie Street. The call was placed by an anonymous person from a nearby pay phone. On arrival, you find that the residence is quiet. You go to the door, and a teenage boy who identifies himself as Chris Wilson answers and invites you inside. You ask whether there is any problem, but before Chris can answer, a man who identifies himself as Chris's father, Tex, shouts, "What the hell are you doing here? How did you get in? Leave the boy alone!" Chris remains silent and walks away as his father approaches.

Tex appears extremely agitated. You ask whether anything is wrong. He tells you, "Everything is fine. What the hell are you doing here?" You explain that you received a disturbance call. He becomes enraged and begins shouting at you, "Get the hell out! I don't want you in my house! Damn police! Who the hell do you think you are! I'm going to sue you! Get out! Get out!" Tex crosses the room and opens the front door, yelling, "get the hell out of my house and don't come back! I can look after my family!"

What do you do in this situation? Explain your obligations as a police officer and be sure to mention the relevant laws.

Case 5.3

John and Jane have divorced. A custody order has been issued allowing Jane visitations with their daughter, Jill, on Saturdays from 10 a.m. to 6 p.m.

You, a police officer, receive a call at 7 p.m. on Saturday from John. Jane has not returned with Jill. You attend the scene. Upon your arrival at 9:15 p.m., Jane is just pulling into the driveway. John is incensed and wants Jane charged with child abduction in contravention of a custody order. Jane tells you that she knows she is late, but the service at the pizza place where they had dinner was slow. She tells you that the child prefers to be with her anyway.

What will you do in this situation? Be sure to quote authorities.

Case 5.4

You are a police officer responding to a call for assistance at 456 Perth Street, the residence of Ruthie and George Smith. You are met by Ruthie Smith and Hazel Taylor. Ruthie tells you that her husband, George Smith, is in the living room and that she wants him to leave. You enter the living room, where you meet two males, later identified as George Smith and Harry Wesson.

George appears to be very upset; he asks you why you are there and says that he doesn't want any trouble. You ask about the situation. George tells you that Ruthie is leaving him for Hazel. Hazel interjects: "Ruthie and I have been together for two years. He knew and didn't care!" George replies: "I don't care what you both do, I just want my boys!"

Hazel tells George that she and Ruthie are going to raise his sons. George replies: "There is no way I am going to allow my sons to be raised in a homosexual home!"

Harry then begins to shout at Hazel, telling her that what she is doing is immoral and unnatural and that she is going to hell.

George tells Ruthie that she can have the house, the cars, all their retirement money, and whatever else she wants. All he wants is to have his sons with him. Ruthie tells him that he can't have the children and that she and Hazel will give them a good home. He can come and visit when all the support details have been ironed out. She tells him that there is nothing wrong with a homosexual relationship and that she loves Hazel more than she ever loved him. George doesn't reply. But Harry does. He tells Ruthie that she is sick and that she disgusts him.

George then asks Ruthie: "Where are the boys?" She tells him that they are safe and that he can see them when they get the support payments sorted out and she is granted custody. George replies: "You are never going to get custody! Where are the boys?" Ruthie refuses to tell him, saying only that they are in a safe place. George is extremely upset and says, "You sent them to your mother's, didn't you?" Ruthie again replies: "They are in a safe place." George turns to you and states: "Her mother lives in England. She must have sent the boys to England!"

You ask Ruthie about the location of the children. Ruthie replies: "I can't tell you until we settle some legal matters such as support. Also, George hits the kids. I can't protect them if he knows their location."

George protests: "I never hit my sons!"

Harry shouts, "You're a liar! George never hit the boys!"

Explain what you will do in this situation. Be sure to quote authorities.

Case 5.5

You are a police officer. You have been dispatched to 123A Portage Street regarding a call of possible domestic violence. The information was received from a neighbour in the adjoining townhouse at 123B Portage Street. The caller reported that she heard screaming and what sounded like furniture being overturned.

Upon arrival at 123A Portage Street, you are unable to hear anything out of the ordinary. All is quiet except for the sound of a television. You ring the doorbell. Mr. James MacKinnon answers the door.

You ask whether there is anything wrong. He tells you that nothing is going on and tells you to "go away."

You ask to speak with Mrs. MacKinnon.

He tells you, "She doesn't want to speak with any cops. Now get out of here!"

What will you do in this situation? Be sure to quote authorities.

Case 5.6

You are a police officer responding to a domestic dispute at 789 Main Street, the Furr residence. A check of the local records management system reveals that police have attended the residence regarding similar complaints nine times in the past six months; no one has been charged.

Upon arrival you hear shouting and swearing from inside the residence. You knock on the door but receive no answer; the shouting and swearing continue. You again knock on the door. This time a male, later identified as Jack Furr, answers the door. He appears to be highly intoxicated. His speech is slurred when he asks you: "What the hell do you want?" You tell him that you received a call for assistance from this residence. He replies, "Nobody from this house called the police. Now get the fuck off my property!"

You hear a voice in the background asking, "Who is at the door?"

Jack replies, "It's the fucking police. They said that someone called." The voice, later identified as Lucy Furr, replies, "I called, let them in!" Jack says to you, "Then come on in, you fucking pig!"

You enter the home. The living room is a mess. There are beer bottles and cans everywhere. Pizza and takeout food containers are littered across the floor and furniture. Sitting in the corner of the room is Lucy. She beckons you to come and speak with her.

As you speak with Lucy, it becomes obvious that she is highly intoxicated. She asks you to come and sit beside her. You decline and ask her why she called. She tells you that her husband, Jack, is abusing her. He shouts and swears at her and calls her "a lazy bitch." She is sick of it and wants him out. Jack interjects, saying that all she does is sit around drinking and ordering takeout food. He adds, "She's a lazy bitch."

The two begin to argue. You interrupt and tell Lucy that you are not going to take her husband from the home because no offence has taken place. She replies that Jack is abusing her. You explain that what has happened is not a police matter, because insulting someone is not illegal. She replies, "Well then. He slapped me across the face a couple of weeks ago!" Jack protests: "I never hit you!"

What will you do in this situation? Be sure to quote authorities.

Case 5.7

Joe Smiley moved to a small community to retire. While buying groceries, he met Janice Burke, a cashier at the store. During the course of their conversation at the checkout, Burke told Smiley that she lived in a farmhouse approximately 20 kilometres from town. He commented about how frightening it must be to live alone, but not to worry, he was not a stalker.

Three days later Smiley again spoke with Burke while paying for groceries. They met again at a community breakfast event two days later. That same afternoon, Smiley arrived at Burke's house. She was alone, preparing to go out for the evening. Burke invited Smiley in, but told him that she had to leave soon.

Smiley talked about his repeated visits to the farmhouse when she was not there, and how glad he was to have found her at home. He spoke again of her isolated setting and her vulnerability to attack. He accurately described her activities with her friends that day.

After approximately one-half hour, Burke told Smiley that he had to leave because she was going out. Smiley left the house. Burke noticed that he did not take his jacket. Burke then went to the home of Joan Paul, a friend. She told Paul that Smiley was "creeping her out" and that she felt uncomfortable when he was around her.

That evening, while attending a community gathering, Paul met Smiley. She told him that Burke was upset by his visit.

The following morning, Smiley showed up at Burke's home. He knocked on the door but received no answer. Burke was at home but was afraid to answer the door. She hid in an area away from the windows until he departed. Smiley began to depart, then stopped and parked his vehicle behind Burke's car. He returned and banged loudly on the door. After approximately 10 minutes, he drove off. Burke then called the police.

Police then interviewed Smiley. He provided a statement indicating that he was new in town, single, and lonely, and that Burke was friendly. He had run into her accidentally at the store, and later at a community event. When he came to visit, she invited him in for a drink. He believed that they were "getting along quite well." When he left Burke's home, there was no indication that she was upset. He was quite puzzled when he later heard that she was upset with him.

He explained in his statement that he had gone to her house the next day to find out why she was upset and to retrieve his jacket. He knocked on the door a couple of times, but it appeared that no one was at home. As he was leaving, he saw a curtain move. He stopped his vehicle and ran back to see if she was at home and if anything was wrong. After receiving no answer, he left.

You are the investigating officer. What will you do? Explain your rationale.

APPENDIX 5A POLICING STANDARDS MANUAL (2000): DOMESTIC VIOLENCE OCCURRENCES

February 2000 LE-024 1/12
Ontario Ministry of the Solicitor General

Legislative/Regulatory Requirements

Section 29 of the Adequacy Standards Regulation requires a police services board to have a policy on investigations into domestic violence occurrences. In addition, section 12(1)(d) requires the Chief of Police to develop and maintain procedures on and processes for undertaking and managing investigations into domestic violence occurrences.

The focus of these policies and procedures should be on domestic violence occurrences. For the purposes of this guideline, domestic violence occurrence means:

> Domestic violence is any use of physical or sexual force, actual or threatened, in an intimate relationship, including emotional/psychological abuse or harassing behaviour. Although both women and men can be victims of domestic violence, the overwhelming majority of this violence involves men abusing women.
>
> Intimate relationships include those between the opposite-sex and same-sex partners. These relationships vary in duration and legal formality, and include current and former dating, common-law and married couples.
>
> *Criminal Code* offences include, but are not limited to homicide, assault, sexual assault, threatening death or bodily harm, forcible confinement, harassment/stalking, abduction, breaches of court orders and property-related offences.
>
> These crimes are often committed in a context where there is a pattern of assaultive and/or controlling behaviour. This violence may include physical assault, and emotional, psychological and sexual abuse. It can include threats to harm children, other family members, pets and property. The violence is used to intimidate, humiliate or frighten victims, or to make them powerless. Domestic violence may include a single act of abuse. It may also include a number of acts that may appear minor or trivial when viewed in isolation, but collectively form a pattern that amounts to abuse.

Sample Board Policy

Board Policy #_____

It is the policy of the _____ Police Services Board with respect to domestic violence occurrences that the Chief of Police will:

a) in partnership with the police service's local Crown, Probation and Parole Services, Victim/Witness Assistance Programme (VWAP), Victim Crisis and Referral Service (VCARS), municipalities, local Children's Aid Societies and other local service providers and community representatives responsible for issues related to domestic violence, including women's shelters, work to establish and maintain one or more domestic violence coordinating committees that cover the geographic areas that fall within the jurisdiction of the police service;

b) implement one or more of the models set out in Ministry guidelines for the investigation of domestic violence occurrences and ensure that the police service has access to trained domestic violence investigators;

c) develop and maintain procedures for undertaking and managing investigations into domestic violence occurrences that address:

    i) communications and dispatch;

    ii) initial response;

    iii) enhanced investigative procedures;

    iv) the mandatory laying of charges where there are reasonable grounds to do so, including in cases where there is a breach of a bail condition, probation, parole or a restraining order;

    v) the use of a risk indicators tool;

    vi) children at risk;

    vii) high risk cases and repeat offenders;

    viii) occurrences involving members of a police service;

    ix) post-arrest procedures;

    x) victim assistance; and

    xi) safety planning;

d) ensure that the police service's response to domestic violence occurrences are monitored and evaluated; and

e) ensure that officers and other appropriate members receive the appropriate Ministry accredited training.

Police Service Guidelines

1. Every Chief of Police, in partnership with the local Crown, Probation and Parole Services, VWAP, VCARS, local Children's Aid Society, municipalities, and other local service providers and community representatives responsible for issues related to domestic violence, including women's shelters, should work to establish one or more domestic violence coordinating committees that cover the geographic areas that fall within the jurisdiction of the police service. The suggested terms of reference for the domestic violence coordinating committee include:

    a) establishing a protocol for the operation of the committee;

    b) establishing criteria for case and/or systems review;

    c) reviewing cases that meet the established criteria, and subject to confidentiality requirements, sharing case specific information among relevant member organizations in order to provide a coordinated response;

    d) monitoring and evaluating the response to cases by organizations participating on the domestic violence coordinating committee;

    e) reviewing the availability of services to victims of domestic violence, including the provision of safety planning;

f) coordinating the development of local written protocols on domestic violence that address:

　　i) the roles and responsibilities of organizations involved in providing services to victims, including notifying and informing the victim about release of the accused, bail conditions, and the criminal justice process;

　　ii) information sharing among the organizations; and

　　iii) referrals for service, including the provision of assistance to victims and children in cases which do not proceed to court, or where no charges have been laid;

g) developing local community strategies and responses to address and prevent repeat victimization, including promoting and supporting follow-up with victims of domestic violence; and

h) developing initiatives/programs for the prevention and early intervention, including:

　　i) Domestic Violence Emergency Response System (DVERS), where practical;

　　ii) addressing the needs of child witnesses of violence; and

　　iii) awareness and information programs on domestic violence occurrences for students and other service providers.

2. Every police service should ensure that it has access to trained domestic violence investigators.

3. Domestic violence investigators will have the primary responsibility for undertaking, managing or reviewing the investigation of domestic violence occurrences, except where the type of occurrence involves an offence which is addressed by the police service's criminal investigation management plan established pursuant to section 11 of the *Regulation on the Adequacy and Effectiveness of Police Services* or is a threshold major case as defined in the *Ontario Major Case Management Manual*.

4. A Chief of Police should not designate a person as a domestic violence investigator unless that person is a police officer and has successfully completed the required training accredited by the Ministry or has equivalent qualifications and skills as designated by the Ministry.

5. A police service may meet its obligations under paragraph 2 by either:

a) ensuring that an adequate number of patrol officers are designated as domestic violence investigators;

b) establishing a specialized unit of domestic violence investigators that will be responsible for undertaking, managing or reviewing the investigation of domestic violence occurrences;

c) designating a domestic violence occurrence as a threshold occurrence under the police service's criminal investigation management plan, thereby requiring that the investigation be undertaken or managed by a criminal investigator; or

   d) designating patrol supervisors as domestic violence investigators who will be responsible for undertaking, managing or reviewing all domestic violence occurrence investigations.

6. Where a police service decides to meet its obligations under paragraph 2 by one of the methods set out in paragraph 5(b)-(d), it should also ensure that its patrol officers receive the required training accredited by the Ministry on the police response to domestic violence occurrences.

7. Every police service, in conjunction with the domestic violence coordinating committee and local community and social service agencies, should consider the need for, and the feasibility of, implementing a multi-disciplinary follow-up support for victims of domestic violence in the their jurisdiction. This support could focus on victims' assistance, counselling, attendance at court, children who witness violence, and intervention strategies, such as safety planning, in cases where there is repeat victimization or high risk to the victim.

8. Every police service's procedures should:

   a) require that all domestic violence occurrence calls be responded to as a priority call for service even if the call is withdrawn, including calls relating to a possible breach of a bail, parole or probation condition, peace bond or a restraining order;

   b) require that when a call is received and the suspect has threatened violence and there is reason to believe that the suspect intends to go to the victim's location the police will go to the victim's location;

   c) set out the number of police officers to attend at the scene, with two as a minimum;

   d) indicate the type of information to be gathered by communications and dispatch personnel and provided to responding officers, including at minimum:

      i) caller's name, address, telephone number and relation to the incident (e.g., witness, victim);

      ii) information about the suspect (e.g., relationship to victim, current location, description, any known mental illnesses, suicidal threats, history of abuse/violence);

      iii) extent of injuries, if known;

      iv) whether the suspect or other residents of the household are under the influence of drugs or alcohol;

      v) whether firearms or other weapons are known to be present at the scene or accessible to the suspect from some other location;

      vi) whether the suspect or anyone in the household has been issued or refused an authorization to acquire a firearm, Firearms Licence or registration certificate;

      vii) whether the suspect is known to have access to firearms;

viii) whether children or other persons are present in the household and their location within the dwelling;

ix) whether there has been one or more previous domestic violence occurrence calls to the address, the nature of previous incidents and whether weapons have been involved; and

x) whether a current peace bond/restraining order or bail/probation condition exists against anyone in the household or suspect; and

e) require communications and dispatch personnel to be provided with a checklist or reference sheet that sets out the information to be gathered and provided to responding officers.

9. The procedures should provide that whenever possible at least one of the minimum two officers responding to a domestic violence occurrence should be a patrol officer who has received training on the police response to domestic violence occurrences or a domestic violence investigator.

10. The procedures should provide that upon arrival at the scene the officers should:

a) try to quickly separate the parties;

b) assist any party in obtaining medical assistance, if necessary;

c) ensure that any children at the scene are provided with appropriate support/assistance; and

d) gather and preserve evidence in accordance with the police service's procedures on the collection, preservation and control of evidence and property.

11. The procedures should provide that:

a) all officers responding to a domestic violence occurrence should make detailed notes, including on the actions and utterances of the parties; and

b) a detailed occurrence report should be completed for every domestic violence occurrence regardless of whether any charges were laid or an offence alleged.

12. The procedures should address the interviewing of the victim(s), suspect and witnesses, including:

a) where available, practical and appropriate, the use of audio or video taping of statements in accordance with the *R v. KGB* guidelines;

b) separate interviews where practical and safe for officers and the parties;

c) if required, the use of an interpreter by a person outside the family where practical;

d) that the officers should ask the victim and other witnesses direct questions about:

i) any history of abuse/violence and stalking/criminal harassment;

ii) any history of personal threats, including threats to life;

      iii) any concerns over the safety of the victim;

      iv) the presence of, or access to, firearms and registration certificates;

      v) the previous use of weapons;

      vi) any history of drug or alcohol abuse; and

      vii) any history of mental health or stability issues;

e) the processes and considerations for interviewing child witnesses, including the appropriateness of asking the child any of the questions set out in (d);

f) that the officer should ask the victim any other questions relevant to the completion of the risk indicators part of the domestic violence supplementary report form;

g) requesting that the victim review and sign the officer's record of their statement, or any other statement that has been provided, and the statements should include the date; and

h) interviewing third party witnesses, including neighbours, other emergency personnel who have responded to the scene and medical personnel who treat the victim.

13. The procedures should address the gathering and documenting of evidence, including:

a) asking whether the victim was physically assaulted and whether any internal or external injuries occurred and noting their response (including where possible on a diagram);

b) photographing the crime scene (e.g., overturned furniture or destroyed property), including the use of video taping, where available and practical;

c) with the victim's consent, photographing the victim's injuries and taking additional photographs within 24-48 hours of the initial occurrence when the injuries are more visibly apparent (if possible by a member of the same gender; consideration should be given to using Polaroid photographs when appropriate);

d) gathering any other evidence, including answering machine tapes, hospital records, torn and/or blood stained clothing, or fingerprint evidence if the suspect has broken into the victim's residence (including any evidence obtained for a Sexual Assault Treatment Centre whose mandate has been expanded to include domestic violence);

e) the review and preserving of 911 tapes that record the call for service;

f) the names and date of birth of all children present, or who normally reside, in the home; and

g) the use of search warrants to obtain relevant evidence.

14. The procedures should provide that in any domestic violence occurrence, which is a threshold major case, the investigation will be in accordance with the Ministry's designated *Ontario Major Case Management Manual.*

15. The procedures should provide that in all domestic violence occurrences an officer is to lay a charge where there are reasonable grounds to do so, including:

    a) where a person has breached a condition of bail, parole, probation or a peace bond;

    b) for any offence committed under the *Criminal Code*, including obstruction of justice (i.e., dissuading the victim from testifying); or

    c) when there is a contravention of a valid order under sections 24 and 46 of the *Family Law Act* and section 35 of the *Children's Law Reform Act*.

16. A decision to lay charges should not be influenced by any of the following factors:

    a) marital status/cohabitation of the parties;

    b) disposition of previous police calls involving the same victim and suspect;

    c) the victim's unwillingness to attend court proceedings or the officer's belief that the victim will not cooperate;

    d) likelihood of obtaining a conviction in court;

    e) verbal assurances by either party that the violence will cease;

    f) denial by either party that the violence occurred;

    g) the officer's concern about reprisals against the victim by the suspect; or

    h) gender, race, ethnicity, disability, socioeconomic status or occupation of the victim and suspect.

17. The procedures should provide that an officer should explain to both the victim and the suspect that it is their duty to lay a charge when there are reasonable grounds to believe that an offence has been committed, and that only a Crown can withdraw the charge.

18. The procedures should address the use of warrants to enter a dwelling house for the purpose of arrest or apprehension in accordance with the relevant sections of the *Criminal Code*.

19. The procedures should provide that if the suspect is not present when officers arrive, and reasonable grounds exist to lay a charge, a warrant for the arrest of the accused should be obtained as soon as possible. Once obtained, a warrant should be entered on CPIC as soon as practicable and no later than within 24 hours. Every reasonable effort should be made to locate and apprehend the suspect.

20. The procedures should address dual arrest, as well as the laying of counter-charges, and highlight the importance of determining the primary offender in order to distinguish assault from defensive self-protection.

21. The procedures should provide that in all domestic violence occurrences, officers should consider whether there is any evidence of criminal

harassment, and should also follow the police service's procedures on criminal harassment investigations.

22. The procedures should provide that in all domestic violence occurrences the officers involved will:

    a) follow the police service's procedures on preventing/responding to occurrences involving firearms, regardless of whether any charges are laid; and

    b) where appropriate, determine whether there is compliance with the sections of the *Criminal Code* and *Firearms Act* relating to safe storage of firearms.

23. The procedures should provide that, as soon as possible, whenever a charge is laid in a domestic violence occurrence, the domestic violence supplementary report form will also be completed, including the part of the report relating to the risk indicators checklist. Where a suspect has been arrested, the procedures should provide that the risk indicators part of the report will be completed prior to any decision to release the suspect or detain for a bail hearing, and will be included with the Crown brief/ show cause report.

24. The procedures should address the use of behavioural science services in domestic violence occurrences if the circumstances of the case require a risk assessment, and how these services can be accessed in accordance with the requirements of the *Regulation on the Adequacy and Effectiveness of Police Services.*

25. The domestic violence supplementary report should be based on the Ministry's designated report form and should include, at minimum, the risk indicators set out by the Ministry.

26. The procedures should require police officers to address issues relating to children, who are under 16, in accordance with the police service's procedures on child abuse and neglect and the police service's protocol with the local Children's Aid Societies.

27. The procedures should address the investigative supports that may be available to assist in cases determined to be high risk, or where there is a repeat offender with a history of domestic violence with the same or multiple victims, including:

    a) the use of physical surveillance;

    b) electronic interception;

    c) video and photographic surveillance; and

    d) victim/witness protection services.

28. The procedures should provide that in cases involving high risk, or where there is a repeat offender, that the offender should be entered into the "SIP" category on CPIC as soon as possible, and no later than within 24 hours.

29. The procedures should provide that where an offender has engaged in a pattern of offending that may indicate hate/bias motivation towards

women, that the domestic violence investigator raise with the Crown the possibility of introducing evidence of hate/bias motivation as an aggravating factor for the purposes of sentencing the offender if convicted.

30. The procedures should set out the steps to be followed when a domestic violence occurrence involves a member of its police service or another police service.

31. The procedures should provide that in all domestic violence occurrences officers will comply with the police service's procedures relating to bail and violent crime.

32. The procedures should provide that in all domestic violence occurrences where there has been a breach of bail, or there is about to be a breach, officers will comply with the police service's procedures relating to breach of bail.

33. Consistent with local protocols, the procedures should set out the roles and responsibilities for notifying and informing the victim as soon as possible about the release of the accused, time and location of bail hearing, bail conditions and the criminal justice process.

34. The procedures should provide that officers who respond to domestic violence occurrences will provide assistance to the victim based on the police service's local procedures, including:

    a) assisting the victim in obtaining medical assistance, if necessary;

    b) remaining at the scene until they are satisfied that there is no further immediate threat to the victim;

    c) addressing any special needs of the victim (e.g., dealing with communication barriers);

    d) addressing the needs of child witnesses of domestic violence occurrences, including encouraging the child's primary caregiver to consider obtaining assistance for the child from a counsellor with experience in assisting child witnesses of domestic violence;

    e) if requested by the victim, attending the residence of the victim to ensure peaceful entry when the victim or accused returns to take possession of personal belongings and when concerns for the victim's safety exist because of the presence of the accused in the residence, unless peaceful entry of the residence cannot be achieved, or the removal of certain property is contested by either party, in which case the officers should advise the parties of the need to seek a civil remedy;

    f) arranging for transportation to a shelter or place of safety, if necessary, with the location remaining confidential to the suspect/accused and third parties; and

    g) providing information to the victim on services that are available, and offer to make initial contact with victims' services.

35. Police services should provide, in conjunction with local victims' services, a localized pamphlet on domestic violence that includes information on local resources to assist victims.

36. The procedures should provide that officers who respond to domestic violence occurrences should ensure that issues surrounding the victim's safety are addressed, including directly providing the victim with information on safety planning or providing information to the victim on the availability of safety planning information and assistance within the community.

37. The procedures should provide in cases where it is determined that there is a high risk, or repeat victimization, a domestic violence investigator or another member of the police service, should warn the victim about the potential risk to the victim or any children, and offer to meet with the victim to assist in developing or reviewing the victim's safety plan and to identify other measures that may be taken to help safeguard the victim and any children.

38. Every police service shall require supervisors to monitor, and ensure, compliance with the police service's procedures related to domestic violence occurrences.

39. Every police service should designate a domestic violence coordinator who will be responsible for:
    a) monitoring the response to, and investigation of domestic violence occurrences, including compliance with the police service's procedures by supervisors, officers and other members;
    b) monitoring and evaluating follow-up to domestic violence cases;
    c) liaising with the Crown, Probation and Parole Services, VWAP, VCARS, the local Children's Aid Society, and other local services and community representatives responsible for responding to issues related to domestic violence occurrences;
    d) informing the public and media about the police service's domestic violence occurrences procedures; and
    e) ensuring that statistical data are kept on domestic violence occurrences and provided to the Ministry in the form designated by the Ministry.

40. Every police service should periodically review the police service's procedures to ensure consistency with legislative and case law changes.

41. Every police service should ensure that persons who provide communications and dispatch functions are trained regarding domestic violence occurrence calls for service.

42. Every police service should ensure that its domestic violence investigators have successfully completed Ministry accredited training, or have the equivalent qualifications and skills designated by the Ministry, that addresses:

a) the dynamics of abusive relationships including the effects of physical assault and psychological abuse;

b) the initial police response to domestic violence occurrences, including officer safety;

c) interviewing, including interviewing child witnesses;

d) collection, care and handling of evidence;

e) search, seizure and warrants;

f) firearms seizures and legislation;

g) the mandatory charge policy, dual arrest and counter-charging;

h) court orders (e.g., restraining orders), judicial interim release orders, parole certificates, other relevant legislation and probation;

i) victim assistance and local victim services, as well as victims with special needs;

j) risk indicators and assessment, including the completion of the domestic violence supplementary report form;

k) procedures relating to post-arrest;

l) strategies for addressing repeat victimization and high risk cases;

m) safety planning; and

n) issues relating to children who witness violence.

43. Where a police service decides to meet its obligations under paragraph 2 by one of the methods set out in paragraph 5(b)-(d), it should also ensure that an adequate number of its patrol officers have received Ministry accredited training on the police response to domestic violence occurrences that addresses:

a) the dynamics of abusive relationships including the effects of physical assault and psychological abuse;

b) the initial police response to domestic violence occurrences, including officer safety;

c) preservation of the crime scene, and initial collection of evidence and interviewing;

d) court orders (e.g., restraining orders), judicial interim release orders, parole certificates, other relevant legislation and probation;

e) firearms seizures and legislation;

f) the role of the domestic violence investigator;

g) procedures relating to children at risk;

h) the completion of the domestic violence supplementary report, including risk indicators;

i) procedures relating to post-arrest;

j) victims' assistance and local victim services, as well as victims with special needs; and

k) issues relating to children who witness violence.

Elder Abuse

6

INTRODUCTION

Elder abuse is the term for any violence or mistreatment directed toward an elderly person by someone on whom the elderly person depends for food, shelter, or other aid. An **elderly person**, for the purpose of this chapter and most of the studies discussed in this chapter, is a person 65 years of age or older.

A common feature of elder abuse is isolation of the victim by the abuser. Isolation allows the abuser to exert his or her power over the victim without fear of repercussions.

It is not possible to know the full extent of abuse of elderly adults. Elder abuse is usually not reported by the victims themselves, but rather by others, or comes to light when the police investigate some other matter.

According to the Department of Justice (2003), elderly persons who are being abused may be unwilling, or unable, to report it for any of the following reasons:

- dependence on the abuser (emotional, physical, or economic);
- fear of being put in an institution;
- fear of retaliation or abandonment;
- fear of outside intervention (and loss of independence and control);
- fear of not being believed;
- pressure to maintain the family/community reputation;
- beliefs about importance of marriage and family;
- cognitive impairment or disability, including dementia or Alzheimer's;
- physical frailty or disability;
- social or geographic isolation;
- literacy, language, or cultural barriers; and
- shame or stigma.

In general, seniors (aged 65 years and older) tend to have lower rates of police-reported violent victimization than younger age groups. See Figure 6.1.

> ## CHAPTER OBJECTIVES
>
> After completing this chapter, you should be able to:
> - Describe the types of elder abuse.
> - Describe techniques for police intervention in elder abuse situations.
> - Identify some of the mental health problems faced by the elderly and explain how they can complicate police intervention in elder abuse situations.
> - Identify and provide for the needs of the elder abuse victim.

elder abuse
any violence or mistreatment directed toward an elderly person by someone on whom the elderly person depends for food, shelter, or other aid

elderly person
a person 65 years of age or older

Figure 6.1   Victims of Violent Crime, by Age Group, Canada, 2009

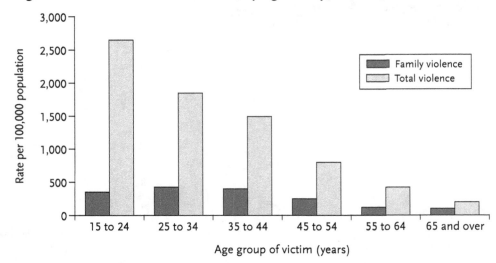

Notes: Excludes incidents where the victim's sex and/or age were unknown. In 2009, data from the Incident-based Uniform Crime Reporting Survey covered 99 percent of the population of Canada. Rates are calculated on the basis of 100,000 population. Populations based upon July 1 estimates from Statistics Canada, Demography Division.

Source: Statistics Canada, Canadian Centre for Justice Statistics, Incident-Based Uniform Crime Reporting Survey. Adapted from Statistics Canada (2011).

INCIDENCE OF VIOLENT CRIMES AGAINST ELDERLY PERSONS

The statistics presented in this section on violent incidents against seniors are based on police-reported data collected as part of the Incident-Based Uniform Crime Reporting (UCR2) Survey. These data represent the number of crimes against elderly persons that have been reported to, and substantiated by, Canadian police services. These statistics do not include emotional or psychological abuse unless a criminal offence had been identified in relation to the emotional or psychological abuse (Statistics Canada, 2011).

Policing data presented in this section may underestimate the true extent of violence against seniors because many cases may not come to the attention of legal authorities. According to results of the 2009 General Social Survey (GSS), about 70 percent of violent incidents were not reported to police because victims did not believe the incident was important enough or they dealt with the incident in some other way. Note also that other types of family violence such as criminal harassment, abduction, emotional or psychological abuse, neglect, and maltreatment are not included in the GSS analysis.

There were 7,871 incidents of violent crime against seniors reported to police in 2009. The perpetrator of 2,427 (31 percent) of these crimes was a member of the victim's family. Another 2,429 (31 percent) were committed by a friend, acquaintance, or a person known through a business relationship. Assaults by strangers accounted for 25 percent or 1,997 occurrences. See Table 6.1.

In 1,080 (13 percent) of these occurrences, the nature of the relationship with the assailant was not identified by the victim.

Table 6.1   Senior Victims (65 Years and Older) of Violent Crime by Sex and Accused–Victim Relationship, Canada, 2009

Accused–victim relationship	Total		Sex of victim			
			Female		Male	
	Number	Rate[a]	Number	Rate[a]	Number	Rate[a]
Total family	**2,427**	**54**	**1,467**	**59**	**960**	**48**
Grown child[b]	785	18	461	19	324	16
Spouse or ex-spouse[c]	680	15	466	19	214	11
Sibling[d]	270	6	156	6	114	6
Parent[e]	249	6	131	5	118	6
Extended family[f]	443	10	253	10	190	9
Total friends, acquaintances, others	**2,429**	**54**	**908**	**37**	**1,521**	**75**
Friend or acquaintance[g]	2,044	46	799	32	1,245	62
Business relationship	373	8	105	4	268	13
Criminal relationship	12	0	4	0	8	0
Stranger	1,997	45	802	32	1,195	59
Unknown	1,018	23	440	18	578	29
Total violence against seniors	**7,871**	**176**	**3,617**	**147**	**4,254**	**211**

Notes: Excludes incidents where the victim's sex and/or age was unknown. In 2009, data from the Incident-based Uniform Crime Reporting Survey covered 99 percent of the population of Canada.

a Rates are calculated on the basis of 100,000 seniors (65 years and older). Populations based upon July 1 estimates from Statistics Canada, Demography Division.

b Includes biological, step, adoptive and foster children.

c Includes current and former legally married and common-law spouses.

d Includes biological, step, adoptive and foster brothers and sisters.

e Includes biological, step, adoptive and foster parents.

f Includes all other family members related by blood, marriage or adoption. Examples include grandchildren, uncles, aunts, cousins and in-laws.

g Includes friends, current or former boyfriends or girlfriends, neighbours, authority figures and casual acquaintances.

Sources: Statistics Canada, Canadian Centre for Justice Statistics, Incident-Based Uniform Crime Reporting Survey. Adapted from Statistics Canada (2011).

The most common violent *Criminal Code* offence committed by family members against seniors in 2009 was common assault (s. 266), the category of least serious physical harm to victims (see Table 6.2). Common assault accounted for more than half (53 percent) of all incidents. This was followed by uttering threats (s. 264.1), which accounted for 21 percent of incidents, major assaults (ss. 267 and 268), which accounted for 13 percent of incidents, and criminal harassment (s. 264), which accounted for 4 percent of incidents. The remaining 9 percent of incidents involved various violent offences, including sexual assault, robbery, and extortion.

Elder Abuse in Institutions

Older adults who are either physically frail or disabled, and those who are cognitively impaired, may be more vulnerable to abuse, especially if they are residents

Table 6.2   Senior Victims (65 Years and Older) of Violence by Sex and Offence Type, Canada, 2009

| | Total | | Sex of victim | | | |
| | | | Female | | Male | |
Type of offence	Number	Rate[a]	Number	Rate[a]	Number	Rate[a]
Homicide or attempted homicide	18	0	10	0	8	0
Sexual assault (levels 1, 2, 3)	25	1	24	1	1	0
Major assault (levels 2, 3)	304	7	163	7	141	7
Common assault (level 1)	1,284	29	774	31	510	25
Robbery	20	0	12	0	8	0
Extortion	18	0	7	0	11	1
Criminal harassment	103	2	79	3	24	1
Uttering threats	520	12	304	12	216	11
Other violent offences[b]	135	3	94	4	41	2
Total	**2,427**	**54**	**1,467**	**59**	**960**	**48**

Notes: Excludes incidents where the victim's sex and/or age was unknown. In 2009, data from the Incident-Based Uniform Crime Reporting Survey covered 99 percent of the population of Canada.

[a] Rates are calculated on the basis of 100,000 seniors (65 years and older). Populations based upon July 1 estimates from Statistics Canada, Demography Division.

[b] Includes, for example, indecent/harassing telephone calls, criminal negligence causing bodily harm, discharge firearm with intent, using firearm/imitation of firearm in commission of offence, pointing a firearm, trap likely to cause or causing bodily harm, kidnapping, unlawfully causing bodily harm, and other violent offences.

Sources: Statistics Canada, Canadian Centre for Justice Statistics, Incident-Based Uniform Crime Reporting Survey. Adapted from Statistics Canada (2011).

of long-term care facilities. These individuals may be more vulnerable to elder abuse because they already require the protective environment of an institution.

There are no available national studies on the prevalence of institutional abuse in Canada. However, in 1997, the College of Nurses of Ontario conducted a survey of nurses that provided some anecdotal evidence of the prevalence of abuse in elder care institutions (College of Nurses of Ontario, 1997).

The survey identified that 56 percent of nurses working in community care witnessed or heard about at least one incident of abuse by a nurse since 1993. The survey found that over 90 percent of these incidents were personally witnessed by the respondent. The most commonly mentioned types of abuse witnessed were roughness (31 percent); yelling and swearing (28 percent); offensive/embarrassing comments (28 percent); and hitting/shoving (10 percent).

The Canadian Network for the Prevention of Elder Abuse (2010) cites the following reasons why elder abuse may occur in an institution:

- *Mismatch of skills.* Staff may not know how to properly care for elderly people with different medical needs, particularly when the elderly person is cognitively or physically impaired.

- *Ageism.* Society places considerable value on being young and active. As people grow older or develop medical conditions that impair their abilities, they may become less valued by others. Some consider the institutions that the elderly persons are living in to be the last place they will live before they die and, because they are much closer to the "end of their life," the elderly person is often devalued.

- *Systemic problems.* Problems may stem from a number of sources: the facility's culture (whether or not staff recognize the dignity and worthiness of their patients as expressed by upper management); inadequate staffing (insufficient number of staff or lack of appropriate training); staff minimization of abuse and rationalization of abuse; policy deficiencies (lack of clear policies for handling difficult situations); financial constraints (contributes to poor quality of care); poor enforcement of standards of adequate care for the institution; work-related stress and staff burnout; staff retaliation (particularly in response to aggressive behaviours in people with dementia).

SIGNS OF ELDER ABUSE

There are some behaviours and signs that may indicate elder abuse. However, the majority of these indicators are generally not observed by police. Police must rely on reports of abuse by concerned individuals before they can intervene. This poses a quandary because the persons most able to report these indicators of abuse are likely to be the abusers.

Indicators of elder abuse include the following (Winnipeg Police Service, 2000):

- repeated occurrences of unexplained physical injuries or accidents;
- a history of changing hospitals and/or doctors;
- dehydration and/or malnutrition;
- unexplained delays in seeking treatment for injuries;
- rent, mortgage, or utility bills that are unpaid or in arrears;
- bedsores, worsening personal hygiene, untreated wounds, and absence of wound dressings;
- insufficient money to purchase clothing, food, medications, or other necessities even though income appears adequate;
- feelings of hopelessness and resignation, withdrawal, and suicidal thoughts;
- depression, fearfulness, anxiety, and low self-esteem in the older person;
- inappropriate use of medication, withholding of needed medications, and oversedation; and
- an occurrence of unusual activity in the older person's bank account, including a change in the amount or frequency of withdrawals, many withdrawals being made by bank card rather than at the teller, and the opening of joint bank accounts.

AGE AS AN AGGRAVATING FACTOR AT SENTENCING

Note that s. 718.2 of the *Criminal Code* recognizes that in crimes committed against elderly persons where the perpetrator of the crime was motivated by bias or prejudice based on age or physical or mental disability, the bias or prejudice will be considered to be an aggravating factor at sentencing. This principle applies to all types of criminal offences.

Other Sentencing Principles: Criminal Code, Section 718.2

718.2 A court that imposes a sentence shall also take into consideration the following principles:

(a) a sentence should be increased or reduced to account for any relevant aggravating or mitigating circumstances relating to the offence or the offender, and, without limiting the generality of the foregoing,

(i) evidence that the offence was motivated by bias, prejudice or hate based on race, national or ethnic origin, language, colour, religion, sex, age, mental or physical disability, sexual orientation or any other similar factor, ...

shall be deemed to be aggravating circumstances.

TYPES OF ELDER ABUSE

There are five specific types of elder abuse: physical abuse, sexual abuse, financial abuse, neglect, and emotional/psychological abuse.

Physical Abuse

Physical abuse includes any violent act, even if it does not result in physical injury. Physical coercion, such as forced feeding and the use of restraints, also constitutes physical abuse.

Physical abuse includes the following (Department of Justice Canada, 2003):

- scalding or burning,
- spitting,
- beating,
- shoving or pushing,
- handling roughly, and
- slapping or hitting.

Physical abuse against elderly persons may also include the following actions (Department of Justice Canada, 2003):

- confining them to chairs or beds;
- confining them to rooms, including locking them in;
- tying them to pieces of furniture;
- using and misusing physical restraints; and

- using tranquillizers, alcohol, or medication as a means of making them more manageable or subduing them.

Signs of Physical Abuse

Signs that a person might be experiencing physical abuse include:

- physical injuries such as bruises, welts, cuts, or burns;
- head injuries that cannot be explained or for which an unlikely explanation is given;
- confusion or tiredness, which may be a result of overmedication;
- loss of mobility, which may be a result of being restrained;
- marks on furniture where restraints might have been used;
- locks on entrance/room doors; and
- locks in areas where food is kept.

Criminal Offences Related to Physical Abuse

As with any unauthorized application of force, there are criminal offences under the *Criminal Code* that may apply. The offence will depend on the nature of the application of force:

- criminal negligence causing bodily harm or death (ss. 220 to 221),
- unlawfully causing bodily harm (s. 269),
- manslaughter (ss. 234 and 236),
- murder (ss. 229 to 231 and s. 235), and
- assault (ss. 265 to 268).

The act of overmedicating the elderly person with the intent to overcome resistance is a criminal offence as defined in s. 246 of the *Criminal Code*.

Overcoming Resistance to Commission of Offence: Criminal Code, Section 246

246. Every one who, with intent to enable or assist himself or another person to commit an indictable offence, ...

(b) administers or causes to be administered to any person, or attempts to administer to any person, or causes or attempts to cause any person to take a stupefying or overpowering drug, matter or thing,

is guilty of an indictable offence and liable to imprisonment for life.

Forcible confinement is another criminal offence that can arise when the elderly are under the care of others, as described in s. 279(2) of the *Criminal Code*.

Forcible Confinement: Criminal Code, Section 279(2)

279(2) Every one who, without lawful authority, confines, imprisons or forcibly seizes another person is guilty of

(a) an indictable offence and liable to imprisonment for a term not exceeding ten years; or

(b) an offence punishable on summary conviction and liable to imprisonment for a term not exceeding eighteen months.

The offence under this subsection does not require proof of total physical restraint of the victim: *R v. Gratton* (1985), 18 CCC (3d) 462 (Ont. CA), leave to appeal to SCC refused [1985] 1 SCR viii. [*Martin's Annual Criminal Code, 2012*, p. 607]

Illegal restraint of the elderly can include being locked in a room or tied to a bed, chair, or other object. The elderly person's physical condition may prevent him or her from calling for assistance or escaping. Note that a charge of forcible confinement is sustainable even if the victim offered no resistance, as stated in s. 279(3) of the *Criminal Code*.

Non-Resistance: Criminal Code, Section 279(3)

279(3) In proceedings under this section, the fact that the person in relation to whom the offence is alleged to have been committed did not resist is not a defence unless the accused proves that the failure to resist was not caused by threats, duress, force or exhibition of force.

Counselling or helping an elderly person to commit suicide is also an offence that may be considered physical (and possibly psychological) abuse, as stated in s. 241 of the *Criminal Code*.

Counselling or Aiding Suicide: Criminal Code, Section 241

241. Every one who
  (a) counsels a person to commit suicide, or
  (b) aids or abets a person to commit suicide,
whether suicide ensues or not, is guilty of an indictable offence and liable to imprisonment for a term not exceeding fourteen years.

Sexual Abuse

Sexual abuse is any form of engaging in sexual activity with a person without the full consent of that person. The elderly person may not have the ability to give consent due to dementia or the effects of prescription drugs. Or consent may have been obtained through fear of repercussions, in which case it is invalid, as was shown in the case of *R v. Ewanchuk*, discussed below.

Sexual abuse includes unwanted sexual touching; sexual relations without voluntary consent; or the forcing or coercing of degrading, humiliating, or painful sexual acts. It also includes incidents of sexual exploitation and sexual harassment.

Regardless of the type of sexual abuse, the key issue in determining whether abuse has occurred is consent, as discussed in ss. 273.1(1) and 273.1(2) of the *Criminal Code*.

Meaning of "Consent": Criminal Code, Section 273.1(1)

273.1(1) Subject to subsection (2) and subsection 265(3), "consent" means, for the purposes of sections 271, 272 and 273, the voluntary agreement of the complainant to engage in the sexual activity in question.

Where No Consent Obtained: Criminal Code, Section 273.1(2)

273.1(2) No consent is obtained, for the purposes of sections 271, 272 and 273, where

(a) the agreement is expressed by the words or conduct of a person other than the complainant;

(b) the complainant is incapable of consenting to the activity;

(c) the accused induces the complainant to engage in the activity by abusing a position of trust, power or authority;

(d) the complainant expresses, by words or conduct, a lack of agreement to engage in the activity; or

(e) the complainant, having consented to engage in sexual activity, expresses, by words or conduct, a lack of agreement to continue to engage in the activity.

No Consent Where Fear of Harm: R v. Ewanchuk

There is no consent where the complainant consents because she honestly believes that she will otherwise suffer physical violence. While the plausibility of the alleged fear and any overt expressions of it are relevant in assessing the complainant's credibility that she consented out of fear, the approach is subjective: *R v. Ewanchuk*, [1999] 1 SCR 330, 131 CCC (3d) 481. [*Martin's Annual Criminal Code, 2012*, p. 582]

Sexual abuse may also include the following activities (Winnipeg Police Service, 2000):

- engaging in acts that are physically intrusive, including sexualized kissing and/or fondling, oral and/or genital contact, digital penetration, and vaginal and/or anal intercourse;
- engaging in exhibitionist and voyeuristic behaviour or engaging in offensive verbal and non-verbal sexual behaviours;
- forcing an unwilling person to view pornographic materials;
- involving the victim in the production of pornographic materials; and
- allowing other people sexual access to the individual.

There may be *Criminal Code* offences that apply in cases of sexual abuse of elderly persons, including sexual assault (ss. 271 to 273) and sexual exploitation of a person with a disability (s. 153.1).

Sexual Exploitation of Person with Disability: Criminal Code, Section 153.1(1)

153.1(1) Every person who is in a position of trust or authority towards a person with a mental or physical disability or who is a person with whom a person with a mental or physical disability is in a relationship of dependency and who, for a sexual purpose, counsels or incites that person to touch, without that person's consent, his or her own body, the body of the person who so counsels or incites, or the body of any other person, directly or indirectly, with a part of the body or with an object, the body of any person, including the body of the person who so invites, counsels or incites and the body of the person with the disability, is guilty of

(a) an indictable offence and liable to imprisonment for a term not exceeding five years; or

(b) an offence punishable on summary conviction and liable to imprisonment for a term not exceeding eighteen months.

Definition of "Consent": Criminal Code, Section 153.1(2)

153.1(2) Subject to subsection (3), "consent" means, for the purposes of this section, the voluntary agreement of the complainant to engage in the sexual activity in question.

When No Consent Obtained: Criminal Code, Section 153.1(3)

153.1(3) No consent is obtained, for the purposes of this section, if

(a) the agreement is expressed by the words or conduct of a person other than the complainant;

(b) the complainant is incapable of consenting to the activity;

(c) the accused counsels or incites the complainant to engage in the activity by abusing a position of trust, power or authority;

(d) the complainant expresses, by words or conduct, a lack of agreement to engage in the activity; or

(e) the complainant, having consented to engage in sexual activity, expresses, by words or conduct, a lack of agreement to continue to engage in the activity.

The definition of consent in s. 153.1 and the limits of the defence of belief in consent are similar to the provisions of ss. 273.1 and 273.2 of the *Criminal Code* (respecting sexual assault).

Signs of Sexual Abuse

The following signs may indicate sexual abuse:

- presence of a sexually transmitted disease in an elderly person who is not known to be sexually active;
- bleeding, pain, or bruises in the genital area; or
- depression, fear, anxiety, withdrawal, or passivity (these signs may also indicate other kinds of abuse).

Financial Abuse

Financial abuse includes financial manipulation or exploitation through fraud, theft, forgery, or extortion. It means using elderly people's property or money dishonestly. It could also mean failing to use elderly people's assets for their welfare. When someone acts without consent in a manner that financially benefits one person at the expense of another, financial abuse has occurred.

Common forms of financial abuse of the elderly are theft or misuse of money; extortion of money or property; and forcing someone to sell his or her property. Any of these actions can lead to criminal charges.

Caregivers, because of their power over the elderly, often have the opportunity to extort money or property from their charges. For example, a caregiver might threaten to withdraw care from an elderly person unless title to real estate is signed over. Using an elderly person's property without his or her permission (as in appropriating an elderly person's vehicle for one's own use) is another form of financial abuse.

Financial abuse can also include wrongful use of a power of attorney. A **power of attorney** is a legal instrument that authorizes a person to carry out specific acts on behalf of another person. Elderly people who have difficulty managing their financial affairs often grant a power of attorney to a family member. Typically, the power of attorney gives the family member access to bank accounts, investment property, and so forth, which can create the potential for abuse.

power of attorney
legal instrument that authorizes a person to carry out specific acts on behalf of another person

In Ontario there are three types of power of attorney:

- A *continuing power of attorney for property* (CPOA) is a legal document in which a person gives someone else the legal authority to make decisions about their finances if they become unable to make those decisions themselves. The person who is named as the attorney does not have to be a lawyer. The power of attorney is called "continuing" because it can be used after the person who gave it is no longer mentally capable.

- A *non-continuing power of attorney for property* covers financial affairs but can't be used if the conveyer becomes mentally incapable. This power of attorney could be used by a person needing someone to look after their financial transactions while they are away from home for an extended period of time.

- A *power of attorney for personal care* (POAPC) is a legal document in which one person gives another person the authority to make personal-care decisions (for example, decisions concerning housing and health care) on their behalf if they become mentally incapable.

The attorney is entitled to take payment at a rate specified by law unless otherwise stated in the CPOA. Section 40 of the *Substitute Decisions Act, 1992* sets out the law relating to compensation:

Compensation: Substitute Decisions Act, 1992, Section 40

40(1) A guardian of property or attorney under a continuing power of attorney may take annual compensation from the property in accordance with the prescribed fee scale.

Same

(2) The compensation may be taken monthly, quarterly or annually.

Same

(3) The guardian or attorney may take an amount of compensation greater than the prescribed fee scale allows,

(a) in the case where the Public Guardian and Trustee is not the guardian or attorney, if consent in writing is given by the Public Guardian and Trustee and by the incapable person's guardian of the person or attorney under a power of attorney for personal care, if any; or

(b) in the case where the Public Guardian and Trustee is the guardian or attorney, if the court approves.

If the CPOA document does not specify the rate of payment, the attorney will be entitled to the amount specified s. 1 of regulation 26/95 of the *Substitute Decisions Act*:

1. For the purposes of subsection 40(1) of the Act, a guardian of property or an attorney under a continuing power of attorney shall be entitled, subject to an increase under subsection 40(3) of the Act or an adjustment pursuant to a passing of the guardian's or attorney's accounts under section 42 of the Act, to compensation of,

(a) 3 per cent on capital and income receipts;

(b) 3 per cent on capital and income disbursements; and

(c) three-fifths of 1 per cent on the annual average value of the assets as a care and management fee.

Some other examples of financial abuse include:

- stealing possessions;
- selling property without permission;
- refusing to pay back borrowed money when requested;
- charging exorbitant prices for goods or services;
- refusing to move out of the elderly person's home when asked;
- sharing a home with an elderly person without paying a fair share of the household expenses; and
- unduly pressuring the elderly person to buy drugs or alcohol.

There are several *Criminal Code* offences that may be present in situations of financial abuse. These offences include:

- theft (ss. 331, 332, and 334)
- criminal breach of trust (s. 336);
- extortion (s. 346);
- forgery (s. 366);

- theft, forgery, etc., of credit card (s. 342);
- use, trafficking or possession of forged document (s. 368); and
- fraud (s. 380).

Neglect

Neglect is failing to care for or meet the needs of elderly persons who are dependent and cannot meet their own needs. Neglect can be intentional or unintentional. Unintentional neglect may occur when a caregiver does not meet the needs of an elderly person because of a lack of skill or information.

neglect
failing to care for or meet the needs of elderly persons who are dependent and cannot meet their own needs

Neglect may include failing to provide the following (Department of Justice Canada, 2003):

- adequate personal care (for example, failing to turn over a bedridden elderly person frequently to prevent bedsores);
- comfortable and safe living conditions;
- a clean home environment;
- items essential for personal cleanliness;
- transportation to required appointments;
- adequate clothing, nutrition, and other necessities; and
- prescribed or other medications necessary to maintain health.

Although the first five examples above do not constitute criminal offences, the final two examples—failing to provide necessities—may be an offence.

Withholding the necessaries of life (food, shelter, clothing, health care, etc.) from an elderly person can be an offence under s. 215(1) of the *Criminal Code*.

Duty of Persons to Provide Necessaries: Criminal Code, Section 215(1)

215(1) Every one is under a legal duty ...

(c) to provide necessaries of life to a person under his charge if that person

(i) is unable, by reason of detention, age, illness, mental disorder or other cause, to withdraw himself from that charge, and

(ii) is unable to provide himself with necessaries of life.

Signs of Neglect

Signs of neglect can include the following (Legal Resource Centre, University of Alberta, 2008):

- dry lips, pale complexion, or unhealthy weight loss, which may indicate malnourishment;
- clothing that is dirty or inappropriate for the weather;
- an absence of dentures, glasses, or hearing aids, when these items are needed;

- physical appearance that indicates infrequent bathing (for example, matted, oily hair);
- untreated incontinence;
- mental or physical deterioration with no apparent medical reason;
- confinement;
- wandering;
- lack of food items in the house;
- inadequate medication or overmedication; and
- meal preparation or housekeeping standards that could cause illness or accident.

It is important to distinguish between neglect and self-neglect. Neglect is caused by someone else, whereas self-neglect is caused by the older person not taking care of himself or herself.

Emotional/Psychological Abuse

Emotional or psychological abuse may be defined as behaviour intended to control a person, instill fear in a person, cause a person to fear for his or her safety, or diminish a person's sense of self-worth (Nova Scotia Department of Community Services, 2002a). It may include frequent verbal aggression; social isolation (for example, refusing to allow access to grandchildren and other family members or friends); humiliation; degradation; threats to institutionalize the person; and actions that deliberately frighten the victim.

Emotional/psychological abuse can also include the removal of decision-making power; the removal of or refusal to provide aids for mobility (for example, wheelchair or cane); the use of restraints or threats to use restraints; and the infantilization of the elderly person (treating the elder like a child).

Although it is not a criminal action to humiliate, insult, or belittle someone, threatening can be a criminal offence under s. 264.1 of the *Criminal Code*.

Uttering Threats: Criminal Code, Section 264.1

264.1 Every one commits an offence who, in any manner, knowingly utters, conveys or causes any person to receive a threat
 (a) to cause death or bodily harm to any person;
 (b) to burn, destroy or damage real or personal property; or
 (c) to kill, poison or injure an animal or bird that is the property of any person.

Emotional/psychological abuse may involve other offences under the *Criminal Code*: criminal harassment (s. 264); harassing phone calls (s. 372); and intimidation (s. 423).

Signs of Emotional/Psychological Abuse

Signs that an elderly person might be experiencing emotional/psychological abuse include the following (Legal Resource Centre, University of Alberta, 2008):

- apathy, withdrawal, or depressed state without any apparent reason;
- physical indicators of imposed isolation (for example, locks on doors and no phone, television, or radio);
- evidence that the older person is being consistently ignored, treated passively, or treated like an infant by a caregiver;
- fear of particular family members, friends, or caregivers;
- low self-esteem;
- feelings of hopelessness and helplessness;
- deference to the caregiver (for example, waits for the caregiver to respond to all questions);
- significant change in weight;
- difficulty visiting, calling, or otherwise contacting the elderly person; and
- the elderly person makes excuses for social isolation.

Learning Activity 6.1

Read the following scenario. Then answer the questions below.

You are a police officer responding to a call for assistance. The caller, Jay Apple, reports that his mother, Joan Apple, is having some mental health problems. He requests that police meet him at his mother's residence.

Upon arrival you are met by Jay. He tells you that his mother has been behaving strangely and that he is worried about her. He asks you to come into the residence with him to talk with his mother. He enters the residence. You do not follow. You ask Mr. Apple if he would please have his mother come to the door to give you permission to enter. He shouts to his mother. A female, identified as Joan Apple, comes to the door. You ask her whether you may come in and you explain to her that her son is concerned about her well-being.

She tells you that she is all right and invites you to come in. Mrs. Apple asks you to join her and her son in the living room to discuss her son's concerns. You enter the living room and sit with Mrs. Apple and her son.

Jay begins the conversation. "My mother has given away her car and donated the family cottage to a charity to be auctioned. She has given the title to this house to charity to be sold when she dies, and has given all of her savings to a hospice. I don't believe that she is acting rationally. She has donated or given away all the family's inheritance, about five and a half million dollars! There is nothing left! All she has to live on is her pensions!"

Joan interjects, "My husband, Edgar, died of cancer two years ago; he was only 74 years old.

"Edgar worked hard to accumulate all these things. He told me that he was sorry that he had worked so much and didn't take more time to enjoy life.

"All the things we accumulated were worthless in the end. I am saddened when I think of all the years we wasted trying to get ahead. Ahead of what, or whom? I don't know. I just know that all these things did not bring us any more happiness or time together.

"The people from the Palliative Care Centre were incredibly kind to us and helped Edgar die with dignity. I will be eternally grateful to them and want to help them help others in our situation."

Joan continues, "I am 79 years old. I won't be around much longer. Edgar and I spoke of what we would leave for our children when we were gone. My children have good careers. We paid for their education. They have homes and families. How much more does a person need?

"There are so many others who have nothing. We decided that we would give all our worldly possessions to charity. Our children didn't need them anymore."

Jay interrupts, "That is extremely selfish! How can you say what I need? I need to work every day! I'm almost 40 years old and I don't have a cottage! I have to keep my boat docked at a public marina! My BMW and Mercedes are almost three years old, hardly new! My house is only half the size of this house! I don't have any savings! I have only been to the Caribbean once this year! My kids need to go to private school! Who is going to pay for that? Do you want them in a public school?"

Joan begins to cry. She says, "I am sorry that I raised you to believe that 'more' is what you need. It is my fault. I didn't know. I am so sorry."

Jay turns to you and says, "See. I told you that she wasn't making sense! She is suffering from some form of dementia! She doesn't realize what she is doing! You can't just give away five and a half million dollars! She needs to see a doctor and a lawyer to get this fixed! There will be nothing left!"

Joan says, "I am sorry that you feel that way. I have spoken with Jane. As you know, she has been our lawyer for the past 30 years. She completed all the necessary legal documentation and assisted me with the donations. I am quite sane. This is all legal."

Jay says, "This is all a conspiracy. Jane Bassett never liked me. She was one of those 'hippie' types from the sixties! I don't know how she became a lawyer. She can't be much of a lawyer anyway! She doesn't even own a cottage or a house! She doesn't even own a car! She uses public transit! She lives in an apartment over a pizza shop! She doesn't even have an office! She works out of a legal aid clinic! My mother can't take advice from her. That woman is a loser!"

Joan interjects, "Au contraire. She is perhaps the biggest winner that I know! I just wish that your father and I had realized what we were doing wrong 30 years ago!"

Jay Apple turns to you and says, "Are you going to do anything about this? She is obviously out of her mind. I think that she is going to kill herself. Isn't giving away your possessions one of the signs that you might commit suicide?"

> Before you can answer, Joan says to you, "If I was going to kill myself, I would have done it when Edgar died. I thought that the world would end. But it didn't. The more I thought about what we had discussed while he was sick, the more I wanted to try to make a difference and try to help those less fortunate. I wish that Jay could understand, but it is my fault that he doesn't. I am not going to kill myself. I'm getting up in years, and I want to live the rest of my days as simply as possible."
>
> Jay says to you, "You have to do something. She has lost her mind! She is not competent!"
>
> Has any type of abuse occurred? If yes, what would you do in this situation? Provide reasons to support your answer.

REASONS FOR ELDER ABUSE

Elder abuse occurs because the elderly are often vulnerable. Some abusers suffer from psychological or emotional problems that contribute to their actions, but others simply act out of greed, self-indulgence, or the desire to exert control.

Abuse can be inflicted by family members, professional caregivers, and any other person in a caregiving role.

In home care settings where the elderly person is ill, primary care is often provided by the family, with limited assistance from part-time professionals. The stress of looking after an ill parent or other relative can trigger abuse by the family member.

Financial dependence can lead to elder abuse. The caregiver may be financially dependent on the elderly person because of unemployment or other problems. Financial dependence can cause the caregiver to attempt to dominate a vulnerable elderly relative who is no longer able to look after himself or herself. Domination may take the form of the caregiver having the elderly person turn over total control of his or her bank account, with the threat of withdrawal of care if the elderly person does not comply.

Abuse can take place in institutional settings as well. Abusive acts by staff may be caused by stress. The abuse may include assault and theft, although institutional abuse more commonly takes the form of neglect, substandard care, and lack of respect for the elderly.

Listed below are some common factors that appear to contribute to elder abuse (Nova Scotia Department of Community Services, 2002b). Although these factors may contribute to abusive behaviour, they are not reasons to excuse the behaviour.

1. *Stress.* Abuse can stem from stresses in a caregiver's life. Adult children who care for their parents often face the additional demands of careers, children, and the financial burden of providing for an adult in their home. Note, however, that the majority of caregivers are not abusive no matter how stressful their lives are.

2. *Substance abuse/psychological problems.* Some caregivers may suffer from substance abuse, poor impulse control, and other issues that affect their ability to care for the elderly. These behavioural problems are likely to

manifest themselves in other areas of their life, including their care of an elderly person.

3. *Unresolved family conflict/abusive behaviour patterns.* If an adult child was abused at a young age, he or she may repeat the abuse. Although this may be a contributing factor, the majority of abused children are not abusive in adulthood.

4. *Increased vulnerability.* As adults age, they may increasingly have to rely on a caregiver for daily care and emotional support if they suffer from physical or cognitive impairment, or if they lack mobility. Elderly persons who become increasingly powerless, vulnerable, and dependent on their caregivers may be at higher risk for abuse.

5. *Societal factors.* Canadian and American cultures in general have been conditioned to have negative social attitudes about aging. Many members of the public perceive that the elderly are generally frail, dependent, sick, and unproductive. This belief, called **ageism**, could lead to discrimination against older adults and may contribute to abuse.

ageism
discriminatory belief that the elderly are generally frail, dependent, sick, and unproductive

Persons who are at increased risk of becoming abusive may also share the following characteristics:

- psychological or financial dependence on the elderly person,
- long-standing history of spousal violence or a poor marital relationship,
- history of mental illness,
- inexperience at care-giving, and
- isolation (the caregiver spends all of his or her time with the elderly person).

Again, none of these justify abusive behaviours.

PUBLIC AWARENESS OF ELDER ABUSE

Research conducted by Environics Research Group (2008) for Human Resources and Social Development Canada has shown that there is widespread awareness among Canadians concerning the issue of elder abuse:

- 95 percent of Canadians believe that most of the abuse experienced by older adults is hidden or goes undetected.
- 22 percent of Canadians believe that a senior they know personally might be experiencing abuse.
- 90 percent of Canadians believe that the abuse experienced by an older person often gets worse over time.
- 87 percent of Canadians believe that raising awareness among seniors about their right to live safely and securely is the most important priority for governments when it comes to elder abuse.
- 67 percent of Canadians believe that older women are more likely to be abused than older men.

- 12 percent of Canadians have sought out information or help about a situation or suspected situation of elder abuse or about elder abuse in general.
- 5 percent of Canadians have searched the Internet for specific information about elder abuse.

REPORTING ABUSE OR NEGLECT

Although there appears to be a consensus that elder abuse is a problem in Canada, there is disagreement about whether reporting abuse should be mandatory where the abuse takes place outside of an institution—for example, in an elderly person's home. (There is currently no legal obligation to report elder abuse occurring in a non-institutional setting.)

Proponents of mandatory reporting argue that society has an obligation to protect its elderly citizens and that it is important to demonstrate that abuse of seniors is a serious issue. They draw a comparison with the mandatory reporting of child abuse. All should have equal protection under the law.

Opponents argue that mandatory reporting would be inappropriate because it's paternalistic. Elderly persons are adults and have the right to choose how they want to live their lives. Those in disagreement put forward that mandatory reporting of elder abuse would result in discriminatory application of the law because there is no requirement to report the abuse of non-elderly adults.

Both sides agree that there should be mandatory reporting of abuse in institutions, citing much of the same reasoning.

- The operators of long-term care facilities have a legal obligation to provide care.
- Elderly persons living in long-term care facilities may be more vulnerable to abuse and neglect because they may have a disabling mental or physical condition.
- The long-term care facilities tend to be away from community scrutiny because of the isolated location or lack of community interaction with the facility.

In Ontario, regulation 79/10 of the *Long-Term Care Homes Act, 2007*, sets out the obligations of a residential long-term care facility. The regulation stipulates the minimum level of care that is legally acceptable in the following areas:

- safe and secure home,
- nursing and personal support services,
- recreational and social activities,
- nutritional care and hydration programs,
- medical services,
- religious and spiritual practices, and
- prevention of abuse and neglect.

Section 96 of the regulation requires long-term care facilities to have a policy of zero tolerance of abuse and neglect.

Policy to Promote Zero Tolerance: Ontario Regulation 79/10, Section 96

96. Every licensee of a long-term care home shall ensure that the licensee's written policy under section 20 of the Act to promote zero tolerance of abuse and neglect of residents,

(a) contains procedures and interventions to assist and support residents who have been abused or neglected or allegedly abused or neglected;

(b) contains procedures and interventions to deal with persons who have abused or neglected or allegedly abused or neglected residents, as appropriate;

(c) identifies measures and strategies to prevent abuse and neglect;

(d) identifies the manner in which allegations of abuse and neglect will be investigated, including who will undertake the investigation and who will be informed of the investigation; and

(e) identifies the training and retraining requirements for all staff, including,

(i) training on the relationship between power imbalances between staff and residents and the potential for abuse and neglect by those in a position of trust, power and responsibility for resident care, and

(ii) situations that may lead to abuse and neglect and how to avoid such situations.

Section 97 sets out the notification requirements in cases of alleged, suspected, or witnessed abuse or neglect.

Notification Re Incidents: Ontario Regulation 79/10, Section 97

97(1) Every licensee of a long-term care home shall ensure that the resident's substitute decision-maker, if any, and any other person specified by the resident,

(a) are notified immediately upon the licensee becoming aware of an alleged, suspected or witnessed incident of abuse or neglect of the resident that has resulted in a physical injury or pain to the resident or that causes distress to the resident that could potentially be detrimental to the resident's health or well-being; and

(b) are notified within 12 hours upon the licensee becoming aware of any other alleged, suspected or witnessed incident of abuse or neglect of the resident.

(2) The licensee shall ensure that the resident and the resident's substitute decision-maker, if any, are notified of the results of the investigation required under subsection 23(1) of the Act, immediately upon the completion of the investigation.

Section 98 of the regulation requires the licensee of the facility to contact police immediately if there is a suspected incident of abuse or neglect that may be a criminal offence.

Police Notification: Ontario Regulation 79/10, Section 98

98. Every licensee of a long-term care home shall ensure that the appropriate police force is immediately notified of any alleged, suspected or witnessed incident of abuse or neglect of a resident that the licensee suspects may constitute a criminal offence.

POLICE INTERVENTION

The goals of police intervention are to stop the abuse and improve the quality of life of the victim. With those goals in mind, police should ask themselves the following questions before beginning the intervention:

- In what way will the intervention empower the victim?
- In what way will the intervention deprive the victim of power?
- In what way will the intervention enhance the victim's safety?
- In what way will the intervention reduce the safety of the victim?

With these points in mind, the officer must intercede in a manner that meets the victim's needs but also fulfills his or her duty to investigate possible offences. The abuse complaint will probably not have been initiated by the victim, and the victim may hesitate to provide information.

Officers should not become exasperated in situations where the abused elder does not wish to cooperate. If the person is not suffering from a mental disorder and is able to make logical decisions, he or she may choose to do nothing.

Seniors are adults, not children. Because they are adults, they have the right to choose how they live. However unlikely it may seem to the officer that anyone would want to live in an abusive situation, the choice belongs to the victim. Officers must allow victims of elder abuse to choose the form of help, and the degree of help, that they want. Some victims will choose to live in abusive situations even after the officer explains their options for leaving or getting out of the abusive situation.

Where the victim may be relying on the abuser for daily care and charges have been laid, alternative care arrangements will be necessary. The need for alternative care should not prevent the officer from charging the abuser if charges are warranted, for the abuser must not be allowed to continue his or her abusive behaviour. If the officer fails to act, this may reinforce the abuser's control over the victim. Alternative care may involve removing the abuser from the home and making arrangements with a community agency. This may be against the wishes of the victim.

Communicating with the Elderly Victim

If the victim is hesitant to speak, but does wish to provide a statement, there are a few suggestions that may be helpful:

- Reassure the victim that you are there to help and that you will do everything possible to assist him or her.
- Talk with the victim alone. The victim is not likely to talk about possible abuse when there is a chance that the abuser could overhear.

- Don't rush the victim. Allow the victim time to get his or her thoughts together and respond to your questions before you speak again.

Officers can also facilitate communication by being sensitive to the victim's feelings:

- Empathy and kindness must be displayed. If the allegations of abuse are true, the elderly victim has reason not to trust persons who claim that they want to help. The victim may have led a fearful, isolated life for a long time and have lost faith in the idea that things can get better. An officer who responds with courtesy, empathy, and kindness may be able to reduce the victim's level of distrust.
- The officer should not assume that all elderly persons have physical difficulties. Assuming, for example, that the elderly are always hard of hearing can embarrass both parties if an officer speaks too loudly to someone with normal hearing.
- If a radio or television is on in the room, the elderly person should be asked whether it may be turned off. The officer should not turn it off without permission, for this may lead the person to believe that the officer is trying to control his or her environment, which in turn will reinforce the person's feelings of helplessness.

Communication with the victim may be difficult if he or she has health problems such as diminished eyesight or hearing. In such situations the following approaches can help:

- On first encountering an elderly person, the officer should speak normally but look for any signs of hearing difficulty such as a puzzled facial expression, leaning to one side to favour a "good" ear, and responding to questions in a way that indicates the questions were not properly understood. If there is a question of this or any other physical disability, the officer should ask the victim if indeed there is a problem.
- The officer should speak directly to the elderly person. This may enhance the accuracy of communication. If the person is wearing a hearing aid, the officer can politely ask whether it is properly adjusted.
- If the elderly person has eyesight problems, the officer should try to ensure that any written information provided to the person is in large print.

With the permission of the victim, the officer should obtain statements from neighbours, family, and others with pertinent information. A thorough investigation may include consulting medical records (with the permission of the victim) and speaking with health-care professionals to obtain information on possible previous abuse.

PERSONS WITH ALZHEIMER'S DISEASE

As with many other elderly persons who depend on others for their care, people with Alzheimer's are at risk for elder abuse. **Alzheimer's disease** is a progressive, degenerative disease that destroys brain cells and causes dementia. It can strike adults at any age, but it is most common in persons 65 and older. Some of the signs of Alzheimer's disease include the following (Alzheimer Society, 2005):

Alzheimer's disease
a progressive, degenerative disease that destroys brain cells and causes dementia

- memory loss that affects day-to-day functioning;
- difficulty performing familiar tasks;
- problems with language;
- chronological and spatial disorientation;
- decreased powers of judgment;
- problems with abstract thinking;
- tendency to misplace possessions;
- changes in mood or behaviour;
- personality changes; and
- loss of initiative.

Conversing with a person with Alzheimer's disease to determine whether he or she has been abused may be difficult. The officer should use communication techniques that enhance the person's ability to understand the situation. The following techniques may be helpful:

- *Get the person's attention.* Approach slowly and if possible from the front. Gently touch the person to get his or her attention if the person appears unresponsive. Although the person's cognitive abilities may be greatly reduced, he or she may still be able to communicate by touch, emotion, or facial expression.
- *Make eye contact.* Making eye contact will help the person know who is speaking and may help the person concentrate on the message. Be aware of your body and facial expressions. Your non-verbal language may convey messages more powerfully than your verbal communication.
- *Speak slowly and clearly.* Use simple words and short sentences. Take your time and allow the person time to respond. Interrupting may discourage further communication.
- *Communicate one message at a time.* Keep the conversation simple. Too many thoughts or ideas may be confusing. Try to limit your questions to those that can be answered with a "yes" or a "no."
- *Pay attention to the person's reactions and body language.* Remember, although the person's cognitive abilities may be diminished, he or she may still be able to express emotions that convey meaning. Respond to the person's body language and emotions, even if they do not appear to match the person's verbal communications.
- *Use actions to illustrate your message.* Examples include pointing to a door or showing the person an article of his or her clothing to illustrate what you mean.

Although it may be frustrating to try to communicate with a person suffering from Alzheimer's disease, if the disease has not progressed to the later stages, the victim may be able to identify possible abusive behaviours.

THE MENTAL HEALTH OF THE ELDERLY

The mental health of any individual is difficult to assess during a short conversation. Common mental disorders of the elderly such as depression, dementia, and Alzheimer's disease make assessing the mental health of an elderly person much more difficult for police officers. Not only may the person be unaware of his or her disorder, the disorder itself may cause communication difficulty. Or, the person may be aware that he or she has a mental disorder but try to hide that fact because he or she fears social stigmatization or removal from the home.

Depression

depression
an illness involving one's body, mood, and thoughts; characterized by persistent feelings of sadness and loss of interest

Depression is an illness involving one's body, mood, and thoughts, and is characterized by persistent feelings of sadness and loss of interest. Depression is not the same as having a bad day. The feeling of being "down" may last for days, weeks, months, or years.

The symptoms of depression include the following (Canadian Mental Health Association, 1992):

- feelings of worthlessness, helplessness, or hopelessness;
- cognitive problems such as confusion, loss of memory, and inability to concentrate;
- prolonged sadness or unexplained crying spells;
- loss of interest in formerly enjoyable activities;
- withdrawal from friends;
- loss of or increase in appetite;
- persistent fatigue and lethargy;
- insomnia or need for increased sleep;
- aches and pains that cannot otherwise be explained; and
- suicidal thoughts.

The officer responding to a complaint of abuse may not recognize these symptoms and not understand that the elderly person is too depressed to recognize the abuse. The elderly person may fail to recognize that the abuser has contributed to the depression. (In some cases the depression is not the result of abuse, but the abuser takes advantage of the person's depressed state.)

Dementia

dementia
mental deterioration characterized by confusion, memory loss, and disorientation

Dementia is characterized by confusion, memory loss, and disorientation (American Psychiatric Association, 2004). Most kinds of dementia are caused by Alzheimer's disease. Other causes include chronic high blood pressure, stroke, Parkinson's disease, and Huntington's disease. Dementia-like symptoms can be caused by adverse drug interactions, which are more common among the elderly. The possibility that an elderly abuse victim may be suffering the effects of over-medication by his or her caregiver should be considered, although it can be difficult to substantiate. The symptoms of dementia can also be mimicked by the symptoms of malnutrition (possibly caused by caregiver neglect) or insufficient blood flow or blood oxygenation related to heart disease, lung disease, or other conditions.

The investigating officer may have difficulty communicating with a victim of abuse who is also suffering from dementia. The victim may be withdrawn, unable to concentrate, and confused. The officer's ability to obtain clear and concise information in such circumstances will be greatly diminished. The officer should place all of what he or she observes into context.

It may not be possible to obtain concise or even intelligible answers from a person suffering from dementia. This creates a difficult situation for police officers. The victim may not be able to recognize that he or she is being abused. Physical indications of abuse such as bruises, lacerations, bedsores, emaciation, and lack of cleanliness may be the only evidence an officer can obtain.

If possible, the names of any medications in plain sight should be recorded. It may be possible that the dementia has been induced intentionally through medication.

The officer must use his or her judgment to determine whether the apparent dementia is the result of abuse or simply of physical or mental conditions unrelated to improper treatment. The officer's lateral thinking skills should enhance his or her ability to arrive at a decision.

Delirium

A person experiencing **delirium** is in a state of confusion accompanied by disorientation and an altered level of awareness. Delirium develops quickly over a period of hours or days. The symptoms of delirium may be transient and are often worse at night. Delirium is a medical condition caused by difficulties in brain functioning. It is usually caused by an illness or a reaction to medications.

delirium
state of confusion accompanied by disorientation and an altered level of awareness

Delirium is more common among older people (over 65) than younger people and is very common among hospitalized elderly people who are taking medications required to treat physical illnesses.

Some symptoms are easier to recognize than others. These symptoms are not likely to be recognized by a police officer responding to a call for assistance, but may be described to the officer by a family member. *Note: Police officers should not provide medical advice or diagnose illnesses. If you suspect that medical assistance may be required, contact paramedics.*

Older people with delirium may display the following symptoms (Canadian Coalition for Seniors' Mental Health, 2009):

- restlessness and anxiousness,
- agitation and hostility, and
- anger or aggressiveness.

They may also:

- hear voices or see people or things that do not exist,
- show fear and believe that others are trying to hurt them,
- not know where they are,
- show an inability to concentrate,
- slur their speech,
- speak but not make any sense,
- lack bladder control,
- not get up, or, if they do get up, not walk as well as they did previously,
- appear to have vivid dreams or nightmares,
- seem drowsy, have trouble staying awake,
- sleep during the day and be awake at night,
- be inactive and quiet, and
- respond slowly when asked questions.

Delirium is usually caused by a combination of factors. Age is one of the risk factors for delirium. A person who has suffered a brain injury or illness such as Alzheimer's disease is also at a higher risk for delirium. Some medical illnesses such as stroke, cancer, diabetes, or heart disease can make the brain more susceptible to delirium. As well, persons who have had previous episodes of delirium are at increased risk for future episodes.

A person experiencing delirium needs medical assistance but may not have the cognitive ability to make decisions about his or her health care. This may be a permanent or temporary condition. The provisions of the *Substitute Decisions Act, 1992* may be applicable.

COMMUNITY SERVICES

Stopping the abuse is the best long-term solution for the elderly victim. However, because ending the abuse may mean removing the primary caregiver, the elderly person may be faced with the immediate problem of having no one to look after him or her. As a result, the victim's fears of institutionalization may be realized, prompting him or her to ask that charges not be laid or withdrawn. This request may or may not be granted. There is no directive or legislation that requires police to lay charges in cases of elder abuse, nor is there a policy requiring the Crown prosecutor to prosecute the accused.

In seeking to solve these problems, the Department of Justice Canada, through the National Crime Prevention Strategy and the Justice Partnership and Innovation Fund, now supports community-based initiatives to address the issue of elder abuse. These projects focus on awareness-raising activities, peer counselling programs, advocacy programs, and the establishment of community-based networks to consult and take action on the issue of abuse of elderly persons.

Police can contact local seniors' advocacy groups to obtain information about how to receive in-home care, which they can then pass on to the victims to allay their concerns. Police can inform victims that there are provincial programs in place that provide in-home care for seniors depending on the level of care needed. In most communities, homemaking services that assist the elderly person with cooking, cleaning, and personal care are available, as are home health-care services that assist with in-home medical treatment.

KEY TERMS

ageism

Alzheimer's disease

delirium

dementia

depression

elder abuse

elderly person

neglect

power of attorney

REFERENCES

Alzheimer Society. (2005). *Alzheimer disease: 10 warning signs.* Retrieved from http://www.alzheimer.ca/english/disease/warningsigns.htm.

American Psychiatric Association. (2004). *Mental health of the elderly.* Washington, DC: Author.

Canadian Coalition for Seniors' Mental Health. (2009). *Delirium in older adults: A guide for seniors and their families.* Retrieved from http://www.ccsmh.ca/pdf/ccsmh_deliriumBooklet.pdf.

Canadian Network for the Prevention of Elder Abuse. (2010). *Abuse in institutions.* Retrieved from http://www.cnpea.ca/abuse_in_institutions.htm.

Canadian Mental Health Association. (1992). *1992 COMPAS survey of Canadians about mental health, mental illness and depression.* Toronto: Author.

College of Nurses of Ontario. (1997). *Abuse of clients by RNs and RNAs: Report to council on result of Canada Health Monitor Survey of Registrants.* Toronto: Author.

Criminal Code. (1985). RSC 1985, c. C-46, as amended.

Department of Justice Canada. (2003). *Abuse of older adults: A fact sheet from the Department of Justice Canada.* Ottawa: Author.

Environics Research Group. (2008). *Awareness and perceptions of Canadians toward elder abuse.* Report prepared for Human Resources and Social Development Canada.

Legal Resource Centre of Alberta. (2008). *Abuse of older adults: Frequently asked questions* (3rd ed.). Retrieved from www.law-faqs.org/docs/AbuseThird-EdAugFINAL.pdf.

Long-Term Care Homes Act, 2007. (2007). SO 2007, c. 8.

Martin's Annual Criminal Code, 2012. (2012). Aurora, ON: Canada Law Book.

Nova Scotia Department of Community Services. (2002a). *Fact sheet 7: Elder abuse.* Halifax: Author.

Nova Scotia Department of Community Services. (2002b). *Fact sheet 8: Abuse of persons with disabilities*. Halifax: Author.

Statistics Canada. (2011). *Family violence in Canada: A statistical profile* (catalogue no. 85-224-X). Ottawa: Minister of Industry.

Substitute Decisions Act, 1992. (1992). SO 1992, c. 30.

Winnipeg Police Service. (2000). *Elder abuse*. Retrieved from http://www.winnipeg.ca/police/takeaction/elder_abuse.stm.

EXERCISES

TRUE OR FALSE

_____ 1. Abusers of the elderly are often family members.

_____ 2. Elder abuse is often reported by the victim.

_____ 3. Isolation from friends and family is common in elder abuse.

_____ 4. When attempting to communicate with a possible victim of elder abuse, police officers should always assume that the elderly person will be unable to communicate properly because of physical disabilities such as hearing loss.

_____ 5. The elderly rarely suffer from depression.

_____ 6. Withholding the necessaries of life from an elderly person can be a *Criminal Code* offence.

_____ 7. The victim of elder abuse must initiate a complaint before the police can investigate.

SHORT ANSWER

1. Briefly define elder abuse.

2. Identify the five types of elder abuse discussed in this chapter and give an example of each.

    a.

    b.

    c.

    d.

    e.

3. Explain why victims of elder abuse seldom report being abused.

4. List four signs of possible physical elder abuse.

    a.

    b.

    c.

    d.

5. List two signs of possible sexual elder abuse.

    a.

    b.

6. List four signs of possible financial abuse of elders.

    a.

    b.

    c.

    d.

7. List four signs of possible neglect of elders.

    a.

    b.

c.

d.

8. List four signs of possible emotional/psychological abuse of elders.

a.

b.

c.

d.

9. Describe five factors that may contribute to the abuse of elders.

    a.

    b.

    c.

    d.

    e.

10. Summarize the problems a police officer can face in obtaining information from a suspected victim of elder abuse. Be sure to mention depression and dementia in your answer. What approaches can the officer adopt to facilitate communication?

CASE ANALYSIS

Case 6.1

You are a police officer. You have received a complaint of elder abuse from a health-care agency. The complaint alleges that a client is being abused by her son, the primary caregiver. The agency provides in-home care for the alleged victim, an 80-year-old woman. The alleged victim has had a stroke and is unable to care for herself. The agency reports that when one of its employees went to the client's house, the son refused to allow her in. He told the agency employee that his mother was too sick to see anyone and that he would look after her. The agency also reports that its employees have suspected on previous occasions that the son is emotionally abusing the mother.

Using the CAPRA system discussed in Chapter 3, describe what you will do in this situation.

Case 6.2

You are a police officer. You have just stopped at a convenience store to buy a package of chewing gum. In front of you is an elderly man buying a package of pipe tobacco. He is dressed in dirty clothes and smells of urine. He does not produce any money but tells the clerk to put it on his tab. He then walks out. You approach the clerk to pay for your gum. He begins a conversation with you about the old man. The clerk, a male in his sixties, tells you that he used to work for the old man, Mr. Todd. Todd was once a successful businessman and is quite wealthy, but for the past three years he has never seemed to have any money. His sister is looking after him; she comes in and pays his tab three or four times a year.

Another older gentleman, Mr. Pitt, who has been listening to the conversation, interrupts. He tells you that he is a friend of Todd. He went to visit Todd last week after being unable to reach him by telephone. He found some notices informing Todd that his telephone service would be cut off if he did not pay an outstanding bill of $65. The notices indicated that Todd's cable service had already been cut off for non-payment. Pitt says that there was no food in the house and that the entire house was filthy. According to Pitt, Todd suffers from dementia and has difficulty carrying on a conversation. Pitt tells you that he is concerned about the well-being of his friend. He asks you to look into the matter and see whether anything can be done.

Using the CAPRA system discussed in Chapter 3, describe what you will do in this situation.

Case 6.3

You are a police officer. You have been called to a residence regarding possible abuse of an elderly person. You speak to Mr. Smith, who tells you that there is nothing wrong and that no abuse has taken place. You hear someone call from another room, "Who is there?" Smith yells, "Be quiet!" You ask who is in the other room.

Smith replies, "My grandfather." You ask to speak to the grandfather. Smith replies, "Sure."

You enter the room, where you find an elderly gentleman, identified as Mr. George Jacobs, 88 years old. He is tied to a large chair with a bed sheet. The bed sheet has been put around him under his arms and tied at the back of the chair. Jacobs begins shouting at his grandson, "Now you are in trouble, the police are here!"

You ask Smith why Jacobs is tied to the chair. Smith tells you that his grandfather has Alzheimer's disease and has trouble with his hips and knees. If he doesn't tie him to the chair, he wanders around the house. Smith explains that he can't watch him all the time and he fears that his grandfather will fall and hurt himself. He ties him to the chair for a few hours each afternoon so that he can get the housework done and prepare dinner for his grandfather.

Smith assures you that the sheet does not hurt his grandfather. The chair is very comfortable and Jacobs has the remote for the television, so he can watch whatever he wants. Smith assures you that he provides him with drinks and snacks in case he gets hungry or thirsty. As well, he puts the telephone beside the chair so that Jacobs can call anyone he wants.

Jacobs confirms that the sheet does not hurt, but he says that he doesn't want to be tied. He tells you that he does have some problems with his memory, but his knees and hips work most of the time.

Using the CAPRA system discussed in Chapter 3, explain what you will do in this situation.

Mental Illness and Personality Disorders

7

INTRODUCTION: THE STIGMA OF MENTAL ILLNESS

Society feels uncomfortable with mental illness. It is human nature to fear what we don't understand. When a person appears to be different, society may view him or her in a negative stereotyped manner. Persons that society perceives negatively are said to be stigmatized. Stigma is a reality for people with a mental illness. Because of stigma, a typical reaction encountered by someone with a mental illness (and his or her family members) is fear and rejection. The stigma experienced by persons with a mental illness can be more destructive than the illness itself.

Canadians' attitudes toward people with mental illness are reflected in the following statistics (Canadian Medical Association, 2008):

- Only 50 percent of Canadians would tell friends or co-workers that they have a family member with a mental illness, compared with 72 percent who would discuss diagnoses of cancer and 68 percent who would discuss diabetes in the family.
- Only 12 percent of Canadians said that they would hire a lawyer who has a mental illness.
- Only 49 percent said that they would socialize with a friend who had a serious mental illness.
- Approximately 46 percent of Canadians think that people use the term "mental illness" as an excuse for bad behaviour.
- Approximately 27 percent are fearful of being around people who suffer from a serious mental illness.

According to Statistics Canada (2003), 70 percent of mental health problems and illnesses begin during childhood or adolescence. Because the onset of most mental illnesses occurs during adolescence and young adulthood, the individual may experience the societal stigma throughout much of his or her life. This affects educational achievement, occupational or career opportunities and successes, and the formation and nature of personal relationships.

The serious stigma and discrimination attached to mental illness are among the most tragic realities facing persons with mental illnesses. Stigma and discrimination result from a lack of knowledge and empathy, along with a tendency to fear and exclude people who are perceived to be different. This stigmatization may convince people that it is in their best interests to remain quiet about their mental illness. This may cause a delay in seeking help. As well, they may avoid sharing their symptoms with family, friends, co-workers, employers, health service providers, and others in the community.

This can cause serious problems. Most mental illnesses can be treated. Timely intervention through treatment is essential. Untreated mental illness may result in lasting disability. A variety of interventions, such as psychotherapy and cognitive behavioural therapy, can improve an individual's functioning and quality of life. Because mental illnesses involve disorders of brain functioning, medication often forms an important part of treatment. Receiving and complying with effective treatment and having the security of strong social supports, adequate income, housing, and educational opportunities are essential elements in minimizing the impact of mental illness.

It is important that police officers not act upon any stereotypical or preconceived notions of mental illness they may hold. Such actions will only further reinforce the social stigma of mental illness.

Police officers are often the first point of access to services for persons with mental illness. A Canadian Mental Health Association study found that over 30 percent of persons with serious mental illness had contact with police while making, or trying to make, their first contact with the mental health system. Further stigmatization through prejudicial or discriminatory actions by responding officers will greatly diminish the possibility that the person will seek assistance.

HOSPITAL-BASED VERSUS COMMUNITY-BASED TREATMENT

Since 1995, the Ontario government has undertaken major initiatives to update Ontario's mental health system to reflect modern practices and philosophies of hospital and community care. One of these initiatives involved a decrease in the proportion of funding for hospital-based treatment and an increase in the proportion of funding for community-based treatment. In 1994–95, 75 percent of these funds went to hospital-based treatment and 25 percent went to community-based treatment. By 1999–2000, only 60 percent of these funds went to hospital-based treatment while 40 percent went to community-based treatment. This trend has continued in recent years.

The Canadian Mental Health Association has identified that waiting lists for services across the province of Ontario have grown significantly. Thousands of people in Ontario have no access to mental health services, possibly because funding for community mental health services has not been significantly increased over the past ten years (Canadian Mental Health Association, 2005a). Complicating these problems is the government's policy of deinstitutionalization, in which hospital beds are closed and mentally ill patients are discharged into the community.

According to Statistics Canada and the Canadian Institute for Health Information (2005), hospitalization for mental illness in Canada has been declining. The number of psychiatric hospital "in patient treatment" per 100,000 population was 150 in 1982–83, 116 in 1992–93, and 81 in 2002–2003. Because fewer people are being treated in health-care facilities, there are more persons with mental health issues receiving treatment in the community, if they are receiving treatment at all.

Deinstitutionalization, along with no significant increase in community care funding, may be why there has been an increase in the frequency of interactions between police and mentally ill persons. Police have to stand in as front-line mental health-care workers. People with mental illness are increasingly coming into contact with police for nuisance crimes because of an apparent lack of mental health care.

Because the likelihood of contact with mentally ill persons has substantially increased for police officers, it is important that officers be able to recognize the symptoms and behaviours that may indicate mental illness. A basic understanding of mental illness may help officers decide which response option they choose.

This chapter will examine mental illness from the perspective of police intervention. It will show how officers can identify mental illness, and it will discuss intervention strategies.

FACTS ABOUT MENTAL ILLNESS

The following are facts about mental illness in Ontario (Canadian Mental Health Association, 2005b):

- 1 percent of Ontarians suffer from schizophrenia.
- 3 percent of Ontarians suffer from bipolar disorder.
- 5 to 12 percent of men and 10 to 25 percent of women in Ontario will have at least one episode of major depressive disorder in their lifetime.
- More than 90 percent of suicide victims have a diagnosable psychiatric illness.
- Persons who have depressive illness carry out 80 percent of all suicides.
- Both major depression and bipolar disorder account for 15 to 25 percent of all deaths by suicide in patients with severe mood disorders.
- Suicide is the most common cause of death for people with schizophrenia.
- 15 percent of people who have significant depressive illness commit suicide.

DETERMINING MENTAL ILLNESS

The following information may be used in determining whether a person is likely to be suffering from a mental illness within the meaning of the *Mental Health Act* (MHA) of Ontario.

Mental illness, for the purpose of police intervention, may be defined as a departure from "normal" thinking that affects a person's ability to interact with his or her environment. There are two general categories of mental disorders encompassed

mental illness
for the purpose of police intervention, a departure from "normal" thinking that affects a person's ability to interact with his or her environment

by this definition: those that cause psychotic symptoms (for example, hallucinations and delusions) and those that do not (for example, depression, neuroses, and phobias). Both kinds of mental disorder may be equally debilitating.

In deciding whether to apprehend a person who appears to be mentally ill, the officer must form reasonable grounds to believe that the person is suffering from a mental disorder and that as a result of the disorder is or will be a danger to himself or herself or to others. The officer also has grounds to apprehend if he or she concludes that the person is unable to care for himself or herself as a result of a mental disorder.

The MHA recognizes that it is unlikely that the attending officer will have the time or the necessary expertise to diagnose a specific mental illness. Police need only conclude that, on the basis of the actions of the person, the person is likely suffering from a mental illness.

Hallucinations, delusions, and psychosis are three of the more easily observed symptoms of mental disorders.

hallucination
sensory perception that is real only to the person experiencing it

delusion
defect in belief or thought processes that is not reasonable

psychosis
disturbance in brain functioning, during which the person experiences loss of contact with reality

Hallucinations are experienced when a person senses (sees, hears, feels, smells, tastes) things that do not exist. Persons experiencing **delusions** hold personal beliefs that are false, inaccurate, or exaggerated, such as beliefs that they are a specific celebrity or well-known person such as a politician. It is possible that the affected person may simultaneously experience hallucinations and delusions.

Psychosis is a disturbance in brain functioning, during which the person experiences loss of contact with reality. It is characterized by changes in the person's way of thinking, perceptions, and behaviour.

Hallucinations, delusions, and psychosis can be symptomatic of a number of different mental illnesses. They may also be drug induced. Police need only recognize the behaviours exhibited, not the underlying cause. It is not likely that a layperson could distinguish between drug-induced hallucinations, delusions, or psychosis and those caused by a mental illness.

Hallucinations

The most common type of hallucination is the auditory hallucination. It often includes hearing voices that tell the person to do something (known as command hallucinations). Persons experiencing auditory hallucinations may appear to be preoccupied and unaware of their surroundings. They may audibly talk to themselves, and may have difficulty understanding or following conversations with others. They may isolate themselves or try to use a radio or other sounds in an attempt to "tune out" the voices.

Other sensory hallucinations may occur. These types of hallucinations may be identified by observing the person's interaction with the hallucination. The person may be visually focused on something that others cannot see. Persons experiencing visual hallucinations may touch, scratch, or brush things off themselves that are not visible to others. Persons who sniff or hold their nose may be experiencing an olfactory hallucination. Continual spitting could indicate a hallucination involving taste.

Hallucinations can be frightening for both the person experiencing them and for those who come in contact with that person. Ensuring everyone's safety and providing calm, clear, and consistent messages that you want to help is the best immediate response.

A person experiencing hallucinations needs medical assistance and should be taken to a hospital or mental health service provider for treatment.

Delusions

Common delusions include delusions of grandeur or delusions of being a famous person. Some people may experience paranoid delusions of persecution and may be afraid of authority figures. It is important to reassure the person that he or she is safe, and that you are not going to harm him or her. Inform the person that the uniform and equipment you carry are for protecting yourself and others. Helping the person get treatment, while at the same time maintaining safety for all, is the purpose of the intervention.

Careful observations of the person's behaviours and verbal and non-verbal communications may assist with identifying the delusion being experienced. Questions about what they are experiencing and whether they intend to harm themselves or others may be posed. Asking the person what they are experiencing may not be particularly effective in identifying the delusion. Persons experiencing delusions may not always be honest about what they think or believe, especially if the delusions are paranoid.

Paranoid delusions are usually evidenced by extreme suspicion, fear, isolation, insomnia (for fear of being harmed while asleep), and avoidance of medications (for fear of poisoning). A person experiencing paranoid delusions is extremely distrustful of others. She or he may misinterpret others' words and actions, and may view persons or things in the surroundings as a threat. A violent reaction is possible to this perceived threat. Maintaining a safe distance that allows you time to react will enhance your safety.

In any situation involving a delusional person, it is important to keep yourself safe from potentially violent reactions and provide a comfort zone for the person experiencing delusions. The use of distance or barriers will assist with ensuring officer safety. It is not advisable to approach or touch the delusional person, unless you are apprehending him or her.

Psychosis

Psychosis is a disturbance in brain functioning. There is no one specific cause of psychosis. A psychotic person experiences loss of contact with reality, characterized by changes in their way of thinking, perception, and behaviour. The person is generally conscious of their surrounding environment. This consciousness may cause further disorientation and distress as a result of the inability to distinguish between differing realities.

Psychosis can happen to anyone. Symptoms of psychosis most often begin between 16 and 30 years of age. Both males and females can be affected. Males tend to experience symptoms a few years earlier than females. Persons with a family history of serious mental illness are at increased risk of developing psychosis.

The person experiencing the psychotic episode is confused and may also be concurrently experiencing hallucinations and delusions. It is unlikely that the person will be able to communicate effectively with police. Confusion and the inability to deal with the severe distress of the episode may result in outbursts of violence.

There may be a relationship between violent behaviour and uncontrollable symptoms of psychosis. The person could experience specific symptoms such as command hallucinations or the belief that outside forces are controlling their thoughts. This is not to insinuate that persons experiencing psychosis are inherently violent, but like anyone, they have a threshold of stress tolerance that may be exceeded.

Note: The following information is sufficient only to identify that a mental illness may be present and must not be used to attempt to diagnose specific disorders.

Bipolar Disorder

bipolar disorder
illness characterized by alternating periods of mania and depression

Bipolar disorder (also called manic depression) is an illness characterized by alternating periods of mania and depression. A chemical imbalance in the brain is believed to be the cause of this illness. Mood swings may be mild, moderate, or severe. Not all people experience only the extremes of depression or mania; they may have one episode of mania and then have many periods of depression interspersed with periods of normal mood. Many people who suffer from bipolar disorder are able to control the illness with the assistance of medication.

In the manic phase, the person may feel "on top of the world" and believe that he or she does not require sleep. Thought processes may be accelerated, and the person may perceive that he or she is in a highly productive state. This perceived productivity may lead the person to maintain that nothing is wrong. The person may show dangerous lapses in judgment, experience feelings of invincibility, or display impulsive behaviour, potentially leading him or her to take chances or make decisions that may be injurious. Other symptoms include an exaggerated sense of self-esteem, continual talking, or an inability to concentrate. In its most severe form, the manic stage of the illness could involve extreme agitation and loss of reason (psychosis), delusions, or hallucinations.

In the depressed phase, the person suffers from feelings of sadness, hopelessness, and helplessness and experiences many other debilitating symptoms (described below). Suicide is a real threat, especially during an episode of depression.

Recognizing Bipolar Disorder

The following sections provide a brief description of some of the signs and symptoms that may be displayed by a person with bipolar disorder.

Note: These descriptions must not be used by a layperson to suggest or diagnose that any person may have bipolar disorder. They indicate only that the person may have a mental illness.

Manic or "High" Phase

Persons with bipolar disorder may show the following signs and symptoms when in the manic phase of the illness (Patient Health International, 2005):

- excessively high or euphoric feelings;
- extreme irritability;
- unrealistic belief in capabilities and powers;
- increased libido;

- uncharacteristically bad judgment;
- decreased need for sleep;
- refusal to admit that anything is wrong;
- intrusive, provocative, or aggressive behaviour;
- increased energy, restlessness, activity, racing thoughts, rapid speech; and
- drug abuse.

Depressed or "Low" Phase

Persons with bipolar disorder may show the following signs and symptoms when in the depressed phase of the illness (Patient Health International, 2005):

- persistent anxious, sad, or empty mood;
- feelings of hopelessness or pessimism;
- withdrawal from social contacts such as family and friends;
- preoccupation with failure or inadequacies;
- feelings of guilt, worthlessness, or helplessness;
- loss of interest in ordinary activities, including sex;
- decreased energy, feelings of fatigue;
- difficulty concentrating, remembering, and making decisions;
- restlessness or irritability;
- sleep disturbances (too little or too much);
- loss of appetite, and weight loss or weight gain;
- chronic pain; and
- thoughts of death or suicide, or occasionally thoughts of homicide.

A person with bipolar disorder may slowly cycle through the mood phases or may rapidly cycle through the phases, causing severe mood changes in a short time period. The intervals between episodes and duration of manic or depressed stages may last for days, months, or, in rare cases, for years. This cycling of moods, extended depressed state, feelings of invincibility, and risk-taking behaviour may increase the risk of accidental death or injury or of suicide. There does not appear to be a significant risk of increased violent behaviour toward others, although the possibility exists.

Depressive Disorders

Depression is a mood disorder—a medical condition that is common and treatable. Depression occurs in all economic, geographic, social, and cultural settings.

Statistics Canada's *National Population Health Survey* (1997) reported that the total number of people who felt sad, blue, or depressed or had lost interest in ordinary activities was 1,314,000.

Approximately 15 percent of the population suffer from moderate to severe depression during some time in their life. It is often difficult to predict when a depressive episode will occur, how long it will last, or what will trigger it.

clinical depression
an illness that is characterized by a continually low, sad, and depressed mood and that interferes with the individual's ability to work, sleep, eat, and enjoy once-pleasurable activities

Clinical depression (also called major depression or unipolar disorder) is an illness that is characterized by continually low, sad, and depressed mood that interferes with the individual's ability to work, sleep, eat, and enjoy once-pleasurable activities. Disabling episodes of depression can occur once, twice, or several times in a lifetime. Approximately 1 percent of Canadian men and 2 percent of Canadian women are clinically depressed at any one point in time, and about 5 percent of men and 10 percent of women experience clinical depression at some point in their life. Regardless of gender, once a person has had one experience of clinical depression, they are at a higher risk for repeated experiences.

A chronic illness, a severe loss, a difficult relationship, a financial problem, or any unwelcome change in life patterns can trigger a depressive episode. Depression may be related to dysfunctional regulation of the brain's chemistry, causing it to send "depressed" signals. Very often, a combination of genetic, psychological, and environmental factors is involved in the onset of a depressive disorder. Psychological makeup also plays a role in depression. People who have low self-esteem, who consistently view the world with pessimism, or who are easily overwhelmed by stress may be prone to depression.

The social stigma of having a mental illness prevents many people from seeking help, although a variety of effective treatments are available. When a proper diagnosis is made and effective treatment and advice are followed, most people recover. It is imperative that someone experiencing depression seek help. Without effective treatment, approximately 30 percent of persons with severe depressive disorders will attempt suicide. Of these, 15 percent will eventually take their life. This group accounts for almost 80 percent of all suicides.

There does not appear to be a substantial risk of violent behaviour toward others, although as with all police–public interactions, police officers must consider their own safety.

Symptoms

The symptoms of depression may be difficult for police officers to identify given time constraints and the nature of the symptoms associated with the illness. Even so, officers should be aware that depressed individuals may show the following symptoms (Depression and Manic Depression Association of Alberta, 2005):

- a marked decrease in interest in usual activities, and often withdrawal from activities;
- feelings of sadness, emptiness, hopelessness, and anxiety;
- difficulty falling asleep and/or early awakening;
- thoughts about suicide;
- fatigue and energy loss;
- irritability;
- changes in eating habits; and
- difficulty with concentration, decision making, and memory.

Children and adolescents can also develop depression, often resulting in learning problems, school failure, disturbed relationships with other people, tendency to illness or psychosomatic disorders, or suicidal thoughts. Symptoms are similar to those in adult depression but children express them through different behaviours such as disruptiveness, fighting, delinquency, bed wetting, and substance abuse.

Postpartum Depression

Many women experience symptoms of depression after childbirth. These symptoms can range from a brief attack of the "baby blues" to clinical depression. This experience is referred to as **postpartum depression**. About 80 percent of new mothers will experience a mild form of postpartum depression, usually within a few days or weeks after giving birth (MediResource Inc., 2005). These feelings will usually disappear in a few weeks.

Women who experience the baby blues commonly feel sad, angry, irritable, and insecure. They may experience self-doubts about being a competent mother, which may contribute to these feelings. They may burst into tears, often without apparent reason. Baby blues may also trigger the occasional negative thought about the baby. Although these feelings are upsetting to the mother, they are normal.

A more severe form of postpartum depression will affect about 20 percent of new mothers. This type of depression is more common with first pregnancies, and can affect women who were not previously depressed. Approximately 20 to 40 percent of women will also experience postpartum depression with subsequent births.

Severe postpartum depression is longer lasting than the baby blues. It includes the symptoms described above, as well as more serious symptoms. Postpartum depression resembles other forms of depression but has a somewhat unusual combination of symptoms that often include confusion and sometimes features of schizophrenia.

Some of the more common indicators of severe postpartum depression include:

- constant fatigue,
- a lack of interest in daily activities,
- withdrawal from friends and family,
- a lack of concern or overconcern for self and baby,
- insomnia,
- a lack of sexual responsiveness,
- severe mood swings, and
- a sense of failure and inadequacy.

There is no single definable cause of postpartum depression, although there are several possible contributing factors:

- hormonal changes,
- disappointment in the birth experience,
- a sense of loss from no longer being pregnant,
- marital dissatisfaction,
- the stress of caring for a demanding baby,
- a lack of family and social support,

postpartum depression
symptoms of depression that can range from a brief attack of the "baby blues" to clinical depression

- physical and mental exhaustion, and
- a family history of postpartum depression.

Although a few women may have a more persisting experience with postpartum depression, about 95 percent of women will improve within two to three months.

The most severe form of postpartum depression is postpartum psychosis. Postpartum psychosis usually develops within a few weeks after childbirth. A woman experiencing this form of depression becomes severely depressed and may experience hallucinations, acute anxiety, paranoia, and hysteria. She may have thoughts related to harming herself or the baby. Postpartum psychosis is relatively rare but requires immediate treatment by a qualified health-care provider.

The *Criminal Code* recognizes the significant impact that postpartum depression may have upon the psyche of the sufferer. In some instances a new mother may behave violently toward her newborn child. (Section 2 of the *Criminal Code* defines a newborn child as being less than one year old.)

According to the *Criminal Code*, if a mother's actions cause the death of her child and at the time she was not fully recovered from the effects of childbirth (which includes postpartum depression), she should not be subjected to as severe a penalty as would otherwise be imposed. Section 233 of the *Criminal Code* acknowledges that the effects of childbirth are a mitigating factor in cases where a mother has caused the death of her newborn, and s. 237 describes the punishment for this offence.

Infanticide: Criminal Code, Section 233

233. A female person commits infanticide when by a wilful act or omission she causes the death of her newly-born child, if at the time of the act or omission she is not fully recovered from the effects of giving birth to the child and by reason thereof or of the effect of lactation consequent on the birth of the child her mind is then disturbed.

Punishment: Criminal Code, Section 237

237. Every female person who commits infanticide is guilty of an indictable offence and liable to imprisonment for a term not exceeding five years.

Homicide Versus Infanticide: R v. L.B.

The Ontario Court of Appeal, in the case of *R v. L.B.*, 2011 ONCA 153, heard an appeal regarding the applicability of the defence of infanticide in a case involving a young mother who killed two of her children. The trial judge had previously ruled that the accused was guilty of the offence of infanticide. The Crown disagreed, arguing that the accused should be convicted of homicide. Excerpts from the decision are included to help you understand the distinction between homicide and the often misunderstood offence of infanticide. Although police officers are not likely to be involved in arguing this distinction in court, it is useful for you to have an understanding of the court's conclusion regarding the distinction between the offences.

SUMMARY OF THE TRIAL DECISION

The accused, L.B., was charged with two counts of first degree murder. The Crown alleged that she murdered two of her children, Alexander in 1998 and Cameron in 2002. She was 17 years old at the time of the first homicide and subject to the terms of the *Youth Criminal Justice Act* (YCJA). She was an adult at the time of the second homicide, and subject to the procedures and sentencing principles under the *Criminal Code*. Charges for both offences were laid after the second homicide. The two charges were tried before the trial judge without a jury.

The trial judge acquitted the accused on the murder charges and convicted her of the included offence of infanticide on both charges.

EXCERPTS FROM THE COURT OF APPEAL DECISION

R v. L.B.
2011 ONCA 153 (footnotes omitted)

DOHERTY JA:

[1] Infanticide has been part of the criminal law of Canada for over 60 years. Homicides for which a conviction for infanticide is a possible verdict are rare. Most of the few convictions for infanticide are the product of guilty pleas. There is no Canadian appellate decision that has examined the infanticide provisions in the *Criminal Code*, RSC 1985, c. C-46 in any detail. This appeal raises an issue that goes to the very nature of those provisions. Is infanticide both a substantive offence and a partial defence to a murder charge, or is it exclusively a substantive offence that may in appropriate cases be an included offence in a murder charge to be considered by the trier of fact if, and only if, the Crown fails to prove murder?

. . .

[56] Murder and manslaughter are distinguished by the mental element required to prove murder. Murder requires proof of an intention to kill (s. 229(a)(i)) or an appreciation that one's acts are likely to cause death (s. 229(a)(ii), s. 229(c)). Manslaughter does not require either an intention to kill or an appreciation that death may be caused by one's acts, but instead requires objective foreseeability of the risk of bodily harm: *R v. Creighton*, 1993 CanLII 61 (SCC), [1993] 3 SCR 3, at pp. 44-45. The requisite mental element required to prove murder is what makes murder more morally culpable than manslaughter and justifies the more punitive sentence.

[57] Unlike murder and manslaughter, infanticide and murder are not distinguished by the required mental element. Infanticide requires a "wilful act or omission" that causes death. The conduct must also be culpable homicide within s. 222(5), meaning, in most cases, that the conduct must constitute either an unlawful act or criminal negligence: *Criminal Code*, ss. 222(5)(a) and (b). As will be explained later in these reasons, although the mental element of infanticide is not limited to the intention to kill, an act or omission done with the intent necessary for murder will satisfy the *mens rea* component of infanticide. The distinction between murder and infanticide lies more in the *actus reus* than the *mens rea*.

[58] Infanticide, as defined in s. 233, targets a very particularized form of culpable homicide. The section has potential application only where a mother kills her newborn child, defined in the *Criminal Code* as a child under one year of age. The potential application of infanticide is further limited by requiring that at the time of the homicide, the mother's mind must be "disturbed," either because she is not fully recovered from the effects of giving birth or by reason of the effect of lactation.

[59] The definition of infanticide focuses on two things. First, it requires a mother-child relationship between the perpetrator and the victim. Second, the mental state of the perpetrator/mother must be disturbed and that disturbance must be connected to the effects of giving birth or lactation. Unlike other mental states that may mitigate criminal responsibility, infanticide does not require any causal connection between the disturbance of the mother's mind and the decision to do the thing that caused her child's death: *R v. Guimont*, 1999 CanLII 13354 (QC CA), (1999), 141 CCC (3d) 314 (QCA), at p. 317; E. Cunliffe, "Infanticide: Legislative History and Current Questions" (2009) 55 Crim. LQ 94, at pp. 112-113; I. Grant, D. Chunn & C. Boyle, *The Law of Homicide*, loose-leaf (Scarborough: Carswell, 1995), at p. 4-91. Because the mother's mental "disturbance" is not connected to the decision to kill, that "disturbance" is better considered as part of the *actus reus* and not a *mens rea* component of the crime of infanticide.

[60] The drastically different penalties available upon conviction for murder, manslaughter or infanticide reflect the very different levels of moral blameworthiness attached to each offence. Clearly murder is regarded as the most blameworthy and infanticide as the least blameworthy. Manslaughter occupies that vast middle ground of blameworthiness between the two extremes of murder and infanticide. The very different penalties prescribed by Parliament for the offences of murder and infanticide leave no doubt that a mother who commits a culpable homicide that constitutes infanticide is regarded as having committed a much less serious crime than someone who committed murder.

. . .

[98] Treating infanticide as a partial defence to murder is consistent with the distinction drawn between infanticide and murder by Parliament. It allows juries to draw that distinction in cases where mothers are charged with murdering their children and evidence brings the homicide within the very narrow factual confines of infanticide. Eliminating infanticide as a partial defence effectively allows the Crown to remove the distinction between infanticide and murder through the exercise of its charging discretion.

[99] My application of the "modern principle" of statutory interpretation leads me to conclude that Parliament intended to make infanticide a partial defence to murder when it introduced infanticide into the *Criminal Code* in 1948. Parliament did not intend to alter the status of infanticide by the 1954 amendments. Infanticide was initially, and still is, both a stand alone indictable offence and a partial defence to a charge of murder.

. . .

[113] The five-year potential maximum penalty for infanticide is far removed from the mandatory minimum life sentence for murder and is significantly less

than even the maximum penalty of life imprisonment available for manslaughter. To the extent that the potential penalty provides insight into the requisite *mens rea*, the five-year maximum penalty for infanticide strongly suggests a *mens rea* closer to the manslaughter requirement of foresight of harm than to the murder requirement of an intention to kill or foresight of probable death.

[114] Considering the homicide provisions as a whole and the obvious hierarchy created by those provisions, I do not think that the infanticide provision can be read as requiring proof of the same *mens rea* as that required for murder. Instead, a *mens rea* for infanticide akin to that for manslaughter is much more consistent with the hierarchy of culpable homicides established in the *Criminal Code*. In my view, infanticide as a form of culpable homicide, should require the *mens rea* required for manslaughter. There is nothing inherent in the seriousness of the offence or the stigma attached to it which requires the imposition of a higher *mens rea* like that required for murder. That, of course, is not to say that a mother who intends to kill her child is, therefore, not guilty of infanticide. Clearly, a person who intends to kill foresees the risk of bodily harm to the child and, therefore, has the required *mens rea* for either manslaughter or infanticide.

[115] If infanticide was read as requiring proof of the same *mens rea* as murder, circumstances could produce anomalous results. For example, if infanticide requires the *mens rea* for murder, a mother who intends to kill her child but whose conduct comes within the meaning of infanticide would be convicted of infanticide, the least culpable form of culpable homicide. A second mother, whose conduct also comes within the meaning of infanticide, but who was so emotionally distraught as to be incapable of forming the intention for murder, could not be convicted of infanticide but would instead be convicted of manslaughter, a more serious offence. Surely, a mother who does not intend to kill her child should not be regarded as having committed a more culpable homicide than the mother who did have that intention. This anomaly disappears if the *mens rea* for infanticide captures both the mother who intends to kill and the mother who unlawfully assaults her child in circumstances where bodily harm to the child is foreseeable.

[116] There is a second, and I think significant, practical problem with treating the *mens rea* for infanticide as the same as that required for murder. Infanticide requires evidence that the mother's mind was "disturbed" at the time of the homicide. Evidence proffered by the defence to meet the evidentiary burden on that issue will, in some cases, cast doubt on whether the mother intended to kill her child. If infanticide operates as a partial defence to murder only where the *mens rea* for murder exists, the very same evidence offered to bring the mother within the infanticide defence could push her outside of that defence by negating the intention to kill or the existence of foresight as to the likelihood of death. If the *mens rea* for infanticide is interpreted as including the *mens rea* required for murder or manslaughter, the defence is not put in the position of offering evidence of the mother's mental state that could simultaneously support and undermine the infanticide defence.

[117] I think treating the *mens rea* for infanticide as reaching not only an intention to kill, but also objective foresight of bodily harm, provides a coherent

and comprehensive reading of the homicide provisions that best reflects the relative seriousness of the three levels of culpable homicide created in the *Criminal Code*. This approach does give the word "wilful" a meaning that is somewhat inconsistent with its customary meaning. I am satisfied, however, that a coherent and workable reading of s. 233 in the context of the homicide provisions supports my interpretation of the word "wilful" in this context.

. . .

[121] For the reasons set out above, I do not think that the *mens rea* for infanticide can be equated with the *mens rea* for murder. In my view, to prove infanticide, the Crown must establish the *mens rea* associated with the unlawful act that caused the child's death and objective foreseeability of the risk of bodily harm to the child from that assault. On this approach, it is the unique *actus reus* of infanticide that distinguishes it from murder and manslaughter. Those distinctions are what caused Parliament to treat infanticide as a culpable homicide, but one that was significantly less culpable than murder and even manslaughter. The presence of the *mens rea* for murder, while not negating the partial defence of infanticide, is not a condition precedent to the existence of that partial defence.

. . .

[140] Applying the approach outlined above to the facts of this case, it was conceded that the respondent caused her children's deaths and that in doing so she committed a culpable homicide. Those concessions take one to the point where the culpable homicide must be categorized. The trial judge found on the balance of probabilities that the respondent met the criteria for infanticide in respect of both homicides. That finding negated any argument that the Crown had proven beyond a reasonable doubt that at least one of the elements of infanticide was not present. The trial judge, therefore, returned the proper verdicts—not guilty of murder but guilty of infanticide.

The Court of Appeal agreed that the finding of guilt for the offence of infanticide was correct. This ruling reinforces the legitimacy of the defence of infanticide but is unlikely to affect the way police will proceed with laying charges in situations where there are reasonable grounds to believe that the mother is responsible for the death of the newborn child. A charge of homicide is likely to be pursued by police with the Crown having the option of accepting the defence of infanticide.

Schizophrenia

The term "schizophrenia" comes from two Greek words: "schizo," which means split, and "phrenia," which means mind (Schizophrenia Society of Ontario, n.d.). People who suffer from this illness do not, however, have a split or multiple personality, which is an entirely different condition. The term **schizophrenia** describes a family of psychological disorders characterized by psychotic thoughts, feelings, perceptions, and actions.

schizophrenia
a family of psychological disorders characterized by psychotic thoughts, feelings, perceptions, and actions

The cause of schizophrenia is unknown. It may be caused by a chemical imbalance within the brain, but these chemicals have not been specifically identified. Schizophrenia is often described as the most chronic and disabling of the mental illnesses.

Schizophrenia affects 1 in every 100 Canadians. There are approximately 300,000 people who suffer from schizophrenia in Canada, of whom 100,000 live in Ontario. The symptoms appear in late adolescence and early adulthood. In males the average age of onset is 18; in women it is 25. It is not possible to accurately describe all the symptoms that may be exhibited by persons diagnosed with schizophrenia, although some generalized symptoms may be observed.

The most dramatic and disabling symptoms involve reality distortion and disorganization of thinking. These symptoms can appear rapidly and include delusions of persecution or grandiosity, and hallucinations. These symptoms are usually treatable with medication.

The initial symptoms of schizophrenia usually appear well before the person's first psychotic episode. Parents may notice that a child who was once ambitious and outgoing has become withdrawn from friends and family, has lost interest in his or her usual activities, and has become unfeeling. Parents may find it difficult to decide whether something is really wrong with their child. The adolescent experience that all teenagers go through can involve similar periods of moodiness and withdrawal.

Psychotic episodes, with their attendant distortion of reality and altered brain function, often result in the psychotic person being hospitalized because they are deemed to be a danger to themselves and possibly to others. Someone experiencing a psychotic episode can be unpredictable and dangerous, especially when he or she has a concurrent substance abuse problem. Approximately 50 percent of persons diagnosed with schizophrenia develop a substance abuse problem that requires medical attention at some point in their life. The substance abuse may develop as the symptoms of schizophrenia worsen, perhaps as an escape for the sufferer or a way to deal with the fear of what he or she is beginning to experience.

The psychotic episodes that the schizophrenic person experiences may take the form of unusual realities, hallucinations, and delusions. Each type of psychotic episode is discussed below.

Unusual Realities

To the person experiencing **unusual realities**, the world may appear distorted or changeable, possibly causing anxiety and confusion. This person may seem detached, distant, or preoccupied and may even sit without moving for hours, not uttering a sound. Alternatively, the person may be constantly moving, wide awake, vigilant, and alert.

unusual realities
perceptions of reality and views of the world that are sharply different from those of people who are not mentally ill and that may cause anxiety and confusion

Hallucinations

To determine an appropriate response in dealing with a hallucinating person, officers should calmly ask the person whether he or she is seeing or hearing anything. It may be possible to appeal to the person's logic if he or she is not totally immersed in the hallucination.

Even if the person cannot respond logically, the officer may be able to determine the nature and substance of the hallucination. Doing so is important because the hallucination could be directing the person to hurt someone, including the officer.

Knowledge of the person's perception of their surroundings may assist the officer in choosing an appropriate response and in alleviating confusion about the person's apparently illogical display of agitation or fear.

Delusions

Persons suffering from schizophrenia may experience delusions of grandeur or may have paranoid delusions of extreme distrust.

delusions of persecution
false and irrational beliefs that a person is being harassed, cheated, poisoned, or conspired against

Delusions of persecution are another frightening and possibly threatening form of delusion experienced by persons suffering from schizophrenia. This type of delusion usually manifests as false and irrational beliefs that the person is being harassed, cheated, poisoned, or conspired against. Persons suffering from this type of delusion may become hostile, suspicious, reclusive, and uncooperative. They may also be dangerous. If they are convinced that they are about to be harmed, they may respond violently in an attempt to protect themselves. Therefore, officers must exercise extreme caution when dealing with these individuals. The officers' actions should be slow, and prior warning should be given before an action is taken—for example, "I am moving across the room. I am not going to hurt you." Officers should ensure that they do not touch the person or invade his or her personal space unless they need to apprehend the individual or protect themselves.

Most schizophrenic individuals, however, are not violent. Some acutely disturbed persons may become violent, but this is relatively infrequent. Persons experiencing a psychotic episode may show an increased propensity toward violence.

Other Symptoms of Schizophrenia

The other major group of schizophrenic symptoms consists of deficits in the person's social and/or cognitive abilities. These symptoms may involve a decrease in motivation, initiative, and emotional response. The symptoms resemble those of clinical depression. Approximately 40 percent of people diagnosed with schizophrenia also experience depression, which can go untreated because of the similarity of the symptoms.

Cognitive deficit symptoms are generally distinct from negative symptoms. Cognitive deficits may impair memory, abstract thinking, vigilance, and other brain functions essential for most employment and social situations. These symptoms usually precede the onset of the first psychotic symptoms.

Some of these cognitive symptoms include disordered thinking and inappropriate emotional expression, which are discussed below.

DISORDERED THINKING

The person may endure hours of being unable to think straight. Thoughts may come and go so rapidly that it is impossible to "catch them." The person may not be able to concentrate on one thought for very long, may be easily distracted, and may be unable to focus. The person may be unable to order thoughts into logical sequences. The person's thoughts may become disorganized and fragmented, making conversation difficult.

INAPPROPRIATE EMOTIONAL EXPRESSION

People with schizophrenia sometimes exhibit what is called "inappropriate affect." This means showing emotion that is inconsistent with the person's speech or thoughts—for example, giggling while verbally expressing extreme despair.

Often people with schizophrenia show "blunted" or "flat" affect. They may not show the signs of normal emotion. Instead, they speak in a monotonous tone of voice and show little facial expression.

Treating Schizophrenia

One of the major difficulties in treating schizophrenia is that the affected individual rarely recognizes his or her symptoms as a disease process. Treatment often depends on the individual recognizing these symptoms as being those of schizophrenia. Without an awareness of his or her illness, the sufferer does not have any motivation to take medication to treat the illness. This poses a perplexing situation. During a delusional or hallucinatory episode, the person does not perceive that anything is out of the ordinary with his or her thought patterns. The delusion or hallucination is perceived as reality. The schizophrenic person finds no reason to believe that medication is needed to control his or her allegedly abnormal thoughts and perceptions.

Relapse is a common problem among schizophrenic people who are receiving treatment. The rate of relapse requiring hospitalization to treat psychotic episodes is about 80 percent in the first year of treatment. The major factor contributing to the relapse is the failure of the person to take his or her prescribed medication.

COMMUNITY TREATMENT ORDERS

With the objective of preventing recurrence of psychotic episodes, the *Mental Health Act* (MHA) was amended in 2000 to include the use of community treatment orders. Community treatment orders may assist in ensuring that the mentally ill person follows his or her prescribed treatment plan (see Appendix 7D at the end of this chapter: Form 45, MHA). Community treatment orders may be useful in helping physicians provide treatment for patients who are unwilling to submit themselves for treatment. Such orders are legal documents that outline the conditions under which individuals with a serious mental illness may be treated within the community.

The purpose of community treatment orders is described in s. 33.1(3) of the MHA:

> 33.1(3) The purpose of a community treatment order is to provide a person who suffers from a serious mental disorder with a comprehensive plan of community-based treatment or care and supervision that is less restrictive than being detained in a psychiatric facility. Without limiting the generality of the foregoing, a purpose is to provide such a plan for a person who, as a result of his or her serious mental disorder, experiences this pattern: The person is admitted to a psychiatric facility where his or her condition is usually stabilized; after being released from the facility, the person often stops the treatment or care and supervision; the person's condition changes and, as a result, the person must be re-admitted to a psychiatric facility.

These orders are somewhat controversial in that the person named in the order may be seen as not voluntarily submitting to therapy, but agreeing to the conditions of the order so that he or she will not be hospitalized, or so that he or she will be released from a psychiatric facility. Specific criteria must be met before authorization to issue a community treatment order is granted. These conditions are set out in s. 33.1(4) of the MHA.

Criteria for Order: Mental Health Act, Section 33.1(4)

33.1(4) A physician may issue or renew a community treatment order under this section if,

(a) during the previous three-year period, the person,

(i) has been a patient in a psychiatric facility on two or more separate occasions or for a cumulative period of 30 days or more during that three-year period, or

(ii) has been the subject of a previous community treatment order under this section;

(b) the person or his or her substitute decision-maker [see Appendix 7F at the end of this chapter: *Health Care Consent Act, 1996*], the physician who is considering issuing or renewing the community treatment order and any other health practitioner or person involved in the person's treatment or care and supervision have developed a community treatment plan for the person;

(c) within the 72-hour period before entering into the community treatment plan, the physician has examined the person and is of the opinion, based on the examination and any other relevant facts communicated to the physician, that,

(i) the person is suffering from mental disorder such that he or she needs continuing treatment or care and continuing supervision while living in the community,

(ii) the person meets the criteria for the completion of an application for psychiatric assessment under subsection 15(1) or (1.1) where the person is not currently a patient in a psychiatric facility,

(iii) if the person does not receive continuing treatment or care and continuing supervision while living in the community, he or she is likely, because of mental disorder, to cause serious bodily harm to himself or herself or to another person or to suffer substantial mental or physical deterioration of the person or serious physical impairment of the person,

(iv) the person is able to comply with the community treatment plan contained in the community treatment order, and

(v) the treatment or care and supervision required under the terms of the community treatment order are available in the community;

(d) the physician has consulted with the health practitioners or other persons proposed to be named in the community treatment plan;

(e) subject to subsection (5), the physician is satisfied that the person subject to the order and his or her substitute decision-maker, if any, have consulted with a rights adviser and have been advised of their legal rights; and

(f) the person or his or her substitute decision-maker consents to the community treatment plan in accordance with the rules for consent under the *Health Care Consent Act, 1996.*

The order may be used as an alternative to institutionalization for individuals who suffer from a serious mental disorder, who have a history of repeated hospitalizations, and who meet the criteria for committal as set out in the MHA.

Involuntarily institutionalized psychiatric patients who agree to a treatment plan may enter into a community treatment order as a condition of their release from a psychiatric facility. The *Health Care Consent Act* (see Appendix 7F at the end of this chapter) allows a substitute decision-maker to accept the conditions of the order on behalf of the patient if the substitute decision-maker believes that he or she can provide the necessary care.

A community treatment order may be issued by a physician where the following conditions are met (Ministry of Health and Long-Term Care, 2005):

1. the individual may be committed under the committal criteria;

2. it will benefit the person subject to the community treatment order;

3. appropriate supports exist in the community to meet the conditions of the community treatment order;

4. it is less restrictive and less intrusive to provide treatment/supervision for the individual in the community rather than in a psychiatric facility; and

5. consent has been obtained from the individual or substitute decision-maker, if the individual is found incapable with respect to treatment.

Community treatment orders are initiated for a period of six months and are thereafter renewable for six-month intervals. They include a treatment plan as well as review, appeal, and cancellation mechanisms.

Safeguards for Patients

Community treatment orders may be seen as a form of coercive treatment and, as such, must have safeguards to protect the interests of the patient. A number of rights flow from the designation of a community treatment order, including:

- a right of review by the Consent and Capacity Board with appeal to the courts each time a community treatment order is issued;

- a right to request additional reviews by the Consent and Capacity Board in the event of a material change;

- a right to request a re-examination by the issuing physician to determine whether the community treatment order is still necessary for the person to live in the community;

- a right of review of findings of incapacity to consent to treatment; and

- provision for rights advice and an entitlement to counsel appointed by the board.

A person entering into a community treatment order has an obligation to follow the conditions of the order. Failure to follow the conditions may result in the examining physician issuing an order for examination (see Appendix 7E at the end of this chapter: Form 47, MHA). Section 33.3(3) of the MHA states that the order is valid for 30 days and directs police to apprehend the named person and escort the person to the issuing physician for examination.

Return to Physician: Mental Health Act, Section 33.3(3)

33.3(3) An order for examination issued under subsection (1) is sufficient authority, for 30 days after it is issued, for a police officer to take the person named in it into custody and then promptly to the physician who issued the order.

Where a community treatment order is not in force and the person has displayed behaviours, as a result of a mental illness, that have caused or are likely to cause serious bodily harm to the person or to others, the physician may issue an application by physician for psychiatric assessment (see Appendix 7A at the end of this chapter: Form 1, MHA). Foreknowledge of this behaviour should alert the police that officer safety must be a primary consideration when apprehending a person under the authority of an order for examination.

Once the person is apprehended, police are required to bring him or her to the issuing physician for assessment. Under s. 33.4(5) of the MHA, the issuing physician is required to examine the named person and decide whether a psychiatric assessment should be made, another community treatment order should be issued, or the person should be released.

Assessment on Return: Mental Health Act, Section 33.4(5)

33.4(5) The physician shall promptly examine the person to determine whether,

(a) the physician should make an application for a psychiatric assessment of the person under section 15;

(b) the physician should issue another community treatment order where the person, or his or her substitute decision-maker, consents to the community treatment plan; or

(c) the person should be released without being subject to a community treatment order.

If the physician requires a psychiatric assessment authorized by s. 15 of the MHA, police are required by s. 33 to remain with the person until the person is admitted to the psychiatric facility.

Self-Injury

self-injury
the act of attempting to alter a mood state by self-inflicting physical harm serious enough to cause tissue damage to the body

Self-injury, also referred to as self-harm, self-abuse, self-inflicted violence, self-mutilation, and para-suicide, is the act of attempting to alter a mood state by self-inflicting physical harm serious enough to cause tissue damage to the body. "Tissue damage" refers to injuries that break, bruise, or burn the skin.

The rarest and most extreme form is major self-mutilation occurring during a psychotic state and resulting in permanent disfigurement—for example, castration or limb amputation. A second type of self-injury involves less serious injury such as bone breaking, head banging, eyeball pressing, and biting. The third and most common form is superficial self-mutilation, which usually involves acts such as cutting, burning, hair-pulling, self-hitting, and interference with wound healing. The majority of self-inflicted injuries are not life threatening and do not require medical treatment.

In some instances the sexual organs may be deliberately injured as a way to deal with unwanted feelings of sexuality, or as a means of self-punishment, possibly in response to childhood sexual abuse. If the person was abused, he or she may feel ashamed and guilty, and blame themselves for the abuse, which in turn causes them to feel the need to punish themselves by inflicting pain on their bodies.

Whatever form of self-injury is used, the person is usually left with a peaceful and calm feeling afterward. Because these feelings are only temporary, the person will probably continue to self-injure until they deal with the underlying issues and find healthier ways to cope.

A misconception regarding self-harm is that it is an attention-seeking behaviour. In most cases, this is inaccurate. Many self-harmers are very self-conscious of their wounds and scars and feel guilty about their behaviour. This leads them to go to great lengths to conceal their wounds from others. Individuals who choose cutting as a method of self-injury usually apply cuts to their wrists, upper arms, and inner thighs—locations that can be covered with clothing and hidden to avoid detection. If their injuries are detected, they may offer alternative explanations for them.

Who Self-Injures?

Statistics regarding the prevalence of self-injury tend to be unreliable due to the private nature of the act. Therefore, the incidents will not likely reach the attention of professionals.

There is some information that appears to be reliable although much of it is anecdotal or non-specific.

Self-injurers come from all walks of life and all socio-economic backgrounds. They can be male or female, gay, straight, or bisexual, PhDs or high school drop-outs, or rich or poor. They may be able to manage to function effectively in demanding jobs. They may be teachers, therapists, medical professionals, lawyers, professors, or engineers.

It is often assumed that females engage in self-injurious behaviour more than males do, but not all studies support this (Whitlock, 2010). There is evidence that males and females differ in their methods used to self-injure. For example, some research suggests that more males may use self-injurious behaviours that lead to self-bruising. They may punch objects, other people, or parts of their own body with the intention of hurting themselves.

Females, in contrast, are more likely to use better-recognized forms of self-injury, such as cutting, scratching, or burning. A study of 240 women aged 14 to 71 by Favazza and Conterio (1989) found that cutting was the most common type of self-injurious behaviour among women in this age group, although multiple methods of self-injury were often used. See Figure 7.1.

It's also uncertain whether race and ethnicity have any bearing on rates of self-injury. Some studies suggest that it may be more common among Caucasians. Other studies show similarly high rates in minority samples. Some even show

Figure 7.1   Self-Injury Among Women Aged 14 to 71

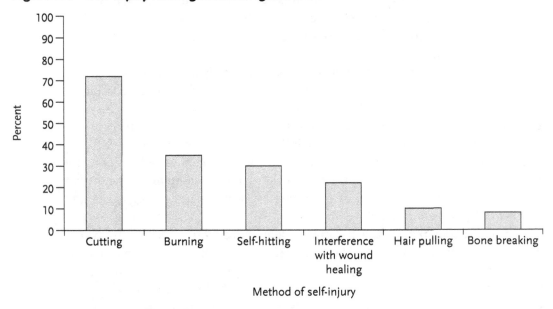

Note: In 78 percent of cases, multiple methods of self-injury were used.

Source: Based on data from Favazza and Conterio (1989).

regional variation in the relationship between self-injury and race and ethnicity. At the time of writing, there has not been any definitive study that identifies an increased risk of self-injurious behaviours based on ethnicity or race.

Although a history of abuse is common among self-injurers, not everyone who self-injures was abused. One factor common to most people who self-injure is invalidation. Emotionally invalidating environments where parents punish children for expressing sadness or hurt can contribute to increased rates of self-harm. The self-abuser may have been taught at an early age that their beliefs and feelings were bad and wrong. At the same time, they may not have had role models to help them develop effective coping skills to deal with distress.

Little is known about the relationship between self-injury and sexual orientation. Being a member of a sexual minority may increase the risk for self-injurious behaviours, possibly due to society's marginalization of persons within the minority sexual orientation groups. This marginalization in combination with the external invalidation of the person's beliefs and feelings experienced early in life could lead to the increased possibility of self-injurious behaviours.

There seem to be parallels between eating disorders and self-injury. Eating disorders are more prevalent in middle- and upper-income groups, leading to speculation that self-injury is likely to be more prevalent in these socio-economic classes. However, no existing research supports this speculation.

Self-injurious behaviours can start early in life. Research suggests that for those with early onset, self-injury may start around the age of 7, although it can start at an earlier age. Most often, self-injury begins in middle adolescence, between the ages of 12 and 15 (Whitlock, 2010). It can last for weeks, months, or even years. In many cases, self-injury is cyclical rather than linear. It may occur for certain periods of time, stop, and then resume.

Some studies suggest that well over 25 percent of those who self-injure began the behaviour at 17 years of age or older and that the behaviour can last well into adulthood.

Some psychological characteristics appear to be common among persons who self-injure including (Herpertz, 1995):

- they strongly dislike and/or invalidate themselves;
- they are overly sensitive to rejection;
- they are chronically angry;
- they tend to suppress feelings of anger;
- they experience strong feelings of aggression, which they disapprove of strongly and often suppress or direct inward;
- they lack impulse control;
- they tend to act according to the mood they are in at the moment;
- they tend not to plan for the future;
- they experience depression and may have self-destructive or suicidal thoughts;
- they suffer from chronic anxiety;
- they tend to be irritable;
- they feel that they are not skilled at coping and do not have a flexible repertoire of coping skills;
- they tend to be avoidant; and
- they feel disempowered.

Although it may not be apparent to an outside observer, self-injury is serving a function for the person who does it. Persons who self-injure have chosen this maladaptive method of coping as a mechanism to provide temporary relief from intense feelings such as anxiety, depression, stress, emotional numbness, and a sense of failure or self-loathing.

Why Do People Self-Injure?

Some of the reasons given for the self-injurious behaviours include (Favazza & Rosenthal, 1993; American Self-Harm Information Clearinghouse, n.d.):

- to ease tension and anxiety;
- to escape feelings of depression and emptiness;
- to escape feelings of numbness;
- to relieve feelings of anger and aggression;
- to relieve or distract from intense emotional pain, lessening a desire to commit suicide;
- to regain control over their body;
- to maintain a sense of security or feeling of uniqueness;
- to obtain a feeling of euphoria;
- to express or cope with feelings of alienation;

- to maintain control and distract themselves from painful thoughts or memories;
- to punish themselves because they believe they deserve punishment for having undeserved good feelings;
- to express things they can't put into words (displaying anger, showing the depth of their emotional pain, shocking others, seeking support and help); and
- to express feelings for which they have no label (this phenomenon, called alexithymia, is common in people who self-harm).

Self-injurious behaviours may also be

- a response to self-hatred or guilt;
- a continuation of previous abusive patterns; or
- a symptom of a more severe mental disorder (for example, borderline personality disorder).

Self-harm is not typically suicidal behaviour, although there is the possibility that a self-inflicted injury may be life-threatening. The behaviour is a maladaptive response that the self-injurious person developed to release their unbearable feelings and pressures. Self-injuring persons who do make a suicide attempt use means that are usually different from their preferred methods of self-injury.

Intervention

The immediate goal of intervention in cases of self-injury is to prevent the person from further harm. Remember that there is little that police will be able to do to provide a long-term solution for the problem.

When intervening in situations of self-harm, keep in mind the following points:

- Although the person is experiencing emotional distress, it is unlikely that he or she is experiencing any unusual realities or a psychotic episode. It is also unlikely that the self-harm is directed toward committing suicide, although this may be a possibility.
- It is important that you validate the person's feelings by accepting that the emotional distress they are experiencing is real. Remember that this is different from validating the behaviour.
- Remember that the person may find the presence of a police officer stressful while they are in a state of distress. Recognize that direct questions may feel invasive and frightening at first—particularly when coming from a person in authority. Make eye contact and be respectful when speaking. Offer reassurance and speak in calm and comforting tones.
- Ask the person if there is anything that you can do to help them with the immediate problem. But realize that your offer of assistance may be rejected. The person believes that he or she has developed a coping method that will relieve the feelings of distress. Self-injury, although destructive, does appear to lessen the person's immediate distress.

Keep in mind that people who self-injure often have difficulty verbalizing their emotions. The person may choose not to speak to you or may have difficulty expressing how they are feeling. If the person is not ready to address the self-harm issue, choose another topic of conversation.

- Don't shout, lecture, or give ultimatums you don't intend to carry out, such as "Stop hurting yourself or I will ..."
- Avoid making statements that can make the person feel as if their problems are trivial, such as, "How can you be so crazy to do this to yourself?" Avoid comments such as: "I know how you are feeling." You likely don't know how he or she feels.

If you determine that the person is self-harming or poses a danger to themselves or others as a result of a mental disorder, the provisions of the Ontario *Mental Health Act* may be applicable. You may need to apprehend the person and bring him or her to a physician. This type of action may be necessary as an interim measure to prevent further harm.

Treatment

There are several treatment options available to help the self-injurer control his or her behaviour:

- *Therapy.* Therapies usually focus on helping the person to tolerate greater intensities of emotions without resorting to self-harm and to develop the ability to articulate emotions and needs. The patient learns alternative, healthy means for discharging his or her feelings of distress through problem solving, conflict resolution, anger management, and assertiveness training.
- *Mediation.* Persons who self-harm and suffer from moderate or severe clinical depression may respond to treatment with antidepressant drugs.
- *Hospitalization.* This type of treatment is a last resort. The main goal of hospitalization is to prevent self-injurers from hurting themselves, albeit in an artificially safe environment. However, in such a controlled environment, the person has less freedom and more supervision. This may be viewed as taking away any remaining semblance of self-control over their lives.

    Treatment in such an environment is not likely to be effective. The person needs to learn to cope with his or her feelings of distress and react in a less destructive manner without external control.

Although these treatment options may offer some benefit, none has been proven to effectively prevent recurrence of self-harm.

PERSONALITY DISORDERS

Personality disorders, although not classified as a mental illness, should be of concern to police officers. Knowledge of personality disorders may assist in officer safety, although it must be remembered that any personality type may present a danger. Caution must always be taken when dealing with any individual—regardless of apparent compliance. There are situations, such as repeated domestic disputes and execution of arrest warrants, where officers are called to the scene, or are engaged in circumstances in which they have prior knowledge of the type of person they will be encountering. Such information may help officers identify whether the person has a personality disorder, and allow the officer to approach the situation accordingly.

The two most frequently encountered personality disorders are the antisocial and the dependent personalities. These disorders, as well as other, less frequently encountered disorders, are discussed below. (Note that the material presented below is for information purposes only and must not be used to attempt to diagnose any specific disorder.)

Antisocial Personality Disorder

antisocial personality disorder
condition whose essential feature is a pervasive pattern of disregard for, and violation of, the rights of others that begins in childhood or early adolescence and continues into adulthood

Antisocial personality disorder is a condition whose essential feature is "a pervasive pattern of disregard for, and violation of, the rights of others that begins in childhood or early adolescence and continues into adulthood" (American Psychiatric Association, 2000). The vast majority of persons with antisocial personality disorder are male.

The terms "sociopath" and "psychopath" are often used to describe antisocial personality disorders. The term "sociopath" stresses a pathological relationship with society. The sociopath is not only alienated from society, but also engaged in a negative relationship with members of the smaller social relationships of family and acquaintances. The term "psychopath" suggests that the psyche of the person is pathological. This is made evident through the psychopath's lack of conscience and lack of positive regard or feeling for others.

Regardless of the term used, it must be stressed that persons with an antisocial personality (ASP) are not insane. These individuals may want others to believe that their behaviour is beyond their control—that they act only because of their inability to control their behaviours—but this is a deception. Such a belief may allow them to continue their antisocial behaviour without having to accept responsibility or to face any repercussions for their conduct. The antisocial personality knows that much of what he or she does is considered both inappropriate and wrong by society. However, the person does not incorporate what society judges to be correct into his or her behaviour. He or she knows right from wrong, but chooses not to conform to socially accepted behaviours. The person's judgment as to what is appropriate behaviour is guided only by his or her need for immediate gratification.

Antisocial personality types tend to project upon others the negative consequences of their behaviour. This may include blaming individuals, groups, or society at large for their antisocial conduct. Rarely will they concede that they are responsible for their actions. Another noteworthy aspect of this personality is the propensity for high levels of aggression along with a low tolerance for frustration—a potentially violent mix.

Typically, antisocial personality traits also include a disregard for social obligations. These individuals easily enter into relationships if they perceive that the relationship may be advantageous for them. As soon as the relationship becomes inconvenient, or there is no gain to be had, or they no longer receive the behavioural reinforcement, they terminate the relationship. The relationships may last days or years, but nonetheless will be immediately and callously discontinued when either the relationship no longer provides benefit, or another person gains their attention.

Knowledge of some of the characteristics of the antisocial personality may be useful beyond safety considerations. Knowing the personality type may assist officers in directing the way in which the individual is questioned and treated. As with any investigation, certain approaches may be more effective in eliciting information.

Description of the Antisocial Personality

Note: Antisocial behaviour may occur during the course of schizophrenia or during manic episodes. Such occurrences do not indicate that the person has an antisocial personality disorder, but are symptoms of the person's illness.

The following is a brief description of some of the characteristics that may be displayed by an antisocial personality.

The person, generally male, is at least 18 years old. Evidence of disorderly conduct is exhibited before age 15, including truancy, initiation of physical confrontations, physical cruelty to people or animals, and acts of vandalism. There is also evidence of irresponsible and antisocial behaviour after the age of 15, including the inability to maintain consistent employment, repeated criminal acts, aggressive or assaultive acts including spousal and/or child abuse, repeatedly failing to honour financial obligations, impulsive behaviour including the inability to maintain a consistent address, no specific immediate goals, reckless regard for personal safety, non-committed personal relationships, and a lack of remorse for wrongs committed.

Interviewing Antisocial Personality Types

The major obstacle in interviewing the antisocial personality is his or her need to control the conversation (US Department of Justice, FBI Uniform Crime Reports, 1992). At the beginning of the interview, the ASP may be testing his or her limits, observing the reaction of the interviewer, and internally establishing that he or she has control over the interview. Clearly, control of the conversation must always be securely located with the interviewer. However, it may be advantageous for the interviewer to consciously relinquish a small amount of control to the interviewee. This may be accomplished by allowing the ASP to vent his or her feelings about law enforcement, society in general, or whatever group he or she believes is responsible for his or her behaviour. Any lashing out, or show of distaste for the comments of the ASP or the inappropriateness of his or her behaviour, is likely to be based on societal norms and should be avoided: the interviewer must recognize that the ASP does not consider societal normalcy in his or her decision-making process. Such displays may lead the ASP to conclude that, as a result of the interviewer's lack of understanding and intelligence, further discussion would be meaningless.

One of the more successful ways to create an effective rapport with the ASP is to let him or her know early in the interview process that he or she is assisting the interviewer. The interviewer should convey to the ASP that, with his or her help, the interviewer will obtain information that he or she otherwise could not obtain. This is, in all likelihood, not true, but it establishes in the mind of the ASP his or her importance. Compliance thereafter is more easily received.

Dependent Personality

Dependent personalities (DPs) are people who are overreliant on others for their physical and emotional needs. These individuals have a history of poor social interaction. They may be described as "weak and ineffective, passive, lacking energy, compliant to a fault, nice but totally inadequate." Typically, these individuals have maintained a relationship well into adulthood with a significant member of their immediate family. These relationships are often identified as "uncomfortable" by the dependent personality—but they maintained the relationship nonetheless. The DP often feels some animosity toward this significant family member. In most instances this family member has made most, if not all, decisions for the DP.

The mental status of the DP reflects the patterns of behaviour one would suspect, including dependency, submissiveness, anxiety, and an overall need to please others. During interviews, the low self-esteem of DP offenders will be apparent. Also noteworthy is the inability of the DP to deal with his or her anger, frustration, and hostility.

The emotional life of these types of individuals can be described using the analogy of a coiled spring. This coil, at the time of birth, begins to be compressed within the person. As he or she experiences situations in which frustration, anger, and hostility are involved, the "spring" compresses more and more. Each time the person is involved in situations that cause stress and anxiety, the tension of this emotional coil increases. Accompanying this increase, a trigger develops that can release the emotional turmoil. Once the trigger has developed, the person is at risk of an explosive episode. There is little or no way to anticipate exactly what will trigger this release. The individual will reach a point when "they have had enough." All the hostility and rage that had been repressed during previous years are vented.

Description

The following is a brief description of some of the characteristics that may be displayed by a dependent personality.

People with dependent personalities show a pervasive pattern of dependent and submissive behaviour beginning in early adulthood. Some indicators include the following:

- the inability to make everyday decisions without reassurance;
- allowing others to make major decisions for them;
- agreeing with others through fear of rejection;
- difficulty doing things by themselves;
- volunteering to do unpleasant or demeaning tasks to get people to like them;
- going to great lengths to avoid being alone;
- feelings of devastation when close relationships end;
- frequent preoccupation with fears of abandonment; and
- susceptibility to emotional injury from criticism.

Interviewing Dependent Personality Types

The interviewer must keep in mind that the DP will not generally take initiative throughout the interview process. This individual has a history of following commands and deferring to the wishes of others. If the correct approach is used, it will be relatively easy to elicit responses from him or her—with one caveat. Although the individual has been conditioned to be compliant, he or she has also developed a resentment to individuals representing authority. Under the apparent calm and docile surface, the dependent personality is a storm of anxiety and fear. His or her inability to deal with years of feelings concerning his or her sense of inadequacy and low self-worth has resulted in inordinate levels of anxiety. This level of anxiety must be reduced in the initial stages of the interview for the interview be productive.

The first technique used to alleviate the DP's fears and anxiety is for the interviewer to state at the beginning of the questioning that he or she understands that the process can sometimes cause anxiety. This allows the DP to consciously recognize his or her anxious feelings. The second technique used to reduce anxiety is to tell the person that the interviewer is not there to pass judgment, only to obtain information. Once the DP's level of anxiety is diminished, the interview can proceed with material directly related to the occurrence in question.

The interviewer must use caution when giving weight to the responses of DPs. In an interview, DPs may demonstrate the same psychological dynamics that they employ when interacting with others outside the interview setting. Consequently, they may sometimes do and say things they feel they should do and say rather than what they actually want to do and say. Therefore, the interviewer must continually verify and corroborate their statements.

OTHER PERSONALITY DISORDERS

This section will give a brief overview of four other personality disorders that are less frequently encountered in policing. The following information must not be used to diagnose any specific disorder.

Borderline Personality Disorder

People with borderline personality disorder display a pervasive pattern of instability of mood (not to be confused with bipolar disorder), interpersonal relationships, and self-image. The disorder begins in early adulthood and expresses itself in a variety of ways:

- a pattern of unstable and intense interpersonal relationships characterized by extremes of excess idealization and devaluation;
- potentially self-damaging behaviour;
- inappropriate, intense anger;
- self-mutilating behaviour;
- uncertainty of self (sexual orientation, goals, friends, etc.); and
- chronic feelings of boredom.

Narcissistic Personality Disorder

Narcissistic personality disorder is characterized by a pervasive pattern of grandiosity in thought or behaviour. The disorder begins in early adulthood. The narcissistic personality exhibits the following traits:

- reacts to criticism with feelings of rage or shame;
- is interpersonally exploitive;
- has an exaggerated sense of self-importance;
- believes that his or her problems are unique and can only be understood by "special" people;
- is preoccupied with fantasies of unlimited success, power, or brilliance;
- has a sense of entitlement; and
- requires constant attention and admiration.

The narcissistic personality is also egocentric, will display a lack of empathy, and is hypersensitive to the evaluation of others.

Passive–Aggressive Disorder

Beginning in early adulthood, the passive–aggressive personality displays a general pattern of passive resistance to demands for adequate social and occupational performance. This pattern is displayed in a variety of ways:

- procrastination;
- becoming sulky, irritable, or argumentative when asked to do something they do not want to do;
- working extremely and deliberately slowly on tasks they do not enjoy;
- protesting when others make demands of them;
- avoiding obligations by claiming to have forgotten them;
- believing that they are doing a much better job than others think they are doing;
- resenting suggestions from others about being more productive; and
- being highly critical of those in authority.

POLICE INTERVENTION

Police officers who must intervene with persons experiencing symptoms of mental illness face several challenges. The majority of symptoms experienced by mentally ill persons may be difficult for officers to identify. It may be difficult to communicate with persons experiencing altered states of mind. Some mentally ill persons may become violent. The following are some suggestions that may be useful in engaging in effective and safe interactions.

Interacting with Persons in a Hallucinatory/ Delusional State

Delusions and hallucinations may be experienced simultaneously by the subject. Interaction with a person in a delusional/hallucinatory state may prove difficult for police. The following are some suggestions to ensure the safety of the officer and the subject during such interactions.

- *Remain aware that the delusion or hallucination is perceived as real to the subject.* The person believes that he or she is experiencing everything he or she sees or feels in the hallucination. If the person is delusional, the departure from normal, rational thought processes convinces the person that the delusion is real. Trying to convince the person otherwise will likely be unproductive.

- *Tell the person that you are there to help.* The person is attempting to interact within separate realities. Allow for delays in responses. If the person asks whether you are experiencing the hallucination or delusion, do not mislead the person by telling him or her that you are. This will reinforce the reality of the experience or lead the person to believe that you are deceiving him or her when you are unable to interact with the imaginary persons or objects in the hallucination. This loss of credibility will hamper your ability to positively interact with the subject.

- *Always make officer safety a major consideration.* Do not become complacent. It is unlikely that the presence of police officers will calm the person. More likely, if the person is delusional or paranoid, he or she will interpret the presence of police officers as evidence of conspiracies against him or her.

- *Watch for rapid movement of the eyes or head, which may indicate that the person is visually hallucinating.* Ask the person whether he or she is seeing or hearing anything or anyone. If so, ask what he or she is seeing or hearing. Try to determine the "message" that the person is receiving. Ask yourself: Is the person likely to react violently to the message?

- *Ask the person what type of assistance he or she requires.* Reassure the subject that police are there to help, provided that the person is not so deeply involved in the delusion that such reassurance will be ineffective. If the person indicates that he or she cannot control his or her actions, explain that police can help if required. If requests for assistance are not forthcoming, offer suggestions such as seeing a doctor or other persons who may be able to help.

- *If the person begins to speak rapidly, request that he or she slow down.* Such a request may reinforce delusions of intellectual superiority, but it is necessary to try to ascertain the direction of the person's thoughts. If the person does not respond to the request, ask specific questions such as his or her name, address, date of birth, or other questions that require specific answers. The purpose of such questioning is to try to force the person to slow down and think about the question.

- *Pay particular attention to the person's non-verbal messages.* Clenched fists, clenched teeth, and stiff or rapid movements may be indicators of potential violence. Or, if the person is non-responsive, he or she may display passive behaviour, not speak, and may stand motionless.
- *If the decision is made to apprehend the person under the authority of s. 17 of the MHA, tell the person of your intention.* Inform the person that he or she is being apprehended but keep in mind that there is the possibility of a violent reaction or refusal to cooperate. If safety precautions have been adhered to, such as removing access to weapons, and ensuring the availability of backup, the level of potential violence should be more easily managed. If the person is unwilling to accompany police to the hospital, explain that the issue is not debatable. Police may allow the person to retain some semblance of control by allowing them to make non-crucial decisions such as the choice of transportation by ambulance or police vehicle.

If the individual is not exhibiting the more obvious psychotic symptoms such as hallucinations and delusions, detecting mental illness may be more difficult. Speaking with the person may assist in determining whether a mental disorder is present. As you speak with the person, ask yourself the following questions:

- Is the person able to conduct a conversation, or are speech and thought patterns disjointed and confused? Is the person able to focus on the question posed?
- Is the person aware of his or her surroundings? Can he or she provide his or her name and address, provide the date, or answer common-knowledge questions?

Interacting with Psychotic Persons

Police may be called by concerned family members or other persons when someone is experiencing a psychotic episode. Psychosis is most notably found in persons with bipolar disorder or schizophrenia. However, officers should give consideration to other possible causes of the behaviour when attempting to interact with a subject in a state of psychosis. Psychotic episodes may be caused by medical conditions such as brain tumours, severe fevers, or epilepsy. Reactions to alcohol or other drugs, head injuries, or acute stress could also induce psychotic behaviour.

Hallucinations and delusions are the most frequently encountered symptoms of psychosis, although there are several others, including:

- extreme anxiety, fear, or panic for no apparent reason;
- withdrawal from family or friends;
- rapid mood swings (also a symptom of bipolar disorder);
- loss of ability to verbally interact;
- disordered, fragmented speech;
- loss of logical reasoning;
- flat affect (lack of emotion) in responses; and
- agitation.

Effective verbal interaction with a psychotic person may be extremely difficult because of his or her loss of ability to reason or think logically. The officer should try to listen to the person empathetically and respond in a calm, reassuring manner. The officer must also be aware of his or her proximity to the person. Invading the psychotic person's personal space can escalate the situation.

If the psychotic person becomes aggressive, it is in the best interests of all concerned to isolate and contain the person. Containment may be achieved by not allowing the person to leave his or her immediate surroundings. This can be achieved by restricting access to exits or by setting artificial boundaries using other officers and having non-essential persons leave the area. If there is a potential for violence, officers can more easily focus on the psychotic person without having to deal with the safety of others. Containment and isolation limits the options of the aggressor, restricts access to potential weapons, and confines the person to a designated area. However, the subject may also react negatively to isolation and containment by becoming more aggressive, particularly if the psychosis is accompanied by paranoia. If such behaviour is exhibited and the scene is safely contained, officers may consider the option of disengagement.

It is unlikely that psychotic behaviour induced through means other than a mental illness will be identified by non-mental health professionals. Within the provisions of the MHA, an officer who has reasonable grounds to believe that the psychotic behaviour was caused by a mental illness is justified in apprehending the person if he or she displays violent behaviours. Section 17 refers to behaviours caused by an apparent mental disorder. The use of the word "apparently" in this section of the Act removes the requirement for police to prove that a specific mental illness is causing the identified behaviour.

RESPONSE OPTIONS

Regulation 3/99 of the *Police Services Act*, s. 13, requires police services to establish procedures on dealing with persons who are emotionally disturbed or have a mental illness. Police officers will follow the procedures of their respective police services.

The following information identifies some possible response options for police officers dealing with mentally disturbed persons. This section is to be used for information purposes only.

No Further Police Action

This may occur in situations where the reported behaviour is disturbing but not dangerous, such as a person walking on the sidewalk calmly talking to imaginary people. Such people appear to be mentally disturbed but do not pose a danger to themselves or the public and are able to care for themselves. The officer forms the opinion that the person is not likely to pose any danger.

Release to Family or Friends

This may be an option where the officer is somewhat concerned about the ability of the subject to care for himself or herself. The person has not displayed any dangerous behaviour, but may be somewhat hindered in his or her ability to interact effectively. The person may show signs of confusion, such as not knowing where he or she is, or not knowing the time, date, year, etc. These signs could lead the officer to believe that the person's ability to care for himself or herself is compromised but that he or she poses no immediate physical danger. Release to the person's family or friends may be a viable option if the officer is able to obtain the information required to contact a family member.

In this situation, the person may not be suffering from a mental illness but may be suffering from a condition such as Alzheimer's disease (see Chapter 6 and the discussion below). The person may exhibit many of the same symptoms and behaviours as a person with a mental illness, but not be suffering from a mental illness within the meaning of the MHA.

Response Where Person Has Alzheimer's

Alzheimer's disease is a progressive, degenerative disease that destroys brain cells and causes dementia. It can strike adults at any age, but is most common in persons 65 and older. Some of the signs of Alzheimer's disease include:

- memory loss that affects day-to-day functioning,
- difficulty performing familiar tasks,
- problems with language,
- chronological and spatial disorientation,
- decreased powers of judgment,
- problems with abstract thinking,
- misplacement of possessions,
- changes in mood or behaviour,
- changes in personality, and
- loss of initiative.

The officer should check to see whether the person is registered in the Alzheimer Wandering Registry. The registry, which is stored in the Canadian Police Information Centre (CPIC) database, contains the names, addresses, physical descriptions, and contact information of the registrants. Each registrant is issued an identification bracelet and card on which pertinent information is recorded. The information will identify the person(s) to contact if the registrant needs assistance. If the person is not in the registry and is unable to articulate his name and address and appears to be unable to care for himself, he may require assistance. The provisions of the *Mental Health Act* may be applicable. It is difficult for a non-medical professional to distinguish between the symptoms of Alzheimer's disease and a mental illness. When in doubt, be cautious and protect the person from possible harm by apprehending and bringing him to a physician for examination.

Voluntary Admittance

If a person is displaying indicators that lead the officer to suspect that a psychiatric assessment may be needed, but the person is not exhibiting behaviours that would allow the officer to use the authorities of s. 17 of the MHA, the officer could ask the person to voluntarily submit to a psychiatric assessment. This option may be applicable in situations where the officer does not believe that an immediate danger exists but is unable to release the person into the custody of family or friends. If the person agrees, he or she may be transported to a medical facility to be examined by a physician. The physician will make the determination whether or not the person should have a psychiatric evaluation.

Under s. 12 of the MHA, the subject may agree and be admitted for evaluation as an informal or voluntary patient.

Admission of Informal or Voluntary Patients: Mental Health Act, Section 12

12. Any person who is believed to be in need of the observation, care and treatment provided in a psychiatric facility may be admitted thereto as an informal or voluntary patient upon the recommendation of a physician.

As a voluntary patient, the person may leave the psychiatric facility at any time, according to s. 14 of the MHA.

Informal or Voluntary Patient: Mental Health Act, Section 14

14. Nothing in this Act authorizes a psychiatric facility to detain or to restrain an informal or voluntary patient.

A problem occurs where the person refuses to be admitted and family or friends are not available. With no other legal options available, the officer must unconditionally release the person. Detailed notes of the interaction should be kept.

Order for Examination Issued by a Justice

An order for examination may be applicable in instances of unconditional release to family or friends. If the family or any person believes, on the basis of their observations, that as a result of a mental disorder, the person poses a danger to themselves or the public, or has caused or is causing a person to fear for their safety, or is unable to care for themselves, the person may appear before a justice seeking an order for psychiatric evaluation. This order is used in situations where the subject will not voluntarily submit himself or herself to a physician for evaluation and the police have not formed reasonable grounds to believe that the person poses an immediate danger to, or is unable to care for, himself or herself.

The justice will hear sworn information from the concerned parties and decide, based on the information presented, whether the subject should be brought to a physician to determine whether a psychiatric evaluation is necessary.

A Form 2, MHA, Order for Examination (see Appendix 7B at the end of this chapter), is issued by the justice authorizing police to apprehend the named person within seven days and bring him or her to a physician for assessment, as set out in ss. 16(1) and 16(3) of the MHA.

Justice of the Peace's Order for Psychiatric Examination: Mental Health Act, Section 16(1)

16(1) Where information upon oath is brought before a justice of the peace that a person within the limits of the jurisdiction of the justice,

(a) has threatened or attempted or is threatening or attempting to cause bodily harm to himself or herself;

(b) has behaved or is behaving violently towards another person or has caused or is causing another person to fear bodily harm from him or her; or

(c) has shown or is showing a lack of competence to care for himself or herself,

and in addition based upon the information before him or her the justice of the peace has reasonable cause to believe that the person is apparently suffering from mental disorder of a nature or quality that likely will result in,

(d) serious bodily harm to the person;

(e) serious bodily harm to another person; or

(f) serious physical impairment of the person,

the justice of the peace may issue an order in the prescribed form for the examination of the person by a physician.

Authority of Order: Mental Health Act, Section 16(3)

16(3) An order under this section shall direct, and, for a period not to exceed seven days from and including the day that it is made, is sufficient authority for any police officer to whom it is addressed to take the person named or described therein in custody forthwith to an appropriate place where he or she may be detained for examination by a physician.

The examining physician will determine whether the person needs to have a psychiatric evaluation. If an evaluation is deemed necessary, the person may voluntarily submit to the evaluation or be required to submit to evaluation. Section 15 of the MHA, below, authorizes the examining physician to order the person to be evaluated at a psychiatric facility.

The order is issued as a Form 1, MHA, Application by Physician for Psychiatric Assessment (see Appendix 7A at the end of this chapter). The order authorizes police to apprehend the named person within seven days and bring him or her to a psychiatric facility for evaluation.

Application for Psychiatric Assessment: Mental Health Act, Section 15(1)

15(1) Where a physician examines a person and has reasonable cause to believe that the person,

(a) has threatened or attempted or is threatening or attempting to cause bodily harm to himself or herself;

(b) has behaved or is behaving violently towards another person or has caused or is causing another person to fear bodily harm from him or her; or

(c) has shown or is showing a lack of competence to care for himself or herself, and if in addition the physician is of the opinion that the person is apparently suffering from mental disorder of a nature or quality that likely will result in,

(d) serious bodily harm to the person;

(e) serious bodily harm to another person; or

(f) serious physical impairment of the person,

the physician may make application in the prescribed form for a psychiatric assessment of the person.

Section 33 of the MHA requires that police stay with the person until the person is admitted to the facility.

Duty to Remain and Retain Custody: Mental Health Act, Section 33

33. A police officer or other person who takes a person in custody to a psychiatric facility shall remain at the facility and retain custody of the person until the facility takes custody of him or her in the prescribed manner.

Immediate Apprehension

In some situations, the immediate apprehension of a mentally disturbed person is necessary—for example, where he or she is suicidal or violent. The person may be experiencing episodes of psychosis, as described earlier. Such persons may pose a risk to the safety of intervening officers. Refer to the previously discussed guidelines for dealing with these occurrences.

Apprehension of a person without prior judicial authorization is allowable only in situations where the safety of the individual or another person is, or is likely to be, in imminent jeopardy. Section 17 of the MHA allows for the immediate apprehension of the person only in circumstances where the officer does not have time to apply for judicial authorization through the provisions of s. 16 of the MHA, as a result of the immediacy of the danger.

Action by Police Officer: Mental Health Act, Section 17

17. Where a police officer has reasonable and probable grounds to believe that a person is acting or has acted in a disorderly manner and has reasonable cause to believe that the person,

(a) has threatened or attempted or is threatening or attempting to cause bodily harm to himself or herself;

(b) has behaved or is behaving violently towards another person or has caused or is causing another person to fear bodily harm from him or her; or

(c) has shown or is showing a lack of competence to care for himself or herself,

and in addition the police officer is of the opinion that the person is apparently suffering from mental disorder of a nature or quality that likely will result in,

(d) serious bodily harm to the person;

(e) serious bodily harm to another person; or

(f) serious physical impairment of the person,

and that it would be dangerous to proceed under section 16, the police officer may take the person in custody to an appropriate place for examination by a physician.

Disengagement

Officers may use disengagement when the situation needs to be reassessed after initial contact with the mentally ill person. This option is available when the subject has been isolated and poses no danger to himself or herself or to the public. If possible, removal of potential weapons will assist in officer safety when the subject is to be removed or other options used. While awaiting backup, officers should make containment of the person their primary concern. The negative behaviour of a person experiencing a psychotic episode is unlikely to diminish while the officers wait for backup to arrive. A detailed description of the behaviour of the subject should be provided to other officers upon their arrival. The sharing of information is crucial in determining the next course of action.

Learning Activity 7.1

You are a police officer responding to a call from Josephine Dane. She tells you that she is concerned that her son, Joe Dane 18 years old, is having some mental health issues. He does not have a history of mental illness.

Joe is in his room. Mrs. Dane tells you that she has heard Joe talking to himself for the past 45 minutes. He appears to be having a conversation. The door to his room is locked.

You knock on the door to Joe's room. You tell him that you are a police officer.

He shouts, "Go away!"

Mrs. Dane tells you that he is alone in the room.

You ask Joe if you can come in to speak with him.

He replies, "If you must. Be careful not to step on the flowers."

You open the door. Joe is sitting on his bed. He is staring at the wall.

He shouts, "Be careful, you almost stepped on a rabbit!"

Mrs. Dane begins to cry.

Joe looks at her and says, "Why are you crying? Everything is great! Your tears are blue! That's the colour tears should be!"

Joe looks at you and begins to laugh. "You have a funny face. You look like the Joker! Look out! Lucy almost hit your head! Lucy is a vulture. She always finds me! You must be careful, her claws are sharp. She caught a rabbit last time I was here!"

You ask Joe if everything is all right.

He replies, "Who is this Joe? I am Madd Haberdasher. I live in this forest!"

Mrs. Dane continues to cry, "My poor little boy! He has lost his mind! It is my fault for protecting him from the world!"

Joe looks at you and says, "Why is the Queen crying? Her tears burn holes in the grass! Please ask her to stop!"

You ask Joe if he is angry with the Queen.

He replies, "I could never be angry with the Queen! She is my mother! She brings life to the world! I worship the Queen!"

You ask Joe how often he comes to the forest.

He replies, "I live in the forest! Sometimes I visit other places. Lucy is from the other place. She follows me everywhere I go. I try to hide. Lucy always finds me, but here in the forest I have help. Life is good here!"

You ask Joe how he got to the forest.

He replies, "Just like you did! You just lick the stamps and come in through the door!"

You ask Joe if he comes out of the forest very often.

He replies, "I try to stay in the forest. I don't like the other place! It is not peaceful like the forest; too many vultures!"

Mrs. Dane asks you to help her son.

Joe is becoming agitated.

He says, "I wish these vultures would leave me alone! Everywhere I go they follow me! They even find me in the forest! All their taunting, humiliation, constantly after me! I need to escape!"

You ask Joe to tell you more about the "vultures."

He replies, "You must know them! Didn't you come to the forest to escape them? The Queen told me that if I ignore them, they will go away. But they have been following me for a long time. They always humiliate me! They won't stop! I can't escape in the forest anymore! I don't know what to do!"

You ask what he plans to do to escape the vultures.

He replies, "No matter where I go, they find me! Maybe they are in my head. Yes, that's it! They are in my head! If I take my head off, they will go away! You have a weapon on your belt. Will you please take my head off?"

You tell Joe that you are not there to hurt him.

He replies, "It won't hurt! If you take my head off, the vultures will go away! I will be all right! If you won't help me, the Queen will. She always helps me."

You tell Joe that the Queen doesn't think that the vultures are in his head.

He replies, "This time she is wrong! I can see them! They are always there! If you won't help, I will do it myself!"

What will you do in this situation? Be sure to refer to the appropriate authorities.

EXCITED DELIRIUM

In some situations it is possible that a person may die suddenly and unexpectedly while in police custody. There does not appear to be any apparent injury or cause of death. These deaths may be attributed to a group of symptoms called **excited delirium**. Death as a result of excited delirium occurs once a subject is "successfully" restrained, possibly within five minutes of the subject becoming quiet. There are no indicators preceding the death.

Death due to excited delirium is not a police-specific phenomenon. Similar deaths occur in psychiatric and geriatric care facilities where patients are required to be restrained for their safety. Persons suffering from a psychiatric illness may be at higher risk of death as a result of excited delirium. Persons experiencing

excited delirium
state of acute agitation and hyperactivity, usually accompanied by violent behaviour

excited delirium are in a state of acute agitation and hyperactivity, usually accompanied by violent behaviour. There has not yet been a definitive cause identified, but persons experiencing psychotic episodes and persons under the influence of drugs, most notably cocaine, appear to be at greater risk.

Police officers should be aware that persons experiencing manias as a result of a psychiatric illness or drug-induced psychosis often present the same symptoms and behaviours as persons experiencing excited delirium. It is therefore almost impossible to accurately determine causation during an encounter.

There are some signs and symptoms that may indicate excited delirium:

- violent/aggressive behaviour;
- disorientation;
- hallucinations;
- panic;
- paranoia;
- impaired thinking;
- diminished sense of pain;
- unexpected physical strength;
- apparent ineffectiveness of oleoresin capsicum (OC) spray, or pepper spray (a second application may be detrimental to the subject);
- profuse sweating; and
- sudden tranquility after aggressive actions.

The final six of these symptoms appear to be common in individuals deemed to be experiencing excited delirium.

There is no set of criteria for establishing a diagnosis of excited delirium. However, there is some useful information that may assist with identifying the possibility of excited delirium occurring.

1. *Pre-encounter descriptions from witnesses.* Information may be available prior to the police encounter that suggests that excited delirium may be present, particularly if the incident is violent in nature. This information may include:
   - known history of schizophrenia, psychosis, or mania; or
   - known or suspected history of substance abuse.

2. *Officer's observations upon arrival at the scene.* Once the officer is on the scene, any or all of the following may be observed:
   - bizarre, purposeless, and violent behaviour;
   - hyperactivity;
   - incoherent shouting or screaming;
   - failure to recognize or acknowledge police presence;
   - extreme aggression; or
   - paranoia (previously discussed).

3. *Physical contact with the individual.* Upon physical contact, the officer may note any or all of the following:

- The subject demonstrates unbelievable strength that appears to be outside his or her physical characteristics.
- The subject is apparently impervious to pain. There is no response to pain compliance techniques.
- The subject is able to physically resist multiple officers without becoming tired.
- The subject is sweating profusely or the subject's skin is extremely dry.

When apprehending a person with a mental disorder, officers should be aware of the increased possibility of excited delirium. In situations involving extremely agitated people, physical restraint is often necessary but should be used only when the situation clearly justifies it and when there is no other way to prevent physical harm to the person or to others. Restraint is not harmless; some of those who are restrained may experience the adverse effects of excited delirium. The time spent under restraint should be minimized. Successfully placing the person in restraint is not an end in itself, but rather the first step in a process of calming the person and resolving the situation. Appropriate techniques for restraint that minimize the use of chest compression and the prone position and that maintain an open airway should be used whenever possible. The restraining officers must take care to not induce positional asphyxia. Positional asphyxia may occur when a person is restrained in the prone position with the officer using his or her bodyweight on the subject's chest or back as a method of control.

It may be that people in a state of excited delirium have a greater oxygen requirement, predisposing them to rapid asphyxiation if placed in a position that inhibits their breathing, such as the prone position. This belief has been reinforced through coroners' rulings of positional asphyxiation as the cause of death in suspected cases of excited delirium. Positional or postural holds are the restraints most frequently associated with unexpected death in persons susceptible to excited delirium.

The position that appears to be most detrimental is face down with feet and hands cuffed together behind the person (commonly referred to as "hog-tying"). If possible, police should not use this restraint method to control people showing signs of excited delirium. Positioning the restrained person in a manner that allows unrestricted breathing, such as sitting, may be helpful in preventing unanticipated death.

The reasons for sudden and unexpected excited delirium deaths are complex. Chris Lawrence (Ontario Police College), working with medical experts such as Wanda Mohr (Associate Professor, Psychiatric Mental Health Nursing, University of Medicine and Dentistry of New Jersey), has been conducting groundbreaking research into the medical literature on excited delirium.

According to the medical literature reviewed for the report *Investigator Protocol: Sudden In-Custody Death*, there appear to be three specific groups of people who are most prone to sudden and unexpected death attributed to excited delirium (Lawrence & Mohr, 2004):

1. individuals who are suffering from psychiatric illness, specifically bipolar disorders and schizophrenia (this is also noted in a study where both agitated and non-agitated subjects suffering from schizophrenia died suddenly and unexpectedly (Rosh, Sampson, & Hirsch, 2003));
2. individuals who are chronic illicit stimulant users; and
3. individuals who combine the two previous risk factors.

As noted previously, the deaths of some individuals while in police custody have been attributed to excited delirium. Evidence, while inconclusive, suggests that physical restraint in certain positions may contribute to such deaths. The use of OC spray may also be a contributing factor in some of these deaths.

In most instances, excited delirium was likely the result of a pre-existing psychiatric illness. In a significant number of cases, it resulted from recent use of cocaine. Other factors contributing to death during excited delirium include heart disease and obesity.

Lawrence (2004) suggests that there are some measures that may be taken to enhance the safety of a person who is about to be, or who has been, taken into custody through physical restraint and is exhibiting signs or symptoms of excited delirium:

- If possible, advanced life support paramedics should be on standby prior to the physical restraint of a person who appears to be experiencing excited delirium.
- Excited delirium is a medical emergency—all subjects should be transported to hospital via ambulance.
- From a control and safety perspective, it is best to control the subject as quickly as possible. It may be that the longer the physical confrontation goes on with a subject experiencing excited delirium, the higher the risk of an in-custody death.
- Given the correlation between the maximal restraint position (hog-tie) and sudden and unexpected death, the use of this restraint position should be used with extreme caution. (Follow your police service guidelines.)
- Once in custody and awaiting transport via ambulance, or while being transported in the ambulance, the restrained subject should be placed in a supine position. If the subject must be maintained on their side, it is recommended that they be placed resting on their left side if possible.
- If the restrained subject suddenly becomes quiet and stops resistance, advanced life support should be summoned where available, and preparation for CPR should be made.

KEY TERMS

antisocial personality disorder
bipolar disorder
clinical depression
delusion
delusions of persecution
dependent personality
excited delirium

hallucination
mental illness
postpartum depression
psychosis
schizophrenia
self-injury
unusual realities

REFERENCES

American Psychiatric Association. (2000). *Diagnostic and statistical manual of mental disorders* (4th ed.). Washington, DC: Author.

American Self-Harm Information Clearinghouse. (n.d.). *About self-harm.* Retrieved from http://www.selfinjury.org.

Canadian Institute for Health Information. (2005). *Hospital mental health services in Canada 2002-2003.* Ottawa: Author.

Canadian Mental Health Association. (2005a). *CAMIMH—Canadian Alliance on Mental Illness and Mental Health: Frequently asked questions.* Ottawa: Author.

Canadian Mental Health Association. (2005b). *Mental health system.* Ottawa: Author.

Criminal Code. (1985). RSC 1985, c. C-46, as amended.

Depression and Manic Depression Association of Alberta. (2005). *Primary unipolar recurrent type of depression.*

Favazza, A.R., & Conterio, K. (1989). Female habitual self-mutilators. *Acta Psychiatrica Scandinavica, 79,* 283–289.

Favazza, A.R., & Rosenthal, R.J. (1993). Diagnostic issues in self-mutilation. *Hospital & Community Psychiatry, 44*(2), 134–140.

Herpertz, S. (1995). Self-injurious behaviour: Psychopathological and nosological characteristics in subtypes of self-injurers. *Acta Psychiatrica Scandinavica, 91,* 57–68.

Lawrence, C.W. (2004, June). Prone position linked to sudden death in suspects. *Blue Line Magazine,* 24–25.

Lawrence, C.W., & Mohr, W.K. (2004). Investigator protocol: Sudden in-custody death. *The Police Chief, 71*(1), 44–52.

MediResource Inc. (2005). *Women's health: Disease information.* Toronto: Author.

Mental Health Act. (1990). RSO 1990, c. M.7.

Ministry of Health and Long-Term Care. (2005). *Mental health: The next steps— Strengthening Ontario's mental health system.* Retrieved from http://www.health.gov.on.ca/english/public/pub/mental/consultation.html.

Patient Health International. (2005). *Bipolar disorder.* London, UK: AstraZeneca.

Police Services Act. (1990). RSO 1990, c. P.15.

Rosh, A., Sampson, B.A., & Hirsch, C.S. (2003). Schizophrenia as a cause of death. *Journal of Forensic Sciences, 48*(1), 164–167.

Schizophrenia Society of Ontario. (n.d.). *About schizophrenia.* Toronto: Author.

Statistics Canada. (1997). *National population health survey.* Ottawa: Author.

Statistics Canada. (2003). *Canadian community health survey: Mental health and well-being.* Ottawa: Author.

U.S. Department of Justice. FBI Uniform Crime Reports. (1992). *Killed in the line of duty: A study of felonious killings of law enforcement officers.* Washington, DC: Author.

Whitlock, J. (2010). *What is self-injury?* Retrieved from Cornell Research Program on Self-Injurious Behavior in Adolescents and Young Adults: http://crpsib.com/factsheet_aboutsi.asp.

EXERCISES

SHORT ANSWER

1. Define "mental illness" for the purpose of police intervention.

2. Identify some common symptoms of mental illness.

3. Describe the authorities of a Form 1, MHA from the perspective of police intervention.

4. Identify the authorities contained in a Form 2, MHA.

5. Describe the authorities contained in s. 17 of the MHA.

6. Explain excited delirium and list some of the common symptoms.

CASE ANALYSIS

Case 7.1

You are a police officer responding to a call of a disturbance in a shopping mall. Upon arrival you are met by mall security guard, Jane Star.

She tells you that she has received a complaint about a male sitting on one of the public benches. He keeps staring at everyone who passes. The store owners are complaining that he is bad for business. Star walks with you to the person's location. She points to the male in question, later identified as Rob Allan, sitting on a bench in front of a ladies' clothing store. You speak to Mr. Allan.

He tells you that he is just sitting on the bench talking to his friend and "checking out the ladies." He continues: "If you sit right here, you can see into the back changing area. Sometimes ladies come out wearing only their underwear! Look, Robert, there's one now!" It appears as if he is speaking to an unseen person to his right.

You ask, "Who is Robert?" Allan replies: "He is my friend, my best friend."

He then introduces you to Robert: "Robert, this is ... Sorry I didn't get your name." You tell him that you are Constable Steeves. He continues: "Robert, this is Constable Steeves. Constable Steeves, this is my best friend, Robert."

He then begins a conversation with his unseen friend. The conversation focuses on where they should go next to see some ladies.

What will you do in this situation? Explain your authorities.

Case 7.2

You are a police officer responding to a call for assistance at 789 Main Street. Upon arrival you are met by Pete Herman and Wendy Herman. Pete is very emotional and is crying.

Wendy tells you that she is scared of Pete. He has been having delusions and hallucinations for the past three days.

You speak to Pete.

He explains to you that he sometimes sees a black dog. The dog talks to him and tells him that he should be having sex with children. He is confused because the dog has never lied to him before, but he doesn't think it is right for adults to have sex with children. Pete tells you that he went to Dr. Kay about a year ago to get help. He told Dr. Kay about his hallucinations and that he believes that he may have sexually touched his two-year-old daughter.

Dr. Kay began counselling Pete and prescribed anti-psychotic drugs for him.

Pete tells you that it has been almost a year and nothing has changed. The therapies aren't working. The dog is around more than ever. It won't shut up.

What will you do in this situation? Explain your authorities.

Case 7.3

You are a police officer on foot patrol of the downtown area of the city. It is 5 p.m. You observe a person lying beside a dumpster behind a restaurant. As you approach the person, you recognize him as Joe Keith. Keith is homeless and an alcoholic. You shout to get his attention. He sits up. You ask him what he is doing.

He tells you that sometimes restaurants throw away their empty liquor bottles. If you can find a few of them and pour the liquor that is still in the bottom of the bottle together with the liquor in the other bottles, you can get a good drink. He tells you that the most beautiful sight he has seen was a half bottle of wine he found last week when he was checking dumpsters.

You ask him to stand up. He tells you that he has a bad leg and can't stand or walk very well. He pulls up his pant leg and shows you a large cut on his calf. He tells you that a rat told him that blood was just like red wine, so he cut himself to find out. He tells you that the "eff'n rat was lying!"

You ask if he wants to go to the hospital to get his leg checked. He replies: "Maybe in a few days. It's Friday night, the best night of the week to get booze. I don't want to go to the hospital tonight." He asks you if you can lend him a few dollars to get a drink. He hasn't had a drink since last night and is feeling pretty rough. He just needs a couple of drinks to "take the edge off."

What will you do in this situation? Explain your answer. Be sure to quote authorities.

APPENDIX 7A   FORM 1, MENTAL HEALTH ACT

| Ministry of Health Ontario | **Form 1** *Mental Health Act* | **Application by Physician for Psychiatric Assessment** |

Name of physician _____

(print name of physician)

Physician address _____

(address of physician)

Telephone number (   ) _____   Fax number   (   ) _____

On_____ I personally examined _____

(date)   (print full name of person)

whose address is _____

(home address)

*You may only sign this **Form 1** if you have personally examined the person within the past seven days.*
*In deciding if a Form 1 is appropriate, you must complete **either** Box A (serious harm test) **or** Box B (persons who are incapable of consenting to treatment and meet the specified criteria test) below.*

Box A – Section 15(1) of the Mental Health Act
Serious Harm Test

The Past / Present Test *(check one or more)*

I have reasonable cause to believe that the person:

☐ has threatened or is threatening to cause bodily harm to himself or herself

☐ has attempted or is attempting to cause bodily harm to himself or herself

☐ has behaved or is behaving violently towards another person

☐ has caused or is causing another person to fear bodily harm from him or her; or

☐ has shown or is showing a lack of competence to care for himself or herself

I base this belief on the following information *(you may, as appropriate in the circumstances, rely on any combination of your own observations and information communicated to you by others.)*
My own observations:

Facts communicated to me by others:

The Future Test *(check one or more)*

I am of the opinion that the person is apparently suffering from mental disorder of a nature or quality that likely will result in:

☐ serious bodily harm to himself or herself,

☐ serious bodily harm to another person,

☐ serious physical impairment of himself or herself

6427–41 (00/12)   *(Disponible en version française)*   *See reverse*   7530–4972

(Appendix 7A is continued on the next page.)

APPENDIX 7A   FORM 1, CONTINUED

Box A – Section 15(1) of the Mental Health Act
             Serious Harm Test *(continued)*

I base this opinion on the following information *(you may, as appropriate in the circumstances, rely on any combination of your own observations and information communicated to you by others.)*

My own observations:

Facts communicated by others:

Box B – Section 15(1.1) of the Mental Health Act
             Patients who are Incapable of Consenting to Treatment and Meet the Specified Criteria

Note: The patient *must* meet the criteria set out in *each* of the following conditions.

I have reasonable cause to believe that the person:

1. Has previously received treatment for mental disorder of an ongoing or recurring nature that, when not treated, is of a nature or quality that likely will result in one or more of the following: *(please indicate one or more)*

   ☐ serious bodily harm to himself or herself,

   ☐ serious bodily harm to another person,

   ☐ substantial mental or physical deterioration of himself or herself, or

   ☐ serious physical impairment of himself or herself;

AND

2. Has shown clinical improvement as a result of the treatment.

AND

I am of the opinion that the person,

3. Is incapable, within the meaning of the *Health Care Consent Act, 1996,* of consenting to his or her treatment in a psychiatric facility and the consent of his or her substitute decision-maker has been obtained;

AND

4. Is apparently suffering from the same mental disorder as the one for which he or she previously received treatment or from a mental disorder that is similar to the previous one;

(Disponible en version française)

6427–41 (00/12)   7530–4972

(Appendix 7A is concluded on the next page.)

APPENDIX 7A FORM 1, CONCLUDED

Box B – Section 15(1.1) of the Mental Health Act
Patients who are Incapable of Consenting to Treatment and Meet the Specified Criteria
(continued)

AND

5. Given the person's history of mental disorder and current mental or physical condition, is likely to: *(choose one or more of the following)*

☐ cause serious bodily harm to himself or herself, or

☐ cause serious bodily harm to another person, or

☐ suffer substantial mental or physical deterioration, or

☐ suffer serious physical impairment

I base this opinion on the following information *(you may, as appropriate in the circumstances, rely on any combination of your own observations and information communicated to you by others.)*

My own observations:

Facts communicated by others:

I have made careful inquiry into all the facts necessary for me to form my opinion as to the nature and quality of the person's mental disorder. I hereby make application for a psychiatric assessment of the person named.

Today's date _____   Today's time _____

Examining physician's signature _____
(signature of physician)

This form authorizes, for a period of 7 days including the date of signature, the apprehension of the person named and his or her detention in a psychiatric facility for a maximum of 72 hours.

For Use at the Psychiatric Facility

Once the period of detention at the psychiatric facility begins, the attending physician should note the date and time this occurs and must promptly give the person a Form 42.

_____   _____
(Date and time detention commences)   (signature of physician)

_____   _____
(Date and time Form 42 delivered)   (signature of physician)

(Disponible en version française)

APPENDIX 7B   FORM 2, MENTAL HEALTH ACT

Ministry of Health
Ontario

Form 2
Mental Health Act

Order for Examination under Section 16

To the police officers of Ontario.

Whereas information upon oath has been brought before me, a justice of the peace in and for the province of Ontario

by _____
(print full name of person bringing information)

of _____
(address of person bringing information)

in respect of _____
(print full name or other description of person to be examined)

of _____
(home address, if known)

Part A or Part B must be completed

Part A – Subsection 16 (1)

Information has been brought before me that such person

☐ has threatened or attempted or is threatening or attempting to cause bodily harm to himself or herself;

☐ has behaved or is behaving violently towards another person or has caused or is causing another person to fear bodily harm from him or her; or

☐ has shown or is showing a lack of competence to care for himself or herself.

In addition based upon the information before me I have reasonable cause to believe that the person is apparently suffering from mental disorder of a nature or quality that likely will result in,

☐ serious bodily harm to the person;

☐ serious bodily harm to another person, or

☐ serious physical impairment of the person.

Part B – Subsection 16 (1.1)

Information has been brought before me that such person

a) has previously received treatment for mental disorder of an ongoing or recurring nature that, when not treated, is of a nature or quality that likely will result in serious bodily harm to the person or to another person or substantial mental or physical deterioration of the person or serious physical impairment of the person; and

b) has shown clinical improvement as a result of the treatment;

In addition based upon the information before me I have reasonable cause to believe that the person,

c) is apparently suffering from the same mental disorder as the one for which he or she previously received treatment or from a mental disorder that is similar to the previous one;

(Appendix 7B is continued on the next page.)

APPENDIX 7B   FORM 2, CONTINUED

Part B *(continued)*

d) given the person's history of mental disorder and current mental or physical condition, is likely to

☐ cause serious bodily harm to himself or herself;

☐ cause serious bodily harm to another person,

☐ suffer substantial mental or physical deterioration of the person, or

☐ suffer serious physical impairment of the person; and

e) is apparently incapable within the meaning of the *Health Care Consent Act*, 1996 of consenting to his or her treatment in a psychiatric facility and the consent his or her substitute decision-maker has been obtained.

Now therefore, I order you, the said police officers, or any of you, to take the said person in custody forthwith to an appropriate place for examination by a physician.

_____
(date of signature)

_____   _____
(Municipality where order signed)   (signature of Justice of the Peace)

                                                    _____
                                                       (print name of Justice of the Peace)

6428–41 (00/12)   7530–4973

(Appendix 7B is concluded on the next page.)

APPENDIX 7B   FORM 2, CONCLUDED

Notes for Applicant / Informant

1. You may wish to provide your telephone number on this form so that you can be contacted by the police or the examining physician after this order is issued. This is entirely voluntary. *You are not required to give this information for the order to be issued or for the order to be legally valid.*

_____   _____
(print name)   (telephone number)

2. You may wish to seek legal advice concerning this order, including the effect of this order and your legal rights.

3. You may wish to inform the police, the examining physician and/or an appropriate health care professional of the evidence you gave to the justice of peace, if you consider it appropriate in all the circumstances to do so. If you decide to do so, please use the space provided below. Use the back of this form if necessary. *You are not required to give this information for the order to be issued or for the order to be legally valid.*

APPENDIX 7C   FORM 3, MENTAL HEALTH ACT

Ministry
of
Health

Form 3
Mental Health Act

**Certificate of Involuntary
Admission**

Name of patient _____
(print name of patient)

Name of physician _____
(print name of physician)

Name of psychiatric facility _____
(name of psychiatric facility)

Date of examination _____
(date)

I hereby certify that the following three pieces of information are correct:

1. I personally examined the patient on the date set out above.

2. I am of the opinion that the patient named above is not suitable for voluntary or informal status.

3. Complete one or more boxes as appropriate.

    ☐ I am of the opinion that the patient named above meets the criteria set out in Box A.
    (please complete Box A below)

    ☐ I am of the opinion that the patient named above meets each of the criteria set out in Box B.
    (please complete Box B below)

Box A –   Risk of Serious Harm

Note: Check one or more boxes as appropriate.

The patient is suffering from mental disorder of a nature or quality that likely will result in:

☐ serious bodily harm to the patient,

☐ serious bodily harm to another person

☐ serious physical impairment of the patient

unless he or she remains in the custody of a psychiatric facility.

Box B –   Patients who are Incapable of Consenting to Treatment and Meet the Specified Criteria

Note: The patient *must* meet *all* of the following five criteria.

1. The patient has been found incapable, within the meaning of the *Health Care Consent Act, 1996* of consenting to his or her treatment in a psychiatric facility and the consent of his or her substitute decision-maker has been obtained.

2. The patient has previously received treatment for mental disorder of an ongoing or recurring nature that, when not treated, is of a nature or quality that likely will result in one or more of the following: *(please indicate one or more)*

    ☐ serious bodily harm to the patient,

    ☐ serious bodily harm to another person,

    ☐ substantial mental or physical deterioration of the patient, or

    ☐ serious physical impairment of the patient;

(Disponible en version française)

6429–41 (2000/12)   ©Queen's Printer for Ontario, 2000

See reverse.

7530–4974

(Appendix 7C is concluded on the next page.)

APPENDIX 7C   FORM 3, CONCLUDED

Box B – Patients who are Incapable of Consenting to Treatment and Meet the Specified Criteria
       (continued)

3.   The patient has shown clinical improvement as a result of the treatment.

4.   The patient is suffering from the same mental disorder as the one for which he or she previously received
     treatment or from a mental disorder that is similar to the previous one.

5.   Given the person's history of mental disorder and current mental or physical condition, is likely to:
     (please indicate one or more)

     ☐ cause serious bodily harm to himself or herself, or

     ☐ cause serious bodily harm to another person, or

     ☐ suffer substantial mental or physical deterioration, or

     ☐ suffer serious physical impairment

_____
(Date of signature)

_____
(signature of attending physician)

Notes

1) This certificate is valid for *14 calendar days*, including the day upon which it was signed.

2) The following actions must be taken promptly after this form is signed:

   a)   The signing physician must give the patient a properly executed Form 30 notice and notify a rights adviser.

   b)   The rights adviser must meet with the patient and explain to him or her the significance of the certificate
        and the right to have it reviewed by the Consent and Capacity Board.

(Disponible en version française)

429–41 (2000/12)   ©Queen's Printer for Ontario, 2000   7530–4974

APPENDIX 7D   FORM 45, MENTAL HEALTH ACT

Ministry
of
Health

Form 45
Mental Health Act

Community Treatment Order

Part 1 – To be Filled Out by Examining Physician

Name of person _____
(print name of patient)

Name of physician _____
(print name of physician)

Name of substitute decision-maker *(if applicable)* _____
(print name of substitute decision-maker)

Name of psychiatric facility *(if applicable)* _____
(name of psychiatric facility)

Date of examination _____
(date)

This community treatment order for the above named person is the:

☐ first for this person   ☐ _____ renewal
(no. of times CTO has been renewed)

Date of issue of previous community treatment order *(if applicable)* _____
(date)

Date of expiry of previous community treatment order *(if applicable)* _____
(date)

During the previous three year period, the person named above:

☐ has been a patient in a psychiatric facility on two or more separate occasions or for a cumulative period of 30 days or more during that three year period, OR

☐ has been the subject of a previous community treatment order.

Criteria for Community Treatment Order

(Note: All the criteria set out below must be met for this order to be valid)

I am of the opinion that

a)   the person is suffering from mental disorder such that he or she needs continuing treatment or care and continuing supervision while living in the community, AND

b)   if the person does not receive continuing treatment or care and continuing supervision while living in the community, he or she is likely, because of mental disorder, to: (choose one or more of the following)

☐ cause serious bodily harm to himself or herself, OR

☐ cause serious bodily harm to another person, OR

☐ suffer substantial mental deterioration of the person, OR

☐ suffer substantial physical deterioration of the person OR

☐ suffer serious physical impairment of the person,

   AND

c)   the person is able to comply with the community treatment plan contained in the community treatment order, AND

(Appendix 7D is continued on the next page.)

APPENDIX 7D FORM 45, CONTINUED

d) the treatment or care and supervision required under the terms of the community treatment order are available in the community, AND

e) If the person is not currently a patient in a psychiatric facility, the person meets the criteria for the completion of an application for psychiatric assessment under subsection 15(1) or (1.1).

The facts on which I formed the above opinion are as follows:

Rights Advice

Note: The person and his or her substitute decision–maker, if applicable, must receive rights advice before the order is issued.

I am satisfied that the substitute decision-maker of the person, if applicable, has consulted with a rights adviser and been advised of his or her legal rights, AND

I am satisfied that the person:

☐ has consulted with a rights adviser and been advised of his or her legal rights, or

☐ has not consulted with a rights adviser because he or she has refused to consult a rights adviser.

Community Treatment Plan

Note: A copy of the community treatment plan must be attached to this order.

I am satisfied that a community treatment plan has been devised for the person.

I have consulted with all the persons named in the community treatment plan.

I am satisfied that:

☐ the person OR

☐ the person's substitute decision-maker, if the person is incapable, consents to the community treatment plan.

The community treatment plan for the person is

(Describe the community treatment plan. Use back of this form if necessary. The community treatment plan must be attached to this order.)

(Appendix 7D is concluded on the next page.)

APPENDIX 7D FORM 45, CONCLUDED

Part 2 – To be Filled Out by the Person or the Person's Substitute Decision-Maker

Undertaking of Person or Person's Substitute Decision-Maker
(to be completed by the person or the person's substitute decision maker, if applicable)

I am

☐ the person named above. I promise to comply with all my obligations as set out in the community treatment plan, OR

☐ the person's substitute decision-maker. I promise to use my best efforts to ensure that the person named above complies with all the obligations as set out in the community treatment plan.

By my signature at the bottom of this order, I signify that I consent to the community treatment plan, and I consent to, and am assuming my undertakings as stated in, the community treatment plan.

Part 3 – Time in Force – To be Completed by the Examining Physician

This community treatment order is in force for 6 months, including the day upon which it is signed, and expires at midnight on the _____ unless it is terminated at an earlier date.
(date) (day / month / year)

Part 4 – Patient Right to Apply to Consent and Capacity Board

A person who is subject to a community treatment order, or any person on his or her behalf, may apply to the Board using a *Form 48* to inquire into whether or not the criteria for issuing or renewing this community treatment order have been met.

Signed at _____
(name of psychiatric facility, or name of place [eg. doctor's office, hospital] where community treatment order signed)

_____   _____
(Date)   (signature of physician)

_____   _____
(signature of person)   (signature of substitute decision-maker) *(if applicable)*

Notes:

The following actions must be taken by the physician who signs this order immediately after the order is signed:

1. A copy of this order, including the community treatment plan must be given to:

    a) the person,
    b) the person's substitute decision-maker, if applicable,
    c) the officer in charge of a psychiatric facility, if applicable,
    d) any other health practitioner or other person named in the community treatment plan.

2. A notice in the approved form *(Form 46)* must be given to the person that he or she is entitled to a hearing before the Consent and Capacity Board.

APPENDIX 7E FORM 47, MENTAL HEALTH ACT

Ministry
of
Health

Form 47
Mental Health Act

**Order for Examination
Sections 33.3(1) and 33.4 (3)
of the Act**

To the police officers of Ontario

WHEREAS _____
(print name of person subject to a community treatment order)

of _____
(address of person subject to community treatment order)

is subject to a community treatment order issued or renewed on _____
(date of order)

by _____
(name of issuing or renewing physician)

of _____ and
(business address of issuing or renewing physician)

WHEREAS such person has

☐ failed to attend appointments or comply with treatment in accordance with ss.33.1(9) of the
Mental Health Act, or

☐ failed to permit _____ to review his/her condition,
(name of iphysician)

in accordance with ss.33.4 (2) of the *Mental Health Act*; and

WHEREAS I have reasonable cause to believe that such person

(i) is suffering from mental disorder such that he/she needs continuing treatment or care and continuing supervision while living in the community;

(ii) meets the criteria for the completion of a Form 1 [an application for psychiatric assessment under ss.15 (1) or (1.1) of the *Mental Health Act*] and is not currently a patient in a psychiatric facility; and

(iii) if the person does not receive continuing treatment or care and continuing supervision while living in the community, he/she is likely, because of mental disorder, to *(choose one or more of the following)*

☐ cause serious bodily harm to himself / herself

☐ cause serious bodily harm to another person

☐ suffer substantial mental or physical deterioration of the person

☐ suffer serious physical impairment of the person.

Now therefore, I hereby issue this Order for Examination for any of you to take such person in custody forthwith to _____
(address of physician, agency or psychiatric facility where the person will be examined)

for an examination by me or by a physician named below appointed to carry out this responsibility in accordance with ss. 33.5 (2) of the *Mental Health Act*.

_____
(name of physician, agency or psychiatric facility responsible for examination of the person

This order is in force for 30 days after the date upon
which it is issued and will expire at midnight on _____
(date order will expire)

Dated at _____ on _____
(name of municipality / city / town)   (date) (day / month / year)

_____   _____
(signature of physician)   (print name of physician)

3761–41 (00/12)

7530–5577

(Appendix 7E is concluded on the next page.)

APPENDIX 7E   FORM 47, CONCLUDED

Notes:

1. The physician who issues an order for examination shall ensure that the police have complete and up-to-date information about the name, address and telephone number of the physician responsible for completing the examination required under an order for examination and shall ensure that the police have such information at all times that the order for examination is in force.

2. The physician who issues an order for examination shall ensure that the police are immediately notified if the person who is subject to the order for examination voluntarily attends for an examination or, for any other reason, the order for examination is cancelled prior to its expiry date.

3. The police may need a physical description of the person named in your Order for Examination so that the person may be located and returned to you for an examination. Please use the space below to provide the police with relevant information about the person's physical description.

4. The police may ask you for information about the person's physical description, in addition to the information you have provided below.

APPENDIX 7F EXCERPTS FROM THE HEALTH CARE CONSENT ACT, 1996

Meaning of "substitute decision-maker"

9. In this Part,

"substitute decision-maker" means a person who is authorized under section 20 to give or refuse consent to a treatment on behalf of a person who is incapable with respect to the treatment.

List of persons who may give or refuse consent

20(1) If a person is incapable with respect to a treatment, consent may be given or refused on his or her behalf by a person described in one of the following paragraphs:

1. The incapable person's guardian of the person, if the guardian has authority to give or refuse consent to the treatment.

2. The incapable person's attorney for personal care, if the power of attorney confers authority to give or refuse consent to the treatment.

3. The incapable person's representative appointed by the Board under section 33, if the representative has authority to give or refuse consent to the treatment.

4. The incapable person's spouse or partner.

5. A child or parent of the incapable person, or a children's aid society or other person who is lawfully entitled to give or refuse consent to the treatment in the place of the parent. This paragraph does not include a parent who has only a right of access. If a children's aid society or other person is lawfully entitled to give or refuse consent to the treatment in the place of the parent, this paragraph does not include the parent.

6. A parent of the incapable person who has only a right of access.

7. A brother or sister of the incapable person.

8. Any other relative of the incapable person.

Requirements

20(2) A person described in subsection (1) may give or refuse consent only if he or she,

(a) is capable with respect to the treatment;

(b) is at least 16 years old, unless he or she is the incapable person's parent;

(c) is not prohibited by court order or separation agreement from having access to the incapable person or giving or refusing consent on his or her behalf;

(d) is available; and

(e) is willing to assume the responsibility of giving or refusing consent.

Meaning of "spouse"

20(7) Subject to subsection (8), two persons are spouses for the purpose of this section if,

(Appendix 7F is continued on the next page.)

(a) they are married to each other; or

(b) they are living in a conjugal relationship outside marriage and,

(i) have cohabited for at least one year,

(ii) are together the parents of a child, or

(iii) have together entered into a cohabitation agreement under section 53 of the *Family Law Act*.

Not spouse

20(8) Two persons are not spouses for the purpose of this section if they are living separate and apart as a result of a breakdown of their relationship.

Meaning of "partner"

20(9) For the purpose of this section,

"partner" means,

(a) Repealed.

(b) either of two persons who have lived together for at least one year and have a close personal relationship that is of primary importance in both persons' lives.

Meaning of "relative"

20(10) Two persons are relatives for the purpose of this section if they are related by blood, marriage or adoption.

Meaning of "available"

20(11) For the purpose of clause (2)(d), a person is available if it is possible, within a time that is reasonable in the circumstances, to communicate with the person and obtain a consent or refusal.

Principles for giving or refusing consent

21(1) A person who gives or refuses consent to a treatment on an incapable person's behalf shall do so in accordance with the following principles:

1. If the person knows of a wish applicable to the circumstances that the incapable person expressed while capable and after attaining 16 years of age, the person shall give or refuse consent in accordance with the wish.

2. If the person does not know of a wish applicable to the circumstances that the incapable person expressed while capable and after attaining 16 years of age, or if it is impossible to comply with the wish, the person shall act in the incapable person's best interests.

Best interests

21(2) In deciding what the incapable person's best interests are, the person who gives or refuses consent on his or her behalf shall take into consideration,

(a) the values and beliefs that the person knows the incapable person held when capable and believes he or she would still act on if capable;

(b) any wishes expressed by the incapable person with respect to the treatment that are not required to be followed under paragraph 1 of subsection (1); and

(c) the following factors:

(Appendix 7F is concluded on the next page.)

1. Whether the treatment is likely to,

      i. improve the incapable person's condition or well-being,

      ii. prevent the incapable person's condition or well-being from deteriorating, or

      iii. reduce the extent to which, or the rate at which, the incapable person's condition or well-being is likely to deteriorate.

2. Whether the incapable person's condition or well-being is likely to improve, remain the same or deteriorate without the treatment.

3. Whether the benefit the incapable person is expected to obtain from the treatment outweighs the risk of harm to him or her.

4. Whether a less restrictive or less intrusive treatment would be as beneficial as the treatment that is proposed.

Information

22(1) Before giving or refusing consent to a treatment on an incapable person's behalf, a substitute decision-maker is entitled to receive all the information required for an informed consent as described in subsection 11(2).

Conflict

22(2) Subsection (1) prevails despite anything to the contrary in the *Personal Health Information Protection Act, 2004.*

Suicide

8

INTRODUCTION

Suicide is an action, not an illness. Underlying the suicidal action is a chain of causal and triggering factors. These are likely to be highly unique to the suicidal individual. Ideally, a health-care professional or other concerned person will identify and address these factors to prevent the suicidal action. Police officers are generally not in a position to do this, and usually are not involved with the person until suicidal actions have taken place or suicidal behaviour has been reported. The task of police officers is to intervene when necessary to stop the action and save lives. With the proper intervention, one-half to two-thirds of all suicide attempts are probably preventable. Police officers, however, are usually not psychiatrists or psychologists. However, they are typically the first individuals offering assistance that a suicidal person encounters. Knowing the signs of suicide, being able to assess a person's risk of suicide, knowing who commits suicide, and understanding why goes a long way toward ensuring that police intervention is successful.

CHAPTER OBJECTIVES

After completing this chapter, you should be able to:

- Explain how age, gender, and other factors affect suicidal behaviour.
- Identify reasons why people commit suicide.
- Identify methods used to commit suicide.
- Identify the provisions of the *Criminal Code* and Ontario *Mental Health Act* that apply to suicide.
- Describe techniques for police intervention in suicide situations.

WHO COMMITS SUICIDE?

Statistics Canada identifies suicide as the 7th leading cause of death among Canadian males and the 12th leading cause of death among Canadian females in 2007. See Table 8.1.

Certain age groups are at higher risk for dying by suicide. In 2007, suicide was the second leading cause of death for people aged 15–24 and 25–34. See Table 8.2.

However, in 2007, the greatest number of suicides were committed by people aged 45–49. See Table 8.3. The overall number of suicides per year in Canada is relatively consistent, averaging 3,649 per year for the years 2003–2007.

The number of suicides by males was relatively consistent for the years 2003–2007, averaging 2,783 per year. See Table 8.4.

The number of females who died by suicide was relatively stable for the years 2003–2007, averaging 866 per year. See Table 8.5.

Table 8.1 Ranking, Number, and Percentage of Male and Female Deaths for the Ten Leading Causes, Canada, 2007

Cause of death	Males			Females		
	Rank	Number	Percent	Rank	Number	Percent
All causes of death	...	118,681	100.0	...	116,536	100.0
Malignant neoplasms (cancer)	1	36,569	30.8	1	33,026	28.3
Diseases of heart (heart disease)	2	26,381	22.2	2	24,118	20.7
Accidents (unintentional injuries)	3	6,015	5.1	6	3,936	3.4
Cerebrovascular diseases (stroke)	4	5,719	4.8	3	8,262	7.1
Chronic lower respiratory diseases..............	5	5,572	4.7	4	5,087	4.4
Diabetes mellitus (diabetes).................	6	3,906	3.3	7	3,488	3.0
Intentional self-harm (suicide)	7	2,727	2.3	12	884	0.8
Influenza and pneumonia. .	8	2,438	2.1	8	3,014	2.6
Nephritis, nephrotic syndrome, and nephrosis (kidney disease)	9	1,877	1.6	9	1,926	1.7
Chronic liver disease and cirrhosis (liver disease)	10	1,756	1.5	11	895	0.8
All other causes..........	...	25,721	21.7	...	31,900	27.4

Note: The order of the causes of death in this table is based on the ranking of the ten leading causes for males.
... = not applicable.

Sources: Statistics Canada. *Leading causes of deaths in Canada, 2007*, CANSIM Table 102–0561. Adapted from Statistics Canada (2010a).

Table 8.2 Ranking of Suicide Among the Ten Leading Causes of Death, by Age Group, Canada, 2007

Age	Rank
10–14..	4
15–24..	2
25–34..	2
35–44..	3
45–54..	4
55–64..	8
65–74..	...
74–84..	...
Over 85	...

... = not in the top ten causes of death.

Source: Based on data from Statistics Canada (2010a).

Table 8.3   Number of Suicides, by Age Group, Canada, 2003–2007

	2003	2004	2005	2006	2007
	Number of suicides, both sexes				
All ages[a]	3,765	3,613	3,743	3,512	3,611
10 to 14	27	28	43	31	33
15 to 19	216	210	213	152	185
20 to 24	306	270	296	265	290
25 to 29	245	275	228	237	282
30 to 34	295	316	283	243	235
35 to 39	434	390	381	318	325
40 to 44	463	409	495	418	403
45 to 49	454	446	476	459	486
50 to 54	404	393	407	369	410
55 to 59	292	275	294	328	307
60 to 64	187	174	166	209	203
65 to 69	142	121	138	145	115
70 to 74	105	108	99	104	102
75 to 79	85	88	113	113	103
80 to 84	53	63	66	62	76
85 to 89	34	36	31	39	42
90 and older	23	11	13	20	14

[a] "All ages" includes suicides of children under age ten and suicides of people of unknown age.

Sources: Statistics Canada, CANSIM, table 102-0551 and catalogue no. 84F0209X. Adapted from Statistics Canada (2010b).

The number of males dying by suicide versus females dying by suicide was higher among all age groups.

Males and females choose differing methods of suicide with males opting for "more violent" means of death. See Table 8.6 and Figure 8.1.

Suicide is not restricted to a particular age, race, gender, or income group, although the statistics indicate that some people are at higher risk than others.

People with mood disorders are at a particularly high risk of suicide. Studies indicate that more than 90 percent of suicide victims have a diagnosable psychiatric illness. Nearly 80 percent of those who commit suicide are suffering from a serious depressive illness (Mood Disorders Association of Ontario, n.d.). Suicide is the most common cause of death for people with schizophrenia. Both major depression and bipolar disorder account for 15 to 25 percent of all deaths by suicide in patients with severe mood disorders.

The following are some additional facts about those who commit suicide:

- Men commit suicide at a rate four times that of women.

- Women attempt suicide at a rate three to four times that of men and are hospitalized for attempted suicide at a rate one and a half times that of men.

- Estimates of attempted suicide indicate that the number of suicide attempts is 8 to 10 times greater than the number of deaths by suicide.

Table 8.4   Number of Male Suicides, by Age Group, Canada, 2003–2007

	2003	2004	2005	2006	2007
All ages[a]	2,903	2,734	2,857	2,695	2,727
10 to 14	19	17	18	13	18
15 to 19	161	161	147	112	131
20 to 24	248	218	231	219	228
25 to 29	197	218	195	175	223
30 to 34	229	259	220	187	181
35 to 39	343	282	296	257	255
40 to 44	357	319	375	329	293
45 to 49	331	325	377	349	367
50 to 54	286	284	293	267	309
55 to 59	231	206	221	253	224
60 to 64	154	126	130	174	151
65 to 69	109	82	105	103	88
70 to 74	87	83	83	69	76
75 to 79	69	71	86	91	83
80 to 84	44	48	47	46	61
85 to 89	22	27	23	34	30
90 and older	16	8	9	17	9

[a] "All ages" includes suicides of children under age ten and suicides of people of unknown age.

Sources: Statistics Canada, CANSIM, table 102-0551 and catalogue no. 84F0209X. Adapted from Statistics Canada (2010b).

Table 8.5   Number of Female Suicides, by Age Group, Canada, 2003–2007

	2003	2004	2005	2006	2007
All ages[a]	862	879	886	817	884
10 to 14	8	11	25	18	15
15 to 19	55	49	66	40	54
20 to 24	58	52	65	46	62
25 to 29	48	57	33	62	59
30 to 34	66	57	63	56	54
35 to 39	91	108	85	61	70
40 to 44	106	90	120	89	110
45 to 49	123	121	99	110	119
50 to 54	118	109	114	102	101
55 to 59	61	69	73	75	83
60 to 64	33	48	36	35	52
65 to 69	33	39	33	42	27
70 to 74	18	25	16	35	26
75 to 79	16	17	27	22	20
80 to 84	9	15	19	16	15
85 to 89	12	9	8	5	12
90 and older	7	3	4	3	5

[a] "All ages" includes suicides of children under age ten and suicides of people of unknown age.

Source: Statistics Canada, CANSIM, table 102-0551 and Catalogue no. 84F0209X. Adapted from Statistics Canada (2010b).

Table 8.6   Methods of Suicide in Canada, 2001

Method	Males (% of deaths)	Females (% of deaths)
Self-poisoning	10.3	36.9
Gases	10.7	7.7
Hanging	42.9	33.9
Drowning	2.5	4.0
Firearms	21.5	4.3
Burning	0.7	0.6
Cutting	2.9	1.5
Jumping	6.8	8.4
Motor vehicle	0.9	0.6
Other	0.9	2.2

Source: Statistics Canada (2001).

Figure 8.1   Methods of Suicide in Canada, 2007

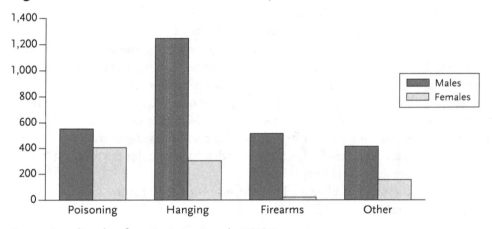

Source: Based on data from Statistics Canada (2010a).

- Studies indicate that there is a significant correlation between a history of sexual abuse and the lifetime number of suicide attempts. This correlation is twice as strong for women as for men.
- Aboriginal people commit suicide at a rate seven times the national average.
- The suicide rate is believed to be higher among the homosexual population than among the heterosexual population, although there are no statistics to substantiate this belief because death records are not categorized by sexual orientation. The risk seems to be higher when a person first identifies their sexual preference, possibly because of lack of acceptance by their families and society.
- Suicide accounts for 18 percent of deaths among alcoholics (87 percent of the victims are male).
- Alcoholism is a factor in 30 percent of all suicide attempts.
- People with AIDS have a suicide risk 20 times greater than that of the general population.

- In many suicides involving people 50 and older, physical illness is an important contributing factor (American Foundation for Suicide Prevention, n.d.).

WHY DO PEOPLE COMMIT SUICIDE?

From the perspective of police intervention, the person's reason for considering suicide is not relevant except as a means for the officer to initiate dialogue. The objective of police intervention is to address the suicidal action. Time constraints generally prohibit any effective discussion of the reason for the behaviour.

Although the person's rationale for wanting to commit suicide is inconsequential to police intervention, the method of death chosen by the suicidal subject is of great concern. For example, if the person has chosen to use a firearm, police interaction is limited. A face-to-face conversation is not possible because of officer safety concerns. If a person has chosen to end their life through the use of barbiturates, there may be more time for close contact intervention.

Suicide is usually an act of desperation carried out by a person who believes that there is no other way to cope with unbearable emotional or sometimes physical pain. The emotional pain can be caused by a variety of problems, both real and perceived. The problem giving rise to the emotional pain may seem insignificant to others, but not to the sufferer. Money or relationship problems, loss of enthusiasm for life, debilitating diseases, and other troubles can all create what the sufferer perceives as insurmountable problems, with no resolution other than suicide. At the same time, the sufferer is often ambivalent about living or dying and their suicide attempt is often a cry for help. (See the discussion under the heading "Commonalities Among Suicidal People," below.)

Although this may sound absurd to someone with good coping skills, everyone has a stress threshold beyond which the ability to cope is lost. Suicide can seem like an attractive option to someone who believes that life will not get better. Police officers usually have stable personalities, and may find it difficult to understand why someone would go to such an extreme to escape what others might view as an insignificant or a manageable problem.

It is difficult to gauge another person's stress threshold, even when one is intimately familiar with the other's thoughts and feelings. Moreover, different people react differently to the same stressors. The latter point is illustrated by the following story:

Four people were imprisoned for their political views. The conditions of their incarceration were deplorable. Each was kept in solitary confinement. Food and water were scarce. There was no toilet and no sunlight. Hours, days, weeks, and months went by. There was no way for any of the four to know how long they had been imprisoned.

Two committed suicide by hanging themselves with their shoelaces. A third went insane, never to recover. The fourth decided that no matter what cards life dealt him, he would prevail.

When he was released, he emerged with a book about the experience. Using a pencil stub and writing on scraps of paper to record his thoughts, he was able to draw on his positive attitude to do something constructive during his months of imprisonment.

Why was one man able to endure when the others were not? No one can give a complete answer to this question. Everyone has his or her stress threshold.

A police officer must not allow personal views and prejudices to hamper his or her duty toward suicidal people, most of whom are looking for help, not death. The officer is often the first ray of hope they encounter. The officer needs to put aside any prejudices about suicide and intervene in an unbiased, constructive manner. Familiarity with the intervention techniques and risk assessment procedures discussed later in this chapter can help the officer develop the proper attitude.

Commonalities Among Suicidal People

Character traits and life experiences cannot be accurately identified by police during interventions of suicidal behaviour. If possible, police should try to obtain information regarding previous suicidal actions by the subject. As will be discussed later in this chapter, past history of suicidal behaviour is an indicator of future behaviour.

There appear to be some common traits, behaviours, and experiences among suicidal people (Shneidman, 1996).

1. *They see suicide as a solution.* Suicide is not a random act. It is a way out of a dilemma, a problem, a bind, a crisis, or a situation that is unbearable. Suicide becomes the answer to the problem of suffering. It answers the questions: "How can I get out of this situation? What can I do?"

2. *They seek cessation of consciousness.* Suicidal people want to end consciousness and unendurable pain. Doing so is seen by the suffering person as the solution to life's painful and unsolvable problems.

3. *They see suicide as a way to escape from psychological pain.* Suicide is a combined movement away from unbearable psychological pain, intolerable emotion, and mental anguish.

4. *They have frustrated psychological needs.* Suicide stems from thwarted or unrealized psychological needs. These unfulfilled needs are what cause the pain and push the suicidal person to act. All suicidal acts reflect a specific psychological need that has not been fulfilled.

5. *They feel hopeless/helpless.* Suicidal people experience pervasive feelings of helplessness and/or hopelessness: "Things will never get better. There is no one who can help me."

6. *Their cognitive state in suicide is ambivalence.* People who commit suicide are ambivalent about living and dying, even as they are committing the act. They both want to die, and wish to be saved. For example, an individual might cut his wrists and cry for help at the same time.

7. *Their perceptual state in suicide is constriction.* Suicidal people have a narrow or constricted view of their options: "There is nothing else I can do but kill myself. The only way out is death."

8. *They communicate their intention to commit suicide.* Many individuals intent on committing suicide emit clues of intention, consciously or unconsciously—signs of distress, pleas for intervention, or whimpers of helplessness.

9. *Their decision to commit suicide is consistent with their lifelong styles of coping.* People react consistently to certain aspects of life throughout its span. There is a connection between an individual's decision to commit suicide, how that individual has coped with previous setbacks, and the individual's capacity to endure psychological pain. For example, suicidal people may show a tendency toward constriction or a tendency to throw in the towel.

The main thrust of these commonalities is that suicidal people are unable to deal with their psychological pain and choose suicide as a means to end their pain. This "surcease" type of suicide is generally accepted as the most common type of suicide involving police intervention.

There are several factors that can challenge a person's will to live and precipitate his or her suicide. The most common of these factors are discussed below.

Relationships

Loss of a close emotional attachment can increase suicide risk. Moreover, some people try to change the nature of an existing relationship through threats of suicide. This sort of manipulative behaviour can have disastrous consequences when actions merely intended to mimic suicide and frighten the other partner in the relationship accidentally cause death.

Revenge and Expression of Anger

Suicide can be a means of teaching others a lesson, a hostile act intended to make others sorry for a perceived insult or injury.

Control

Someone who feels that his or her life is spinning out of control may see suicide as the only remaining option. Self-injury can be an attempt to regain control. This need for control sometimes expresses itself as murder–suicide or as seemingly random murder. The perpetrator of such acts has an intense need to control his or her life and possibly the lives of others.

Avoidance

Some people do not cope well with life's pressures. Built-up tension may find its release in self-destructive behaviour. Generally this takes the form of non-fatal self-mutilation—a cry for help—although the result is sometimes unintentional death.

Exit

A person plagued by a terminal illness, chronic pain, depression, feelings of guilt, or other seemingly intolerable afflictions may choose death as his or her means of escape.

Mental Illness and Personality Disorders

People experiencing debilitating symptoms of mental illness are at risk of committing suicide. Recall that more than 90 percent of suicide victims have diagnosable psychiatric illness. (See also Chapter 7, Mental Illness and Personality Disorders.)

The risk increases with the delay in receiving assistance, more so if the person is experiencing a psychotic episode. The suicide usually occurs through the person's efforts to stop the psychotic episode. This is referred to as "psychotic suicide."

Impulsive Behaviour

Persons prone to impulsive behaviour may be more likely to attempt suicide. Impulsivity may be defined as the inability to resist impulses, or behaviours that occur without reflection or consideration for the consequences of such behaviour. Although not definitive, there have been several studies that appear to substantiate this theory.

An examination of 350 suicide attempts (Plutchik & van Praag, 1995) revealed that 40 percent of those who attempted suicide spent less than five minutes contemplating their act. Plutchik and van Praag concluded that both suicidal and violent people exhibited significantly higher levels of impulsivity. Persons who committed violent acts were found to be considerably more impulsive than those who did not commit violent acts. The study concluded that there is a relationship between suicide, violence, and impulsive acts. In other words, when the relationship between impulsivity and violence was examined, impulsive behaviour increased the risk of suicide attempts by an impulsive individual to 22 times more than that of a non-impulsive individual.

Study results of suicide in the general Quebec population released in 2005 appears to support the Plutchik and van Pragg study. The Quebec study found higher levels of impulsivity and related behaviours in people attempting suicide than in healthy people in a control group (Dumais et al., 2005).

More extreme levels of impulsivity were observed among people who committed suicide. The study found that subjects who used the more violent methods of suicide tended to have notably higher levels of impulsivity than those who used non-violent suicide methods.

A study of 102 suicide deaths in New Brunswick between April 2002 and May 2003 suggests that there is a correlation between suicide and impulsive–aggressive behaviours, further substantiating the belief that impulsive behaviour is a significant contributing risk factor (Séguin et al., 2005).

VICTIM-PRECIPITATED SUICIDE

victim-precipitated suicide
the use of police to commit
suicide, achieved by
challenging police with a
lethal or apparently lethal
weapon, giving them no
choice but to use lethal force
to stop the threat; often
referred to as "suicide
by cop"

Victim-precipitated suicide, often referred to as "suicide by cop," is a relatively new phenomenon whereby a suicidal person uses a police officer as a means of death.

Traditional methods of suicide, such as jumping from a high structure, crashing a speeding vehicle, or causing a self-inflicted wound, require a decision and commitment on the part of the victim. In victim-precipitated suicides, the difficult decision to end one's life is made by someone else. The disturbed or distraught individual, with a lethal or apparently lethal weapon, challenges law enforcement officers in a manner that leaves the officers no choice but to use lethal force to stop the threat.

Van Zandt (1993) states that the police are specifically singled out because they are the only community agency equipped with firearms and the training to react to potentially life-threatening situations with accurate and deadly force. In addition, people who commit suicide by cop may feel that the stigma and social taboos associated with suicide can be absolved if they are killed by an external mechanism such as the police. Police officers, as agents of the state, may represent to them a faceless means of ending their life in a somewhat dignified manner.

Gerberth (1993) has theorized that the police can symbolically represent the social conscience. Gerberth notes that, at times, suicidal individuals may have feelings of guilt, real or imagined. Police officers traditionally represent law and order within society. A guilt-ridden, suicidal individual may enter into an interaction with the police in an attempt to relieve his or her guilt-ridden conscience through punishment that may include death.

In other instances, the suicidal individual may not have the determination to end his or her own life. In these cases, the suicidal individual cannot "pull the trigger" and, therefore, seeks assistance in accomplishing his or her death.

Richard Parent (2004), a leading expert in the field, estimates that at least one-third of police shootings across the continent are precipitated by the victim. Parent's research is based on examinations of more than 400 police shootings in Canada and more than 400 others in the United States between 1980 and 2002. Parent's research also involved interviews with police officers who used deadly force, and prison inmates who survived police shootings.

Hostage-Taking

Suicidal individuals may use hostage-taking incidents to bring about their demise. In these situations, the suicidal individual may adopt a confrontational posture with the police. They will often announce their intention to die. In addition, these individuals may set a deadline for their own death or begin talking about people who are dead as if they are still alive. In following this course of action, the individual accomplishes his or her own self-destruction while going out in a "blaze of glory."

The person may believe that being shot by the police will bring them notoriety they did not have in life. Even if the police shoot, but do not kill the person, the objective of notoriety has been achieved. This may sound absurd, but remember that the person has decided that his or her life is worthless; what does he or she have to lose?

Commonalities Among Persons Seeking Suicide by Cop

People who initiate suicide by cop appear to share some common characteristics. However, as with all incidents of suicidal behaviour, there is no definitive characteristic that all initiators will share.

- They are overwhelmingly male. In the cases studied by Hutson et al. (1998), 98 percent of initiators were male.
- They put a lot of thought and preparation into their own deaths (Van Zandt, 1993).
- They are under the influence of drugs or alcohol.
- They are between the ages of 21 and 35 years.
- They are in possession of a handgun or knife.
- In the majority of situations, the weapon used by the initiator was either not loaded, was not working properly, or was an imitation, indicating that the subject had no real intention of hurting others.

Persons seeking to commit suicide by cop may also exhibit the following behaviours:

- They may make requests or demands such as "Kill me!" or "Shoot me!"
- They may give a deadline for their death. The officer should ignore the deadline and not allow the person to control the situation.
- They may refuse to listen to any requests from police and refuse to discuss the issue.
- They may verbally communicate that they no longer want to live but are unwilling to take their own life.

Response Options

When confronted with a situation of victim-precipitated suicide, the officer should evaluate the danger posed by the subject and respond with the least amount of force necessary to ensure the officer's safety.

If forced to use a firearm to control the person, the officer may experience feelings of remorse or may feel anger at knowing that the person has manipulated him or her into using a firearm. These feelings can be addressed through critical incident stress debriefings, where officers are able talk about stressful incidents with the knowledge that anything they say will remain confidential.

The effects experienced by police officers after an incident of suicide by cop are closely related to symptoms of post-traumatic stress disorder. Officers have reported a range of symptoms, including:

- anger (including anger at being manipulated by the suicidal person, particularly if the weapon brandished was found to be an imitation or was unloaded),
- depression,
- resentment and disbelief,
- preoccupation with the incident,

- nightmares,
- anxiety,
- hypersensitivity,
- diminished self-confidence,
- changes in eating and sleeping patterns,
- feeling a loss of control, and
- memory difficulties.

Learning Activity 8.1

Identify the following as true or false:

_____ 1. During police intervention, the reason for suicidal behaviour should not be discussed with the subject.

_____ 2. A suicidal person suffering from depression will not be able to engage in a rational conversation.

_____ 3. The chosen methods of suicide vary by gender.

_____ 4. The majority of people in Canada that die by suicide are male.

_____ 5. Suicide is the leading cause of death among adults 25 to 34 years old.

_____ 6. Approximately two-thirds of police shootings may be identified as suicide by cop.

_____ 7. Police officers should take considerable time to carefully determine whether a person is trying to commit suicide by cop in situations where the suspect is pointing a firearm at the officer.

LEGISLATION REGARDING ASSISTED SUICIDE

There has been extensive debate in Canada regarding the issue of assisted suicide, with supporters arguing that the practice should be allowed in certain cases, such as when a person suffers from an incurable illness that leaves them in constant pain. Despite this, assisted suicide remains illegal. Section 241 of the *Criminal Code* prohibits anyone from aiding or counselling a person to commit suicide.

Counselling or Aiding Suicide: Criminal Code, Section 241

241. Every one who
(a) counsels a person to commit suicide, or
(b) aids or abets a person to commit suicide,
whether suicide ensues or not, is guilty of an indictable offence and liable to imprisonment for a term not exceeding fourteen years.

The constitutional validity of this section has been argued before the Supreme Court of Canada in the case of *Rodriguez v. British Columbia (Attorney General)*,

1993 CanLII 75 (SCC). Rodriguez, a 42-year-old woman who suffered from a debilitating and terminal illness, amyotrophic lateral sclerosis (ALS), argued that s. 241 deprived her of her right to liberty and security of the person under s. 7 of the *Canadian Charter of Rights and Freedoms.*

However, in a 5 to 4 ruling, the Supreme Court upheld the decision of the Appeal Court of British Columbia that s. 241 of the *Criminal Code* does not violate the Charter.

The minority dissenting opinion was presented by Chief Justice Lamer. In the dissenting opinion, Lamer differentiates between the situations of a physically disabled person and a person suffering from a terminal illness. Lamer also states that to "decriminalize *completely* the act of aiding, abetting or counselling suicide would therefore not be a valid legislative policy."

Although the minority opinion did not prevail, it is important to remember that four of the nine Supreme Court justices agreed that assisted suicide may be allowable. If one more justice had agreed with the dissenting opinion, assisted suicide would now be legal in Canada.

While the legality of assisted suicide will likely continue to be debated, the law in Canada is still clear—assisted suicide is not legal.

LEGISLATION REGARDING SUICIDE

Parliament removed the offence of attempted suicide from the *Criminal Code* in 1972. As a result, suicide and attempted suicide are not viewed as a criminal matter in Canadian law. The aim of legislation, both federally and provincially, is to prevent the act of suicide from occurring. Relevant sections of the Ontario *Mental Health Act* are discussed in the next section. Relevant sections of other provincial legislation and federal legislation are dealt with under the heading "Suicide and Police Intervention" below.

Ontario Mental Health Act

Sections 15, 16, and 17 of the Ontario *Mental Health Act* (MHA) authorize that a person who poses a danger to himself or herself or others, because of a mental disorder, may be apprehended and brought to the appropriate medical facility for assistance.

The Act appears to presume that any person wishing to commit suicide is not mentally stable and should be apprehended for his or her protection.

Section 15(1) of the MHA sets out the authority for a physician to compel a person to submit to psychiatric examination if the physician believes that the person may be a danger to himself or herself or others.

Application for Psychiatric Assessment: Mental Health Act, Section 15(1)

15(1) Where a physician examines a person and has reasonable cause to believe that the person,

(a) has threatened or attempted or is threatening or attempting to cause bodily harm to himself or herself;

(b) has behaved or is behaving violently towards another person or has caused or is causing another person to fear bodily harm from him or her; or

(c) has shown or is showing a lack of competence to care for himself or herself,

and if in addition the physician is of the opinion that the person is apparently suffering from mental disorder of a nature or quality that likely will result in,

(d) serious bodily harm to the person;

(e) serious bodily harm to another person; or

(f) serious physical impairment of the person,

the physician may make application in the prescribed form for a psychiatric assessment of the person.

The prescribed form is referred to as a Form 1 MHA (reproduced in Chapter 7, Appendix 7A). A Form 1 directs police to apprehend the named person and bring him or her to a psychiatric facility for assessment.

Section 16(1) of the MHA sets out the authority of a justice of the peace to issue an order for examination.

Justice of the Peace's Order for Psychiatric Examination: Mental Health Act, Section 16(1)

16(1) Where information upon oath is brought before a justice of the peace that a person within the limits of the jurisdiction of the justice,

(a) has threatened or attempted or is threatening or attempting to cause bodily harm to himself or herself;

(b) has behaved or is behaving violently towards another person or has caused or is causing another person to fear bodily harm from him or her; or

(c) has shown or is showing a lack of competence to care for himself or herself,

and in addition based upon the information before him or her the justice of the peace has reasonable cause to believe that the person is apparently suffering from mental disorder of a nature or quality that likely will result in,

(d) serious bodily harm to the person;

(e) serious bodily harm to another person; or

(f) serious physical impairment of the person,

the justice of the peace may issue an order in the prescribed form for the examination of the person by a physician.

This order is referred to as a Form 2 MHA (reproduced in Chapter 7, Appendix 7B). Any person may appear before a justice and provide sworn testimony that establishes reasonable grounds to believe the named person is a danger to himself or herself or others. The justice may issue an order for examination, Form 2, authorizing police to apprehend the named person and bring him or her to a physician for examination. The examining physician will determine whether the person needs a psychiatric assessment.

Section 17 of the MHA sets out the authority for police to apprehend a person without previous authorization.

Action by Police Officer: Mental Health Act, Section 17

17. Where a police officer has reasonable and probable grounds to believe that a person is acting or has acted in a disorderly manner and has reasonable cause to believe that the person,

(a) has threatened or attempted or is threatening or attempting to cause bodily harm to himself or herself;

(b) has behaved or is behaving violently towards another person or has caused or is causing another person to fear bodily harm from him or her; or

(c) has shown or is showing a lack of competence to care for himself or herself,

and in addition the police officer is of the opinion that the person is apparently suffering from mental disorder of a nature or quality that likely will result in,

(d) serious bodily harm to the person;

(e) serious bodily harm to another person; or

(f) serious physical impairment of the person,

and that it would be dangerous to proceed under section 16, the police officer may take the person in custody to an appropriate place for examination by a physician.

This section authorizes police to immediately apprehend a person. Apprehension is authorized where reasonable grounds exist to believe that the person is a danger to himself or herself or others as a result of a mental disorder.

Upon apprehension, the person is brought to a physician for examination. The physician will decide whether further assessment is required.

PERSONAL ATTITUDES ABOUT SUICIDE

A police officer will answer many calls for assistance in his or her career. Suicide calls can be some of the most emotionally difficult for an officer, whether the calls involve someone threatening suicide or someone who has already committed the act. The emotions felt, and sometimes repressed, by officers are real and can affect their judgment and behaviour on suicide calls. It is therefore necessary for prospective officers to understand their own views on suicide before they become involved in suicide calls. See Box 8.1.

SUICIDE AND POLICE INTERVENTION

There have been many ethical and philosophical debates about the appropriateness of the state intervening in situations where a person has chosen to end his or her life. Yet without police intervention, the suicidal person might make a rash and ill-considered decision. The majority of suicidal people dealt with by police are irrational and seeking immediate relief from a short-term problem. Most have not considered the finality of their actions because of their emotional and psychological imbalance. Police intervention may stop an irreversible mistake.

For a police officer, intervening in a situation where a person believes that he or she has no reason to live is extremely dangerous and stressful. A suicidal person can be extremely unpredictable and is usually irrational. Police officers must therefore

Box 8.1   Class Discussion: Personal Attitudes About Suicide

The following exercise will help you assess your personal attitudes toward suicide. For each of the statements below, place a checkmark in the box that corresponds most closely with your belief. Answer as truthfully as possible.

Then, as a class, discuss your answers and their implications for police work.

1. Suicide is wrong. ☐ strongly agree ☑ agree ☐ disagree ☐ strongly disagree

2. Suicide is all right for some people. ☐ strongly agree ☐ agree ☑ disagree ☐ strongly disagree

3. Anyone who commits suicide is mentally unstable. ☐ strongly agree ☑ agree ☐ disagree ☐ strongly disagree

4. A person who commits suicide is a coward. ☐ strongly agree ☐ agree ☑ disagree ☐ strongly disagree

5. I would attempt to stop anyone who tries to commit suicide. ☑ strongly agree ☐ agree ☐ disagree ☐ strongly disagree

6. Suicide is a sin. ☐ strongly agree ☐ agree ☑ disagree ☐ strongly disagree

7. I would feel shame if I ever considered suicide. ☐ strongly agree ☐ agree ☑ disagree ☐ strongly disagree

8. I would feel shame if anyone in my family attempted suicide. ☐ strongly agree ☐ agree ☑ disagree ☐ strongly disagree

9. Anyone who contemplates suicide is a loser. ☐ strongly agree ☐ agree ☑ disagree ☐ strongly disagree

10. Police officers must remain emotionally detached from a suicidal person. ☐ strongly agree ☐ agree ☐ disagree ☑ strongly disagree

follow guidelines designed to minimize the risk to their safety and expedite getting help for the suicide attempter.

The following information may be useful in assisting police officers to effectively and safely intervene with suicidal people (improvisation may be necessary, however).

Officer Safety

It is the duty of the police to help people in crisis, but a more pressing duty is returning home at the end of the shift. An injured officer is a liability on the scene and cannot assist anyone. Safety precautions must be foremost in the officer's mind.

A successful intervention begins with the officer taking proper precautions to ensure his or her own safety. Persons contemplating suicide can be dangerous. Most will be thinking and acting irrationally. In most interventions the person is looking for help, but there are some circumstances where the person is intent on self-destruction and possibly on eliminating those around him or her.

Most officers are not prepared to face situations of suicidal behaviour. When they find themselves interacting with a suicidal person, the officers may shift their attention from personal safety to subject preservation. Officers may perceive that their job is to preserve the life of the person at any cost. If the subject dies, the intervening officer may inaccurately perceive this outcome as a failure to "do their job." In an effort to avoid this "failure," officers may make tactically unsound decisions such as hesitating to take action in situations that clearly threaten the officer, moving too close to the subject in an effort to de-escalate the situation, or taking unnecessary risks in an effort to disarm the subject.

A peaceful, non-violent resolution is clearly the desired outcome, but it must not be achieved through any compromise of officer safety.

Suicidal behaviour involving weapons or assaultive actions is the most obvious threat to officer safety, but there are other dangers as well. A suicidal person with a blood-borne pathogen, such as HIV or hepatitis B or C, poses a substantial risk to anyone who has direct contact with that person's blood or, less dangerously, other bodily fluids.

Some suicidal people are drug abusers. An intravenous drug user may be carrying a number of harmful viruses in his or her body. The combination of drug abuse and suicidal behaviour presents serious health risks to officers.

There are other, less obvious dangers such as the possibility of an officer being attacked by a dog that is trying to protect its master. Or, a family member or friend may attempt to prevent police interference with a suicidal person's desire to die.

Suicide intervention is therefore a dangerous situation for police officers. Observing and quickly assessing the suicidal person and his or her surroundings are imperative for an effective intervention.

Obtaining Background Information

The information obtained before encountering the suicidal person is possibly more important than the information obtained on the scene. However, owing to time constraints or lack of information sources, it is not always possible to obtain background information.

The officers must use their discretion to determine whether (1) their response at the scene must be immediate or (2) the person can be better helped by obtaining a history of the situation. The circumstances surrounding the original call for assistance may help determine the degree of urgency. A few minutes spent speaking with someone who is knowledgeable about the situation may help the officers identify the suicidal person's problem and increase officer safety by giving the officers more preliminary information. In many cases the person's suicidal thoughts are a manifestation of his or her need for help. If a person calls someone to say that he is considering suicide, he may be crying out for help.

Interviewing relatives and friends of the suicidal person can be extremely helpful in determining the seriousness of the situation. But the information obtained should not be relied on exclusively, especially when safety concerns such as the availability of weapons arise. However, the information can be used to help plan a course of action.

Interviews with relatives and friends can provide information on changes in the person's behaviour. These behavioural changes can provide clues as to how the person is feeling and serve as warning signs of possible suicidal action, as shown in the table below:

Feelings	Warning signs
Desperation	Giving away possessions
Anger	Loss of interest in physical appearance, sexual activity, and life itself
Loneliness	Self-mutilation
Worthlessness	Reckless behaviour
Irritability	Negative comments about self
Depression	Change from depression to a feeling of being at peace (as a result of deciding to commit suicide)

The list in the table above is far from comprehensive. Many other warning signs may exist. Occasionally, a suicidal person provides no warning signs at all.

There are some questions that may help officers assess the person's risk of suicide:

- *How old is the person?* Certain age groups are more suicide prone than others.

- *Has the person previously attempted suicide?* Subsequent suicide attempts are more likely to be successful than first-time suicide attempts.

- *Has a family member or friend previously attempted or completed suicide?* The suicidal person may have a positive or negative reaction to this incident.

- *Has there recently been a death in the family?* The suicidal person may want to join a loved one.

- *Has the person recently suffered a significant loss?* The loss of a job, a home, or a romantic partner may make the person feel abandoned, without hope, or depressed.

- *Does the person have any religious beliefs?* Religious people are less likely to commit suicide.

- *Is the person an alcoholic?* Alcoholics are more likely than non-alcoholics to commit suicide.
- *Is the person under the influence of drugs?* Drugs are involved in many suicides.
- *Does the person have a history of depression?* Depression is a major contributor to suicidal behaviour.
- *Is the person involved in a stable romantic relationship?* Where marital status is concerned, single people are the highest-risk group, whereas married people with children face the lowest risk.

Entry

Entry into public places should not pose a legal problem for officers. Although legality of entry is an important consideration, officer safety should be the foremost consideration.

In situations where the suicidal person is armed or where a hostage is involved, responding officers shall adhere to the direction given by regulation 3/99 of the *Police Services Act.*

Section 22 of regulation 3/99, below, states that officers shall not enter an area where the situation requires the use of a tactical unit, unless it is necessary to prevent the loss of life or serious bodily harm.

22(1) Every chief of police shall establish procedures on preliminary perimeter control and containment.

(2) A police force may include a containment team using police officers and, if it does, the chief of police shall develop procedures for it.

(3) Police officers who are not members of a tactical unit and who are deployed in a containment function, including members of a containment team, shall not, before the arrival of members of a tactical unit, employ offensive tactics unless the police officers believe, on reasonable grounds, that to do so is necessary to protect against the loss of life or serious bodily harm.

Section 23 of regulation 3/99, below, identifies the composition and duties of a tactical unit.

23(1) A tactical unit or hostage rescue team, whether provided by a police force or on a combined or regional or co-operative basis, shall consist of a minimum of 12 full-time tactical officers, including the supervisor.

(2) A tactical unit shall be able to perform the following functions:

1. Containment.

2. Apprehension of an armed barricaded person.

(3) A tactical unit may perform explosive forced entry if it uses the services of a police explosive forced entry technician.

(4) A hostage rescue team shall be able to perform the functions set out in subsection (2) and hostage rescue.

(5) The functions of a tactical unit and hostage rescue team may be provided by one unit or team that is capable of performing the functions of both a tactical unit and a hostage rescue team.

(6) For the purposes of this section,

"full-time tactical officer" means a police officer assigned and dedicated to the tactical unit or hostage rescue team, but who, when not training or undertaking tactical or hostage rescue activities, may undertake community patrol.

As previously stated, officer safety is the first concern when entering a place where a suicidal person may be. The officers must use approach-and-entry techniques that will ensure safe access. The next concern should be legality of entry. The information received by the police may be incorrect, although in most circumstances the police should respond as if the information is accurate, especially if the information cannot be verified. It is possible that there may not be anyone in crisis, and therefore the legality of the entry must be considered. Entering a place other than a dwelling should not pose any legal difficulty. Legal entry into a dwelling is more complicated. If circumstances and safety considerations permit, the easiest method of entry is to knock on the door and ask permission to enter.

If invited entry is unsafe or otherwise unfeasible, officers should ensure, whenever possible, that entry is legally justified. The *Criminal Code* provides a right of entry under certain circumstances. Section 117.04(2) permits officers to enter to search and seize.

Application for Warrant to Search and Seize: Criminal Code, Section 117.04(2)

117.04(2) Where, with respect to any person, a peace officer is satisfied that there are reasonable grounds to believe that it is not desirable, in the interests of the safety of the person or any other person, for the person to possess any weapon, prohibited device, ammunition, prohibited ammunition or explosive substance, the peace officer may, where the grounds for obtaining a warrant under subsection (1) exist but, by reason of a possible danger to the safety of that person or any other person, it would not be practicable to obtain a warrant, search for and seize any such thing, and any authorization, licence or registration certificate relating to any such thing, that is held by or in the possession of the person.

To rely on this section, one needs to establish reasonable grounds that a person has a weapon and that there is a danger that the person will use the weapon to harm himself or herself or others. There also must be such an urgent need for entry that there is no time to obtain a warrant. The search should be used only to find the person and the weapon or weapons in question. Once the objects of the search have been found, the search must cease. This section cannot be used as an all-embracing authority to enter. Reasonable grounds must be ascertained in every situation, and one cannot automatically assume that a person who possesses a weapon does so in a manner that jeopardizes safety.

Extreme caution must be used when it has been reasonably established that a person possesses a weapon and is a danger to himself or herself or others. A simple precaution that can enhance officer safety is to have dispatch call the person and if possible keep him or her on the telephone while the premises are being entered.

A judicial decision on s. 103(2), the predecessor to s. 117.04(2), stated that s. 103(2) did not infringe s. 8 of the *Charter of Rights and Freedoms*: *R v. Smith* (1988), 5 WCB 164 (Ont. Prov. Ct.).

As discussed in Chapter 5, s. 529.3 of the *Criminal Code* authorizes police to enter a dwelling, without warrant, to effect an arrest in exigent circumstances where it would not be practical to obtain a warrant.

Authority to Enter Dwelling Without Warrant: Criminal Code, Section 529.3(1)

529.3(1) Without limiting or restricting any power a peace officer may have to enter a dwelling-house under this or any other Act or law, the peace officer may enter the dwelling-house for the purpose of arresting or apprehending a person, without a warrant referred to in section 529 or 529.1 authorizing the entry, if the peace officer has reasonable grounds to believe that the person is present in the dwelling-house, and the conditions for obtaining a warrant under section 529.1 exist but by reason of exigent circumstances it would be impracticable to obtain a warrant.

Section 529.3(2) identifies the exigent circumstances in which a police officer may enter without warrant.

Exigent Circumstances: Criminal Code, Section 529.3(2)

529.3(2) For the purposes of subsection (1), exigent circumstances include circumstances in which the peace officer

(a) has reasonable grounds to suspect that entry into the dwelling-house is necessary to prevent imminent bodily harm or death to any person; or

(b) has reasonable grounds to believe that evidence relating to the commission of an indictable offence is present in the dwelling-house and that entry into the dwelling-house is necessary to prevent the imminent loss or imminent destruction of the evidence.

If the suicidal person poses a threat to anyone other than himself or herself, entry may be gained under the authority of s. 27 of the *Criminal Code*.

Use of Force to Prevent Commission of Offence: Criminal Code, Section 27

27. Every one is justified in using as much force as is reasonably necessary

(a) to prevent the commission of an offence

(i) for which, if it were committed, the person who committed it might be arrested without warrant, and

(ii) that would be likely to cause immediate and serious injury to the person or property of anyone; or

(b) to prevent anything being done that, on reasonable grounds, he believes would, if it were done, be an offence mentioned in paragraph (a).

This section can be used to justify the use of force to prevent the suicidal person from harming anyone else on the premises. The authority to use as much force as is reasonably necessary can include forcible entry into a dwelling to prevent an offence that would likely cause immediate and serious harm to a person. This authority applies only to an offence for which a person can be arrested without a warrant. Because attempting suicide is not illegal, s. 27 cannot be relied on as providing authority to enter when it has not been established that the suicidal person is a danger to someone other than himself or herself.

R v. Custer appears to give police officers the authority to forcibly enter private premises when there are reasonable grounds to believe that a person's life is in danger. Although this is a provincial court decision, and therefore not binding authority, it has been relied upon for many years without legal repercussions.

> An officer would be in the execution of his duty in forcibly entering private premises where he believes on reasonable and probable grounds that he is confronted with an emergency situation involving the preservation of life of a person in the dwelling-house, or the prevention of serious injury to that person, and if a proper announcement is made prior to entry: *R v. Custer* (1984), 12 CCC (3d) 372, [1984] 4 WWR 133 (Sask. CA). [*Martin's Annual Criminal Code, 2012*, p. 259]

The authority allowed by the Saskatchewan court seems to go beyond that of s. 27 of the *Criminal Code* by stating that it is the duty of a police officer to intervene in a situation involving the preservation of life. Apparently, this applies to people who may be a danger to themselves. The permission is given to officers only after proper announcement of their intentions has been made.

Similarly, the Supreme Court of Canada's decision in *R v. Godoy* appears to give police officers the authority to enter a home by force if necessary if there is articulable cause to believe that a person's life is in danger. Articulable cause means suspicion based on some discernible fact. *R v. Simpson* addresses the issue of articulable cause:

> In the absence of statutory authority to stop a vehicle, the stopping and detention of the occupants for the purpose of determining whether they were involved in criminal activity can only be justified if the detaining officer has some articulable cause for the detention. There must be a constellation of objectively discernible facts which give the detaining officer reasonable cause to suspect that the detainee is implicated in the activity under investigation. A "hunch" based entirely on intuition gained by experience cannot suffice: *R v. Simpson* (1993), 79 CCC (3d) 482, 20 CR (4th) 1, 43 MVR (2d) 1, 12 OR (3d) 182 (Ont. CA). [*Martin's Annual Criminal Code, 2005*]

Articulable cause appears to be referred to in *R v. Godoy* as well:

> In *R v. Godoy*, [1999] 1 SCR 311, 131 CCC (3d) 129, the Supreme Court of Canada held that forced entry into a dwelling house in response to a disconnected 911 call did not violate s. 8. The common law duty of police to preserve life is engaged whenever it may be inferred that the 911 caller may be in distress. In this case, the accused had refused entry to the police responding to the 911 call. The forced entry of the apartment to locate the caller and determine the reason for the call

constituted a justifiable use of police powers. The police do not, however, have a further authority to search the premises or otherwise intrude on a resident's privacy or property. The court did not consider the applicability of the plain view doctrine in such circumstances. [*Martin's Annual Criminal Code, 2012*, p. 1073]

In *R v. Godoy*, the officers did not have reasonable grounds to enter the dwelling house but did have articulable cause based on the phone call from the residence. The court cited the duty of police to preserve life and ruled that the forced entry was legal.

In situations where legal authority appears to be absent, the officer must use ingenuity to determine a method of entry. In some circumstances, possibly involving the elderly or people with infirmities, there may be a person with power of attorney who can be contacted for permission to enter the residence. The legality of this approach can be questionable, however. The person contemplating suicide may consider himself or herself to be competent and able to make rational decisions, and think that the attorney does not have the authority to make decisions on his or her behalf. The *Mental Health Act* considers all people contemplating or attempting suicide to be incompetent and acting irrationally. It does not make allowances for people who possibly may be making an informed and, in the person's eyes, reasonable choice. The *Mental Health Act* does not contain provisions that allow police officers to enter a dwelling for investigative purposes.

In some cases, relatives or neighbours will have keys to the residence and the authority to use them in times of emergency. It can be argued that allowing the police to enter exceeds the authority granted by the homeowner, but it helps establish that the police made reasonable efforts to enter the residence without using force.

If no other recourse is readily available, it may be necessary to forcibly enter the home. The officers should enter in a manner that causes the least amount of property damage. If all other options have been exhausted and the officers are acting under a good-faith belief that the person is in danger, there is little chance of prosecution.

Intervention After Entry

Once entry has been gained, the officers must establish whether the person is a danger to himself or herself or others. As always, officer safety is a primary concern.

Unconscious Person

If the person is obviously injured and is unconscious, the first priority is medical assistance. The officers must be careful to avoid direct contact with blood-borne pathogens if administering first aid. The use of safety equipment such as latex gloves and barrier devices used when giving artificial respiration is necessary.

Deceased Person

If on arrival at the scene the officers find that the person is obviously dead, they should not move or touch the body. The signs of obvious death are decomposition, decapitation, and rigor mortis. Each is discussed below.

Decomposition

If the body has begun to decompose, medical assistance is obviously not required. Decomposition may be determined visually or through a very distinct smell that will emanate from the body.

Decay of the body takes place through two processes. In the first process, the body's own enzymes break down tissue. In the second process, bacteria breaks down tissue. The bacteria may be present in the body or the surrounding environment. Bacterial decomposition is usually accompanied by the liquefaction of body tissues and the production of large volumes of gases. The body becomes bloated, which results in the expulsion of fluids, usually from body orifices.

Analyzing the rate of decomposition as a means of establishing time of death is not very accurate. High environmental temperatures may accelerate the process to the degree that decomposition may be advanced to a stage where time of death is indeterminable. Decomposition tends to occur rapidly in areas of the body that are engorged with blood at the time of death. Decay may also be unusually rapid in cases where bacteria are present in the blood at the time of death.

Decapitation

When a human body has been decapitated, the head is severed from the body. There is no possibility of providing any effective medical assistance in cases of decapitation.

Rigor Mortis

Rigor mortis is the stiffening of the body after death. It results from a chemical reaction that takes place in muscle tissue. Consequently, rigor mortis appears sooner and lasts longer in muscular, well-developed males. Conversely, it may develop more slowly in a person with less muscle mass. Infants show the effects of rigor mortis sooner than adults.

Investigation Where Person Is Deceased

Immediately upon discovery of a dead body, the scene must be secured for investigation. If the responding officers are not in charge of crime scene investigation, their duty is to secure the scene for the police investigators and the coroner. No one may enter the area and nothing must be removed from the scene until responsibility for the investigation is handed over to the officers who will be in charge.

Treating the scene as a "worst-case scenario" (homicide) will assist in preventing the destruction of potential evidence. This topic is discussed in greater detail under the heading "Homicide or Suicide?" below.

Section 10(1) of the Ontario *Coroners Act* requires that police officers immediately notify the coroner in all cases of "unexpected or sudden death."

Duty to Give Information: Coroners Act, Section 10(1)

10(1) Every person who has reason to believe that a deceased person died ...

(d) suddenly and unexpectedly ...

shall immediately notify a coroner or a police officer of the facts and circumstances relating to the death, and where a police officer is notified he or she shall in turn immediately notify the coroner of such facts and circumstances.

The coroner or designate will generally attend the scene. On the basis of his or her observations and the information provided by the investigating officer(s), the coroner will determine whether it is necessary to continue an investigation, called an **inquest**, separate from a police investigation.

inquest
investigation by a coroner into the cause of a unexpected or sudden death

The purposes of a coroner's inquest are set out in s. 31(1) of the *Coroners Act* and are quite specific.

Purposes of Inquest: Coroners Act, Section 31(1)

31(1) Where an inquest is held, it shall inquire into the circumstances of the death and determine,

(a) who the deceased was;

(b) how the deceased came to his or her death;

(c) when the deceased came to his or her death;

(d) where the deceased came to his or her death; and

(e) by what means the deceased came to his or her death.

The inquest cannot be used to determine criminal culpability, as stated in s. 31(2) of the *Coroners Act*.

Purposes of Inquest: Coroners Act, Section 31(2)

31(2) The jury shall not make any finding of legal responsibility or express any conclusion of law on any matter referred to in subsection (1).

Homicide or Suicide?

If the cause and nature of death are not readily apparent or if there are some unanswered questions regarding the circumstances of death, officers should treat the death as a homicide, the worst-case scenario. This entails treating the scene of death as a crime scene, which reduces the likelihood that potential evidence will be contaminated or that a possible homicide will not be investigated. The hypothesis that the death is a homicide allows the investigators the opportunity to establish evidence that supports the hypothesis. If the evidence does not support homicidal death, other avenues may be investigated.

There are several indicators that should arouse an officer's suspicion that a sudden death may be a homicide:

- multiple wounds;
- the absence of a weapon that caused the wounds;
- wounds on areas of the body not easily accessible to the victim (for example, a stab wound in the back is unlikely to be self-inflicted);
- signs of a struggle (for example, overturned furniture);
- signs of forcible entry to a home or room;
- the body is found outdoors, inappropriately dressed for the season, or a considerable distance from home; or
- missing wallet, jewellery, or other effects that are usually carried or worn.

There may be other situational indicators that appear to be out of context with circumstances of suicide or natural death.

The investigating officer must carefully examine the evidence before concluding that the sudden death was a suicide. It is possible that the deceased is the victim of a carefully crafted homicide. Using the worst-case scenario context, the investigator must find evidence at the scene to support the theory that death was the result of action taken by the victim, and not the result of the actions of another person. This evidence may include:

- handwritten notes explaining the suicide that are consistent in content with the opinions of others who knew the person. Mechanically produced documents are less reliable.
- information, obtained through interviews with people having knowledge of the deceased, confirming that the victim had a problem that may have led to suicide.
- the manner of death, position of weapons used, position of the body, and bloodstain patterns.
- post-mortem lividity, which refers to the changes in skin colour that appear where blood has pooled. This pooling of blood can be used to determine whether the body has been moved and an approximate, although not very accurate, time of death. The colour of the area of lividity may be useful in initially identifying the cause of death. In instances of heart failure, the area of lividity is bluish-grey in colour. Carbon monoxide poisoning produces a pinkish-red colour. Cyanide poisoning produces a similar but more reddish colour.

Conscious Person

If the person is conscious, the officer must use verbal intervention techniques and his or her powers of observation to determine whether a danger of suicide or serious bodily harm exists. A conversation with the person may help. The officer must remember that the person is not a suspect in an investigation. Therefore, the tone of the conversation should not be that used in an interrogation.

The goals of intervention are to reduce the person's feeling of isolation through the use of effective communication, and to assess the seriousness of the threat to the person.

At this stage the officer should attempt to make contact with the suicidal person. From a position of safety, the officer should let the person know that he or she is not alone and help is available. The officer's demeanour and the degree of understanding and empathy he or she displays have an important influence on the outcome of the intervention. Officers should keep in mind the following tips for dealing with a potentially suicidal person:

- Try to be non-judgmental, non-threatening, non-critical, calm, sympathetic, and helpful.
- Show concern for how the person feels. Ask: "How do you feel about things right now? What thoughts are you having?"
- Engage the subject in conversation if possible. Remarks should be kept short and simple.
- Try to address one key problem. Ask: "What is the one problem that is overwhelming right now?" Focus on the ability to manage the problem.
- Try to get the person to identify the problem and put it in perspective.

The officer should be direct and ask whether the person intends to hurt or kill himself or herself. This is important because such questioning immediately establishes the seriousness of the dialogue and possibly allows the officer to make an immediate decision about the nature of his or her intervention. The question should be succinct—for example, "Do you intend to kill yourself?" A question of this kind will not lead the person to entertain fresh thoughts of suicide. If the person indicates that he or she does wish to commit suicide, the officer may decide to rely on the arrest provisions of s. 17 of the MHA.

The Act authorizes the officer to take into custody a person who is a danger to himself or herself or others because of a mental illness.

However, the MHA does not address the manner in which such apprehensions are carried out. Use of force authorities pertaining to all provincial legislation of Ontario, including the MHA, are found in s. 146 of the *Provincial Offences Act* of Ontario.

Use of Force: Provincial Offences Act, Section 146(1)

146(1) Every police officer is, if he or she acts on reasonable and probable grounds, justified in using as much force as is necessary to do what the officer is required or authorized by law to do.

If the person answers no to suicide or is noncommittal, further conversation with the person is essential for assessing the risk of suicide.

While speaking to the suicidal person, the officer should not lecture, criticize, or preach. The pros and cons of suicide should not be discussed, and the person's beliefs and rationale should not be challenged, because his or her reaction can be unpredictable.

The problem that caused the suicidal person to consider suicide is real to that person, and the officer must not express ridicule or deny that the problem exists. Above all, officers must remain calm and in control. The suicidal person has lost control of his or her life and may believe that his or her world is crumbling. The officer's calm reassurance may help the person put the problem into perspective.

Strategies for Verbal Intervention

The following 10 strategies may assist with officer safety and reduce the risk to the suicidal person. Points 1 and 2 deal with building a rapport and making the area safer. Points 3 through 8 involve helping the person identify his or her problems, developing solutions, and settling on a method of assisting the person with his or her problems. Points 9 and 10 involve making a referral and evaluating suicide potential. Assistance could be provided through community agencies, mental-health care facilities, or family. Note the reference to "his or her problems." Police officers should not allow the person's problems to become their problems. Empathy is necessary but the officer's emotional health demands that the problems remain with the suicidal person.

1. *Build a rapport.* The ability to develop a rapport differs among officers and depends upon the officer's communication skills and life experiences. Regardless of their ability, officers must attempt to develop a positive rapport with the suicidal person. The conversation should focus on the problem(s) that led to the suicidal behaviour. If the person does not wish to immediately address their problem(s), any type of positive conversation is better than silence. As long as the person is listening, there is a chance that they will reconsider their suicidal behaviour.

   - Let the person know that you are there to help.
   - Tell the person that you take the threat seriously.
   - Listen actively.
   - Do not argue about the person's reason for contemplating suicide.
   - Talk about the suicide plan.
   - Remember that negotiation is not an option. The person does not have anything to offer. Offering options in exchange for the person's agreement to not end his or her life may not be effective. (The person may believe that his or her life is worthless.)
   - Carefully consider requests made by a suicidal person before fulfilling them. Requests for alcohol or other drugs that interfere with the person's ability to reason should be refused.
   - If you are the officer in charge of the scene, carefully consider requests to talk to a relative, friend, or clergy. The request may be a legitimate cry for help, or the person may be planning to apologize for the hardship he or she is about to impose—and then commit suicide.

2. *Make the area safer.*
   - Remove any readily accessible weapons.
   - If the person is holding a weapon, ask him or her to put it down.

3. *Try to have the person identify the problem(s).*

4. *Focus the conversation on the problem(s).* If the person is not ready to talk about their problem(s), choose another topic and return to the problem(s) later.

5. *Ask the person what he or she has done to address the problem(s).*

6. *Try to assist in helping or offering a solution to the problem(s).*

7. *Be positive when discussing solutions.* Try to instill a sense of hope in the person.

8. *Ask the person for an agreement to try the proposed solution(s).*

9. *If the person ceases his or her suicidal actions, provide immediate medical or psychological assistance through the appropriate referrals.*

10. *Evaluate suicide potential.*

    • Evaluate background information and risk factors.

    • Use the three Ps (plan, past, and partners) to determine immediate risk. The three Ps will be explained in the next section of this chapter.

These strategies may be categorized in order of importance as:

1. Addressing safety issues.

2. Building a rapport.

3. Assessing the risk of suicide.

4. Providing assistance.

Assessing the Risk of Suicide

The next step, after acquiring information from conversations with the suicidal person and possibly friends and relatives, establishing a rapport with the person, and ensuring officer safety, is to assess the risk of suicide. Police need to use a method that can be applied quickly and effectively. The luxury of time is usually not available.

There are many different methods of assessment. None of them are completely reliable. Nevertheless, if an assessment indicates that the person is at risk of committing suicide, the officer should err on the side of caution and take appropriate action.

One method of assessment is the **three Ps (plan, past, and partners)**, outlined below. The three Ps can help officers analyze the situation and determine whether there is an immediate risk of suicide.

• *Plan.* How does the person plan to commit suicide? Does he or she have the means to carry out the plan? A plan suggests that the person is serious about ending his or her life. If there is a plan and steps have been taken to obtain the resources necessary to carry it out, the situation is serious. If the person has implemented a time frame, the situation needs immediate attention.

• *Past.* Has the person tried suicide before? A history of suicide attempts greatly increases the likelihood that the person will achieve the desired end. First-time attempts are less likely to end in death.

**three Ps
(plan, past, and partners)**
a risk assessment tool that determines whether there is a plan for suicide, a past history of suicide attempts, and partners who can reduce the risk of suicide by helping the person solve his or her problems

- *Partners.* Who is available to help the suicidal person overcome his or her personal difficulties? Are friends, family, and community and social services agencies available? Although police officers provide the initial intervention, long-term assistance is required. A network of these partners greatly reduces the risk that the person will commit suicide in the future.

If there is a plan, the risk is high. If the person has taken steps to carry out the plan, the risk has escalated. A combination of a developed plan and a history of suicide attempts creates a very high risk that the person will kill himself or herself. When the first two Ps are present and the third is unavailable, either literally or according to the accused's perception, the person is in extreme danger. Officers faced with these circumstances should take the person into custody and deliver him or her to an appropriate medical or psychiatric facility.

The first two Ps do not have to be present for an officer to take a person into custody. The provisions of s. 17 of the MHA allow an officer to use his or her judgment. In arriving at a decision, the officer needs to consider how the safety of the person and of society itself can best be protected.

Officers must take the following factors into consideration when trying to determine the risk of suicide:

- *Gender.* Males are more likely than females to kill themselves.
- *Stress.* The amount of real or perceived stress in a person's life influences the degree of risk. The more stress, the greater the risk.
- *Signs.* The more signs of suicidal tendencies displayed, the greater the risk.

If it is determined that the person is not at immediate risk of committing suicide, the officers should refer him or her to an appropriate community or social services agency. Ideally, the officers should provide the address, telephone number, and name of a contact person at the agency. One officer should make a follow-up call the next day to let the person know that the police are concerned and are available to help. If instead an immediate threat is identified, the provisions of s. 17 of the MHA may be applicable.

In situations where a person is experiencing a psychotic episode, officers will be unable to reason with him or her. Although the psychotic person is not rational, it may be possible to reach the person on some cognitive level. The person may be able to recognize that police are there to help even though he or she is unable to interact rationally. In such cases, the use of non-lethal force may be a viable last option to prevent the psychotic person from harming himself or herself. Anecdotal evidence appears to confirm that the use of conductive energy devices such as the Taser, which causes temporary paralysis, may be a more effective non-lethal control option than oleoresin capsicum (OC) spray. The use of OC spray appears to be less effective on people experiencing psychosis and may contribute to excited delirium.

Some recent controversy has arisen regarding the use of the Taser to control violent, mentally ill people. There have been reports of 60 deaths in Canada and the United States where a Taser has been used. It should be noted that in none of these deaths was the Taser ruled to be the cause of death. In all, the subjects were mentally ill and/or under the influence of a drug when they were Tasered.

In 2004, the president of the BC Schizophrenia Society, Fred Dawe, endorsed the use of Tasers by police as a method of saving lives (Lee, 2004). "The schizophrenia movement across this country believes in the Taser," he said. "We support the appropriate use of the Taser as a life-saving means of force in emergency police interventions."

If the situation escalates and the suicidal person becomes violent, disengagement from the scene may be a viable option. Although the safety of the person is an important concern, officer safety is foremost.

If the intervention is not successful and the person takes his or her life, the intervening officers must not consider their actions to be unsuccessful. The act of attempting to render assistance is all that can be expected. The police had, at the least, offered some solace to the person in their final moments.

Intervention Summary

1. Officer Safety
   - *First* priority.
   - Persons contemplating suicide may be dangerous because of irrational/self-destructive thinking.
   - Weapons may be present.
   - There is a risk of the intervening officer contacting bodily fluids that may contain blood-borne pathogens.

2. Obtaining Background Information
   - The officer should try to obtain as much background information about the person as possible.
   - Time constraints may not allow the gathering of much information, but any information obtained is helpful.
   - If time is an issue, the officer should immediately check for the presence of weapons and any history of suicide attempts.
   - If time permits, the officer then may obtain information regarding the person's behaviour before the crisis.
   - The officer's questions should establish whether any warning signs are present, although warning sign(s) will not always be present.
   - Other information, such as the person's age and religious beliefs, can help officers assess the risk of suicide.

3. Entry
   - The primary concern should be officer safety.
   - The next concern should be the legality of the entry.
   - If safe, knocking on the door and asking permission to enter is the preferred method of entry.
   - If unsafe, the officer should try to ensure that entry is legal.
   - Possible *Criminal Code* provisions that could allow entry are ss. 117.04(2), 529.3, and 27.
   - The cases of *R v. Custer* and *R v. Godoy* discuss the legality of entry.

4. Intervention After Entry

• The primary concern should be officer safety.

• If the person is obviously injured or unconscious, assistance should be rendered if the situation is safe. The officer should take necessary precautions by using latex gloves and other safety equipment.

• If the person is conscious, the officer should be direct in questioning—"Do you intend to kill yourself?" "Why do you want to die?" Such questioning may have a psychological effect on the person by allowing him or her to realize the seriousness of the situation.

• Officers should try to ask questions and elicit answers that address the three Ps: plan, past, and partners.

• The three Ps also allow the officer to establish reasonable grounds allowing the use of s. 17 of the MHA if necessary.

• Negotiation is not an option. The person does not have anything to offer. (The person may believe that his or her life is worthless.)

• Officers should carefully consider requests made by a suicidal person before fulfilling them. Requests for alcohol or other drugs that interfere with the person's ability to reason should be refused.

• Requests to talk to a relative, friend, or clergy should be carefully considered by the officer in charge of the scene. The request may be a legitimate cry for help or the person may be planning to apologize for the hardship that he or she is about to impose—and then commit suicide.

Learning Activity 8.2

Read the following scenario. Then answer the question that follows.

You are a police officer responding to an emergency call for assistance at 123 Main Street. On arrival you are met by Albert Rose, who lives next door at 125 Main Street. He believes that his neighbour, Hazel Malcolmson, is going to injure herself. Hazel called and asked him to wait an hour, then call the police. Her words were, "My life is over." He immediately called the police. Albert tells you that he knows Hazel quite well. She does not own any firearms, nor has she ever indicated a desire to die. Albert offers to stay around in case Hazel needs to talk to someone she knows. You thank him and ask him to remain in the area.

You cautiously approach the front door of Hazel's house. The door is unlocked. You open it and call out Hazel's name. There is no reply. You believe that you have reasonable grounds to enter the house. You enter and continue to call out her name while searching the house for her. In an upstairs bedroom, you find her sitting in a chair with a straight razor in her hand.

She looks at you and says, "You are not supposed to be here yet." She tells you not to come closer or she will cut herself and you. You ask her to tell you about her problems. She says that you would not understand, that the matter is very personal. When pressed for details, she becomes withdrawn and does not speak.

Albert suddenly enters the room, which enrages Hazel, who begins screaming, "This is your fault!" You tell Albert to leave the room. Hazel says that she wants him to stay so that he can "see what he has done." Her speech is becoming slurred. You ask whether she has taken any drugs, and she replies, "Two bottles of sleeping pills about twenty minutes ago."

You start to approach her, calmly speaking to her as you advance. She shouts, "Stop or I'll cut both of us. I want to die. My life is over anyway!" She holds the razor to her throat and makes a small cut. Blood begins to flow. She shouts, "Touch me and you are dead!" You retreat.

Using the CAPRA system discussed in Chapter 3, describe what you will do in this situation.

SUICIDE INTERVENTIONS AND OFFICER STRESS

The stress of suicide interventions can be enormous. However, interventions that prevent a person from taking his or her life can be extremely rewarding. In such cases, the officers have fulfilled one of the greatest responsibilities that society has bestowed on them—the responsibility of saving people's lives.

It is not always possible to prevent a person from committing suicide. The stress of an intervention can be greatly amplified when the intervention fails to prevent a suicide. Police officers are taught that they are able to handle any situation. Their personalities usually reinforce this teaching. Most police officers have a "helping" personality—they want to assist anyone in trouble. Unsuccessful interventions can cause officers to question their abilities and how well they are fulfilling their obligation to society.

The duty of officers is to diligently provide assistance where circumstances permit. They must remember that although the person may have committed suicide, an intervention that ends in death does not necessarily mean that the officers were unsuccessful. If all reasonable attempts to prevent the person from harming himself or herself are made, the officers have carried out their duties diligently.

The final phase of any intervention is assessment. The officers must assess their response and decide whether their course of action was appropriate. If all that could have been done was done properly, but death occurred nevertheless, the proper conclusion is that the outcome was unavoidable. But an assessment can reveal a different strategy to follow the next time a similar situation arises. Because each situation is unique, the response must be unique. This uniqueness makes it impossible to determine one course of action that will be effective in all situations. The officers must remember that they are not infallible and that even if they do everything right, the outcome may be beyond their control. The officers must learn from the incident and then put it behind them. This does not necessarily mean that they must forget all about the victim to have closure. Although some officers believe that forgetting is the best way to cope with the stress, others believe that holding on to a compassionate memory of the victim facilitates coping. Police officers are individuals who must develop coping mechanisms tailored to their individual needs; it cannot be said that one coping method is superior to another.

Failure to successfully deal with the stress caused by suicide interventions may lead to post-traumatic stress disorder. Police officers should be aware of the early indicators of this disorder in order to prevent its development. Episodes where officers relive the incident in their thoughts or dreams or re-experience feelings of anxiety when thinking of or responding to similar occurrences may be early indicators of the disorder. (Chapter 1 discusses these indicators in detail.) If these early indicators are identified, the officer may, through proper treatment, be able to diminish their effect.

KEY TERMS

inquest
three Ps (plan, past, and partners)
victim-precipitated suicide

REFERENCES

American Foundation for Suicide Prevention. (n.d.). *Facts and figures: National statistics.* Retrieved from http://www.afsp.org.

Coroners Act. (1990). RSO 1990, c. C.37.

Criminal Code. (1985). RSC 1985, c. C-46, as amended.

Dumais, A., Lesage, A.D., Lalovic, A., Seguin, M., Tonsignant, M., Chawky, N., et al. (2005). Is violent method of suicide a behavioral marker of lifetime aggression? *American Journal of Psychiatry 162*(7), 1375–1378.

Gerberth, V. (July 1993). Inviting death from the hands of a police officer. *Law and Order,* 105–109.

Lee, J. (2004, July 24). Man's death after Taser jolt fuels growing safety debate. *Vancouver Sun.*

Martin's Annual Criminal Code, 2005. (2005). Aurora, ON: Canada Law Book.

Martin's Annual Criminal Code, 2012. (2012). Aurora, ON: Canada Law Book.

McMains, M.J., & Mullins, W.C. (1996). *Crisis negotiations: Managing critical incidents and hostage situations in law enforcement and corrections.* Cincinnati, OH: Anderson Publishing.

Mental Health Act. (1990). RSO 1990, c. M.7.

Mood Disorders Association of Ontario. (n.d.). *Frequently asked questions—Suicide.* Retrieved from http://www.mooddisorders.ca/faq/suicide.

Parent, R.B. (2004). Aspects of police use of deadly force in British Columbia: The phenomenon of victim-precipitated homicide. PhD dissertation, Simon Fraser University.

Plutchik, R., & van Praag, H.M. (1995). The nature of impulsivity: Definitions, ontology, genetics and relations to aggression. In F. Hollander and D.J. Stein (Eds.), *Impulsivity and aggression* (pp. 7–24). New York: Wiley.

Police Services Act. (1990). RSO 1990, c. P.15.

Provincial Offences Act. (1990). RSO 1990, c. P.33.

Séguin, M., Lesage, A., Turecki, G., Daigle, F., & Guy, A. (2005). *Research project on deaths by suicide in New Brunswick between April 2002 and May 2003.* Retrieved from New Brunswick Department of Health website: http://www .gnb.ca/0051/index-e.asp.

Shneidman, E. (1996). Commonalities of suicide. In *The suicidal mind* (pp. 129–137). Oxford: Oxford University Press.

Statistics Canada. (2001). Causes of death, shelf tables. Data year—2001. ICD-10 X60-X84 and Y87.0. Ottawa: Author.

Statistics Canada. (2010a). *Leading causes of death in Canada, 2007* (catalogue no. 84-215-XWE). Ottawa: Author.

Statistics Canada. (2010b). *Summary tables.* Retrieved from Statistics Canada website: http://www40.statcan.ca/l01/cst01/hlth66a-eng.htm.

Van Zandt, C.R. (July 1993). Suicide by cop. *The Police Chief,* 24–30.

EXERCISES

TRUE OR FALSE

_____ 1. Persons contemplating suicide always signal their intention by providing various warning signs.

_____ 2. The behaviour of people with schizophrenia is usually quite predictable, which makes assessing the suicide risk of specific people with schizophrenia an easy task.

_____ 3. Alcohol use is rarely a factor in suicidal behaviour.

_____ 4. Gender has little bearing on suicide rates.

_____ 5. Depressive illnesses are a contributing factor in a substantial number of suicides.

_____ 6. As males enter old age, their risk of suicide drops dramatically.

SHORT ANSWER

1. Dorothy Williams calls 911 to report that her husband, Robbie, is attempting to hurt himself. On arriving at the Williams house, the responding officer learns from Dorothy that Robbie is schizophrenic and is acting irrationally. Dorothy says that he has threatened to kill himself. The officer speaks to Robbie, who rationally tells the officer that his wife is not telling the truth, and that he does not wish to harm himself.

   Explain what the officer should do. Refer to the appropriate legislation in your answer.

2. Summarize the procedure for obtaining a physician's order for a psychiatric assessment under s. 15 of the *Mental Health Act*.

3. How does a justice of the peace's order for psychiatric examination under s. 16 of the *Mental Health Act* differ from a physician's order under s. 15?

4. What should be the primary concern of police officers on being called to a location where a person is threatening suicide?

5. How should officers cope with the stress of suicide interventions?

CASE ANALYSIS

Case 8.1

You are a police officer responding to a call for assistance. The information you have received is that Thelma Smith is worried that her former husband, Tom, will injure himself. Further details from dispatch are requested. Thelma called to report that Tom called her about five minutes ago. He seemed depressed over their divorce and loss of access to their children. Thelma lives in a community 500 kilometres away from Tom. Tom has never, to Thelma's knowledge, attempted suicide. He has never owned a firearm.

You, along with another officer, arrive at Tom's apartment. You knock on his door and identify yourself as a police officer. A person who identifies himself as Tom Smith answers the door and asks what you want. You tell him that you are concerned for his safety. He tells you that nothing is wrong and that you can leave. You ask to come inside so you can talk privately. He invites you in.

Once inside, you tell Tom about Thelma's concerns. He tells you that he did call her, adding that perhaps he is a little down because he hasn't seen his children in six months. He is unemployed and living on disability insurance he collects for a back problem. He doesn't have enough money to visit his children, nor does his wife have enough money to send the children to visit him. You continue to speak to Tom while observing the surroundings for any indication of a suicide plan. There are several empty beer bottles but nothing out of the ordinary is noted.

Tom begins to become upset, telling you that he doesn't believe that Thelma wants him to see the children. He tells you that he hasn't been able to send the children any gifts because he doesn't have any money. He has filed a claim with the workers' compensation board but has been denied benefits. He thinks he may have to go on social assistance. He can't make ends meet with the insurance money he receives.

You ask whether he intends to hurt himself. He tells you, "No, I just want an end to my problems." He also tells you that he doesn't own any firearms. You ask whether he would like to talk to someone about his problems. He tells you that he doesn't really have any friends in town and that he moved to town only a month ago. He is becoming agitated and says, "Please leave. I want to be alone." You tell him that you are only trying to help. He replies, "There's nothing wrong. I don't want help." He is becoming increasingly agitated and tells you to get out.

Using the CAPRA system discussed in Chapter 3, describe what you will do in this situation.

Case 8.2

You are a police officer responding to a 911 call for assistance from an anonymous caller. On arrival at the address given by dispatch you are met at the door by Harold Bryant. He tells you that there is no problem and that he did not call. You ask Harold whether he wants to talk about anything and whether anything is wrong. He says that everything is fine but he wouldn't mind talking to someone for a while. He invites you inside and you cautiously accompany him to the living room. Harold asks, "Do you believe in God? Do you believe that you will go to hell if you commit a sin?" You tell him that you don't know.

After some prodding you learn that Harold is 33 years old and a high school teacher. He has been married five years and has daughters aged two and three.

Harold resumes his former line of conversation by asking, "Could you forgive your spouse for doing something really wrong?" You respond by telling him that you do not want to discuss your beliefs on that point. Harold says that he understands and does not speak for a couple of minutes. He then says, "Do you ever wonder what it would be like to die?" You ask him whether he intends to harm himself. He replies, "No. I don't think so. I just have some personal problems that I'm having difficulty dealing with. I did something that I'm not proud of and it has gotten me into serious trouble." You again ask whether he wants to talk about his problem. He replies, "No. It's between me and God." He thanks you for listening and tells you to leave.

Using the CAPRA system discussed in Chapter 3, describe what you will do in this situation.

Case 8.3

You are a police officer responding to a call for assistance from Tim Jackson. He invites you into his house and tells you that his wife, Louisa, recently died of cancer. A lawyer has just sent him a letter that was written by Tim's wife shortly before her death and given to the lawyer on the understanding that it would be sent to Tim after she died. The letter states that she gave her permission to their family physician, Dr. Jane Wells, to administer a lethal dose of morphine if her suffering became unbearable and there was no possibility of recovery. Tim remarks that his wife had been suffering terribly but was able to talk rationally most of the time. He has asked Dr. Wells to come over. She should be arriving shortly. Tim feels betrayed by his wife's decision not to consult him before making her arrangement with Dr. Wells.

Dr. Wells arrives. Tim invites you and her into his living room. Dr. Wells states that the letter was written by Louisa about a week before she died. It was written with a lawyer present and was notarized to verify Louisa's signature. Louisa did not want to involve Tim in the decision because she knew that he would not want to let her go. Dr. Wells states that she had known Louisa for about 30 years and that Louisa "fought a good fight" but was suffering immensely and wanted to end her life on her own terms. Louisa, whose condition was terminal, had asked to be given something to allow her to "go gently." Dr. Wells states that she gave Louisa a large dose of morphine to allow her to end her life without further suffering. Dr. Wells begins to cry and says that she lost a true friend. Tim puts his arms around her and tells her that he forgives her.

Using the CAPRA system discussed in Chapter 3, describe what you will do in this situation.

Case 8.4

You are a police officer responding to a call for assistance at 321 North Avenue, Smith Pharmaceuticals Company. Upon arrival you are met by the owner, Mr. Smith. Smith tells you that he is worried about the well-being of Dan Bayer, a sales representative whom he fired this morning. Bayer had been given two prior warnings about his alcohol consumption while making sales calls. Smith had received several further complaints from doctors and pharmacists about Bayer smelling of alcohol when he came to their offices.

Bayer told Smith that he has very large debts to pay and doesn't know how he will pay them. He begged Smith to reconsider. He said he would stop drinking if given another chance. Smith replied that he was not willing to jeopardize his business by keeping Bayer and told him he would not reconsider. Bayer became very upset and exclaimed, "Where else can I make a hundred thousand a year? I sold a lot of your drugs and this is what I get?"

Bayer then stormed out of Smith's office. About three hours later Smith received a call from Bayer, who was now at home. He sounded intoxicated. Bayer again asked Smith to reconsider and was told by Smith that he would not rehire him. Bayer began crying and said that he didn't know what he was going to do.

You attend Bayer's condominium, where the door is answered by Dan Bayer. He appears to be intoxicated and smells strongly of alcohol. You tell him that Smith is concerned about his well-being. He replies, "Then he should give me my job back!" You ask whether you can come in and talk. He tells you, "OK, come in."

Bayer offers you a drink, which you politely refuse. Bayer then pours himself a large glass of liquor and sits down. He begins to tell you about his financial problems: "I was making over a hundred thousand a year selling Smith's drugs. I bought this condo, new furniture, a new Porsche, and a few other toys. I drink a bit but that's not illegal. How am I going to pay all these bills? I'm not married and live alone. That's probably a blessing. At least I'm not hurting anyone else."

While he continues to tell you about how unfair it is that Smith fired him, he drinks another large glass of liquor. He tells you that he was good at his job and Smith will miss him. He is becoming more intoxicated and incoherent. He soon begins to fall asleep.

What will you do in this situation? Explain your answer. Be sure to quote authorities.

Case 8.5

Brian is a 14-year-old male in grade 9. He is having problems at school with other boys pushing him around and teasing him. He is very concerned about his small stature and has been using anabolic steroids for the past month in an effort to increase his weight. He has gained weight but has experienced many of the common side effects of steroid use. The worst, at least for Brian, is acne. He is now teased about his small stature and about his severe acne.

Brian tells his parents that he doesn't know whether he can take the humiliation anymore. He tells his father, "I'm a loser. I'm never going to grow. You are small. Mom is small. I'll always be small!"

His father tells him about great achievers who were also of small stature such as Napoleon Bonaparte and Alexander the Great. Brian replies, "So what! I'll bet that no one pulled their pants down in the hallway at school! The bullying is driving me crazy! I can't take it anymore! I going to end it all! I'll, I'll, I'll ... chop off my foot with an axe and bleed to death! That will show them!" Brian then runs out of the house and locks himself in the garage.

You are a police officer called to the scene. What will you do?

Crime Victims

9

INTRODUCTION

There are two major national surveys that present a statistically accurate portrayal of the number of crime victims and the types of crimes committed in Canada. The first of these studies is the yearly Uniform Crime Reporting Survey compiled by Statistics Canada. (Another version of this survey, the UCR Survey, was discussed in earlier chapters.) The UCR Survey reflects the number and types of crimes reported to police each year. See Table 9.1. The statistics reflect the number of crimes reported, but not the actual number of victims. It is possible that a crime victim may be the victim of numerous crimes; this is not reflected in the UCR Survey.

The second major survey is the General Social Survey (GSS). (Recall that the GSS was discussed in Chapters 5 and 6 in the context of spousal abuse and elder abuse.) The GSS collects information every five years from the personal experiences of the interviewees. The information relates to eight crime categories: assault, sexual assault, robbery, break-and-enter, theft of motor vehicles, theft of household property, theft of personal property, and vandalism (mischief).

In 2009, the GSS collected data from 19,500 respondents living in the ten provinces of Canada. Information was also collected from the three territories, but had not yet been processed at the time of writing.

The GSS data are based on the information obtained from the interviewee and identifies the percentage of respondents reporting victimization, whether or not the crime has been reported to police.

The 2009 GSS on victimization revealed that 27 percent of Canadians aged 15 and older said that they had been a victim of a crime in the year preceding the survey (Statistics Canada, 2010). This percentage was unchanged from 2004, the last time the victimization survey was conducted.

The majority of self-reported crimes were non-violent. About 36 percent consisted of incidents such as break-and-enters, theft of motor vehicles, vandalism (mischief), and theft of household property. Approximately 34 percent of respondents

Table 9.1   Police-Reported Crime for Selected Offences, Canada, 2009 and 2010

Type of offence	2009[a] Number	Rate	2010 Number	Rate	Percent change in rate 2009 to 2010	Percent change in rate 2000 to 2010
Total crime (excluding traffic)— crime rate	**2,172,960**	**6,444**	**2,095,921**	**6,145**	**−5**	**−19**
Violent crime						
Homicide.....................	610	2	554	2	−10	−9
Other violations causing death[b]	101	0	91	0	−11	−18
Attempted murder............	801	2	693	2	−14	−19
Sexual assault— level 3—aggravated	119	0	188	1	56	−7
Sexual assault—level 2—weapon or bodily harm..............	352	1	388	1	9	−11
Sexual assault—level 1	20,450	61	21,604	63	4	−17
Sexual violations against children[c]	2,693	8	3,648	11	...	...
Assault—level 3— aggravated.................	3,619	11	3,410	10	−7	20
Assault—level 2—weapon or bodily harm..............	53,383	158	51,340	151	−5	14
Assault—level 1..............	180,564	535	173,843	510	−5	−18
Assault police officer[d]	11,837	35	17,377	51	45	105
Other assaults	3,427	10	3,257	10	−6	−36
Firearms—use of, discharge, pointing....................	1,736	5	1,952	6	11	−21
Robbery	32,463	96	30,405	89	−7	−11
Forcible confinement or kidnapping	4,791	14	4,308	13	−11	80
Abduction	435	1	446	1	1	−46
Extortion....................	1,718	5	1,548	5	−11	−29
Criminal harassment..........	19,860	59	21,108	62	5	−5
Uttering threats..............	78,652	233	75,927	223	−5	−28
Threatening or harassing phone calls.......................	23,186	69	21,436	63	−9	−36
Other violent *Criminal Code* violations..................	3,736	11	3,793	11	0	−11
Total	**444,533**	**1,318**	**437,316**	**1,282**	**−3**	**−14**
Property crime						
Breaking and entering.........	206,069	611	196,881	577	−6	−40
Possess stolen property	30,712	91	29,823	87	−4	−6
Theft of motor vehicle.........	107,992	320	92,683	272	−15	−48
Theft over $5,000 (non–motor vehicle)	15,795	47	15,790	46	−1	−33
Theft under $5,000 (non–motor vehicle)	559,155	1,658	536,151	1,572	−5	−27
Fraud	90,731	269	88,491	259	−4	−7
Mischief....................	362,326	1,075	339,831	996	−7	−6
Arson	13,404	40	12,241	36	−10	−19
Total	**1,386,184**	**4,111**	**1,311,891**	**3,846**	**−6**	**−26**

(The table is concluded on the next page.)

Table 9.1   Concluded

Type of offence	2009[a]		2010		Percent change in rate 2009 to 2010	Percent change in rate 2000 to 2010
	Number	Rate	Number	Rate		
Other *Criminal Code* offences						
Counterfeiting	818	2	820	2	−1	−46
Weapons violations.	14,987	44	14,861	44	−2	3
Child pornography[e].	1,587	5	2,190	6	36	123
Prostitution	3,534	10	3,043	9	−15	−46
Disturb the peace	117,644	349	117,903	346	−1	32
Administration of justice violations.	171,848	510	176,560	518	2	9
Other violations.	31,825	94	31,337	92	−3	−25
Total	**342,243**	**1,015**	**346,714**	**1,016**	**0**	**10**
***Criminal Code* traffic violations**						
Impaired driving[f].	88,303	262	84,397	247	−6	−4
Other *Criminal Code* traffic violations.	57,839	172	55,604	163	−5	46
Total	**146,142**	**433**	**140,001**	**410**	**−5**	**11**
Drug offences						
Possession—cannabis	49,151	146	56,870	167	14	13
Possession—other drugs . . .	8,224	24	9,462	28	14	91
Trafficking, production, or distribution—cannabis. . . .	16,404	49	18,256	54	10	−21
Trafficking, production, or distribution—cocaine.	10,027	30	9,729	29	−4	11
Trafficking, production, or distribution—other drugs .	6,543	19	6,956	20	5	38
Total	**97,963**	**291**	**108,529**	**318**	**10**	**11**
Other federal statute violations						
Youth Criminal Justice Act . . .	12,461	37	13,036	38	3	−45
Other federal statutes	19,279	57	19,684	58	1	33
Total	**31,740**	**94**	**32,720**	**96**	**2**	**−15**
Total—all violations.	**2,448,805**	**7,262**	**2,377,171**	**6,969**	**−4**	**−17**

Notes: Counts are based upon the most serious violation in the incident. One incident may involve multiple violations. Data for specific types of crime are available (in most cases) beginning in 1977. Rates are calculated on the basis of 100,000 population. Percent change based on unrounded rates. Populations based upon July 1 estimates from Statistics Canada, Demography Division. ... = not applicable.

[a] Revised.

[b] Includes, for example, criminal negligence causing death.

[c] Sexual offences against children is a relatively new crime category with only partial data available prior to 2010. As a result, numbers and rates should not be directly compared to data from previous years.

[d] In 2009, legislation was introduced to create the offences of assault with a weapon or causing bodily harm to a peace officer (level 2) and aggravated assault to a peace officer (level 3). As a result, the large increase in assaults against police officers may be the result of increased reporting and should be interpreted with caution.

[e] In 2002, legislative changes were made to include the use of the Internet for the purpose of committing child pornography offences. As such, the percent change in this offence is calculated from 2003 to 2010.

[f] Includes alcohol and/or drug impaired operation of a vehicle, alcohol and/or drug impaired operation of a vehicle causing death or bodily harm, failure or refusal to comply with testing for the presence of alcohol or drugs, and failure or refusal to provide a breath or blood sample.

Sources: Statistics Canada, Canadian Centre for Justice Statistics, Uniform Crime Reporting Survey. Adapted from Brennan and Dauvergne (2011).

were victims of theft of personal property. Violent incidents accounted for 30 percent of self-reported incidents.

The 2009 GSS asked victims whether the incident was reported to the police. If the respondent did not report the incident to the police, the survey did not question why the incident was not reported.

For the eight crime types covered by the 2009 GSS on victimization, the proportion of incidents reported to the police by respondents dropped from 34 percent in 2004 to 31 percent in 2009.

Of those people who were victims of household crime, only 36 percent reported the incident to the police. Among the 36 percent of respondents who reported household crimes, break-and-enter was the most often reported (54 percent), followed by theft of motor vehicles (50 percent). For incidents of theft of personal property, 28 percent were brought to the attention of the police, again similar to the proportion of incidents reported to police in 2004.

Victims of violent crimes reported 29 percent of incidents to the police in 2009, essentially the same as in 2004. Robberies (including attempted robberies) were most likely to be reported to police (43 percent), followed by physical assaults (34 percent). About 74 percent reported that they had been victimized once in the previous 12 months. An additional 16 percent said they had been violently victimized twice, while 10 percent reported three or more violent experiences.

POLICE RESPONSE

Police officers responding to calls have the dual role of trying to gather facts while, at the same time, addressing the needs of the victim. To the victim, the officer may appear to be remote, uninterested, or unconcerned. There are several reasons for this. First, it is not uncommon for police officers to develop a protective emotional detachment to help shield themselves from being overwhelmed by the occurrences that they routinely encounter. Second, the machismo of the police subculture with its emphasis on toughness, suspicion of outsiders, and cynicism may further inhibit the ability of the officer to display emotion. Finally, police officers can become so involved in a criminal investigation that they forget the needs of the victim or victims.

Victims often feel fear, depression, helplessness, powerlessness, anger, and possibly guilt, all at the same time. Police officers are expected to calm and console the victim and help restore the victim's sense of equilibrium. If the response of the officer is viewed as callous or skeptical, the victim may feel let down, rejected, or betrayed. Officers should make a genuine effort to recognize and respond to the needs of the victim by listening attentively, showing concern, and refraining from challenging the victim's version of the crime, at least until further evidence is obtained.

Politicians have tried to address the needs of victims through legislation such as Ontario's *Victims' Bill of Rights, 1995*, but legislation cannot teach an officer compassion. Compassionate officers are able to draw on experience and knowledge to relate to crime victims in a caring, professional manner.

Nevertheless, knowledge of the applicable legislation is an important part of addressing a victim's needs. Officers should know what a victim's rights are and be able to advise victims on restitution, compensation, and victim assistance programs. Officers are expected to meet the needs of victims in all respects, if not personally then through referrals to the appropriate community or social services agencies.

The following section discusses the rights of crime victims under federal and Ontario victims' rights legislation. Later sections focus in more detail on specific rights such as the rights to compensation and restitution.

VICTIMS' RIGHTS LEGISLATION

On October 1, 2003, Federal, Provincial, Territorial Ministers Responsible for Justice endorsed a new *Canadian Statement of Basic Principles of Justice for Victims of Crime, 2003*. The statement sets out ten principles that "are intended to promote fair treatment of victims and should be reflected in federal/provincial/territorial laws, policies and procedures" (Department of Justice Canada, 2003). The principles read as follows:

1. Victims of crime should be treated with courtesy, compassion, and respect.

2. The privacy of victims should be considered and respected to the greatest extent possible.

3. All reasonable measures should be taken to minimize inconvenience to victims.

4. The safety and security of victims should be considered at all stages of the criminal justice process and appropriate measures should be taken when necessary to protect victims from intimidation and retaliation.

5. Information should be provided to victims about the criminal justice system and the victim's role and opportunities to participate in criminal justice processes.

6. Victims should be given information, in accordance with prevailing law, policies, and procedures, about the status of the investigation; the scheduling, progress and final outcome of the proceedings; and the status of the offender in the correctional system.

7. Information should be provided to victims about available victim assistance services, other programs and assistance available to them, and means of obtaining financial reparation.

8. The views, concerns and representations of victims are an important consideration in criminal justice processes and should be considered in accordance with prevailing law, policies and procedures.

9. The needs, concerns and diversity of victims should be considered in the development and delivery of programs and services, and in related education and training.

10. Information should be provided to victims about available options to raise their concerns when they believe that these principles have not been followed.

The Victims' Bill of Rights, 1995 (Ontario)

The *Victims' Bill of Rights, 1995* (VBR) was proclaimed in force in June 1996. The VBR recognizes and supports the needs and rights of crime victims in both the criminal and civil justice systems. It establishes principles to support victims throughout the criminal justice process and makes it easier for victims to sue their assailants in civil actions. The VBR's statement of principles (in s. 2(1)) specifies how victims should be treated by judicial officials at different stages of the criminal justice process.

Principles: Victims' Bill of Rights, Section 2(1)

2(1) The following principles apply to the treatment of victims of crime:

1. Victims should be treated with courtesy, compassion and respect for their personal dignity and privacy by justice system officials.

2. Victims should have access to information about,

   i. the services and remedies available to victims of crime,

   ii. the provisions of this Act and of the Compensation for Victims of Crime Act that might assist them,

   iii. the protection available to victims to prevent unlawful intimidation,

   iv. the progress of investigations that relate to the crime,

   v. the charges laid with respect to the crime and, if no charges are laid, the reasons why no charges are laid,

   vi. the victim's role in the prosecution,

   vii. court procedures that relate to the prosecution,

   viii. the dates and places of all significant proceedings that relate to the prosecution,

   ix. the outcome of all significant proceedings, including any proceedings on appeal,

   x. any pretrial arrangements that are made that relate to a plea that may be entered by the accused at trial,

   xi. the interim release and, in the event of conviction, the sentencing of an accused,

   xii. any disposition made under section 672.54 or 672.58 of the Criminal Code (Canada) in respect of an accused who is found unfit to stand trial or who is found not criminally responsible on account of mental disorder, and

   xiii. their right under the Criminal Code (Canada) to make representations to the court by way of a victim impact statement.

3. A victim of a prescribed crime should, if he or she so requests, be notified of,

   i. any application for release or any impending release of the convicted person, including release in accordance with a program of temporary absence, on parole or on an unescorted temporary absence pass, and

   ii. any escape of the convicted person from custody.

4. If the person accused of a prescribed crime is found unfit to stand trial or is found not criminally responsible on account of mental disorder, the victim should, if he or she so requests, be notified of,

    i.   any hearing held with respect to the accused by the Review Board established or designated for Ontario pursuant to subsection 672.38(1) of the *Criminal Code* (Canada),

    ii. any order of the Review Board directing the absolute or conditional discharge of the accused, and

    iii. any escape of the accused from custody.

5. Victims of sexual assault should, if the victim so requests, be interviewed during the investigation of the crime only by police officers and officials of the same gender as the victim.

6. A victim's property that is in the custody of justice system officials should be returned promptly to the victim, where the property is no longer needed for the purposes of the justice system.

Section 3(1) of the VBR states that a person convicted of a crime prescribed by regulation by the lieutenant governor in council is liable for damages to the victim for emotional distress, and for bodily harm resulting from the distress.

Damages: Victim's Bill of Rights, Section 3(1)

3(1)   A person convicted of a prescribed crime is liable in damages to every victim of the crime for emotional distress, and bodily harm resulting from the distress, arising from the commission of the crime.

The prescribed crimes are identified in Ontario regulation 456/96:

1. All crimes described in the *Criminal Code* (Canada) are prescribed for the purposes of paragraphs 3 and 4 of subsection 2(1) of the Act.

2. The crimes described in the following provisions of the *Criminal Code* (Canada) are prescribed for the purposes of subsection 3(1) of the Act:

    1.   Section 151. [sexual interference]
    2.   Section 152. [invitation to sexual touching]
    3.   Section 153. [sexual exploitation]
    3.1. Section 153.1. [sexual exploitation of person with disability]
    4.   Section 155. [incest]
    5.   Section 159. [anal intercourse (found to violate s. 15 of the Charter)]
    5.1. Section 163.1. [child pornography]
    6.   Section 170. [parent or guardian procuring sexual activity]
    7.   Section 171. [householder permitting sexual activity]
    8.   Section 172. [corrupting children]
    8.1 Section 172.1. [luring a child]
    9.   Section 220. [causing death by criminal negligence]
    10. Section 221. [causing bodily harm by criminal negligence]

11. Section 235. [murder]

12. Section 236. [manslaughter]

13. Section 239. [attempt to commit murder]

14. Section 240. [accessory after fact to murder]

15. Section 244. [discharging firearm with intent]

16. Section 264. [criminal harassment]

17. Section 264.1. [uttering threats]

18. Section 266. [assault]

19. Section 267. [assault with a weapon or causing bodily harm]

20. Section 268. [aggravated assault]

21. Section 269. [unlawfully causing bodily harm]

22. Section 271. [sexual assault]

23. Section 272. [sexual assault with a weapon, threats to a third party or causing bodily harm]

24. Section 273. [aggravated sexual assault]

25. Section 279. [kidnapping]

26. Section 279.1. [hostage taking]

27. Section 280. [abduction of person under sixteen]

28. Section 281. [abduction of person under fourteen]

29. Section 283. [abduction]

29.1 Section 318. [advocating genocide]

29.2 Section 319. [public incitement of hatred]

30. Section 344. [robbery]

31. Section 372. [false messages, indecent telephone calls, harassing telephone calls]

32. Subsection 430(4.1). [mischief relating to religious property]

33. Any provision of the *Criminal Code* (Canada), if the court that imposes a sentence in respect of a crime described in the provision finds that the crime was motivated, in whole or in part, by any factor listed in subclause 718.2(a)(i) of that Act.

Section 3(2) of the VBR makes it clear that a victim of domestic assault, sexual assault, or attempted sexual assault is presumed to have suffered emotional distress.

Presumption: Victims' Bill of Rights, Section 3(2)

3(2) The following victims shall be presumed to have suffered emotional distress:

1. A victim of an assault if the victim is or was a spouse, within the meaning of section 29 of the *Family Law Act*, of the assailant.

2. A victim of a sexual assault.

3. A victim of an attempted sexual assault.

And subject to judicial discretion, the VBR applies the following provisions to civil actions brought by crime victims:

- An offender's sentence should not be considered when the court awards compensatory damages for the offender's crime.
- Victims who are successful in their lawsuits are presumed to be entitled to reimbursement for most of their legal costs by their assailant.
- Victims are entitled to receive interest on awards from the date of the crime to the date of trial.
- Victims who live outside Ontario and who are commencing a lawsuit usually should not have to post security at the outset of the proceeding.

The victim assistance fund account referred to in s. 60.1(4) of the *Provincial Offences Act* (POA) is continued as the victims' justice fund account in the VBR so that money collected under the VBR will be dedicated solely to providing services for victims.

The money for the fund is collected through fine surcharges, which have been applied to all fines under the POA (except parking violations) since January 1, 1995. *Criminal Code* fine surcharge revenues are also added to this fund.

VICTIM FINE SURCHARGES

Victim fine surcharges are collected through the courts within the authority of the Ontario *Provincial Offences Act*, the *Criminal Code*, and the *Youth Criminal Justice Act*. The surcharges are not punitive, but rather are used to enhance the services available to victims of crime.

Victim fine surcharges are provided for in s. 60.1 of the *Provincial Offences Act*, s. 737 of the *Criminal Code*, and s. 53 of the *Youth Criminal Justice Act*.

Provincial Offences Act (Ontario)

Surcharge: Provincial Offences Act, Section 60.1(1)

60.1(1) If a person is convicted of an offence in a proceeding commenced under Part I or III and a fine is imposed in respect of that offence, a surcharge is payable by that person in the amount determined by regulations made under this Act.

The *Provincial Offences Act* supplies a surcharge grid that is to be followed by the courts and by police officers when issuing a Part I offence notice. This grid is found in regulation 161/00 of the *Provincial Offences Act*. See Table 9.2.

Collection: Provincial Offences Act, Section 60.1(2)

60.1(2) The surcharge shall be deemed to be a fine for the purpose of enforcing payment.

Table 9.2 Provincial Offences Act Surcharge Grid

Fine range	Surcharge
dollars	
0–50	10
51–75	15
76–100	20
101–150	25
151–200	35
201–250	50
251–300	60
301–350	75
351–400	85
401–450	95
451–500	110
501–1,000	125
Over 1,000	25% of actual fine

Source: *Victim Fine Surcharges* (2000).

Priorities: Provincial Offences Act, Section 60.1(3)

60.1(3) Any payments made by a defendant shall be credited towards payment of the fine until it is fully paid and then towards payment of the surcharge.

Part X Agreements: Provincial Offences Act, Section 60.1(3.1)

60.1(3.1) When an agreement made under Part X applies to a fine, payments made by the defendant shall first be credited towards payment of the surcharge, not as described in subsection (3).

Special Purpose Account: Provincial Offences Act, Section 60.1(4)

60.1(4) Surcharges paid into the Consolidated Revenue Fund shall be credited to the victims' justice fund account and shall be deemed to be money received by the Crown for a special purpose.

Criminal Code

Victim Surcharge: Criminal Code, Section 737(1)

737(1) Subject to subsection (5), an offender who is convicted or discharged under section 730 of an offence under this Act or the *Controlled Drugs and Substances Act* shall pay a victim surcharge, in addition to any other punishment imposed on the offender.

Amount of Surcharge: Criminal Code, Section 737(2)

737(2) Subject to subsection (3), the amount of the victim surcharge in respect of an offence is

(a) 15 per cent of any fine that is imposed on the offender for the offence; or

(b) if no fine is imposed on the offender for the offence,
   (i) $50 in the case of an offence punishable by summary conviction, and
   (ii) $100 in the case of an offence punishable by indictment.

Increase in Surcharge: Criminal Code, Section 737(3)

737(3) The court may order an offender to pay a victim surcharge in an amount exceeding that set out in subsection (2) if the court considers it appropriate in the circumstances and is satisfied that the offender is able to pay the higher amount.

Amounts Applied to Aid Victims: Criminal Code, Section 737(7)

737(7) A victim surcharge imposed under subsection (1) shall be applied for the purposes of providing such assistance to victims of offences as the lieutenant governor in council of the province in which the surcharge is imposed may direct from time to time.

Youth Criminal Justice Act

The *Youth Criminal Justice Act* includes a victim surcharge in s. 53 of the Act.

Funding for Victims: Youth Criminal Justice Act, Section 53(1)

53(1) The lieutenant governor in council of a province may order that, in respect of any fine imposed in the province under paragraph 42(2)(d), a percentage of the fine as fixed by the lieutenant governor in council be used to provide such assistance to victims of offences as the lieutenant governor in council may direct from time to time.

Victim Fine Surcharge: Youth Criminal Justice Act, Section 53(2)

53(2) If the lieutenant governor in council of a province has not made an order under subsection (1), a youth justice court that imposes a fine on a young person under paragraph 42(2)(d) may, in addition to any other punishment imposed on the young person, order the young person to pay a victim fine surcharge in an amount not exceeding fifteen per cent of the fine. The surcharge shall be used to provide such assistance to victims of offences as the lieutenant governor in council of the province in which the surcharge is imposed may direct from time to time.

Learning Activity 9.1

Check your comprehension of the previous reading by completing this learning activity.

1. Broadly categorize the types of offences that have been identified by the Ontario *Victims' Bill of Rights, 1995* that hold the offender liable to the victim for damages. These broad categories may be useful when providing information to the victim of a crime regarding the possibility of civil action. (Note: Police officers do not provide legal advice, only information.)

2. The Ontario *Victims' Bill of Rights, 1995* sets out a number of principles that should be followed regarding victims of crime. These principles address the right of victims of crime to have access to information regarding the services and remedies available to them, as well as access to information regarding the prosecution, court disposition, and punishment of the offender. Application of these principles has resulted in the formation of agencies to assist victims of crime. Referring to the previous reading, how are these agencies partially funded? (Tax dollars are also used to fund these programs.)

THE INITIAL POLICE RESPONSE TO THE NEEDS OF CRIME VICTIMS

Victims expect thorough investigations. Victim dissatisfaction may arise whenever officers give the impression that the victim's complaint is not serious enough to justify the expenditure of police resources.

Crime victims have the right to courteous and compassionate treatment by the police. Their dignity and privacy must be respected. The qualities that allow an officer to behave in the appropriate way toward crime victims rest on the officer's integrity and life experience. Officers learn that more is required of them than simply responding to a victim's needs in a manner that is consistent with policy and addresses all of the legal aspects of an investigation.

Police want the cooperation of persons who report crimes. Without their help, the crime is probably not going to be solved. There may, however, be areas of conflict between police and victim expectations. Responding officers may seem remote, detached, uninterested, or unconcerned about the victim's plight. The victim may feel susceptible to further violation through the belief that the police will not provide any comfort. The victim may be reacting to the protective shield of emotional detachment often displayed by police officers who remain detached as a way of dealing with the daily encounters of policing.

If the officer fails to acknowledge the victim's emotional state, his or her actions may be construed as a lack of compassion. The officer can greatly enhance the victim's recovery by offering compassion, empathy, and timely advice at the outset.

The officer must try to preserve the victim's dignity by asking as few questions as possible, while still taking care to obtain the information needed to start an investigation. Asking too many personal questions may be interpreted by the victim as an indication that the victim is a suspect. If all the information needed to start an investigation is obtained during the initial contact with the victim, the officer can return later to seek further details, thus giving the victim the opportunity to at least partially recover from his or her turmoil.

Victims of crime often have many questions about the criminal justice system and their involvement in it. Victims may want to know the status of an investigation and how the police are handling the matter. Has a suspect been arrested? Have criminal charges been laid? Will the matter go to court? Will it be necessary to testify in court?

This information can be provided by the investigating officer or through a referral to the office of the Crown.

The officer must be aware of the community and social services agencies that may be available to help the victim. Officers cannot help everyone with every problem, but they can at least provide information about where help can be obtained. The public relies on them for this information.

VICTIM AND WITNESS ASSISTANCE PROGRAMS
Victim Crisis Assistance and Referral Service Program

Ontario has various programs for offering assistance to crime victims. One such program is the Victim Crisis Assistance and Referral Service program (VCARS).

Victim services are available through community-based VCARS programs or independent police-based victim assistance programs that operate 24 hours a day, seven days a week, 365 days a year. In 2009, there were 48 VCARS organizations providing crisis support to victims of crime, tragedy, and disaster in Ontario (Ontario Network of Victim Service Providers, n.d.).

Each VCARS program is unique, and the services offered can vary. Selected VCARS sites provide Domestic Violence Emergency Response System (DVERS) portable home alarms to persons at very high risk of domestic violence and sexual assault. The DVERS allows women or men whose lives are threatened to immediately alert police by simply pressing a silent alarm. The alarms are monitored 24 hours a day, seven days a week.

Some VCARS programs include SupportLink, a program that provides wireless telephones pre-programmed to dial 911 in an emergency for persons at high risk of domestic violence, sexual assault, harassment, and stalking.

The services provided by VCARS programs are free of cost to the victim and are confidential unless there is evidence of suicidal or homicidal behaviour, or suspected child abuse. In these circumstances, police will be contacted.

VCARS programs work in partnership with local police services and other emergency service providers and provide immediate on-site service to victims of crime and tragic circumstances. The programs provide immediate short-term emotional support and practical assistance to victims of crime. This may include transporting and accompanying the victim to emergency services such as a shelter or hospital, making phone calls upon request, or performing other helpful tasks.

Such assistance can allow police to concentrate on investigational procedures or to leave the scene to attend to other calls for service, knowing the victim's needs are being met.

Victim/Witness Assistance Program

The goal of the Victim/Witness Assistance Program (V/WAP) is to enhance victims' and witnesses' understanding of and participation in the criminal justice process (Ontario Ministry of the Attorney General, 2008-2010). V/WAP offers courtroom orientation sessions, information about the criminal justice process generally, case-specific information (for example, the offender's bail and probation terms), and courtroom accompaniment services. It also acts as a liaison between victims and witnesses on the one hand and police officers and Crown attorneys on the other, provides referrals to community agencies for counselling and other support services, provides a public education and coordination function for government agencies and other government bodies within the community, and seeks community participation through the operation of an active volunteer program.

The program gives priority to acutely traumatized victims and witnesses. The groups who most frequently receive assistance are victims of and witnesses to spousal assault (particularly female spouses), sexual assault, and child abuse.

V/WAP provides training for Crown attorneys on the issues of spousal assault, sexual assault, and child abuse. It has developed an information and activity book for child witnesses that is available in both French and English. The V/WAP brochure itself is available in 13 languages.

The program has 45 offices in Ontario.

- *North:* For offices in North Region, contact 705-564-7269.
- *West:* For offices in West Region, contact 519-453-8973.
- *East:* For offices in East Region, contact 613-239-0392.
- *Central:* For offices in Central Region, contact 905-853-4852.
- *Central West:* For offices in Central West Region, contact 905-521-7590.
- *Toronto:* For offices in Toronto Region, contact 416-212-1310.

Victim Support Line

The Victim Support Line (VSL) is a province-wide, toll-free information line for crime victims in Ontario. It is sponsored by the Ministry of the Attorney General. The VSL offers service in 13 languages. By calling 1-888-579-2888 (or 416-314-2447 in Toronto), crime victims can obtain the following information from 8 a.m. to 10 p.m., 7 days a week:

- advice from a counsellor on appropriate services available in the victim's community (such as women's shelters and sexual assault counselling services);
- tape-recorded information on arrest and release procedures, the court system, probation and parole, and other subjects of interest to crime victims;
- information on how victims can ensure that their concerns are heard when a decision about releasing an offender is to be made; and
- the release status of any adult offender in the provincial corrections or parole system (available to the victim by registering with an automated callback system).

The Ministry of the Attorney General is responsible for all victim assistance programs. If a victim is unable to locate or access a regional or local program, he or she can contact the Office of the Attorney General at the following address and telephone number:

Ministry of the Attorney General
Victim/Witness Assistance Program
720 Bay Street, 9th Floor
Toronto, ON M7A 2S9
Telephone: 416-326-2429

THE VICTIM'S ACCESS TO INFORMATION ON OFFENDERS IN THE FEDERAL SYSTEM AFTER SENTENCING

(The following information does not apply to an accused who is a young offender.)

Section 26 of the *Corrections and Conditional Release Act* gives victims access to certain information about the offender after sentencing. If the National Parole Board decides that the victim's interests clearly outweigh the invasion of the offender's privacy, the victim or his or her agent may request information about the offender. The information that may be released includes:

- whether the offender is in custody, and if not, why;
- where the offender will be released;
- when the offender will be released;
- what type of release the offender has been released on—for example, parole, day pass, or work release; and
- any conditions attached to the offender's release.

The victim will not automatically be given this information. Application for the release of the information must be made by the victim or his or her agent. The victim or agent may also request ongoing information such as any movement of the offender from one correctional facility to another.

VICTIM PARTICIPATION IN PAROLE HEARINGS

At any time, but preferably as soon as possible after the offender is sentenced, victims may also provide a **victim impact statement** to the National Parole Board. (Note that victim impact statements may also be presented to a judge before sentencing. This topic is discussed below under the heading "Victim Impact Statements.") The statement should contain a written description of any harm done to the victim, any loss that he or she has suffered as a result of the offence, and any additional information that the victim feels may be important for the board to consider.

If the victim wants to present additional information to the court after the statement has been completed, an addendum may be added to the original statement through the investigating officer or the Crown attorney responsible for the case.

victim impact statement
a written description of any harm to a victim or loss suffered by a victim because of an offence; it is considered by the courts in sentencing and by parole boards at parole hearings

Once the offender begins his or her sentence with the correctional service, the victim may add to the victim impact statement at any time.

The board will use the information in its assessment of the likelihood of the offender reoffending or whether additional release conditions should be placed on the offender to enhance the protection of the victim.

The victim should be made aware that all the information provided will be disclosed to the offender with the exception of personal information such as the victim's address or phone number.

Victims can attend parole board hearings as observers, or may read a statement, in person or via audiotape or videotape, at a National Parole Board hearing. Applications to be an observer and/or to read a statement should be submitted to the board as far in advance of a hearing as possible. Victims may apply for funding to cover expenses associated with their attendance at parole hearings by calling the Victims Fund Manager toll-free at 1-866-544-1007.

For more information on parole, or to submit a victim impact statement, the victim can contact the National Parole Board at one of the following five regional offices:

1. Atlantic Region
   National Parole Board
   1045 Main Street, 1st Floor, Room 101
   Moncton, NB E1C 1H1
   Telephone: 1-800-265-8644 or 1-888-396-9188
   Fax: 506-851-6926

2. Ontario Region
   National Parole Board
   516 O'Connor Drive
   Kingston, ON K7P 1N3
   Telephone: 1-800-518-8817
   Fax: 613-634-3861

3. Pacific Region
   National Parole Board
   32315 South Fraser Way, Suite 305
   Abbotsford, BC V2T 1W6
   Telephone: 1-888-999-8828
   Fax: 604-870-2498

4. Prairies Region
   National Parole Board
   101–22nd Street East, 6th Floor
   Saskatoon, SK S7K 0E1
   Telehone: 1-888-616-5277
   Fax: 306-975-5892

5. Quebec Region
   National Parole Board
   Guy-Favreau Complex
   200 René-Lévesque Blvd. West
   10th Floor, Suite 1001, West Tower
   Montreal, QC H2Z 1X4
   Telephone: 1-877-333-4473
   Fax: 514-283-5484

CRIMINAL INJURIES COMPENSATION

A victim injured as a result of a criminal act should be informed that he or she may be entitled to monetary compensation. This compensation does not prohibit the victim from seeking damages in civil court.

The Criminal Injuries Compensation Board is a quasi-judicial tribunal that provides compensation to victims of violent crime in Ontario (or their survivors). Applications may be made by victims who have been injured by a criminal act as defined under the *Criminal Code*, or by the survivors of persons killed as a result of such an act. An application for compensation must be made within two years of the date of the incident.

When deciding whether to make an award for compensation, the board considers the following (Criminal Injuries Compensation Board, n.d.):

- Whether a violent crime under the *Criminal Code* or an arrest has occurred, or whether the injured or deceased person was assisting a peace officer with his or her law enforcement duties, or trying to prevent a crime from occurring. The board considers the provisions of the *Criminal Code* in effect at the time of the incident.
- Whether there is enough reliable information available to support the claim.
- All of the relevant circumstances, including any behaviour of the injured or deceased person that caused or contributed to the injuries or death.
- Whether the applicant refused reasonable cooperation with the police or failed to report the offence promptly to the police.
- Whether the applicant received any benefits paid by private insurance, the Workplace Safety and Insurance Board or any other source, as a result of the crime (not including Ontario Works or the Ontario Disability Support Program).

For the board to properly adjudicate a claim, credible evidence must be provided. Proof that the offender was convicted of a criminal offence as described in s. 11 of the *Compensation for Victims of Crime Act* constitutes credible evidence.

Compensation may be awarded for

- expenses actually and reasonably incurred as a result of the victim's injury or death;
- emergency expenses such as medical expenses, funeral expenses up to $9,000, and interim counselling expenses up to $5,000;

- lost wages up to $250 a week, when the monetary loss is a consequence of a total or partial disability affecting the victim's capacity to work;
- financial losses suffered by the dependants of a deceased victim;
- pain and suffering; and
- maintenance of a child born as a result of a sexual assault.

When one person is injured or killed as a result of a violent crime, the *maximum* amount that may be awarded as a one-time payment is $25,000.

When more than one person has been injured or killed as the result of a violent crime, a *maximum* of $150,000 as a one-time payment may be awarded.

Ongoing monthly periodic payments can be awarded in cases where there is an ongoing financial loss (for example, lost income or childcare expenses). When a periodic award is made, the amount of the lump-sum component cannot exceed $12,500. The *maximum* amount awarded as a periodic payment is $1,000 per month. Periodic payments cannot exceed a total of $365,000. Periodic awards are reviewed annually to determine whether the victim still qualifies for the funds.

More information can be obtained from the board's office:

Criminal Injuries Compensation Board
439 University Avenue, 4th Floor
Toronto, ON M5G 1Y8
Telephone: 1-800-372-7463 (or 416-326-2900 in the Toronto calling area)

THE COURT PROCESS

The victim has the right to know the name of the accused unless the accused is a young offender. Also, information about the offence with which the accused is charged, and when and where court proceedings will commence, must be provided if requested.

Court procedures should be explained to victims in plain language. Victims benefit from an understanding of the judicial process, and having this information can help them decide whether they wish to attend the proceedings. The possibility that a victim may see the accused in a public place while the accused is at large under the conditions of a judicial interim release or other release order should be explained to the victim. Conditions requiring the accused to abstain from contact with the victim should also be disclosed and explained.

If a victim is to be called as a witness, the procedures for testifying should be explained, including the possibility of cross-examination. The fact that the accused will be present in court should also be mentioned. Assuring a victim that he or she will be safe and that the accused will not be allowed to harm or harass him or her in court may alleviate a possible fear of testifying.

Victims should also be advised about their rights under s. 722 of the *Criminal Code*, which allows a victim to submit a victim impact statement before a convicted person is sentenced.

Victim Impact Statements

A victim impact statement allows an opportunity for participation in the sentencing and post-sentencing stages of the criminal justice process (Victims of Violence, 2008). The statement provides the victim with a voice through which they can express to the offender, the judge, and correctional and parole authorities how the crime has affected their life. The victim impact statement may affect the terms of an offender's sentence, as well as decisions for conditional release. In some cases, the judge may also order payment for losses or expenses that the victim outlines in their statement. This could include the value of damaged property, health-care costs, and income lost as a result of the crime.

A victim impact statement is a written statement that describes the harm or loss suffered by the victim of an offence. The statement may contain information describing the physical, emotional, and financial impact of the crime. The victim impact statement is completed by any individual to whom harm has been done or who has suffered physical or emotional loss as a result of the crime.

The statement may be completed by the victim or someone on their behalf. One person can act as a "spokesperson" for the rest of the family, or all members of the family may be able to fill out a statement. These options should be discussed with the Crown beforehand.

The victim or their family may obtain assistance in preparing the statement from law enforcement, the Crown, court-based victim/witness programs, community based agencies, and/or victim advocacy organizations.

A "victim" is defined in s. 722(4) of the *Criminal Code*.

Definition of "Victim": Criminal Code, Section 722(4)

722(4) For the purposes of this section and section 722.2, "victim," in relation to an offence,

(a) means a person to whom harm was done or who suffered physical or emotional loss as a result of the commission of the offence; and

(b) where the person described in paragraph (a) is dead, ill or otherwise incapable of making a statement referred to in subsection (1), includes the spouse or common-law partner or any relative of that person, anyone who has in law or fact the custody of that person or is responsible for the care or support of that person or any dependant of that person.

While the preparation and submission of a victim impact statement is the victim's choice, consideration of the statement by the judge is mandatory. The *Criminal Code* is clear; where a victim impact statement has been prepared, the sentencing judge must consider the statement.

Victim Impact Statement: Criminal Code, Section 722(1)

722(1) For the purpose of determining the sentence to be imposed on an offender or whether the offender should be discharged pursuant to section 730 in respect of any offence, the court shall consider any statement that may have been prepared in accordance with subsection (2) of a victim of the offence describing the harm done to, or loss suffered by, the victim arising from the commission of the offence.

Procedure for Victim Impact Statement: Criminal Code, Section 722(2)

722(2) A statement referred to in subsection (1) must be
(a) prepared in writing in the form and in accordance with the procedures established by a program designated for that purpose by the lieutenant governor in council of the province in which the court is exercising its jurisdiction; and
(b) filed with the court.

The victim will be allowed to read the statement in court if he or she so chooses.

Presentation of Statement: Criminal Code, Section 722(2.1)

722(2.1) The court shall, on the request of a victim, permit the victim to read a statement prepared and filed in accordance with subsection (2), or to present the statement in any other manner that the court considers appropriate.

Upon conviction, if a victim impact statement has not been presented, the presiding judge will ask the Crown, the victim, or a representative of the victim whether a victim impact statement has been prepared. If a statement has not been prepared and the victim wishes to prepare one, the judge may adjourn proceedings if such an adjournment would be consistent with the proper administration of justice.

Inquiry by Court: Criminal Code, Section 722.2(1)

722.2(1) As soon as practicable after a finding of guilt and in any event before imposing sentence, the court shall inquire of the prosecutor or a victim of the offence, or any person representing a victim of the offence, whether the victim or victims have been advised of the opportunity to prepare a statement referred to in subsection 722(1).

Adjournment: Criminal Code, Section 722.2(2)

722.2(2) On application of the prosecutor or a victim or on its own motion, the court may adjourn the proceedings to permit the victim to prepare a statement referred to in subsection 722(1) or to present evidence in accordance with subsection 722(3), if the court is satisfied that the adjournment would not interfere with the proper administration of justice.

The *Youth Criminal Justice Act* includes provisions allowing the use of victim impact statements following the same procedures as the *Criminal Code.*

Application of Part XXIII of Criminal Code: Youth Criminal Justice Act, Section 50(1)

50(1) Subject to section 74 (application of *Criminal Code* to adult sentences), Part XXIII (sentencing) of the Criminal Code does not apply in respect of proceedings under this Act except for paragraph 718.2(e) (sentencing principle for aboriginal offenders), sections 722 (victim impact statements), 722.1 (copy of statement) and 722.2 (inquiry by court), subsection 730(2) (court process continues in force) and sections 748 (pardons and remissions), 748.1 (remission by the Governor in Council) and 749 (royal prerogative) of that Act, which provisions apply with any modifications that the circumstances require.

RESTITUTION

Victims should also be informed of the availability of a **restitution order** as described in s. 738 of the *Criminal Code*.

restitution order
a court order that instructs an offender to make a payment to a victim to compensate him or her for property damage and/or bodily harm

Restitution to Victims of Offences: Criminal Code, Section 738(1)

738(1) Where an offender is convicted or discharged under section 730 of an offence, the court imposing sentence on or discharging the offender may, on application of the Attorney General or on its own motion, in addition to any other measure imposed on the offender, order that the offender make restitution to another person as follows:

(a) in the case of damage to, or the loss or destruction of, the property of any person as a result of the commission of the offence or the arrest or attempted arrest of the offender, by paying to the person an amount not exceeding the replacement value of the property as of the date the order is imposed, less the value of any part of the property that is returned to that person as of the date it is returned, where the amount is readily ascertainable;

(b) in the case of bodily or psychological harm to any person as a result of the commission of the offence or the arrest or attempted arrest of the offender, by paying to the person an amount not exceeding all pecuniary damages incurred as a result of the harm, including loss of income or support, if the amount is readily ascertainable;

(c) in the case of bodily harm or threat of bodily harm to the offender's spouse or common-law partner or child, or any other person, as a result of the commission of the offence or the arrest or attempted arrest of the offender, where the spouse or common-law partner, child or other person was a member of the offender's household at the relevant time, by paying to the person in question, independently of any amount ordered to be paid under paragraphs (a) and (b), an amount not exceeding actual and reasonable expenses incurred by that person, as a result of moving out of the offender's household, for temporary housing, food, child care and transportation, where the amount is readily ascertainable; and

(d) in the case of an offence under section 402.2 or 403, by paying to a person who, as a result of the offence, incurs expenses to re-establish their identity, including expenses to replace their identity documents and to correct their credit history and credit rating, an amount that is not more than the amount of those expenses, to the extent that they are reasonable, if the amount is readily ascertainable.

Restitution may be ordered in [four] circumstances. Under para. (1)(a), the offender can be required to pay to persons whose property was lost or destroyed the replacement value of the property, provided that the damage or loss or destruction of the property was the result of the commission of the offence or the arrest or attempted arrest of the offender. The amount to be paid cannot exceed the replacement value of the property at the time the order is made less the value of any of the property that has been returned to the person. Under para. (1)(b) the offender may be required to pay an amount not exceeding all pecuniary damages, including loss of income and support, to any person who suffered bodily harm [or psychological harm] as a result of the commission of the offence or the arrest or attempted arrest of the offender. Paragraph (1)(c) allows the court to order the offender to pay an amount not exceeding the actual and reasonable expenses incurred by a spouse, [common-law partner,] child or other person who was a member of the offender's household, as a result of moving out of the offender's household, for temporary housing, food, child care and transportation. Paragraph (1)(c) only applies in the case of bodily harm or threat of bodily harm to the offender's spouse, [common-law partner,] child or any other person as a result of the commission of the offence or the arrest or attempted arrest of the offender. [Under paragraph 1(d), in the case of an offence under s. 402.2 or 403, where as a result of the offence a person incurs expenses to re-establish their identity, the court may order the offender to pay an amount not exceeding those expenses, to the extent that those expenses are reasonable.] In all cases the amount must be "readily ascertainable." [*Martin's Annual Criminal Code, 2012*, pp. 1492-1493]

SPECIAL SITUATIONS

The following sections discuss certain situations that can be traumatic for victims and others: the aftermath of a break-and-enter, and injury and death notifications. The information provided below is intended for general guidance only. Individual police services may have their own policies regarding the situations described below.

Break-and-Enter

The crime of break-and-enter is common in many places. The frequency of its occurrence may lead an investigating officer to treat the crime as routine and forget how devastating it can be for the victim.

The property taken may, even if its monetary value is insignificant, have great sentimental value for the victim. And in addition to the property loss, the victim may feel violated because his or her personal space has been encroached upon. The victim may experience feelings of insecurity, shock, fear, and outrage.

The attending officer must, of course, perform his or her investigative duties, but should try to remain sensitive to the victim's needs. The officer should be empathetic and seek to view the event from the victim's perspective. And the officer should not create an unrealistic expectation that the property will be returned, because in many instances it cannot be recovered.

Information about preventing future break-and-enters may help alleviate some of the victim's fear and apprehension. The police can provide information on programs such as Neighbourhood Watch, on security devices such as alarm systems, and on security measures such as remembering to lock all doors and windows. This advice may seem insignificant, but imparting it may allow the victim to regain a sense of control over his or her domestic space.

A follow-up call by the police, and having an officer visibly present in the neighbourhood, will also help reinforce positive contact with the victim.

Restitution of Property

A person whose stolen property has been recovered may feel greatly inconvenienced and also revictimized if the property is withheld by the police for use as evidence. For this reason, the property should be returned as soon as possible once it is no longer needed for court proceedings or to preserve the continuity of evidence. The *Criminal Code* addresses restitution of property in ss. 489.1, 490, and 491.2, below. The latter section concerns the use of photographs in court in lieu of the property itself.

Restitution of Property or Report by Peace Officer: Criminal Code, Section 489.1(1)

489.1(1) Subject to this or any other Act of Parliament, where a peace officer has seized anything under a warrant issued under this Act or under section 487.11 or 489 or otherwise in the execution of duties under this or any other Act of Parliament, the peace officer shall, as soon as is practicable,

(a) where the peace officer is satisfied,

(i) that there is no dispute as to who is lawfully entitled to possession of the thing seized, and

(ii) that the continued detention of the thing seized is not required for the purposes of any investigation or a preliminary inquiry, trial or other proceeding,

return the thing seized, on being issued a receipt therefor, to the person lawfully entitled to its possession and report to the justice who issued the warrant or some other justice for the same territorial division or, if no warrant was issued, a justice having jurisdiction in respect of the matter, that he has done so; or

(b) where the peace officer is not satisfied as described in subparagraphs (a)(i) and (ii),

(i) bring the thing seized before the justice referred to in paragraph (a), or

(ii) report to the justice that he has seized the thing and is detaining it or causing it to be detained

to be dealt with by the justice in accordance with subsection 490(1).

Detention of Things Seized: Criminal Code, Section 490(1)

490(1) Subject to this or any other Act of Parliament, where, pursuant to paragraph 489.1(1)(b) or subsection 489.1(2), anything that has been seized is brought before a justice or a report in respect of anything seized is made to a justice, the justice shall,

(a) where the lawful owner or person who is lawfully entitled to possession of the thing seized is known, order it to be returned to that owner or person, unless the prosecutor, or the peace officer or other person having custody of the thing seized, satisfies the justice that the detention of the thing seized is required for the purposes of any investigation or a preliminary inquiry, trial or other proceeding; or

(b) where the prosecutor, or the peace officer or other person having custody of the thing seized, satisfies the justice that the thing seized should be detained for a reason set out in paragraph (a), detain the thing seized or order that it be detained, taking reasonable care to ensure that it is preserved until the conclusion of any investigation or until it is required to be produced for the purposes of a preliminary inquiry, trial or other proceeding.

In all situations, the officer must report the disposition of seized property through the use of a Report to a Justice, Form 5.2 of the *Criminal Code*. A copy of Form 5.2 is found in Appendix 9A at the end of this chapter.

Photographic Evidence: Criminal Code, Section 491.2(1)

491.2(1) Before any property that would otherwise be required to be produced for the purposes of a preliminary inquiry, trial or other proceeding in respect of an offence under section 334 [theft under $5,000], 344 [armed robbery], 348 [break-and-enter], 354 [possession of stolen property], 355.2 [trafficking in property obtained by crime], 355.4 [possession of property obtained by crime—trafficking], 362 [false pretences] or 380 [fraud] is returned or ordered to be returned, forfeited or otherwise dealt with under section 489.1 or 490 or is otherwise returned, a peace officer or any person under the direction of a peace officer may take and retain a photograph of the property.

Certified Photograph Admissible in Evidence: Criminal Code, Section 491.2(2)

491.2(2) Every photograph of property taken under subsection (1), accompanied by a certificate of a person containing the statements referred to in subsection (3), shall be admissible in evidence and, in the absence of evidence to the contrary, shall have the same probative force as the property would have had if it had been proved in the ordinary way.

Statements Made in Certificate: Criminal Code, Section 491.2(3)

491.2(3) For the purposes of subsection (2), a certificate of a person stating that
   (a) the person took the photograph under the authority of subsection (1),
   (b) the person is a peace officer or took the photograph under the direction of a peace officer, and
   (c) the photograph is a true photograph

shall be admissible in evidence and, in the absence of evidence to the contrary, is evidence of the statements contained in the certificate without proof of the signature of the person appearing to have signed the certificate.

Secondary Evidence of Peace Officer: Criminal Code, Section 491.2(4)

491.2(4) An affidavit or solemn declaration of a peace officer or other person stating that the person has seized property and detained it or caused it to be detained from the time that person took possession of the property until a photograph of the property was taken under subsection (1) and that the property was not altered in any manner before the photograph was taken shall be admissible in evidence and, in the absence of evidence to the contrary, is evidence of the statements contained in the affidavit or solemn declaration without proof of the signature or official character of the person appearing to have signed the affidavit or solemn declaration.

At times it is not feasible to physically bring evidence to court (for example, if an object is large or perishable). In these cases a photograph that meets the requirements of s. 491.2 will be admissible.

Learning Activity 9.2

Determine in the following scenarios whether property should be returned, retained by police, or photographed and then returned (where a photograph of the evidence is sufficient for the purposes of an investigation and court proceedings). Note: Police services may have specific policies regarding the procedures to be followed when returning property. Officers are required to follow the policies of their respective police services.

Scenario 1
Police investigating an incident of theft under $5,000 seize 50 unopened CDs and DVDs from a suspect. The suspect is charged with theft under $5,000. The store owner wants the items returned to her.

Should the items be returned to the store owner?

Scenario 2
While executing a search warrant, police seize 1 gram of cocaine. The person in possession of the drug is charged and fined $1,000. The person pays the fine and asks that the cocaine be returned.

Should the cocaine be returned?

> **Scenario 3**
> Police are investigating an incident of assault with a weapon. A knife used in the assault has been seized. Forensic evidence concludes that the knife was used in the assault. A trial date has been set for the accused. The victim of the assault is also the owner of the knife. He asks that the knife be immediately returned because it is one of a set of 12 that was given to him as a gift.
>
> Should the knife be returned?
>
> **Scenario 4**
> A homicide has occurred. The victim died as a result of injuries sustained through an assault with a baseball bat. At the conclusion of the trial and the period allowed for appeal, the owner of the bat requests that it be returned to him. He wants to auction the baseball bat on the Internet.
>
> Should the baseball bat be returned to the owner?

Injury and Death Notifications

Injury and death notifications are a necessary but unpleasant aspect of policing. The reaction of the friend or relative who receives the news can range from calm acceptance to hysteria. Officers can prepare themselves to handle these situations and alleviate some of the turmoil experienced by those who receive the news by following the guidelines in this section.

The responding officer should ensure that he or she has all the pertinent information and that it is accurate. The following information is required:

- The name of the injured or deceased person. If the person has not been positively identified, a friend or family member may be required to identify him or her.
- The facts surrounding the injury or death.
- The exact location of the incident.
- The names of the attending officers (if the responding officer was not at the scene).

Once this information has been obtained, the officer attends the residence of the victim's partner or relative to notify him or her of the situation. Information should not be released to the media before notification. The following are some suggestions that may help alleviate the mental anguish experienced by friends and family:

- The officer must ensure that he or she is attending the proper address.
- If possible, another officer or resource person should attend at the residence along with the primary responding officer.
- The officer should introduce himself or herself and any others in attendance.
- The persons receiving the news should be asked to sit down (if they are outside the residence, they should be asked to go inside). In most instances, people are upset by the arrival of a police officer at their

residence. An officer should not worsen matters by walking into a residence without first asking to be invited in.

- The officer must be polite, patient, respectful, and professional. The information relayed by the officer will be regarded as truthful, accurate, and sincere.

- Information about the incident should be relayed truthfully, but need not be graphic. If the case is a homicide and it is possible that details of a graphic nature will be discussed in court, the officer should, sometime before the trial date, disclose the details to the affected persons before they hear them in court.

- The officer should not speculate about what happened, but simply relay the facts.

- The officer should listen and respond to questions as truthfully as possible, and remain empathetic and compassionate. The officer should not rush matters.

- Within the limits of police service policies, all possible assistance should be provided to the persons being notified.

- The persons being notified should not be left alone. With their permission, a relative, friend, or representative of a service such as the Victim Crisis Assistance and Referral Service can be asked to stay.

- A follow-up call will help confirm that the police are compassionate and concerned.

KEY TERMS

restitution order
victim impact statement

REFERENCES

Brennan, S., & Dauvergne, M. (2011, July). Police-reported crime statistics in Canada, 2010. *Juristat* (catalogue no. 85-002-X). Ottawa: Minister of Industry.

Corrections and Conditional Release Act. (1992). SC 1992, c. 20.

Criminal Code. (1985). RSC 1985, c. C-46, as amended.

Criminal Injuries Compensation Board. (n.d.). *Board considerations.* Retrieved from http://www.cicb.gov.on.ca.

Department of Justice Canada. (2003). *Department of Justice Canada—Victims of crime.* Retrieved from http://www.justice.gc.ca.

Martin's Annual Criminal Code, 2012. (2012). Aurora, ON: Canada Law Book.

Ontario Ministry of the Attorney General. (2008-2010). *Programs and services for victims of crime.* Retrieved from http://www.attorneygeneral.jus.gov.on.ca.

Ontario Network of Victim Service Providers. (n.d.). *History of VCARS*. Retrieved from http://www.victimservicesontario.ca/page.asp?idpage=8127&webaddress=onvsp.

Provincial Offences Act. (1990). RSO 1990, c. P.33.

Statistics Canada. (2010, September 28). General Social Survey: Victimization, 2009. *The Daily* (catalogue no. 11-001-XIE).

Victim Fine Surcharges. (2000). O. Reg. 161/00.

Victims' Bill of Rights, 1995. (1995). SO 1995, c. 6.

Victims of Violence. (2008). *Victim impact statements*. Retrieved from http://www.victimsofviolence.on.ca/rev2/index.php?option=com_content&task=view&id=364&Itemid=54.

Youth Criminal Justice Act. (2002). SC 2002, c. 1.

EXERCISES

SHORT ANSWER

1. How are victim services programs funded in the province of Ontario?

2. Explain when photographs of seized property may be introduced into court as evidence.

3. Explain the purpose of the Victim Crisis Assistance and Referral Service program.

4. What is the purpose of the Victim/Witness Assistance Program?

5. How can a victim of crime ascertain the release status of an incarcerated adult offender?

6. What is the maximum monetary compensation available through the Criminal Injuries Compensation Board?

7. What is a restitution order?

APPENDIX 9A FORM 5.2, CRIMINAL CODE

FORM 5.2

(Section 489.1)

REPORT TO A JUSTICE

Canada,

Province of . . . . ,

(territorial division).

To the justice who issued a warrant to the undersigned pursuant to section 256, 487 or 487.1 of the Criminal Code (or another justice for the same territorial division or, if no warrant was issued, any justice having jurisdiction in respect of the matter).

I, *(name of the peace officer or other person)* have *(state here whether you have acted under a warrant issued pursuant to section 256, 487 or 487.1 of the Criminal Code or under section 489 of the Criminal Code or otherwise in the execution of duties under the Criminal Code or other Act of Parliament to be specified)*

1. searched the premises situated at . . . . ; and

2. seized the following things and dealt with them as follows:

Property Seized *(describe each thing seized)*	Disposition (state, in respect of each thing seized, whether *(a) it was returned to the person lawfully entitled to its possession, in which case the receipt therefor shall be attached hereto, or* *(b) it is being detained to be dealt with according to law, and the location and manner in which, or where applicable, the person by whom it is being detained).*
1.	. . . .
2.	. . . .
3.	. . . .
4.	. . . .

In the case of a warrant issued by telephone or other means of telecommunication, the statements referred to in subsection 487.1(9) of the *Criminal Code* shall be specified in the report.

Dated this . . . . day of . . . . A.D. . . . . at . . . .

. . . .

Signature of peace officer or other person

Glossary

abuse

in the *Child and Family Services Act*, a state or condition of being physically harmed, sexually molested, or sexually exploited

active listening

devoting complete attention to a message to ensure full and accurate understanding

acute stress

a reaction to one or more specific critical incidents that are beyond the individual's ability to cope

ageism

discriminatory belief that the elderly are generally frail, dependent, sick, and unproductive

aggressiveness

in the context of conflict situations, attacking a person's perspective in an antagonistic manner

Alzheimer's disease

a progressive, degenerative disease that destroys brain cells and causes dementia

antisocial personality disorder

condition whose essential feature is a pervasive pattern of disregard for, and violation of, the rights of others that begins in childhood or early adolescence and continues into adulthood

articulable cause

suspicion based on some discernible fact

assertiveness

in the context of conflict situations, confidently stating a position in a forceful but non-aggressive manner

bipolar disorder

illness characterized by alternating periods of mania and depression

CAPRA

a problem-solving system with five components: clients (and communication skills), acquiring and analyzing information, partnerships, response, and assessment

child sexual abuse

any activity or behaviour that is sexual in nature and directed toward a child

child

generally, a person under the age of 18; under some legislation, a person under the age of 16 or 14

client

anyone directly or indirectly involved in an occurrence, or in any way affected by it

clinical depression

an illness that is characterized by a continually low, sad, and depressed mood and that interferes with the individual's ability to work, sleep, eat, and enjoy once-pleasurable activities

coerce

use threats or force to require another person to do something against his or her will

cognitive behavioural therapy

psychological treatment to change maladaptive thoughts, feelings, beliefs, and habits

conflict

a dispute in which the goals or motives of the involved parties are incompatible; a conflict may not require police intervention

criminal harassment

conduct that makes a person fear for his or her safety or for the safety of someone he or she knows; also called stalking

crisis

a situation in which the parties involved in a conflict can no longer effectively deal with the stress of the conflict

 cumulative stress

stress that is caused by long-term, frequent, low-level stress; also called chronic stress

delirium

state of confusion accompanied by disorientation and an altered level of awareness

delusion

defect in belief or thought processes that is not reasonable

delusions of persecution

false and irrational beliefs that a person is being harassed, cheated, poisoned, or conspired against

dementia

mental deterioration characterized by confusion, memory loss, and disorientation

dependent personality

person who is overreliant on others for his or her physical and emotional needs

depression

an illness involving one's body, mood, and thoughts; characterized by persistent feelings of sadness and loss of interest

elder abuse

any violence or mistreatment directed toward an elderly person by someone on whom the elderly person depends for food, shelter, or other aid

elderly person

a person 65 years of age or older

emotional/psychological abuse

behaviour intended to control or instill fear in a person, cause a person to fear for his or her safety, or diminish a person's sense of self-worth

excited delirium

state of acute agitation and hyperactivity, usually accompanied by violent behaviour

fight or flight response

the body's physiological response to a perceived threat; chemicals are released into the bloodstream, producing mental and physical changes that increase the person's ability to fight or flee from the threat

financial abuse

actions that result in financial loss or financial harm to a person

hallucination

sensory perception that is real only to the person experiencing it

indictable offence

a crime that is more serious than a summary conviction offence, that carries heavier penalties, and that may be tried by a judge or a judge and jury

influence

use effective communication techniques to affect another person's thought process and behaviours with the objective of persuading the person to change his or her perspective

inquest

investigation by a coroner into the cause of a unexpected or sudden death

 intervention

for the purposes of this text, any verbal or physical interference by police for the purpose of managing the course of events in an effort to change or modify any negative outcome

intrapersonal stress

stress that can occur when a person believes that his or her abilities do not coincide with his or her position in life

mediation

assisted negotiation in which a third party helps the disputants resolve their disagreement themselves

mental illness

for the purpose of police intervention, a departure from "normal" thinking that affects a person's ability to interact with his or her environment

neglect

caregiver omissions in providing adequate care that result in actual or potential harm to a child; failing to care for or meet the needs of elderly persons who are dependent and cannot meet their own needs

organizational stress

stress that emanates from the police service itself, including policies and procedures that govern and direct the officer's actions

 PARE

a problem-solving system with four components: problem identification, analysis, response, and evaluation

pedophile

a person who is sexually attracted to children

person in crisis

a person pushed beyond his or her ability to cope with stress from any source

physical abuse

the use of force in a way that injures a person or poses a risk of injury to a person

postpartum depression

symptoms of depression that can range from a brief attack of the "baby blues" to clinical depression

post-traumatic stress disorder (PTSD)

a disorder in which a person is unable to recover from physical, emotional, and psychological stress caused by exposure to a "psychologically traumatic event involving actual or threatened death or serious injury to self or others"

power of attorney

legal instrument that authorizes a person to carry out specific acts on behalf of another person

psychosis

disturbance in brain functioning, during which the person experiences loss of contact with reality

restitution order

a court order that instructs an offender to make a payment to a victim to compensate him or her for property damage and/or bodily harm

SARA

a problem-solving process with four components: scanning, analysis, response, and assessment

schizophrenia

a family of psychological disorders characterized by psychotic thoughts, feelings, perceptions, and actions

self-injury

the act of attempting to alter a mood state by self-inflicting physical harm serious enough to cause tissue damage to the body

sexual abuse

engagement in any form of sexual activity with a person without the full consent of that person; includes all forms of sexual assault, sexual harassment, or sexual exploitation

spousal abuse

the physical, sexual, emotional/psychological, or financial abuse of one spouse by another

spouse

any person involved in a relationship of cohabitation

stress

a response to a perceived threat or challenge or change; a physical or psychological response to a demand

stressor

something that causes a stress reaction or response

sudden infant death syndrome (SIDS)

the sudden, unexpected, and unexplained death of an infant during sleep

summary conviction offence

a crime that is less serious than an indictable offence and that is tried without a jury or preliminary hearing

three Ps (plan, past, and partners)

a risk assessment tool that determines whether there is a plan for suicide, a past history of suicide attempts, and partners who can reduce the risk of suicide by helping the person solve his or her problems

unusual realities

perceptions of reality and views of the world that are sharply different from those of people who are not mentally ill and that may cause anxiety and confusion

victim impact statement

a written description of any harm to a victim or loss suffered by a victim due to an offence; it is considered by the courts in sentencing and by parole boards at parole hearings

victim-precipitated suicide

the use of police to commit suicide, achieved by challenging police with a lethal or apparently lethal weapon, giving them no choice but to use lethal force to stop the threat; often referred to as "suicide by cop"

violence

any unwanted act of aggression resulting in physical contact

Index

Credits

Page 97: Figure 4.1, Rates of Violent Victimization Highest Among Youth Aged 15 to 17. Source: *Child and Youth Victims of Police-reported Violent Crime, 2008*, 85F0033MWE2010023, no. 23, March 2010; http://www.statcan.gc.ca/bsolc/olc-cel/olc-cel?catno=85F0033MWE&lang=eng.

Page 97: Figure 4.2, Rates of Violence Steadily Increase, Peaking at Age 17 for Both Girls and Boys, 2008. Source: *Child and Youth Victims of Police-Reported Violent Crime, 2008*, 85F0033MWE2010023, no. 23, March 2010; http://www.statcan.gc.ca/bsolc/olc-cel/olc-cel?catno=85F0033MWE&lang=eng.

Page 100: Figure 4.3, Sexual Assault Rates Highest Among 13- to 15-Year-Old Girls, 2008. Source: *Child and Youth Victims of Police-Reported Violent Crime, 2008*, 85F0033MWE2010023, no. 23, March 2010; http://www.statcan.gc.ca/bsolc/olc-cel/olc-cel?catno=85F0033MWE&lang=eng.

Page 102: Table 4.1, Child and Youth Victims of Violence by Method of Violence Causing Injury and Sex of Victim, Reported to a Subset of Police Services, 2008. Source: *Child and Youth Victims of Police-Reported Violent Crime, 2008*, 85F0033MWE2010023, no. 23, March 2010; http://www.statcan.gc.ca/bsolc/olc-cel/olc-cel?catno=85F0033MWE&lang=eng.

Page 104: Table 4.2, Victims of Violence by Age Group and Offence Type, Reported to a Subset of Police Services, 2008. Source: *Child and Youth Victims of Police-Reported Violent Crime, 2008*, 85F0033MWE2010023, no. 23, March 2010; http://www.statcan.gc.ca/bsolc/olc-cel/olc-cel?catno=85F0033MWE&lang=eng.

Page 132: Table 4.3, Appropriateness of Sexual Behaviours: Toddlers and Preschoolers. *Understanding Your Child's Sexual Behavior: What's Natural and Healthy* by JOHNSON, TONI C. Copyright 1999. Reproduced with permission of NEW HARBINGER PUBLICATIONS in the format Textbook via Copyright Clearance Center.

Page 133: Table 4.4, Appropriateness of Sexual Behaviours: School-Aged Children. *Understanding Your Child's Sexual Behavior: What's Natural and Healthy* by JOHNSON, TONI C. Copyright 1999. Reproduced with permission of NEW HARBINGER PUBLICATIONS in the format Textbook via Copyright Clearance Center.

Page 195: Appendix 4A, Information in Support of a Warrant to Apprehend and Return a Child Who Has Withdrawn from a Parent's Control. © Queen's Printer for Ontario, 2011. Reproduced with permission.

Page 197: Appendix 4B, Warrant to Apprehend and Return a Child Who Has Withdrawn from a Parent's Control. © Queen's Printer for Ontario, 2000. Reproduced with permission.

Page 201: Table 5.1, Victims of Self-Reported Spousal Violence in Current Relationships Within the Past 12 Months, by Sex and Selected Demographic Characteristics, 1999, 2004, and 2009. Source: Statistics Canada, *Family Violence in Canada: A Statistical Profile*, 85-224-XIE2010000, January 2011; http://www.statcan.gc.ca/bsolc/olc-cel/olc-cel?catno=85-224-X&chropg=1&lang=eng.

Page 202: Table 5.2, Victims of Self-Reported Spousal Violence Within the Past Five Years, by Type of Violence, 1999, 2004, and 2009. Source: Statistics Canada, *Family Violence in Canada: A Statistical Profile*, 85-224-XIE2010000, January 2011; http://www.statcan.gc.ca/bsolc/olc-cel/olc-cel?catno=85-224-X&chropg=1&lang=eng.

Page 203: Figure 5.1, Victims of Self-Reported Spousal Violence, by Most Serious Form of Violence, by Sex, 2009. Source: Statistics Canada, *Family Violence in Canada: A Statistical Profile*, 85-224-XIE2010000, January 2011; http://www.statcan.gc.ca/bsolc/olc-cel/olc-cel?catno=85-224-X&chropg=1&lang=eng.

Page 204: Figure 5.2, Reasons for Not Reporting Spousal Violence to Police, by Sex, 2009. Source: Statistics Canada, *Family Violence in Canada: A Statistical Profile*, 85-224-XIE2010000, January 2011; http://www.statcan.gc.ca/bsolc/olc-cel/ olc-cel?catno=85-224-X&chropg=1&lang=eng.

Page 206: Table 5.3, Victims of Spousal Violence by Offence Type and Sex of Victim, Reported to a Subset of Police Services, 2007. Source: Statistics Canada, *Family Violence in Canada: A Statistical Profile 2009*, October 2009; http://www.statcan.gc.ca/bsolc/olc-cel/ olc-cel?catno=85-224-X&chropg=1&lang=eng.

Page 207: Figure 5.3, Level 1 Assault the Most Common Offence Against Current and Former Spouses, Criminal Harassment and Threats More Common Among Ex-Spouses, 2007. Source: Statistics Canada, *Family Violence in Canada: A Statistical Profile*, 85-224-XIE2009000, October 2009; http://www.statcan.gc.ca/bsolc/olc-cel/ olc-cel?catno=85-224-X&chropg=1&lang=eng.

Page 212: Figure 5.4, Danger Assessment Instrument. Campbell, J.C. (2004). *Danger Assessment*. Retrieved November 25, 2011, from http://www.dangerassessment .org. Campbell J.C., Webster, D.W., Glass N. (2009). The danger assessment: Validation of a lethality risk assessment instrument for intimate partner femicide. *Journal of Interpersonal Violence, 24*(4): 653–674.

Page 219: Figure 5.5, Victims of Self-Reported Emotional and Financial Abuse, by Sex and Type of Abuse, 2009. Source: Statistics Canada, *Family Violence in Canada: A Statistical Profile*, 85-224-XIE2010000, January 2011; http://www.statcan.gc.ca/bsolc/olc-cel/ olc-cel?catno=85-224-X&chropg=1&lang=eng.

Page 243: Figure 5.7, Information. Copyright Ontario Ministry of the Attorney General (2011). Current at the time of publication. Readers should refer to current section 810 of the *Criminal Code*.

Page 256: Table 5.4, Criminal Harassment, by Province and Territory, 2008 and 2009. Source: Statistics Canada, Criminal Harassment in Canada, 2009, *Juristat Bulletin*, 85-005-XIE2011001, June 2011; http://www.statcan.gc.ca/bsolc/olc-cel/ olc-cel?catno=85-005-XIE&lang=eng#formatdisp.

Page 257: Figure 5.8, Criminal Harassment, by Relationship of Accused to Victim, Canada, 2009. Source: Statistics Canada, Criminal Harassment in Canada, 2009, *Juristat Bulletin*, 85-005-XIE2011001, June 2011; http://www.statcan.gc.ca/bsolc/olc-cel/ olc-cel?catno=85-005-XIE&lang=eng#formatdisp.

Page 266: Table 5.5, Victims of Violent Crime Perpetrated by Dating Partners, by Sex of Victim and Relationship to Accused, 2008. Source: Statistics Canada, Police-Reported Crime Statistics in Canada, 2009, *Juristat*, 85-002-XWE2010002, vol. 30, no. 2, September 2010; http://www.statcan.gc.ca/bsolc/olc-cel/ olc-cel?catno=85-002-x&lang=eng.

Page 267: Figure 5.9, Females Most Likely Victims of Dating Violence, 2008. Source: Statistics Canada, Police-Reported Crime Statistics in Canada, 2009, *Juristat*, 85-002-XWE2010002, vol. 30, no. 2, September 2010; http://www.statcan.gc.ca/bsolc/olc-cel/ olc-cel?catno=85-002-x&lang=eng.

Page 268: Table 5.6, Victims of Dating Violence by Offence Type and Sex of Victim, 2008. Source: Statistics Canada, Police-Reported Crime Statistics in Canada, 2009, *Juristat*, 85-002-XWE2010002, vol. 30, no. 2, September 2010; http://www.statcan.gc.ca/bsolc/ olc-cel/olc-cel?catno=85-002-x&lang=eng.

Page 284: Appendix 5A, *Policing Standards Manual (2000): Domestic Violence Occurrences*. © Queen's Printer for Ontario, 2000. Reproduced with permission.

Page 296: Figure 6.1, Victims of Violent Crime, by Age Group, Canada, 2009. Source: Statistics Canada, *Family Violence in Canada: A Statistical Profile*, 85-224-XIE2010000, January 2011; http://www.statcan.gc.ca/bsolc/olc-cel/ olc-cel?catno=85-224-X&chropg=1&lang=eng.

Page 297: Table 6.1, Senior Victims (65 Years and Older) of Violent Crime by Sex and Accused–Victim Relationship, Canada, 2009. Source: Statistics Canada, *Family Violence in Canada: A Statistical Profile*, 85-224-XIE2010000, January 2011; http://www.statcan.gc.ca/ bsolc/olc-cel/olc-cel?catno=85-224-X&chropg=1& lang=eng.

Page 298: Table 6.2, Senior Victims (65 Years and Older) of Family Violence by Sex and Offence Type, Canada, 2009. Source: Statistics Canada, *Family Violence in Canada: A Statistical Profile*, 85-224-XIE2010000, January 2011; http://www.statcan.gc.ca/bsolc/olc-cel/ olc-cel?catno=85-224-X&chropg=1&lang=eng.

Page 396: Table 8.1, Ranking, Number, and Percentage of Male and Female Deaths for the Ten Leading Causes, Canada, 2007. Source: Statistics Canada, Leading Causes of Death, *The Daily*, 85-002-XWE2010002, vol. 30, no. 2, September 2010; http://www.statcan .gc.ca/bsolc/olc-cel/olc-cel?catno=85-002-x&lang=eng.